CONSUMERISM

THE ETERNAL TRIANGLE

*

Business,
Government,
and Consumers

EDITED BY

BARBARA B. MURRAY Ph.D
UNIVERSITY OF DETROIT

GOODYEAR PUBLISHING COMPANY, INC.
PACIFIC PALISADES, CALIFORNIA

Current printing (last digit):
10 9 8 7 6 5 4 3 2 1

ISBN: 0-87620-194-X

Library of Congress Catalog Card Number: 72-91154

Y-194X-4

Printed in the United States of America

To Sharron and Kevin

CONTENTS

Contents

VII. BUSINESS AND CONSUMERISM

VIII. MARKETING AND CONSUMERISM

IX. ADVERTISING AND CONSUMERISM

X. WARRANTIES AND PRODUCT LIABILITY

CONTENTS

PREFACE

IN OUR day, the consumer is coming into his own; his rights and needs are being expressed, paid attention to in places of power, and are giving him influence in business and in government. The increased interest in consumerism has put emphasis on the maxim *caveat venditor*, let the seller beware, rather than on the traditional maxim *caveat emptor*, let the buyer beware. The shift in focus has occurred because consumerists now question the operationality of the consumer sovereignty assumption for the marketing concept of the competitive market.

It has generally been accepted, that in a competitive economy, the consumer decides the success or failure of business by his decision whether or not to buy products.

Traditionally, business has responded by saying that "consumer sovereignty" is sufficient to protect the consumer. Government has responded by trying to keep the assumption operating through legislation and various regulating agencies. The consumer's response was that he not only needed sufficient information for rational decision making but also that he wanted the right to be heard and represented.

Organized around business, government, and consumers, this book emphasizes the social, economic, and marketing aspects of consumerism as related to government legislation (i.e., Truth-in-Lending and Packaging); to institutions (particularly the Federal Trade Commission) and enforcement; to business and its marketing and advertising functions (with particular emphasis upon warranties and product liabilities); and to the low-income consumer with whom many issues of consumerism are most visible.

The section on business provides a framework for understanding why there has been a lack of dialogue between business and the consumerist, and why business should not view the consumerist as an adversary but rather as a partner. The emphasis of the marketing section is upon the various marketing strategies that would promote this partnership relationship and make it profitable within the free enterprise system.

The advertising function of marketing has been under considerable attack from consumers and the government. The questions concern not only the "want creation" aspects of advertising, and the private and social costs associated with advertising, but also the form it should take in its informational role. A current thrust of the consumer movement is the effect of advertising on market structures and pricing policies that deviate from the competitive norm.

ix

Inasmuch as the Federal Trade Commission is a primary agency for the enforcement of consumer legislation and the regulation of advertising, a special section is devoted to the controversy surrounding its effectiveness in protecting the consumer and the criteria it should adopt for regulation.

The sections on credit and lending, and on packaging, are designed to explain the legislation and to provide an understanding of its effects on consumer and business behavior. The empirical studies indicate that, although much of the legislation was designed to protect the low-income consumer, he has had little benefit. In order to develop policies that will assist him, it is necessary to understand the behavior of the low-income consumer, rather than to use the traditional assumption that he is irrational. The low-income consumer has often been the focal point of the abuses, issues, and problems with which the consumer movement is concerned.

Only by viewing the interrelationships among the concepts, analyses, and strategies of business, government, and consumers, can an objective analysis of consumerism be gained. This book is designed so that each section builds upon and reinforces the previous sections. This organization is necessary because the output of one section is the input for another section. Consumerism is a system with major informational flows and feedback effects among the three major sectors: business, government, and consumers. One should not view each of the parts in isolation, but rather as a complex system that is constantly changing in response to changes in its components.

INTRODUCTION

CONSUMERISM, with its emphasis on the rights of the consumer, has become a respectable topic of concern for business, government, and consumers.[1] Basically government and business accept the marketing concept of consumer sovereignty—that the rational consumer decides the success or failure of business through his dollar votes in the marketplace.[2] But government and business do not agree about the concept's operationality, about the availability of information, or about the degree of imperfection in the information available to the consumer.[3] Business has argued that the concept *is* operational and sufficient for consumer protection.[4] Government has argued that it must strive to maintain the operationality of the concept to protect the consumer's interest. Thus government passed antitrust legislation to ensure that, by maintaining competition, the consumer has the right to choose;[5] that by guaranteeing sufficient information via the Fair Packaging and Labeling Act and the Truth in Lending Act, the economic man could be rational in his choice. Now, in the middle of the controversy, the consumer himself questions his own ability to make rational choices from among the profusion of products[6] with their increasing complexity.[7]

GOVERNMENT FOCUS

The original focus of government was to protect the consumer against adulterated and unsafe products in the food and drug industries. Its first piece of consumer legislation, the Food, Drug, and Cosmetic Act of 1906, was passed in response to public demands to curb these abuses. The next phase of government interest centered on the consumer's right to choose and his right for protection against unfair competition. Out of this phase came the rationale for the Wheeler-Lea Amendment to the Federal Trade Commission Act. The amendment made the Federal Trade Commission responsible not only for policing, regulating, and enforcing the provisions of the act with respect to false and misleading advertising, but also for protecting the consumer against unfair competitive acts.

Basically the thrust of government has been toward maintaining consumer sovereignty assumptions—witness the passage of the Fair Packaging and Labeling Act[8] and the Truth-in-Lending Act. The purpose of these acts and "similar statutes is to facilitate attainment of a higher level of consumer satisfaction.

To accomplish this the government seeks to assure a supply of information which permits an individual to evaluate more objectively the goods available for purchase."[9]

With Ralph Nader's investigation of the automobile industry,[10] the emphasis of government concern shifted to protecting the consumer from himself—witness the legislation eventually passed as the National Traffic Motors Safety Act of 1966. The implicit assumption of the act was that the concept of consumer sovereignty is inadequate if there are external costs in the consumption and/or production of the product which the consumer does not account for in his consumption decision. As a result of these "market failures," there is increased pressure for government intervention to "internalize the externalities." The usual method is to increase legislative controls. As Stanley Cohen[11] indicates, current government interest in externalities may turn into government controls on quality standards and more government regulation to upgrade product quality and repairability.

MAJOR ELEMENTS OF CONSUMERISM

Consumerism in the 1960s and 70s has been attributed to the facts that public standards of business conduct are rising and that consumers have become more aware of their rights. These changes were brought by increasing levels of education and consumer sophistication. Robert Herrmann argues that better variables for understanding the course and timing of consumer unrest are the inflationary forces reducing the consumer's real income.[12]

Traditionally, the scope of and interest in consumerism has been associated with increased government activity in the marketplace. The marketplace concern of consumers with respect to fraud, excessive prices, exorbitant credit changes, poor quality of merchandise and service, and lack of information are most visible among low-income groups.[13] Historically, the response has been that this group of consumers are irrational in their buying behavior. But, ". . . to indict poor consumers as irrational is too simple an explanation . . ."[14] "Many of the solutions for improving information and product quality provide little benefit for the poor who lack the marketing behaviorial characteristics of the middle income groups for which the proposals and legislation are directed."[15]

In addition to the catalyst provided by the low-income consumer and the ghetto market, the current surge in consumerism

> has been enhanced by several major factors . . . First, increased leisure time, rising levels of income, higher educational levels, and general affluence have tended to magnify and intensify the forces of consumerism. Second, inflation has made purchase behavior even more difficult. Third, unemployment has been low. Therefore, the marginal laborer has been employed even though he has fewer skills. Such workers reduce output quality. Fourth, demands for product improvement have led to increased product complexity. Further, the

complexity has been stimulated by the emergence of new technology. This has led to service difficulties and reliability problems. Finally, the popular success achieved by individuals such as Ralph Nader, in his crusade for consumerism, and the political support now developed for the forces of consumerism certainly reinforce the fact that the entire area must become a more important factor in business policy.[16]

Others, like William Kaye, emphasize that, to be rational, business policy must recognize the interest of consumers as a means of profit maximizing.[17]

PRESIDENTIAL INTEREST

Another important factor underpinning the stronger focus on consumerism has been the interest expressed in it by the executive branch of the government. "Organized labor, business, and farmers have representatives at the Cabinet level to plead their cases before the President and Congress, but the consumer has no spokesman of such rank."[18] The impetus at the presidential level began with President Kennedy's efforts to establish the rights of the consumer not only to choose but also to be heard.[19] President Johnson[20] initiated an eight-point program for consumer protection which included in addition the areas of product warranty and product liability. President Nixon[21] proposed a "Buyer Bill of Rights" to provide an office of consumer affairs, greater consumer representation in the regulatory process, a consumer Fraud Prevention Act utilizing class action suits, and a consumer Product Test Methods Act.

THE REGULATORY PROCESS

There are increasingly interested government and consumer advocates in the regulatory process (particularly the Federal Trade and Federal Drug commissions) because it is through the regulatory commissions that implemented and enforced consumer interests can be brought to focus among business, government, and consumers.

Some consumer advocates have mixed feelings about the effectiveness of the Federal Trade Commission.[22] Most supporters of consumer interest—for example, Senator William Proxmire[23] and Miles Kirkpatrick[24]—would like to see increased consumer representation on the FTC, and a broader interpretation of the commission's regulation of advertising. Others feel that a strong central consumer agency is required for enforcement and representation of consumer interest.[25] Basically the issue is whether regulatory agencies have the *interest* and *ability* to implement the consumer programs and legislation. Those who argue that the interest of these agencies lies elsewhere say that the FTC has been used as a training ground for corporate lawyers and businessmen rather than for representing consumer interest.[26] The ability element of the argument is that "the agencies are made to operate on a starvation budget,"[27] with a limited staff to engage in enforcement. In general there is a consensus for greater consumer representation and greater attention on the economic aspects of consumerism—particularly the cost to consumers of oligopoly market structure and its advertising expenditures.[28]

FEDERAL TRADE COMMISSION AND ADVERTISING

One of the primary functions of the Federal Trade Commission is its regulation of advertising for the protection of consumers against false and misleading advertising. The criteria for regulation of advertising by the FTC is aptly put by Dorothy Cohen. "In broad terms, the commission's judgements have been consistent with an 'economic man' concept of consumer purchase behavior. The basic assumptions of the commission's regulatory design or criteria are maximization of the consumer's utilities and rational choice."[29] But she argues that the consumer is selective in the information provided to him. Because of the difference between his "subjective and objective environments," the consumer does not measure value in economic terms alone.[30] Consequently for the commission to improve protection of the consumer, who may be a "satisficing animal rather than a maximizing animal,"[31] its members must understand the consumer's behavior.

CONSUMER CRITICS AND ADVERTISING

Of all the marketing functions of business, advertising has probably been the subject of the most controversy by government and consumers. "Advertising has been under attack for years. But the years when advertising was criticized it was generally in terms of its 'truthfulness.' Now, however, the attacks have broadened. Today critics are more often raising fundamental questions about advertising influence over the structure of the economy, its social responsibilities, its ethics, its morality, its esthetics."[32]

Although advertising may be a more visible and, as some have argued, an economical source of information,[33] does it provide the basic information that the consumer needs?[34] "Marketing, as a unique and definable management function and as it relates to the problem of consumer interest, should receive special attention. . . . Since a majority of consumer problems (packaging, product testing and pricing, advertising policies, and so forth) directly involve marketing policies and practices, marketing is the one management area in which the question will most often be raised—Is it good for the consumer?"[35]

As Weiss[36] notes, the consumer's right to truthful information and performance criteria—"freedom of information"—has been turned into an argument against governmental intervention, the consumer's "freedom to be wrong." This latter interpretation is a restatement of the original argument by business (when consumerism was viewed as an attack upon the free enterprise system) that consumer sovereignty protects the consumer. But because some businessmen equate responsible behavior with the producer's legally acceptable behavior, reliance upon consumer sovereignty will inhibit changes in business operations.[37] If business fails to meet consumer's needs, government will. "If business managers want to avoid such new governmental regulations (with the attendant possibilities of excessive and punitive legislation), they will have to take positive action to demonstrate that the business interest is in more general accord with consumer needs and wants."[38]

EXTENSION OF IMPLIED WARRANTIES AND PRODUCT LIABILITY

Galbraith[39] has attacked the "want creation" aspects of advertising—i.e., that advertising creates a demand for a product that the consumer does not inherently have. His "countervailing power" concept has been used as an explanation for the legal expansion of implied warranties and product liability. Essentially the argument is that an imbalance of power between manufacturers and consumers will generate a countervailing power. David Rados[40] and Arthur Southwich, Jr.,[41] feel that the judiciary has been the countervailing power in the warranty and product liability areas. Judiciary influence has given rise to legal reforms toward the elimination of privity of contract and expansion of implied warranties, via court decisions rather than legislation.

The landmark case for the extension of implied warranty and product liability was *Henningsen* v. *Bloomfield Motors*.[42] "The decision held unequivocally that a contractual relationship is not necessary to create liability for breach of an implied warranty of quality. In reaching this decision, the court relied heavily on the fact that the privity rule was developed at a time when marketing was relatively unsophisticated, when the buyer and seller were in relatively equal bargaining terms, when the buyer had an opportunity to inspect the merchandise, and when the primary demand for goods was created by the retailer-seller rather than the manufacturer."[43]

"THE DIALOGUE THAT NEVER HAPPENS"

Is there an objective framework for understanding the lack of communication between business and the consumer advocate? Raymond Bauer and Stephen Greyser provide two models for explaining why 'the dialogue never happens."[44] They hold that the consumer advocate argues from a pure competitive model composed of: (1) price competition, (2) a simple basic product, i.e., bread rather than rolls, (3) a corresponding matching of the basic product to the consumer's basic needs, (4) rationality on the part of the consumer with respect to his expenditures, and (5) any objective information that facilitates a more informed and rational decision on the part of the consumer with respect to the product. Business argues from a monopolistic model composed of the ideas that (1) products are differentiated, (2) product differentiation occurs through style differences and packaging, (3) consumer needs are any consumer desire with which the product can be associated and therefore separated from its basic use, (4) any customer decision that serves the customer's own self-interest is rational, and (5) that subjective as well as objective information is that data which will enhance the attractiveness of the product in the eyes of the customer.

NOTES

1. "Need to Protect Consumers," *U.S. News and World Report*, February 2, 1970, pp. 44-47.
2. "Consumerism—An Interpretation," Richard H. Buskirk and James T. Rothe, *Journal of Marketing*, October 1970, p. 61.
3. Richard H. Holton, "Government-Consumer Interests—The University Point of View," in *Changing Market Systems*, American Marketing Association, 1967; Ralph Nader, "Consumer Protection and Corporate Disclosure, *Business Today* (Autumn 1968), p. 70.
4. E. B. Weiss, "The Consumers Freedom to Be Wrong," *Advertising Age*, March 4, 1968, p. 53.
5. The antitrust laws, primarily the Clayton Act, Federal Trade Commission Act and Wheeler-Lea Amendment.
6. E. B. Weiss, "Line Profusion in Consumerism," *Advertising Age*, April 1, 1968, p. 72.
7. "Rattles Pings, Dents, Leaks, Cracks and Cost," *Newsweek*, November 25, 1968, p. 93.
8. The lobbying efforts of industry to prevent and finally to comprise the Packaging and Labeling Act are presented by Jerry Main, "Industry Still Has Something to Learn about Congress," *Fortune*, February 1967, pp. 123-135.
9. Robert L. Birmingham, "The Consumer as King: The Economics of Precarious Sovereignty," *Case Western Reserve, Law Review*, 20 (1967), p. 377.
10. Ralph Nader, *Unsafe at Any Speed* (New York: Pocket Book, 1969).
11. Stanley E. Cohen, "Pollution Threat May Do More for Consumers than Laws, Regulation," *Advertising Age*, March 2, 1970, p. 72.
12. Robert Herrmann, "Consumerism: Its Organization and Future," *Journal of Marketing*, October 1970, pp. 55-60.
13. David Caplovitz, *The Poor Pay More* (New York: The Free Press, a Division of Macmillan, 1963) and "Exploitation of Disadvantaged Consumers by Retail Merchants," Report of the National Commission on Civil Disorders, (New York: Bantam Book, 1968), pp. 274-277.
14. Louise G. Richards, "Consumer Practices of the Poor," in *Low Income Life Styles*, Lola M. Irelan, ed., (Washington, D.C.: U.S. Department of Health, Education and Welfare, 1967).
15. Lewis Schnapper, "Consumer Legislation and the Poor," *Yale Law Journal*, 1967, p. 76.
16. Buskirk, Richard H. and Rothe, James T., "Consumerism: An Interpretation," *Journal of Marketing*, October 1970, p. 63.
17. William Kaye, "Take in a New Partner—The Consumer," *Nation's Business*, February 1970, pp. 54-57.
18. Senator Phillip A. Hart, "Can Federal Legislation Affecting Consumer Interest Be Enacted?" *Michigan Law Review*, May 1966, p. 1255.

19. President John F. Kennedy, "A Special Message on Protecting the Consumer Interest," Message to Congress, March 15, 1962.

20. President Lyndon B. Johnson, "The American Consumer," Message to Congress, February 6, 1968.

21. President Richard M. Nixon, "Consumer Protection," Message to Congress, March 24, 1971.

22. "FTC Gets a Nader Needling," *Business Week*, January 11, 1969, p. 34.

23. Senator William Proxmire, "Qualifications for FTC Chairmanship," and Harvey Frazier, "Consumers and the FTC," *Antitrust Law and Economic Review*, Spring 1970.

24. Miles Kirkpatrik, "ABA Report: A Summary," *Antitrust Law and Economic Review*, Spring 1970.

25. Richard J. Barber, "Government and Consumer," *Michigan Law Review*, May 1966.

26. Senator William Proxmire *Antitrust Law Review*, Spring 1970, and Ralph Nader, "The Great American Gyp," *New York Review of Books* (November 21, 1968), p. 28.

27. Ralph Nader, "Great American Gyp," p. 28.

28. Paul P. Scanlon, "Anti Competitive Advertising and the FTC," and "Oligopoly and 'Deceptive Advertising,' " *Antitrust Law and Economic Review*, Spring 1970.

29. Dorothy Cohen, "The Federal Trade Commission and the Regulation of Advertising in the Consumer Interest," *Journal of Marketing*, January 1969, p. 40.

30. Herbert A. Simon, "Economics and Psychology," in *Psychology: A Study of a Science*, Simon Koch, ed. (New York: McGraw-Hill, 1963). Vol. 6.

31. Ibid., p. 710.

32. E. B. Webb, "Advertising Crises of Confidence," *Advertising Age*, June 26, 1967.

33. Jules Backman, "Is Advertising Wasteful?" *Journal of Marketing*, January 1968, pp. 2-8.

34. Buskirk and Rothe, *Journal of Marketing*, October 1970.

35. Tom Hopkinson, "New Battleground Consumer Interest," *Harvard Business Review*, October 1964, p. 101.

36. E. B. Weiss, "The Consumers Freedom to Be Wrong," *Advertising Age*, March 4, 1968, pp. 53-55.

37. E. B. Weiss, "Marketeers Fiddle While Consumers Burn," *Harvard Business Review*, July-August 1968, p. 45-53.

38. Hopkinson, *Harvard Business Review*, October 1964, p. 97.

39. John Kenneth Galbraith, *The Affluent Society* (Boston: Houghton-Mifflin, 1958).

40. David L. Rados, "Product Liability," *Harvard Business Review*, July-August 1969, pp. 144-152.

41. Arthur F. Southwich, Jr., "Mass Marketing and Warranty Liability," *Journal of Marketing*, April 1963, pp. 9-14.

42. Henningsen v. Bloomfield Motors, Inc., 32 N.J. 358 (1960).

43. Southwich, "Mass Marketing," *Journal of Marketing*, April 1963, p. 12.

44. Raymond Bauer and Stephen Greyser, "The Dialogue That Never Happens," *Harvard Business Review*, January-Feburary 1969, pp. 122-128.

PART ONE

*

Economics
and
Consumerism

INTRODUCTION

Economics and Consumerism

THE SELECTION by Jerome Rothenberg sets the scene for this entire book. He explains the concept of consumer sovereignty and the problems associated with its interpretation. The common interpretation of consumer sovereignty, also termed the marketing concept, is that the way the consumer spends his income (dollar votes) determines what will be produced—consumption is the ultimate end of all production.

Rothenberg presents an alternative—freedom of choice—which he feels is more representative of the real world. Here the consumer is not assumed to be all knowing; his tastes are not necessarily accurately known (he can be subjected to the want creation aspects of advertising). Under freedom of choice, the consumer has the right to be wrong.

To make the choice between consumer sovereignty and freedom of choice, one must determine which tastes are relevant; one must understand how endogenous and exogenous changes in products and in taste affect normal use; and one must be able to differentiate between the descriptive use of consumer sovereignty and its normal use.

The problems and issues raised by Rothenberg form the basis of the various viewpoints presented in the other sections of this book.

1. CONSUMERS' SOVEREIGNTY REVISITED AND THE HOSPITALITY OF FREEDOM OF CHOICE

Jerome Rothenberg

It is now twenty-five years since W. H. Hutt, in his book, *Economists and the Public*, coined the title, if not the substance of the concept of "consumers' sovereignty." In the intervening period, developments have occurred which affect both the interpretation and the ethical persuasiveness of the concept. In this paper I shall first raise some issues connected with the scope of the concept; following this I shall consider how changes in products and tastes affect the ethical status of the concept. My conclusion is that consumers' sovereignty is incomplete and ambiguous. In order to make it operational, a series of highly controversial, partly normative decisions have to be made. Further the extent to which consumers *can* be truly sovereign is questionable. In view of this, the concept loses attractiveness. By contrast a principle which is distinguished from consumers' sovereignty but which has often been treated indistinguishably—freedom of choice—gains attractiveness. The analysis indicates that the two are likely to be competitive to some extent; so we must examine our preferences between them more closely than we have done.

Consumers' sovereignty was early used in two senses; one descriptive, the other normative. In its descriptive sense it simply signified that the consumer was in fact the ultimate king: production in a market economy is ultimately oriented toward meeting the wants of consumers. Production is the means, consumption the end. More particularly, market performance is responsive to consumer demands. If we should ask the more interesting question of how responsive this performance is, we move over to the normative sense. In its normative sense consumers' sovereignty asserted that the performance of an economy should be evaluated in terms of the degree to which it fulfills the wants of consumers. Different institutional systems, and even different market structure under a market system, fulfill these wants in different degree. Thus, despite the fact that consumers' sovereignty in this normative sense has

Reprinted from *American Economic Review*, vol. 52, No. 2 (May 1962), pp. 260-268; by permission of the author and the American Economic Association.

from the beginning been intimately associated with a belief in the optimality of the free market, even Hutt finds the responsiveness of the market to consumer demands to be less than ideal where monopolistic elements are present. It is on the normative usage, as a keystone of welfare economics, that we shall focus in this paper.

THE SCOPE OF CONSUMERS' SOVEREIGNTY

The principle of consumers' sovereignty as presently employed is a value judgment which stipulates that we should take the degree of fulfillment of consumers' wants—or the degree to which performance accords with consumers' taste—as a criterion for evaluating the social desirability of different social situations and, through these, the desirability of the various public policies or institutional structures which give rise to them. The form such a criterion should take is not obvious. For one thing, the central fact of scarcity means that no combination of social structure and public policy can lead to a satiation of all wants. The possible is limited by available resources and state of technological knowledge. Our criterion therefore becomes: how good is performance relative to the best it might conceivably be? Optimality consists in maximizing consumers' utilities subject to the constraints of available resources and techniques.

The first problem which must be faced in interpreting consumers' sovereignty has been recognized for some time. The criterion must be able to compare situations in which the well-being of a large number of individuals is involved. What does it mean to satisfy the potentially differing tastes of a numerous group? Does the principle itself determine a unique function of these tastes which is to be maximized? The answer is not clear. Indeed, even its epistemological status is not clear. . . .

The fact that consumers' sovereignty does not imply a unique complete criterion is serious. The family of functions possessing the property that the first partial derivative of social welfare with respect to every individual welfare argument is positive is very large. The leap from consumers' sovereignty to a complete criterion is accordingly substantial. The decision to use one particular function instead of another even only moderately different can make a bigger difference to social welfare evaluations than the most radical changes in the tastes of several individuals.

WHICH TASTES ARE RELEVANT?

The second problem in defining consumers' sovereignty as a criterion is that it is not obvious which tastes are the relevant ones to consult. Three dimensions of the problem can be distinguished: which tastes, whose tastes, and tastes for what. First, if an individual is obviously uninformed about certain kinds of commodities, are his expressed preferences the right ones to consider? Since he himself would change his preferences if he were better informed,

4

should not his present evaluations be considered the wrong tastes—not really his—and be substituted for in the light of his "true" tastes?

How much information and experience concerning commodities is necessary to make an individual "correctly" informed? A conceivable empirical test would be to expose an individual to more and more information (experience) about the relevant consumption area so long as he keeps changing his preferences. Well-informedness would be the state of preference stability. Such a process *might* lead to a limit set of tastes.[1] But this cannot generally be expected. Accumulating exposure over time changes the individual; his expressed preferences may continue to change because his "true" tastes are changing. In these cases it is impossible in principle to distinguish "correctional" changes from "real" changes. Any judgment about well-informedness here would be a value judgment.

The second dimension involves a deeper problem. Psychologists believe in the existence of "erroneous preferences" which cannot be "corrected" by simply providing information or experience. Feeble-mindedness, psychosis, neurosis, dope addiction, immaturity, and perhaps criminality are such states where the individual wants what he does not "really" want. Does consumers' sovereignty require that individuals in these states be disenfranchised, or that an attempt be made to discover their "true preferences"? Psychiatrists claim to know what unconscious motives really impel some neurotics and psychotics; but these motives are often pathological and are unacceptable to the patients themselves. Also, the physician's concept of normality intervenes. It is felt that only when the patient is cured can his motives be said to be truly his. But while the practitioner can often understand existing unconscious complexes of motivation, he is likely to be far less capable of predicting what the person will—or would—be like when cured.

Thus, "correction" of the preferences of sick people is neither objectively straightforward nor ridiculous. Its possibilities rather depend on opinion which, given the empirical uncertainties and the emotive implications, are likely to be value-saturated. This conclusion is even stronger for children and, possibly, criminals. But what about the claim of psychologists that even most normal law-abiding adults do things they do not really want to? To be serious about sovereignty requires evaluating this claim and substituting corrected preferences in the criterion wherever it can be substantiated. Perhaps the enormity of the task and the controversiality of the objective grounds for correctly performing it would lead one to wish to confine it only to those cases where the existing distortion of tastes is substantial. But application of such a principle is likely to be at least as much value-laden as the decisions about the immature, the sick, the outlaw—and much more controversial.

The third dimension of the problem of defining relevant tastes concerns not which are the true preferences but rather what are the alternatives to which the preferences refer. This is probably the area where recent speculation differs most from the context envisaged by those who first proposed consumers' sovereignty. Welfare analysis has usually assumed that each individual's well-being, therefore his preferences, depends only on the commodities which he himself consumes. In this formulation, tastes are completely distinct from the function which joins them into a welfare criterion. But a number of economists have recently emphasized that an individual's well-being depends importantly on consumption by others as well as himself. There are three types of dependency. First, specific acts of consumption by others directly affect the individual; for example, the growing of roses by the neighbor of a man with a severe allergy. Second, the standard of living of specific other persons either angers him because of envy or pleases him because of empathy. Third, he has strong opinions about what should be the general shape of the frequency distribution of income. I have argued in the *Measurement of Social Welfare* [2] that the welfare impact on the individual of these external relations is psychologically of the same type as that of most of his own consumption, being a matter of social interaction. Thus, it seems reasonable to include them in spelling out the alternatives of choice to which tastes refer. Consumer sovereignty should concern consumer "values" rather than tastes, in Friedman's and Arrow's terms.

These external effects deserve consideration because they affect the individual's utility. Does any variable, therefore, deserve consideration if it affects utility? Individuals often have strong feelings about the kind of institutions they want to make social decisions about economic matters. Since these institutions reflect social rules or criteria for adjudicating among the various claims of the population, a concern about them can be treated as a concern about social welfare criteria. This is an external effect intimately related to attitudes about income distribution: it represents a concern about the principles which ought to govern that distribution. The allegiance to "free markets" or to "planning" is often considerably stronger than preferences about the exact composition of one's own consumption. Should these effects be included? . . .

The analysis suggests that preferences about welfare criteria be excluded after all as arguments of the individual utility functions on our original decision level. But then perhaps general attitudes toward income distribution should also be excluded, since they are so intimately related to preferences about welfare criteria. Do such attitudes have relevance for resource allocation independently of their relevance for the choice of welfare criteria? If so, how could such independent influence be partitioned to the appropriate decision levels? I cannot answer these questions. Indeed, here too I am not even sure of the epistemological status of the answer. My conclusion is tentatively to suggest, as before, that controversial value judgments are probably involved. Consumers' sovereignty here too can only be defined by recourse to complex and controversial normative assumptions.

A final complication on this dimension. We have just questioned the inclusion of "impartial" judgments about the consumption of others on methodological grounds. What about "partial" judgments? If individual A begrudges high income to individual B because he dislikes B or is simply envious, does this have the same ethical status as his allergic complaint over B's roses? Personal experience suggests that many persons would wish to separate the two ethically. Some complaints about others' behavior seem justifiable, others do not. On what criterion should such a distinction rest: real versus unreal injury (or benefit)? The person feels just as "really" injured through envy as through asthma. Yet an outsider would often want to say that the first type of complaint, but not the second, is unjustified because it is just none of his business. Perhaps the implied desideratum is that individual A cannot help himself in regard to his asthma but can in regard to his envy. This too is a slender reed. Can an individual really help himself for his tastes—for his personality? The typical link in all these external effects is psychological, not physical. Again, any criterion in this area will be largely a normative one.

To summarize this section, we have indicated that consumers' sovereignty does not make clear exactly which structures of individual tastes are to be consulted, or which individuals, or even what are the appropriate types of alternatives to which these tastes are to refer. Each area involves thorny problems whose resolution requires making controversial normative assumptions. Consumers' sovereignty, even if unqualifiedly accepted, must be a variable patchwork of value judgments; it will therefore mean different things to different people.

ENDOGENOUS CHANGES IN COMMODITIES

The above complexities affect the ethical persuasiveness of consumers' sovereignty as we shall see, but indirectly. Now we shall consider problems which have a more direct effect. Up to now, tastes—however finally specified—have been implicitly held to furnish a criterion external to and autonomous of the situations being evaluated. Moreover, the conceivable alternatives of choice have been assumed to be clearly delineated. The resulting evaluational process has an "integrity" which is important to its attractiveness. I suggest that in fact both of these assumptions are at variance with the real world.

The problems stem from the economy's use of substantial resources deliberately to change products and consumer tastes. Product development and advertising, as representative of these uses, employ considerable resources which have been increasing both absolutely and as a percentage of total output in the postwar period.

Product development affects our criterion in two ways: first, through an impact on the set of feasible output alternatives; second, through an effect on tastes. We postpone consideration of the latter to the next section. The first has the effect of making less clear how the criterion can be used to evaluate the efficiency of resource allocation. If all commodities remain unchanged over time, the alternatives of choice are simply different output combinations of the given commodities. Efficiency can be evaluated by the criterion through traditional welfare analysis. Suppose, now, given known modifications can be produced in these commodities by specified known modifications of resource use. Call this the modification model. It is not now enough to compare all the different possible output combinations of the single pattern of product modifications chosen at a given time. One must be able to compare the whole set of different feasible product modifications. This still can be done in principle—by applying our criterion to traditional analysis—since each investment for modification is specific and its outcome is specific in terms of the modification achieved and its estimated effect on demand. Besides, external effects will be minimal since we have assumed that all modifications depend on known processes and not on the results of possible unforeseen developments elsewhere.

Let us now, however, admit true innovations. Call this the innovation model. Unlike predictable modifications, innovations typically result from unpredictable outcomes of investment policies. One commits resources to try to bring about a particular product change or develop new products without knowing beforehand what will occur. The cost and benefit categories of traditional analysis apply here, but with an important distinction: costs are for the project as a whole (justified by its expected returns) while the benefits are for the unpredictable successful outcomes only. In addition, innovations typically carry substantial external effects in production and consumption—also largely unpredictable. These properties substantially complicate the problem of comparing the desirability of all possible ways of using resources, both for producing commodities under existing technology and for changing that technology in various ways. To appeal to "expected values" for comparability of different projects is hampered by the lack of grounds for ascribing probabilities and pay-offs except in a small minority of possible investment directions, since most possible innovating directions have probably never been tried. The attempt to bypass this by confining comparisons to the actual outcome of a particular pattern of innovating investment on one hand and either a no-innovation situation or one with some alternative investment pattern calculated in terms of expected outcome on the other, would be extremely misleading.

The trouble is that the existence of investments for innovation makes unclear just what is the set of alternative feasible outcomes. This trouble affects the integrity of many welfare criteria. But it especially affects consumers' sovereignty because, when applied to a free market system, performance is typically evaluated not directly by examining individual utilities but indirectly by looking at the degree of competitiveness of the system and the special provisions introduced in areas where external effects are significant. It is assumed that the market makes all feasible outcomes implicitly open to consumer choice and the degree of competitiveness determines the responsiveness of the market to these choices. The argument of this section is that the link between the resource implications of what the consumers think the alternatives are and those of what the producers think the alternatives are, becomes very loose. It becomes more hazardous to assume that actual market choices strictly "reveal" relevant preferences.

ENDOGENOUS CHANGES IN TASTES

What causes most trouble is endogenous changes in tastes. Consider the most extreme case first. There is only one firm. It uses part of its resources to produce some output without considering consumers' tastes. Then it uses the remaining part successfully to persuade the consumers that this output is exactly what they want. Are consumers sovereign here when their tastes change accommodatingly to output, not because of some inner dynamic of personality, but at the influence of resources deliberately used by the producer to gain acceptance of his output? It is not taste changes per se, accommodating or otherwise, that damage the normative integrity of consumers' sovereignty. It is endogenous taste changes—changes induced by producer investments designed to effect just such changes.

Few would insist that the consumer in this case is sovereign in any useful sense. The real world diverges from this, however, in a variety of pertinent ways. First, persuasiveness is not invariably effective. While consumers can be easily persuaded to some things, it is much more difficult or impossible (within the relevant range of persuasive techniques) to persuade them to others. Second, the degree of persuasiveness is a function of the resources used for persuasion. Greater persuasiveness requires using more resources. Third, there exist many producers, whose combined persuasive efforts to some extent cancel or to some extent complement, one another. Fourth, some portion of these efforts consists largely in giving information or making available a new product. In the former, their effect is to "correct" tastes. In the latter, they induce tastes to be realigned with a new set of consumption opportunities.

Given the incidence of attempted persuasion in the real world, how much damage is done to our criterion? The answer depends partly on how strongly tastes are actually influenced by producers' persuasive efforts. That we should expect to find some such influence is indicated by the large and increasing expenditures on product development and advertising. Most economists agree that advertising can shift market shares for different brands within a given commodity class. But this may not seriously damage consumers' sovereignty. In an opulent society with thousands of types of commodities available, preference changes among brands of a single type of commodity may have only trivial effects on individual welfare. The billions of dollars of annual resources spent to accomplish such changes may not so much discredit the welfare criterion as suggest considerable waste in terms of that criterion.

Are important taste changes brought about by producer persuasion? Product development *in toto* has radically changed some patterns of consumption. But much of this stems from the information content of substantial changes in consumption possibilities brought about by innovation. A large part of "informational" advertising is linked to such major product advances. For these the dominant effect on tastes is "correction," not change. Other product development, however, represents only slight modification and is amenable to linkage with the kind of persuasive differentiation which is believed to be the mainstream of modern advertising. For this highly persuasive area of development and advertising taste change is the battlefield—whether a firm's aim is to prevent already-attached customers from detaching or induce otherwise attached customers to become attached. There is no definitive evidence available as to the importance of changes here.[2] One may speculate; but it is easy to exaggerate in this area. Advertising is not the only, nor even the strongest, influence on tastes. Personality core, social role identifications, social mobility,

9

and informal interpersonal relationships are important determinants. One should not expect advertising to do very radical things. Of course, some of the indirect effects of advertising—on market structure, technological changes—may have stronger influence on over-all consumption patterns.

While advertising is probably not accountable for drastic changes, it is reckless to assume only trivial impact. The complex of product development and advertising has produced most of the economy's atomistic product differentiation as well as the larger configurational swings known as fashion. Consumption has changed variously and frequently under their flailing. Critics and advocates of advertising alike claim that advertising changes tastes. To the extent that they are true, these claims damage the acceptability of consumers' sovereignty.

One attempt to salvage consumers' sovereignty, despite the presence of endogenous persuasion, emphasizes that the consumer is not passive but selective under the buffetings of the persuasive assaults aimed at him. Advertisers propose—and often in contradictory fashion—but the consumer disposes. Besides, when he allows himself to be persuaded it is because he is improving his tastes, not simply changing them [3]. Thus advertising is not at all destructive of consumers' sovereignty. Instead of making consumers less discriminating it makes them more so.

In evaluating this it is helpful to link some types of product development with advertising. Atomistic product differentiation probably does show instances of improved consumer discrimination, largely in areas where the desire for variety is important. In many other instances even in these areas, though, the differentiation is illusory, adding nothing to the consumers' sensorium. The fact that a consumer is pleased when he consumes a persuasively advertised brand does not imply that he would not be just as pleased if he were to consume other brands. Differentiation associated with fashion, on the other hand, is likely to boast far less development of tastes. Individuals here are not chiefly interested in variety but in social distinction.[3] Fashion leaders cast off the old and set the new fashions chiefly as a competitive search for prestige and status by appearing distinctive rather than because of taste elevation or need for variety. The content of new fashions is chosen to prevent easy emulation, not to display improvement of wants. This is especially clear where fashion content changes cyclically, the styles of, say, ten years ago reappearing as the latest. Fashion behavior of style followers has much the same competitive motivation. Prestige here is obtained by emulating the leaders, conforming rather than seeking variety.

Thus, correctional effects do not seem to bulk large enough to mitigate much of the damage to consumers' sovereignty. Ironically, in fact, the occurrence of any such effects raises a new question which may weaken the criterion from a different direction.

To say that tastes are "improved" implies there exists a criterion which can judge between better and worse tastes. To be consistent with consumers' sovereignty this criterion would have to be part of the consumers' own evaluative apparatus. It thus would enable them to criticize their own and possibly others' present preferences. This would raise more urgently the question whether present revealed tastes are the appropriate representatives for what the consumers want to want. But here the problem itself becomes fuzzy. Should "improvements" be envisaged as simply broadly defined corrections within stable tastes, in which case the criticism would not be criticism of tastes but only of uninformedness; or should they be considered true taste changes? Any appearance of taste criticism from within the tissue of consumer sovereignty strikes at the foundation of the doctrine that tastes shall be the final arbiter, not subject to scrutiny.

The discussion suggests a further problem, possibly the most basic of all. Why are an individual's tastes deemed worthy of serving as a criterion of his welfare? In an earlier era his tastes could be thought to be a unique representation of what was indissolubly his. The membrane distinguishing the individual from his environment was deemed solid. Social science in the last thirty years has changed this view. Tastes, even personality itself, are now seen made and unmade by the social nexus. The bounding membrane is alarmingly porous. The tastes of an individual—even if we depreciate the effect of advertising—are not nearly so heroically his. They, and he himself, are "only" a relatively stable structure of organized interchanges with a social environment.

IMPLICATIONS AND PREJUDICES

As welfare criterion, consumers' sovereignty is incomplete, highly ambiguous, and lacks independence. In order to apply it with precision, a variety of decisions must be made which are extremely complicated and at least partly normative. These conclusions modify the attractiveness of the criterion for me.

If consumers knew more, knew better, were cured, were not as gullible, they would regret many of their present choices. So the preferences they reveal on the market are "wrong" in many respects. To give them what they "truly" want, they would have to be diagnosed by authorized experts and prescribed for through a monopolization of persuasive information. The ability to accomplish this with any degree of accuracy depends on the capacities of the social sciences. It is far from clear that many individuals would entrust such a burden to the social sciences at anything like their current stage of underdevelopment.

The undesirability of the prospect stems from more than its questionable feasibility, however. As so conceived, consumers' sovereignty is antipathetic to freedom of choice. The presumed alienation of consumers' choices from their own true tastes makes it unlikely that sovereignty could be efficiently implemented by free choice. Central authoritative prescription and co-ordinated "correct" distribution is more efficient than a multiplicity of conflicting pleas for attention and idiosyncratic partly erroneous choices. Thus, one may have to choose between consumers' sovereignty and freedom of choice, or at least have to express the rate at which one would be willing to sacrifice degrees of attainment of one for the other.

Freedom of choice entails accepting the voluntary choices of consumers on whatever markets exist. Since freedom exists in degrees and is related to the range of alternatives available to choice, it will be largely illusory if the market has no responsiveness to consumer choices. A totalitarian state can reduce free choice to a triviality by presenting only a narrow and biased range of alternatives. Besides it can resort to monopolized persuasion to change consumers' choices. Freedom of choice, no less than consumers' sovereignty, must bear up under analysis.

Yet our argument up to now lends attractiveness to it. Consumers' choices may not reflect their true tastes; but we have suggested that maybe these tastes cannot accurately be known; or that they are not really "owned" but only "loaned" tastes anyway, passed on from one person to another. What really can belong to the self and be accurately known is the experience of making and taking responsibility for choices, whether right or wrong, and seeking to know by this continuing dialogue across the permeable boundary of the self what if anything is worth preserving. It is possible that this quest, given any reasonable degree of responsiveness in the outside world, is what consumers want more than being given what they are told they really want. I suggest that when the doctrine of consumers' sovereignty was first presented, perhaps inadvertently attached to freedom of choice, an important part of its appeal rested really with freedom of choice. If forced to choose between them, our present visit may cause one to pause before automatically picking consumers' sovereignty. Might one not even actually prefer freedom of choice—the right to be often wrong, always wheedled and imperfectly hearkened to? It may be easier to hear the still small voice under the babble of TV hawkers than over the public address system.

NOTES

1. Indeed, I myself have argued that it sometimes would [1].
2. My own attempt to rectify this lack led to a highly inconclusive empirical study.
3. This analysis owes much to Robinson [4].

References

1. Jerome Rothenberg, "Welfare Comparisons and Changes in Tastes," *American Economic Review* (December 1953), pp. 885-889.

2. Jerome Rothenberg, *Measurement of Social Welfare*, Englewood Cliffs, N.J.: Prentice-Hall, 1961, Chapter 2.

3. Harry G. Johnson, "The Political Economy of Opulence," Unpublished paper.

4. Dwight E. Robinson, "The Economics of Fashion Demand," *Quarterly Journal of Economics* (August 1961), pp. 376-393.

PART TWO

*

Consumerism

INTRODUCTION

Consumerism

As THE *Wall Street Journal* selection indicates, consumers are frustrated when products do not work, when products deteriorate in quality, when company services and warranty policies do not meet their expectations. Although these frustrations are popularly associated with consumerism, they are only the symptoms, not the causes.

Consumerism is not a new phenomenon. Historically we have long been concerned with the health and safety of products and with legislation designed to protect the consumer. In the sixties the focus was shifted toward questioning the consumer sovereignty assumption for consumer protection and toward questioning the quality and quantity of information available to the consumer for rational decision making.

All the writers in this section tend to view consumerism as a result of the operationality of consumer sovereignty, or as Buskirk and Rothe define it the "prostitution of the marketing concept."

The question of operationality raised by consumerism can be viewed in terms of the failure of communication and informational flows between business and consumers to implement the consumer's right to be heard. Ralph Nader's selection focuses upon the weakness of the concept's operationality by identifying three myths: (1) the omniscient discerning consumer, (2) the general honorability of most firms in meeting consumer preferences, and (3) the adequacy of regulatory agencies in maintaining and protecting the consumer interests.

The consumer unrest of the 1960s has generally been attributed to the increasing affluence and sophistication of the consumer. This view could be regarded as somewhat contradictory—on the one hand the claim is made that the consumer is better educated and, on the other, that products are so complex he cannot evaluate them.

Robert Herrmann makes a case for inflation as a primary cause for the timing of consumer movements. In periods when prices are increasing faster than consumer's incomes, the consumer's real purchasing power is reduced. Consequently, the consumer cannot maintain and/or increase his standard of living—he's frustrated.

Buskirk and Rothe define consumerism "as the organized efforts of consumers seeking redress, restitution and remedy for dissatisfaction they have accumulated in the acquisition of their standard of living." In addition to inflation and increasing affluence, they feel other factors have contributed to the consumer movement. These are (1) that low levels of unemployment tend to adversely affect product quality because of the employment of marginal workers, (2) the interrelationship between improving product quality and product complexity, (3) the leadership provided by consumer advocates like Ralph Nader, and (4) the political support for the consumer from the White House. The writers in this section generally agree that the success of the consumer movement in defining and attaining its objectives depends upon the emergence of leadership from individuals, professional organizations, and the government.

The consumer movement does not appear to have an overall philosophy or program of action, but rather a conglomerate of separate groups ranging from Consumer Union to Nader's Raiders. Herrmann provides a typology of groups that make up the consumer movement. These are: (1) the Adaptationists, who emphasize consumer education as a means of maintaining the consumer sovereignty concept; (2) the Protectionists, the oldest portion of the consumer movement, concerned with health and safety issues; and (3) the Reformers, who want to increase the role of the consumer in government. Ralph Nader's article provides an excellent example of the philosophy and policies of the reformer group.

The future of consumerism will be concerned with the relative roles of business and government in providing the opportunities and organizations for communications, the quality and quantity of information, and protection for the consumer. Not only will health and safety issues continue to be of concern, but also increasing legal responsibility with respect to product liability and environmental issues. Marketing and management will increasingly recognize and formalize the consumer's role in corporate decision making. Marketing and management will no longer be content with determining consumer preferences through his dollar votes. As Herrmann points out, in the past marketing may have been guilty of too narrow a view of its role. Once the two-way flow of information between business and consumers is instigated the major question then becomes —what kind of information should the firm seek from the consumer and the consumer from the firm?

2. *CAVEAT EMPTOR* (MANY PEOPLE COMPLAIN THE QUALITY OF PRODUCTS IS DETERIORATING RAPIDLY)

The Wall Street Journal

ROOFS LEAK. Shirts shrink. Toys maim. Toasters don't toast. Mowers don't mow. Kites don't fly. Radios emit no sounds, and television sets and cameras yield no pictures.

Isn't *anything* well made these days?

Yes, some things are. A man at Consumers Union, the publisher of *Consumer Reports* magazine, says that refrigerators are better than ever, for instance, and that wringer washing machines are becoming much safer. But he agrees that shoddy goods abound, and *Wall Street Journal* reporters' talks with Americans from coast to coast indicate that quality of merchandise is worse than ever.

Price is no factor. Expensive goods fall apart or fail to work or have missing parts with the same regularity as cheap goods, buyers say. What's more they complain that it's often a long, hard fight—sometimes a long, hard, costly fight—to get the merchandise repaired or replaced. They say salesmen and factory representatives have become masters of doubletalk and artists of the runaround.

For their part, sellers and manufacturers see things differently. Most companies contacted say their complaints are actually declining (though most Better Business Bureaus report the opposite), and they say that many of the complaints they do get are due to stupid customers. "Customer knowledge isn't as good as it should be. People don't read instructions. They just try to plug things in and make them work," maintains L. G. Borgeson, a vice president of RCA Service Co.

A BUZZ, A BLUR AND A HISS

But Mr. and Mrs. Howard C. Tillman of Memphis aren't dumb, and they say it isn't their fault that their Magnavox television set hasn't worked right since they bought it three years ago. They paid $1,200 for their console, but Mrs. Tillman says the world of color hasn't been so wonderful for them.

"The longest we've gone without a service call is three months," she says. The problem: "When you turned the set on, it sounded like a buzzer at a basketball game. You could see the picture, but it was like the times in a movie when the picture just flips up and down. We had to keep it unplugged, because it hissed whenever it was plugged in, even if it was off."

The people at Scott Appliances Inc., where the Tillmans bought the set, refused to replace it, Mrs. Tillman says, and so finally the Tillmans hired a lawyer this spring. No suit was filed, but the lawyer did get some action. Three weeks ago Magnavox replaced everything in the set except the speakers. Mrs. Tillman isn't completely happy—she says the speakers were a major problem—but so far she has no more complaints. "So far, it's been working fine," she says. "But I haven't really played it much. We've been out of town."

A spokesman at Scott Appliances won't comment on Mrs. Tillman's case, except to say that Scott stands behind its product even though "it's a headache and a cost to us." A spokesman at Magnavox in Skokie, Ill., says he is aware of the Tillman case. He doesn't explain the Tillman's long wait for replacement parts, but he says, "We try to show interest in a customer's inquiry."

WHY ARE THINGS SO SHODDY?

It isn't difficult to find people like the Tillmans who have complaints. Not so long ago, eight employees in a small Chicago office of CNA Financial Corp. were comparing notes on new purchases they had recently made. The most common thread: Six of them had bought defective goods. The *Consumer Reports* man to the contrary, the finish on a $425 GE refrigerator was peeling. A $400 Admiral color TV set required a two-week factory overhaul. A $20 pair of women's shoes ripped at the seam during the first wearing. The chain fell off a $32 training bike. A Roper dishwasher was installed incorrectly and had a defective timer. And a Roper gas range had a defective pilot light.

Why does this happen? Morris Kaplan, technical director of Consumers Union, says there are a couple of reasons for quality deterioration. First of all, he says, there is simply less quality control at many factories. He blames this in part on "the annual model change" in appliances and other goods. "The drive to get the new model out will frequently make it impossible for the manufacturer to do anything in the way of quality control," he says.

A second reason for poor quality is tough price competition, Mr. Kaplan says. "Makers try to reduce quality as much as possible to reduce price," he says. As an example, he cites black and white television sets, which recently have come down in price but "precious few" of which now have horizontal control knobs or knobs to adjust brightness levels.

Mr. Kaplan, a 58-year-old man who has been at Consumers Union for 23 years, says it is very difficult to generalize and say that products are shoddier now than in the past. In some areas, quality has improved, he asserts. But he maintains that those products that are bad seem worse than ever, and he says that among bad products a greater percentage of the output is faulty now than in the past.

"A NEW PHENOMENON"

He says, for instance, that Consumers Union bought 25 or so instant-load, automatic-exposure cameras not so long ago. They cost $30 to $70, he says, and they included brands made by 15 to 20 manufacturers. "One half of them as received were not operable or became inoperable shortly after we got them," he says. Similarly, he says, the organization recently bought 15 or so hi-fi tape recorders, costing several hundred dollars each, and discovered that one third of them were faulty.

"This is a new phenomenon—so many bad items," says Mr. Kaplan.

Mr. Kaplan will reel off a list of products that he says are better than ever. Clothes washers have improved, he says, and he maintains that the durable press innovation has made clothing better. But he also will list what he considers bad products. "Frozen fish has been lousy for a long time and is still lousy," he says. "The quality is abominable."

MRS. ESPOK'S LEAKY IRON

Mrs. Michael J. Espok of Irwin, Pa., isn't too concerned about frozen fish, but you won't find her singing the praises of GE irons or K-Mart discount stores. Last Feb. 13, Mr. Espok bought his wife a GE steam iron, which K-Mart had marked down to $8.97 from its regular price of $11.97. After a week of use, says Mrs. Espok, "all the water ran out the bottom and spotted my clothes."

She called a local GE service center, where a "very nice" man told her to take it back to K-Mart. She did. But K-Mart refused to take it back, since it had been sold more than 10 days before. "He told us to take it back to GE," says Mrs. Espok. Mrs. Espok finally did mail it to GE, and four weeks later she received a replacement, which she says is working fine. But she still isn't happy. She was without an iron for a month, and she had to make a special trip to the K-Mart.

The manager of the K-Mart store now says the store should have taken back the iron. "There was a slight misunderstanding," he says. "If she had come to me, we would have exchanged it. GE probably should have taken it, too." Mrs. Espok says the man she talked to at K-Mart had a bad attitude. "My husband never swears," she says, "but he said, 'We'll never buy another God-damned thing at K-Mart again.' "

Though General Electric replaced the iron, a GE service representative can't get too excited about Mrs. Espok's complaint. "It's a cheap iron. People expect too much from them," he says.

1 IN A MILLION? OR 74 OUT OF 100?

But expensive things aren't faultless. A Boston salesman says his Brooks Brothers suit began to deteriorate two weeks after he bought it. The store took it back and gave him credit. Similarly, a woman says that she bought a skirt at posh I. Magnin in Los Angeles and that after two hours it became completely wrinkled. "It looked like I'd slept in it. The belt became completely shriveled," she says. The store returned her money.

Another Los Angeles store, when asked about a customer's complaint about a bedspread, confirms the problem but says "this kind of thing is really one in a million." Perhaps, but other statistics indicate the ratio is a bit different. In the May issue of *Consumer Reports*, for example, the magazine discloses results of a survey of 90,000 owners of color TV sets. Seventy-four per cent of the color sets reported on "had required repairs of some sort," the magazine says. Most of the sets were three years old or less. The article also says that 6% of the sets bought in 1968 had to have their picture tubes replaced before the year was out.

If the magazine "had a dime for every complaint we've received about color TV . . . well, we could afford another color set. But we wouldn't be anxious to take on the headaches that seem to come with color," the article states.

TV sets have lots of parts, and it's possible to understand how they can break down. You'd think kites would be different, but William Ryder of Findlay, Ohio, says that isn't the case. He plunked down a dollar not so long ago for a plastic kite shaped like a bat. The first time he and his five-year-old son tried the kite, the keel, to which the string is attached, tore off and the kite plummeted earthward.

Back to the toy store, where he got another one free. Another try, another torn-off keel, and another kite crash. Back to the toy store for a third one, which he tried in gentler breezes. When the keel began to tear away, he patched it with plastic tape—and it's been flying great ever since.

A spokesman for the kite maker, Gayla Industries of Houston, says Mr. Ryder probably didn't read the directions, which admonish users not to fly the kite in high winds or cold weather, both common to Ohio. And he adds, "You expect kites to break up sometimes." He says, however, that complaints have declined while sales have quadrupled.

A much more serious complaint comes from some doctors who implant pacemakers in patients to regulate their heart beats. For a while, some pacemakers made by the Electrodyne subsidiary of Becton, Dickinson & Co. were inferior, some doctors allege.

"The problem was that the pacemaker, which was supposed to operate for 18 to 24 months, would stop in three or four months," says a Texas doctor. "The patient would then have to undergo surgery for us to replace the defective instrument, and sometimes the new one we put in would stop after two or three days.'' The new operation would cost the patient $3,000 to $4,000, this doctor says, not to mention the pain and suffering.

An official of Electrodyne concedes the company had trouble with its pacemakers, but he says that this is ''ancient history'' now and that it's been ''well over a year'' since the company received complaints about the instruments. The Texas doctor says he and his colleagues complained repeatedly before anything was done. The Electrodyne official replies: ''If something is wrong with a piece of equipment, that does not mean we can immediately correct it. We took immediate action to find what was causing the problem. We found it and corrected it.''

There was little the heart patients could do, of course, but submit to a new operation. In other areas, though, consumers have found ways to get back at the manufacturers or sellers. Many, like Mrs. Espok, the dissatisfied K-Mart shopper, simply refuse to shop any more at the store where they bought the faulty merchandise. Many complain to Consumers Union or to Better Business Bureaus in hopes of giving the offender a bad name. And many just start word-of-mouth campaigns against the stores or products.

An Iowa grandfather, for instance, who has been arguing for years with Sears-Roebuck about what he says is a leaky roof the retailer put on his house, signs all of his frequent letters to his children this way:

''Love, and don't buy anything at Sears.''

3. CONSUMERISM: ITS GOALS, OR- GANIZATION, AND FUTURE

Robert O. Herrmann

THE PRESENT era of consumer unrest is not unique in history. It follows two previous periods of consumer unrest, in the early 1900s and the 1930s. In each of these periods, consumer boycotts erupted in response to rising food prices, new consumer organizations appeared, and journalistic exposés of the dangers of widely used products created a rising demand for new consumer protection legislation. The common feature of the three periods provide a new perspective on the consumer movement of the 1960s, and may help in identifying the causes of consumer unrest, the forms it will take, and its probable course.

THE CAUSES OF CONSUMER UNREST

E. B. Weiss and others who have examined the consumer movement of the 1960s have attributed consumer unrest to rising public standards of business conduct and social responsibility brought about by increasing education and sophistication.[1] While increasing education and sophistication help to explain the public's growing awareness of consumer problems, these increases have been gradual and have occurred over a long period of time. They do not, however, explain why the present era of unrest began exactly when it did nor do they provide one with much help in understanding the cause or the timing of the consumer unrest of the early 1900s or the 1930s.

The three eras of consumer unrest do, however, have an important characteristic in common. Each occurred during a period of serious economic and social dislocation—periods in which rising consumer prices meant declining real incomes for a significant proportion of the population. Hard-pressed by their declining purchasing power, consumers in each era began to examine more carefully both the products which they were being offered and business behavior.

The unrest of the early 1900s came after several decades in which con-

Reprinted from *Journal of Marketing*, Vol. 34 (October 1970), 55-60, published by the American Marketing Association.

sumers' real incomes increased substantially as prices fell. This trend was reversed when new gold discoveries and refining methods led to an upturn in prices, beginning in 1897. These price increases left fixed-income groups hard-pressed and resentful of the power of the booming trusts and the growing union movement. In the early 1930s, declining consumer prices eased the public's adjustment to declining incomes, but in 1935 prices began to move upward again. In protest against increases in meat prices, housewives in Detroit began a meat buying strike which spread to several other cities and later led to a series of consumer conferences on the high cost of living.

In the 1960s, pressures on real income have also coincided with rising consumer unrest. After a gradual price rise of about 1% a year in the early 1960s, the 5% increase in food prices in 1966 was a major jolt to consumers. The increases were especially visible since they came on a number of frequently purchased items such as beef, pork, eggs, and lettuce. The buying power of many groups in the population had increased only gradually or just kept pace with price increases following the recession of the early sixties. Suddenly, these groups were faced with an actual decline in purchasing power.[2] Consumer discontent found open expression in a wave of supermarket picketing which began in Denver in October 1966. A flurry of consumer legislation began the same fall.

The rise in prices since 1966 has continued to be a major source of consumer unrest. In a recent interview, Mrs. Virginia H. Knauer, Special Assistant to the President for Consumer Affairs, noted that complaints about "high prices, especially for products that don't hold up" were, next to complaints about product warranties, the most frequent subject of the complaints received by her office.[3] Recent price increases have been felt particularly strongly since consumers' incomes are also under pressure from rising taxes.

The pattern of the three eras suggest that the pressure of rising prices on incomes has been an important cause of consumer unrest. Not all periods of rapid price increase have necessarily resulted in this unrest, however. Consumer prices rose rapidly during World War I, World War II, and the Korean War, but the shortage of consumer goods, rising incomes, and patriotic fervor seem to have blunted protests during these wartime periods.

While frustrations affecting many people are a necessary prerequisite for the appearance of a mass movement, the existence of such frustrations does not necessarily result in the formation of a movement. For a movement to grow, there must be both (1) a vision of a better state of affairs and a belief that it can be attained, and (2) the emergence of leadership and the development of organizations for attaining the goals of the movement.[4] The goals of the consumer movement and its organizational structure will be discussed in the following two sections.

THE GOALS OF CONSUMERISM

Some of the proposals for improving the consumer's position have come from radicals who believe that the consumer's present situation is the inevitable result of an exploitative system. These radicals call for a fundamental reorganization of the entire economic system, but their views have won little support. Most of the proposals by less radical consumer spokesmen deal only with a specific problem or are so vague that they have provided little basis for action.[5] No overall view of the consumer's needs has ever been widely accepted and, as a result, the philosophical basis necessary for formulating a program of action has not developed.

Because of the lack of an overall philosophy and program of action, there is in a sense no real consumer movement. Consumerism is instead a conglomeration of separate groups, each with its own particular concerns, which sometimes form temporary alliances on particular issues. The constituent groups in these coalitions include labor organizations, consumer cooperatives, credit unions, consumer educators, the product-testing and consumer education organization (Consumers Union), state and local consumer organizations, plus other organizations with related interests such as senior citizens' groups and professional organizations. The interest and involvement of these groups on a particular issue—for example, the setting of public utility rates—may vary widely. Because of its diverse composition, the problem of maintaining coalitions in the consumer movement is difficult and the desire to preserve harmony places certain issues beyond the pale. Any discussion, for example, of the monopoly power of labor unions and its impact on consumer prices is taboo.

In addition to the diversity of views about problems and priorities, there is also a diversity of views about the type of remedial action needed and about methods for obtaining it. These differences are reflected in the following, perhaps oversimplified typology of groups which make up the consumer movement:

1. *The Adaptationists*, who emphasize educating the consumer to avoid fraud and deception and seek to prepare him to deal intelligently with the market as it is. This group sees little need for new consumer protection legislation and gets along comfortably with consumer service specialists in industry, and business and trade association representatives. Many consumer educators fall into this category.

2. *The Protectionists*, whose primary concern is with health and safety issues involving the possibility of physical harm to the individual. This group includes scientists, physicians, nutritionists, and other professionals.

3. *The Reformers*, who like the adaptationists want to improve consumer education and who like the protectionists want to insure the individual's health and safety, and who, moreover, seek to increase the consumer's voice in government and the amount of product information available to him. This group consists chiefly of political liberals with a variety of professional affiliations.

THE CHOICE OF ISSUES

Since the consumer movement lacks a carefully planned program of action, its choice of issues is largely the result of historical accidents. In some cases issues have arisen because journalistic exposés, like Rachel Carson's *Silent Spring*, have aroused public concern. In other cases, clear threats to health and safety, such as the side effects of thalidomide, have demanded action, while in some cases issues have arisen simply because someone in a place of influence felt they were important. Senator Hart is reported to have developed the Truth-in-Packaging Bill after observing that the net weight of the contents of cereal packages on his breakfast table had declined while their price had not. One can imagine a very different result if the senator had instead become concerned about the nutritional value of the contents.

Even Ralph Nader does not seem to be guided by any systematic program of action. When he was asked how he selects the areas in which he becomes involved, Nader asserted:

> I've developed three criteria to determine my selection of an issue; I ask myself first how important it is; second, what kind of contribution I can make; and third, how many people already are working in the area . . . I can only handle four, or at the very most, five major issues at one time without dissipating whatever effectiveness I may have.[6]

His stated criteria and his record suggest that Nader has given little weight to the interrelationships between issues or the possibility of achieving some cumulative effect when selecting issues.

The hit-and-miss manner in which issues are adopted by the consumer movement concerns some of its leaders. Colston Warne, president of Consumers Union and a leading figure in the consumer movement, has expressed concern that the fight for Truth-in-Packaging and Truth-in-Lending during the 1960s diverted the consumer movement from more important issues, such as the creation of a Department of the Consumer, which he feels would have produced more important long-run benefits.[7]

LEADERS, ORGANIZATIONS, AND SUPPORTERS

In any organized group, the setting of goals and priorities is a key function of the leadership. The erratic manner in which the issues arise and are taken up by the consumer movement reflects lack of overall leadership.

Not only has the consumer movement lacked intellectual leaders able to develop a comprehensive philosophy and program of action, it also has lacked charismatic leaders able to translate this program into simple terms and dramatize it so as to catch the public's attention. During the 1960s, only three individuals—Ralph Nader, Esther Peterson, and Betty Furness—gained the public exposure necessary to exercise this kind of leadership. More recently,

Virginia Knauer has become increasingly conspicuous and influential despite close supervision and control of her activities by the White House staff.[8]

Leaders in the consumer movement and concerned professionals often have recognized problem areas and have attempted to arouse public interest in corrective measures years before scandal and crisis ultimately aroused public opinion and brought legislative action. Attempts to obtain Pure Food legislation dealing with specific foods began in the 1880s. Legislation did not come until 1906 when public indignation was aroused by Upton Sinclair's *The Jungle*, an exposé of working conditions in the Chicago packinghouses. The need for updating the Pure Food and Drug Act was well recognized by FDA staff members by the early 1930s. The needed legislation requiring proof of the safety of new drugs did not come until 1938, after more than 100 died when *Elixir Sulfanilamide*, a liquid form of a new sulfa wonder drug, proved lethal. Although Senator Kefauver began hearings on further increasing FDA powers in 1959, the need for such legislation did not become apparent to the general public until 1962, when a mass tragedy was only narrowly averted by Dr. Frances Kelsey of the FDA who used bureaucratic delaying tactics to prevent the marketing of thalidomide.

WHITE HOUSE LEADERSHIP CRUCIAL

Although scandal and crisis have been important factors in generating public support for the passage of new health and safety legislation, White House leadership and pressure have also played an important role in the passage of new consumer legislation. When it has lacked White House support, consumer legislation seldom has had much success. In 1906, new meat inspection legislation was obtained only after Theodore Roosevelt resorted to a form of blackmail—the threat that he would release additional information on packinghouse conditions—to force House action on the Senate-passed bill. A bill strengthening FDA powers was submitted early in the New Deal, but Franklin Roosevelt failed to give the bill full support, apparently because he felt he needed to preserve his political capital for more important measures. It took the *Elixir Sulfanilamide* tragedy to finally produce congressional action on the bill.

John F. Kennedy indicated a long list of needed legislation in his "Consumer Message" of March, 1962. The "New Frontier" administration was, however, too involved in international crises and economic problems at home to produce much action on the program. Liberal support in the Congress for new consumer protection legislation was insufficient, moreover, to overcome the resistance of conservative opponents and the inertia produced by the general preference for avoiding controversial issues.[9] Increased powers were given to the FDA after the thalidomide scandal but the remaining program made little progress. Despite his appointment of Esther Peterson, a well-known figure in the labor movement, as his Special Assistant for Consumer Affairs in January, 1964, and his consumer message to Congress in February of that year, Lyndon Johnson exerted little real pressure for new consumer legislation in the early years of his administration. It was not until March, 1966, when he sent his

"Consumer Interests Message" to Congress that he became actively involved in support of new legislation. A wave of activity followed, spurred on by special consumer messages and the State of the Union messages in 1967 and 1968.

ORGANIZATIONS

The consumer movement has produced only a few enduring organizations. The most important and influential is Consumers Union. From its inception in 1936, CU has concerned itself with a wide range of issues beyond product testing. In recent years, it has increasingly come to view itself as an organization to promote consumer education. CU has undertaken to inform consumers about all phases of their relationship with the marketplace including such topics as interest rates, guarantees, and warranties, life insurance, product safety, and the selection of a doctor. As a result of its sizable membership (1.6 million) and annual budget ($10 million in 1969-70),[10] CU is an important source of financial assistance for other parts of the consumer movement. It has helped to finance a variety of activities, including David Caplovitz's research on the problems of the low-income consumers,[11] the development of an international organization of product-testing associations, the International Organization of Consumers Unions, and the provision of expert testimony at regulatory and legislative hearings.[12]

Attempts to organize individual consumers on a national basis for political action have met with little success and have been shortlived. Organizations of individual consumers at the state and local level have proved somewhat more durable and effective. In early 1969, there were 29 state consumer organizations and local organizations in 9 major cities or counties; the Louisiana Consumer League and the Arizona Consumers Council with chapters in Tucson, Phoenix, and Flagstaff are currently among the most active of these organizations. State and local organizations have achieved some success in obtaining legislation on specific issues. They also have proven useful in providing group support for consumer representatives in state and local governments, and have become increasingly skilled at putting together temporary coalitions to advance the cause of consumers in state legislatures. Most of these organizations are, however, dependent on part-time leadership and volunteer staff and have had difficulty in maintaining continuing programs.

In late 1967, a new attempt was made to form a viable national consumer organization. The new organization, the Consumer Federation of America, is a national federation of organizations with consumer interests and includes labor unions, state and local consumer organizations, the National Council of Senior Citizens, and the National Consumers League. Its purposes include fact-finding and analysis of consumer issues and the provision of an information clearinghouse on the consumer-related activities of its member groups. The new federation has taken the leadership in the organization of the Consumer Assembly, an annual Washington conference for the discussion of consumer problems and legislative needs. Although the strength and durability of CFA remain to be determined, its chances appear good. By mid-1970, its membership included 160 organizations.

SUPPORTERS

Historically, consumer problems seem to have aroused most concern among middle- and upper-middle-income families. George Gallup reported in 1940 that this was the group which had been most influenced by the ideas of the consumer movement of the 1930s.[13] Over the years, Consumers Union members have been drawn chiefly from this same group, despite continued efforts to recruit low-income and working-class families. The subscribers responding to CU's most recent annual questionnaire had a median income of $14,000 and 58% were college graduates.[14] [The available evidence indicates that leadership of the 1966 supermarket protests also was above average income and education.] In a nationwide survey of leaders of local protest groups, Monroe Friedman found that the majority was under 35, had one or more years of college, and had family incomes of more than $8,000.[15] The nature of the support for consumer organizations seems to bear out E. B. Weiss' argument that concern with consumer issues will increase as income and education rise.

PREDICTING THE COURSE OF CONSUMERISM

The history of the consumer movement suggests that the present era of unrest will continue due to the pressure of further inflationary price increases and rising taxes on consumers' purchasing power. The consumer movement also will be aided by the increasing use of consumer issues by politicians seeking voter support. Lyndon Johnson found consumer legislation an "inexpensive" way to build a domestic legislative record and cool consumer ire in a period of rapid price increases. The continued burden of Viet Nam war costs and the new wave of consumer price increases apparently had induced President Nixon to adopt a similar strategy. The President has made consumer protection part of his legislative program; in October, 1969 he forwarded a consumer message to Congress calling for the establishment of a permanent Office of Consumer Affairs in the Executive Offices of the President, a new Division of Consumer Protection in the Justice Department to represent consumer interests in regulatory hearings, and legislation to permit class group actions by consumers after the successful completion of governmental action.[16] However, without active support from the White House, whatever its motivation, significant new consumer legislation seems unlikely.

The increasing number of organizations in the consumer movement also increases the likelihood that consumer unrest will persist. In the past, only Consumers Union performed the role of raising and dramatizing consumer issues. In the future, CU's activities will be supplemented by those of the Consumer Federation of America and by Ralph Nader's new Center for the

Study of Responsive Law. The movement will also draw somewhat more cautious support from the new consumer protection agencies being created at all levels of government.

Consumerism may also experience the sort of acceleration effect which occurred both in the early 1900s and 1930s. In each of these periods consumer activity in creating an awareness of one consumer problem also created sensitivity to others. With the solution of each problem, through either legislation or other means, the consumer movement was encouraged in its attempts to resolve others.

In the future, consumer issues seem likely to continue to be selected by historical accident. Health and safety problems will probably continue to erupt as unpredictably as in the past. As noted, concerned professionals in both government and industry frequently have pointed out problem areas years before they became a public issue and public opinion forced corrective action. Unless management becomes more attentive to these early warnings, it likely will continue to be taken by surprise on health and safety issues. The recent controversy over the effects of cyclamates suggest that there are still many problem areas waiting only for a journalistic exposé or a Ralph Nader to turn them into full-scale issues. Given the present climate of opinion, both in Congress and among the public, new legislation on critical health and safety issues is likely to be approved relatively easily and quickly.

Along with health and safety, two additional themes underlie most of the new consumer legislation now being proposed. One group of bills seeks to increase the consumer's voice in government. The proposals in this area range from the creation of a Department of Consumer Affairs to more modest ones, such as the creation of a permanent office to review and coordinate all federal programs affecting consumers, and the provision of consumers' counsels to represent consumer interest in federal regulatory hearings. The other group of proposals concerns consumer information and education. The most far-reaching of these is Senator Hart's plan for the creation of a federally chartered corporation to serve as an ombudsman for consumer complaints and to dispense product information. The less revolutionary proposals in this category include a bill providing for federal matching funds for state and local consumer protection programs.

Legislation on both consumer representation and consumer information historically has had a more difficult time than that on health and safety issues. The idea of a Department of the Consumer was first proposed almost 40 years ago and has been revived from time to time. Passage of legislation in the consumer information area has also typically been slow and difficult. The Truth-in-Lending Bill, for example, took eight years for passage; Truth-in-Packaging took five. New legislation in these areas moves through Congress so slowly that it is unlikely business will be taken unaware.

IMPLICATIONS FOR MARKETING

Responsibility for dealing with product design and safety issues raised by consumerists falls mostly to areas outside of marketing. Marketing professionals are more directly concerned with the issues of product information and the consumer's right to be heard.

Increased product information for consumers has been widely prescribed as a remedy for consumerism. This prescription is too general to be of much use, and specific aspects of it need examination by marketing educators and corporate marketing managers. There is, for example, the issue of just what rights consumers have to product information. Just how much is the manufacturer or retailer obliged to tell? Where do a firm's responsibilities end? With the provision of full technical information on the product in a form which will facilitate comparisons with other brands? With a full evaluation of its suitability and safety for various likely uses? With comprehensive comparisons of its composition and performance to recognized governmental or industry standards? With comparison of its performance and composition to other similar products? While these questions will be decided partly by legal requirements and partly by pragmatic considerations, their ethical implications deserve attention both in university courses on the social responsibilities of marketing and in corporate committee meetings.

Another problem involving product information is the determination of what information is really useful and meaningful to consumers. Consumers could easily be inundated with a flood of technical details. The firm which wants to provide better product information to consumers must first discover which product attributes consumers consider salient. Are these really appropriate measures of quality and effectiveness or should consumers be educated about other important product attributes? How do consumers interpret product information which is presently available? Is it comprehensible and meaningful to the poor and less-educated? How are consumers likely to interpret the new product information which the firm plans to provide?

Marketing also has a role to play in helping the consumer's voice to be heard within the firm. Up to now, consumer research within marketing has focused, in large part, on unmet consumer needs and their implications for product development, and on the decision process surrounding brand choice. Preoccupation with these specific problems may have caused other important problem areas, such as consumer expectations and perceptions of product performance, to be neglected. What problems have customers experienced in using a product? How do they think these problems should be remedied? Who do they feel is responsible for making the necessary changes? Are consumers' expectations about product performance unrealistic? If so, how did they get that way and what can be done about changing them? An expansion of the range of questions asked of consumers by marketing researchers can aid in providing answers to many of these questions. A program of research on consumer expectations and perceptions of product performance could well begin with a systematic analysis of consumers' letters to individual firms, consumer agencies in government, and the Better Business Bureaus—information sources which are easily accessible and inexpensive.

In the past, marketing may have been guilty of too narrow a view of its role. Marketing is a principal channel of information between consumers and the firm, in which information should flow in both directions. Marketing educators and corporate practitioners must reconsider what kinds of information should be moving in this channel, and also the forms in which this information will be most useful and meaningful. The challenge of consumerism may prove to be less of a threat to marketing than it has often appeared. It may, instead, be an opportunity to expand the services and relationships which are considered to be part of the marketing concept.

NOTES

1. E. B. Weiss, *A Critique of Consumerism* (New York: Doyle Dane Bernbach, Inc., 1967), p. 8.

2. George Katona, Eva Mueller, Jay Schmiedeskamp, and John A. Sonquist, *1966 Survey of Consumer Finances* (Ann Arbor, Michigan: Survey Research Center, University of Michigan, 1967), pp. 245, 247.

3. "The Consumer Revolution; Interview with Mrs. Virginia H. Knauer, Special Assistant to the President," *U.S. News and World Report*, 67 (August 25, 1969), pp. 43-46.

4. Lewis M. Killian, "Social Movements" in *Handbook of Modern Sociology*, Robert E. L. Faris, ed. (Chicago: Rand McNally, 1964), p. 433.

5. Richard J. Barber, "Government and the Consumer," *Michigan Law Review*, 64 (May, 1966), p. 1219.

6. "Playboy Interview: Ralph Nader," *Playboy*, 15 (October 1968), p. 224.

7. Colston E. Warne, "Is It Time to Re-evaluate the Consumer Activities of the Federal Government?" *Journal of Consumer Affairs*, 1 (Summer 1967), pp. 26-27.

8. Andrea F. Schoenfeld, "CPR Report/Mrs. Knauer, Consumer Envoy—both for and to the White House," *National Journal*, 2 (January 10, 1970), pp. 90-98, at pp. 90-91.

9. Richard Harris, *The Real Voice* (New York: Macmillan, 1964), pp. 139-153.

10. Robert L. Smith, Assistant Director of Consumers Union, personal communication dated September 23, 1969.

11. David Caplovitz, *The Poor Pay More* (New York: The Free Press of Glencoe, 1963).

12. "This is Consumers Union," *Consumer Reports*, 26 (May 1961), pp. 259-290.

13. George Gallup, "An Analysis of the Study of Consumer Agitation," February 9, 1940 (courtesy of American Association of Advertising Agencies).

14. Robert L. Smith, Assistant Director of Consumers Union, personal communication dated September 23, 1969.

15. Monroe Peter Friedman, "The 1966 Consumer Protest against Rising Food Prices: A Survey of the Participants and Their Actions," paper presented to the 15th Annual Conference of the American Council on Consumer Interest, Greeley, Colorado, April 18, 1969.

16. Richard Nixon, "Message from the President on Consumer Affairs and Protection," *Congressional Record—Senate* (October 30, 1969), pp. S13471-S13474.

4. CONSUMERISM—AN INTERPRETATION

Richard H. Buskirk and James T. Rothe

CONSUMERISM HAS received much attention in recent business literature.[1] Most articles and editorials dealing with the topic have commented on its importance, its underlying causes, its implications, or what interested parties (consumer, government, firms) should do, but most discussions have failed to deal with the topic in a total sense. This article attempts to (1) determine what consumerism is, (2) reveal what has caused it, (3) study its implications and potential dangers, and (4) develop guidelines for corporate policy in dealing with consumerism.

Peter Drucker offers the following definition of consumerism: "Consumerism means that the consumer looks upon the manufacturer as somebody who is interested but who really does not know what the consumers' realities are. He regards the manufacturer as somebody who has not made the effort to find out, whodoes not understand the world in which the consumer lives, and who expects the consumer to be able to make distinctions which the consumer is neither willing nor able to make."[2]

Another definition of consumerism has been developed by Mrs. Virginia H. Knauer, special assistant to the President for Consumer Affairs. She stated that the watchword for the new militant mood among American consumers is simply "Let the seller beware," in comparison to the age-old *caveat emptor* or "Let the buyer beware."[3]

Both of these definitions provide some insight into this current phenomenon referred to as *consumerism*. Perhaps it would be most relevent to relate consumerism to what has been popularly accepted as the marketing concept for the past 20 years. The marketing concept, simply stated, suggests that the purpose of a business is to provide customer satisfaction. Thus, it is anticipated that the firm will maximize long-term profitability through customer orientation. The marketing concept is primarily a post-World War II development, produced largely by economic conditions which changed a seller's market to a buyer's market. The marketing concept was hailed as being the essential fulcrum with which business resources could be allocated to best enhance profitability for the firm in a buyer's market. Consequently, much has been written and said about the marketing concept—how it can be utilized and what it

Reprinted from *Journal of Marketing*, Vol. 34 (October 1970), 61-65, published by the American Marketing Association.

means. However, the marketing concept and the forces labeled *consumerism* are incompatible. If consumerism exists, the marketing concept has not worked. It may be that consumerism actually is the result of prostitution of the marketing concept, rather than a malfunction of it.

Examples of customer dissatisfaction are not difficult to find. For example, a recent article in the *Wall Street Journal* noted that roofs leak, shirts shrink, toys maim, mowers do not mow, kites do not fly, television sets burn up, service is difficult or impossible to obtain, and warranties are not honored.[4]

Certainly each of us, as a consumer, has experienced the cumulative frustration associated with products that do not conform to expectations. It is this sense of frustration and bitterness on the part of consumers, who have been promised much and have realized less, that may properly be called the driving force behind consumerism. Accordingly, consumerism is defined as *the organized efforts of consumers seeking redress, restitution and remedy for dissatisfaction they have accumulated in the acquisition of their standard of living*.

CAUSE OF CONSUMERISM

There are two major opposing theories about the role of the consumer in the market place of a free enterprise system. One theory suggests that the consumer is "king." It is his dollar choice in the market which decides success or failure of producers; consequently, the consumer plays a decisive role in the entire process. This concept is referred to as "consumer sovereignty."

A completely opposite approach suggests that the consumer is a pawn in the entire process. The brilliance of Madison Avenue, sparked by research conducted by skilled behavioral scientists, has been used to deceive the consumer to the extent that he is incapable of intelligent selection. His dollar vote does not come across in any rational manner to decide who should be producing what; consequently, the consumer is not playing a decisive role in the process.

According to the marketing concept, the first of these two theoretical approaches would be correct: the consumer is viewed as the dominant force since his purchases determine market success for competing firms.

There is some truth in both theories. This can best be explained by relating purchase behavior to the type of product purchased. When consideration is given to the importance of the product purchased, the frequency of the purchase, and the information sources used, both theories are partially correct. For example, if a product is purchased frequently, the consumer has an outstanding information source—his previous experience with it. In such a situation he is capable of judging the product's effectiveness and how well it has lived up to his expectations, both physically and psychologically. Thus, the consumer is capable of exhibiting more rational behavior when buying frequently purchased products than when acquiring "once-in-a-lifetime" items. Collective consumer behavior of this type results in the market process being served appropriately. Competition for the consumer's choice is then the determinant which leads to congruity between perceived and received quality on the part of the buyers. This is, in essence, a fulfillment of the marketing concept and accurately reflects a situation in which the consumer plays a major role in deciding who is successful in the market place.

On the other hand, the situation in which the consumer purchases a product he has not bought before (or at best, infrequently) and which is of sufficient importance, often finds his attempt at rational behavior stymied by the lack of information. Since he has not previously purchased this product, his own experience is negligible. Another possible source of information is his peer group, but the limited accuracy of this type of information reduces its role in the transaction. Also, independent concerns' ratings of products are not widely used. This leaves the consumer with a basic information source—the company's marketing program. Evidently many marketing programs are not providing the information necessary for rational purchase behavior. This may be the result of short-term orientation on the part of management whose performance is judged on an annual basis. Top management's insistence on quarterly and annual budgeting performance may force operational management to make short-run decisions detrimental to the consumer because the impact of such decisions will not be reflected during operational management's tenure in that position. Consequently, when a product revision is needed, the response may be increased advertising and promotion expenditures rather than the more appropriate effort.

CATALYSTS IN CONSUMERISM MOVEMENT

The current wave of consumerism is not unprecedented in the history of business.[5] However, this time consumerism is enhanced by several major factors which were not evident in earlier expressions of consumerism. First, increased leisure time, rising incomes, higher educational levels, and general affluence have tended to magnify and intensify the forces of consumerism. The consumer's expectations with respect to the products he purchases are founded in a quest for individuality; yet, the market provides mass-consumption products with which the individual is not completely satisfied.

Second, inflation has made purchase behavior even more difficult. Rising prices have led consumers to increased quality expectations which are not achieved; thus, again contributing to the frustration of consumers.

Third, unemployment has been low. Therefore, the marginal laborer has been employed even though he has fewer skills. Such workers reduce output quality.

Fourth, demands for product improvement have led to increased product complexity. Further, this complexity has been stimulated by the emergence of new technology. This has led to increased service difficulties as well as performance and reliability problems. Moreover, society has been thoroughly conditioned to expect perfection from its technology. Moon landings, miracle drugs, organ transplants, and jet transportation make the housewife wonder why zipper manufacturers cannot make one that will not jam. The high degree of perfection that has been reached in recent years in a few fields only serves to disguise the higher *average* level of technical proficiency of present-day

33

manufacturing. Yet, it is apparent that the consumer is demanding better products than those presently available, regardless of the economic and technical ability of the firm to provide it.

Finally, the popular success achieved by individuals such as Ralph Nader, in his crusade for consumerism, and the political support now developing for the forces of consumerism certainly reinforce the fact that this entire area must become a more important factor in business policy.

IMPLICATIONS OF CONSUMERISM

It seems apparent that consumerism will affect industries, firms, governments, and, if it is effective, the consuming public.

The consumerism movement will develop more power as its forces become more coordinated and as it develops more leadership and organization. This will be partly manifested in legal remedies, such as class suits, that the consumer willseek.

At present, it appears the success of consumerism will depend largely on governmental involvement, the beginnings of which are already evident. For example, truth in lending, truth in packaging, product safety standards, and other recent legislative efforts, as well as a great number of consumer protection and awareness bills, indicate that the role of government will be much greater. (Over 100 "consumer protection" bills have already been introduced in the 91st Congress since January, 1969.)[6]

The role of the federal government in consumerism was first set forth by President John F. Kennedy's directive to the Consumer Advisory Council in March of 1962. He said:

Additional legislative and administrative action is required, however, if the federal government is to meet its responsibility to consumers in the exercise of their rights. These rights include: (1) the right to safety; (2) the right to be informed; (3) the right to choose; and (4) the right to be heard.[7]

It is apparent that the right to be informed, as well as the right to be heard, is of major importance. In fact, if all consumers were informed and were heard, this would then represent the fulfillment of the marketing concept as it was initially developed. The responsibility President Kennedy mentioned above should be industry's in a free society, not the government's. However, consumerism rightly claims industry has neglected its responsibility.

The relative role the government will play, and that which industry should play, is a critical aspect in the resolution of the consumerism issue. Given industry's traditional negative or complacent reaction to such issues, the result may be a coalition of consumer and government forces versus industry, which could lead to federal standards for industry. The resulting standardization and bureaucracy may stifle the economic process. It is imperative that industry recognize the message and seriousness of the consumer movement and take positive action *now* rather than having to live with legislation that may not be in the long-run best interest of society.

The basic premise is that consumerism is primarily the result of a lack of information on the part of consumers which hinders their ability to buy certain products. This reflects itself in an ever-increasing gap between product expectations and product performance. Moreover, consumers must be heard, which indicates the need for an industry or company *ombudsman*. An excellent example of the *ombudsman* concept in action is that of the Whirlpool Corporation which has established a "cool line." The "cool line" enables owners to call the customer service director at all times.[8] A direct communication contact of this nature will greatly enhance consumer-company relationships; it represents the first step toward solution of owner problems.

The owner problem is not fraudulent or deceptive practices for the most part; rather, the problem is improper or nonexistent communication. This seems to be incongruous since communication efforts—primarily advertising—exist in great abundance. However, communications between the firm and the consumer emphasize *imagery* at the expense of *information*.

Consumerism is attempting to tell industry something their research has not found, or that management has rejected or ignored. Appropriate information flow from the firm to the market in the form of product performance characteristics, simple-language warranty specifications, and safety standards will improve the basic customer-firm relationship, particularly for the infrequently purchased item where long, low service life is a major objective of the consumer. Product performance characteristics must be improved for competitive success if communication is predicated on an information basis. Thus, the poor product quality problem will be largely eliminated.

The other link in this communication structure, that of the consumer to the firm, should be explored. It is imperative that some mechanism be developed which will enable the consumer to communicate more directly with management. The consumer *does* have something to say, but management must learn to listen and translate this information into action.

FALLOUT FROM CONSUMERISM—LOCUS OF LIABILITY

While it is easy for consumers' advocates to talk about "class suits" against manufacturers, it is not completely clear how these would work. If consumers as a group were damaged by an automobile made by General Motors, then General Motors would be the defendant in the class suit, and if it lost the case there would be some hope of collecting the resulting judgment.

But let us examine several other cases. Suppose consumers are damaged by an automobile produced by a small foreign automobile manufacturer. Who would be sued if the parent corporation did not do business in the United States, but rather operated through an independent agent, a corporate front set up to absorb such liabilities?

What about situations in which the manufacturer of a product is not

35

apparent? Suppose a sales agency imports a product made by an unknown manufacturer. The sales agent takes the product and sells it. Later, a class suit is levied against the sales agent, who has taken care to have his corporate entity contain few assets.

It would seem that if class suits became a great risk businessmen would take steps to limit their personal liability and leave successful plaintiffs with judgments against nothing. Class suits strongly discriminate against the large, reputable American manufacturers to the benefit of the fly-by-night operator who is, from a practical standpoint, beyond the reach of such judgments. It is conceivable that a successful class suit against a significant U.S. corporation could bankrupt it. Who would benefit from such a development—competitors or consumers? Is this legal situation in the consumer's best interests? It is doubtful. Clearly, the class suit must be examined closely by all parties beforebeing used.

WHO PAYS THE PRICE?

State and federal governments now pay more than half the cost of a class suit, because the defense costs and judgments are legitimate business expenses. The remainder comes from earnings. The economic facts of life indicate that if class suits and other costs of consumerism become a fact of corporate life, then management will have to budget for such costs because those costs must be covered by the price obtained for the products the company sells. The result of imposing more stringent legal and quality control regulations on industry will be to raise prices. This should not be underestimated. Evidence from the space industry indicates that the marginal costs of increased quality are high. The consumer has been conditioned to expect perfection from technology but not to the price this perfection costs.

A valid question can be asked concerning the economic wisdom of consumerism: Is it socially wiser to accept the present market-determined rate of consumer dissatisfaction than to pay the marginal costs that will be incurred in reducing consumer dissatisfaction by government decree? Is the market willing to pay for these consumer recommendations? It may not be.

Only the well-established, reputable firm that fully intends to meet its costs and obligations under consumerism would be forced to raise its prices. Again, fly-by-night operators who are beyond the reach of the law from a practical standpoint would not have to include the costs of consumerism in their prices; therefore, such operators may become competitively stronger if consumers fail to discriminate between the reputable firm and the fly-by-night operation. Further, this problem will become increasingly acute in private label situations where the producing firm is unknown.

GUIDELINES FOR CORPORATE POLICY

Consumerism is here, and businesses should respond thoughtfully and rationally to the issues rather than react negatively or not at all. Several guidelines are developed below which businesses should follow in their response to consumerism.

* *Establish a separate corporate division for consumer affairs.* This division would participate in all corporate decisions that have consumer implications. It would participate in research and design, advertising, credit, pricing, quality assurance, and other similar decisions.
  It would respond to all consumer inquiries and complaints and would have the authority to make appropriate adjustments.
  It would be responsible for the development and dissemination of factual product and service information.
  It would work with industry or trade associations in the development of a consumer education program.
  The division must be given the status and power necessary for it to fulfill its mission. It should not be placed in a position in which either marketing or production forces could dilute its effectiveness. Possibly the wisdom of placing all quality assurance programs in the division should be carefully examined.
* *Change corporate practices that are perceived as deceptive.* The consumer affairs division should identify corporate practices that are perceived as deceptive and/or antagonistic by consumers. These practices should be reviewed and a viable resolution of the problem developed. Examples of such corporate practices include packaging, credit, advertising, warranties, and the like.
* *Educate channel members to the need for a consumerism effort throughout the channel system.* Recognition of the need for a consumerism effort by all members of the channel will aid in the development of an industry consumerism program which will enhance performance of the channel system and provide better customer satisfaction. Moreover, a firm must be willing to eliminate an organization from its overall channel system if that organization is unwilling or unable to work within the constraints of corporate policy.
* *Incorporate the increased costs of consumerism efforts into the corporate operating budget.* Unless the consumer affairs division is budgeted sufficient money to carry out its mission, it will be little more than a facade and its effectiveness will be hampered. These costs will be reflected either in higher prices or lower margins unless the consumer program affects sales sufficiently to lower costs commensurately. To date little or no research exists to document the market responses to such programs. However, it does seem apparent that substantial costs will be incurred by firms not meeting their responsibilities to the consumer because of both governmental and legal actions.

An analysis of the above guidelines suggests that an effective consumerism program will be directed primarily at the communications problem between firms and consumers. The main purpose of the consumerism program will be to enhance the quality of communications between the consumer and the firm and to incorporate valid complaints into corporate decisions.

The corporate leader has two basic options: He may take positive action in this matter, or he may ignore it. If he ignores it, he must be prepared for a government program. It would seem that the corporate decision maker should prefer to develop a consumerism program of his own. The alternative course of action, with its attendant governmental regulation and bureaucracy, would not be in the best interest of either the consumer or the firm because of its impact upon competition, prices, and consumer satisfaction.

NOTES

1. "Business Responds to Consumerism," *Business Week*, 2088 (September 6, 1969), pp. 94-108. "And Now, a Message From the Consumers," *Fortune*, 80 (November 1969), p. 103. "Buckpassing Blues," *Wall Street Journal*, 174 (November 3, 1969).

2. Peter Drucker, "Consumerism in Marketing," a speech to the National Association of Manufacturers, New York, April 1969.

3. "The Consumer Revolution," *U.S. News & World Report,* 68 (August 25, 1969), pp. 43-46.

4. "Caveat Emptor," *The Wall Street Journal*, 173 (June 26, 1969), p. 1.

5. Stuart Chase and F. J. Schlink, *Your Money's Worth* (New York: Macmillan, 1934).

6. "The Rush to Help Consumers," *U.S. News & World Report,* 67 (August 25, 1969), p. 47.

7. *Consumer Advisory Council, First Report*, Executive Office of the President (Washington, D.C.: United States Government Printing Office, October 1963), pp. 5-8.

8. "Appliance Maker Comes Clean," *Business Week*, 2088 (September 6, 1969), p. 100.

5. THE GREAT AMERICAN GYP

Ralph Nader

LAST JANUARY a confidential nationwide survey by the Opinion Research Corporation spread considerable alarm among its corporate subscribers. The poll concluded "that seven Americans in ten think present Federal legislation is inadequate to protect their health and safety. The majority also believe that more Federal laws are needed to give shoppers full value for their money." To many businessmen, this finding merely confirmed what speakers had been telling them at trade gatherings during the previous year—that consumers were beginning to fall prey to "consumerism."

"Consumerism" is a term given vogue recently by business spokesmen to describe what they believe is a concerted, disruptive ideology concocted by self-appointed bleeding hearts and politicians who find that it pays off to attack the corporations. "Consumerism," they say, undermines public confidence in the business system, deprives the consumer of freedom of choice, weakens state and local authority through Federal usurpation, bureaucratizes the marketplace, and stifles innovation. These complaints have all been made in speeches, in the trade press, and in Congressional testimony against such Federal bills as truth-in-lending, truth-in-packaging, gas pipeline safety, radiation protection, auto, tire, drug, and fire safety legislation, and meat and fish inspection.

But what most troubles the corporations is the consumer movement's relentless documentation that consumers are being manipulated, defrauded, and injured not just by marginal businesses or fly-by-night hucksters, but by the U.S. blue-chip business firms whose practices are unchecked by the older regulatory agencies. Since the consumer movement can cite statistics showing that these practices have reduced real income and raised the rates of mortality and disease, it is not difficult to understand the growing corporate concern.

That the systematic disclosure of such malpractice has been so long delayed can be explained by the strength of the myths that the business establishment has used to hide its activities. The first is the myth of the omniscient consumer who is so discerning that he will be a brutal taskmaster for any

Reprinted with permission from *The New York Review of Books*, Vol. 11 (November 21, 1968), 27-34. Copyright 1968; The New York Review.

firm entering the market. This approach was used repeatedly to delay, then weaken, the truth-in-packaging bill. Scott Paper Co. ran an advertising campaign hailing the American housewife as "The Original Computer: . . . a strange change comes over a woman in the store. The soft glow in the eye is replaced by a steely financial glint; the graceful walk becomes a panther's stride among the bargains. A woman in a store is a mechanism, a prowling computer. . . . Jungle-trained, her bargain-hunter senses razor-sharp for the sound of a dropping price. . . ." John Floberg, Firestone's General Counsel, has been even more complimentary, arguing that consumers can easily discriminate among 1,000 different brands of tires.

However, when companies plan their advertising, they fail to take advantage of the supposed genius of the consumer. Potential car buyers are urged to purchase Pontiacs to experience an unexplained phenomenon called "wide-tracking before you're too old to know what it is all about." Sizable fees are paid to "Motivation" experts like Ernest Dichter for such analysis as this: "Soup . . . is much more than a food. It is a potent magic that satisfies not only the hunger of the body but the yearnings of the soul. People speak of soup as a product of some mysterious alchemy, a symbol of love which satisfies mysterious gnawings. . . . The term 'pea soup'—mystery and magic—seem to go together with fog. At the same time we can almost say soup is orgiastic. Eating soup is a fulfillment."

A second myth is that most American businesses perform honorably but are subjected to undeserved notoriety because of a few small unscrupulous merchants and firms. This notion is peddled by so-called consumer protection agencies as well as by the business-dominated Better Business Bureaus. But the detailed Congressional hearings on drug hazards, unsafe vehicles, vicious credit practices, restraints on medically useful or dollar-saving innovations, auto insurance abuses, cigarette-induced diseases, and price-fixing throughout the economy have made it clear that this argument will not hold up.

Most misleading of all is the myth that irresponsible sellers are adequately policed by local, state, and Federal regulatory agencies. Years ago, corporations learned how to handle these agencies, and they have now become apologists for business instead of protectors of the public.

First, the agencies are made to operate on a starvation budget. The combined annual budget of the Federal Trade Commission and the Antitrust Division of the Justice Department in 1968 was $23 million, the highest amount yet appropriated. With this sum, they were supposed to collect data, initiate investigations, and enforce the laws dealing with deceptive and anticompetitive practices of a $350 billion economy.

Secondly, political patronage has undermined local and state consumer protection agencies; it has, for example, helped to make the Federal Trade Commission as ineffectual as it is.

Thirdly, business lobbying—including campaign contributions, powerful law firms, trade associations, and public relations—works against vigorous enforcement.

Finally, so many regulatory officials resign to go into high-paying jobs in the industries they were once supposed to regulate that these government posts are viewed as on-the-job training by cynical appointees.[1] The Federal Aviation Agency, Interstate Commerce Commission and the Federal Communications Commission all carry on a tradition that inhibits officials from action and attracts appointees who are temperamentally reluctant to act.

The increasing irrelevance of these older agencies was made apparent by the unprecedented consumer legislation enacted under the Johnson Administration. After the dismal spectacle of the cigarette labeling act of 1964—which foreclosed action by the states and the FTC in return for a paltry warning on the package that could serve as a company's defense in liability suits—Congress passed a string of important bills and has other legislation near passage. A shift of responsibilities for consumer protection to the Federal government now seems to be taking place: state and local governments have for years defaulted on these obligations to the consumer.

In no other period of history have the safety and prices of marketed products and services received remotely comparable legislative treatment. Sensing this climate, President Johnson allowed his consumer adviser, Betty Furness, to speak openly to business groups. In 1964, her predecessor, Esther Peterson, could not get White House clearance even to make a public statement about rigged odometers which misled motorists about the accuracy of mileage traveled, enriched car rental companies to the amount of $4 million a year, and encouraged automobile sales. In 1968, Miss Furness was urging appliance manufacturers to tell their customers how long they can expect their products to last. In 1969, President Johnson established the post of Consumer Counsel in the Justice Department—a first small step toward the creation of a Federal office which would have powers to intervene in cases before the courts and regulatory agencies as the representative of consumer interests.[2] In July, 1969, Vice-President Humphrey said he favored enlarging the counsel's powers to include making complaints about dangers to public health. He also became the first government official to endorse public disclosure of information about consumer products now in the files of the General Services Administration and the Department of Defense. These agencies test hundreds of consumer products—from light bulbs and bed sheets to washing machines—in order to determine which have the best value. But they have refused thus far to release the data that would rank products by quality—a refusal naturally supported by the business community.

The business world, meanwhile, has become increasingly adept in dealing with the rising pressures for consumer legislation. Tutored by their well-connected Washington lawyers, the large corporation and their trade associations can sense the critical moment at which it is wise to stop opposing a bill and begin to cooperate with Congressional committees in order to shape legislation to their liking. For example, after opposing the passage of any auto safety bill whatever, the auto manufacturers relented in the spring of 1966 and hired Lloyd Cutler, an experienced Washington lawyer, who succeeded in weakening the disclosure provisions of the bill and in eliminating all criminal penalties for willful and knowing violations of the law.

Although consumer measures may be weakened in this way, they do at least commit the government to the idea of consumer protection and they lay the groundwork for the stronger legislation that may be feasible should the consumer movement gain more strength. The attack on corporate irresponsibility which produced the recent flurry of legislation in Congress has not, it must be said, been the work of a broad movement but rather of tiny ad hoc coalitions of determined people in and out of government armed with little more than a great many shocking facts. They have gotten important support from Senator Warren Magnuson, Chairman of the Senate Commerce Committee, whose interest in consumer problems set in motion a little-noticed competition with the White House to promote legislation.

What has taken place during the last few years may be seen as an escalating series of disclosures. The charges made by independent Congressmen and people like myself almost always turn out to be understatements of the actual conditions in various industries when those industries are subsequently exposed in Congressional hearings and investigations. As these charges get attention, demands for new legislative action increases. This, at least, has been the case with the exposure of defects in vehicles, industrial and vehicle pollution, gas pipelines, overpriced or dangerous drugs, unfair credit, harmful pesticides, cigarettes, land frauds, electric power reliability, household improvement rackets, exploitation in slums, auto warranties, radiation, high-priced auto insurance, and boating hazards. How many people realized, for example, that faulty heating devices injure 125,000 Americans a year or that poorly designed stoves, power mowers, and washing machines cause substantial injury to 300,000 people annually? Or that, as Rep. Benjamin Rosenthal recently revealed, the food rejected by Federal agencies as contaminated or rotting is often rerouted for sale in the market? These abuses are now starting to be discussed in the press and in Congress.

One result of the detailed Congressional hearings has been a broader definition of legitimate consumer rights and interests. It is becoming clear that consumers must not only be protected from the dangers of voluntary use of a product, such as flammable material, but also from *involuntary* consumption of industrial by-products such as air and water pollutants, excessive pesticide and nitrate residues in foods, and antibiotics in meat. A more concrete idea of a just economy is thus beginning to emerge, while at the same time, the assortment of groups that comprise the "consumer's movement" is moving in directions that seem to me quite different from the ones that similar groups have followed in the past. Their demands are ethical rather than ideological. Their principles and proposals are being derived from solid documentation of common abuses whose origins are being traced directly to the policies of powerful corporations.

This inquiry is extending beyond the question of legal control of corporations into the failure of business, labor, and voluntary organizations to check one another's abuses through competition and other private pressures. It is becoming apparent that the reform of consumer abuses and the reform of corporate power itself are different sides of the same coin and that new approaches to the enforcement of the rights of consumers are necessary. There are, I would suggest, at least ten major forces or techniques that now exist in some form, but greatly need to be strengthened if we are to have a decent consumer society.

Consumerism

1. Rapid disclosure of the facts relating to the quantity, quality, and safety of a product is essential to a just marketplace. If companies know their products can quickly be compared with others, the laggard will be goaded to better performance and the innovator will know that buyers can promptly learn about his innovation. On the other hand, buyers must be able to compare products in order to reject the shoddy and reward the superior producer. This process is the great justification for a free market system. Manufacturers try to avoid giving out such information and instead rely on "packaging" or advertising. Auto companies refuse to tell the motorist the safety performances of his car's brakes and tires, and concentrate on brand names—Cougar, Baracuda, Marauder—and vehicle "personality": "Mustang makes dull people interesting. . . ." From cosmetics to soaps and detergents, the differences emphasized are emotional and frivolous and have no relation to functions. This practice permits the producer with the largest advertising budget to make matters very difficult for a smaller competitor or potential entrant into the market who may have a superior product. The anti-competitive effects of such advertising led Donald F. Turner, the former head of the Anti-trust Division of the Justice Department, to suggest that the government subsidize independent sources of consumer information. Senator Philip Hart has gone a step further in proposing a National Consumer Service Foundation to provide product information to consumers at the place of purchase. Computers could help to assemble such information cheaply and quickly. One can, for instance, imagine machines dispensing data on individual products at shopping centers, a plan which Consumer's Union has begun to study.

2. The practices of refunding dollars to consumers who have been bilked and recalling defective products are finally becoming recognized as principles of deterrence and justice. More than six million automobiles have been recalled since September, 1966—the date of the auto safety law. The Food and Drug Administration now requires drug companies to issue "corrective letters" to all physicians if their original advertisements were found to be misleading. Nearly 30 such letters were sent out by drug companies during the first 20 months of FDA action. The threat of liability suits and the willingness of the press and television to mention brand and company names in reporting on defects are causing companies to recall products "voluntarily" even where no law or regulation exists. Earlier this year, for instance, Sears-Roebuck recalled some 6,000 gas heaters after public health officials warned of lethal carbon monoxide leakage. After similar warnings by U.S. Public Health officials and the threat of disclosure by a major newspaper, General Electric made changes in 150,000 color TV sets which had been found to be emitting excessive radiation. Some insurance companies are beginning to offer "defect recall" insurance.

The duty to refund remains even less well recognized than the duty to recall a product because of defects. Orders to "cease and desist," the usual decree of the Federal Trade Commission after it catches swindlers, at best stop the defrauder but do not require him to pay back the funds. Without this sanction a major deterrent is lost. The mere order to "go and sin no more," which replaces it, is easily evaded.

The only enforcement action made by the FTC is pertinent here. For 30 years, the Holland Furnace Company used scare tactics and routinely deceived the public. Its salesmen were encouraged to pose as "safety inspectors" and were trained to be merciless: one elderly and ailing woman was sold nine new furnaces in six years, costing a total of $18,000. Following up on complaints beginning in the Thirties, the FTC secured a stipulation from the company that it would stop its misleading advertising. This had little if any effect. A cease and desist order was entered in 1958 but it was not until January, 1965, that the company was fined $100,000 for violating the order and an ex-president was sent to jail. At that point, the Holland Furnace Co. decided to file a petition for bankruptcy. But as Senator Warren Magnuson said: "In the meantime Holland Furnace at the height of its business cost the American public $30 million a year." The FTC's ponderous procedures and anemic enforcement powers (it has no power of preliminary injunction, no criminal penalties, and no power of its own to fine, assess, or award damages) encourage the unscrupulous businessman to continue his abuses; if he is caught later on, he will merely be told to stop.

Two developments in recent years have strengthened private actions against malpractices by established corporations with large assets. The first is the growing practice of filing treble damage suits against violators of antitrust laws. In the early Sixties, corporate and government customers of G.E., Westinghouse, and other large companies collected about $500 million in out-of-court settlements after these companies and their officers were convicted for carrying on a criminal antitrust price-fixing conspiracy. Although such punitive damage payments were tax-deductible as "ordinary and necessary business expenses,"[3] the deterrent was an effective one. Cases brought by both private and government procurement agencies have multiplied in many other industries recently—from drugs to children's books—and these will increase, especially with tougher antitrust action by the Justice Department and by the states.

The second development is in the use of "class actions" in which suits are filed on behalf of large numbers of people who have been mistreated in the same way. In modern mass merchandising, fraud naturally takes the form of cheating a great many customers out of a few pennies or dollars: the bigger the store or chain of stores, the greater the gain from gypping tiny amounts from individuals who would not find it worthwhile to take formal action against the seller. Class actions solve this problem by turning the advantage of large volume against the seller that made predatory use of it in the first place. Poverty lawyers, supported by the U.S. Office of Economic Opportunity, are just beginning to use this important technique.

A case of great potential significance for developing broad civil deterrence has been brought in New York City against Coburn Corp., a sales finance company, by two customers who signed its retail installment contracts. They are being assisted by the NAACP Legal Defense and Educational Fund. The plaintiffs charge that Coburn violated Section 402 of the New York Personal Property Law by not printing its contracts in large type as specified by law. They are asking recovery of the credit service charge paid under the contracts for themselves and all other consumers similarly involved. If the plaintiffs win, consumers in New York will be able to bring class actions against any violations of law contained in any standard form contracts.

3. Disputes in courts and other judicial forums must be conducted under fairer ground rules and with adequate representation for buyers. Here the recent appearance of neighborhood legal service attorneys is a hopeful sign. These poverty lawyers—now numbering about 2,000 and paid by the Office of Economic Opportunity—are representing the poor against finance companies, landlords, auto dealers, and other sellers of goods and services. Because of their work, the law of debtors' remedies and defenses is catching up with the well-honed law of creditors' rights that generations of law students studied so rigrously. These lawyers are bringing test cases to court and winning them. They are gradually exposing the use by slum merchants of the courts as agents to collect from poor people who are uninformed or cannot leave their jobs to show up in court. For the first time, poverty lawyers are challenging the routine contract clauses that strip the buyers of their legal defenses in advance, as well as those involving illegal repossession, unreasonable garnishment, undisclosed credit, and financing terms, and a great many other victimizing practices.

But even many more poverty lawyers could handle only a few of the cases deserving their services. What is important is that recent cases are documenting a general pattern of abuses and injustices in the legal system itself. This is beginning to upset influential lawyers; it may prod law schools to more relevant teaching as well as guide legislatures and courts toward much-delayed reform of laws, court procedures, and remedies. At the same time, wholly new and more informed ways of resolving conflicts are being considered—such as neighborhood arbitration units which are open in the evenings when defendants need not be absent from their work. However, if such developments seem promising they must not obscure the persisting venality of the marketplace and the generally hopeless legal position of the consumer who is victimized by it.

4. The practice of setting government safety standards and periodically changing them to reflect new technology and uses is spreading, although it is still ineffective in many ways. Decades after banking and securities services were brought under regulation, products such as automobiles (53,000 dead and 4-1/2 million injured annually), washing machines and power lawn mowers (200,000 injuries annually), many chemicals, and all pipelines did not have to adhere to any standards of safety performance other than those set by the companies or industries themselves. With the passage of the auto safety law in 1966, other major products have been brought under Federal safety regulation. To avoid continuing a piecemeal approach, Congress in 1967 passed an act establishing the National Commission on Product Safety to investigate many household and related hazards, from appliances to household chemicals. Moreover, the Commission must recommend by this year a more detailed Federal, state, and local policy toward reducing or preventing deaths and injuries from these products.

The Commission's recommendations will probably go beyond household products to the problem of a safer man-made environment. So far, most state

45

and Federal efforts to set meaningful safety standards and enforce them have failed miserably. The only organized and effective pressures on the agencies responsible for setting standards have come from the same economic interests that are supposed to be regulated. Two illustrations of this failure have been the Flammable Fabrics Act of 1953 and the Oil Pipeline Safety Act of 1965. In both cases, little has happened because the laws have not been administered. It took three-and-a-half years before the Federal government even proposed oil pipeline standards, and these were taken almost verbatim from the pipeline industry's own code. Similarly, when the General Accounting Office recently reviewed the enforcement of the pesticide law by the Department of Agriculture it found that repeated mass violations of the laws between 1955 and 1965 were never reported to the Department for prosecution. This is a typical example of how consumers are deprived of legal protection in spite of a statute intended toprotect them.

5. If the government is to impose effective standards, it must also be able to conduct or contract for its own research on both the safety of industrial products and possible methods of improving them. Without this power, the agencies will have to rely on what is revealed to them by industry, and their efforts will be crippled from the start. They will, for example, be unable to determine whether a better vehicle handling system is required or to detect promptly the hidden dangers in apparently harmless drugs. The government could also bring strong pressures on business by using its own great purchasing power and by developing its own prototypes of safer products. The existing safety laws, however, do not even permit the government to find out quickly and accurately whether industry is complying with the law. The National Highway Safety Bureau, for example, had little idea whether or not the 1968 automobiles met all the safety standards since no Government testing facilities existed.

But full enforcement of the law also depends on the existence of effective penalties, and in this respect the recent safety laws are feeble, to say the least. There are no criminal penalties for willful and knowing violation of the auto safety, gas pipeline, radiation control, and similar laws. The civil fines are small when considered against the possibility of violations by huge industries producing millions of the same product. Of course, the Washington corporation lawyers who lobby to water down the penalties in these safety laws have no interest in the argument that stronger sanctions would not only act as a deterrent to industry but make enforcement cheaper.

6. In the ideology of American business, free competition and corporate "responsibility" are supposed to protect the consumer; in practice both have long been ignored. Price-fixing, either by conspiracy or by mutually understood cues, is rampant throughout the economy. This is partly revealed by the growing number of government and private antitrust actions. Donald Turner, the former head of the Antitrust Division, has despaired of effectively enforcing the law against price-fixing with the existing manpower in the Justice Department. Price-fixing, of course, means higher prices for consumers. For example, the electrical price-fixing conspiracy, broken by the Justice Department in 1960, involved not only G.E., Westinghouse, Allis Chalmers, but several small

companies as well; the overcharge to the direct purchasers of generators and other heavy duty equipment was estimated at more than a billion dollars during the ten-year life of the conspiracy that sent several executives to short jailterms.

Even greater dangers arise when the failure of large industry to compete prevents the development of new products that might save or improve the lives of consumers. When such restraint is due to conspiracy or other kinds of collusion, it should be the task of antitrust enforcement to stop the practice of "product-fixing." Traditional antitrust enforcement has been slow to grasp the fact that the restraint of innovation is becoming far more important to big business than the control of prices. New inventions—steam or electric engines, longer lasting light bulbs and paints, and cheaper construction materials—can shake an industry to its most stagnant foundations. For 18 months the Justice Department presented to a Los Angeles grand jury its charges that the domestic auto companies conspired to restrain the development and marketing of vehicle exhaust control systems. When and if it files its complaint, a pioneering case of antitrust enforcement in a health and safety issue could reveal much about this as yet unused weapon for public protection.

Ideally, one of the most powerful forces for consumer justice would be the exercise of corporate responsibility or private "countervailing" and monitoring forces within the corporate world. Unfortunately for believers in a pluralist economic system recent decades have shown that the economics of accommodation repeatedly overwhelms the economics of checks and balances.

The casualty insurance industry is a case in point. Logically it should have a strong interest in safer automobiles. In fact it has chosen to raise premiums instead of pressuring the auto industry to adopt safety measures that have been available for a long time. The casualty insurance industry has not demanded legislation to improve the design and inspection of motor vehicles; nor has it encouraged the rating of vehicles according to their safety. It has been equally indifferent to the need to reform methods of fire prevention (where the U.S. is far behind Japan and England) or standards of industrial safety and health. What the industry has done instead is to spend large sums on advertising assuring the public it is concerned about the consumer safety it has declined to pursue in practice.

7. Professional and technical societies may be sleeping giants where the protection of the consumer is concerned. Up to now, such groups as the American Society of Mechanical Engineers, the American Chemical Society, and the American Society of Safety Engineers have been little more than trade associations for the industries that employ their members. It is shocking, for example, that none of these technical societies has done much to work out public policies to deal with the polluted environment and with such new technological hazards as atomic energy plants and radioactive waste disposal. Except in a few cases, the independent professions of law and medicine have done little to fulfill their professional obligations to protect the public from victimization. They have done less to encourage their colleagues in science and engineering to free themselves from subservience to corporate disciplines.

47

Surely, for example, the supersonic transport program, with its huge government subsidies and intolerable sonic boom, should have been exposed to careful public scrutiny by engineers and scientists long before the government rather secretively allowed it to get under way.

The engineers and scientists, however, had no organization or procedure for doing this. None of the professions will be able to meet its public responsibilities unless it is willing to undertake new roles and to create special independent organizations willing to gather facts and take action in the public interest. Such small but determined groups as the Committee for Environmental Information in St. Louis, headed by Professor Barry Commoner, and the Physicians for Automotive Safety in New Jersey have shown how people with tiny resources can accomplish much in public education and action. If such efforts are to be enlarged, however, the legal, medical, engineering, and scientific departments of universities must recognize the importance of preparing their graduates for full-time careers in organizations devoted to shaping public policy; for it is clear that professionals serving clients in private practice will not be adequate to this task. Had such organizations existed two or three decades ago, the hazards of the industrial age might have been foreseen, diagnosed, exposed, and to some extent prevented. During the recent controversy over auto safety, I often speculated that the same kind of reform might have occurred 30 years ago had a handful of engineers and physicians made a dramatic effort to inform politicians about scandals that even then took more than 30,000 lives a year and caused several million injuries. Instead the doctors were busy treating broken bones and the engineers were following corporate orders, while their technical journals ignored a major challenge to their profession. For all the talk about "preventive medicine" and "remedial engineering," this is what is happening now.

8. During the past two decades, the courts have been making important if little noticed rulings that give injured people fairer chances of recovering damages. These include the elimination of "privity" or the need to prove a contractual relation with the person sued; the expansion of the "implied warranty" accompanying items purchased to include not only the "reasonable" functioning of those items but also the claims made in deceptive advertising of them; and the imposition of "strict liability" which dispenses with the need to prove negligence if one has been injured through the use of a defective product. At the same time, the laws of evidence have been considerably liberalized.

This reform of the common law of "bodily rights"—far in advance of other common-law nations such as Great Britain and Canada—has been followed by some spectacular jury verdicts and court decisions in favor of the injured. These are routinely cited by insurance companies as a rationale for increasing premiums. The fact is, however, that these victories still are rare exceptions, and for obvious reasons. Winning such cases requires a huge investment in time and money: the plaintiff's lawyer must collect the evidence and survive the long and expensive delays available to the corporation defendant with its far superior resources. But now the rules give the plaintiff at least a decent chance to recover his rights in court or by settlement. It remains for the legal profession to find ways to cut drastically the costs of litigation, especially in cases where a single product, such as a car or drug, has injured many people.

However, the law of torts (personal injuries) still does not protect the consumer against the pollution of the environment which indiscriminately injures everyone exposed to it. Pollution in Los Angeles is a serious health hazard, but how may the citizen of that besmogged metropolis sue? A group of eighty-eight residents of Martinez, California, is suing Shell Oil's petroleum refinery for air pollution and its "roaring noises, recurring vibrations and frightening lights." In an increasingly typical defense, Shell claims that it meets the state's mild pollution-control regulation. But such standards are largely the result of political pressures from corporations whose profits are at stake. Thus, increasingly, justice in the courts must be paralleled by justice in the legislatures. However, there are some signs that the courts are beginning to take account of the right to a decent environment in cases against industrial pollutants. In 1967, a lady in Pennsylvania recovered about $70,000 for injuries sustained from living near a beryllium plant which emitted toxic fumes daily. (The case was appealed.)

9. One of the more promising recent developments is the growing belief that new institutions are needed within the Government whose sole function would be to advocate consumer interests. As I have pointed out, the Johnson Administration has done no more than create in 1968 an Office of Consumer Counsel in the Justice Department. The Executive Branch has been hostile to a proposal by Congressman Rosenthal and others for a new Department of Consumer Affairs on the Cabinet level. This proposal has been criticized by Federal officials on grounds that it would duplicate what government agencies are now doing. The fact is, however, that most of the government agencies that are supposed to be concerned with the health and safety of consumers are also promoting the interests of the industries that cause the consumer harm. The U.S. Department of Agriculture represents the farmers and processors first and the consumer second—whether in controversies over the price of milk or over the wholesomeness of meat and poultry. The regulatory agencies themselves at best merely act as referees and at worst represent business interests in government.

Clearly it would be useful if a new bureau within the Government itself could both expose these regulatory agencies and challenge them to take more vigorous action. Senator Lee Metcalf has introduced legislation to create an independent Office of Utility Consumer's Counsel to represent the public before regulatory agencies and courts. This approach is different from that of Congressman Rosenthal and it remains to be seen which scheme can best avoid the dangers of bureaucratization and atrophy. What is not generally appreciated however is that, if they are to succeed, such new governmental units will badly need the vigorous support of organizations outside the government which would have similar concern for the consumer and would also be able to carry on their own research and planning.

10. I have already pointed out the need for independent organizations of professionals—engineers, lawyers, doctors, economists, scientists, and others

—which could undertake work of this kind. But they do not as yet exist. Still, we can draw some idea of their potential from the example of people like Dr. Commoner and his associates who have managed to stir up strong public opposition to Government and private interests while working in their spare time. Similarly, other small groups of professionals have saved natural resources from destruction or pollution; they have stopped unjust increases in auto-insurance rates; they have defeated a plan for an atomic explosion to create a natural gas storage area under public land, showing that excessive safety risks were involved.

Is there reason to hope that the high energy physicists who lobbied successfully for hundreds of millions of dollars in public funds might be emulated by other professionals seeking to improve the quality of life in America? Certainly there is a clear case for setting up professional firms to act in the public interest at Federal and local level. While thousands of engineers work for private industry, a few hundred should be working out the technical plans for obtaining clean air and water, and demanding that these plans be followed. While many thousands of lawyers serve private clients, several hundred should be working in public interest firms which would pursue legal actions and reforms of the kind I have outlined here. Support for such firms could come from foundations, private gifts, dues paid by consumers and the professions, or from government subsidies. There is already a precedent for the latter in the financing of the Neighborhood Legal Services, not to mention the billions of dollars in subsidies now awarded to commerce and industry. In addition, groups that now make up the consumers' movement badly need the services of professional economists, lawyers, engineers, and others if they are to develop local consumer service institutions that could handle complaints, dispense information, and work out strategies for public action.

Notwithstanding the recent alarm of industry and the surge of publicity about auto safety and other scandals, the consumer movement is still a feeble force in American power politics. The interests of consumers are low on the list of election issues; the government's expenditure to protect those interests are negligible. Some would argue that this situation will inevitably prevail in view of the overwhelming power of American corporations in and out of government. But, as I have tried to show, new approaches to judging and influencing corporate behavior have begun to emerge in the last few years. It seems possible that people may begin to react with greater anger to the enormity of their deprivation—each year consumers lose half a billion dollars in securities frauds and a billion dollars in home repair frauds, to name only two of thousands of ways in which their income is being milked. The current assault on health and safety of the public from so many dangerous industrial products, by-products, and foods has resulted in violence that dwarfs the issue of crime in the streets. (In a recent three-year period, about 260 people died in American cities; but every two days, 300 people are killed, and 20,000 injured, while driving on the highways.) What the consumer movement is beginning to say—and must say much more strongly if it is to grow—is that business crime and corporate intransigence are the really urgent menace to law and order in America.

NOTES

1. Two recent chairmen of the Interstate Commerce Commission later became President of the National Association of Motor Business Carriers and Vice-President of Penn-Central. Both industries are supposedly regulated by the ICC.
2. The first appointee to this job was Mr. Merle McCurdy who died in May, 1969.
3. Starting in 1970, only one-third of such damages are deductible.

PART THREE

*

Government
and
Consumerism

INTRODUCTION

Government and Consumerism

IN THE previous section, we saw that leadership from the White House is necessary for the implementation of the objectives and legislation of consumerism. White House support for the consumer movement began with President John F. Kennedy's March 15, 1962 message to Congress. Providing the broad outline of the consumer movement goals, the message stated consumer rights: (1) The right to safety; (2) The right to be heard; (3) The right to be informed; and (4) The right to choose.

President Lyndon Johnson reaffirmed these rights and expanded the federal government's area of interest to specifics, i.e., sales rackets, automobile insurance, and product warranties. There was also increased emphasis upon the health and safety issues associated with the meat, fish, and poultry industries. During Johnson's administration a great deal of consumer legislation was passed—in the food area the Wholesome Meat Act of 1967 and the Wholesome Poultry Act of 1968; in the area of truthful disclosure the Fair Packaging and Labeling Act of 1966 (Truth-in-Packaging), the Fair Credit and Lending Act of 1968 (Truth-in-Lending), and the Interstate Land Sales Disclosure provisions of 1968.

President Richard Nixon also supported the rights of consumers with his "Buyers Bill of Rights." Under his administration the Office of Consumer Affairs came into existence; its function was to coordinate federal activities in the field of consumer protection and to establish guidelines for consumer education.

The primary thrust of the Nixon Administration was to increase the scope and power of the Federal Trade Commission. This was to be accomplished by ensuring that consumer interest was represented in the regulatory process and by seeing that the commission enforced consumer legislation for which it was responsible.

The Murray article traces the development of federal consumer legislation. Historically the concern of the federal government, as the Bralove article indicates, was with health and safety issues of the food and drug industries—usually after exposé of the dangers and health hazards as in Upton Sinclair's *The Jungle*. With the passage of the Federal Trade Commission Act of 1914, the FTC was to protect the consumer against unfair competitive acts. The extended interpretations of the power of the commission, provided within the act, has expanded the commission's role so that it is the primary regulatory agency concerned with consumer protection. Some of the acts that the commission is responsible for administering are: (1) Wool Products Labeling Act 1939, (2) Fur Products Labeling Act 1951, (3) Textile Fiber Labeling Act 1958, (4) Cigarette Labeling and Advertising Act 1966, and (5) Fair Packaging and Labeling Act 1968.

Other agencies responsible for the enforcement of consumer legislation are: (1) the Department of Transportation for the National Traffic and Motor Vehicle Act of 1966, (2) the Department of Housing and Urban Development for the Interstate Land Sales, and (3) the Federal Reserve Board for the Fair Credit and Lending Act of 1968.

States also are becoming involved in consumer protection. As the Bylin article indicates, the state interest has been primarily with respect to repair services. The overall emphasis of the federal legislation has been to maintain the operationality of the consumer sovereignty assumption by maintaining information flows to the consumer. The thrust of the legislation has been to require disclosure of accurate and truthful information to the consumer so that he can make rational purchase decisions.

6. AN AGENCY IN CALIFORNIA IS MODEL IN CAMPAIGN TO CURB REPAIR FRAUDS

James E. Bylin

A STATE agent lurked in the background while an undercover operative, a housewife, waited for the suspect to arrive at the stakeout in El Monte, a Los Angeles suburb.

For months, the agent had dogged the man, a television repairman named Lawrence A. Goldberg, but he would continually drop out of sight, keeping one step ahead of the authorities. This time, though, Mr. Goldberg drove up on time in a Lincoln Continental, entered the house and unwittingly committed his crime in front of witnesses.

He "repaired" a TV set—by installing two tubes it didn't need. Mr. Goldberg subsequently was arrested. He pleaded guilty to charges of petty theft and operating without a license and was fined, placed on probation and ordered not to engage in TV repair. But he later violated the order and was rearrested, convicted and fined again.

This cloak-and-dagger operation was engineered by a small California agency that is looming big these days in the consumer-protection field, not only here but nationally. Charged with ferreting out fraud in the repair of TV sets, radios and record players, the agency—known as the Bureau of Repair Services—asserts that it saves California consumers more than $15 million annually. And that's a very conservative estimate, officials maintain. The bureau employs only 11 people and spends a relatively miniscule $300,000 a year, all collected in registration fees by repair dealers.

"AT THE END OF THE TUBE"

Last July, *Consumer Reports*, the consumer-affairs magazine, investigated the bureau in detail and decided its approach might represent the "light at the end of the tube" in the war against TV repair fraud. *Consumer Reports* recommended that other states "could well pattern regulation on California's." Several states already have enacted similar laws in recent years, including Florida, Oregon, Indiana, Louisiana, Massachusetts and Connecticut, though some don't go as far as a 1970 Florida law that was copied almost exactly from California's.

"At least a dozen more states are considering such laws," says a bureau official.

The Bureau of Repair Services' influence is spreading in other ways, too. Using it as a prototype, the California legislature recently enacted after a three-year fight what is generally considered to be the stiffest crackdown by any state on auto-repair fraud. This law could also become a forerunner for consumer legislation in other states. It establishes a self-financed Bureau of Automotive Repair that, like the Bureau of Repair Services, will investigate customer complaints and inspect repair shops, with violators being subject to fines up to $1,000 and six months in jail.

Auto repair dealers must register with the state by next June 30, at which time the Bureau of Auto Repair will be in full swing. The stakes in the auto-repair field will be much higher than in TV repairs. There are an estimated 40,000 auto-repair outlets in California, compared with 6,200 TV-radio-phonograph repair dealers currently registered with the Bureau of Repair Services. (TV-repair complaints account for about 90% of the bureau's work-load.)

CONSUMERISM'S DARK AGES

The Bureau of Repair Services was spawned in what now could be considered the dark ages of consumer legislation. In the late 1950s, officials in the TV repair industry proposed that the state test and then license repairmen for competency. The legislature, though, rejected the motion several times on the ground that it could lead to a closed shop. Meanwhile, state officials became increasingly aware that the real problem was fraud, not a repairman's competency. The result, in 1963, was the bureau's establishment, with its powers to investigate and bring criminal charges as well as to administratively revoke dealer registrations.

The TV-repair industry, realizing shady dealers were hurting the entire industry, supported creation of the bureau. In fact, the industry fought a 1968 move by the administration of Gov. Ronald Reagan to abolish the bureau in an economy move. "We felt it was somewhat like taking a lighthouse off a reef," recalls Ralph Johonnot, executive director of the California State Electronics Association, a 1,500-member trade group. However, much of the auto repair industry, especially oil companies with their vast networks of service stations, fought registration of auto-repair shops until this past legislative session, when they adopted a neutral stance. "What looked like a turkey three years ago now looked like a motherhood issue," says an aide to state Sen. Anthony Beilenson, sponsor of the auto-repair bill.

The Bureau of Repair Services, which has processed some 19,000 complaints, figures it has slashed the instances of fraud by at least one-third. But it still has plenty to do.

Incidences of TV-repair fraud are most prevalent in the urban areas like Los Angeles and San Francisco, according to William J. Hayes, the bureau's assistant chief. Shady dealers "like to prey on the elderly," Mr. Hayes says. "They feel they're vulnerable." Paradoxically, he adds, the elderly also are the ones who "have the time to write us with detailed complaints." The fraud itself, of course, can come in many forms.

RANSOMED SETS

Dealers may charge for parts they haven't installed or labor they haven't done, or they may put in unneeded parts. Some will hold sets for ransom—"setnapping," in the trade parlance. In such a case, a dealer finds an excuse to take the set to the shop and then demands an exorbitant price for the customer to get it back. Others misleadingly advertise low-priced service calls that, it turns out, don't include any labor or parts, just the repairman coming to the house.

"We had one dealer who charged low for a house call, but he also charged for everything he did once he got there," recalls Mr. Hayes. "He would even charge so much a screw as he took them out of the back of the set." As a result, his bill would run as high as 10 times normal, Mr. Hayes says.

The bureau has no jurisdiction over prices charged, but at times it can evoke a "gross negligence" stipulation in the law to settle a dispute. "We had one dealer who charged $18 for an 80-cent part," Mr. Hayes says. "Now, we consider that gross negligence." The dealer was persuaded to make compensation.

Under the law, a dealer must supply an estimate, orally or in writing, if requested, and his bill can't exceed the estimate without prior approval. Donald Peacock, the bureau's chief, laments that too many people skip this safeguard. "The public is gullible as hell," he sighs. "We're trying to educate them, but it's the consumer's own fault if he doesn't ask for an estimate."

As an example, officials point to a dealer who is the target of a large number of complaints. He openly charges $24.50 for a service call, compared with an average of $15. The man's repairmen are also trained salesmen who can "sell tubes like crazy," says Mr. Peacock. "It's all legal, but it is overselling. After they leave, people realize, 'My God, this guy got to me.' People should shop around more."

Mr. Hayes says the bureau is more interested in compliance with the law than in prosecution, and thousands of complaints have been informally adjusted through negotiations to the benefit of the consumer. Sometimes, of course, the repairman isn't at fault; about 20% of the complaints are termed unjustified.

But the bureau has helped jail about a dozen repairmen over the years, and nearly 200 others have received suspended sentences and been placed on three years' probation. Mr. Hayes says he usually prefers probation to a 30-day or 60-day jail sentence because then "we can hold the probation over his head for three years. If he even spits on the sidewalk, he's back in jail." Dozens of other dealers have had their registrations revoked.

The bureau's mere existence is a major deterrent to fraud, officials feel. Not long ago, an agent stopped at a repair shop in Santa Cruz, where he fell into conversation with the owner, who was congratulating himself for "outwitting" a state agent. The dealer explained that a well-dressed customer driving a new car had stopped by a few days earlier with a brand new set that worked perfectly. The dealer said he immediately spotted it as a state "plant" and didn't do any work on it. The agent had the last laugh, however; the customer had had nothing to do with the state.

Five field agents work for the bureau. All are trained repairmen. Their chief weapons are well-equipped electronic laboratories in both Sacramento and Los Angeles and about 100 TV sets. Parts in the sets are carefully marked and intentional malfunctions noted, and the sets then are taken to dealers who have been the subject of complaints. Usually, at least two cases of fraud by a dealer are documented before action is taken.

Officials find that some repairmen have become adept at spotting state sets. One Southern California dealer recognized a state-owned set and left a card inside it reading "Hello George" as a greeting to an agent.

To combat this, agents have devised ways to replace dust and cobwebs in their sets to make them seem untouched for years. In preparing a set, agents try to find one that matches the decor of the home or apartment used for a stakeout. The agents prefer to have them serviced in the home in order to know what individual did the work. Wives of state employees or local policemen are usually enlisted as undercover operators to handle this chore.

Not all shady dealers are master crooks. One was prosecuted three times—he kept returning to the same town under the same name even though he wasn't registered. "He was real easy to catch," Mr. Peacock says. "The third time the judge banned him from the state. I didn't know he could do that."

7. THE AMERICAN CONSUMER

Lyndon B. Johnson

To the Congress of the United States:

SPEAKING FOR every American, I present to the Congress my fourth Message on the American Consumer.

President Truman once observed that while some Americans have their interests protected in Washington by special lobbying groups, most of the people depend on the President of the United States to represent their interests.

In the case of consumer protection, however, the President—and the Congress—speak for every citizen.

A hundred years ago, consumer protection was largely unnecessary. We were a rural nation then: a nation of farms and small towns. Even in the growing cities, neighborhoods were closely knit.

Most products were locally produced and there was a personal relationship between the seller and the buyer. If the buyer had a complaint, he went straight to the miller, the blacksmith, the tailor, the corner grocer. Products were less complicated. It was easy to tell the excellent from the inferior.

Today all this is changed. A manufacturer may be thousands of miles away from his customer—and even further removed by distributors, wholesalers and retailers. His products may be so complicated that only an expert can pass judgment on their quality.

We are able to sustain this vast and impersonal system of commerce because of the ingenuity of our technology and the honesty of our businessmen.

But this same vast network of commerce, this same complexity, also presents opportunities for the unscrupulous and the negligent.

It is the government's role to protect the consumer—and the honest businessman alike—against fraud and indifference. Our goal must be to assure every American consumer a fair and honest exchange for his hard-earned dollar.

Reprinted from "The American Consumer," President Lyndon B. Johnson's message to Congress, February 6, 1968 (Washington: Library of Congress, Legislative Reference Service).

THE RECORD OF PROGRESS

Thanks to the work of the last two Congresses, we are now much closer to that goal than ever before. In three years, we have taken historic steps to protect the consumer against:

> Impure and unwholesome meat.
> Death and destruction on our highways.
> Misleading labels and packages.
> Clothing and blankets that are fire-prone, rather than fire-proof.
> Hazardous appliances and products around the house.
> Toys that endanger our children.
> Substandard clinical laboratories.
> Unsafe tires.

In addition to these, the first session of this Congress took important steps toward passage of other consumer proposals we recommended last year, including the Truth-in-Lending, Fire Safety and Pipeline Safety bills which passed the Senate, and the fraudulent land sales, mutual funds and electric power reliability measures.

This session of the Congress should complete action on these vitally needed proposals to protect the public. It has already begun to do so.

In passing the Truth-in-Lending Bill last week, the House of Representatives brought every American consumer another step closer to knowing the cost of money he borrows. I urge the House and Senate to resolve their differences promptly and to give the consumer a strong Truth-in-Lending law.

A NEW PROGRAM FOR 1968

But that record alone, as comprehensive as it is, will not complete our responsibility. The needs of the consumer change as our Society changes, and legislation must keep pace.

For 1968, I propose a new eight-point program to:

> Crack down on fraud and deception in sales.
> Launch a major study of automobile insurance.
> Protect Americans against hazardous radiation from television sets and other electronic equipment.
> Close the gaps in our system of poultry inspection.
> Guard the consumer's health against unwholesome fish.
> Move now to prevent death and accidents on our waterways.
> Add new meaning to warranties and guarantees, and seek ways to improve repair work and servicing.
> Appoint a government lawyer to represent the consumer.

SALES RACKETS

Every Spring, when families turn their thoughts to household improvements, the shady operator goes to work.

His office may be a telephone booth, a briefcase which he carries from door to door, or a car which he drives from state to state. His sales brochure may be a catchy newspaper advertisement.

With false and deceptive offers of attractive home repairs or items that are more promise than product, he preys most of all on those who are least able to protect themselves: the poor, the elderly, the ignorant.

Too often—and too late—the victim discovers that he has been swindled: that he has paid too much, that he has received inferior work, and that he has mortgaged himself into long-term debt. Some even lose their homes. A recent Report of the National Better Business Bureau estimates that deceptive practices in the home improvement field alone cost the consumer between $500 million and $1 billion yearly.

Sales rackets are not limited to home improvements. And sales rackets of all types are on the increase.

As the law now stands, there is no effective way to stop these unscrupulous practices when they are discovered. The legal machinery may drag on for two or three years before the violator can be ordered to cease and desist. In the meantime, countless more Americans are cheated.

In matters so flagrantly deceptive, the consumer and the honest businessman deserve greater—and speedier—protection.

I recommend that the Congress enact the Deceptive Sales Act of 1968 to give new powers to the Federal Trade Commission.

Under this Act, the FTC would be able to obtain Federal court orders to stop fraudulent and deceptive practices immediately while the case is before the Commission or the courts.

With this measure we can complete the cycle of protection for the consumer in fraud cases—by adding Federal court injunctions to the administrative and criminal processes which now exist.

AUTOMOBILE INSURANCE

One area of major concern to the consumer is automobile insurance. Every motorist, every passenger, and every pedestrian is affected by it—yet the system is overburdened and unsatisfactory.

Premiums are rising—in some parts of the country they have increased by as much as 30 percent over the past six years.

Arbitrary coverage and policy cancellations are the cause of frequent complaint—particularly from the elderly, the young, the serviceman, and the Negro and Mexican-American.

A number of "high risk" insurance companies have gone into bankruptcy—leaving policyholders and accident victims unprotected and helpless.

Accident compensation is often unfair: Some victims get too much, some get too little, some get nothing at all.

Lawsuits have clogged our courts. The average claim takes about two and one-half years just to get to trial.

This is a national problem. It will become even more of a problem as we license more drivers, produce more automobiles and build more roads.

With more than 100 million drivers and 96 million motor vehicles in the United States, the insurance system is severely strained today.

While many proposals have been made to improve the system, many questions remain unanswered. The search for solutions must be pressed.

I propose legislation to authorize the Secretary of Transportation to conduct the first comprehensive study of the automobile insurance system. He will undertake this review with the full cooperation of the Federal Trade Commission and other appropriate agencies of the Executive Branch.

In recent months we have acted to make our cars and our highways safer. Now we must move to streamline the automobile insurance system—to make it fair, to make it simple, and to make it efficient.

HAZARDOUS RADIATION

It has been said that each civilization creates its own hazards. Ours is no exception. While modern technology has enriched our daily lives, it has sometimes yielded unexpected and unfortunate side effects.

Recently it was discovered that certain color television sets emit radiation which exceeds accepted safety limits.

We also know that poorly designed X-ray equipment is unnecessarily exposing some patients to the danger of radiation.

Such defects have introduced a new element into the problem of radiation hazards.

Intensive research has already probed this area. But those efforts have dealt primarily with radiation from medical equipment, isotopes, and nuclear devices.

We have long known that large doses of radiation can be fatal. But we have much more to learn about the harmful effects of lesser doses—effects which may not show up for many years.

Now modern science must be put to work on these hazards—particularly the hazards which confront the consumer.

I recommend enactment of the Hazardous Radiation Act of 1968. This measure will give the Secretary of Health, Education, and Welfare authority to

Conduct intensive studies of the hazards and set and enforce standards to control them.

Require manufacturers to recall defective equipment and devices.

The proposed legislation sets penalties for those who ignore the standards established by the Secretary of Health, Education, and Welfare.

WHOLESOME POULTRY

Last year, the Congress enacted the Wholesome Meat Act to insure the quality and safety of the food that American housewives put on their tables.

This year, the scope of that protection must be extended.

In 1967, Americans consumed over 12 billion pounds of poultry, most of it inspected under Federal law. But the 1.6 billion pounds which did not cross state lines received no Federal inspection. And State inspection is minimal at best. Thirty-one States have no poultry inspection laws. Of the remaining 19, only four have effective laws in operation.

The American consumer is paying for this neglect. He pays for it in poor quality, and in potential danger to his health.

In poultry processing plants that are Federally inspected, four percent —over 400 million pounds—of the poultry is rejected because it is diseased and contaminated. There is every reason to believe that the percentage of rejection would be even higher in uninspected plants.

There is no way of knowing how much unwholesome poultry is processed by these plants and passed on to the unsuspecting buyer. But we do know that:

Conditions in many of these plants are poor and that quality control is far below Federal standards.

Poultry can be seriously adulterated by impure water and unsanitary processing conditions.

There is a practice among some poultry producers of sending to uninspected plants inferior poultry flocks which, under Federal inspection, would face rejection.

The housewife receives protection for the poultry that comes from a neighboring state. Why should she not receive the same protection when the poultry is processed and sold in the state where she lives?

I recommend the Wholesome Poultry Products Act of 1968.

This legislation follows the pattern of the Wholesome Meat Act. It will help the States develop their own programs and train inspectors.

At the end of two years, if the States do not have inspection programs at least equal to Federal standards, the Federal inspection requirements will prevail.

In the meantime, the Act will require those intrastate plants which pose a health hazard to clean up or close down.

WHOLESOME FISH

If poultry inspection is spotty today, fish inspection is virtually non-existent.

Each year, Americans consume about two billion pounds of fish—nearly 11 pounds per person. A common item in every family's diet, fish can also be an all-too-common carrier of disease if improperly processed and shipped.

Last summer, the Senate Subcommittee on Consumer Affairs heard testimony which disclosed that a substantial amount of the fish sold in this country exposes the consumer to unknown and unnecessary dangers to his health.

It is impossible to show every link between contaminated fish and illness. Yet these links do exist: links to botulism, hepatitis, and other diseases. About 400 cases of food poisoning, reported on a single weekend in 1966, were traced to fish processed in dirty plants.

Despite these facts, the Nation has no adequate program for continuous fish inspection—either at the Federal or State level. Nor is there any systematic program for inspecting imported fish and fish products, which account for more than 50 percent of our annual consumption.

I propose the Wholesome Fish and Fishery Products Act of 1968.

The bill would authorize the Secretary of Health, Education, and Welfare to:

Develop a comprehensive Federal program for consumer protection against the health hazards and mislabeling of fish, shellfish and seafood products.

Set standards and develop continuous inspection and enforcement.

Support research, training, and inspection programs.

Help the states develop their own fish inspection programs.

Assure that imported fish products are wholesome.

RECREATIONAL BOAT SAFETY

Until recently, boats were reserved for commerce, or were owned by the very wealthy. But in our changing pattern of leisure, more and more Americans are taking to the water.

Today, boating has become a major form of recreation, with more than eight million small boats now in operation. Everywhere we see them: on our shores, in our bays, in our lakes, and on our rivers.

In these waters, Americans find rest and relaxation. But some find unexpected tragedy as well.

Last year, boating accidents claimed more than 1,300 lives—about as many as were lost in aircraft accidents.

This problem, as tragic as it is, has not yet reached major national proportions. It has not yet reached the level of automobile accidents, which cost us 53,000 lives annually. But if the Nation had begun its highway safety campaign years ago, there is no way of knowing how many American lives could have been saved. That is all the more reason why we should start now.

I propose the Recreational Boat Safety Act of 1968:

To help the states establish and improve their own boat safety programs. These programs could include the removal of hazardous debris from our lakes and rivers, boat operators education and licensing, safety patrols and inspections, testing of boats, and accident investigations.

To authorize the Secretary of Transportation to set and enforce safety standards for boats and equipment.

This program would be directed by the Secretary of Transportation. But its ultimate success will depend on the cooperation of industry, State and local governments, and boat owners themselves.

REPAIRS, WARRANTIES AND GUARANTEES

"I wish I could buy an appliance that would last until I've finished paying for it."

That complaint, familiar to every American housewife, was recently passed on to my Special Assistant for Consumer Affairs. It is a complaint that cannot be ignored.

The products of American industry save us hours of work, and provide unmatched convenience and comfort.

But they can be a source of annoyance and frustration.

Consumers have no way of knowing how long these products are built to last.

Guarantees and warranties are often meaningless—written in vague and complex language.

Repair work is sometimes excellent, sometimes shoddy, and always a gamble.

These are not problems that can be solved by legislation at this time. But they are problems that need attention now.

The Special Assistant to the President for Consumer Affairs, the Chairman of the Federal Trade Commission, the Secretary of Commerce and the Secretary of Labor will begin work immediately with the industry to:

Encourage improvements in the quality of service and repairs.
Assure that warranties and guarantees say what they mean and mean what they say.
Let the consumer know how long he may expect a product to last if properly used.
Determine whether federal legislation is needed.

A CONSUMER'S LAWYER

Less than two months after assuming office, I reaffirmed these basic rights of the American consumer:

The right to safety.
The right to be fully informed.
The right to choose.
The right to be heard.

To give added meaning to these rights, the first Special Presidential Assistant on Consumer Affairs and a Presidential Committee on Consumer Interests were appointed.

I said at the time that the voice of the consumer must be "loud, clear, uncompromising, and effective" in the highest councils of Government.

Now it is time to move closer to that goal. It is time to appoint a lawyer for the consumers.

I plan to appoint a Consumer Counsel at the Justice Department to work directly under the Attorney General and to serve the Special Assistant to the President for Consumer Affairs.

But most important, he will act in the interest of every American consumer.

He will seek better representation for consumer interests before administrative agencies and courts. He will be concerned with the widest range of consumer matters—from quality standards to frauds.

TO PROTECT THE CONSUMER'S DOLLAR

One thing, above all, should be clear to us today. We *can* encourage safety and wholesomeness by law. We *can* curb abuses and fraud.

But all our actions will be in vain if we fail to protect the buying power of every American consumer.

The Nation is now in its 84th month of historic economic growth. More Americans are at work than ever before—earning more, and buying more.

But in the midst of prosperity there are signs of danger: clear and unmistakable signs. Prices are rising faster than they should. Interest rates are climbing—and indeed have passed their peaks of 1966.

A year ago, we asked the Congress for a modest but urgently needed tax increase to curb inflation. That request was repeated last August in a Special Message calling for an average tax of about a penny on a dollar of income.

This is a fair request. Your Government is asking for only about half of what it returned to the taxpayer in the tax reduction of 1964. A penny on the dollar tax now will be much less painful than the far more burdensome tax of accelerating inflation in the months ahead.

And so today—as part of this consumer message—I again call for action on the tax request.

Business and labor leaders, consumers all, must respond to this Nation's call for restraint and responsibility in their wage-price decisions.

TO ADVANCE THE CONSUMER INTEREST

For 1968, this message proposes eight new steps to advance the consumer interest.

This is not a partisan program or a business program or a labor program. It is a program for *all* of us—all 200 million Americans.

8. CONSUMER PROTECTION

Richard M. Nixon

To the Congress of the United States:

THE HISTORY of American prosperity is the history of the American free enterprise system. The system has provided an economic foundation of awesome proportions, and the vast material strength of the nation is built on that foundation. For the average American, this strength is reflected in a standard of living that would have staggered the imagination only a short while ago. This constantly rising standard of living benefits both the consumer and the producer.

In today's marketplace, however, the consumer often finds himself confronted with what seems an impenetrable complexity in many of our consumer goods, in the advertising claims that surround them, the merchandising methods that purvey them and the means available to conceal their quality. The result is a degree of confusion that often confounds the unwary, and too easily can be made to favor the unscrupulous. I believe new safeguards are needed, both to protect the consumer and to reward the responsible businessman.

I indicated my deep concern for this matter in my special message to the Congress of October 30, 1969. At that time I urged the Congress to enact a legislative program aimed at establishing a "Buyer's Bill of Rights." This proposal found little success in the 91st Congress. But putting the remedies aside has not sufficed to put the problems aside. These remain. They must be dealt with.

Accordingly, I am again submitting proposals designed to provide such a Buyer's Bill of Rights by:

Creating by Executive Order a new Office of Consumer Affairs in the Executive Office of the President which will be responsible for analyzing and coordinating all Federal activities in the field of consumer protection;

Recognizing the need for effective representation of consumer interests in the regulatory process and making recommendations to

Reprinted from "Consumer Protection," President Richard M. Nixon's message to Congress, February 24, 1971 (Washington: Library of Congress, Legislative Reference Service).

accomplish this after full public discussion of the findings of the Advisory Council on Executive Organization;

Establishing within the Department of Health, Education, and Welfare a product safety program. The Secretary of Health, Education, and Welfare would have authority to fix minimum safety standards for products and to ban from the marketplace those products that fail to meet those standards;

Proposing a Consumer Fraud Prevention Act which would make unlawful a broad but clearly-defined range of practices which are unfair and deceptive to consumers and would be enforced by the Department of Justice and the Federal Trade Commission. This act, where appropriate, would also enable consumers either as individuals or as a class to go into court to recover damages for violations of the act;

Proposing amendments to the Federal Trade Commission Act which will increase the effectiveness of the Federal Trade Commission;

Calling upon interested private citizens to undertake a thorough study of the adequacy of existing procedures for the resolution of disputes arising out of consumer transactions;

Proposing a Fair Warranty Disclosure Act which will provide for clearer warranties, and prohibit the use of deceptive warranties;

Proposing a Consumer Products Test Methods Act to provide incentives for increasing the amount of accurate and relevant information provided consumers about complex consumer products;

Resubmitting the Drug Identification Act which would require identification coding of all drug tablets and capsules;

Encouraging the establishment of a National Business Council to assist the business community in meeting its responsibilities to the consumer; and by

Other reforms, including exploration of a Consumer Fraud Clearinghouse in the Federal Trade Commission, increased emphasis on consumer education and new programs in the field of food and drug safety.

NEW OFFICE OF CONSUMER AFFAIRS

The President's Committee on Consumer Interests has made important gains on behalf of the American consumer in the past two years.

It has brought a new and innovative approach to the problem of keeping the consumer informed and capable of handling the complex choices presented to him in today's commercial world. One such measure involves the dissemination of information which the United States Government, as the nation's largest single consumer, collects on the products it uses. In my message of October 30, 1969, I announced that I was directing my Special Assistant for Consumer Affairs to develop a program for providing the buying public with this information.

On the strength of her recommendations, on October 26, 1970, I signed Executive Order 11566 which establishes a means for making available to the public much of the product information which the Federal Government acquires in making its own purchases. A Consumer Product Information Coordinating Center has been established in the General Services Administration with continuing policy guidance from my Special Assistant for Consumer Affairs to make these data available to the public through Federal information centers and other sources throughout the country.

In addition, the Committee on Consumer Interests has made significant strides in developing Federal, State and local cooperation in consumer programs, encouraging establishment of strong State and local consumer offices, and advising on the enactment of effective consumer laws and programs.

Nevertheless, further cooperation among Federal, State and local governments is essential if we are truly to insure that the consumer is properly served. Therefore, I am asking my Special Assistant for Consumer Affairs to intensify her efforts on behalf of the consumer at the State and local level. I am also directing her to conduct regional meetings with State officials concerned with consumer issues, with consumer groups, and with individual consumers to discuss common problems and possible solutions.

But I believe the greatest overall accomplishment of this office has been to give the consumer new assurance of this administration's concern for his and her welfare in the marketplace. In manifesting this concern during the past two years, the responsibility of the President's Committee on Consumer Interests has grown, as has its impact on consumer problems. I have therefore signed today a new Executive Order creating a new Office of Consumer Affairs in the Executive Office of the President. I am appointing my Special Assistant for Consumer Affairs to be Director of this new Office. This change reflects the increasingly broad scope of responsibilities assigned to the Special Assistant for Consumer Affairs and will increase the effectiveness of the Office. The Office will advise me on matters of consumer interests, and will also assume primary responsibility for coordinating all Federal activity in the consumer field.

Finally, while I am deeply concerned with obtaining justice for all consumers, I have a special concern to see justice for those who, in a sense, need it most and are least able to get it. Therefore, I am directing my Special Assistant for Consumer Affairs to focus particular attention in the new Office on the coordination of consumer programs aimed at assisting those with limited income, the elderly, the disadvantaged, and minority group members.

A CONSUMER ADVOCATE

In my message of October 30, 1969, I pointed out that effective representation of the consumer requires that an appropriate arm of the government be given the tools to serve as an advocate before the Federal agencies. I proposed then that this function be performed by a Consumer Protection Division created for the purpose and located within the Department of Justice. That proposal was not acted on.

Since that time my Advisory Council on Executive Organization has completed its Report on Selected Independent Regulatory Agencies. This report makes sweeping recommendations on the reorganization of those agencies for the purpose of helping them better serve the interests of the consumer.

One specific recommendation involves the creation of a new Federal Trade Practices Agency dealing exclusively with matters of consumer protection. This Agency would result from a general restructuring of the Federal Trade Commission. The report specifically suggests that a consumer advocate might be placed within the Federal Trade Practices Agency.

I believe that this is a better approach than the creation of still another independent agency which would only add to the proliferation of agencies without dealing with the problems of effectiveness to which the Advisory Council report addresses itself.

As I indicated at the release of the Advisory Council's report, I am delaying legislative proposals on these issues pending full public discussion of the findings and recommendations of the Council. I urge that those who comment on the Advisory Council recommendations also focus on the manner in which the consumer interest can best be represented in Federal agency proceedings. I further urge the Congress to view the problems of consumer advocacy and agency structure as part of the general problem of making the Federal Government sufficiently responsive to the consumer interest.

After April 20, when comments have been received, I will make the recommendations I consider necessary to provide effective representation of consumer interests in the regulatory process. If the Congress feels it must proceed on the matter of consumer advocacy prior to receiving my recommendations, then I strongly urge and would support, as an interim measure, the placement of the advocacy function within the Federal Trade Commission.

A PRODUCT SAFETY ACT

Technology, linked with the American free enterprise system, has brought great advantages and great advances to our way of life. It has also brought certain hazards.

The increasing complexity and sophistication of many of our consumer goods are sometimes accompanied by the increasing possibility of product failure, malfunction, or inadvertent misuse resulting in physical danger to the consumer.

Therefore, I propose legislation providing broad Federal authority for comprehensive regulation of hazardous consumer products.

This product safety legislation will encompass five major responsibilities which would be assigned to a new consumer product safety organization within the Department of Health, Education, and Welfare. Through this organization the Secretary of Health, Education, and Welfare will:

1. Gather data on injuries from consumer products;
2. Make preliminary determinations of the need for particular standards;
3. Develop proposed safety standards with reliance on recognized private standards setting organizations;
4. Promulgate standards after a hearing and testimony on the benefits and burdens of the proposed legislation; and
5. Monitor industry compliance and enforce mandatory standards.

The mechanisms which will be included in this bill provide for full participation on the part of private organizations and groups in the development of standards.

NATIONAL ATTACK ON CONSUMER FRAUD

Consumer fraud and deception jeopardize the health and welfare of our people. They cheat consumers of millions of dollars annually. They are often directed against those who can least afford the loss, and are least able to defend themselves—the elderly, the handicapped, and the poor.

At the same time, the honest businessman is damaged by fraud and deceptive practices every bit as much as the consumer—and perhaps more. He is subjected to the unfair competition of the unscrupulous businessman, and he loses money. He is subjected to the opprobrium of those who have suffered at the hands of unscrupulous businessmen, and he loses the goodwill of the public. For it is a fact, however unfortunate, that in the area of business especially, the many are commonly judged by the actions of the few.

Efforts to eliminate these unethical business practices have not been successful enough. It is commonly profitable for unscrupulous businessmen to operate in defiance of the enforcement authorities, to accept whatever penalties and punishments are incurred, and to continue to operate in spite of these. The penalty is just part of the overhead. I want these practices brought to an end.

With this message I am committing this administration to a full and forceful effort to see that they are brought to an end.

CONSUMER FRAUD PREVENTION ACT

I am again submitting and I urge prompt attention to a bill to make unlawful a broad but clearly defined range of practices which are deceptive to consumers. The legislation would provide that the Department of Justice be given new powers to enforce prohibitions against those who would victimize consumers by fraudulent and deceptive practices.

It would give consumers who have been victimized by such practices the right to bring cases in the Federal courts to recover damages, upon the successful termination of a government suit under the Consumer Fraud Prevention Act.

I am also recommending civil penalties of up to $10,000 for each offense in violation of this act.

The Department of Justice has created a new Consumer Protection Section within the Antitrust Division, which has centralized the Department's enforcement in the courts of existing statutes designed to protect the consumer interest. Thus the Department of Justice is prepared to enforce promptly the proposed Consumer Fraud Prevention Act.

FEDERAL TRADE COMMISSION

While there is a need for new legislation to insure the rights of the consumer, there is also a need to make more effective use of the legislation we already have, and of the institutions charged with enforcing this legislation.

A principal function of the Federal Trade Commission has historically been to serve as the consumers' main line of resistance to commercial abuse. In the past year the Commission, under new leadership, has been substantially strengthened. A major organizational restructuring has produced within the Commission a Bureau of Consumer Protection, a Bureau of Competition, and a Bureau of Economics. An Office of Policy Planning and Evaluation has been created to establish a more effective ordering of priorities for the Commission's enforcement efforts.

In order to make FTC procedures more responsive to the needs of consumers, responsibilities of the eleven Commission field offices have been extended to include trying cases before hearing examiners in the field, negotiating settlements, conducting investigations, and referring complaints to the Commission. Six Consumer Protection Coordinating Committees have been established in selected metropolitan areas.

I am submitting today legislation which would provide the FTC with the authority to seek preliminary injunctions in Federal courts against what it deems to be unfair or deceptive business practices. The present inability to obtain injunctions commonly results in the passage of extended periods of time before relief can be obtained. During this time the practices in question continue, and their effects multiply.

The proposed bill would expand the jurisdiction of the Commission to include those activities "affecting" interstate commerce, as well as those activities which are "in" interstate commerce.

Finally, I recommend that the penalty schedule for violation of a Commission cease-and-desist order be adjusted from a maximum of $5,000 per violation to a maximum of $10,000 per violation.

GUARANTEES AND WARRANTIES

A constant source of misunderstanding between consumer and businessman is the question of warranties. Guarantees and warranties are often found to be unclear or deceptive.

In 1970, I submitted a proposal for legislation to meet this problem. I am submitting new legislation for this purpose.

This proposal would increase the authority of the Federal Trade Commission to require that guarantees and warranties on consumer goods convey adequate information in simple and readily understood terms.

It would further seek to prevent deceptive warranties; and it would prohibit improper use of a written warranty or guarantee to avoid implied warranty obligations arising under State law.

CONSUMER FRAUD CLEARINGHOUSE

My Special Assistant for Consumer Affairs is examining the feasibility of a consumer fraud clearinghouse—a prompt exchange of information between appropriate Federal, State and local law enforcement officials which can be especially helpful in identifying those who perpetrate fraudulent, unfair and deceptive practices upon the consumer and deprive the honest businessman of his legitimate opportunities in the marketplace.

Upon her recommendation, I am asking the FTC to explore with State and local consumer law enforcement officials an effective mechanism for such an exchange.

CONSUMER EDUCATION

Legislative remedies and improved enforcement procedures are powerful weapons in the fight for consumer justice. But as important as these are, they are only as effective as an aware and an informed public make them. Consumer education is an integral part of consumer protection. It is vital if the consumer is to be able to make wise judgments in the marketplace. To enable him or her to do this will require a true educational process beginning in childhood and continuing on.

The Office of the Special Assistant for Consumer Affairs has established guidelines for consumer education suggested for use at the elementary and high school level. Those guidelines have been sent to every school system in the country, and their reception has been encouraging. I believe they mark an effective step toward developing an informed consumer. The Office has also begun the development of suggested guidelines for adult and continuing education with particular emphasis on special socioeconomic groups and senior citizens.

Now, in order to expand and lend assistance to Consumer Education activities across the nation, I am asking the Secretary of Health, Education, and Welfare, in coordination with my Special Assistant for Consumer Affairs, to work with the nation's education system to (1) promote the establishment of consumer education as a national educational concern; (2) provide technical assistance in the development of programs; (3) encourage teacher training in consumer education; and (4) solicit the use of all school and public libraries as consumer information centers.

I am also asking the Secretary of Health, Education, and Welfare, in coordination with my Special Assistant for Consumer Affairs, to develop and design programs for the most effective dissemination of consumer information, and particularly to explore the use of the mass media, including the Corporation for Public Broadcasting.

ADDITIONAL PROPOSALS

CONSUMER REMEDIES

As we move to shape new consumer legislation, I believe we must also review all consumer remedies. Although this is primarily a matter of State and local responsibility, I believe that the problem is also of national concern. Accordingly, I am asking the Chairman of the Administrative Conference of the United States to join with other interested citizens representing a broad spectrum of society to undertake a thorough study of the adequacy of existing procedures for resolving disputes arising out of consumer transactions.

The study would (1) focus particularly on the means of handling small claims and explore methods for making small claims courts more responsive to the needs of consumers; (2) examine existing and potential voluntary settlement procedures, including arbitration, and potential means of creating incentives to voluntary, fair settlements of consumer disputes; (3) address the difficult and troublesome questions presented by mass litigation; (4) examine problems and solutions at the State as well as the Federal level; and (5) draw on the experience of other nations in improving consumer remedies.

The purpose of this study will be to gather those facts needed to determine the means of gaining the greatest benefit to consumers with the least cost to production processes and to the country. I urge Federal, State, local and private bodies to cooperate in this effort. I also ask that recommendations to the President, the Congress, the courts and the general public be made within the shortest practicable time.

FOOD AND DRUG PROGRAMS

Events in the past year have reconfirmed the need for urgent action to insure thorough and effective quality control through the Food and Drug Administration over the food Americans consume and the drugs they take.

In my message of October 30, 1969, I called for stronger efforts in the field of food and drug safety.

At that time I announced that the Secretary of Health, Education, and Welfare had initiated a thorough study of the Food and Drug Administration. As a result of that study, a number of management reforms have contributed to a more effective functioning of the FDA.

Food.

During the past two years consumer concern about the quality of certain foods in this nation has become acute. I have instructed the Food and Drug

Administration to develop new and better methods for inspecting foods —domestic and imported—to insure that they are entirely free from all natural or artificial contamination. In addition, a major study is under way reviewing the safety of all food additives. Finally, because too many Americans have no understanding of the most basic nutritional principles, the Food and Drug Administration has developed programs of nutritional guidelines and nutritional labeling. Different approaches to labeling are presently being tested for method and effectiveness.

Drugs.

In the past year the Food and Drug Administration has been engaged in an extensive program to insure the effectiveness of the drugs Americans use. Decisions have been made on some 3,000 drugs marketed between 1938 and 1962 and representing 80% of the most commonly prescribed drugs.

In addition, the Food and Drug Administration will expand its research efforts aimed at insuring that all drugs available on the market are capable of producing the therapeutic effects claimed for them.

I have resubmitted legislation requiring the identification coding of drug tablets and capsules to prevent those poisonings which result from the use of drug products of unknown or mistaken composition.

A CONSUMER PRODUCT TEST METHODS ACT

Consumers are properly concerned with the reliability of the information furnished them about the goods they buy, and I believe they have a right to such information.

Accordingly, I again propose legislation aimed at stimulating product testing in the private sector. Under this legislation, the Secretary of Commerce, through the National Bureau of Standards, in consultation with my Special Assistant for Consumer Affairs, would identify products that should be tested. Competent Federal agencies would identify product characteristics that should be tested and would approve and develop, where necessary, testing methods to assess those characteristics. Suppliers of goods would be permitted to advertise their compliance with government approved testing standards. In addition, interested private organizations may receive accreditation indicating their competence to perform the approved tests, and the use of an accredited organization in testing a product may be advertised.

NATIONAL BUSINESS COUNCIL FOR CONSUMER AFFAIRS

Most businessmen recognize and accept their responsibility to the consumer, and in many cases they have voluntarily undertaken efforts to assure more fully that these responsibilities are met throughout the business community.

To emphasize and encourage such voluntary activity, a National Business Council for Consumer Affairs will be organized by the Secretary of Commerce. It will work closely with my Special Assistant for Consumer Affairs, the Federal Trade Commission, the Justice Department and others as appropriate in the further development of effective policies to benefit American consumers.

The Council will be a vehicle through which Government can work with business leaders to establish programs for accomplishing the goal I stated in my 1969 message on consumer protection of fostering "a marketplace which is fair both to those who sell and those who buy." And it will encourage everyone who does business to do an even better job of establishing competitive prices for high quality goods and services.

CONCLUSION

In submitting the foregoing proposals, I want to emphasize that the purpose of this program is not to provide the consumer with something to which he is not presently entitled; it is rather to assure that he receives what he is, in every way, fully entitled to. The continued success of our free enterprise system depends in large measure upon the mutual trust and goodwill of those who consume and those who produce or provide.

Today, in America, there is a general sense of trust and goodwill toward the world of business. Those who violate that trust and abuse that goodwill do damage to the free enterprise system. Thus, it is not only to protect the consumer, but also to protect that system and the honest men who have created and who maintain it that I urge the prompt passage of this legislative program.

9. MAJOR FEDERAL CONSUMER PROTECTION LAWS, 1906-1970

Barbara B. Murray

MANY PEOPLE are unaware of how much consumer protection legislation the federal government has passed. There are three primary views regarding this legislation. One view is that existing legislation is adequate to protect consumer's interest. A second view is that more adequate funding for existing enforcement agencies would ensure better consumer protection. A third view is that existing enforcement agencies are unable to provide consumer protection and that further legislation and consolidation of consumer activities into a central agency is required to protect the consumer and represent his interest.

Therefore, it seems appropriate to identify the major federal consumer protection legislation. The legislation can be divided into four categories: (1) food, drugs, and cosmetics; (2) truthful disclosure; (3) safety; and (4) automobiles.

FOOD, DRUGS, AND COSMETICS

FOOD, DRUGS, AND COSMETICS ACT OF 1906

This act is generally considered the first significant piece of consumer protection legislation in the United States. The Federal Drug Administration was formed to administer and enforce the provisions of the act. Basically, the law forbade adulteration and misbranding of food sold in interstate commerce.

ADULTERATION

Food was defined as adulterated if (1) it contained decomposed or putrid animal or vegetable substances or parts of diseased animals; (2) it had been mixed or colored so as to conceal its inferiority; (3) ingredients had been added that made it injurious to health; and (4) if valuable constituents had been removed and others substituted or mixed with it so as to impair its quality or strength.

Drugs were adulterated if they fell below the standards specified in the

Paper prepared especially for this volume.

United States Pharmacopoeia or the National Formulary or any other standards under which they were sold.

MISBRANDING

Food and drugs were declared to be misbranded if their packages or labels bore statements which were "false or misleading in any particular," if one were sold under the name of another, if the contents of the package had been removed and other contents substituted, or if the presence of certain narcotics or stimulants were not revealed. Food was also considered misbranded if its weight or measure was not plainly shown, and drugs if their packages or labels bore false claims of curative effects.

THE FEDERAL FOOD, DRUG, AND COSMETICS ACT OF 1938

This act strengthened the earlier definitions of adulteration and misbranding. Food was now defined as adulterated if (1) it contained any poisonous or deleterious substance; (2) it was colored with coal tars not approved by the Food and Drug Administration; (3) it was prepared under conditions that might result in contamination with filth or injury to health; or (4) if it was packed in containers composed of substances that might make it injurious.

Under an amendment to the 1906 Act, the Food and Drug Administration was authorized to establish standards of "quality, condition, and/or fill of container" for canned goods. Such goods were said to be misbranded if failure to meet the standards was not disclosed. The administration was also empowered to set up minimum standards of identity and fill for all foodstuffs, and disclosure of failure to meet them was required. For drugs, the law required (1) the variations from the standards to be included on the label; (2) directions for use; and (3) directions for use and warning against misuse.

The scope of the law was extended to cover adulteration and misbranding of cosmetics and therapeutic devices, excluding soap. The rules for cosmetics were less stringent than those for foods and drugs. For cosmetics, no provision was made for the establishment of standards, and the disclosure of ingredients was not required.

The Food and Drug Administration was authorized to inspect factories producing foods, drugs, and cosmetics. The administration was empowered to license manufacturers and establish standards of sanitation for granting licenses when the processing of foodstuffs might involve a risk of contamination so as to be a menace to public health. Drug firms developing new drugs were required to obtain approval from the Food and Drug Administration before putting them on sale, and the administration was authorized to deny approval of drugs that had not been tested and to those that were found to be unsafe.

1962 DRUG AMENDMENTS TO THE FOOD, DRUG,
AND COSMETIC ACT OF 1938

Basically the amendments provided that under the existing law: (1) All drug factories were to be inspected at least biennially; (2) Drug manufacturers must maintain quality by following manufacturing practices defined by the Food and Drug Administration; (3) The administration can forbid the testing of drugs on humans if it finds that clinical testing on animals is not adequate; (4) A physician must have the consent of his patients before giving them an experimental drug, unless he decides that getting consent is not feasible or not in a patient's best interest; (5) All antibiotics must be tested, batch by batch, for strength and purity; (6) A manufacturer applying for approval of a drug must prove that it is not only safe but also effective; (7) No drug can be put on the market until it is specifically approved by the Food and Drug Administration; (8) Drug manufacturers must keep records on clinical experiences with respect to the drugs and report this information upon request; (9) Drug labels and advertisements must contain information on injurious side effects of the drug; (10) Generic names of drugs must be presented in type at least half as large as that used for the trade name of the drug; (11) The Food and Drug Administration was authorized to review all generic names and establish simpler ones where needed; (12) The Food and Drug Administration can remove a drug from the market if it has evidence that it carries an imminent threat to health.

MEAT INSPECTION ACT OF 1907

The United States Department of Agriculture is the enforcement agency for the provisions of this act. The act provides that a veterinarian, from the U.S. Department of Agriculture, inspect the slaughtering, packing, and canning plants that ship meat in interstate commerce. Animals are inspected before slaughter and the carcasses after slaughter. Diseased meat is destroyed. Pure meat is stamped U.S. GOVERNMENT INSPECTED.

WHOLESOME MEAT ACT OF 1967

Essentially this act, which is an amendment to the 1907 Act, was designed to force states to raise their inspection standards to those of the federal government. If the states failed to achieve federal standards within two years, the U.S. Department of Agriculture was to impose federal standards and inspection.

POULTRY PRODUCTS INSPECTION ACT OF 1957

The Department of Agriculture was authorized to inspect poultry sold in interstate commerce. The department was to examine each lot before slaughter and each bird after slaughter. Approved poultry was stamped U.S. GOVERNMENT INSPECTED. In addition the Department of Agriculture was to supervise the sanitation and processing of poultry for sale in interstate commerce.

WHOLESOME POULTRY ACT OF 1968

This legislation followed the pattern of the Wholesome Meat Act of 1967. It provides federal aid to the states so that they can develop their own inspection program for intrastate poultry plants, to meet federal inspection standards. If at the end of two years, the states' programs do not equal federal standards, the federal standards will prevail for poultry sold in intrastate as well as interstate commerce. Those intrastate poultry processing plants that pose a health hazard were to be cleaned up or they would be shut down.

TRUTHFUL DISCLOSURE

FEDERAL TRADE COMMISSION ACT OF 1914
The act provided for the creation of the Federal Trade Commission to enforce its provisions. The heart of the act is Section 5, which prohibits "unfair methods of competition in interstate commerce. . . . Whenever the commission shall have reason to believe that any such person, partnership, or corporation has been using or is using unfair methods of competition in commerce, and if *it shall appear to the commission that a proceeding by it in respect thereof would be in the interest of the public*, it shall issue and serve . . . a complaint."

WHEELER-LEA AMENDMENT OF 1938
The need for providing *consumers* with protection against unfair and injurious competitive practices led to the enactment of the Wheeler-Lea amendment to the Federal Trade Commission Act. Section 5 was amended to prohibit "unfair or deceptive acts or practices" in interstate commerce. In addition, the law specifically prohibits "false advertising" which was designed to induce purchases of foods, drugs, devices, or cosmetics.
This amendment made of equal concern before the law the consumer who may be injured by an unfair trade practice and the merchant or manufacturer injured by the unfair methods of a dishonest competitor.

FEDERAL CIGARETTE LABELING AND ADVERTISING ACT OF 1966
The provisions of the act are administered by the Federal Trade Commission. The law requires that cigarettes sold in interstate commerce be packaged and labeled with the following warning: *Caution: Cigarette smoking may be hazardous to your health.* In addition, advertising of cigarettes on television was to be eliminated.

WOOL PRODUCTS LABELING ACT OF 1939
The act is administered by the Federal Trade Commission. The primary purpose of the act was to protect manufacturers, merchants, and consumers against deception and unfair competition in articles made in whole or in part of wool. The law provides that all products containing wool, which are sold in interstate commerce—except carpets, rugs, mats, and upholsteries—must disclose on a label attached to the merchandise the type and percentage of "wool," "reprocessed wool," and "reused wool." The name of the manufacturer or distributor must also appear on the label. The label must remain on the merchandise until it is delivered to the consumer.

THE FUR PRODUCTS LABELING ACT OF 1951
This legislation, modeled after the Wool Products Labeling Act of 1939,

is administered by the Federal Trade Commission. Its purpose was to protect consumers and industry members against the misbranding, false advertising, and false invoicing of furs and fur products in interstate commerce.

The widespread use of deception and false advertising in the sale of furs —for example, the use of the term "mink blended coney" for rabbit fur—gave rise to demands within the industry for corrective action. Manufacturers and distributors are now required to attach labels to the garment showing the name of the animal that produced the fur; the country of origin; and whether the fur is bleached or dyed, or composed of paws, tails, bellies, or waste furs. Retailers may substitute their own labels, but they must retain the information from the original label for three years.

TEXTILE FIBER IDENTIFICATION ACT OF 1958

This act, administered by the Federal Trade Commission, covers the labeling and advertising of all textile fibers not required to be labeled under the Wool Act. It requires disclosure on the label and in advertising of the exact fiber content of all textile fiber products, other than wool, marketed in interstate commerce. Products included are: (1) wearing apparel; (2) draperies; (3) floor coverings, (4) yard goods; (5) blankets; and (6) sheets. All such products must show the exact fiber content in percentage terms. Imported products must in addition carry on the label the name of the country in which the product was manufactured or processed.

FAIR PACKAGING AND LABELING ACT OF 1966

Also administered by the Federal Trade Commission, this act contains both mandatory and discretionary provisions designed to assure more accurate labeling and informative packaging of most "kitchen and bathroom" products. The Secretary of Health, Education, and Welfare administers that portion relating to a commodity which is a device or cosmetic; the Federal Trade Commission administers the portion that relates to any consumer commodity which is not a "food, drug, device, or cosmetic, and shall constitute an unfair or deceptive act. . . ."

Essentially the law requires the commodity to have a label specifying the identity of the commodity and the name and place of business of the manufacturer, packer, or distributor. The net quantity of contents are required to be separately and accurately stated in a uniform location upon the display panel of the label.

CONSUMER CREDIT PROTECTION ACT OF 1968

This act requires disclosure of credit terms, annual rates of finance charges on loans and installment credit in dollars and cents as well as percentages, and annual as well as periodic disclosure of charges on revolving credit accounts. The law requires meaningful disclosure of interest on first mortgages and permits persons to exempt themselves from second mortgages used as collateral within three business days of the agreement. It restricts garnishment of wages by creditors. In addition, it provides for penalties for exorbitant credit charges (loan sharking).

Enforcement of the act is spread among nine different federal agencies: (1) the Federal Reserve, (2) the Federal Deposit Insurance Corporation, (3) the Comptroller of the Currency, (4) the Federal Home Loan Bank Board, (5) the Bureau of Federal Credit Unions, (6) the Interstate Commerce Commission, (7) the Civil Aeronautics Board, (8) the Agriculture Department, and (9) the Federal Trade Commission.

INTERSTATE LAND-SALES FULL DISCLOSURE

This legislation relating to interstate land sales is Title XIV of the Housing and Urban Development Act of 1968, and is administered by the Department of Housing and Urban Development.

Title XIV provides for the regulation of interstate land sales (of the sale of interests in subdivisions in commerce or through the mails). It requires a statement from the seller which includes: (1) the name and address of each person having an interest in the land, (2) the condition of title to the land, (3) the terms and condition of the proposed disposal of the land, (4) the condition of access to utilities, (5) any blanket encumbrances, (6) a copy of the articles of incorporation, (7) a copy of the deed, (8) a copy of council or title insurance policy, (9) copies of all forms of conveyance to be used in selling parcels, and (10) other information that may be deemed necessary.

FAIR CREDIT REPORTING ACT OF 1970

The act, enforced by the Federal Trade Commission, provides consumers with the legal right of access to their credit dossiers. Consumers also have the opportunity to force credit reporting firms to correct inaccurate, misleading, or obsolete information, or at least to force the firm to report the consumer's side of any disputed credit information case.

SAFETY

THE FLAMMABLE FABRICS ACT OF 1953

This act contains prohibitions which are placed on: (1) manufacturing, (2) importing or (3) transporting for sale of any wearing apparel "so highly flammable as to be dangerous when worn by individuals." The Federal Trade Commission enforces the provisions of the act.

FLAMMABLE FABRICS ACT OF 1967

This amendment to the 1953 law includes interior furnishings, fabrics, and materials.

FEDERAL HAZARDOUS SUBSTANCES LABELING ACT OF 1960

This law became effective in 1962. If the Food and Drug Administration finds household products such as cleaning agents, paint removers, and polishes to be hazardous, warning must be printed on the labels.

CHILD PROTECTION ACT OF 1966

This act, which strengthens the Hazardous Substances Labeling Act of

1960, prevents the marketing of potentially harmful toys and articles intended for children. The Food and Drug Administration is to remove inherently dangerous products from the market.

NATIONAL COMMISSION ON PRODUCT SAFETY 1967

This law established a National Commission on Product Safety composed of seven members. The commission is (1) to conduct a study of the scope and adequacy of measures now used to *protect consumers from unreasonable risk of injuries* which may be caused by hazardous household products and (2) to submit such interim reports to the President and Congress as the committee deems advisable before its final report which was due not later than January 1, 1969.

FIRE RESEARCH AND SAFETY ACT OF 1969

This law expresses the desire of Congress to cooperate with and assist public and private agencies in fire research and safety programs, and in the reduction of death, personal injury, and property damage caused by fire.

Funds were provided to collect, analyze, and disseminate information on fire safety and to conduct fire prevention education programs. In addition, projects were to be conducted to improve the efficiency of fire-fighting techniques.

Although the Department of Commerce was to carry out the provisions of the act, a National Commission on Fire Prevention and Control was established to study the problem and submit a report to the President within two years of its establishment.

MOTOR VEHICLES

AUTOMOBILE INFORMATION DISCLOSURE ACT OF 1958

The act requires automobile manufacturers to post the suggested retail price on all new passenger vehicles. The purpose of the act was also to prevent dealers from misrepresenting the value of cars and the value of trade-in allowances.

NATIONAL TRAFFIC AND MOTOR VEHICLE SAFETY ACT OF 1966

This law directed the Secretary of Transportation to issue safety standards for new and used motor vehicles and for motor vehicle equipment.

Under the provisions of this law, temporary federal safety standards for new 1968 automobiles were established by January 31, 1967. Incorporating standards already established by the General Service Administration for any 1968 model automobile purchased by the government, these GSA standards include such features as an impact-absorbing steering wheel and column, safety door latches and hinges, safety glass, dual braking system, impact resistant gasoline tanks and connections.

Manufacturers or dealers must equip vehicles with tires that meet load standards for fully loaded vehicles (including luggage). Tires must be labeled with the name of the manufacturer or retreader and with certain safety information, including the maximum permissible load for the tire. In accordance with the law, a uniform quality grading system was established in 1968.

10. DOES YOUR PAPRIKA GET UP OFF THE PLATE AND JUST WALK AWAY?

SPICES WITH INSECTS OR MOLD ARE COMING UNDER ATTACK; IS SOME FILTH ACCEPTABLE?

Mary Bralove

CLYDE CHRISTENSEN likes a dash of pepper on his breakfast eggs. But since he discovered that this bit of pepper spices his eggs with 60,000 colonies of fungus, his enjoyment has dwindled.

Mr. Christensen is a mycologist—that is, a man who studies fungi—at the University of Minnesota. In a study of pepper diligently collected from grocery stores, posh restaurants, pizza parlors and even airliners, Mr. Christensen found that every single sample contained a large amount of mold. "The relative moldiness of the pepper had nothing to do with the price of the restaurant," says Mr. Christensen. "We even found moldy pepper in the first-class sections of airplanes." Some of the pepper has 850,000 tiny colonies of fungus per ounce, he says.

The findings add to the criticism that is mounting against the spice industry. Of the 250 million pounds of ginger, marjoram leaves, thyme and other spices, herbs and seeds that arrive in this country each year, a huge share comes diced with mold, insect parts, rat excreta, larvae and dirt. Despite efforts of the industry and the Food and Drug Administration, part of these unsavory morsels are ground in with the spices, critics contend.

FDA officials are quick to point out that this filth—euphemistically called "extraneous matter"—isn't usually a health hazard but rather is merely an "esthetic consideration." In other words, eating insect parts won't make you sick, although the thought might.

CLEANING WITH TWEEZERS?

The industry is aware of the problem. "Even with today's technology, it's impossible to get spices wholly clean," says Thomas Burns, president of the American Spice Trade Association (ASTA). He adds, "Sure you could get spices wholly clean by using a high-power microscope and taking it out with tweezers, but it would cost you a million dollars a pound."

But the Consumers Union and other watchdog groups are pressing the spice industry to come clean—or at least cleaner. "People don't want to put paprika on their plate and see it walk away," says one sympathetic FDA official.

Moreover, dirty spices really may pose a health problem despite assurances to the contrary. Scientists have recently discovered that under certain conditions mold can turn into aflatoxin, a chemical found to induce cancer in rats. Last November, the FDA recalled 87 tons of corn-meal mix; the corn from which it was made was found to contain aflatoxin which developed from mold.

For esthetic reasons, the FDA had earlier clamped down on the amount of mold that was tolerable in spices and foods. The Consumers Union has been pressuring the FDA lately to make public the allowable levels of filth in imported spices, which account for 90% of all spices used in the U. S.

It may seem strange to talk about acceptable amounts of filth. Indeed, the Food, Drug and Cosmetic Act technically prohibits any filth at all in foods and spices. But since spice men say that's impossible, the FDA has established its own filth allowances.

These FDA standards are secret—at least to the consumer. The spice industry knows the FDA contamination levels, and the FDA knows that the spice industry knows. "It's a game," says George Pollack, head of the Consumers Union foods division. "The only one left in the dark is the public."

But according to the ASTA standards for imported spices, which are said to be "close" to the secret FDA allowances, between 0.5% and 2% of "extraneous" material is allowed. These figures, which vary according to the spice involved, seem lenient to some critics. But on one point the ASTA is indignantly adamant: "No live insects are permitted," admonishes the trade group. "Provisions (for importing filth) are made only for whole dead insects."

Since 1968, spice importers in New York (which account for over 75% of all spice imports) have operated a self-policing program. When a shipment arrives, the FDA sometimes still makes a cursory inspection. But in any event, the importer then sends random samples of his lot to laboratories certified by the FDA. If the spice doesn't meet the ASTA standard, the importer must reclean the lot until it does. In addition, the FDA still spot-checks warehouses and spice processors for contamination.

ARE INSECTS GOOD FOR YOU?

The filth sometimes originates in the growing field, where such insects as grasshoppers, ants and beetles are harvested along with the spices. And sometimes it comes from the warehouse, where roaches, weevils and rats crawl through the sacks. At some seaports, too, spices may be stored in damp conditions where mold can readily form.

"There's no way of preventing contamination of insects in the field, no matter how sophisticated your harvesting methods," says Richard Hall, vice president for research and development at McCormick & Co., a large New York spice concern. "You could drench the area with more insecticides, but then no one would eat the spices."

Consumers Union recognizes this problem, but is stressing the need to clean up warehouse contamination. "You know a cockroach didn't get into the spices in the fields in Madagascar," insists the group's Mr. Pollack. "We have the know-how and the technology to keep our warehouses clean."

Partly under pressure from critics, spice importers have improved their cleaning techniques. They use all sorts of methods including vacuuming of spice bags, passing spices through filter screens and just plain washing with water.

Moreover, there are signs the FDA may respond to the public pressure. The government agency says that until now it has hesitated to make filth standards public for fear of tying its inspectors to rigid, unenforceable regulations. But an FDA official suggests that in the near future the organization will indeed make the standards public so that consumers will know how many "extras" are allowed in their spices.

Of course, if those "extras" are removed, the consumer could be hurt. Explains the ASTA's Mr. Burns: "Insect fragments won't make you sick—in fact, they're protein."

PART FOUR

*

Federal Trade Commission and Consumerism

INTRODUCTION

Federal Trade Commission and

Consumerism

THE FEDERAL Trade Commission is one of the primary agencies for the enforcement of consumer legislation. The commission has also been the subject of a great deal of controversy from consumer advocates and from business. All writers in this section tend to agree that the FTC has not been entirely effective in its efforts to protect the consumer. The reasons why and the proposed changes by the writers vary widely.

The American Bar Association (ABA) report tends to emphasize that the FTC is managed inefficiently. The primary reasons for the inefficiency—and Senator Proxmire tends to concur—are: ´(1) emphasis on recruiting commissioners from business rather than from groups more directly tied to the consumer's interest; and (2) the commissioners' lack of technical competence in the area of economics.

Richard Posner agrees that the FTC is inefficient, concentrates on trivia, and is slow to act—but on rather different grounds. He feels that there has been very little consumer protection for the funds allocated to the commission, and questions why there should be a Federal Trade Commission. His thesis is that private remedies for fraudulent practices and conduct already exist and are enforced by the judiciary. Therefore, the Federal Trade Commission is unnecessary.

Senator Proxmire, the members of the ABA Commission, and Paul Scanlon would like to see greater regulation of oligopolistic industries and market structures by the Federal Trade Commission. The reason for their position is the cost of oligopolistic market structures in terms of higher prices for the products the consumers purchase. Scanlon analyzes the factors that determine market concentration and oligopolistic market structures; his focus is primarily on the interrelationship between advertising expenditures and concentration levels in industries. He would like to see the commission devote its efforts to industry studies rather than "petty commercial practices."

Dorothy Cohen criticizes the assumptions that the FTC uses in its regulatory design, particularly its criteria that the consumer is maximizing his utility and making rational choices. For the regulation of advertising and consumer protection activities, she proposes a behavioral model of consumer preferences that encompasses not only the consumer's objective environment but also his subjective environment. As she says, even if it were possible to provide the consumer with complete information based on economic criteria, the individual may still be unable to exercise informed choice, because the consumer does not appraise his interest solely in economic terms.

11. QUALIFICATIONS FOR FTC CHAIRMANSHIP: COMPETENCE, CONCERN, AND CONSUMER CONFIDENCE

Senator William Proxmire

REPRESENTATION FOR PUBLIC INTEREST

Honorable Frank E. Moss
Chairman, Consumer Subcommittee
Commerce Committee
Washington, D.C.

I WANT to make it clear at the outset that this letter is not intended to reflect in any personal way on the nominee you are considering for FTC Chairman. I have no reason to believe he is anything other than a lawyer of the highest standing in his profession and a man of intelligence and integrity. I do want to present for your consideration, however, a number of qualifications that I think the chairman of the Federal Trade Commission ought to have, qualifications that your Committee ought to direct its attention to in its hearings.

The chairmanship of the Federal Trade Commission requires, it seems to me, at least three highly important characteristics: First, technical competence; secondly, a will to perform in the interests of the consuming public; and, thirdly, the confidence and support of the country's consumer movement.

These are all obviously related. The first, technical competence, refers simply to the capacity of the man to *recognize* and accurately appraise the public interest, to avoid the common error of honestly confusing public and private interests. The second refers to a willingness to *act* on that perception, to pursue the public interest in the face of the inevitable pressures that effective

Reprinted by permission *Antitrust Law & Economics Review*, Vol. 3, No. 3 (Spring 1970), pp. 34-41.

public-interest action always generates. And the third refers to the important principle that government officials, like Caesar's wife, should not only serve the public interest faithfully but should clearly be *seen* by the public as a faithful servant of public rather than narrow, private interests.

REQUEST FOR CONSUMER REPRESENTATION

Let me take the last of these first.

A short while ago, the President was asked to consult with the country's various organized consumer groups in the selection of the next Chairman of the FTC. Ralph Nader and his associates; the Consumer Federation of America, an organization that includes many state consumer groups with, I am told, some 20 million consumer-members; and the editors of a scholarly antitrust publication, the *Antitrust Law & Economics Review,* all sent the President a formal request that the country's consumer groups be given the same voice in the selection of the head of the nation's principal consumer agency that business, for example, is given in the selection of the Secretary of Commerce and that organized labor is given in picking the Secretary of Labor.

These requests were not honored. The name under consideration now for this office was never mentioned to any of these consumer groups prior to the public announcement of that name in the press. They were not asked to propose names for the President's consideration. In short, the decision has apparently been made that consumers do not have the same rights in these matters as business and labor, the right to have a voice in the selection of the men who are to represent *them* in the councils of government and in the courts.

FTC NOT CONSUMER REPRESENTATIVE?

Like a number of our other regulatory agencies, the FTC has been subjected to some increasingly severe criticisms in recent months, one of the most troublesome of these being the charge that it really does not represent the consumer at all. We are now beginning to witness, for example, the phenomena of the student-advocate, the law-school student group that comes before our federal agencies asking for an opportunity to intervene and present the *consumers* case. It is understood in these matters—and I gather there is indeed quite widespread agreement on the point—that the agency itself does *not* represent the consumer. In short, we have reached a point in our national life when the citizen candidly acknowledges a lack of faith in these regulatory agencies. No one would claim, I suspect, that the American consumer regards the FTC as a consumer-advocate in the sense that it regards, say, Mr. Nader in that role.

My point here, then, is that the public is entitled to an FTC chairman that enjoys its full, affirmative confidence and support, not simply one that is not suspected of some specific anti-consumer bias. The consumer wants—and, in my view, is entitled to have—a powerful advocate for its own interests,

93

a man who is not only pro-consumer in the full meaning of that word but is fully accepted as such by the consuming public and its representatives, the organized consumer movement.

FORMER BUSINESS LAWYERS AS FTC COMMISSIONERS

I am of course profoundly skeptical of the fairness of appointing to the country's major consumer agency men who have devoted their professional lives to the representation of precisely those interests that the consumer is currently demanding protection *from*. Many such men do of course turn out well in public office. But to pass over the consumer's own chosen representatives in favor of their former opponents—to put business advocates in charge of consumer protection—seems to me a most inappropriate way to win the confidence of the American consumer in the sincerity and gravity of the Federal Trade Commission's work. I think the time has come to recognize the consumer movement in America as the power it is rapidly becoming and that it fully deserves to become.

AN ECONOMIST FOR FTC CHAIRMANSHIP?

The most difficult part of my argument to you today has to do with the question of technical competence, with the technical knowledge and intellectual capacity to accurately distinguish public from private interests in the complex industry situations that come before the Federal Trade Commission. How does one measure the "performance" of an agency like the FTC and thus the performance of the men that head it up? What technical skills are required in order to turn out an acceptable performance in this area?

One of the groups that I mentioned a moment ago, the editors of the *Antitrust Law & Economics Review,* argues that the responsibilities of the Federal Trade Commission are so heavily *economic* in character that only a highly qualified professional economist—one of the stature normally associated with, say, the Chairmanship of the Federal Reserve Board or the Council of Economic Advisers—can really be expected to adequately represent the consumer there. As they argued in their wire to the President: "We urge you to consider the selection of a non-lawyer for this post. There is no statutory requirement that this agency be headed by lawyers and, in view of its key role in carrying out the nation's economic policy in such vital areas as the preservation of competitive industrial structures, in the prevention of monopoly pricing, and thus in supplementing the country's other anti-inflation policies, we think the same factors that argue for the appointment of professional economists to the Federal Reserve Board and the Council of Economic Advisers call for their appointment to the Chairmanship of the FTC."

LAWYERS AND ECONOMIC "TRIVIA"

Many others have urged the putting of at least one professional economist on this five-man Commission, the argument being that only the presence of at least one technically qualified person of equal status could provide the other four commissioners with a sharp enough incentive to make them give up their alleged current preoccupation with economically trivial matters.

There is much to be said for all of these arguments, particularly, it seems to me, for the latter one: I would very much favor putting at least one professional economist on the FTC. It might very well be, as many economists have suggested, that this would be the single most important step that could be taken toward a genuine reformation of this agency.

And while I am well aware that the chairmanship involves administrative as well as substantive duties—and that some competence in economic analysis can be acquired without formal economic training—I would not dismiss out of hand the suggestion that the chairman of the FTC should be a professional economist with special competence in the antitrust and consumer-protection branch of the discipline, industrial organization. I have recently become seriously concerned with the question of whether a non-economist, no matter how able he might otherwise be, can really be expected to cope with the technical demands of that office.

FTC DOESN'T KNOW WHICH INDUSTRIES IT IS INVESTIGATING?

I recently requested the present chairman of the agency, Mr. Weinberger, to conduct an economic study of the country's major oligopolies—the more highly concentrated of our major manufacturing industries—the objective of that study being a direct factual determination of which industries, if any, are noncompetitive in character and are thus charging the consumer prices that exceed competitive levels. A copy of that request to the FTC, together with Mr. Weinberger's reply, is attached to this letter for your consideration. Because I was not entirely sure what the FTC was trying to tell me, I then sent Mr. Weinberger another letter, one in which I asked for such details as: (1) what industries the Commission is spending its $20 million budget on; (2) the level of concentration in those industries it is investigating; (3) whether the public is being charged a higher-than-competitive price in those industries; and (4) what the FTC expects to get for the consumer in those industries in return for the tax dollars being spent there. A copy of that letter and Mr. Weinberger's response are also attached for your consideration. As I read this correspondence, the FTC *doesn't know* which industries it is currently spending its money on—and, what is more, I gather that it doesn't think the answer is very important.

NO OLIGOPOLY STUDY

In addition, I have also concluded that the Commission does not intend to conduct the oligopoly study that I requested. Some mention is made in these FTC papers of studies already underway in six industries—steel, autos, drugs, electrical machinery, the energy industries, and chemicals—but I am advised that, while such an inquiry was in fact *proposed* some 2 years ago, in 1968, not a cent has been spent on it to date and that, in good bureaucratic terms, the project holds a "very low priority" at the FTC.

I have prepared a further request for this information on the agency's work and am hopeful that I will ultimately be able to persuade it that the public has a right to know which industries, if any, are charging higher-than-competitive prices. The FTC was created precisely for the purpose of investigating these things and informing the Congress, the Executive, and the public in that regard. If it doesn't know the answers to some of these questions, then it has, it seems to me, the duty to find out. It has the power to summon evidence—that, is, the subpoena power—and it has the resources, a budget, as noted, of some $20 million and the authority to hire whatever economists it needs. In short, I am hard-pressed to find an acceptable reason for the FTC to be, as it seems to be claiming, uninformed on the question of whether the American consumer is being overcharged for its automobiles, its gasoline, and its bread, and I am hoping that I will be able to persuade its chairman in due course that the agency is going to have to prepare for us and for the public at large a full report on the state of competition in our oligopoly industries, a report that will tell the consumer whether she is paying a competitive price or a higher-than-competitive price to these 100 or so concentrated industries.

FTC TECHNICALLY INCOMPETENT

Until the FTC has demonstrated that it is prepared to give the public this kind of a report, its technical competence seems to me to be seriously in doubt. The capacity to do this kind of work for the consumer—to hire and supervise a staff of genuinely competent economists who can develop the kind of data we have to have if we are going to have a rational consumer-protection pro-gram—is at the heart of the professional skills required of the men who head up this agency.

In short, I would not vote to confirm any man as chairman of the FTC until he was able to persuade me that he would in fact give the very highest priority at the agency—with a commitment of a very substantial part of its total resources—to an immediate, full-scale economic study along the lines of my recent request for the oligopoly investigation that I mentioned earlier.

COSTS OF OLIGOPOLY

Mr. Chairman, the FTC is a small agency but it is a very important one. Recent estimates by Mr. Nader, Senator Hart, and others have put the cost of monopoly and related industrial crimes at some $100 billion or more each year—more than 20% of every dollar spent by the consumer. As several commentators have written in recent weeks, some of our other great national problems seem almost small by comparison with this enormous figure. For example:

The country's total *crime bill* was $32 billion last year;

Removing the major sources of *pollution* would cost $15 billion per year; and

Eliminating poverty ($3,000 minimum income for all families) would cost $11 billion per year.

EVALUATING FTC COMMISSIONERS

As one commentator has put it: "If the public is in fact being overcharged by $100 billion or more each year for the goods it buys, and if the five commissioners that sit on the FTC are in fact seriously charged with the duty of seeing that such overpricing doesn't occur, then they are five very important men indeed. Few men have it in their power to cost their fellow countrymen, by lack of technical skill, social concern, or of any other intellectual or human shortcoming, anything near $20 billion a year."[1]

The FTC *is* supposed to protect the American consumer from that $100 billion overcharge and future commissioners—particularly future chairmen—should be evaluated by this Committee in terms, it seems to me, of their *capacity* and their *willingness* to get on with the job of stopping it. It is a job that demands, I believe, an extraordinarily high order of technical competence, of dedication to consumer interests, and of support and confidence by the American consumer and his chosen representatives.

NOTES

1. Editor's Foreword, 2 *Antitrust Law & Economics Review* 17 (Summer 1969).

12. THE ABA REPORT ON THE FTC: CONSUMER PROTECTION OR CONSUMER EXPLOITATION
Miles W. Kirkpatrick et al.

Frederick M. Rowe John D. French
Jack Greenberg Carl A. Auerbach
Thomas E. Harris Carl H. Fulda
Ellen Ash Peters Jesse W. Markham
Paul G. Bower Betty Bock
Allen C. Holmes Charles E. Stewart, Jr.
Ira M. Millstein Harlan M. Blake

DELAY, TRIVIA, AND INEFFICIENCY

THE FEDERAL Trade Commission, an independent regulatory agency established in 1914, is assigned the responsibility of administering a wide variety of antitrust and trade regulation laws. Over the past 50 years, a succession of independent scholars and other analysts have consistently found the FTC wanting in the performance of its duties by reason of inadequate planning, failure to establish priorities, excessive preoccupation with trivial matters, undue delay, and unnecessary secrecy.

This present ABA Commission was appointed by President William T. Gossett of the American Bar Association, at the request of President Nixon, to undertake an appraisal of the "present efforts of the Federal Trade Commission in the field of consumer protection, in its enforcement of the antitrust laws, and of the allocation of its resources between these two areas."

The FTC of the 1960s is probably superior to most of its predecessors, but continues to fail in many respects. Through lack of effective direction, the FTC has failed to establish goals and priorities, to provide necessary guid-

Reprinted by permission from *Antitrust Law& Economics Review*, Vol. 3, No. 3 (Spring 1970), pp. 58-62.

ance to its staff, and to manage the flow of its work in an efficient and expeditious manner.

All available statistical measures of FTC activity show a downward trend in virtually all categories of its activities in the face of a rising budget and increased staff. Moreover, present enforcement activity rests heavily on a voluntary compliance program devoid of effective surveillance or sanctions. It thus appears that both the volume and the force of FTC law enforcement have declined during this decade.

INCOMPETENT FTC STAFF

We believe that the FTC has mismanaged its own resources. Through an inadequate system of recruitment and promotion, it has acquired and elevated to important positions a number of staff members of insufficient competence. The failure of the FTC to establish and adhere to a system of priorities has caused a misallocation of funds and personnel to trivial matters rather than to matters of pressing public concern.

The primary responsibility for these failures must rest with the leadership of the Commission. In recent years, bitter public displays of dissension among Commissioners have confused and demoralized the FTC staff, and the failure to provide leadership has left enforcement activity largely aimless.

Turning to specific areas of FTC efforts, we find, first, that in the field of consumer protection, the agency has been preoccupied with technical labeling and advertising practices of the most inconsequential sort. This failing derives in large part from a detection technique which relies almost exclusively on the receipt of outside complaints.

RETAIL FRAUD "TASK FORCES"

At the same time, the FTC has exercised little leadership in the prevention of *retail marketing frauds*. In this important field, the FTC has failed to build upon its most imaginative undertaking, the District of Columbia pilot project. Although emphasizing the need for state and local effort, the FTC has kept its Federal-State Coordination program patently understaffed. Unjustified doubts within the FTC as to its power or effectiveness in dealing with local frauds have caused it to remain largely passive in this area of enforcement.

We recommend a new and vigorous approach to consumer fraud. The FTC should establish task forces in major cities to concentrate exclusively on this problem. These task forces should be given ample manpower and authority to pursue localized frauds expeditiously and effectively.

We see in this project a source not only of improved enforcement but of substantially expanded knowledge as to the nature and significance of consumer fraud. We would expect the project to generate both new initiatives in the enforcement of the Federal Trade Commission Act and proposals for new legislation in the field of fraudulent and deceptive practices. Furthermore it would establish new lines for communication and cooperation with state and local agencies. We also believe that effective law enforcement in this area requires the creation of new procedural devices, including a right in the FTC, in appropriate situations, to seek preliminary injunctions against deceptive practices, and some form of private relief for or on behalf of consumers injured by such practices.

ANTITRUST POLICY—BUREAU OF ECONOMICS

In the antitrust field, we believe that the FTC can perform valuable service in bringing the administrative process to bear on difficult and complex problems. We therefore propose that the concurrent jurisdiction of the FTC and the Department of Justice in antitrust enforcement be retained. We urge, however, that the present allocation of enforcement resources be reexamined and realigned in a manner more nearly consistent with the objectives of antitrust policy.

The work of the FTC's Bureau of Economics has been of substantial value. We think, however, that its public acceptance would be improved by a structural division into two separate units—one to provide support to the enforcement work of the FTC, and the other to engage in fundamental economic research.

PLANNING—DELEGATION OF AUTHORITY—EX PARTE COMMUNICATIONS

Finally, we believe that several serious and pervasive deficiencies at the FTC must be acknowledged and corrected.

First, it is imperative that the FTC embark on a program to establish goals, priorities, and effective planning controls. We recommend establishment of a special staff committee to review the current backlog of pending matters and to recommend to the Commission the closing of files of marginal significance. We further propose the immediate expansion and invigoration of the Office of Program Review to take primary responsibility for proposing to the Commission ways and means of coordinating future operations.

Second, the agency must recognize that some of its most serious problems —such as excessive delay and the conflict at the Commissioner level between the functions of prosecutor and judge—can be solved by greater delegation of authority to the staff. We recommend that the Commission confer on its bureau directors the authority to issue complaints and close investigations, on its General Counsel the authority to seek preliminary injunctions, and on its projected consumer-protection task forces the authority to initiate and close investigations, issue complaints, and otherwise act as operating bureaus with respect to its own programs.

Third, Commissioners have been criticized for making themselves available to those representing respondents or potential respondents on an *ex parte*, off-the-record basis. The Commission should define and publish criteria concerning the circumstances under which businessmen and their attorneys may confer with Commissioners at all stages of its proceedings.

REFORM OR ABOLITION

In conclusion, this Commission believes that it should be the last of the long series of committees and groups which have earnestly insisted that drastic changes were essential to recreate the FTC in its intended image. The case for change is plain. What is required is that the changes now be made, and in depth. Further temporizing is indefensible. Notwithstanding the great potential of the FTC in the field of antitrust and consumer protection, if change does not occur, there will be no substantial purpose to be served by its continued existence; the essential work to be done must then be carried on by other governmental institutions.

13. SEPARATE STATEMENT OF RICHARD A. POSNER FOR THE ABA REPORT ON THE FEDERAL TRADE COMMISSION

Richard A. Posner

IN A time when "new Philosophy calls all in doubt," it will no longer do to rest upon the old verities regarding the administrative process. If it is to reflect contemporary currents of thinking and awareness, a serious analysis of the FTC must address fundamentals: What is the need, if any, for a government agency charged with protecting consumers from deception or ignorance? Are the benefits of such an agency likely to outweigh its costs: Does the record of performance of the FTC justify its continuation? Are its defects merely accidental and remediable, or inherent? Are there alternatives to administrative regulation that should perhaps be tried? The majority report of this committee largely ignores these questions and confines its attention to the surfaces of problems. It is missed opportunity of major dimensions. This is a uniquely auspicious occasion to conduct a far-ranging examination of the assumptions underlying the entire range of the FTC's activities, not only because of the change in public opinion noted earlier but also because of the extraordinary mood that pervades the Federal Trade Commission today. Deeply shaken by the revelations of mismanagement and demoralization contained in the report sponsored by Ralph Nader,[1] virtually paralyzed by internal dissension, and increasingly conscious of its inability to respond effectively to the growing pressures of the resurgent consumer movement in this country, the Commission is at present in a state of crisis, self-doubt, and self-criticism. The response of the majority report to this anguish consists of homilies on the importance of inspired leadership, good planning, and sensible priorities; and of proposals that amount to tinkering with the details of the Commission's existing operations and organization.

Reprinted from the American Bar Association Commission Report on the Federal Trade Commission, 1969, pp. 983 and 993-1009.

I turn now to an analysis of what I conceive to be the fundamental issues in a serious assessment of the FTC.

* * *

III

Although originally created to grapple with monopoly problems, the FTC, within a few years after it opened its doors, was devoting the bulk of its time and resources to combating false advertising and other deceptive or unfair merchandising practices.[2] The shift is instructive and we shall consider the reason later. A more fundamental question, one rarely put because the answer strikes most people as self-evident, is whether there ought to be a government agency that prosecutes sellers who try to mislead consumers. Even in the absence of any legal remedies, it is unclear that deception would be markedly more frequent than it is. Good preventives against deception are to be found in the incentive of the consumer to exercise reasonable care and commonsense in purchasing, in the incentive of sellers not to antagonize customers, and the incentive of competitors of deceptive advertisers to give consumers prompt and accurate information in order to correct any misrepresentation that might cause a substantial diversion of their sales. The last point is too little stressed. In other areas of discourse we posit a marketplace of ideas in which good ideas can be expected to prevail in open competition with bad. One could quite reasonably take a similar approach to advertising. Individuals probably know a good deal more about household products than about political questions. If we trust them to evaluate competing and often fraudulent claims by political candidates, we should also trust them to evaluate competing product claims. Since other sellers, like rival candidates, have every incentive to counter the misleading representations of a competitor, there seems little danger that false claims will not be exposed. Nor is it clear that occasional, transitory misrepresentations are entirely a bad thing. If a false claim elicits a substantial increase in sales, the industry has learned something about consumer demand, and competitors of the false advertiser will have an incentive to develop a product about which the claim can be truthfully made.

This is not to suggest that market processes afford complete protection against consumer deception. Since the provision of information is not a costless activity, one can imagine cases where the impact of the deceptive practice is so limited that it does not pay competitors to supply correct information, even though some consumers are fooled and switch their business to the deceiver. However, these are doubtful cases for any form of corrective action, public or private; they are cases where the costs of truth appear to outweigh its benefits. A related, but more serious, problem arises when other sellers lack incentive to inform the public of the fraud, not because its impact is very limited, but because exposing it will not significantly increase their sales. What sellers could expect marked gains from telling the public that cigarette smoking is harmful to health? (More on this shortly.)

Most important, there is bound to be a lag between the misrepresentation and the truthful rebuttal. The prospect of a quick killing before consumers are made wise to the fraud by competing sellers may induce a firm that is not concerned to remain in the business to engage in deceptive practices, and when it is exposed switch to another line. If consumers have no legal protection against such a firm, they may resort to all sorts of costly self-protective devices, such as vastly increased expenditures on shopping, blacklists of sellers, and refusing to deal with newly established firms. That is one reason why we have a law of contracts.[3] The provision of legal remedies for breach of contract reduces the cost of transactions by obviating, or at least reducing, the need of buyer or seller to take costly and cumbersome measures to protect himself against the other's bad faith. As an incidental feature of the system of contract rights and remedies, one who is inveigled by fraud or misrepresentation into a transaction may rescind it, or, if it has already been consummated, collect damages from the defrauding party.[4] In this fashion, the legal system protects buyers against sellers who are tempted by the prospect of short-term gains to obtain business by deceit.

As in the case of the FTC's antitrust role, then, there was an existing system of remedies for fraudulent conduct, and the question is why it was thought necessary to supplement these by a scheme of administrative regulation. (As mentioned earlier, apparently it was not thought necessary by the sponsors of the Commission, who envisaged it as an antitrust agency.) The justification that is usually advanced for having the government prosecute deceptive sellers is that the system of private remedies is ineffectual where the injury to any single consumer is small. Although the aggregate injury to the consuming public may be considerable, no individual consumer has an incentive to assume the costs of litigation. The corollary to this is that private remedies should be relatively effective in preventing serious frauds—frauds that endanger health or safety or inflict large monetary loss—for these are cases where the likelihood of a private suit is great. What the point about the small claim ignores, however, is that competitors of the deceptive advertiser should have a substantial incentive to institute judicial proceedings to eliminate a fraud that, if successful, must be diverting appreciable sales from them. In such proceedings, the competitor of the deceptive advertiser (or trade association of competitors) would, in effect, be aggregating the individually insignificant consumer claims. Consumers would not be made whole for past losses but the practice would be stopped, which is all that FTC fraud proceedings can do.

Implicit in the foregoing is the assumption that the courts are capable of evolving reasonably satisfactory legal principles governing consumer fraud. The assumption seems broadly correct, although the courts have been slow to recognize the right of a competitor to sue on the ground of false advertising per se[5] (the occupation of the field by the FTC may provide a partial explanation). Fraud and misrepresentation are familiar concepts in Anglo-American jurisprudence, and their application in the sale context would appear to present neither conceptual nor practical difficulties of moment. In any event, the assumption of judicial lawmaking adequacy is not necessary. If the courts hesitate or stumble in adapting common law principles to novel circumstances, it is open to the Legislature to lend a hand by excising existing defenses or declaring new rights of action.[6] Indeed, Congress in the Lanham Act created a new right of action for competitors injured by misrepresentation that, although little utilized,[7] appears to remedy any deficiencies of the common law in this area.[8]

Procedurally or institutionally, it is doubtful that administrative enforcement of antifraud principles has any comparative advantages over judicial. The nature and complexity of the issues do not argue for an administrative agency. The interpretation of advertising or sales representations and the determination of their truth seem well within the ordinary competence of judges and juries. True, an agency, if given its head, is likely to develop stricter standards of what constitutes unlawful deception than would courts. The agency is more likely to define its mission as one of consumer protection (narrowly conceived), rather than as the neutral resolution of disputes between sellers and buyers. But society may not gain from the stricter standards. Just as the cheapest way to reduce the incidence of certain crimes, such as car theft, is by inducing potential victims to take simple precautions (locking car doors), so possibly the incidence of certain frauds could be reduced at least cost to society by insisting that consumers exercise a modicum of care in purchasing, rather than by placing restrictions on sellers' marketing methods. Whenever the Commission compels a seller to supply additional information to consumers, it increases the consumer's shopping burdens and, since consumers must be nearly saturated with product information already, may force the displacement of other and equally significant product messages. Much advertising that the Commission views as suspiciously inexplicit or elliptical may simply reflect the need to economize on product information, albeit, a byproduct may be that here or there someone is misled. The answer in these cases may be to hold the consumer to a somewhat higher standard of care. But this is a line of thinking that the FTC, which avows a standard of protecting "fools" as well as average or reasonable consumers from deception,[9] seems incapable of grasping.

A system of private remedies for fraud is unlikely to be completely adequate. In particular, it will fail to deter sellers who compound their fraud by ingeniously evading legal processes through concealment of their assets or frequent changes in the locus of their activity and in their corporate identity. Criminal or other punitive sanctions are necessary in such cases. But this is not a problem that having a Federal Trade Commission will cure.

The one area in which the case for an agency is stronger than previously suggested is where no seller has an incentive to furnish correct information, or to sue a seller who misleads the consumer. An example is cigarettes. There are no direct substitutes for cigarettes, except other tobacco products. If cigarette sales declined because people became convinced that smoking was dangerous, the sales of other products or services would rise. However, apart from sellers of other tobacco products, for whom a campaign of disparaging cigarettes would involve a palpable risk of being hoist with their own petard, there is probably no seller or group of sellers who could anticipate a marked rise in sales as a result of a reduction in smoking. There is therefore no "competitor" with an incentive to supply information on the relationship between smoking and health that cigarette companies naturally try to withhold.

Even this case is less clear-cut than at first appears. Competitive pressures should induce cigarette companies to search out ways of making their cigarettes less toxic and should evoke efforts to devise a nontoxic substitute for cigarettes. Both forces have been at work. Cigarette companies have striven to reduce the tar and nicotine content of their tobaccos and to improve filtration, and ingenious people have invented cigarettes that contain lettuce or some other allegedly harmless tobacco substitute. In the ordinary course one would expect cigarette companies to advertise that a particular brand was safer than competitors'—thereby tipping the industry's hand, for such advertising unmistakably implies that there is a health hazard—and for the inventors of nontobacco cigarettes to advertise that their products, unlike tobacco cigarettes, are safe. Competition should thus cause the information barrier eventually to crumble. It is a profound irony that for years the FTC, encouraged by cigarette companies that feared the process I have described, forbade the disclosure in advertising of the tar or nicotine content of any cigarette brands.[10]

It is one thing to identify an area in which free competition may not supply an adequate flow of correct information and another to devise an appropriate remedy. One possibility might be a government agency charged with studying the characteristics and effects of consumer products, especially in the area of health and safety, and publicizing the results to consumers. To explore this avenue, however, would take us too far afield. For present purposes, it is sufficient to observe that, although the most persuasive case for a consumer-protection agency relates to the situation where the fraud embraces all close substitutes of a product, and there is consequently no incentive for competing sellers to furnish correct information or to bring suit, this has not been the emphasis of the FTC. One's strong impression is that most FTC fraud cases are initiated, either directly or indirectly, by the complaint of a competitor (or of the union representing the competitor's employees). These are precisely the cases where private remedies should be adequate. Where competitors do not complain, and private remedies may be inadequate, the FTC usually provides no remedy either. Individual consumers rarely complain to the FTC—they have little incentive, since the FTC cannot give them reparations —and the Commission has never developed effective machinery for independently uncovering frauds. And by hypothesis, in an area where the private market is failing to supply correction information, consumers frequently will not realize that they have been defrauded.

If this is a correct description of the FTC's emphasis in the fraud area, and some corroborative evidence will be provided in a moment, the FTC is doing little or nothing that is not within the competence of courts. But the FTC's fraud activities are not merely redundant. Ordinarily, a firm cannot conduct a lawsuit against a competitor or potential competitor without incurring costs comparable to those of its opponent. This rough equality of burdens is a deterrent to the use of the litigation process to harass. Proceeding against a competitor by way of a complaint to the Trade Commission, in contrast, is a method of imposing the cost of litigation on the competitor at no cost to the complainant. All of the costs of prosecution are borne by the FTC; all of the costs of defense by the respondent. The complainant pays nothing. This arrangement creates an incentive to engage in litigation designed purely to suppress competition, for it enables the complaining party to create a barrier to entry in its exact technical sense: a condition that imposes upon a new entrant a cost not borne by firms already in the market.[11]

I emphasize the effects of the unequal burdens of FTC litigation on entry because it is the new firm or, what is analytically quite similar, the new product sold by an existing firm that is most vulnerable to a charge of deceptive marketing. A new product is generally a substitute for an old one, and to market the new product successfully the seller must convince consumers that it has all or many of the best features of the old, besides being cheaper or otherwise preferable. This gives an opening to the seller of the old product to argue that its attributes are being falsely ascribed to the new. Such arguments are likely to fare better before an administrative agency that conceives its mission as one of protecting fools from being misled than before a court that views its mission as the impartial resolution of disputes between an old and a new seller.

A perusal of FTC rules and decisions reveals hundreds of cases in which prohibitory orders have been entered against practices, not involving serious deception, by which sellers have attempted to market a new, often cheaper, substitute for an existing product. Forced disclosure of the country of origin of watchbands, Christmas tree bulbs, radio components, and scores of other products; prohibition of literally true designations on the ground that they might cause confusion with the same product made by a different process (e.g., charcoal made out of corn cobs); broad prohibitions against comparisons with more expensive substitutes; forced disclosure of facts that are irrelevant to product performance but might alarm consumers (for example, that motor oil has been "reprocessed"): these and other unworthy categories of proceeding constitute a significant part of the FTC's total output over the years.[12] And, in contrast to the antitrust area, reviewing courts have deferred broadly to the judgment of the Commission in fashioning standards of deception (e.g., the fool test), doubtless because the unfair-or-deceptive standard of section 5 of the Federal Trade Commission Act, unlike antitrust provisions, is a purely administrative standard.

Partial confirmation of the judgment that the FTC's efforts in the consumer-fraud field are systematically misdirected is furnished by a survey of the more than 200 decisions and orders in this field issued by the Commission during the 12-month period, July 1, 1962, to June 30, 1963, scanned earlier in connection with the agency's antitrust work. In more than one-third of the cases, there was, so far as one can determine from the allegations of the complaint or, in the few litigated cases, the Commission's opinion, no fraud or unfairness worthy of the name involved. Some of these cases turn on technical issues—the efficacy of vitamin or iron supplements, the salubriousness of yogurt, the efficacy of a "six month" floor wax—on which experts differ. Others involve payola, which is a form of commercial bribery and has nothing to do with fraud; still others, the use of games of chance to sell merchandise. A few involve the practice of collection agencies in smoking out elusive debtors by announcing that a reward or bequest awaits the individual whom they are trying to run to ground. A number of cases involve nondisclosure of the foreign origin of badminton-set components, watchbands, ball bearings, and other products. In one case manufacturers of domestic substitutes were called to testify that consumers prefer American-made products! In no case was there a suggestion that foreign materials or workmanship were inferior in quality to domestic, or otherwise distinguishable save in being cheaper.

A number of the cases in this group involve allegations of fictitious pricing. A sale price is represented to be lower than the seller's regular price or the manufacturer's preticketed or list price. Judging from the cases in which the Commission wrote an opinion, the seller's representation is usually accurate—the sale price is lower than the former price; the compared price is the bona fide manufacturer's list price—and the Commission's complaint is that the seller did not have many sales at the former price, or that, due to widespread discount selling in the local area, the manufacturer's list price is not a common selling price there. However, such representations are not only literally truthful, but unlikely to be understood by consumers in the strained sense insisted upon by the Commission. Consumers realize that price reductions are commonly motivated by the seller's inability to move the item at the former price and that many products are never sold at the manufacturer's list price. These cases serve no purpose other than harassment of discount sellers.

Among the many other cases in which it is hard to believe that a substantial number of consumers would be fooled are cases in which the Commission orders a seller of dime-store jewelry to disclose that its "turquoise" rings do not contain real turquoises, orders a toy manufacturer to disclose that its toy tank does not fire projectiles that actually explode, orders the maker of "First Prize" bobby pins to change the name because a consumer might think his purchase would make him eligible to enter a contest, and orders a manufacturer of shaving cream to cease representing that his product can shave sandpaper without first soaking the sandpaper for several hours. The representation that a product is "guaranteed" is interpreted by the Commission, though I doubt by any consumer, to mean fully guaranteed; furthermore, the term is deemed misleading per se unless all of the conditions of the guarantee are printed in the ad. "Free," as in "buy one and get one free," means, to the Commission, and only to the Commission, a true gratuity. The practice of offering a cheap product in order to get a hearing from the consumer and then trying to switch her to a more expensive one is condemned even where the seller appears perfectly willing to sell the cheaper product if the consumer is unconvinced by his spiel.

In another one-third or so of the year's consumer-protection cases, if there is any fraud, and my guess is that typically there is none, the private legal remedies for the wrong seem plainly adequate and there is no excuse for expending public funds. This group includes cases of passing off one product assomething else and of disparagement of competitors. Typical are false claims that a product is "stone china" or "whole cowhide" or meets the standards of the Aluminum Window Manufacturers Association. The trade association composed of sellers of the genuine article should have no difficulty obtaining an injunction in a private suit. Other cases involve sales not to consumers but to business firms, or to businessmen qua businessmen, who should be held responsible for protecting themselves against deception, either by the exercise of normal caution or by invoking the tort and contract remedies on which business enterprises usually rely in purchasing. The remaining cases in the group, and the vast majority, are those under the Fur Products Labeling Act, the Wool Products Labeling Act of 1939, and the Textile Fiber Products Identification Act.[13] Sellers of fur, wool, or textile products who resorted to fraud could be dealt with under section 5 of the Federal Trade Commission Act. The purpose of the specialized statutes, as disclosed by their terms and the legislative history,[14] is less to combat fraud than to protect the trademarks and goodwill of high-grade furs, wools, and textile fibers against infringement or dilution by sellers of cheap substitutes. Judging from the cases in my sample, much of the Commission's enforcement activity under these statutes consists of springing traps on the unwary: sellers are enjoined for failing to label natural mink "natural"; for using abbreviations instead of the full name; and for other misdeeds of comparable gravity. My point, however, is not that the Commission's enforcement of these curious laws (which it helped get enacted)[15] is frequently aberrational but that the policing of trademarks and quality standards is a job for sellers and their trade associations rather than for the government.

Another group of cases does not involve fraud or information at all. They are cases under the Flammable Fabrics Act,[16] a safety statute, curiously lodged with the FTC, which forbids the sale in interstate commerce of dangerously flammable fabrics. A number of other cases involve hard-core fraud where, if the allegations of the complaint be believed, the number and blatancy of the misrepresentations, combined with the evasive character of the respondent's operations, indicate the kind of malice or wilfulness (in the legal sense of those terms) that would justify criminal proceedings under the federal mail-fraud statute[17] or state criminal fraud laws.[18] These are the freezer-plan, correspondence-school, and other mail-order or door-to-door frauds that have long been the staple of the Commission's fraud docket. The respondents in these cases seem thorough rogues, and I would be astonished if the feeble weapons at the Commission's disposal had much effect on them beyond mild harassment and perhaps inducing some to abandon interstate commerce and prey on intrastate commerce instead.

That leaves a bare handful of cases in which Commission action may have served a useful purpose, although knowledge of the true facts might lead one to revise this estimate, and in only one case is it probable that private legal remedies would be inadequate. Thus we find cases (not marked by evidence of wilfulness) where a seller falsely claimed that a fabric had been imported from Italy; where the length of a tape was misrepresented; and where one brand of bread was falsely advertised as lower in calories than other breads. And these are instances where corrective action against the deception could probably be left to competitors. There is, however, an interesting case in which cheap jewelry was represented as goldplated, when in fact a minute layer of gold had been applied by electrolysis. At first blush, one might think that this, too, is a case where competing sellers, sellers of real goldplate, can be relied upon to correct the deception—until one remembers that the people who buy the cheap jewelry in question may not be potential customers of real goldsmiths.

In fiscal year 1963, one is forced to conclude, the FTC bought precious little consumer protection for the more than $5 million that it expended in the area of fraudulent and unfair marketing practices,[19] and the many millions more that it forced the private sector to expend in litigation and compliance. Besides wasting a good deal of money in tilting at windmills, the Commission inflicted additional social costs of unknown magnitude by impeding the free marketing of cheap substitute products, including foreign products of all kinds, fiber substitutes for animal furs, costume jewelry, and inexpensive scents; by proscribing truthful designations; by harassing discount sellers; and by obstructing a fair market test for products of debatable efficacy.

Before leaving the subject of fraud and the FTC, I should like to say a word about the extent of deception in sales to poor people. The majority report of this committee recommends that the FTC give more emphasis to the protection of poor people from fraud. I am far from satisfied with the evidence that has thus far been adduced to support the proposition that fraud is rampant in the urban slums. It consists, for the most part, of unverified and often incredible assertions by dissatisfied consumers in testimony before legislative committees or in interviews.[20] Nor is it immediately clear why fraud should be prevalent in sales to the poor. Since the poor of any major city represent in the aggregate a substantial market, one would expect sellers to compete in supplying true information about products to poor as to rich consumers. And neither the reported profit rates of slum merchants nor the structure of retail distribution and finance markets support a hypothesis of exploitation. Still, I do not deny the possibility that there may be a serious problem here. Perhaps, as Anthony Downs has argued in another context, the poor "are people who 'fall into the cracks' between the neat logical categories" of economic analysis.[21] Maybe the educational deficiencies of poor people are such that honest sellers find it too costly to educate them to the product misrepresentations of dishonest rivals. At all events, given the state of our knowledge, it is premature to unleash the FTC on the problems of poor consumers. Study should precede action. Having failed in so much else, the FTC is not likely to succeed in making a dent in our most intractable domestic problem, that of poverty, until it is better understood.

I am also concerned lest a campaign of compelling greater disclosure of product claims by slum merchants have results quite different from those intended. To repeat an earlier point, information is not costless. If slum merchants are forced to supply additional information, they will raise their prices; in effect, the careful poor consumer will be insuring his careless neighbor against the consequences of imprudence. This seems a curious way to fight poverty.[22]

IV

My colleagues of the majority, while fully conscious of the Commission's deficient performance of more than 50 years, maintain a resolute air of optimism. With better leadership and better staff, with greater appropriations, with a renewed sense of dedication, and with wise direction from committees such as these, the Commission, in their view, can still be redeemed for socially productive activities. I am not so sanguine. The Commission has done so badly continuously over so long a period of time that it is difficult any longer to regard its failings as accidental and remediable. It is not as if the deficiencies in its performance had gone unobserved until the present committee began its study. The criticisms and recommendations of this committee were anticipated by the Hoover Commission in its 1949 report on the FTC[23] in such detail as to make the present study little more than an updating of that report. And 25 years earlier a perceptive study of the FTC by Gerard Henderson had reached similar conclusions.[24]

The failure of these studies to have a significant impact on the Commission's behavior is rooted in the fact that they were preoccupied, as is the present majority report, with management efficiency. It is tempting to ascribe the deficiencies in the Commission's performance to mismanagement, and hence to focus on leadership, personnel, organization, planning, and other managerial concerns. But it is doubtful that mismanagement is more than a symptom of the agency's underlying problems. Two of these problems that have already been touched on in these pages are the unsoundness of the assumptions that underlie most of the Commission's activities and the remoteness of the Commission from Presidential interest and support. The proposition that supplies the Commission with its raison d'être—that the administrative process has a constructive role to play in supplementing judicial and market remedies against restraints of trade and deceptive practices—is highly questionable. Even if the conceptual foundations of the Federal Trade Commission were stronger than they are, the Commission would still suffer greatly from its isolation from the President. The consumer interest has always been poorly represented in Congress in comparison with organized interest groups. Dependent on Congress to a degree that no Attorney General is, the Commission is naturally influenced by the parochial interests of powerful Congressmen. And Presidents have deemed it statesmanlike to conciliate these Congressmen on appointment, staffing, and other matters relating to the Commission as a means of enlisting their support for legislation more central to the Administration's program. Exhortations by this committee are unlikely to change these stubborn facts of political life.

Another inherent limitation of the FTC arises from the structure of incentives operating on the members and staff of the Commission. Fundamentally, the problem is that the output of a regulatory agency, unlike the output of a private firm, is not sold in any market, and, not being sold, cannot be priced. As a result, regulators lack objective criteria against which to measure the effectiveness with which they pursue the goals of regulation. The absence of such criteria makes it difficult to design a system of rewards for success and punishments for failure that would align the regulators' personal interests with the social interest in effective regulation. Unlike businessmen, whose social product is measured with reasonable precision by profit-and-loss statements, or professionals, whose performance can usually be measured with tolerable accuracy by reference to widely accepted professional standards, regulators' performance cannot be well evaluated, and they are in consequence left with considerable latitude to substitute their personal goals for the social goals of regulation.[25]

This analysis has implications that go far beyond the problems of the FTC. Its relevance here is in reminding that the personal goals of FTC members and staff (power is shared between these groups, not concentrated wholly in the hands of the commissioners) influence the character and direction of the Commission's activity. It has been proposed as a reasonable hypothesis that regulators motivated by self-interest act so as (a) to retain their jobs and (b) to obtain greater appropriations for their agency as a way of augmenting personal power (and frequently remuneration as well).[26] This assumption seems reasonable as to those commissioners who seek reappointment and those members of the staff who make a career of government service. The path of self-interest for such individuals would appear to lie through conciliation of well organized economic interests and influential Congressmen—foci of political power. Zealous pursuit of the consumer interest offers few dividends besides unquiet.

Not every commissioner or staff member makes a career of government service, however. Among the 14 FTC commissioners appointed since 1949 who are not present incumbents, the average tenure was only 4 years, less than a full term (7 years). The majority of these commissioners left the agency to join private law firms. The turnover among staff is also high, and most of those who leave enter the private practice of law too. A commissioner concerned with his future success at the bar will have no greater incentive to promote the consumer interest fearlessly and impartially than one whose guiding principles are job retention and agency aggrandizement. He will receive no bonus upon entry (or reentry) into private practice for the vigorous championing of the consumer interest. The gratitude of consumers—indulging the improbable assumption that such a thing exists—cannot be translated into a larger practice. On the other hand, the enmity of the organized economic interests, the trade associations and trade unions, that a zealous pursuit of consumer interests would engender may do him some later harm, while making his tenure with the Commission more tense and demanding than would otherwise be the case. Exceptional people may rise to the challenge but they are unlikely ever to constitute a sizeable fraction of commissioners.

The picture is much the same with regard to those members of the staff who do not intend to make the Commission a career. The principal attraction of government service to lawyers who wish to use it as a steppingstone to private practice lies in the opportunities it affords to gain trial experience of an amount and at a level of responsibility usually denied young men in private firms. (Thus, it is reported that the recent reduction in the level of the FTC's litigation activity has made it difficult for the Commission to recruit good young lawyers.) The value of their trial experience to future employers is unaffected by whether the cases tried promote or impair the welfare of society. It is the experience of trying cases, the more the better, not the social payoff from the litigation, that improves the professional skills and earnings prospects of government lawyers.

Given the absence of any mechanism for effectively conforming the private interests of FTC personnel to the social interest in consumer protection, it is hardly surprising that over the years the FTC has devoted its principal efforts to bringing cases that, if our sample is at all representative, do not promote any coherent public policy, at the behest of corporations, trade associations, and trade unions whose motivation is at best to shift the costs of their private litigation to the taxpayer and at worst to harass competitors. By takingthe part of well organized economic pressure groups, representing established firms and their employees, rather than of new entrants, foreigners, and the unorganized, largely silent consumer, the FTC commissioners and staff have minimized the friction and work that a genuine dedication to consumer interests would have entailed. By concentrating on trivial fraud cases, the Commission and its staff have created the illusion of tangible results, while minimizing controversy. And by concentrating its antitrust activities not in monopolistic or oligopolistic industries, but in the most competitive industries in the American economy, such as food, textile, and retail and wholesale distribution, and by applying antitrust principles to shield powerful organized economic blocs in those industries (such as food brokers and retail gasoline dealers) from the competitive gale, the Commission has curried favor with the groups whose power to affect the fortunes of Commission personnel is greatest.

V

The alternative to a trade commission is greater reliance on market processes and on the system of judicial rights and remedies that provides the framework of transactions in the market. A comparison of these alternative institutional arrangements reveals some interesting contrasts between courts and the Commission. One is in regard to capacity for modernization and reform. During the more than 50 years that the FTC has been adrift in its backwater, enormous strides in reducing the cost and increasing the efficacy of judicial processes have been made. Judicial procedure has been radically simplified; small claims courts have been created; new rights of action have been declared — recently, at the state level, in one of the areas, protection against fraud, where the FTC has been floundering; and Neighborhood Legal Services have been created to assure meaningful legal remedies for poor people. One can criticize some of these changes, and certainly much remains to be done. In particular, it is shocking that successful litigants are generally unable to recover their legal expenses from the losing party. But the crucial fact is that the updating of the judicial process appears to be proceeding more rapidly than the reform of the administrative process.

A second source of strength in the judicial process is the prestige that judges enjoy in our society. It is significant that judicial appointment is normally a terminal appointment, not a steppingstone. In the federal court system, certainly, it is rare for judges to leave the bench for private practice. I do not mean to imply that members of administrative agencies should be given life tenure. Considering the caliber of the appointees, which I do not think would be materially improved by such a system, the results would be disastrous. For reasons apparently deeply rooted in the attitudes of lawyers, it is impossible to attract many first-rate people to a lifetime career as a member of an administrative agency. Until those attitudes change, life tenure for agency members is out of the question, and judicial enforcement of rules against fraud will continue to have this marked advantage over administrative: in striving to establish a proper balance between the rights of sellers and consumers, judges, with rare exceptions, are not going to be influenced by considerations of the impact of their decision upon a future career at the bar.

It is time to sum up. In the real world, a choice among possible institutional arrangements for dealing with social problems is a choice among highly imperfect alternatives. A free market backed up by private judicial remedies will not eliminate all frauds, nor will the Antitrust Division action through the courts eliminate all restraints of trade. It does not follow that the administrative process should be used as an alternative or supplement to these approaches.

Since many of the basic goals and policies of the institution seem to me misconceived, I cannot regard proposals for improvements in its operational efficiency without mixed feelings. On the other hand, I do not believe that a proposal for abolition of the FTC can be justified on the basis of the kind of evidence that I have been able to assemble for the purposes of this statement. I would propose, however, a policy of (a) freezing the Commission's appropriations at their present level and (b) withholding from it any new responsibilities. It is scandalous to allow so dubious an enterprise to continue to wax in size and power. The procedure that I suggest would at least force the agency and its supporters to attempt to justify its existence and actions. If no justification were forthcoming, the freeze would be maintained and the forces of inflation and economic growth would gradually effect a practical repeal of the regulatory scheme.

NOTES

1. Cox, Fellmuth, and Schulz, The Consumer and the Federal Trade Commission (1969), reprinted in 115 Cong. Rec. E. 370 (daily ed., Jan. 22, 1969).
2. Rublee, "The Origianl Plan and Early History of the Federal Trade Commission," 11 Acad. Pol. Sci. Proc. (1926), 666, 669-70.
3. I do not mean that the only purpose of the law of contracts is to prevent bad faith; another is to resolve peaceably bona fide disputes arising from ambiguity, unforeseen circumstances, and the like.
4. Restatement, Contracts, § 470 et seq. (1932). Fraud and misrepresentation are also torts. Restatement, Torts, § 525 et seq. (1938).
5. See American Washboard Co. v. Saginaw Mfg. Co., 103 Fed. 281 (6th cir. 1900); "Developments in the Law—Competitive Torts," 77 Harv. L. Rev. 888, 905-07 (1964).

6. *See, e.g.*, 45 U. S. C. 51 *et seq*. (1964) (Federal Employers' Liability Act).

7. Perhaps because, as we shall see, the FTC affords a costless remedy to a firm injured by a competitor's deceptive sales practices.

8. *See* 15 U. S. C. 1125 (1964).

9. *See, e.g.*, Aronberg v. FTC, 132 F. 2d 165, 167 (7th Cir. 1942); General Motors Corp. v. FTC, 114 F. 2d 33, 36 (2d Cir. 1940), certiorari denied, 312 U. S. 682 (1941); Exposition Press, Inc. v. FTC, 295 F. 2d 869, 872 (2d Cir. 1961).

10. *See* FTC 1960 Ann. Rep., p. 82.

11. Stigler "The Organization of Industry 67" (1968).

12. Many of these cases are discussed in Alexander, *Honesty and Competition* (1967).

13. 15 U. S. C. 69 (1964); 15 U. S. C. 68 *et seq*. (1964); 15 U. S. C. 71 (1964).

14. Cited in the discussion of the Bureau of Textiles and Furs in Part V.A. of the majority report.

15. *See, e.g.*, Hearings on H. R. 2321 before a Subcomm. of the H. Comm. on Interstate and Foreign Commerce, 82d Cong., 1st Sess. 8 (1951).

16. 15 U. S. C. 1191 *et seq*. (1964).

17. 18 U. S. C. 1341 (1964).

18. Collected in Note, "The Regulation of Advertising," 56 *Colum. L. Rev.* 1018, 1098-1111 (1956).

19. FTC 1963 Ann. Rep.

20. *See* items cited in section V.A. of the majority report. The lawyer's penchant for substituting anecdotal for scientific evidence has been a frequent source of blunders. A relevant case is that of predatory pricing. For many years it was believed that large sellers would frequently sell below their cost in order to destroy their competitors. This belief, sustained by victims' anecdotes much like those we now read about in the fraud area, spurred enactment of section 2 of the original Clayton Act and other statutes. In 1958, a scholarly study of the Standard Oil Trust showed that, even before section 2 was enacted, the most notorious predator of them all had not, in fact, employed predatory pricing; the study also supplied reasons why, as a matter of economic theory, such pricing is rarely a rational strategy for monopolizing. McGee, "Predatory Price Cutting: The Standard Oil (N. J.) Case," 1 *J. Law* & Econ. 137 (1958). This study has never been refuted, and is widely accepted. See Turner "Conglomerate Mergers and Section 7 of the Clayton Act," 78 *Harv. L. Rev.* 1313, 1339-52 (1965). And they are corroborated by the extraordinary paucity of cases over the years in which predatory pricing could plausibly be inferred. Predatory pricing is now regarded by most students of antitrust as very largely a mythical beast. The belief in its reality was based on the same kind of casual, anecdotal evidence now adduced, again without good basis in theory, to create belief in the existence of a serious problem of consumer fraud.

21. Comments, in *Issues in Urban Economics* 419, 426 (Perloff & Wingo, eds. 1968).

22. Equally questionable are proposals to abrogate, as unfair, certain devices used in the financing of consumer purchases, such as the defense of holder in due course. See, e.g., Comment, "Consumer Legislation and the Poor," 76 *Yale L. J.* 745 (1967). Any rule that makes it more costly for merchants or finance companies to do business with poor people is likely to raise the price of products and credit to them, and thereby make it even more difficult for them to obtain the goods they want.

23. Commission on Organization of the Executive Branch of the Government, Task Force on Regulatory Commissions, Appendix N, p. 122 (1949).

24. Henderson, *supra* note 4, ch. VI.

25. Cf. Downs, *Inside Bureaucracy* (1966); Stigler, "The Regulation of Industry" (April 10, 1969, unpublished).

26. Ibid.

14. THE FEDERAL TRADE COMMISSION AND THE REGULATION OF ADVERTISING IN THE CONSUMER INTEREST

Dorothy Cohen

IT IS the purpose of this article to review the present means by which the Federal Trade Commission regulates advertising for the protection of the consumer, as well as the adequacy of the criteria which underlie the regulatory process. Further, it is suggested that additional measures be taken that would increase the effectiveness of the advertising regulatory process.

In implementing its responsibility to regulate advertising for the protection of consumers, the Federal Trade Commission has developed informal decision criteria. In broad terms, the Commission's judgments have been consistent with an "economic man" concept of consumer purchase behavior. It views the consumer as an informed, reasoning decision maker using objective values to maximize utilities. This is essentially a normative concept.

The basic assumptions of the Commission's regulatory design or criteria are maximization of the consumer's utilities and rational choice. A necessary ingredient to fulfill these assumptions is full, accurate information. The Commission, therefore, protects the consumer by identifying and attacking information which is insufficient, false, or misleading. These deficiencies are uncovered by relating the objective characteristics of a product, as determined by the Commission, to its advertising representations.

The Commission, therefore, operates under the legally and economically acceptable premise that the consumer is to be assured full and accurate information which will permit him to make a reasoned choice in the marketplace. Nonetheless, examination of the results of the Commission's activities utilizing this concept reveals the existence of several gaps in its protection. For example, the poor are not always protected from excessive payments because of lack

Reprinted from *Journal of Marketing*, Vol. 33 (January, 1969), 40-44, published by The American Marketing Association.

of information about true cost or true price. The health and safety of the consumer are not always assured, since information concerning the hazards of using particular products is not always available. The belief that added protection is needed was reinforced by a report of the Consumer Advisory Council to President Johnson which states "that although this is an era of abundance . . . there is also much confusion and ignorance, some deception and even fraud. . . ."[1]

The need for added protection does not necessarily suggest discarding the Commission's regulatory framework, because a more effective structure currently does not exist. The elimination of the present regulatory design would in fact create a void in the consumer protection network. It does suggest, however, that steps should be taken as a basis for stronger protection in the future. The current movement to improve regulation through stressing full disclosure, while serving to eliminate some deficiencies, is not sufficient.[2] The Consumer Advisory Council's report, for example, in summarizing the outlook for the future observes:

> Technological change is so rapid that the consumer who bothers to learn about a commodity or a service soon finds his knowledge obsolete. In addition, many improvements in quality and performance are below the threshold of perception, and imaginative marketing often makes rational choice even more of a problem.[3]

Full disclosure of pertinent facts is one step in improving the protection network. Additional steps are needed to assure that the consumer understands the significance of the facts. It has been noted, for example, that the consumer is selective in his acceptance of information offered. This selectivity is due, in part, to a difference between the objective environment in which the consumer "really" lives and the subjective environment he perceives and responds to.[4] The consumer reacts to information not only with his intelligence, but also with habits, traits, attitudes, and feelings. In addition, his decisions are influenced significantly by opinion leaders, reference groups, and so on. There are predispositions at work within the individual that determine what he is exposed to, what he perceives, what he remembers, and the effect of the communication upon him.[5]

It has been noted that appeal to fear (emphasizing the hazards of smoking or of borrowing money) may not deter the chronically anxious consumer, nor will it necessarily protect his health or pocketbook. Valid communications from a non-authoritative source may be readily accepted. Thus, the extensive use of "sufficient" truth may take on an aura of non-believability and be rejected. Attempts to avoid conflicting evidence may result in ignoring the information completely.

The Commission's efforts to provide the consumer with economic information concerning value are not completely effective, since the consumer does not measure value in economic terms alone. Brand loyalties create values in the eyes of the consumer as does the influence of social groups and opinion leaders within these groups. His desire to attain certain levels of aspiration may lead the consumer to be a "satisficing animal . . . rather than a maximizing animal,"[6] that is, one who chooses among values that may be currently suitable, rather than those which maximize utilities. In order for the Commission to improve the consumer protection network, it must reflect an understanding of the behavioral traits of consumers.

Adapting the regulatory design to handle behavioral traits is no easy task. An examination of a behavioral model of consumer performance reveals the existence of many intervening variables, so that the creation of standards for this non-standardized consumer becomes exceedingly difficult. Moreover, current knowledge of the consumer as a behavioralist is far from complete. Indeed, the feasibility and success associated with the practical uses of this model are dependent upon future research.

It is, therefore, recommended that attention be directed toward current and future research in the behavioral sciences to devise means for amending the advertising regulatory framework. This would lead to improvements in the communication process and the elimination of protection gaps. The application of behavioral characteristics to the regulatory model is not intended as a panacea, but is a suggestion for improving some regulatory ailments. In broad policy terms the Commission can initially do little more than establish closer contact with the consumer and analyze behavioral data which may be relevant to the regulation of advertising. Suggestions for improved administrative procedures are limited to applications of current behavioral knowledge of the consumer. Future research may suggest more precise administrative action, for increased knowledge of the consumer's buying behavior should lead to the development of more effective mechanisms for his protection.

RECOMMENDATIONS

The following specific recommendations are suggested as guidelines for future governmental activities relative to consumer advertising.

BUREAU OF BEHAVIORAL STUDIES

A Bureau of Behavioral Studies should be established within the Federal Trade Commission (similar to the Commission's Bureau of Economics) whose function would be to gather and analyze data on consumer buying behavior relevant to the regulation of advertising in the consumer interest.

CONSUMER COMPLAINT OFFICES

The Federal Trade Commission should establish "consumer complaint" offices throughout the United States. One method of gathering more information about the consumer is to provide closer contact between the Federal Trade Commission and the public. Complaints about advertising abuses may originate with consumers, but these have been at a minimum; and lately the Commission has accentuated its industry-wide approach to deceptive practices. Although the industry-wide approach is geared toward prevention and permits the FTC to deal with broad areas of deception, it minimizes the possibility of consumer contact with the Commission. In 1967, awareness of this fact re-sulted in an action in which the Commission's Bureau of Field Operations and its 11 field offices located in cities across the United States intensified its program of public education designed to give businessmen and consumers a better understanding of the work of the agency.[7]

If the Commission is to operate satisfactorily in the consumer interest, it must develop a closer relationship with consumers. Most consumers are still uncertain about the protection they are receiving, and the Federal Trade Commission appears to be an unapproachable body with little apparent contact with the "man-on-the-street."

Consumer complaint offices would identify the Federal Trade Commission's interest in the consumer and act as a clearing house for information. Consumers could be informed about steps to take if they believe they have been deceived, what recourse is open, and how to secure redress for griev-ances. The Commission could secure evidence about deception directly from consumers. Moreover, the complaints of these private individuals might be based on non-economic factors, permitting clearer delineation of the behavioral man and the ways in which he might be protected.

PRIORITY OF PROTECTION

The Federal Trade Commission should establish a definitive policy of priority of protection based on the severity of the consequences of the advertis-ing. While appropriations and manpower for the Federal Trade Commission have increased in recent years, they are still far from adequate to police all advertising. Therefore, the ability to protect is limited and selective. In its recent annual report the Commission did indicate, however, that it had estab-lished priorities:

> A high priority is accorded those matters which relate to the basic necessities of life, and to situations in which the impact of false and misleading advertising, or other unfair and deceptive practices, falls with cruelest impact upon those least able to survive the con-sequences—the elderly and the poor.[8]

Nevertheless, in the same year the Commission reported that approximately 20% of the funds devoted to curtailing deceptive practices were expended on textile and fur enforcement (noting that the Bureau on Textiles and Furs made 12,679 inspections on the manufacturing, wholesaling, and retailing level).[9]

Priority may be established in two ways. First, it may be considered rela-tive to the harmful consequences of deceptive advertising. This approach could suggest, for example, that the Federal Trade Commission devote more of its energies to examining conflicting claims in cigarette advertising than to examining conflicting claims in analgesic advertising (which seems to focus on the question of whether one pain reliever acts faster than the other). Exercis-ing such priorities might accelerate the movement toward needed reforms (such as the current safety reforms in the automobile industry) by pinpointing the existence of inadequately protected consumer areas.

A second method of establishing priority could be to delineate the groups that are most susceptible to questionable advertising. This is where the behavioral model may play an important role. Sociologists are trying to discover common aspects of group behavior, and research has disclosed that each social class has its own language pattern.[10] Special meanings and symbols accentuate the differences between groups and increase social distance from outsiders.[11]

Disclosure of special facets of group behavior should be helpful to the Commission in designing a program of protection. As noted earlier, the poor cannot be adequately protected by the disclosure of true interest rates because their aspirations may provide a stronger motivating influence than the fear of excessive debt. Knowledge of the actual cost of borrowing would offer no protection to the low-income family which knows no sources of goods and credit available to it other than costly ones. Nor would higher cost of borrowing deter the consumer who, concerned mostly with the amount of the monthly payment, may look at credit as a means of achieving his goals. In fact, the Federal Trade Commission concluded, in a recent economic report on installment sales and credit practices in the District of Columbia, that truth-in-lending, although needed, is not sufficient to solve the problem of excessive use of installment credit for those consumers who are considered poor credit risks and are unsophisticated buyers.[12]

The problems of the poor extend beyond the possible costs of credit. They include the hazards of repossession, the prices paid for items in addition to credit costs, and the possibility of assuming long-term debt under a contractual obligation not clear at the outset. It is possible that behavioral studies may disclose a communication system that would be a more effective deterrent to the misuse of credit than the disclosure of exorbitant interest rates. Until then, the Commission should give priority to investigations where the possibility of fraudulent claims, representations, and pricing accompany the offering of credit facilities to low-income groups. For example, advertisements of "three complete rooms of furniture for $199.00, easy payments" continue to appear despite the Commission's ruling that "bait and switch" tactics are unfair. Thus, the possibility exists that the low-income consumer may be "switched" to a much more expensive purchase whose costs become abnormally high due to the exorbitant interest rates included in the "easy payments." In its monitoring and review of advertising the Commission's staff should give precedence to investigations of such "bargain, easy payments" advertising, since much of it is especially designed to attract the low-income groups.

IMPROVEMENT OF THE COMMUNICATION PROCESS

The consumer's cognitive capacity (the attitudes, perceptions, or beliefs about one's environment) and its effect on the communication process should be reflected in designing advertising controls so that the inefficient mechanisms can be improved or eliminated.

Currently the concept of full disclosure is being expanded as the major means of offering the consumer additional protection. This is particularly evident where the objective is to dissuade the consumer from the use of or excessive use of a product or service. Little attention is paid, however, to determining whether the selective consumer is taking note of these disclosures.

An examination of behavioral man reveals that he is less "perfect" than economic man. His values are not based on objective realities alone, nor are his choices always what may be objectively considered as best among alternatives. In legislative design the regulatory authorities should come to grips with the question of whether protection of the consumer includes "protection from himself." There are indications that the latter concept is considered a legitimate area for regulatory activities—as evidenced in legislation affecting cigarette advertising and in some elements of the truth-in-lending and truth-in-packaging bills.

While questions may be raised about the legitimacy of interfering with the consumer's "freedom of choice," there is evidence that the methodology devised for this interference is deficient. In the current regulatory design, the proposed method of securing these different kinds of protection is the same, although the kinds of protection offered to the consumer may differ. For example, the consumer is currently protected against deceptive advertising by laws requiring that he be provided with truthful disclosure as to the product and its features. Where authorities believe that the advertising claims of certain products or services should be minimally used or completely avoided, the consumer is again protected by non-deceptive "full disclosure" as to the product and its features. Yet a quick review of consumer behavior and persuasibility reveals that a strategy designed to change or dissuade must, of necessity, differ from a strategy designed to reinforce. The consumer may be quite willing to accept information which supports his beliefs or preconceptions and yet be unwilling to accept evidence which refutes these same beliefs. Moreover, research has disclosed that adherence to recommended behavior is inversely related to the intensity of fear arousal. Intense fear appeal may be ineffective since it arouses anxiety within the subject which can be reduced by his hostility toward the communication and rejection of the message. It has also been noted that the tendency toward dissonance reduction can lead to failure to understand the information disclosed. Thus "full disclosure" cannot be a completely effective control mechanism when its main purpose is to protect the consumer from using a particular product or service, for the consumer may simply ignore these disclosures.

Based on current research, one approach the Commission might take toward an improved program of dissuasion would be to reinforce the negative information through an authoritative source, such as the Commission itself. Although the agency has a number of publications—*Annual Report, News Summary, Advertising Alert*—none of these is specifically geared to provide the consumer with information. A monthly report to consumers, initially available at "consumer complaint" offices, might serve as an effective mechanism for denoting the existence of hazardous products, excessive claims, questionable representations, and so forth. Specifically, this report could detail information of particular interest to consumers concerning advertising abuses that had been curtailed, cease and desist orders, questionable advertising practices currently under investigation, and so on. It is also suggested that this printed publication occasionally be supplemented by reports through a more pervasive medium—television.

It is not recommended that the Commission become a product-testing service, since the latter implies governmental control over competitive offerings and could place excessive restrictions on freedom of choice. Instead the report is to be considered a communication device, designed to insure that consumers take more note of available information on the premise that the information emanates from an authoritative governmental source.

BEHAVIORAL CRITERIA

The Federal Trade Commission should use behavioral as well as economic criteria in evaluating consumer interest. Subjective as well as objective claims should be examined in determining whether a "tendency to deceive" exists. Due to insufficient knowledge of consumer behavior, an accurate blueprint for defining products in terms of consumer choice is not available. Future research may present more precise propositions about consumer behavior which would facilitate the development and implementation of behavioral criteria. However, currently there are areas wherein the adaptation of behavioral factors in establishing criteria for advertising regulation may provide for more adequate protection in the consumer interest.

Assuming it were possible to provide the consumer with complete information based on economic criteria, the individual may still be unable to exercise informed choice. A recent report by the National Commission on Food Marketing stated: "Given complete price information, the help of computers and all the clerical help needed, it is impossible to say which retailer in a particular community has lower prices."[13] Moreover, as noted earlier, individuals do not choose on the basis of price appeal alone.

Advertising today, to a great extent, stresses non-economic or promotional differences. Products are denoted as being preferred by groups, individuals, society, motion picture stars, sports leaders, and the average man. Since consumers may make their selections on the basis of these promotional representations, adequate protection requires that advertisements be subject to as close an examination for deceptive representation as they are for deceptive price claims.

Insufficient emphasis has been placed in the advertising regulatory design on the importance of testimonials in influencing consumer choice. In the examination of the selective consumer, it has been noted that his choice is influenced by a desire for group membership and by the opinion of leaders within these groups. It has also been noted that the consumer engages in selective exposure and selective perception, suggesting that when the consumer finally does accept an "opinion leader," the latter exerts significant pressure on the consumer's choice.

The use of testimonials in advertising takes account of this fact of consumer behavior, but the regulatory design does not. Those who are deemed to be opinion leaders and dominant members of groups are selected and paid for their "testimonials." Moreover, where the selected figure does not perform well, for example, on television, an actor is used to replace him. The consumer may be deceived into believing an "opinion leader" is evaluating a product or service. These opinions may be used by the consumer to substantiate the suitability of this particular item in his own value structure.

Currently, the basic legal requirement is that testimonials be truthful. However, if someone declares that he prefers "Brand X," validation of this statement is necessarily subjective. Adequate consumer protection requires more stringent regulations which should extend into evidence of truthfulness of this testimonial and disclosure as to the way in which it was secured. It is suggested that in using a testimonial no substitute attestors be allowed; and if payment has been made for the endorsement, the advertisement should so state. If evidence is available that the individual does not use the product (such as a cigar recommendation by a non-cigar smoker), his testimonial should not be permitted.

SUMMARY

In its efforts to protect the consumer against advertising abuse, the Federal Trade Commission has developed a protective network in the consumer interest primarily based on economic standards. There are gaps in this protection network, which result from the fact that the consumer does not appraise his interest solely in economic terms. Rather, the consumer develops patterns of buying behavior that reflect the influence of noneconomic values and the individuals's cognitive capacity. The Federal Trade Commission should take cognizance of this "behavioral" man in its consumer interest activities.

It is recommended that the Commission become more familiar with and establish closer contact with the consumer through a Bureau of Behavioral Research, consumer complaint offices and through the distribution of consumer publications to disclose advertising irregularities. In addition, it is recommended that the Commission adapt regulatory criteria to current knowledge of the behavioral man in order to assure that federal regulation of advertising is accurately functioning in the consumer interest.

NOTES

1. *Consumer Issues '66,* A Report Prepared by the Consumer Advisory Council (Washington, D.C.: U.S. Government Printing Office, 1966), p. 1.

2. *See* The J. B. Williams Co., Inc. and Parkson Advertising Agency, Inc. v. FTC, *5 Trade Regulation Reporter No. 72,182* (Chicago, Ill.: Commerce Clearing House, Inc., August, 1967); and several aspects of truth-in-packaging and truth-in-lending legislation.

3. *Consumer Issues '66,* p. 6.

4. Herbert A. Simon, "Economics and Psychology," in *Psychology: A Study of a Science,* Simon Koch, ed., Vol. 6 (New York: McGraw-Hill Book Co., Inc., 1963), p. 710.

5. Joseph T. Klapper, "The Social Effects of Mass Communication," in *The Source of Human Communication,* Wilbur Schramm, ed. (New York: Basic Books, Inc., 1963), p. 67.

6. Simon, "Economics and Psychology," p. 716.

7. Federal Trade Commission, *Annual Report,* 1967, p. 67.

8. Federal Trade Commission, at p. 17.

9. Federal Trade Commission, at pp. 30 and 81.

10. Leonard Schatzman and Anselm Strauss, "Social Class and Modes of Communication," *American Journal of Sociology,* 60 (January 1955), pp. 329-338.

11. Tamotsu Shibutani, "Reference Groups as Perspectives," *American Journal of Sociology,* 60 (May 1955), p. 567.

12. *5 Trade Regulation Reporter No. 50,205* (Chicago, Ill.: Commerce Clearing House, Inc., July 1968).

13. *Organization and Competition in Food Retailing, Technical Study No. 7,* a report prepared by the National Commission on Food Marketing (Washington, D.C.: U.S. Government Printing Office, 1966), p. 169.

15. OLIGOPOLY AND DECEPTIVE ADVERTISING: THE CEREAL INDUSTRY AFFAIR

Paul D. Scanlon

MARKET STRUCTURE AND PRODUCT PERFORMANCE

MR. CHAIRMAN, members of the Subcommittee: We think it would be most unfortunate if these hearings should end without some discussion of the underlying structural *causes* that have produced the unsatisfactory patterns of behavior in the cereal industry that Mr. Choate has so vividly described for you. The thesis we wish to present is that industrial behavior of this kind —large amounts of promotional (noninformational) advertising accompanied by high prices and product stagnation or deterioration—is largely dictated by certain structural features of an industry and thus can only be cured by reforms addressed to those more basic industrial factors and to the lines of conduct that create and support them.

Some definitional concepts should be noted at the outset, particularly the fact that the terms we employ here are used in their economic rather than their legal sense. By the term "monopoly," for example—and its multi-firm synonym, "oligopoly"—we refer simply to a situation in which the share of an industry's sales held by the 3 or 4 largest firms is so great that, by long-established economic principles and empirical research, the likelihood of prices being set at economically competitive levels is not particularly great. Similarly, when we use such synonymous terms as "monopoly price," "oligopoly price," and "overcharge," we refer merely to a price that exceeds the one that would be expected to prevail if the industry in question was competitively structured (unconcentrated), not one that necessarily offends the Sherman Act of 1890 or any other antitrust statute.

Reprinted by permission from *Antitrust Law & Economics Review*, Vol. 3, No. 3 (Spring 1970), pp. 99-110.

CONCENTRATION RATIO A "COLLUSION INDEX"

In brief, this 4-firm market share or concentration ratio is considered, in the words of the current Economic Assistant to the head of the Antitrust Division, as something of a "collusion index"—the higher it rises, the greater the probability that collusion in one form or another will appear in the industry. The most widely-accepted boundary or dividing line on the structural spectrum at which competitive pricing is believed to significantly give way to noncompetitive or monopolistic pricing is the point at which those 4-largest firms control 50% or more of the industry's total sales.[1] Beyond this point on the concentration scale, few knowledgeable non-industry economists would care to bet too heavily on the consumer's chances of being able to buy the industry's product at a competitive price. Whether accomplished through collusion or otherwise, the fact is that serious price competition seems to lose most of its cutting edge in industries that have been able to achieve this comfortable position the economists call "structural oligopoly."

ADVERTISING AND PRODUCT VARIATIONS

This death of price competition in these higher ranges of concentration tends to produce, in addition to monopoly prices, some other unfortunate side effects. If the product is one that lends itself to "differentiation"—to promotional efforts designed to convince consumers that it is "different" from products that are in fact identical—then high volumes of advertising tend to appear, along with a proliferation of surface variations in the basic product, particularly in matters of style and design.[2] The money expended on advertising and style changes has to be recovered, of course, together with a return on the capital employed in those promotional activities, and this means the price to the consumer must be raised accordingly.

ADVERTISING AS A CAUSE OF HIGH CONCENTRATION

The kinds of high-level advertising expenditures common in industries of this kind—"high levels" being defined generally (and conservatively) as those that amount to approximately 5% of industry sales or more—also tend to have a "feed-back" effect on concentration. By and large it is only the very largest firms in an industry that can afford either the high cost of say TV network advertising or the high risks inherent in gambling such large sums of money on these high-cost advertising campaigns. The result is that, in industries where intensive advertising is the rule, concentration tends to be very high, with the smaller firms being effectively barred from serious growth (and small outside firms from entry) by the high-cost, high-risk nature of that kind of promotion. High-volume advertising tends to increase concentration still further, then, continuously widening the gap between the large and the small, the established firm and the potential entrant.

126

The result is that the phenomenon of rising concentration in American industry is focused primarily on *consumer goods* (rather than producer goods, those sold to businessmen) and, within that broad category, on differentiated consumer goods.[3] In short, most of the increases in concentration in the country at the present time are attributable to product differentiation induced by high-intensity advertising, particularly TV advertising.

CONCENTRATION LEVELS AND ADVERTISING EXPENDITURES

A certain level of concentration, either existing or anticipated, is generally necessary, however, before it becomes exceptionally profitable for a firm to engage in large-scale product promotion. In the very low concentration ranges, the individual firm has so small a share of the total market that it may well be unable to capture enough of the added sales volume its advertising generates to recover its cost. This "leakage" factor diminishes as market share rises, reaching zero at the complete monopoly level, the point at which the firm *is* the industry and thus at which any increase in industry-wide sales accrues solely to the advertiser himself and not to his non-advertising competitors.[4]

In brief, rising concentration in consumer industries tends to be accompanied by rising expenditures on advertising. Lower concentration ranges tend to be associated with smaller expenditures on advertising and of course with lower consumer prices. (In some industries, particularly those in which consumers are the most vulnerable to unverifiable claims—i.e., those in which consumers are technically the least able to make their own evaluations of the properties of the advertised products or to acquire the necessary technical skills—advertising expenditures sometimes account for as much as 40% of the industry's total sales.) Concentration produces high advertising expenditures—and high advertising expenditures produce high concentration. The two feed upon and strengthen each other.

CONCENTRATION AND TECHNOLOGICAL PROGRESS

One other aspect of the product-quality problem should be mentioned here. It was widely believed by economists at one time that technological progress—inventions and innovations—were helped rather than hurt by monopoly. The argument was that, without monopoly profits, there would be neither the *incentive* nor the *wherewithal* to build the expensive laboratories that were thought to be the seedbed of new technological developments. Today, with mounting evidence that the giants of industry contribute *less* rather than more than their share of significant innovations and that they have repeatedly conspired to suppress new inventions, few knowledgeable economists would care to defend the thesis that high concentration is necessary if we are to continue our scientific progress. Indeed, the suspicion is growing that precisely the opposite is the case, that monopoly (and oligopoly) has the same effect on the incentive to compete on *product quality* that it has on the incentive to compete on *price*, namely, a decidedly negative effect. There can be little doubt, for example, that there are today many industries in which lower concentration would result in more strenuous research efforts and thus in better products at lower prices.[5] Monopoly and oligopoly are thus implacable enemies of the consumer interest in product quality as well as in price.

INFLATED PRICES UNDER COLLUSION AND OLIGOPOLY

One final introductory matter might be mentioned here before we turn to the cereal industry. A number of empirical investigations have been conducted by economists specializing in the economics of monopoly in an effort to estimate the quantitative effects of monopoly and oligopoly on the price paid by consumers. The results of some of these studies offer some insight into what we can expect by way of consumer losses under various conditions of monopoly or oligopoly:

> Collusive or price-fixing agreements among competing firms, a type of monopolization that is presumably approximated in terms of its effect on price under conditions of high concentration (oligopoly), tend to inflate consumer prices on the average by some 25% or more above the level that would have prevailed under competitive conditions.[6]
>
> Resale price-fixing or "fair trade," the kind of vertical collusion in which a manufacturer dictates the price to be charged the consumer by his dealer, tends to inflate consumer prices by from 35% to 40% above competitive levels.[7]

INFLATED COSTS UNDER COLLUSION AND OLIGOPOLY

Costs tend to rise sharply under collusion and similarly under oligopoly—e.g. in higher executive salaries and in larger DC-3's for their traveling pleasure—which means that the *profits* retained by the firms in oligopoly industries greatly *understate* the loss to the consumer. (In one case, for example, prices rose by 32% during a price-fixing conspiracy but an accompanying 23% increase in costs left the industry with monopoly profits of only 9 additional percentage points on sales. When the conspiracy was broken up, prices fell by the whole amount, 32%, not by just 9%, the residual monopoly profits. In other words, elimination of collusion or monopoly causes *efficiency* to return to an industry along with competition on price and on product quality.)[8]

"Product differentiation," the development of "consumer franchises" via high-volume advertising and restrictive dealer systems, tends to inflate prices on the average by some 20% or more above the competitive price level.[9]

128

Considering all of these findings together, one might conservatively estimate that consumer prices are, on the average, at least 25% above the competitive level in those industries that are classed as "structural oligopolies," those in which the 4 largest firms account for 50% or more to total industry sales.

Roughly 25% of American manufacturing—about 100 out of a total of 430 manufacturing industries—is so blessed,[10] including the breakfast cereal industry.

CEREAL INDUSTRY—CONCENTRATION AND ENTRY BARRIERS

The essential structural features of the cereal industry and the conduct-performance patterns they have given rise to can be briefly summarized as follows:

1. *Concentration* is exceedingly high in the cereal industry, with the 3 largest firms—Kellogg, General Foods, and General Mills—together accounting for approximately 85% of the industry's total sales. The remaining 15% is shared by some 40-odd firms,[11] all but about 2% of it being held by the next 3 largest firms.

2. Exceedingly high *entry barriers* of the so-called *"product differentiation"* variety are maintained in the industry via the expenditure, by the 3 largest firms, of approximately 15% of each sales dollar on advertising, particularly TV advertising.

CEREAL INDUSTRY PERFORMANCE CHARACTERISTICS

3. *Industry profits* are maintained at super-competitive levels, with Kellogg, the industry leader (over 40% of industry sales) averaging an after-tax return on stockholders' equity of over 20% year-after-year, or more than double the competitive norm.

4. *Advertising expenditures* by the 3 largest firms—expenditures that run, as noted, to 15% or more of every sales dollar—greatly exceed the level that would be expected to prevail if the industry was competitively structured and thus alone add more than 10% to the cost of the final product to the consumer.

5. *Product quality* is, as Mr. Choate has so eloquently described, at a very low level, competitive rivalry having been diverted away from price and quality and over to the proliferation of varieties of brand names and insubstantial product variations.

6. *Consumer prices* are maintained at higher-than-competitive levels, probably at 25% or more above the price that would be expected to prevail under a competitive (unconcentrated) industry structure. With industry sales of nearly $1 billion per year (at retail), the consumer is probably paying at least $250 million per year more

for breakfast cereals than he would be required to pay if the industry were unconcentrated.

7. There are *no "scale-economy"* or "efficiency" justifications for the high degree of concentration present in the cereal industry. All cost savings associated with large firm size are realized in this industry at a volume of output equal to from 1% to 5% of the industry's total sales[12]—which means that the industry could readily support *between 20 and 100 efficient-size firms.*

ADVERTISING AND MONOPOLY IN OTHER INDUSTRIES

It should be emphasized again, however, that, while the cereal industry is one of the more obvious examples of the country's roughly 100 oligopolized industries and the exceedingly poor social performance that this structural condition spawns, it is by no means unique in this respect. Virtually all of the characteristics described here would apply almost equally well to most of the other members of the oligopoly group, including automobiles, gasoline, home electrical appliances, soap, soup, coffee, orange juice, bread, aspirin, cigarettes, cosmetics, razor blades, and so forth. These are all highly concentrated industries; they all spend exceptionally large amounts on product promotion and distribution; and they all charge prices that greatly exceed the levels that would prevail if they were more competitively structured (less concentrated). Indeed, the cost to the consumer from the advertising-induced overpricing in some of these other industries—for example, the super-competitive car prices that stem from the auto industry's annual model changes, TV advertising, elaborate network of trade-restraining dealerships, and 2-firm dominance of the industry—obviously exceeds by a very substantial margin the $250 million or so in higher-than-competitive prices that the $1 billion cereal industry is currently imposing.

PRICE DIFFERENTIAL BETWEEN "BRANDED" AND "PRIVATE-LABEL" PRODUCTS

One of the best measures of an industry's monopoly power—its power to charge the consumer a higher-than-competitive price—is the size of the price differential between the industry's highly-advertised "brand" products and the so-called unbranded or "private-label" products that it produces for its large chain-store customers for resale under their own names. Because these large buyers often have the capacity and incentive to build their own manufacturing plants—to "vertically integrate"—they frequently can and do refuse to pay more than a competitive price for this private-brand merchandise. And, for precisely the same reasons, they are often able to and do insist that the products they sell under their own labels be at least *equal in quality* to the best advertised brands. Private-label prices frequently provide, therefore, some rough approximations of what the competitive price would be on all of an industry's products

Table 1

Comparative Prices of Manufacturer Brand and Private Label Products,
Selected Items, A&P Stores in Washington, D.C., June 10, 1970

Product	"Brand" Product	A&P "Private Label"	Price Difference	Percentage Difference in Price
Laundry Bleach	59¢	45¢	14¢	23.7%
(Gallon Bottle)	(Clorox)	(A&P)		
Scouring Pads	49¢	39¢	10¢	20.4%
(18 in pkg.)	(Brillo)	(A&P)		
Window Cleaner	33¢	27¢	6¢	18.2%
(8 oz.)	(Windex)	A&P)		
Aluminum Foil	65¢	46¢	18¢	27.7%
(18 in. x 25 ft. roll)	(Reynold's)	(A&P)		
Cleanser	2/37¢	2/25¢	12¢	32.4%
(18 oz.)	(Comet)	(Sail)		
Furniture Polish	95¢	49¢	46¢	48.4%
(7 oz. spray can-lemon)	(Pledge)	(A&P)		
Liquid Detergent	57¢	43¢	14¢	24.6%
(22 oz. plastic)	(Ivory)	(Sail)		
Spray Disinfectant	85¢	59¢	26¢	30.6%
(7 oz. can)	(Lysol)	(A&P)		
Golden Cream Corn	29¢	20¢	9¢	31.0%
(17 oz. can)	(Del Monte)	(A&P)		
Canned Dog Food	6/88¢	6/65¢	23¢	26.1%
(15-1/2 oz. can)	(Ken-L-Ration)	(Daily)		
Mouthwash	89¢	59¢	30¢	33.7%
(14 oz. bottle)	(Listerine)	(A&P)		
(12 oz. bottle)	89¢	59¢	30¢	33.7%
	(Scope)	(A&P)		
Spray Deodorant	$1.19	69¢	50¢	42.0%
(7 oz. can)	(Right Guard)	(A&P)		
Liquid Shampoo	95¢	59¢	36¢	37.9%
(8 oz. bottle)	(Breck)	(A&P)		
Shave Cream	95¢	49¢	46¢	48.4%
(11 oz. can)	(Rapid Shave)	(A&P)		
Toothpaste	55¢	29¢	29¢	47.3%
(3.25 oz., with fluoride)	(Colgate)	(A&P)		
Instant Coffee	$1.15	93¢	20¢	17.4%
(6 oz. jar)	(Maxwell House)	(A&P)		
Instant Breakfast	75¢	49¢	26¢	34.7%
(6 envelope pkg.)	(Carnation)	(A&P)		
Pancake Mix	29¢	18¢	11¢	37.9%
(1 lb.)	(Aunt Jemima)	(Sunnyfield)		
Tomato Ketchup	2/59¢	2/43¢	16¢	27.1%
(14 oz. bottle)	(Heinz)	(Ann Page)		
Mayonnaise	79¢	49¢	30¢	37.9%
(Quart jar)	(Kraft)	(A&P)		

Source: A&P Advertisement, *Washington Post*, June 10, 1970.

if it were free of all monopoly elements, particularly of the high concentration and product differentiation created by its high-intensity advertising.

In other words, the deconcentration of an industry and reduction of its advertising expenditures would be expected to lower its overall prices to *at least the approximate level of the prevailing private-label prices*. This would mean, as noted above, an average drop in consumer prices in these industries of at least 20%. Table 1, p. 131, based on a recent advertisement by the A&P Company in Washington, D. C., illustrates the magnitude of these price differentials between the chain's own private-label prices and those charged for the brand-name versions of those same products.

FRESH MEAT INDUSTRY—NO ADVERTISING, NO MONOPOLY

One of the best illustrations of this connection between industry structure, on the one hand, and high-volume deceptive advertising, on the other, is provided by the country's fresh meat industry. Thanks to a compulsory grade-labeling requirement, one under which fresh meats are graded for quality by government inspectors rather than by advertising agencies, product differentiation has been made impossible: no housewife can be persuaded to pay a penny more per pound for Armour's Grade-A sirloin than for Swift's Grade-A sirloin. In thus providing the consumer with the key piece of information needed for intelligent meat-shopping, the government has quite effectively destroyed the ability of the country's meat-packing firms to either oligopolize their industry or to practice deceptive advertising on their customers. The result is that the fresh meat industry is strikingly unconcentrated (its four largest firms—Swift, Armour, Wilson and Cudahy—have less than 25% of the industry's total sales); its advertising costs are pratically nil; its promotional practices are devoid of the kind of misleading advertising so characteristic of our major oligopolies; and, despite the large size of its individual firm-members, its profits are singularly modest in amount. (Swift and the other giants of the industry seldom earn more than 8% after taxes on stockholders' equity, or about one-third of Kellogg's earning rate).

PROPOSED OLIGOPOLY INVESTIGATION

The Federal Trade Commission has recently been urged by Senator William Proxmire and Congressman Benjamin Rosenthal to undertake a preliminary economic study of the country's oligopoly industries and thus provide the consuming public with a list of those that are charging higher-than-competitive prices.[13] It has full power to undertake such an investigation—the subpoena power and the enabling statutory mandate to keep the Congress and the public informed on economic matters of this kind—and it has the resources, a budget of more than $20 million per year, one that, in our view, and in that of many other students of the agency, it has been devoting largely to economic trivia.

FTC REFORM—CONCENTRATION AND DECEPTIVE ADVERTISING

As our journal has emphasized many times in the past, no real reformation of the FTC is possible—and no lasting solution to the consumer abuses found in the breakfast cereal and other such industries can be achieved—until the agency is persuaded to leave the country's competitive industries alone and direct its attention and resources to our non-competitive or oligopoly industries. False advertising and product deterioration stem from the same root causes as super-competitive consumer prices, namely, *high concentration* and *product differentiation*. Those two consumer abuses, deceptive advertising and non-effective product performance are—at least in their socially-significant forms —not the products of atomistic, competitive industry structures but of this nation's major oligopolies, the 100 or so highly-concentrated industries that have the power and the incentive to engage in large-scale practices of that kind.

We urge this Subcommittee to use its influence with the Federal Trade Commission to persuade that agency to choose its industry investigations with a great deal more care in the future, to focus its scarce resources on a smaller number of larger, more-concentrated industries, to direct its efforts toward industry *structures* rather than petty commercial practices, to take on the role of the serious *economic* agency its founders intended it to be and that its friends still hope it will one day become.

NOTES

1. *See The Structure of Food Manufacturing* 205 (Technical Study No. 8, Staff Report to FTC, National Commission on Food Marketing, June 1966).
2. For the standard textbook discussion of this phenomenon, *see* Dr. Frederick M. Scherer, *Industrial Market Structure and Economic Performance* 324-325 (Rand McNally, 1970).
3. *See Studies by the Staff of the Cabinet Committee on Price Stability* 54-63 (January 1969); Dr. Willard F. Mueller, *A Primer on Monopoly and Competition* 56-60 (Random House, 1970); Charles E. Mueller, "Sources of Monopoly Power: A Phenomenon Called 'Product Differentiation,' " 2 *Antitrust Law & Economics Review* 59 (Summer 1969).
4. *See* Scherer, *Industrial Market Structure,* 324-325..
5. *See* Dr. Peter M. Costello, "The Tetracycline Conspiracy," *Antitrust Law & Economics Review* 13-44 (Summer 1968).
6. *See* Dr. Walter B. Erickson, *Price Fixing Under the Sherman Act: Case Studies in Conspiracy* (Michigan State University, 1965) (Ph.D. diss.), presented in part in his recent article, "Economics of Price Fixing," *Antitrust Law & Economics Review* 83, 102-03 (Spring 1969).
7. Dr. William Alfred Sandridge, "The Effects of Fair Trade on Retail Prices of Electrical Housewares in Washington, Baltimore and Richmond, 1952-1959" (University of Virginia, 1960, Ph.D. diss.).
8. Erickson, *Price Fixing.* Product innovation and technological progress began to accelerate immediately after the break-up of the conspiracy in this industry (the folding

seat or bleacher industry), as it did after the legal proceedings in the tetracycline drug case mentioned in "The Tetracycline Conspiracy."

9. Scherer, *Industrial Market Structure*, p. 331. *See also* Table 1, below.

10. *See* W. Mueller, *A Primer on Monopoly*, p. 35.

11. *See Fortune* magazine (December 1967) p. 128; R.C. Meinke, *Barriers to Entry: A Case Study of the Breakfast Cereal Industry* (University of Nebraska, July 1965); and the National Commission on Food Marketing, Technical Study No. 6, *Grocery Manufacturing* 56 (June 1966).

12. National Commission on Food Marketing, *Grocery Manufacturing.*

13. For the texts of these requests for an oligopoly investigation, and the FTC's response, *see Antitrust Law & Economics Review,* Vol. 3, nos. 1 and 2 (Fall 1969 and Winter 1969-70).

PART FIVE

*

Credit and Lending

INTRODUCTION

Credit and Lending

Many consumerists feel that the consumer sovereignty assumption is weakest in the area of credit and lending. Their argument is that the consumer does not have adequate knowledge of alternative sources of credit and the cost of credit. Therefore, the consumer is placed at a disadvantage relative to the lender and there is little incentive for the lenders to compete on rates and terms of credit. Another aspect of the lack of consumer information is with respect to his credit rating. The article by Shaffer points out the weakness in the Credit Reporting Law.

Truth-in-Lending legislation was passed primarily because government and consumerists both wanted to provide protection for low-income consumers in their use of credit. The consumer was given simple information about the cost of credit so that he could more effectively evaluate its use. Many consumerists feel that, although the legislation was designed for the poor, the middle-income consumer tends to benefit most from the legislation.

Since its passage, amendments have extended the scope of the act, i.e., to include limitations on the liability of lost or stolen credit cards. One area under litigation, of primary concern to consumerists, is the use of class action suits for violations of the provisions of the act.

A basic question is whether or not the regulation of credit is in the consumer's best interest. Proponents argue that regulation saves the consumer money; opponents argue that it will produce higher cash prices for merchandise and a lack of credit availability for some consumers. John Wheatley and Guy Gordon examine these two views in their paper, in a study of the state of Washington. They found that retailers responded to credit limitation laws as most economists would have predicted; i.e., they (1) reduced loan maturities; (2) required larger down payments; (3) made rejection ratios higher; (4) added charges for previously free services; and (5) increased prices on merchandise. The negative effects of interest limitation laws were felt primarily by the low income groups who could no longer obtain credit and by cash buyers who paid higher prices. The Federal Reserve Board is studying the implications for cash buyers and interest rates.

Richard Sauter and Orville Walker in a similar follow-up study found that a greater proportion of retailers instigated changes in credit policies when the interest rate ceiling was set at low levels. Retailers tended to favor policy changes that were the least visible to their customers (i.e., more stringent credit requirements). They also concluded that the burden of interest rate limitation laws falls primarily on the low-income, marginal borrower who can no longer obtain credit.

Cooling-off laws (contract recision privileges for goods purchased on credit) are another form of lending regulation designed to protect low-income groups. These laws are directed primarily at the direct selling industry (primarily durable goods). Orville Walker and Neil Ford present the pros and cons of the laws from the perspective of the consumer advocate and the direct selling industry. They indicate the structural problems that inhibit industry self-regulation and enforcement of legislation. They, as the other writers, conclude that here also, although designed to protect the low-income consumer from unethical practices of some retailers, the laws tend primarily to benefit the middle-class consumer.

16. CONSUMERS GRIPE THAT CREDIT REPORTING LAW DOESN'T ALWAYS WORK

Richard A. Shaffer

WOULD YOU sell an automobile insurance policy to this man?

He and his wife, a secretary, together earn only $5,000 a year. And his 18-year-old son, who will be driving the car, is a "hippie-type youth" who is "active in various antiestablishment concerns" and "suspected of using marijuana on occasion."

On the basis of that report, provided by a credit investigation agency, Nationwide Mutual Insurance Co. canceled the policy on one of Robert Meisner's cars.

Now, let the real Bob Meisner family stand up. Mrs. Meisner, who actually is a registered nurse, earns more than $5,000 by herself. Her husband, an Oldsmobile salesman, makes considerably more. Their son Danny says he experimented with marijuana only once, a year ago, and he certainly seems an unlikely drug addict: He lettered in track at high school in Croton-on-Hudson, N.Y., campaigned in a recent election for a Republican candidate, represented the student body on the executive committee of the PTA, won a school award for his work in student government and is considered by his principal a "model student, a straight kid." Antiestablishment concerns? He organized two protests against the war in Vietnam.

PARTIAL CORRECTION

It's not too surprising that such misinformation occasionally creeps into credit reports. But what shocked Mr. Meisner was the difficulty he encountered in straightening things out, despite a new federal credit-reporting law aimed at giving consumers with bad ratings a fair crack at setting their record straight.

When Mr. Meisner protested "this astounding inability to get even the simplest facts right" (the credit reporting firm, Retail Credit Co., Atlanta, said that only one Meisner child lived at home even though three actually do), the company looked into his case again, as required by the new federal Fair Credit Reporting Act.

"Unfortunately," says Mr. Meisner, "it didn't do much good." After Mr. Meisner took his case to the New York Civil Liberties Union, Nationwide Mutual reinstated his car insurance. But, he says, Retail Credit "corrected every mistake except the most important one. It left in the stuff about Danny and drugs, which is nothing but gossip, and they still talk about his politics and hair, which have nothing to do with his driving ability."

Howard H. Nichols, a vice president of Retail Credit, says: "It is company policy not to comment on individual cases, which we regard as confidential between us and the consumer."

To what degree the average consumer shares the Meisners' dissatisfaction won't be gauged until early next year, when studies on the new law's impact are published by the Federal Trade Commission, which enforces it, and the National Academy of Sciences, which is investigating the impact of computerized data banks on individual privacy. But there already are hints that many consumers don't think it is working the way it was supposed to. The FTC has received more than 1,000 complaints under the new law. Critics say the number is impressive considering that the law has been in effect only seven months or so. "What we've seen so far is probably only the tip of the iceberg," says Sheldon Feldman, assistant director for special projects at the FTC. "Most consumers don't yet know their rights under the act."

BIG BROTHER IS WATCHING

Dozens of private companies, such as credit bureaus and detective agencies, collect and sell personal information about nearly everyone who ever has applied for credit, insurance or a job. Retail Credit, one of the biggest of the firms, claims files on 48 million Americans. As the Meisner case shows, the files may deal with matters as detailed as the length of a teen-ager's hair. Until recently, these reports were so confidential that most consumers were in no position to determine their accuracy.

Last April, when the credit reporting act went into effect, consumers won legal access to their dossiers. They also got the opportunity to force credit reporting firms to correct inaccurate, misleading or obsolete information, or at least to make sure that the firms reported the consumer's side in any disputed case. In the main, FTC men say, credit reporting firms are trying to comply with the new law, though not always successfully.

A good many of the current complaints accuse credit reporting outfits of hindering access to their files by consumers. Salvatore Sangiorgi, assistant director the the FTC's New York regional office, says some New York credit bureaus apparently have told inquirers, "We don't have to show you your file, and we aren't going to." Others, he says, have put off consumers with excuses such as "the man who handles that sort of thing isn't here right now and won't be back for three or four days. Come back then."

WHY THE SECRECY?

Sometimes, officials say, the agencies may merely be trying to avoid trouble with credit applicants whose records are blemished, accurately or not. In other cases, they may simply be zealous in guarding their reports against release to unauthorized persons. The result, however, is often the same in either case: The consumer finds it difficult or impossible to see his credit report.

"There is some evidence that credit bureaus are playing a shell game with records," says Arthur Miller, a University of Michigan law school professor who testified during congressional hearings on the credit reporting bill last year. "A guy will come down to the office and say, 'I'd like to see my records,' and the man behind the counter will disappear into the back room and then two minutes later will report that the file is in another office for posting, and that if he comes back in another week or so—you know, it's the war of attrition type of thing," the professor says.

Jim Henderson, a Tulsa newspaper reporter, asked the Tulsa office of Retail Credit for his file. He was told the company didn't have one. A few weeks later, through another source, he obtained a copy of a credit report on himself, and on the basis of the detailed information in it concluded that it had to have been compiled before he made his visit to the firm's office.

"What Mr. Henderson saw was probably an old report no longer in our files that he may have obtained from one of our customers," says Retail Credit's Mr. Nichols. "Retail Credit itself routinely destroys most files 13 months after preparation. It has always been our policy to discuss any file with an individual, upon proper identification, even before the Fair Credit Reporting Act."

In general, says Mr. Nichols, "we've had excellent experience with the consumers who have come to our offices. We have discussed their files in full, and in most instances the consumer has been satisfied. In those instances where there has been disagreement, we have followed the law explicitly, taken the necessary statement and reinvestigated. There have been very few cases in which complete satisfaction was not noticed."

But many consumers have complained that the credit agencies require an unreasonable amount of identification as a condition for disclosing their records. A typical complaint comes from Mr. T, a 35-year-old Dallas systems analyst who couldn't find work for 16 months after a layoff, apparently because of a letter in his credit file from a former employer that Mr. T says is "full of innuendo and vague generalities which seem to say a lot without really saying anything. For example, it said that I'd sometimes exhibited a bad attitude, and that I didn't always take to training."

MORE INFORMATION ASKED

When Mr. T found out about the letter he went to Credit Bureau Services, a division of Chilton Corp., to have it removed from his file or to have his refutation included. In order to see the file, he was told, he would have to complete and sign a two-page identification form.

The form, among other things, asked for his addresses over the prior five years, his employers in the same period, the number of his dependent children, and his wife's name and her employer. The form he was to sign also authorized Credit Bureau Services to investigate him, and it authorized "any business or organization to give full information and records" about him. "In short," he contends, "they were asking me to waive my right to privacy." Mr. T refused to sign the form or to show any identification other than his Social Security card and his driver's license. To date, Credit Bureau Services has refused to show him the file.

General manager Al Ferguson says the firm is simply trying to protect people's privacy. "In order to keep from showing a consumer someone else's file, we've programmed the computers where our files are stored not to print out a record unless we feed in a lot more information than (Mr. T) is willing to give us," he says. But Mr. T is taking the case to court. The damaging letter, he says, "doesn't have a bit of truth in it, but even if it did, I still have the right by law to put my side of the story down there in the file, and they won't let me."

The identification forms that some agencies give consumers reviewing their reports require a consumer, in return, to waive any right to sue the reporting agency for libel, invasion of privacy, or negligence in reporting false information. The federal law itself bars such suits except in the case of "false information furnished with malice or wilful intent to injure."

A FEE MAY FIX IT

Some consumers who experienced little difficulty in seeing their credit files have told the FTC they were charged fees as high as $25. And a Midwesterner—call him Walter—claims a credit agency tried to charge him even more. Walter says he was denied life insurance on the basis of a credit report that he kept unsavory company and had destroyed private property. The first allegation was entirely false, he says, and the second referred to an incident 15 years before when he accidentally broke a plate glass window in a sandlot baseball game. Both charges, he said, came from a neighbor he was suing because her dog bit one of his children.

Once it heard his side of the story, the credit bureau agreed to check it out. But Walter says he was told that the fee would be $10 an hour, with a 15-hour minimum, payable in advance. Only after he took the case to his Congressman and to the FTC did the bureau agree to waive a fee. The bureau said there must have been a misunderstanding.

While most of the difficulties consumers have encountered may seem technical problems that will disappear in time, some critics believe the new law basically is flawed because it is aimed at correcting, rather than preventing, unfair credit reporting; some consumers may never even suspect that their files are inaccurate. An agency still, under the law, isn't prevented from reporting a consumer's race, religion, politics, or neighborhood gossip about his sex life or drinking habits.

Sen. Mark Hatfield (R., Ore.) has introduced a bill that would require credit reporting agencies to furnish consumers copies of their credit reports before they were supplied to business orother subscribers. The opposition to Sen. Hatfield's and like proposals is strong. In Oklahoma, which has such a law on the books, credit agencies are refusing to obey it. Retail Credit argues on legal grounds that "it doesn't apply to us," and the firm says the case is "entirely without merit."

17. ANNUAL REPORT TO CONGRESS ON TRUTH IN LENDING FOR THE YEAR 1971

Board of Governors of the Federal Reserve System

REGULATION Z REFERS TO THE TRUTH-IN-LENDING LEGISLATION. ITS PURPOSE IS TO LET BORROWERS AND CUSTOMERS KNOW THE COST OF CREDIT SO THAT THEY CAN COMPARE THE COSTS WITH OTHER SOURCES AND AVOID THE UNINFORMED USE OF CREDIT.

EDITOR

Amendments and Interpretations of Regulation Z

DURING 1971, the Board issued nine amendments and two interpretations of Regulation Z. The most far-reaching amendment added a new section to the Regulation, section 226.13,[1] which was necessitated by the credit card amendment to the Truth in Lending Act in Public Law 91-508. The new section, which became effective on January 25, 1971, set forth implementing regulations to restrict the issuance of unsolicited credit cards and to limit to a maximum of $50 the cardholder's liability for unauthorized use of his card resulting from loss, theft or other occurrence.

An amendment was issued to section 226.7(e) to provide that creditors must give advance notice of a change in terms of an open end credit account only to those persons whose accounts are active at the time of the change.[2] Inactive account holders must be notified of the change when their accounts

Reprinted from *Annual Report to Congress on Truth in Lending for the Year 1971* (Board of Governors of the Federal Reserve System, January 3, 1972), pp. 2-6, 9-22.

become active. Furthermore, a reduction in the minimum periodic payment, periodic rate or rates, or in any minimum fixed, check service, transaction, activity or similar charge applicable to the account is not a change in terms requiring prior disclosure. The amendment reduced the period of advance notice from 30 to 15 days to allow creditors to provide the notice with any billing statement issued at least 15 days prior to the beginning of the billing cycle in which the change takes place.

Three amendments were issued relating to the customer's right to rescind certain credit contracts as provided in section 226.9. One amendment adds Columbus Day to the list of holidays excluded for the purpose of calculating the time in which a customer may exercise his right to rescind.[3] The second amendment permits creditors to use certain specified substitute wording in the notice of right of rescision to make the notice more meaningful to the customer when the transaction is secured by a parcel of land or a vacant lot which the customer expects to use as his principal residence.[4] The third amendment exempts agricultural transactions from the requirement prohibiting performance by creditors (e.g., the disbursement of loan proceeds) during the rescision period.[5]

An amendment added section 226.10(e) to the advertising requirements of the Regulation which provides a specific means for advertising homes under the FHA Section 235 financing program.[6] Special procedures were found to be necessary to provide meaningful advertisements for this program, because it calls for a variation in monthly payments and annual percentage rates applicable to different customers, depending upon their individual income and family composition.

Proposed amendments to section 226.7, which have been issued for public comment, would require disclosure of an annual percentage rate on periodic billing statements in open end credit plans when no finance charge is imposed.[7] The background for this proposal is described more fully [. . . elsewhere] relating to litigation.

Two formal Board interpretations of Regulation Z were issued during the year. One interpretation, section 226.705, relates to a change in the method of determining the balance on which a customer's finance charge is computed. No advance notice to the customer is required where a creditor changes his method of determining the balance on which finance charges are computed from one in which payments are credits made during the billing cycle are not deducted in determining the balance, to one in which payments and credits are deducted.[8] Such a change in methods generally results in a reduction of the finance charges to those customers who do not pay their accounts in full. The second interpretation, section 226.407, provides that an annual fee charged by a credit card issuer for membership in his credit plan and for the issuance of a credit card is not a finance charge under the Regulation.[9] Such charges are not finance charges, since they are imposed for membership in the credit plan and for issuance of the credit card. They are not related to any specific extensions of credit, and are imposed whether or not the cardholder uses his card.

LITIGATION

The Board is aware of the existence of 71 civil actions which have been brought under section 130 of the Act for damages for alleged violations of the Act, and it is likely that additional suits have been instituted. In 49 of these cases, class action status is sought on behalf of the named plaintiffs and all others similarly situated under Rule 23 of the Federal Rules of Civil Procedure. At least four Courts have refused to allow Truth in Lending suits to proceed as class actions.[10] However, several other Courts have viewed class actions as applicable in such suits.[11] The issue of the appropriateness of class actions for Truth in Lending violations is presently under specific consideration by the United States District Court for the Southern District of New York.[12]

Two actions were brought against the Board by home improvement contractors alleging that the Board exceeded its authority in sections 226.2(z) and 226.9(a) of Regulation Z by providing that the right of recision applied to consumer credit contracts secured by mechanics or material-men's liens on the customer's home, even though no mortgage or deed of trust was executed by the customer.[13] Plaintiffs asked for declaratory judgments of invalidity and injunctions against enforcement of the Regulation in this regard. On January 6, 1971, summary judgment, without opinion, was granted in favor of the Board in one of the sections,[14] but on September 21, 1971, the Court in the second action held that section 226.9(a) was null and void "in so far as it relates to liens which may come into existence by operation of law after midnight of the third business day following the date of consummation of the credit transactions.[15] An appeal has been filed in one case by the home improvement contractors. In the other case, the Department of Justice has authorized the filing of a notice of appeal.

The Department of Justice, on the Board's behalf, filed briefs *amicus curiae* in two cases.[16] A brief in *Garland* v. *Mobil Oil Corp.* was filed on behalf of the Federal Trade Commission as well as the Board pursuant to judicial request for a statement of Board and Commission views on whether the Act and Regulation applied to Mobil's credit card plan during a period when no finance charges were assessed, although authorized by the underlying credit documents. The Government's brief concluded that the plan was not subject to the Truth in Lending disclosure requirements during this period. The Court has not yet ruled on the question. In *Mourning* v. *Family Publications Service, Inc.*, the issue was the validity of the "more-than-four-installment" rule in section 226.2 (k) of Regulation Z. Under the rule, transactions are considered "consumer credit" subject to the Act when, by agreement, they involve more than four installments, although the creditor has not specifically identified any finance charges. The Court held that the rule exceeded the Board's authority and that the rule created a conclusive presumption in violation of constitutional principles. A petition for *certiorari* has been filed with the Supreme Court for review of the decision, and the Board expects the appeal to be supported by briefs *amicus curiae*.

During 1971, several additional important decisions were rendered on

Truth in Lending matters by the Courts. In *Ratner v. Chemical Bank New York Trust Company*[17] the Court held the bank in violation of the Act for failure to disclose the nominal annual percentage rate on plaintiff's open end credit billing statement which showed an outstanding balance but no finance charge yet incurred. Following that decision, the Board, on August 6, 1971, issued for public comment proposed amendments to Regulation Z requiring this disclosure. Final amendments have not yet been adopted by the Board. The Court also ruled that under section 130(a) of the Act a finance charge need not be imposed at the time of the omitted disclosure as a condition to establishing liability. In addition, it held that section 130(c) absolving a creditor from liability who shows that his "violation was not intentional and resulted from a bona fide error notwithstanding the maintenance of procedures reasonably adapted to avoid any such error" applies to clerical errors as opposed to errors of law.[18]

In *Douglas v. Beneficial Finance Co. of Anchorage*,[19] the Court upheld the Board's definition of "security interest" in section 226.2(z) of Regulation Z to include confessions of judgment which allow the creditor to record a lien on the property of the obligor without any opportunity for the customer to enter a defense against such action prior to entry of the judgment. That definition was also supported in *Garza v. Chicago Health Clubs, Inc.*[20]

The Court in *Sapenter v. Dreyco, Inc.*[21] held that a mortgage on an obligor's home was not subject to the Act when executed in connection with an extension of credit for business purposes.

It was held in *Jordan v. Montgomery Ward & Co., Inc.*[22] that section 130 of the Act did not create a private right of action for violation of the Chapter 3 advertising provisions.

In *Bostwick v. Cohen*,[23] the Court considered the issue of whether a customer's election to rescind a transaction under section 125 of the Act precluded recovery under the civil liability provisions of section 130. It concluded that the civil liability provisions were remedial rather than punitive, and that by electing to rescind the contract, the customer had removed himself from the class of persons which section 130 was designed to protect.

COMPLIANCE

The enforcement of the Truth in Lending Act is spread among nine Federal agencies. For the most part, Federal agencies with general supervisory authority over a particular group of creditors were also given Truth in Lending enforcement responsibility over those creditors. Enforcement for all remaining creditors, except in those States which have an exemption from the Act, is the responsibility of the Federal Trade Commission. Consequently, the Commission has the bulk of the enforcement task.

As in the past, information received from the Federal agencies having prior supervisory authority over their creditors indicates no significant problems in the enforcement of Regulation Z. Generally, these agencies point out that the level of compliance is high, and that the errors that are found result from misunderstanding or clerical error, rather than any attempt to evade the requirements of the Act. For the most part, compliance is determined by these agencies during the regular periodic examinations of the creditors under their jurisdiction.

The Federal Trade Commission has conducted two surveys in an attempt to determine the extent of compliance by creditors under its jurisdiction. The results of these two surveys were reported by the Commission in a release titled *Federal Trade Commission Report on Surveys of Creditor Compliance with The Truth in Lending Act* dated April, 1971. A summary of the results shows that of the five classes of creditors sampled, New and Used Automobile Dealers, as a class, ranked highest in overall compliance. (New Automobile Dealers were virtually flawless in their compliance. Used Automobile Dealers, however, were found to be in a state of compliance worse than any of the other classes sampled.) The classes of TV & Appliance Dealers and Furniture Stores together ranked second in overall compliance of each class. Jewelry Stores were the least complying class of creditor. Home Improvement Companies were so inconsistent in their responses that no reliable conclusions could be drawn, although the overall average of their compliance was comparable to the middle two classes.

The Report revealed that 86 percent of all creditors in the five classes surveyed were using contracts which were in either total or substantial compliance. Sixty-nine percent of all creditors in the five classes achieved the total compliance designation which means that they were disclosing all information required by the Act and Regulation and doing so in the proper format. Seventeen percent of all creditors surveyed achieved the substantial compliance designation, which refers to the disclosure of the annual percentage rate and finance charge, using those exact terms, but omitting other requirements. Fourteen percent of all creditors in the five classes were using installment contracts which did not disclose the annual percentage rate and finance charge.

The Commission drew several conclusions from the survey results—among them:

> With all five classes of creditors combined, those with sales volumes of $1 million to $10 million were in the best overall compliance.
> Creditors extending credit in less than 50% of their sales were in a better state of compliance than those who extend credit in 50% or more of their sales.

Reports of substantial compliance have also been received from the four exempt States. Of the States reporting statistical evidence of the degree of compliance, Maine reported 62 percent of creditors under its jurisdiction examined in 1971 were in complete compliance, 14 percent were in substantial compliance, 19 percent were in partial compliance and 5 percent were in noncompliance. Connecticut reported 81 percent of the creditors examined were found to be satisfying their requirements.

Based upon the reports of all enforcement agencies, it is the Board's belief that substantial compliance with Truth in Lending is being achieved.

ISSUES AND RECOMMENDATIONS

There are a number of problem areas within the Truth in Lending Act and Regulation Z which the Board believes should be brought to the attention of Congress. Some of these represent issues which the Board is currently study-ing to determine possible solutions within the regulatory authority now pro-vided. These are discussed under the heading "Issues." Others take the form of formal recommendations for legislation and are discussed under the heading "Recommendations."

Several of the enforcement agencies have brought to the Board's attention certain areas related to the Regulation which they believe should be changed. These suggestions are being studied further and, where necessary, appropriate changes will be made.

ISSUES

Discounts for Prompt Payment
The problems involved with Truth in Lending coverage of discounts for prompt payment continue to exist. Also, questions have arisen with respect to plans involving discounts for cash which have been gaining in popularity recently. These plans often involve "cash cards" which when presented entitle the cardholder to a discount for paying cash. The question arises whether this discount becomes a finance charge to those who do not pay in cash, but, instead, charge their purchases. Staff is currently studying these problems, but no formal action beyond that reported in the previous annual report has been taken.

Disclosures in Foreign Languages
In order to provide uniformity in disclosure of credit terms, Regulation Z prescribes certain English terminology to be used. However, the benefit which such disclosures may bring to those consumers who do not read or understand English is highly questionable. Although disclosures must be given prior to the consummation of a credit transaction and, theoretically, a consumer can obtain an explanation or a translation of the disclosures before committing himself, such translations or explanations are probably rarely obtained in actual practice. The objective of providing meaningful disclosures to all consumers, including non-English speaking, is certainly a desirable one. A number of pos-sible solutions to this problem have been proposed, but none appear feasible. It may be that the only solution is increased education of consumers, and the Board believes that the Spanish translation of the consumer leaflet, *What Truth*

in Lending Means to You, is a step in that direction. However, the Board is still concerned about the problem and will continue to explore potential solutions.

Advertising of Specific Credit Terms

The inclusion of specific credit terms in credit advertising appears to continue at a level lower than desirable to enable consumers to effectively shop for the best credit terms available. However, there are informal indications that the use of more specific advertising is increasing. While creditor complaints against the advertising restrictions have diminished, the Board anticipates reviewing this area to determine whether changes can be made to encourage greater inclusion of specific credit terms.

RECOMMENDATIONS

Class Action Exposure and Civil Liability

Creditors have been expressing increased concern over their possible exposure to class action suits and the potential ruinous liability which may be attached to such suits. While the question of class action liability in the *Ratner* case has not yet been decided, the reported $13 million potential liability has led many creditors to believe that similar suits filed against them could seriously threaten the solvency or future existence of their organizations. Furthermore, the Act's civil liability section does not necessarily preclude liability when a creditor has acted in good faith in conformity with Regulation Z. The Board recommends that the Act be amended to provide for a "good faith" provision, such as contained in the Securities and Exchange Act of 1934, which would apply to both the Board's Regulation Z and formal interpretations of it.[24] It also may be desirable to set a maximum liability, or otherwise restrict the scope of potential class action liability, should it be finally determined that class actions are allowable in Truth in Lending suits.

Section 130 of the Act provides that a creditor is liable for a minimum of $100 for failure to make proper disclosure "in connection with any consumer credit transaction." There is some uncertainty as to the meaning of "transaction" when applying section 130 to a possible error on a periodic statement used in connection with an open end account. It might be contended that each separate purchase for which a credit card is used constitutes a "transaction" for purposes of section 130, or that each periodic statement is a transaction. More likely the opening and use of the account is a single transaction. The Board believes that Congress should clarify the very important meaning of "transaction" in section 130.

Right of Rescision

Section 125 of the Act, implemented by section 226.9 of Regulation Z, provides that in some consumer credit transactions in which a security interest in the customer's residence is involved, the customer has three business days in which to rescind the transaction. The creditor must notify the customer of his right of rescision and provide a form which may be used in exercising that right. The law does not specify any limitation on the period in which the right continues in force where the creditor has failed to notify the customer of his right. Also, even though the required notice is given, there is a question as to whether the rescision period may continue where the other required disclosures of credit terms are given but are incorrect. As a result, the titles to many residential real estate properties may become clouded by the uncertainty regarding these rights of rescision. The Board recommends that Congress amend the Act to provide a limitation on the time the right of rescision may run.

As previously discussed, the Court in *N. C. Freed Company, Inc.*, v. *Board of Governors*,[25] held section 226.9(a) of Regulation Z invalid "in so far as it relates to liens which may come into existence by operation of law after midnight of the third business day following the date of consummation of the credit transaction." That section, which implements section 125 of the Act, grants the customer a three-day right of rescision in transactions involving a security interest in his principal residence. In effect, the Court ruled that the section was inapplicable to transactions in which no mortgage or deed of trust is signed by the customer, but where the transaction is nevertheless secured by lien rights in the customer's home. The Department of Justice has authorized the filing of a notice of appeal in the case.

In a related case, *Gardner and North Roofing and Siding Corp.* v. *Board of Governors*,[26] which attacked the Board's Regulation on identical grounds, the Court ruled in the Board's favor and granted the Government's motion for summary judgment. The case has been appealed.

The right of rescision was designed to allow homeowners a "cooling-off" period before entering into credit transactions involving security interests in their homes, principally as a result of home improvement contracts, and to reduce the likelihood of abuses of homeowners by unscrupulous contractors. The Board believes that successful accomplishment of these goals necessitates the coverage of all transactions in which a customer's home may be lost through foreclosure, whether by mortgage, deed of trust, or other lien rights. It therefore recommends that Congress specifically amend the Act to remove any uncertainty about the coverage of these transactions under section 125.

More-than-Four-Installment Rule

In *Mourning* v. *Family Publications Service, Inc.*,[27] the Court declared the Board's more-than-four-installment rule in section 226.2(k) of Regulation Z invalid. Acting under the statutory directive to issue regulations to effectuate the purposes of the Act and to prevent circumvention or evasion thereof,[28] the Board in Regulation Z defined "consumer credit," to which Truth in Lending applies, to include credit which, pursuant to an agreement, "is or may be payable in more than four installments."[29] By this provision, vendors who may have considered concealing finance charges in the price of goods to evade the Act's requirements, as well as the so-called "no-charge-for-credit" sellers already operating in low income markets, were placed on notice that the Board considered them subject to the Act's requirements. By so doing, the Board insured that they would make certain important disclosures required by Truth in Lending, even when no finance charge or annual percentage rate was disclosed. For example, the Act requires disclosure of the total amount of the consumer's obligation.

The Board's rule was based on the economic fact that installment contracts of more than four installments typically include some component to compensate the creditor for the cost involved in allowing deferred payment, even though that cost may not be separately identified as a finance charge. The Board believes the rule is both within the scope of its authority, and necessary to prevent evasion of the Act. However, the appellate Court held that the Board exceeded its authority, and that the rule is void on the grounds that it creates a conclusive presumption in violation of requirements of the Fifth Amendment.

Should the Court's decision stand, many creditors would not only escape the requirement of Truth in Lending disclosures prior to consummation of their contracts, but would also be free of the Act's prohibitions against "bait" credit advertising.[30] They would also be able to advertise "no down payment" or the amount of the payments without further information, which is prohibited for creditors subject to the Act.[31]

In addition, home improvement contractors might avoid giving customers the right of rescision, even where they obtained a second mortgage on the customer's home, simply by "burying" the finance charges in the price of the contract.

In short, the Board is convinced that invalidation of the "more-than-four-installment" rule would seriously impair the effectiveness of the legislation. The Board believes that Congress should amend the Act to remove any possible doubt that it does include transactions payable in more than four installments.

NOTES

1. 37 Fed. Reg. 1040, 1/22/71.
2. 36 Fed. Reg. 4113, 3/4/71.
3. 36 Fed. Reg. 19671, 10/9/71.
4. 36 Fed. Reg. 4113, 3/4/71.
5. Ibid.
6. Ibid.
7. 36 Fed. Reg. 15130, 8/13/71.
8. Fed. Reg. 16646, 8/25/71.
9. Fed. Reg. 16050, 8/19/71.
10. Buford v. American Finance Company, U.S.D.C., N.D. Ga., Oct. 1, 1971, 4 CCH *Consumer Credit Guide*, ¶99,302; Mourning v. Family Publications Service, Inc., U.S.D.C., S.D. Fla., Nov. 27, 1970, 4 CCH *Consumer Credit Guide*, ¶ 99,632; Allerton v. Century Credit Corporation, Civil No. 70-1614, U.S.D.C., Fla., April 12, 1971; Rogers v. Coburn Finance Corp. Civil No. 14843, U.S.D.C., N.D. Ga., Sept. 22, 1971.
11. Smith v. International Magazine Services, Civil No. 71-16-F, U.S.D.C., N.D. W. Va., Nov. 2, 1971; Martin v. Family Publications Service, Civil No. 5829, U.S.D.C.,

D. Vt., June 30, 1970; Rademacher v. Town & Country Charge, Civil no. 70-C-194, U.S.D.C., N.D. Ill., Oct, 9, 1970; Douglas v. Beneficial Finance Co. of Anchorage, U.S.D.C., D. Ak., Sept, 2, 1971, 4 CCH *Consumer Credit Guide* 99,295; Richardson v. Time Premium Company Civil No. 70-1814-JLK, U.S.D.C., S.D. Fla., February 4, 1971; Givens v. W. T. Grant Company, Civil No. 14296, U.S.D.C., D. Conn., Sept. 22, 1971; Katz v. Carte Blanche Corporation, Civil No. 69-1326, U.S.D.C., W.D. Pa., Nov. 17, 1971; Berkman v. Westinghouse Electric Corporation, Civil No. 69-C-2056, U.S.D.C., N.D. Ill., June 25, 1970.

12. Ratner v. Chemical Bank New York Trust Company, 4 CCH *Consumer Credit Guide* ¶ 99456.

13. Gardner and North Roofing and Siding Corp. v. Board of Governors, D. D.C., 4 CCH *Consumer Credit Guide* ¶ 99621; N.C. Freed Company, Inc. v. Board of Governors U.S.D.C., W.D. N.Y., 4 CCH *Consumer Credit Guide* ¶ 99356.

14. Gardner and North Roofing and Siding Corp. v. Board of Governors, *supra* note 13.

15. N. C. Freed Company, Inc. v. Board of Governors, *supra* note 13.

16. Garland v. Mobil Oil Corporation, U.S.D.C., N.D. Ill., 4 CCH *Consumer Credit Guide* 99,558; Mourning v. Family Publications Service, Inc., 5th Cir., 4 CCH *Consumer Credit Guide* ¶ 99,337.

17. U.S.D.C., S.D.N.Y., June 16, 1971, 4 CCH *Consumer Credit Guide* ¶ 99,456.

18. *See also* Buford v. American Finance Company, *supra* note 10; Douglas v. Beneficial Finance Co. of Anchorage, U.S.D.C., D. Ak., Sept 2, 1971, 4 CCH *Consumer Credit Guide* ¶ 99,295.

19. *Supra* note 18.

20. U.S.D.C., N.D. Ill., July 29, 1971, 4 CCH *Consumer Credit Guide* ¶ 99,384. *(See* Board interpretation 12 C.F.R. 226.202).

21. U.S.D.C., E.D. La., April 27, 1971, 4 CCH *Consumer Credit Guide* ¶ 99,375, 326 F. Supp. 871.

22. 8th Cir., May 3, 1971, 4 CCH *Consumer Credit Guide* ¶ 99,502, *cert denied* Oct 12, 1971, 4 CCH *Consumer Credit Guide* 99,332. But *see* Garza v. Chicago Health Clubs, Inc., *supra* note 20 where the Court assumed, without deciding, that it had jurisdiction to enjoin fraudulent credit advertising, including violations of the Truth in Lending Act and Regulation Z.

23. U.S.D.C., N.D. Ohio, Nov. 24, 1970, 4 CCH *Consumer Credit Guide* ¶ 99,583. However, *see* Douglas v. Beneficial Finance Co. of Anchorage, *supra* note 18 where plaintiff was allowed to rescind her loan as well as collect damages.

24. "No provision of this subchapter imposing any liability shall apply to any act done or omitted in good faith in conformity with any rule or regulation of the Commission, notwithstanding that such rule or regulation may, after such act or omission, be amended or rescinded or be determined by judicial or other authority to be invalid for any reason." 15 U.S.C. §77s (a).

25. *Supra* note 13.

26. *Supra* note 13.

27. *Supra* note 16.

28. 15 U.S.C. §1604.

29. 12 C.F.R. §226.2(k).

30. 15 U.S.C. §1662.

31. 15 U.S.C. §1664.

18. CAN "COOLING-OFF LAWS" REALLY PROTECT THE CONSUMER?

Orville C. Walker, Jr. and Neil M. Ford

IN RECENT years legislative interest at state and national levels has focused upon the protection of consumers from the unethical persuasions of door-to-door salesmen. The most common form of direct sales regulation provides for a *cooling-off period* during which the consumer may rescind a contract to purchase goods or services when the sale is consummated at a place other than the address of the seller. This cancellation privilege provides immediate recourse for the consumer who feels he has been pressured or tricked into making an unwanted purchase.

This paper examines the role of the cooling-off legislation in consumer protection and explores three basic questions: (1) What provisions are included in cooling-off laws and how many states have enacted them? (2) What arguments are advanced by supporters and opponents of such legislation? (3) Are these laws an effective means of protecting consumers from the unethical practices of some sellers? In other words can cooling-off legislation accomplish its stated objectives?

THE MAJOR PROVISIONS OF COOLING-OFF LEGISLATION

Fifteen states have enacted cooling-off period laws. The states in which contract recision statutes have been enacted (on or before July 1, 1969) and the major provisions of each state's statute are presented in Table 1. In 1967 Senator Warren Magnuson of the state of Washington introduced a bill (S. 1599) proposing a federal cooling-off law to the Consumer Subcommittee of the Senate Subcommittee of the Senate Committee on Commerce. The bill was voted out of committee in 1968 but was not acted upon by the Senate

Reprinted from *Jounal of Marketing*, Vol. 34 (April 1970), 53-58, published by the American Marketing Association.

Table 1

CONTRACT RECISION STATUTES ENACTED:

State and Year Enacted	Length of Cooling-off Period	Applicable to Cash Sales as well as Install-ment Sales
Connecticut: 1967 (Amended, 1969)[1]	Three business days	No
Georgia: 1967	One business day	No
Hawaii: 1967 (Amended, 1969)	Three business days	No
Illinois: 1967	Three business days	Yes ($50 minimum)
Indiana: 1969	Two business days	Yes ($50 minimum)
Maine: 1969	Three business days	Yes ($25 minimum)
Massachusetts: 1966	One business day	No
New Hampshire: 1969	Four days	No
New Jersey: 1968	Two business days	No
Oklahoma: 1969 (UCCC)[2]	Three business days	No
Pennsylvania: 1968	Two business days	Yes ($25 minimum)
Rhode Island: 1968	Three business days	No
Utah: 1969 (UCCC)[2]	Three business days	No
Vermont: 1967 (Amended, 1969)	One business day	Yes
Washington: 1967	One business day	No

[1]All statutes and amendments will be in effect on or before October 1, 1969.

[2]The recision statutes are a part of the Uniform Commercial Credit Code adopted by these states.

Table 1

July 1, 1969[1]

Notice to Buyer Required in Contract	Registered or Certified Mail Required to Notify Seller	Delivery Negates Right of Recision	Penalty for Cancellation
Yes	Yes	No	Yes
No	Yes	No	Yes
Yes	Yes	No	Yes
No	No	No	No
Yes	No	No	No
Yes	No	No	No
Yes	Yes	Yes	No
Yes	Yes	No	No
No (Notice to appear on "receipt")	Yes	No	No
Yes	No	No	Yes
No	No	No	No
Yes	Yes	No	Yes
Yes	No	No	Yes
No	Yes	Yes	No
Yes	Yes	Yes	Yes

Source: Mr. F. R. Sherwood, Director, Community and State Relations, American Educational Publishers Institute, Chicago, Illinois.

and, therefore, expired. In 1969, Representative Seymour Halpern of New York introduced the same bill (H.9289) to the House Foreign and Interstate Commerce Committee, but no action is expected on the bill this year. Senator Magnuson states, however, that the bill will be reintroduced to the Senate in 1970.

COVERAGE

The majority of state cooling-off statutes cover only sales of goods or services which involve installment contracts. Those statutes that also cover cash sales usually exempt sales below some minimum amount, generally $25. Thus, the laws focus on sellers of durable goods. Direct sellers of convenience items who rely on customer goodwill for repeat sales are exempt.

All of these state statutes, except Vermont's and Illinois', apply only to sales agreements signed somewhere other than the seller's place of business. Vermont's law applies to all installment sales. The Illinois law applies to all sales resulting from "a salesman's direct contact with or call on the customer at his residence."

LENGTH OF THE COOLING-OFF PERIOD

In most states, the cooling-off period begins with the signing of the sales contract. In Illinois the period begins when the seller provides his address or phone number to the buyer. Length of the period ranges from one to four business days.

In some states, the buyer may not cancel after the receipt or tender of a substantial part of the goods or services. This provision encourages the care and disposition of merchandise received before cancellation.

NOTICE OF THE BUYER'S RIGHTS AND OBLIGATIONS

The majority of state statutes require that the printed sales contract include a notice informing the buyer of his right to cancel and the procedure to follow in doing so. Hawaii's law also requires the seller to provide the buyer with a form to use in making a cancellation. Several states require no printed notice to the buyer.

Most existing laws require the cancellation in writing. Many state laws also insist that notice be sent by registered or certified mail.

PENALITIES FOR CANCELLATION

Several state laws impose a penalty on the buyer for cancelling a sales contract. This allows the seller to retain a percentage of the buyer's payment up to a maximum dollar amount, usually $5 to $15. The penalty reimburses sellers for expenses incurred when contracts are cancelled and discourages buyers from signing sales contracts when they have no intention of honoring them.

ARGUMENTS IN SUPPORT OF COOLING-OFF LEGISLATION

Proponents of direct sales regulation argue that cancellation privileges are necessary to neutralize the high-pressure methods of "hit-and-run" sellers by giving consumers a chance to objectively evaluate their purchases when they are no longer under the influence of the salesman. Although remedies already exist for fraud and misrepresentation, many consumers are unaware of their rights. The low-income buyer, in particular, is especially vulnerable to high-pressure sellers because he often lacks knowledge of alternative products, sources of supply, and sources of professional legal aid. Proponents contend that giving the consumer the ability to cancel would improve the likelihood of his escaping fraudulently induced contracts.

Those who support cooling-off legislation generally agree that most direct sellers honestly perform a useful function by bringing their products to the customer's door. They also agree that unethical operators are found in all forms of retailing—but they believe the cancellation privilege should be restricted to sales made by direct sellers. The contention is that direct selling is inconsistent with the rational consumer decision-making process: the seller initiates contact with the buyer, who has to make a decision about the product on the seller's information alone. The buyer has no opportunity to compare alternative products, prices, and the like.

Direct sellers often discount installment contracts with finance companies. The "holder-in-due-course" doctrine protects these finance companies from legal recourse by the sellers' customers. Because of this protection many money lenders fail to investigate companies from whom they purchase installment contracts, and in some instances they collaborate with fraudulent sellers. The finance companies cannot be held responsible without proof of their complicity in a fraud, and the consumer must pay his debts even when they are fraudulently induced.[1] The protected position of finance companies improves the seller's ability to engage in fraud and misrepresentation because he can readily discount installment contracts without worrying about their collectibility. Rapid discounting of contracts also improves the seller's mobility.

Proponents argue that the direct seller's ability to "short-circuit" consumer decision processes and his high mobility makes his method of selling well suited to high pressure and fraudulent techniques. This is particularly true of the "hit-and-run" seller who is not interested in cultivating repeat customers. Whether or not direct sellers actually employ fraudulent tactics, proponents argue, their invasion of the privacy of the home and their greater *potential* for the use of fraud and misrepresentation should be offset by providing increased protection to their customers through cooling-off legislation.

THE INDUSTRY'S ARGUMENTS AGAINST
COOLING-OFF LEGISLATION

Spokesmen for the direct selling industry also admit that unethical business techniques exist, but argue that these abuses are already dealt with in existing legislation. They suggest that the consumer can be more effectively protected from dishonest sellers by providing regulatory agencies, such as the Federal Trade Commission, with the resources necessary to enforce existing laws.

Opponents claim cooling-off laws dilute the sanctity of the contract and undermine a basic principle of the American legal system, particularly since the consumer is given the right to cancel contracts not involving fraud or misrepresentation. They argue that this amounts to violation of a legal contract without cause.

Although most direct sellers object to cancellation privileges in any form, they are particularly opposed to laws which single out the direct selling industry. They argue that high-pressure tactics are employed in the store as often as in the home, and singling out their industry for separate treatment taints their method of doing business in the public eye. Most direct sellers also argue that cooling-off legislation will have adverse economic consequences for legitimate members of their industry—more sales and promotional expenses will have to be allocated for each "firm sale," and recruiting and maintaining salesmen will be more difficult due to unfavorable public opinion toward the direct selling industry.

THE POTENTIAL EFFECTIVENESS OF COOLING-OFF LEGISLATION

Both supporters and opponents of cooling-off legislation agree on one point—some sellers employ high-pressure and fraudulent tactics. There is nearly universal agreement that the consumer, particularly the unsophisticated, low-income consumer, can and should be protected from these unscrupulous sellers. But will cooling-off legislation provide the most effective solution to the problem? For example, will consumers take the initiative to protect themselves even when they have the right to cancel? Will the threat of cancellation force sellers to adopt more ethical techniques?

RELIANCE UPON THE CONSUMER'S INITIATIVE

No doubt, many consumers ultimately realize they have been victimized by a salesman. The right to cancel makes it easier for them to escape fraudulently induced contracts. However, even the most sophisticated consumer may not discover the fraud within the cooling-off period, particularly when the seller may delay delivery and in other ways conceal his deception.

The low-income consumer is particularly susceptible to such deceit. He is often unwilling or unable to shop outside of his own neighborhood to compare merchandise prices and credit terms.[2] His lack of objective information

158

and experience reduces the probability that he will realize he is being victimized by dishonest salesmen.

Even if an unsophisticated consumer does realize he has agreed to purchase goods on the basis of a false or misleading sales pitch, it is unlikely that he will use the cancellation privilege. Only one-third of Caplovitz's sample of low-income consumers was aware of existing sources of consumer aid.[3] Very few consumers will be aware of cancellation privileges, particularly in states not requiring notice of the buyer's rights in the contract.

And even when the low-income consumer is aware of his rights, he may still be unwilling to rescind the agreement. Caplovitz points out that the low-income buyer faces a dilemma: He desires to purchase the symbols and appurtenances of the "good life," but lacks the means needed to fulfill those desires.[4] Lack of financial resources and the inability to meet credit standards of more legitimate merchants force ghetto consumers to deal with the ghetto retailers or forego the purchase of durable goods. They buy at inflated prices on credit terms featuring low payments, long payback periods, and very high interest rates. Ghetto merchants argue that these and other questionable practices are necessary if they are to stay in business while dealing primarily with very low-income customers. Their margins must be high to cover extremely high losses due to bad debts, theft, and so forth.

In addition to his reliance upon the ghetto merchant as the only available source of durable goods, the low-income consumer often considers these merchants as "friends of the family,"[5] particularly the "customer peddler" who makes regular calls selling and delivering merchandise and collecting payments. Through constant contact and the performance of services, such as check cashing and making small personal loans, the peddler establishes himself as the trusted friend of his customers even though he charges exorbitant prices for poor merchandise, collects endless payments, and works to keep his customers in constant debt. The peddler is a common figure in ghetto retailing. Over half of Caplovitz's sample admitted dealing with peddlers.[6] It is unlikely that ghetto consumers will use cancellation privileges against peddlers they rely on and trust.

THE POSSIBILITY OF AVOIDANCE

Even if consumers can be expected to make effective use of cancellation privileges, the potential effectiveness of cooling-off legislation must still be questioned because many unscrupulous sellers can avoid the law's provisions.

Since coverage is usully limited to sales agreements signed at places other than the sellers' address, direct sellers can avoid the law by establishing "temporary stores." Customers are solicited door-to-door, and then taken to the "store" to sign a sales contract. Similar practices are already employed by merchants in low-income urban areas where they employ peddlers, or canvassers, to solicit customers in the neighborhood and bring them to the store for the final sale.[7] Many independent peddlers operate in a similar way, taking or sending their customers to a local store where the store owner sells the customer the desired merchandise at a price much higher than he would normally charge. The peddler then pays the owner a so-called "wholesale" price which in most instances approaches the normal price, and takes over the responsibility of collecting from his customers. In all of these cases, signing the sales agreement at the seller's address eliminates cancellation rights under cooling-off legislation (exemptions are the Vermont and Illinois laws).

Peddlers may also avoid the law simply by not using written sales or installment contracts and by not informing the buyer of his right to cancel. Many peddlers operate solely on verbal agreements and rely extensively on informal social controls to guarantee payment from their customers.[8]

Several other provisions in existing cooling-off statutes provide ready avenues of escape for unethical sellers. In some states, for example, delivery of a substantial part of the goods or services negates the buyer's right to cancel. Unscrupulous salesmen in these states can simply carry merchandise with them to provide immediate delivery. In other states, sellers may make false claims about the quality of their merchandise and delay delivery of the goods until expiration of the cancellation period.

Some salesmen might attempt to explain away the cancellation right when making a sale. They might tell buyers that by accepting some "free gift" or by taking advantage of a "special offer," they are committing themselves and may not withdraw at a later date.[9]

SUMMARY AND EVALUATION

The question of the potential effectiveness of direct sales legislation is an important and timely one. Frustrations are high in low-income areas with consumers demanding protection from high-pressure, unethical business operators.

But the question remains unanswered. Contract recision privileges may provide a useful tool for the protection of the sophisticated, middle-class consumer. But doubts have been raised about the ability of the low-income consumer to make effective use of cancellation privileges. In addition, sellers can easily avoid the provisions of contract recision statutes by adopting new unethical practices. There is a strong possibility, in other words, that cooling-off legislation will protect those consumers who least need protection.

Cooling-off laws, if effective, would provide increased protection to the consumer without corresponding increases in governmental machinery. If the law is ineffective, however, perhaps a more effective short-run solution would be to increase regulatory activities of government. The financial and manpower resources of the Federal Trade Commission could be expanded, for example, to allow stricter enforcement of existing regulations against unfair and deceptive selling practices. The FTC has already established jurisdiction over such practices.[10]

A recent criticism of the Federal Trade Commission activities suggests that the Commission concentrates too heavily on cases where precedent has already been established instead of expanding the application of existing legislation to new problem areas in consumer protection. The use of the FTC to police the practices of door-to-door sellers would require an even larger expenditure of effort for enforcement as opposed to innovative application of the law. In addition, it has also been suggested that the FTC lacks sufficient machinery to enforce their rulings. To overcome these shortcomings perhaps a new enforcement agency, such as a Consumer Affairs Commission, should be created. These courses of action, however, would increase governmental bureaucracy. Effective cooling-off laws would avoid this problem by relying on individual initiative.

For cooling-off provisions to be universally effective, consumer education, particularly for those in low-income areas, must be accelerated. Retailers should be encouraged to build stores in ghetto areas and to accept the credit of the urban poor through investment and tax incentives or other means in order to provide alternatives to direct sellers and peddlers. These, however, are long-run solutions.

In the short run, the potential effectiveness of cooling-off legislation can be improved by broadening its coverage to reduce the number of avenues of escape open to unscrupulous sellers. Vermont's statute, for example, applies to all sales regardless of where they are consummated. This eliminates the ability of a seller to avoid the law by soliciting customers door-to-door and taking them to his place of business to sign a sales contract. Other "loopholes" can be closed by requiring a clear explanation of the buyer's right to cancel and the procedure for doing so on all sales contracts, and by allowing consumers to cancel even when delivery is made before the cancellation period expires.

Recently proposed changes in existing laws may reduce the need for cooling-off legislation. Elimination of the "holder-in due" course doctrine, for example, would force finance companies to be more careful when discounting installment contracts, since they would no longer be able to collect on contracts induced through fraud or misrepresentation. This would severely reduce the mobility of fraudulent sellers. Similarly, the recent proposal to allow consumers to bring "class actions" in federal courts would allow more consumers to initiate legal actions under existing laws and reduce the enforcement burden faced by government agencies.

For the direct selling industry, the strong interest in legislation designed to protect the consumer should serve as a warning to clean up shoddy practices. Indeed, if the questionable practices continue, stronger legislation may result in substantial restrictions or direct selling activities. Some direct sellers are making efforts to improve their relations with customers. A number of firms allow contract cancellations prior to merchandise delivery. Some reference book sellers are now taking more time to investigate the potential customer's ability to pay before a sale is consummated, and are making follow-up calls to customers to make sure contract terms are understood and acceptable. No doubt, legislative activity prompted some of these changes, while others resulted from the growing realization that satisfied customers represent potential repeat purchases, even for firms selling durables such as reference books and cookware.

A major problem faced by companies in attempting to police themselves, however, is their lack of control over the salesman in the field. They may change their sales training programs to deemphasize high pressure and misleading selling techniques, but changing company policies does not insure that salesmen will change their selling tactics. The use of part-time salesmen and compensation by commission aggravates this problem. Since the salesman is paid for making a sale and the company has no knowledge of how that sale was consummated, many salesmen will continue to employ whatever tactics necessary to produce signed sales contracts.

Some direct sellers are currently attempting to overcome this problem by establishing cooperative programs with local Better Business Bureaus and Chambers of Commerce in order to obtain information about questionable practices by their salesmen in the field.[11]

Some of the arguments for expanding consumer protection through cooling-off legislation are persuasive, but questions concerning the ability of such laws to provide effective protection are equally important. In the final analysis the question of the effectiveness of cooling-off legislation is an empirical one. It will be satisfactorily answered only when objective research findings are available. Thus, empirical research would seem a logical undertaking for legislative bodies contemplating future enactment of cooling-off laws.

NOTES

1. Warren G. Magnuson and Jean Carper, *The Dark Side of the Marketplace* (Englewood Cliffs, N.J.: Prentice-Hall, Inc., 1968), p. 118.

2. Frederick D. Sturdivant, "Better Deal for Ghetto Shoppers," *Harvard Business Review*, 46 (March-April 1968), p. 134.

3. David Caplovitz, *The Poor Pay More* (New York: The Free Press, 1967), Chapter 12.

4. Caplovitz, *The Poor Pay More*, p. 59.

5. William M. O'Brien, statement in *Door-to-Door Sales Regulation*, Hearings before the Consumer Subcommittee, 90th Congress, 2nd Session, on S. 1599, March 4-21, 1968 (Washington: U.S. Government Printing Office, 1968), p. 30.

6. Caplovitz, *The Poor Pay More*, p. 59.

7. Ibid., pp. 25-26.

8. Ibid., pp. 23-25.

9. Byron D. Sher, "The 'Cooling-Off Period' in *Door-to-Door Sales*, Hearings before the Consumer Subcommittee, p. 216.

10. *See* Leon A. Tashoff, et al., FTC Dkt. 8714, CCH ¶ 18,606 (December, 1968).

11. Edward J. McCabe, statement in *Door-to-Door Sales Regulations*, Hearings before the Consumer Subcommittee, p. 143.

19. REGULATING THE PRICE OF CONSUMER CREDIT

John J. Wheatley and Guy G. Gordon

ONE OF the persistent aspects of the consumer movement in this country has been to seek government intervention in the marketplace in order to solve the problems that have produced consumer discontent. The cost of money is one element of a market-oriented economy that affects all consumers. It may create a concern among borrowers because of the intangible nature of the service involved and because of the almost universal use of consumer credit.

Does the regulation of the cost of consumer credit serve the consumers' best interest? This is one question about which considerable disagreement exists. There are claims that such regulation is necessary for consumer protection, and there are opinions that it impairs the free market for credit. An opportunity to empirically examine both sides of this argument recently arose by the passage of a law in the state of Washington in December, 1968, which limits the interest rate that can be charged on various types of consumer credit to 12% per year. It covers installment credit plans, revolving credit arrangements, and credit cards of both retail merchants and banks.

The state also has a general usury law which limits interest rates on most types of loans, including cash loans, to 12% annually. This law had been amended prior to the passage of the December, 1968 statute to permit a charge of 18% per year on retail credit contracts. In an opinion of the state attorney general, bank credit cards were classified as "retail contracts," making them eligible for the 18% charge permitted by the amendment. The primary effect of the 1968 law was to reduce the maximum rate that retailers, sales finance companies, and banks could charge their customers on retail credit transactions from 18% to 12%. However, the new law, Initiative 245, did not affect all financial institutions. Small loan companies, for example, could still charge 36% per year on loans under $300 and 18% per year on loans between $300 and $500.

The basic argument of proponents of the law was that consumers would save money as a result of its passage. The law's opponents responded that all it would produce was higher cash prices for merchandise and a lack of

Reprinted from *Journal of Marketing,* Vol. 35 (October, 1971), 21-28, published by The American Marketing Association.

credit availability for some consumers. Both sides appear to have been at least partially correct in their assessment of the probable impact of the law.

To determine the precise effects of the finance charge limitation law, personal interviews were conducted throughout the state in every city with a population of 10,000 or more, and in several small cities and town near the state's borders. Furniture and appliance dealers, automobile dealers, small loan companies, banks, and department stores were surveyed. The respondents surveyed during the third quarter of 1969 were general managers, owners, or credit managers. All banks, department stores, chain small loan companies, sales finance companies, and large furniture and appliance dealers in these cities were contacted as well as a randomly selected sample of small furniture and appliance merchants and automobile dealers. Chains, particularly in the financial field, were covered by a relatively small number of interviews by obtaining system-wide data at headquarters offices. A total of 145 interviews were completed. The feasibility of surveying consumers was also tested, but the results indicated that useful information could not be readily or easily obtained from this source. In checking a small sample of consumer responses against prior knowledge, it was found that *all* respondents gave incorrect information concerning their credit experience.

The study required data from several sources. To enable price comparisons, three price surveys of specific models of major applicances were conducted in Los Angeles and Seattle. Summary data on the financial operations of all the banks and consumer loan companies in Washington State were obtained from state government sources. A combination of state, trade association, and individual company data provided information on all of the credit insurance business conducted in the state of Washington in 1968 and 1969. A detailed study was also made of two large Seattle automobile dealers' sales contracts, as well as all installment sales contracts registered in King County (which includes Seattle) for 1968 and 1969. In addition, one large car manufacturer provided complete information on dealer pricing and margin experience during the same period for both Washington and Oregon.

Data from secondary sources were also utilized to verify respondent information and to serve as a basis for comparison wherever possible. These included the Federal Reserve, Department of Commerce, National Consumer Finance Association, Institute of Life Insurance, Automobile Manufacturers Association, and, at the state level, the Washington Department of Motor Vehicles, the Washington Department of Revenue, and the Division of Banking.

Unfortunately, the economy of the state was far from stable during the period immediately before and after December, 1968. Early in 1968 the state's economy was in the late stages of a very rapid and substantial expansion. This boom ended in the second half of the year, and rising unemployment began in January, 1969. By mid-1969 the state was in the beginning stages of a fairly substantial economic depression. These developments were coupled with sharp increases in interest rates and retail price levels. Under the circumstances, it was difficult to isolate and quantify the *precise* effects of the new ceiling from aggregate data such as statistical summaries in state government reports.

These problems notwithstanding, the research findings did produce a reasonably clear picture of the effects of the new law.

PROFESSIONAL OPINIONS ON FIXING THE PRICE OF MONEY

Economists typically favor a free market for money or credit as well as for products and services. They generally regard interest rates as a regulating mechanism which should be free to respond to market forces. Many businessmen, politicians, and consumers, on the other hand (even those who favor free market prices as a general policy), tend to favor legal limits on the price (interest rate) which may be paid or received for money or credit. These limits are often set for noneconomic reasons, although justification of such acts is usually couched in economic terms. As Milton Friedman has said (commenting on the writings of Jeremy Bentham in 1787 which opposed interest limitation laws):

> I know of no economist of any standing from that time to this who has favored a legal limit on the rate of interest that borrowers could pay or lenders receive—though there must have been some. I know of no country that does not limit by law the rates of interest—and I doubt that there are any.[1]

Most scholars feel that the hoped-for effects of such statutes not only are unlikely to materialize, but also they produce a number of harmful social and economic side effects. The essence of the economic issue involved in legal limitations on interest rates is simple and straightforward; the regulation of the price of one key component in a market economy inevitably causes dislocations in the system and results in a misallocation of resources.

Other, more specific objections to the regulation of interest rates have also been raised. Each law or regulation on interest strives to favor one side of, or one party to, a financial transaction. For example, the typical usury law is intended to benefit the borrower (or, in the case of consumer credit, the purchaser of goods and services). Since such a law usually takes the form of setting a fixed annual percentage rate, or a fixed scale of rates, it necessarily disregards the overall supply of, and demand for, money or credit.

Another serious limitation of the power of interest limitation laws or regulations is that none really controls the price of money or credit. Taken individually, they typically control only a portion of particular transactions—the portion which formally states an interest rate; however, in any such transaction, the true price of money or credit can often exceed the legal limit. For example, in a mortgage transaction the lender can capture a higher rate than that specified by government regulation by means of "discounting" the loan. In a commercial loan, the bank can insist on a "reserve" (or compensating balance) on a loan which effectively raises the rate on the money actually received by the borrower. On a consumer credit purchase, a seller can raise the price of the goods or services involved. He can also increase the charges for peripheral services and/or add new charges, reduce the allowance on trade-ins (where trade-ins are accepted), change his assortments of goods to increase his average gross margin, or insist on life and/or disability insurance which raises the cost of credit to the consumer and increases the "credit" earnings of the seller.

In setting ceilings too low on small loan interest rates, funds for the poor may become unavailable or may be supplied by loan sharks at very high interest rates. Samuelson has pointed out that the forms of setting ceilings often have done more harm than good, and that loan sharks have lobbied for unrealistic minimum rates in order to increase their business.[2]

In spite of such objections, there is, as Friedman intimates, widespread acceptance outside of the economics profession of the notion that the price of money should not be allowed to respond to the forces of supply and demand in the marketplace.[3] This attitude is based on the fear that retailing and financial institutions will take unfair advantage of consumers. Consumers are thought to lack knowledge concerning the alternative sources and costs of credit, and this lack of knowledge lessens the need for credit grantors to compete on rates. Hence, laws to limit interest and credit service charge rates typically are based on a concept of consumer protection. The effects of these statutes, however, have received scant study.

RESEARCH FINDINGS

Since Initiative 245 reduces the interest income of retailing and financial institutions, they could compensate by reducing their costs, particularly those related to credit transactions. They could also attempt to increase their revenue, or to combine both of these alternatives. The findings of the study suggest that both cost reductions and revenue increases did occur.[4]

ADJUSTING COSTS AND CREDIT POLICIES

The form of the cost reductions varied. Businessmen attempted to lower their costs by making qualitative changes in their consumer-lending activities. Virtually all financial institutions and retailers tightened their lending policies by increasing down-payment requirements and by shortening loan maturities. By the third quarter of 1969, almost all used auto retailers and 25% of nonautomobile retailers had adopted this course of action. One car dealer reduced maturities for marginal buyers from a possible 36 months to a span of only 2-6 months. Retailers made a conscious attempt to shorten maturities in order to reduce the discount rate they had to accept on indirect paper sold to financial institutions. Higher downpayments were sought to minimize the number of high-risk transactions. While customers who can afford large downpayments are not always better credit risks, merchants and bankers believe that large downpayments generally minimize their risks and, consequently, their costs. The impact of these changes has been reflected in operating results.

One bank chain reported that its bad debt losses had been reduced by one-third. Consumers considered to be marginal risks (e.g., new to the community or the job, having a "limited," uncommitted, or discretionary monthly income, or who were "slow payers") were turned down with greater frequency when they applied for retail credit. Of 30 new auto dealers, 22 tightened their eligibility rules for credit; of 46 used car dealers, 36 adopted this policy. Seven dealers cancelled out whole categories of people who might have received credit prior to the passage of the law. In other retail lines, 67% reported rejecting applicants who would have been accepted prior to the enactment of the law; the rejection rate for all retailers increased by 9% by the second quarter of 1969. Bank credit card rejection rates increased in 1969 over 1968 by 2.2% in July, 11.4% in August, 8.4% in September, 10.7% in October, 6.1% in November, and 13.0% in December.

Most large retailers have not found it feasible to eliminate the "free" credit granted to a significant portion of their retail customers on open-book accounts. However, the time period granted to customers on open-book accounts was reduced. Of 37 merchants who were offering 90-day open-book accounts, two reduced this to 60 days, six reduced it to 30 days, and five cancelled the plan. Regular and "slow-pay" accounts were encouraged to switch to sales contracts, revolving credit accounts, or bank cards.

Cash sales were encouraged especially for product categories such as older used cars. Banks have switched small loans (i.e., under $500) to their credit card systems whenever possible. It appears that the latter development reduces the cost of handling small loan transactions. The impact of this and similar policies toward smaller loans is evidenced by the sharp increase in average loan size during 1969 reported later in the article.

Since the reduction in allowable credit charges represented a substantial loss in revenue to retailers, they were under pressure to reduce costs as one means of staying profitable. All respondents tried this partial solution; hence, efficiencies developed which were attributable to the passage of the Initiative.

PRICE INCREASES

Most retailers admitted to raising prices in direct response to the passage of Initiative 245. Moreover, the price increases were not restricted to products usually sold on credit terms. Fifty-six percent of nonautomobile retailers said that they raised prices an average of 5% on *all* merchandise in their stores in response to the passage of the Initiative. In the furniture and appliance field, 64% raised prices on items usually sold on credit (virtually on all of their merchandise). In the auto field, 43% of the new auto dealers reported raising prices an average of 5.3%, and 41% of the used car dealers raised prices an average of 11%. Verification from external sources of the price increases proved to be difficult.

A check of major appliance prices in Los Angeles and Seattle revealed that prices in the latter area advanced somewhat more rapidly in 1969 than they did in the former, in spite of the deterioration of Seattle's economy. A fact that lends credence to the retailers' admission regarding price increases

167

Table 1
Losses on Retail Credit Operations
1968

	Percent of Credit Sales				Dollars Per Active Account			
	All Credit	30-day Credit	Re-volving Credit	Install-ment Credit	All Credit	30-day Credit	Re-volving Credit	Install-ment Credit
United States[a]	(3.41%)	(5.82%)	(2.31%)	(2.41%)	($3.95)	($5.99)	($2.22)	($4.42)
Washington State[b]					($1.92)	($4.64)	($ .05)	($1.54)

aSource: Touche, Ross, Bailey & Smart, "Economic Characteristics of Credit Revenues and Costs in Department Stores," *Economic Characteristics of Department Store Credit* (New York: National Retail Merchants Association, 1969), p. 42.

bSource: Touche, Ross, Bailey & Smart, *Study of Consumer Credit Costs in Retail Stores in Washington: Costs and Service Charges for Credit Activity* (Seattle: Washington Retail Council, 1969), p. 1.

is that wholesale distributors of electrical appliances advised retailers to raise prices 5% when the law took effect (December, 1968). They pointed out that if cash sales amounted to 15% or more of the total sales, a price increase of 5% would recover a loss of 6% in credit revenues. The wholesale prices of older used cars fell in Seattle in 1969 when compared to those prevailing in 1968. This did not occur in Denver, which was used as a control city for this phase of the study. The implication here is that buyers were being offered lower trade-in allowances on new car purchases, at least when older cars were involved. The difficulty in financing older car purchases also undoubtedly contributed to this price depression.

Despite a rapidly deteriorating local economy, automobile dealer margins on both new and used car sales increased more rapidly in Washington in 1969 than in the bordering state of Oregon. This occurred in spite of the fact that total automobile sales grew less rapidly in Washington than in the rest of the country, and almost twice as many Washington dealers went out of business in 1969 than did in 1968.

In responses which were less direct, but which had the net effect of raising prices to consumers, retailers also indicated that they were adjusting their merchandise offerings to obtain higher average mark-ups than those which existed prior to Initiative 245. Such adjustments can be accomplished by changing to suppliers whose suggested retail prices include a higher percentage of gross margin for retailers, by choosing suppliers whose wholesale prices permit a higher rate of gross margin at accepted local retail price levels, or by replacing stocks with items whose unit prices are higher than those of prior offerings. The latter device raises the dollar gross margin per unit without necessarily increasing the rate of gross margin.

ADDITIONAL CHARGES

Some retailers instituted charges for services which were provided "free" prior to Initiative 245. Product-related charges were assessed on check cashing, wrapping and packaging, lay-away, delivery, product installation, product service contracts, and parking. Where charges had existed on such services, the charges were increased. Some stores placed substantial charges on product installation, where this service had formerly been "free." The new charges may not have actually covered the installation costs to the store, but they represented net price increases to consumers. Service charges and other fees, such as those for late payment, were also either raised or instituted by both retailers and banks wherever they were permitted.

In addition to the reduction in the amount of finance charges permitted, retailers had to contend with a reduced ceiling on the amount they could charge consumers for preparing a credit transaction. The amount allowed prior to the enactment of the law was $15; this was reduced to $10 or 1% on the amount of credit granted. On the other hand, the findings indicated that many banks and retailers apparently instituted such charges for the first time in their efforts to generate additional revenues.

Retailers, and particularly automobile dealers, also compensated for their decline in income on credit transactions by selling more of their customers' credit-life, credit-health, and accident insurance policies. Approximately one-third of the auto dealers were trying much harder to sell credit insurance, and in some cases began to require customers to purchase the insurance after the passage of the Initiative. The amount of life and health insurance premiums on automobile sales in Washington increased 23% in 1969, while there was only a negligible increase in neighboring states. The consumer who purchases either a health and accident and/or life insurance contract incurs an additional cost that is determined by the amount of his loan and the applicable rate for the coverage involved.

In addition to a desire to increase their revenues (through receiving 40% of the premiums), there are other reasons why retailers have emphasized the sale of these types of insurance. First, in the event of a consumer's sickness or disability, his payments are made by the insurance company. Second, credit insurance makes the contract between the merchant and the consumer more salable to financial institutions. Otherwise, many financial institutions either reject the paper or discount it an additional point if the purchaser is not insured.

One concluding remark on the behavior of businessmen with reference to the issue of cost and revenue adjustments seems warranted. In spite of these efforts to cut costs and to increase revenues, evidence suggests that their reaction to the passage of Initiative 245 did not necessarily occur immediately after the law went into effect, although it was widely discussed at the time. The adjustments which took place appear to have transpired throughout the year, and it is possible that some adjustments remain to be made. This seems to be partially due to the fact that many businessmen, particularly in the smaller firms, have been unable to ascertain the precise effect of the law on their operations, while others were unable to decide upon their courses of action in the face of the known effect of the law.

One of the reasons why retail businessmen cannot ignore Initiative 245 is that, generally speaking, consumer credit per se is not profitable even in the absence of low-rate ceilings on credit charges.[5] Stores have been found to lose money on all three forms of credit (30-day charge account, revolving credit, and installment accounts). The average losses on various forms of credit found by a 1968 study of department store credit revenues and costs are shown in Table 1.

The costs included in the study consisted of only a 6% cost of capital. Stores in Washington and most stores in the national study were charging 1-1/2% per month (18% annually) for revolving credit and for installment credit. Actual costs of capital for smaller stores in Washington had risen to 9% in 1968. The authors of the study concluded that:

> Providing credit in the department store field was a costly undertaking . . . It is clear, therefore, that credit must be justified economically by the department [store] as a selling tool—not as a separate business venture . . . The small stores had greater deficiencies of revenue over costs.[6]

On the other hand, it seems unlikely that the affected retailers will be able to dispense with their consumer credit arrangements, even if they do incur losses. An accommodation is necessary which permits products such as automobiles, household furnishings, and major appliances to be purchased by consumers who must borrow in order to buy. Borrowing money for a good reason is not only a socially accepted practice in this country, it is also an absolute necessity for the survival of many retail businesses.

Banks are in an equally difficult position. As a cash lender, banks are unable to levy any significant additional charges on borrowers beyond those permitted by law. In spite of the imposition of such fees and charges as are allowed and the potential cost savings in the machine processing loan transactions, personal loans for small amounts are not profitable for banks. This remains true no matter how small the risk associated with the loan, for the high cost of money and the fixed costs of doing business on a credit basis constitute an extremely high percentage of the cost of small credit or loan transactions. Whether the banks actually would raise their rates, if they had the opportunity, is a moot question. Evidence strongly suggests that their rates would have increased since the margin between the primate rate and the 12% ceiling dropped to as low as 3.5%. If the 12% revenue ceiling remains in effect, some banks might drop bank credit cards altogether or resort to an annual charge to the consumer for using bank credit card services. Credit cards are still in use, however, because of the very substantial investment that the sponsoring banks have made in them, because of hopes that either the price of money will come down and/or the interest ceiling will be revised upward, and because of a feeling among bankers that credit cards will increase in importance.

SOME ECONOMIC EFFECTS OF CEILINGS ON FINANCE CHARGES

The effects of interest limitation laws may be expected to vary depending on the nature of the lender's business. Banks have been forced to take more drastic action in the process of adjusting to Initiative 245 than retailers. The volume and nature of business that banks conduct with consumers has been significantly affected, except perhaps for credit cards.

BANKS AND LOAN COMPANIES

Despite the fact that retail sales, including autos, increased in 1969, direct consumer loans made by major Washington banks that year declined relative to 1968.[7] Direct auto loans declined 11.8% in number of contracts and 8.6% in dollar volume. Personal loans declined 25% in number and 12.9% in dollar volume, and direct bank consumer loans declined 20.2% in number and 10.5% in dollar volume. There were similar, though less pronounced, declines in the amount of consumer loans outstanding in 1969 relative to 1968. Total consumer loans outstanding declined 12.4% in number and 6.3% in dollar volume. In all of the above loan categories, there was an increase in the average loan

171

size. Although the average size of auto loans increased only 3.5%, the average size of personal loans increased 16.2%, largely due to the setting of higher minimum loan sizes and an apparent shift toward more affluent customers. This suggests that the decrease in the number of loans was not across the board, but the cutoff mainly affected small loans with the net effect being a smaller number of loans, but of larger average size.

Other financial institutions such as small loan companies have also experienced a significant change in their operating environment and, at least initially, have responded to the new opportunities confronting them in a logical but unexpected manner. Douglas has indicated that the apparent behavior of finance company lenders is such that raising and lowering finance rates may not result in increases or declines in their profit.[8] This observation led to the expectation that the unwillingness of banks and most retailers to make small loans would give loan companies an opportunity to expand their volume of business since they are able to charge up to 36% simple interest. Contrary to expectations, an examination of the operating results of small loan companies in the state did not support this hypothesis. In the face of increased opportunity to lend, there was no appreciable growth in the dollar total of loans made during the year. Instead, the small loan companies apparently took advantage of the opportunity to improve their earnings and the quality of their loan portfolios. Net earnings before interest on borrowed funds in 1969 were up by more than ten times the average increase during the previous three years, while the change in the number and amount of loans charged off was up by about 11% and 14% over 1968.[9]

The price that the banks and finance companies charge the retail dealers with whom they do business increased (it is not controlled by law), reflecting the rising cost of money to these financial institutions. Instead of paying dealers "participation," a practice in which the bank shared the interest proceeds received from a consumer loan with the merchant, the financial institutions began to discount dealer paper. There was a participation rate of 2% in 1968 which changed to a standard 2% discount in 1969. Small used car dealers reported paying discounts as high as 5%.

The principal reason for this shift in policy by the financial institutions was that the paper generated from credit transactions between consumers and retail dealers carried a finance charge rate of only 12%. Prior to the enactment of Initiative 245, retail credit contracts were written with interest charges of up to 18% per annum. Thus, dealers were forced to assume the burden of the mandatory reduction in consumer interest charges through the discounting of their contracts. Understandably, the net result has been a decline in the volume and number of new indirect loans through consumer and sales finance companies and commercial banks.

Indirect loans through banks declined significantly in the state of Washington (40.9% for appliances),[10] even though such loans have risen on the national level. Bank records show that total volume of indirect automobile loans in 1969 handled by Washington banks through automobile dealers declined 10% in number and 5% in volume below the level prevailing prior to the enactment of Initiative 245. At the national level, however, indirect bank auto loans outstanding *rose* by 5.6% in volume.

RETAILERS

Retail merchants were also affected by other changes in the lending policies of the banks with whom they did business. These modifications were not uniform throughout the banking system; for example, many banks will no longer handle indirect loans for older model automobiles, particularly those five years of age and older. When older model cars are still financed on an indirect basis, it is because the automobile dealers involved are especially important customers of the bank. A small number of banks no longer make any indirect loans for amounts less than $500. This particular policy change primarily affects furniture and appliance dealers. One large bank with several branches is no longer handling any indirect paper from household goods dealers in the state, and another bank no longer handles consumer paper from appliance dealers. Still another will handle indirect paper only when it originates with an individual who is also a depositor of the bank as well as a customer of the merchant. Six of the 46 automobile dealers surveyed reported a tightening on recourse arrangements (requirements that the retailer assume liability for loss) with banks, usually by extending the time limit on repurchase agreements from 90 to 120 days.

CONSUMER

The law did benefit consumers in that the cost of direct or indirect merchandise loans, the use of bank credit cards, and interest charged by merchants has been either held at or reduced to 12% per annum. In view of the rapid and substantial increase in the cost of money mentioned earlier and the costs of operating a credit card service and a credit department, it seems likely that the banks would have increased their charges above 12% on direct merchandise loans and stayed at—or raised them to—18% on bank credit cards if the law had not been passed. Further, most retail merchants would probably have kept finance charges at, or raised them to, 18%. The evidence for this statement is, of course, largely circumstantial, but it appears quite convincing. The new law has also benefited consumers by forcing businessmen to strive for greater efficiency in their operations in order to compensate for their reduction in interest revenues.

The effect of the law has been uneven, however, and there appear to be consumer groups who have suffered adversely from its enactment. Cash customers, for example, have received no benefits. They are probably paying higher prices because most retailers contacted had raised prices on *all* merchandise by the third quarter of 1969. At the same time, retailers appear to be switching customers from a credit to a cash basis whenever possible. Customers who continue to buy on open-book accounts have been affected in essentially the same manner as the cash customers, although they are still being subsidized by cash customers to some extent. Another adversely affected group consists of those who were on open-book accounts prior to the passage of the law, but were switched to revolving credit accounts or some other basis which requires them to pay a 12% finance charge in addition to higher prices.

When loan maturities have been shortened, the consumers monthly payments have increased. Therefore, most consumers are able to borrow less than they were prior to the enactment of the law. A reported increase in downpayment requirements has also served to inhibit borrowing in much the same way. Thus, if the consumer does purchase a product, the higher monthly payments may force him to accept lower quality merchandise. Finally, there are those who must forego product purchases that require loans because of an inability to borrow from *any* legal source on terms that would permit the buyer to handle repayment out of future income.

CONCLUSIONS

On the basis of gathered evidence, a number of conclusions appear warranted:

(1) Low-income people who are marginal credit risks seem to have suffered the most from the enactment of Initiative 245 because of the general tightening of credit. Since prices have been raised, customers who pay cash have also suffered. Newcomers and those new on their jobs have always had some difficulty borrowing; their difficulties appear to have increased substantially since loan requirements have been made more stringent. Some consumers (notably the most credit-worthy) may be benefiting from the lower credit charges and the degree of inertia that banks and merchants have displayed in adjusting their business practices.

(2) At the time of the surveys (Summer, 1969), a part of the burden of supplying a service (credit), the cost of which may exceed its price, seemed also to have fallen on the merchants and the banks. The merchants and banks have taken steps to maximize their revenue, but, given the constraints of the new law and a depressed economy, this has proven most difficult. They also appear to have made efforts to reduce their costs, but once again there seem to be limits to what can be done. The merchants and banks seem to be placing their main hope in the passage of an increase in the legal lending rate. If this does not materialize, banks and merchants may have to take additional steps which would, in all likelihood, reduce their volume of business still further and have an adverse effect on a still larger number of borrowers and cash buyers. These steps would involve some additional price rises, tighter credit restrictions, and more frequent decisions not to do business on a credit basis for small sums. Buyers in the last category would be encouraged to borrow directly from personal finance companies, credit unions, or other financial institutions. In fact, merchants might decide to engage in the small loan business themselves to the extent that it can be handled profitably.

(3) It seems unlikely that merchants will be able to institute *dramatic* price increases in order to make up for the revenues lost as a result of the imposition of the 12% rate ceiling. Large price increases would place them at a disadvan-

tage on comparable merchandise vis-a-vis those merchants who stress cash sales and could substantially undersell them. Rather, it is likely that merchants will opt for a combination of moves including some price increases, adjustment of credit practices and merchandise assortments, and raising charges or instituting new charges on ancillary services. These actions will probably occur because a larger part of the cost of credit sales will have to be absorbed by the ultimate consumer. This is not to suggest that it is a matter of indifference how this burden is borne, nor is it meant to suggest that it will ultimately be borne equally by all consumers.

Popular support for laws that restrict interest rates probably springs from the germ of truth in the argument that at least some consumers will save money under such circumstances and from a lack of understanding of the range of options open to businessmen to adjust to such laws. The objectives of interest limitation laws may be laudable, at least from the consumer's viewpoint, but these objectives are, at best, only partially achieved, and many of the side effects of these statutes are objectionable.

More effective pricing restraints could probably be imposed on lenders by a combination of encouraging more competition among merchants and financial institutions and full disclosure of credit costs to borrowers coupled with an educational program designed to show consumers how to make such decisions in their own self-interest. The goals of those in favor of legislation limiting the price of consumer credit could then perhaps be achieved at a lower cost to society. There is every reason to believe that businessmen, however reluctant some of them might be, would also adjust readily and successfully to such a situation. Merchants and financial institutions might even exhibit the same flexibility in setting finance charges on smaller retail credit transactions that they display in their commercial, wholesale activities, and larger retail credit transactions and charge their best (lowest risk) customers less than their high-risk customers.

NOTES

1. Milton Friedman, "On Defense of Usury," *Newsweek*, 75 (April 6, 1970), p. 79.
2. Paul A. Samuelson, statement in *Major Statements in Support of the Uniform Credit Code Filed with the Massachusetts Committee on the Judiciary, January 29, 1969* (Chicago: National Conference of Commissioners on Uniform State Laws, 1969), p. 32.
3. Friedman, "On Defense of Usury."
4. Guy G. Gordon, et al., *The Impact of a Consumer Credit Interest Limitation Law* (Seattle: Graduate School of Business Administration, University of Washington, 1970), pp. v, 132.
5. Robert W. Johnson, "Economic Analysis of Credit Revenues and Costs in Department Stores," in *Economic Characteristics of Department Store Credit* (New York: National Retail Merchants Association, 1969).
6. Johnson, "Economic Analysis of Credit Revenues and Costs," pp. 50-51.

7. Friedman, "On Defense of Usury," p. 48.

8. Paul H. Douglas, statement in *Major Statements in Support of the Uniform Consumer Credit Code Filed with the Massachusetts Committee on the Judiciary,* January 29, 1969 (Boston: National Conference of Commissioners on Uniform State Laws, Chicago, Illinois, 1969), p. 11. Douglas footnotes this comment with a reference to Robert P. Shay, "State Regulation and the Provision of Small Loans," in *Consumer Finance Industry,* John M. Chapman and Robert P. Shay, eds. (New York: Columbia University Press, 1967), p. 100.

9. Unpublished data, Supervisor of Banks, State of Washington, correspondence.

10. Friedman, "On Defense of Usury," p. 48.

20. RETAILERS' REACTIONS TO INTEREST LIMITATION LAWS —ADDITIONAL EVIDENCE

Richard F. Sauter and
Orville C. Walker, Jr.

IN A recent *Journal of Marketing* article, Professors Wheatley and Gordon examined the impact of legislation limiting the rate of interest or service charges on retail credit contracts. They concluded that, while the objectives of interest limitation laws may be laudable, "these objectives are, at best, only partially achieved, and many of the side effects of these statutes are objectionable."[1]

One major reason for the ineffectiveness and adverse consequences of these laws is that they take a static, "all-other-things-equal" approach toward regulating a dynamic economic system. Providing consumer credit programs is often an unprofitable undertaking for retailers even in the absence of low-rate ceilings on interest rates.[2] When interest ceilings are instituted, retailers are motivated to compensate for the loss of this interest income by reducing their costs, increasing their revenues from other sources, or both. Professors Wheatley and Gordon found that many retailers attempted to reduce bad debts and administrative costs by using stricter criteria for evaluating credit applicants, thereby granting credit to fewer "marginal risks," and by eliminating or revising some of their credit programs. Retailers also tried to increase their income by raising prices, adding or increasing charges for peripheral services, reducing trade-in allowance, increasing the size of the down payments, and selling credit life insurance.[3]

The Wheatley and Gordon study of Washington state retailers provides the first empirical examination of reactions to interest limitation legislation; however, it leaves several questions unanswered. Although attempts were made to use retailers in other states and historical operating data as benchmarks, many economic and environmental factors could not be controlled. Con-

Reprinted from *Journal of Marketing,* Vol. 36 (April, 1972), 58-61, published by The American Marketing Association.

sequently, it is difficult to determine: (1) the extent to which various retail policies changed; (2) to what degree those changes were the direct result of the new legal interest ceiling rather than other economic conditions in the state; (3) whether retailers would have reacted differently to a more or less severe interest limit; and (4) what factors influenced retailers responses to the interest ceiling.

The present study, therefore, supplements the information provided by Professors Wheatley and Gordon by examining three questions:

What policy changes are retailers most likely to adopt in response to a legal ceiling on retail interest charges?

What proportion of retailers are likely to adopt each of the alternative policy changes?

What effect does the rate at which the legal interest ceiling is set have upon the retailers' reactions to that ceiling?

Do store and locational characteristics influence retailers' reactions to interest limitation laws?

METHOD

THE SAMPLE

A random sample of 363 retail organizations was drawn from a population of the building materials, apparel, home furnishing, and department stores listed in Minnesota.[4] Self-administered questionnaires were mailed to the credit managers of those organizations, and 174 completed questionnaires were returned; a 48% response rate. Twenty retailers did not offer any consumer credit programs at the time of the survey, and these were deleted from the sample resulting in 154 usable responses.

DATA COLLECTION

The questionnaire presented retailers with a number of policy changes they might make in response to a legislated interest ceiling. These options were:

Increase prices, but only on merchandise frequently purchased on credit.

Increase prices on all or most merchandise in the store.

Require down payments where they are not presently required.

Increase the size of down payments on purchases where they are presently required.

Be more selective in granting credit by using stricter criteria for judging credit applicants.

Eliminate some or all of the credit programs now offered.

Take some other action (specify).

Make no changes in present policies.

Respondents were asked to indicate the likelihood that their firm would initiate each of these policy changes, assuming that an 8% interest limit was passed, by checking the appropriate space on a five-point scale ranging from "extremely likely" to "extremely unlikely." The policy alternatives were then presented a second time, and the respondents were asked to make a second set of likelihood estimates assuming a 12% legal interest ceiling.

Supplementary information was collected concerning: (1) type of merchandise carried by each retailer; (2) size of each organization as indicated by the number of employees and the number of branch stores; (3) size of the city in which the organization was located; (4) types of credit programs offered; and (5) yearly interest rate being charged by the organization at the time of the survey.

At the time of the survey in spring, 1971, the Minnesota Legislature was considering a number of retail interest limitation proposals containing interest ceilings as low as 8%. Minnesota subsequently passed a law in the summer of 1971 limiting interest charges on retail installment and revolving charge accounts to a maximum of 12%. Interest limitation, therefore, was a real issue for the state's retailers, and many had already begun to consider their reaction to the passage of such legislation before the survey was initiated. On the other hand, the timeliness of the issue and the potential for legislative action may have prompted some retailers to overstate their likely reactions to interest limits, even though the survey's cover letter did not suggest that the findings would be made available for legislative use.

RESULTS

RETAILERS' PREFERENCES AMONG ALTERNATIVE COURSES OF ACTION

When retailers are faced with a low-interest ceiling, the vast majority expects to initiate some policy changes in order to compensate for the resulting loss in interest income. Given an 8% maximum yearly interest rate on their credit accounts, only 14% of the respondents believed it was "likely" or "extremely likely" that they would *not* make any changes in their present policies (Table 1).

It was hypothesized that retailers would favor policy changes that are least visible to the majority of their customers and which have the smallest probability of damaging their competitive position. Consistent with this expectation, the largest proportion of retailers indicated it was likely that they would react to an 8% interest limit by employing stricter criteria in evaluating credit applicants (Table 1). While this action would help reduce bad debts and collection costs, it would not be visible to nor affect the majority of their customers. The next most frequent reaction was to require down payments where they were not previously required and also to increase the size of required down payments. The smallest proportion of retailers said it was likely that they would increase prices or reduce the number of consumer credit programs offered.

179

TABLE 1

PERCENTAGE OF ALL RETAILERS LIKELY TO ADOPT SPECIFIC POLICY CHANGES UNDER 8% AND 12% INTEREST CEILINGS
(N = 154)

Alternative Policy Changes	Percentage of Retailers Indicating Policy Change Would be "Likely" or "Extremely Likely" Given an Interest Ceiling of . . . :		Difference Significant at [a]:
	8 Percent	12 Percent	
1) Selective price increases on merchandise frequently purchased on credit	21	12	.05
2) Price increases on all merchandise	41	27	.005
3) Require down payments where not presently required	57	45	.005
4) Increase the size of required down payments	51	42	.01
5) Use stricter criteria for judging credit applicants	79	71	.005
6) Eliminate some or all credit programs	39	22	.005
7) Make no changes in present policies	14	23	.05

[a]A proportions test for matched samples was used to test these findings. See W. Allen Wallis and Harry Roberts, *Statistics: A New Approach* (New York: The Free Press, 1956), pp. 431-433.

Both of these courses of action would be highly visible and could have a major impact on existing store customers.

Among those who expected to increase prices, a larger proportion believed they would institute "across-the-board" price increases rather than institute selective increases on merchandise frequently purchased on credit. This may be explained by the fact that "across-the-board" increases would be operationally simpler to institute. Also, general price increases may have less impact on the retailers' competitive position, since small "across-the-board" increases might be less visible to the consumer than larger increases on selected items.

RETAILERS' SENSITIVITY TO DIFFERENT LEGAL INTEREST CEILINGS

As might be expected, the higher the maximum interest rate specified by interest limitation legislation, the larger the proportion of retailers who are not likely to adjust their policies in response. While only 14% of the retailers thought it was likely that no policy changes would be made under an 8% interest ceiling, 23% did not foresee any policy changes given a 12% maximum rate (Table 1).

A similar pattern of responses was found for each of the alternative policy changes. A significantly smaller proportion of the respondents thought each alternative action was likely under a 12% ceiling rate than under an 8% maximum rate. The relative likelihood rankings of the alternative actions was the same under both the 8% and 12% ceilings; however, with the largest proportion of retailers expecting to use stricter criteria in granting credit and the smallest proportion indicating that selective price increases were likely (Table 1).

DIFFERENCES IN THE REACTIONS OF LARGE AND SMALL RETAILERS

It was expected that a greater proportion of large retail organizations (i.e., more than 25 employees) would change their policies in response to lower interest ceilings than smaller organizations. The rationale for this hypothesis was that larger organizations are more likely to (1) be aware of their credit costs and revenues and be better able to foresee the impact of an interest ceiling; (2) have more expertise and resources to institute policy changes, such as the stricter screening of credit applicants; and (3) be stronger relative to competition so that a policy change would not be as great a threat to their competitive position.

While there was no significant difference between the proportion of large and small retailers who would make no policy changes under an 8% interest ceiling, the proportion of large retailers who believed that they would maintain the status quo in the face of a 12% ceiling was smaller than the proportion of small retailers (Table 2). This suggests that larger retailers are more sensitive to moderate reductions in interest income, whereas all retailers are about equally sensitive to severe interest rate restrictions. This tendency can be observed in the responses of large and small retailers to each of the policy alternatives, although the only statistically significant differences occur between the proportion of large and small firms expecting to employ stricter evaluation criteria (Table 2).

TABLE 2

DIFFERENCES IN PERCENTAGE OF RETAILERS LIKELY TO ADOPT SPECIFIC POLICY CHANGES BY SIZE OF FIRM AND TYPE OF LOCATION

Alternative Policy Changes	Interest Ceiling	Size of Firm			Type of Location		
		Percentage[a] of Large Firms (»25 Employees) (N = 45)	Percentage[a] of Small Firms («25 Employees) (N = 109)	Difference Significant at[b]:	Percentage of Rural Firms (pop. «10,000)[a] (N = 53)	Percentage of Urban Firms (pop. »10,000)[a] (N = 101)	Difference Significant at[b]:
1) Selective price increases	8%	24	20	NS	27	17	NS
	12%	18	11	NS	14	11	NS
2) Price increases on all merchandise	8%	44	40	NS	39	41	NS
	12%	37	25	NS	29	25	NS
3) Require down payments where not presently required	8%	61	57	NS	61	55	NS
	12%	61	42	NS	44	44	NS
4) Increase size of required down payments	8%	61	50	NS	57	48	NS
	12%	56	39	NS	46	39	NS
5) Use stricter criteria for judging credit applicants	8%	90	77	NS	84	77	NS
	12%	88	67	.05	71	70	NS
6) Eliminate some or all credit programs	8%	41	37	NS	49	34	NS
	12%	29	21	NS	23	22	NS
7) Make no changes in present policies	8%	5	15	NS	11	15	NS
	12%	5	25	.01	25	21	NS

NS = difference not significant.

[a] Percentage indicating a policy change is likely.

[b] A test of differences between proportions was used to examine the statistical significance of these findings. See Paul G. Hoel, *Elementary Statistics*, Second Edition (New York: John Wiley & Sons, Inc., 1966), pp. 183-185.

DIFFERENCES IN THE REACTIONS OF URBAN AND RURAL RETAILERS

Although Professors Wheatley and Gordon collected their data primarily from retailers in cities with populations of 10,000 or more,[5] the present study compared the reactions of urban retailers with those of firms in rural and small town locations (i.e., less than 10,000 population). No statistically significant differences were found between the responses of the two groups under either 8% or 12% interest ceiling (Table 2).

CONCLUSIONS

Interest limitation laws will produce lower credit costs for all credit customers only if retailers absorb the resulting reduction in interest income while maintaining prices and services at previous levels. This study indicates, however, that at least three-quarters of all retailers believe they would have to make some policy changes that will affect credit customers in the face of a 12% interest limit; the proportion is even larger when the interest rate restriction is made more severe.

It was found that the largest proportion of retailers expects to react to interest ceilings by becoming more selective in granting credit. While the reaction may reduce the retailers' cost and lead to cheaper credit for many consumers, the burden will be borne by low-income and other "marginal" customers who will be forced to forego credit purchases or turn to more costly sources of funds.

While revenue-increasing actions were found to be less popular, a substantial proportion of retailers believed they would increase prices in response to an interest limit. Such a reaction would negate much of the benefit of lower interest rates for credit buyers. It would also penalize cash buyers by forcing them to subsidize the lower interest rates charged on credit purchases.

These findings, therefore, generally support the conclusion of Professors Wheatley and Gordon that interest limitation laws may reduce credit costs for some consumers, but retailers may react to such laws in ways that negate the benefits of lower interest rates and that may be detrimental to many other consumers.

NOTES

1. John J. Wheatley and Guy G. Gordon, "Regulating the Price of Consumer Credit," *Journal of Marketing,* 35 (October, 1971), p. 28.
2. Touche, Ross, Bailey, and Smart, "Economic Characteristics of Credit Revenues and Costs in Department Stores," *Economic Characteristics of Department Store Credit* (New York: National Retail Merchants Association, 1969).
3. Wheatley and Gordon, "Regulating the Price of Consumer Credit," pp. 23-26.
4. *Dun and Bradstreet Reference Book,* Vol. 480 (New York: Dun and Bradstreet, Inc., 1969).
5. Wheatley and Gordon, "Regulating the Price of Consumer Credit," p. 21.

PART SIX

*

*Truth-
in-
Packaging*

INTRODUCTION

Truth-in-Packaging

THE FAIR Packaging and Labeling Act was designed to improve the objective information provided by the package so that the consumer could make rational package and product comparisons. The basic rationale was that, if consumer sovereignty was to be operational, the consumer had to have sufficient objective information about the contents of the package to make price/quantity comparisons among comparable products.

The article by Dik Warren Twedt provides not only an excellent summary of the provisions of the act but also raises the question of the law's value—because of the omission of the metric system as a unit of measurement. He thinks that not only does the metric system provide a more logical means of measurement than the "archaic English system" but also that the majority of the world uses the metric system.

Jerry Main provides a lucid account of the events and political responses that led up to the final enactment of the legislation. He feels that not only did industry overreact to the legislation but also that industry was politically naive in its responses. Industry has benefited from the experience and will develop greater political sophistication with respect to the issues and legislation of consumerism.

David Gardner's emphasis is upon the shopper-package relationship as a criteria for future legislation. He argues that the criteria for shopper behavior necessary for the Truth-in-Packaging legislation is that, the consumer evaluates all purchases on a price/quantity basis and is concerned primarily with objective information. He, as Dorothy Cohen, feels this is too narrow a view of the shopper and prefers an extended interpretation. The broader view of the shopper is that he is a problem solver with respect to replenishing or extending an assortment of goods to support his expected behavior which is affected by subjective information. This view places greater emphasis upon subjective information and how this information affects the shopper-package relationship. Gardner feels that if the government is to protect the consumer as a shopper, greater understanding of shopper behavior is necessary.

Robert Birmingham also argues that the package is a powerful communication vehicle. But his emphasis is upon objective information within the regulatory design of the Federal Trade Commission. Using economic theory as a frame of reference and the normative view of consumer sovereignty, he concludes that the Truth-in-Packaging Act provides a means of supplying accurate information to the consumer so that he can evaluate products and attain a higher level of satisfaction.

In contrast to Birmingham, George Burditt argues that the act will reduce the consumer's welfare, by reducing his freedom of choice and by making prices higher. He argues that the cost of redesigning and reprinting of commodity labels will be passed forward to the consumer. In addition, the consumer would have to pay higher taxes to provide funds to the agencies responsible for compliance.

21. WHAT EFFECT WILL "FAIR PACKAGING AND LABELING ACT" HAVE ON MARKETING PRACTICES?

Dik Warren Twedt

THE "FAIR Packaging and Labeling Act" (Public Law 89-755) will take effect July 1, 1967 (with the possibility of a 12-month postponement for individual product categories, if the federal agencies involved find such delay to be in the public interest). Marketing people will have to become familiar with the major provisions and implications of this act. Some background information on the act, popularly known as the Hart Act, is included in this article.

A BRIEF LEGISLATIVE HISTORY OF "TRUTH IN PACKAGING"

As a result of investigative hearings held by the Senate Antitrust and Monoply Subcommittee during late 1961 and early 1962, S.387 was offered by Senator Philip Hart of Michigan as an amendment to the Clayton Act. The bill was favorably reported to the full Judiciary Committee, but the committee declined to act on the bill, and therefore it died at the close of the Eighty-eighth Congress in 1964.

In 1965, Senator Hart redrafted the bill (S.985) as an independent act rather than as an amendment to the Clayton Act, and it was assigned to the Senate Commerce Committee. After further extensive hearings (858 pages of testimony and statements before the Senate Commerce Committee, and 1,169 pages before the House Interstate and Foreign Commerce Committee), it became obvious that the House Commerce Committee favored a bill less restrictive than S.985. Such a compromise bill was sustained in the House-

Reprinted from *Journal of Marketing*, Vol. 31 (April, 1967), pp. 58-59, published by The American Marketing Association.

Senate conferences of October, and the bill was signed into law by the President on November 3, 1966.

The purpose of the law is clear, as stated by Report No. 2076 of the House Interstate and Foreign Commerce Committee, Eighty-ninth Congress, Second Session, September 23, 1966:

> More than 8,000 packages containing different consumer commodities now compete for the consumer's dollar. The packages have replaced the salesman. Therefore, it is urgently required that the information set forth on these packages be sufficiently adequate to appraise the consumer of their contents and to enable the purchaser to make value comparisons among comparable products.

WHAT PACKAGES ARE COVERED BY THE ACT?

In general, the Act covers products customarily found in the modern supermarket, with the exception of certain commodities (such as meats, poultry, tobacco, prescription drugs, poisons, seeds, etc.) that are generally subject to federal regulation under other laws. A manufacturer may apply for exemption from the Act's provisions based upon the nature, form, or quantity of the product, or for other good and sufficient reasons.

WHICH FEDERAL AGENCIES WILL ADMINISTER THE ACT?

Regulation of any consumer commodity which is a "food, drug, device, or cosmetic" as defined by the Federal Food, Drug, and Cosmetic Act of 1938 will be a responsibility of the Secretary of Health, Education, and Welfare (HEW). All other domestic packages covered by the act will be regulated by the Federal Trade Commission. HEW'S area of regulatory responsibility is both broader and more specifically defined than that of FTC. Imported packages are subject to regulation by the Secretary of the Treasury.

HOW WILL THE ACT BE ADMINISTERED?

The Act makes provision for both *mandatory* regulation and regulation by administration *discretion*. As part of the mandatory requirements, packages must bear labels specifying:

1. Identification of the commodity.
2. Name and place of business of the manufacturer or distributor.
3. Net quantity of contents (in terms of weight, measure, or numerical count). The statement of quantity must appear in a uniform location upon the principal display panel of the label.

4. If the package weighs less than four pounds (or one gallon if liquid measure), its weight shall be expressed in both ounces (specified as avoirdupois or fluid ounces) *and* in pounds, with any remainder in terms of ounces or common or decimal fractions of the pound. Liquid measure shall be shown in the largest whole unit (quarts or pints as appropriate), with any remainder in terms of fluid ounces or common or decimal fractions of the pint or quart. The law also makes provisions for packages whose contents are commonly specified in length or area, and for random weight packages.
5. Statements about number of servings must include net weight, measure, or numerical count of each serving.

The administrative agencies will have *discretionary* authority to establish regulations determining:

1. Appropriate typographic relationships for type sizes.
2. Standards for characterization of package sizes (such as "small," "medium," and "large"). But the law also specifically states that it "shall not be construed as authorizing any limitation on the size, shape, weight, dimensions, or number of packages which may be used to enclose any commodity."
3. Regulation (but not prohibition) of the use of such promotional devices as "cents off or "large economy size."
4. The extension to all products covered, of the requirement that ingredients be listed by their common or usual names, and in descending order of predominance (except that trade secrets are not required to be divulged).
5. The interpretation of what constitutes illegal slack fill (slack fill not necessitated by product protection or automatic packaging).

If the Secretary of Commerce finds that a product is being sold in quantities which make value comparisons difficult for the average consumer, he is directed to seek voluntary industry standards for packaging. If the industry does not set standards within one year, or the standards are not observed, the Secretary shall report his findings to Congress, along with his recommendation as to whether Congress should enact additional regulatory legislation.

WHAT THE ACT WILL COST

The Department of Health, Education, and Welfare has estimated that its administration of the Act will require an additional $1.5 million of annual budgeted funds. FTC estimates additional costs of about $250,000 a year. The Department of Commerce assumes that annual administrative costs will run between $700,000 and $1 million, with average costs of voluntary standards proceedings estimated at $20,000 per product category.

PENALTIES

Any misbranded food, drug, device, or cosmetic covered by this Act, if it is delivered for interstate shipment, is subject to seizure or injunction under the Federal Food, Drug, and Cosmetic Act (but not to criminal penalties). Manufacturers or distributors of packages regulated by FTC are subject to cease and desist order proceedings.

CONFLICT WITH THE METRIC SYSTEM

Provisions of the Act having to do with specifications of weights and measures are expressed in the archaic English system—despite the fact that 80% of the world's population now uses the metric system (and even Great Britain is scheduled to begin the switch to the metric system in 1970). If, in order to compete in world markets, a package must specify its weight in ounces, pounds, and kilograms—it may prove more, rather than less confusing to consumers.

Frank Archer[1] has pointed out that if products were packaged in fairly even multiples of "metric sizes," it would be considerably easier to calculate values. In the metric system, prices can be determined directly by dividing price by size, whereas with our present system the size must first be converted to pounds before making the division.

"Truth in packaging" and adoption of the metric system are, of course, two quite different topics, and each may be considered separately on its merits. It is relevant to point out, however, that at least some of the difficulties inherent in making value comparisons based upon our present system would be minimized with a more rational metric system.

NOTES

1. Frank Archer, "Marketing's Role in the Change to the Metric System," *Journal of Marketing,* 30 (October 1966), pp. 10-14.

22. INDUSTRY STILL HAS SOME-THING TO LEARN ABOUT CONGRESS

Jeremy Main

FOR SENATOR Philip Hart, the gentlemanly Democrat from Michigan, it started at the breakfast table. The Harts and their eight children all like to eat Nabisco Shredded Wheat in the morning. But in 1961 they discovered that the old, familiar box had changed; it had become taller and narrower. Inside, there were still twelve biscuits, each apparently the same size as before. But a close reading of the new label indicated that here, too something curious had happened. The net weight of the contents had been reduced from twelve ounces to ten and one-quarter. The Harts concluded that they were paying the same price for less cereal and more package.

The Harts didn't stop buying shredded wheat, but the incident helped convince the Senator that the shopper in an American supermarket doesn't always get what the package makes him think he is getting. Thereupon Hart set off on a minor crusade that ended, after five years of lobbying and legislating, with the passage of the Fair Packaging and Labeling Act, commonly called the "truth-in-packaging" law.

The law that finally emerged from Congress has not seriously disrupted industry. Many of its provisions were actually already contained in a series of food and drug laws enacted since the beginning of the century. But industry was concerned, for, as the National Association of Manufacturers Report put it, the law "gives the consumerists the start they need." Hart himself has stated, not entirely accurately, that "this is the first time Congress legislated to protect the economic—rather than the health or safety—interests of the consumer."

One alarmed food maker claimed "consumerism is rampant." And there is evidence to support his statement. There have been three presidential messages on consumer interests in recent years and, in 1964, President Johnson appointed Mrs. Esther Peterson, a persuasive lady of attractive Scandinavian

Reprinted by special permission from *Fortune Magazine*, February 1967, pp. 128-135. © 1967; Time Inc. Jeremy Main is an Associate Editor of *Fortune*.

wholesomeness, the nation's first Special Assistant to the President for Consumer Affairs. The Senate Commerce Committee created a subcommittee on consumer affairs, which will doubtless produce new consumer laws. A "truth-in-lending" bill has been enacted. Another bill regulating warranties and guarantees on consumer goods is a possibility. And the NAM is warning its members to watch out for still other forms of consumer legislation that will affect manufacturers.

Relations between the consumer-products industry and the government are plainly entering a new phase. And the lobbying against the Hart bill—at first petulant and clumsy, later more skillful and to the point, but never really well organized—showed how much industry has to learn about the delicate art of dealing with Congress. The old kind of lobbying that gave the trade such a bad name never appeared during the truth-in-packaging battle. "There was no hanky-panky, no slush funds, no political contributions," claimed one of the lobbyists, and there's no evidence to the contrary in Congress. But the companies concerned were surprisingly backward in the more sophisticated kind of lobbying: presenting sound arguments attuned to political reality in all the right places.

"TOO BUSY OR TOO TIRED OR TOO HARASSED"

Industry's strategic mistake in battling truth in packaging was to adopt an attitude of intransigent opposition. The companies concerned denied any need for the bill, challenged the right of the Federal Government to interfere, and attempted to kill the legislation. They thereby lost a number of opportunities to come to terms with Congress on an early compromise. Five years of lengthy public hearings gave consumerists a public forum for publicizing their cause and complaints. If "consumerism" really is "rampant," then the companies that stock the nation's supermarkets helped make it that way.

The long series of hearings held before Senate and House committees between 1961 and 1966 offered plenty of evidence that food and soap companies were, at times, guilty of deceptive packaging. Proponents of the bill exhibited "giant economy size" cans of coffee selling for more per ounce than the smaller jars; complained of "packaging to price" (reducing the contents of a package without reducing the price or package size); described "cents-off" sales that went on for years and, in fact, did not always represent a saving; and criticized the confusing proliferation of odd-sized packages of the same product. (Potato chips were being sold in 71 different-sized bags, boxes, and cans.) One Senate witness, magazine writer and critic Mary Mannes, summed up the frustrations of many consumers when she said, "most of us are simply too busy or too tired or too harassed to take a computer, a slide rule, and an MIT graduate to market and figure out what we're buying."

The companies concerned did a poor job of meeting such complaints. In most cases they talked in generalities and argued that the bill was an attack on free enterprise. The market, said industry witnesses, was self-policing: the housewife is smart enough not to buy a deceptively labeled item twice. But evidence disproved this. The industry also claimed that existing laws and regulations were adequate to deal with deception. The bill's supporters didn't agree. Moreover, the critics were no longer satisfied with case-by-case action against deception by the Federal Trade Commission and the Food and Drug Administration, which is what the existing laws allowed. They wanted the government to set standards for packaging and labeling so the housewife would know exactly what she was buying.

PRESSURING THE PRESS

At times, industry witnesses were inept as well as vague. D. Beryl Manischewitz, chairman of the NAM's marketing committee, rose to a high cumulus of nonsense when he tried to explain the need for fancy containers. "These examples of individual taste are difficult to explain," he said. "But no more difficult than why more than half a million persons gathered in the city of Washington recently to view the four-hundred-year-old masterpiece portrait, *Mona Lisa*. Those who cannot understand this will not be able to understand why millions of American women find an urn-shaped container of toiletry with a golden stopper more appealing than a standard jug or bottle."

Senators were bored with the industry's witnesses. In fact, they were bored with the bill. During the five years that it dawdled in the Senate, only Hart himself and Oregon's Senator Maurine Neuberger consistently supported the bill. Industry, in turn, was offended by the Senate's lack of interest and apparent lack of understanding. Top executives found themselves testifying before only one or two Senators (which is quite normal to those who know the Senate). Senators were put off by industry's refusal to consider any alternative to killing the bill. Lobbyists were disappointed when they found it difficult to see Senators (which is also normal) and then found it even harder to get them interested in the bill. "These were among the least constructive hearings in my experience," said one Senate staffer.

With the Senate unreceptive, industry turned to the press, a perfectly legitimate maneuver, but in this case badly handled. In 1962, Paul Willis, president of the Grocery Manufacturers of America, boasted in a speech to a television-industry group how he had enlisted the help of national magazines. "We suggested to the publishers that the day was here when their editorial department and business department might better understand their interdependency relationships as they affect the operating results of their company. . . . We invited them to consider publishing some favorable articles about the food industry instead of only singling out isolated cases of criticism." He pointed out that GMA's members were spending $1.2 billion on advertising that year and said threateningly, "We are not aware of any great amount of cooperation that television extended to us."

Willis' remarks set off protests in Congress and the press that delighted supporters of the Hart bill, but the speech apparently had some effect. Hart

194

complained later that several TV appearances he had scheduled were canceled; he says, "I was told off the record that advertisers had objected." It isn't likely, however, that this crude pressure won the grocery manufacturers any close friends.

In any case, industry did not seem to have much to worry about until the beginning of 1965. The bill was blocked in the Senate Judiciary Committee. Although Esther Peterson had been traveling around the country arousing consumers, the Administration, which had never offered any truth-in-packaging bill of its own, gave the Hart bill only tepid support. But then Hart got his bill transferred to the more sympathetic Senate Commerce Committee. At first its chairman, Washington's Senator Warren Magnuson, was not convinced that there was enough support in Congress or the White House to carry the bill. However, in early 1966, President Johnson, having got approval for his priority Great Society legislation, turned to consumerism as a cause—because, say the cynics, he needed a new victory that wouldn't add to the budget. The President told Magnuson that he wanted the Hart law. In a message on consumer interests in March, 1966, the President asked Congress to pass a truth-in-packaging law because "there are instances of deception in labeling. Practices have arisen that cause confusion and conceal information even when there is no deliberate intention to deceive. The housewife often needs a scale, a yardstick, and a slide rule to make a rational choice."

By now it was clear that much of the bill was acceptable to a majority in the Senate committee. The acceptable parts included a ban on meaningless adjectives attached to statements of the quantity of contents such as "giant quart," the establishment of standards for the prominent statement of net quantity on packages, and a requirement that net weights in packages under four pounds be expressed either completely in ounces or in whole pounds.

However, a majority of Magnuson's committee—and all of the industry—were firmly opposed to a section of the bill giving the government the right to standardize package sizes and prohibit odd shapes. Opponents of the bill contended, with some reason, that setting such standards would put an end to competitive, attractive packaging; this section, they said, had to be amended if they were to vote the bill out of committee.

After beating off Republican attempts to strike the standardization section, Magnuson and Hart worked out a compromise that provided for a complicated way of establishing standards with industry participation. Basically, the government could still establish package size standards, but only after allowing industry 18 months to formulate voluntary standards. This compromise concluded an unusually long series of executive sessions (13 in all) and won over the doubtful members of the committee. The bill was reported out of committee 14 to 3 in May, 1966. After another unsuccessful Republican attempt on the floor to extract the standardization section, the Senate passed the bill 72 to 9.

The bill was weaker than Hart had intended it to be. But industry could take little credit for the change. Lobbyists did manage to get specific product exemptions written into the law's provisions. However, they had refused offers

195

by Hart and others to discuss compromises on the main parts of the bill. Senate sources say that before the bill picked up political steam in the Senate, industry could have negotiated half of it away. Instead, the industry stuck to its determination to kill the bill outright in fear that if any of its representatives helped draft a truth-in-packaging law, they would be maneuvered into supporting it. As a result, the major surgery on the legislation was performed by the Senators with little industry guidance. And it was performed not to adjust the law to industry arguments, but as a maneuver to win the support of doubters in the Senate.

Industry continued intransigent until the end. However, by the time the House Interstate and Foreign Commerce Committee opened its hearings on truth in packaging in July, the lobbyists were far .better organized than they had been in the early years of the battle.

Back in 1963, an *ad hoc* committee of some 50 companies and trade associations had been formed in Washington to oppose Hart's bill. The committee limited itself to arousing industry opposition and made no effort to direct lobbying. In early 1966, however, the most active members of the group formed an executive committee, consisting principally of representatives of Procter & Gamble, National Biscuit, the National Canners Association, the NAM, General Foods, the Soap and Detergent Association, Colgate-Palmolive, and Kellogg. The "excom" began coordinating lobbying chores so all of the key people on Capitol Hill would be plied with arguments.

The "excom" had a forceful ally: forty-year-old George Koch, the Sears, Roebuck representative in Washington, who had become president of the Grocery Manufacturers of America. Koch, who knows how to get people to listen to him on Capitol Hill, is credited with being the most effective industry lobbyist in the truth-in-packaging battle. "Who did I see?" Koch says. "Every living soul I could. It was important to get the facts across and important to do it person to person."

A GOOD IDEA BACKFIRES

Koch also helped to organize "district teams" of businessmen in the constituencies of the members of the House committee. The idea that Congressmen would be more likely to listen to businessmen in their own districts than to lobbyists in Washington was a sound one. In practice, it was only a partial success. The lobbyists discovered that it is difficult to arouse local businessmen except with an issue that hits the current year's balance sheet. Congressmen were contacted at home only on a haphazard and occasional basis.

One local effort backfired when the Staten Island Chamber of Commerce passed out leaflets to ferryboat commuters asking them to tell their Congressman, Democrat John Murphy, that they were against the bill. Murphy got a lot of mail on truth in packaging—as much, he says, as on the war in Vietnam—but it ran two to one in favor of the bill. To the chamber's chagrin, many of the letters were written on the back of its leaflets.

196

For the House hearings the industry selected its witnesses more skillfully than it had during the Senate hearings. The executives who testified had more facts and, especially on the question of standardization of packages, they had better arguments. Arthur Larkin, executive vice president of General Foods, for example, explained why his company's 13 regular cake mixes come in different and odd sizes. The mixes have different densities. But the housewife can take any one of them, add two eggs, and produce a cake of a standard size. "If we were bound by a standard requiring all cake mixes to have the same net weight, conceivably the recipe might call for 1 3/4 eggs," Larkin said. "Poor a cook as I am, I know that might be difficult to accomplish in the kitchen." With such arguments presented to attentive and probing Congressmen, and with lukewarm testimony from government witnesses, several of the House committee members became uneasy about the bill.

At this point the bill's fate was focused by circumstances on a freshman Congressman from Ohio, John Gilligan, 45. Gilligan was a member of the committee; he represented Cincinnati, headquarters for one of the biggest lobbyists against the bill, Procter & Gamble; and he was engaged in a difficult campaign for re-election (which he eventually lost).

As a liberal Democrat, Gilligan was expected to support the Hart bill down the line. But he and four other Democrats on the thirty-three-man committee were not convinced by the government witnesses, and became the key swing group. Gilligan decided the government had not made a good case for being given sweeping authority to standardize packages.

A VISIT AT HOME

Before the hearings began, a delegation of about eight local businessmen had called on Gilligan during one of his visits to Cincinnati. "They didn't know much about the legislation," says Gilligan, "but they knew what they were afraid of. When local people come to see you, you tend to give them more attention than you do the professional in Washington." Then, just before Procter & Gamble was scheduled to testify, P. & G. Chairman Neil McElroy and Gilligan spent an hour chatting about the bill at McElroy's invitation. McElroy said he did not want a bill, but if there had to be one he felt something had to be done about the standardization section. Despite the "district team" idea, the two meetings were the only efforts to influence Gilligan in Cincinnati. But, in Washington, Gilligan—and the other swing men—were approached time and again by industry lobbyists as well as supporters of the bill, especially labor representatives.

When the hearings ended and the committee went into executive sessions, the problem facing Chairman Harley Staggers of West Virginia was similar to the one faced by Magnuson and Hart in the Senate: a majority of the committee would oppose the bill unless the standardization section was weakened even more than it had been in the Senate.

By this time Gilligan had decided that a compromise was possible if standardization were made purely voluntary. While campaigning at home one weekend in mid-September, he got a call from Wilbur Cohen, then Under Secretary of Health, Education and Welfare. Cohen asked Gilligan why he couldn't support the bill. Gilligan explained his doubts about standardization and proposed his compromise. Cohen talked to the other swing men, to the White House, and to the Commerce Department. Before the weekend was over, he called Gilligan back to tell him the Administration would back a compromise.

With the Administration and the swing men behind it, an amended bill was easily reported out of committee on September 22. Eleven days later, it passed the House by a vote of 300 to 8. That close to Election Day, only the most adamant opponents were willing to vote against a bill with the built-in voter appeal of "truth in packaging."

"CONSUMERISM" WON'T GO AWAY

Hart claims that 90 percent of his original bill is contained in the final act. Other "consumerists" say it was eviscerated when standardization of package sizes was made purely voluntary. Certainly industry was delighted to see this happen. The act says that when the Secretary of Commerce determines "there is undue proliferation of weights, measures, or quantities" that "impairs the reasonable ability of consumers to make value comparisons," then he can ask industry to develop voluntary standards. If industry fails to do so within a year, he can ask Congress for further legislation.

The rest of the act contains much of what Hart wanted—and much that the industry didn't want. The contents of a package, if it is less than four pounds or one gallon, must be stated in total ounces as well as pounds or quarts. Contents must be printed on the main display panel, in a color that contrasts with the background and in type sizes to be established by government agencies. When the number of servings is given, their size must be given. Exaggerations, such as "giant quart," are prohibited. Government can control "nonfunctional slack fill" and "cents-off" sales.

The law is one that industry can live with. It requires no more than changes in most labels, which are frequently revised in any case. But since much depends on future regulations and since Congress has invited future amendments, the battle over truth in packaging is not necessarily finished. Moreover, Congress will be considering other such laws.

In this time of "consumerism," the experience with truth in packaging offers some simple, important lessons: straight, factual testimony is more effective than oratory; the most telling lobbying begins at home, but an astute Washington representative is also a great asset to a company; cooperation among the companies concerned can be useful even if it is difficult and perhaps undesirable to present a united front that looks like a superlobby; legitimate complaints against industry cannot be shrugged off as attacks on free enterprise.

Most of all, the consumer-goods industry is going to have to face up to the fact that "consumerism" has become politically popular. As industry learned when it tried to kill truth in packaging, "consumerism" cannot be killed. It is part of the Democrats' legislative program; it is strongly supported by organized labor and other groups; and consumers themselves have become more aggressive and articulate.

Truth in packaging was signed into law by President Johnson in November, 1966. At the cermony he handed out several hundred pens. With each was a statement that said, in part: "One of the pens used by the President in signing *S.985*, an Act to regulate interstate and foreign commerce by preventing the use of unfair or deceptive methods of packaging and labeling." In fact, only a dozen or so of the pens had been used. It was a clear case of deceptive labeling.

23. THE PACKAGE, LEGISLATION, AND THE SHOPPER: CUSTOMER BEHAVIOR SHOULD DETERMINE REGULATIONS

David M. Gardner

IN THE last few years, such terms as "deceptive packaging," "mislabeling," "short weights," "nonexistent price reductions," "false advertising," and "truth-in-packaging" have become all too common in the field of marketing. The concern has been that potentially unethical practices lead to confusion and the erosion of competence by the consumer in the marketplace. The result has been charges and countercharges by consumer organizations, legislators, and the marketing industry; on the sideline is the housewife, who tends to view the industry as a usurious, unethical ogre, a view supporting her conviction that gouging middlemen are to blame for cost-of-living increases.

The most recent development is the passage of truth-in-packaging legislation by the Eighty-ninth Congress. It is generally conceded that this legislation, which places considerable reliance on voluntary standards, is mild. Unquestionably, most marketing firms can live with the way it deals with the listing of ingredients for cosmetics and detergents, definition of slack fill, and labeling requirements. The new law is apt to be amended in the near future, however, for two reasons. First, it contains a phrase stating that packaging should be regulated in such a way as to "facilitate value comparison." Congress and the various regulatory agencies will soon try to define exactly what is meant by this phrase and how the idea should be implemented. Second, Senator Warren Magnuson, chairman of the Senate Commerce Committee in his role as champion of the unprotected consumer, is unhappy with the legislation passed

Reprinted from *Business Horizons*, October 1968, pp. 53-58. Copyright 1968 by the Foundation for the School of Business, Indiana University.

by the Eighty-ninth Congress and has promised to keep the subject alive in the Ninetieth.[1]

The goal of present and proposed truth-in-packaging legislation is to "protect" the consumer. Unfortunately, this goal is not stated in operational terms. To do so, it is necessary to look at the shopper in the marketplace. We must have an understanding of how the shopper behaves if we are to provide a sound basis for future legislation and interpret present legislation. (For the purpose of this discussion, "shopper" will be used to describe the person who is the purchasing agent for a family.)

It is not the purpose of this article to offer moral judgment of the marketing industry or governmental bodies. It does seem appropriate, however, to offer a way of thinking about the relationship between the shopper and the package.

IMPORTANCE OF THE PACKAGE

Truth-in-packaging legislation is based on the assumption that consumers are not getting the most value possible for their money due to misleading or inadequate information. Presenting misleading or inadequate information is judged to be a deceptive practice.

To understand the basis for this assumption, it is necessary to look back one generation. Self-service is a rather recent innovation in the marketing of *consumer* goods; in addition, fewer choices for products and brands were offered one generation ago. The usual relationship in the marketplace was between the salesperson in the store and the shopper, who, for the most part, relied on the salesperson's judgment and recommendations. In many cases, the merchandise was measured out to order in front of the shopper.

We have moved away from this type of "personal" merchandising and now emphasize self-service. Self-service has both a cause-and-effect relationship to deceptive packaging because of the attention that now must be given to the package. Instead of a salesperson-shopper relationship, we now often have a package-shopper relationship. The information that was once passed on to the shopper by the salesperson must now be transmitted by the package and its label. If any deception exists, it is now easily documented.

In short, given the absence of salespeople, the package itself has now become a crucial marketing element. The intense competition in most grocery product markets has led many manufacturers to introduce an array of adjectives and labeling practices designed to induce the shopper to buy a particular product. Such descriptive phrases as "the giant pound" and "generous servings for a family of four" produced confusion and skepticism in many shoppers. Any issue of *Consumer Reports* or the mailbox of any congressman contains complaints about the packaging practices of the grocery products industry. This, coupled with complaints in other areas of consumer interest, has led Congress to pass "consumer protection" legislation of which the truth-in-packaging effort has been most notable.

201

This article attempts to give some structure to this rather undefined area of shopper-package relationship by advocating a realistic view of the shopper in the marketplace, by offering a partial checklist against which to evaluate present and future regulations, and a definition of deception in packaging.

SHOPPER IN THE MARKETPLACE

Two distinct views of the shopper in the marketplace can be used to understand the shopper and to form the basis for legislation. The underlying assumptions of each view would produce different types of legislation.

In one view, the shopper evaluates all purchases on a price/quantity basis. The view implicitly assumes that brands are of little or no importance and that the shopper is operating independently of any environmental influences. Therefore, the act of paying additional money is judged to be irrational—whether it is intended to gain the perceived benefits of a branded good, the convenience of a smaller package, or the advantage of a "nondrip" syrup container. That shoppers do not use the price/quantity relationship in many purchase decisions is the finding of forty-six studies conducted by the Creative Research Associates.[2]

Shoppers do seem to perceive values in products other than "most for the least." Not too many years ago, for example, a large cereal company lost a substantial part of the cereal market because of the shape and size of its packages. Therefore, any legislation or interpretation based on this view of the shopper will be based on a rather narrow and static understanding. The result is apt to be legislation and rulings that tend to put emphasis on clear statements of weight so that price/quantity comparisons can be made readily.

The second view is one offered by Wroe Alderson who suggests that the shopper is engaged in problem solving with primary emphasis on replenishing or extending an assortment of goods needed to support expected future behavior.[3] The shopper is a problem solver, not in the sense of getting the most units of breakfast cereal for the least amount of money, but finding that particular breakfast cereal that will be most apt to satisfy the family. This view also holds that an individual item cannot be evaluated on a price/quantity basis; attention must be given to the total assortment of goods into which the item will fit. The assortment of goods that an individual or family assembles is based on the particular values of that individual or family, values determined by reference groups, perception of social class, education, income, influence, and the nature of the assortment. This view is primarily concerned with the quality of the assortment. Cost certainly enters into the decision process, but not necessarily as the most important variable.

This view is more complete and accurate. It takes into account the fact that the shopper is buying items to support a way of life, and "getting the best buy" has entirely different connotations than under the first view of shopper behavior. Any legislation or interpretation based on this view of shopper behavior is apt to be more difficult to write because it must be general, rather than specific. The legislation is more apt to set up rules of reason and guidelines rather than specific do's and don'ts because of the shopper's concern with the "quality" of an assortment of goods, rather than a price/quantity concern for a single item.

SHOPPER-PACKAGE RELATIONSHIP

The shopper-package relationship is basically one in which the package, by its shape, color, size, label, and price, gives information to the shopper, who evaluates the information and considers the possibility of extending or replenishing an assortment. The evaluation process, which ultimately results in an assortment of goods, is the product of various influences. All of these make up the need-value system of the shopper. In the absence of a salesperson, the package must convey the information to be evaluated. The shopper evaluates the information against the needs of the family with the goal of increasing the quality of the assortment of goods.

The information conveyed by the package is both *objective* and *subjective*. Objective information is a factual description of contents, and its weight, volume, and price; subjective information is offered by the brand name, color of the package, size and shape of the container, and design of the label. (There is a very good commonsense argument that price, in many circumstances, is also subjective information.) This type of information is subjective in the sense that it is affected by the biases and background of the shopper.

More specifically, then, how does a shopper decide whether an item should be added to an assortment? A family (or individual) over time tends to value certain groups, certain ideas, and certain objects more highly than others, and to build an assortment of goods that fits this need-value structure. This structure has a specific influence on the assortment of goods and the package-shopper relationship and determines for the shopper whether an item will add quality to an assortment. For instance, a family that values being "modern" will select a different assortment of goods than will a family that values traditional behavior. Therefore, the "modern" family would be quite apt to add frozen dried chicken cubes to its assortment or even a prestuffed and seasoned turkey. The "traditional" family, however, would be less apt to have either in its assortment of goods.

This article adopts the commonsense position that a package's subjective information conveys an image to the shopper. The shopper, in the process of problem solving, decides whether the image "fits" with the need-value system of the family. If it does, the brand is apt to be added to the assortment. Keep in mind, however, that certain objective information, like calorie content or extremely high prices, could override the decision for addition.

The most important fact about the evaluative process is that the information transmitted by the package is filtered or understood by the shopper on the basis of previous contact with a social group and the anticipated contact with this group. The process is also affected by culture, education, experience,

Shopper-Package Relationship

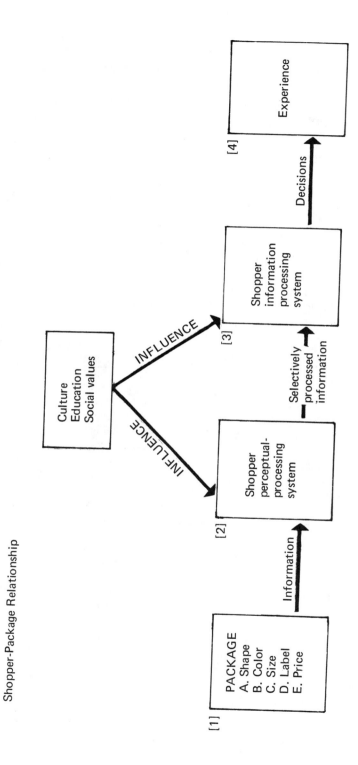

[1]
PACKAGE
A. Shape
B. Color
C. Size
D. Label
E. Price

Information →

[2]
Shopper
perceptual-
processing
system

Selectively
processed
information →

[3]
Shopper
information
processing
system

Decisions →

[4]
Experience

Culture
Education
Social values

INFLUENCE

INFLUENCE

and the physiological makeup of the shopper. The accompanying figure shows this relationship. The information transmitted by the package is seen in a selective way by the shopper. This means, that, because of the need-value system of the shopper, certain words take on value loadings, certain shapes and sizes of containers look larger and more attractive, and certain adjectives denote social and cultural approval. The information is evaluated and decisions are made on the basis of the evaluation. An item is purchased if it will make the assortment of goods more complete in the view of the perceiver, not what it actually does in fact. Experience with a brand or product alters the perception and understanding of future package-shopper relationships.

In replenishing or extending an assortment of goods, a shopper acquires certain brand loyalties but may be induced to alter these loyalties in case of poor experience with a previous purchase or because a package of another brand contains information in the form of shape, color, price, and so on that makes it appear to fit into the assortment of goods. We are primarily concerned with the situation where a shopper alters brand loyalties based on perceptions that produced the feeling that the quality of the assortment would be enhanced, but, in fact, is not.

Given this brief look at the shopper-package relationship, we can now advance a definition of deception in packaging:

> Shoppers purchase an item because they anticipate it will enhance the quality of their assortment of goods. Therefore, if any package transmits information in any form that induces the shopper to purchase, and the value of the item adds less quality to the assortment of goods than expected, then deception in packaging exists.

Note that this definition is quite general—necessarily so. Each package must be examined on an individual basis in relation to the context in which the information will be perceived by the shopper. For this reason, this definition is not meant to include potential deception in packaging.

Based on the preceding discussion, a partial and necessarily general checklist is offered to evaluate present and future legislation and interpretations.

> Have all the relevant influences on shopper behavior been taken into consideration? Has the influence of culture, experience, education, and so on been taken into consideration?
>
> Is the legislation based on an understanding of the individual shopper, or an aggregation of consumer behavior in the macro sense?
>
> Is the emphasis placed on an individual item and its price/quantity relationship or on the item as it fits into a total assortment of goods?
>
> What assumptions about perception and meaning of information to the shopper are being made? Are they realistic or normative?

RECOMMENDATIONS

The understanding of the shopper-package relationship advocated in this article leads to three recommendations. First, the legislation passed by the Eighty-ninth Congress, if understood to be concerned with deception in objective information is certainly a valid piece of legislation. However, I would strongly recommend that further attempts be stopped at once by Miss Betty Furness, the executive branch of government, well-intentioned congressmen such as Senator Magnuson, and organizations such as Consumer Union to facilitate value comparison by reducing or eliminating the subjective information conveyed by packages. This must be done until we are able to document and understand the value of the subjective information to shoppers, and base any further legislation on how shoppers actually do behave, rather than on how we would like them to behave.

The second recommendation follows from the first. It is imperative that the federal government in its assumed role of consumer protector set out to study in detail each phase of the shopper-package relationship shown in the figure. This will not only form an important foundation for potential legislation, but will aid consumer-goods firms in better understanding the shopper-package relationship and hence help them become more efficient. Much of the necessary information for such a study already exists in the files of private firms and in a wide collection of academic papers. However, for various reasons, the information is not public or not readily useful. Therefore, the federal government must take the initiative and motivation for such a study.[4] The actual study can be conducted by private firms and the academic community. One important caution, however: allowance must be made for incorporating and evaluating new evidence as it becomes available. This study must *not* be the study to end all studies.

The final recommendation is directed at Congress itself. Any legislation should contain provisions that make it mandatory for the appropriate regulatory body charged with administering truth-in-packaging legislation to make its rulings and interpretations based on actual consumer behavior evidence, rather than on a normative view that characterizes shoppers as evaluating all purchases on a price/quantity basis.

NOTES

1. "House is 'Adamant', so Senate Accepts Mild Package Bill," *Advertising Age*, 37 (October 17, 1966), p. 1.

2. Irving S. White, "The Perception of Value in Products," in Joseph W. Newman, ed., *On Knowing the Consumer* (New York: John Wiley, 1966), p. 92.

3. Wroe Alderson, *Dynamic Marketing Behavior* (Homewood, Ill.: Richard D. Irwin, Inc., 1965), pp. 144-46, 155-59.

4. Two possible frameworks for this type of study are in existence. For this particular study, modifications would be necessary, but they do represent a point of departure.

They are: Alan R. Andreasen, "Attitudes and Customer Behavior: a Decision Model," in Lee E. Preston, ed., *New Research in Marketing* (Berkeley, Calif.: University of California Institute of Business and Economic Research, 1965), pp. 1-16; and John A. Howard and Jagdish N. Sheth, "The Theory of Buyer Behavior," Mimeographed, Graduate School of Business, Columbia University, 1965.

24. FAIR PACKAGING AND LABELING—THE COST TO CONSUMERS

George M. Burditt

THE PACKAGING Institute's National Packaging Forum is an appropriate occasion to discuss an aspect of the Fair Packaging and Labeling Act (FPLA) which has been sadly neglected: The cost to consumers. A great deal has been said about the merits of the bill—and it certainly does have substantial merit—but, like most legislation, it is going to cost something. This is the subject I would like to consider with you today.

THE STATUTE

The FPLA was passed in November 1966 and went into effect on July 1, 1967. It is administered by three agencies: The Department of Health, Education and Welfare, which means the Food and Drug Administration (FDA) with jurisdiction over food, drugs, devices and cosmetics; the Federal Trade Commission (FTC) with jurisdiction over all other consumer goods covered by the Act, and the Department of Commerce with jurisdiction over any commodity if the Secretary determines there is an undue proliferation of package sizes of that commodity.

The Act requires the promulgation of some regulations and permits the promulgation of others. Time doesn't begin to permit a detailed review of the Act, but let me just mention three of the regulations which are required to be promulgated:

First, a regulation requiring the net quantity of contents of a package to appear "in a uniform location upon the principal display panel" of the label;

Second, a regulation requiring the net quantity on packages of between one pound and four pounds, or between one pint and one gallon, to be stated in two different ways, for example "16 oz. net wt. (1 lb.)";

Reprinted from *Food, Drug, Cosmetic Law Journal,* Vol. 22 (October 1967), pp. 542-547.

Third, a regulation requiring that the net quantity statement be "in a type size which shall be (i) established in relationship to the area of the principal display panel of the package, and (ii) uniform for all packages of substantially the same size."

The regulations permitted include these:

First, to "establish and define standards for characterization of the size of a package";

Second, to "regulate the placement upon any package" of any cents off or similar labeling;

Third, to "prevent the nonfunctional-slack-fill of packages."

All of these regulations are required to be, or may be, promulgated by FDA and FTC. Meanwhile, if the Secretary of Commerce determines that there is an undue proliferation of the weight, measure or quantities in which any consumer commodity is sold, and that the undue proliferation impairs the reasonable ability of consumers to make value comparisons, he is directed to request manufacturers, packers, distributors and consumer representatives to cooperate in the development of "voluntary product standards." If this does not work out satisfactorily, he is directed to report back to Congress with a recommendation as to whether further legislation should be enacted. In fact, the Act is so detailed, complicated and restrictive in solving the problem that I am reminded of the story of the legislator who had a nervous breakdown because he had found the solution to the problem but he's forgotten what the problem was!

REGULATIONS

So much for the statute itself. As to regulations, all three agencies are hard at work. The food regulations are now final; the drug and cosmetic regulations, and the FTC regulations, have been proposed and commented on; the Department of Commerce regulations are partially final, with certain implementing provisions being in the proposal stage.

There are, of course, many similarities between the FDA and FTC regulations, but there are also some differences. For example, the FDA regulations require that the quantity statement appear in the bottom 30 per cent of the label, whereas the FTC regulations require that it appear "in close proximity to the most conspicuous statement of the trade or brand name." The FDA regulations require that the signature copy include the zip code; the FTC regulations merely require "an adequate and sufficient mailing address." In the case of odd shaped containers, FDA requires that the area of the principal display panel be measured by "40% of the total surface of the container," whereas FTC uses the "total actual area of the surface of the principal display panel." The regulations are necessarily complicated; with less reason, they are ambiguous and unduly restrictive in some respects, perhaps because of some unfortunate choices of words in the Act.

THE COST

Now let me get to the cost to the consumer. The first obvious cost is financial. Virtually every package of food, drugs and cosmetics is going to have to be redesigned. And many of the redesigns are substantial. For example, the quantity statement has to be moved to the bottom 30 per cent of the label; it has to appear in the two forms I mentioned a moment ago; it must appear in a new and specific type size which in a good many cases is twice as large as the type size put into effect about two years ago by the National Conference on Weights and Measures; and it must be separated from other printed matter according to a specific formula. Similar, although not identical, changes are going to have to be made on other consumer commodities under the jurisdiction of the FTC.

In terms of dollars, how much will it cost to redesign and reprint virtually every single consumer commodity label in the United States? Obviously it is going to cost many, many millions of dollars. The returns are not all in. Costs can be influenced dramatically by the degree of reasonableness exercised by the regulatory agencies. Haste will be extremely costly because it will necessitate the destruction of unused labels and plates and cylinders which are not worn out. Under any circumstances, the new art work, new sales, production and legal approvals, new plates and cylinders and duplicate inventories necessitated by the signature clause provisions will be expensive. Work on container standards will inevitably be high, since all three agencies will have to add personnel to handle the questions of interpretation, requests for exemptions and the myriad of other administrative problems. So the consumer is going to have to pay, both in terms of higher prices and in terms of increased taxes.

You may have heard the story about the Congressman—and this may have occurred after the FPLA was passed—who was worried about a particular bill which had just been approved and said to one of his colleagues, "We have met the enemy and they are us."

The second cost to consumers is in terms of consumer confusion, one of the very things the Act is designed to prevent. The prime example of this, of course, is in the dual declaration requirement. I simply can't believe that telling a consumer in two different ways how much a package contains is going to be helpful. And what about tray pack displays where the tray covers the bottom 30 per cent of the label where the quantity statement must appear? And is it going to help consumers to see as a signature "The Universal Hospital Supply Corporation" on a can of orange juice concentrate, or "The Tampa Cigar Company" on a package of aspirin?

The third cost to consumers is in a loss of freedom of choice. An inevitable result, sooner or later, is going to be a reduction in the number of package sizes available to consumers. There has been a lot of talk about the number of sizes of potato chip packages. But the complainers seem to forget that if consumers didn't want different package sizes they wouldn't buy them. It's the consumer who benefits by the various sizes of packages and if she doesn't want them they simply won't be on the market very long. So the consumer is going to pay in terms of fewer choices. We are heading for standardization.

The final cost I would like to mention is still problematical. I don't want to be melodramatic about it, but I think it is the most serious of all. It is the kind of thing which must make Patrick Henry twitch a little in his grave. FDA has denied a hearing on the regulations although approximately fifty objections and requests for a hearing were filed. And this is in the face of the specific requirement of both the Federal Food, Drug and Cosmetic Act and the Fair Packaging and Labeling Act that hearings be held on the filing of valid objections. I realize that the FDA, like industry, is highly desirous of getting on with the job of complying with congressional intent as expressed in the Fair Packaging and Labeling Act. But part of this intent is that hearings be held.

The reasons for denying the hearing as set forth in the final FDA order are in large measure unsound. Let me give you two or three examples. A hearing is denied on one issue on the ground that: "Since this was a matter which the Commissioner had to decide, it is not considered as one warranting a public hearing." This is a patent non sequitur. On another issue, a hearing is denied "Since the statute provides that [the decision] should be made by the Commissioner and not by popular vote." The Commissioner has to make the final decision on all regulations. Indeed, this is the very reason a hearing is required—so that every American citizen has an opportunity to present his views, to question and oppose the views of others, and so that a full record can be prepared for a court to make a judicial determination if necessary.

A hearing is denied on another issue, and again I am going to quote, "since the objector did not suggest an alternative." There is no legal requirement that an objector suggest an alternative. If this is a valid ground for denying a hearing, no consumer, and no industry member, could ever get a hearing without suggesting an alternative, which is clearly unsound law.

I am greatly concerned, and a little disappointed and worried, that the final order deprives everyone, consumers and industry alike, of the right to be heard in an administrative tribunal. After all, in our modern society, administrative hearings are in many ways just as important as judicial hearings. Any impairment of the fundamental right to a hearing should be taken most seriously, not only because of the immediate effect, but also because of its ramifications for the future.

So the Packaging and Labeling Act isn't going to give consumers a free ride to anywhere. I imagine some Congressmen are having second thoughts about it.

25. THE CONSUMER AS KING: THE ECONOMICS OF PRECARIOUS SOVEREIGNTY

Robert L. Birmingham

RECENTLY THE Magazine Publishers Association, an association of 365 leading United States magazines, sponsored a group of advertisements advertising advertising. One of the most popular of these, which appeared in many mass-consumption magazines in the spring and summer of 1967, was a Feiffer-like series of sketches set at a cocktail party.[1] A professorial and hence hardly virile-looking simpleton is depicted expounding his views on economic planning to a young woman obviously drawn to illustrate the ease of combining sexual attractiveness with the responsibilities of motherhood:

Professor: Our economy is like a great complicated machine that has too many moving parts!

Matron: We used to have a car like that.

Professor: I say *simplify!* Give the public *one* good TV . . . *one* soap . . . just *one* brand of *everything*.

Matron: I do hope it's a pink soap or maybe a nice yellow or . . .

Professor: Think what we'll *save* on promotion . . . advertising . . . wasteful competition! The mind boggles.

Matron: When that happens to me, I take an aspirin or an "Empirin" or an "Alka-Seltzer." It depends.

Professor: Of course the *government* would see to it every product met a certain *standard*.

Matron: And if they didn't, I'd simply switch to a better brand!

Professor: No, no!! Thousands of brands screaming to be bought is a thing of the *past*. We must go *beyond* that.

Matron: You mean I couldn't choose things to buy the way I pick a movie or a . . .

Professor: You wouldn't need to choose.

Reprinted from *Case Western Reserve Law Review*, Vol. 20 (1969), 354-367, 377.

Matron: My husband and I passed through a *charming* little country just like that.
Professor: Really, which one?
Matron: Albania.

Elaboration is provided in text at the bottom of the page, apparently to aid those missing the point but nevertheless literate:

> If you're laughing at that fellow up above, we've got news for you. He's serious!
> There actually are people—well-meaning people—in this country today who think the government should regulate the number of brands on the market.
> Mrs. Smith is confused by all the varieties of soap on her supermarket shelf, they say. It would simplify things if there were only four or five, they claim. Making shopping a whole lot quicker and easier.
> Of course, poor, little, mixed-up Mrs. Smith won't get to choose which soaps go and which soaps stay. Seventeen years of sharp-eyed, close-fisted comparison shopping and product testing apparently have left Mrs. Smith incapable of that judgment.
> So, now she'll have friends in high places to do her shopping for her. Lucky Mrs. Smith.
> Let's hope they know Mrs. Smith has a 12-year-old with dry skin. And a mauve bathroom.

Even disregarding the permissibility of travel through Albania at the time of the trip, this advertisement raises interesting problems. Our ideology asserts that maximization of satisfaction can best be attained through vigilant protection preventing regulatory adulteration of a largely mythical but nevertheless sacred market mechanism.[2] Consumer choice is held to be inviolable.[3] We blindly assume that each person is endowed with an immutable set of preferences dictating degrees of satisfaction associated with the acquisition and use of various combinations of goods. Since discovery of such pleasure schedules cannot be disassociated from individual selection among proffered bundles of products, interference with this selection is generally deemed to reduce community utility. Claims of efficacy, however, do not stop here: "[W]ithin the model of the free market lies one good chance of smoothing the frictions which develop between men on the score of religion, race, colour or social values. 'The market is a great civilizer.' "[4]

The increasing complexity of the modern market place has rendered the unaided individual almost defenseless against modern merchandising techniques. The head of a large department store has stated: "God created the masses of mankind to be exploited. I exploit them; I do his will."[5] In a message to Congress delivered February 5, 1964, President Johnson noted that "for far too long, the consumer has had too little voice and too little weight in government. As a worker, as a businessman, as a farmer, as a lawyer or doctor, the citizen has been well represented. But as a consumer, he has had to take a back seat.''[6]

In spite of our ideological bias toward nonintervention, concern for consumer impotence has inspired recent legislation designed to redress the imbalance of power. In this article, selected superstitions underlying our economic value judgments are briefly examined. Next, attention is focused on the Fair Packaging and Labeling Act. After briefly describing it I will attempt to evaluate its purpose and impact in the light of economic theory.

EQUILIBRIUM AND OPTIMALITY

Pareto optimality—economic equilibrium such that with given community resources no person can be made better off without injury to another—will result if: perfect competition prevails; there are constant returns to scale; and there are no external economies or diseconomies with respect to production or consumption.[7] The Platonic ideal of a perfectly competitive commodity market requires that:

1. firms produce a homogeneous commodity, and consumers are identical from the sellers' point of view, in that there are no advantages or disadvantages associated with selling to a particular consumer;
2. both firms and consumers are numerous, and the sales or purchases of each individual unit are small in relation to the aggregate volume of transactions;
3. both firms and consumers possess perfect information about the prevailing price and current bids, and they take advantage of every opportunity to increase profits and utility respectively;
4. entry into and exit from the market is free for both firms and consumers.[8]

Perfectly competitive factor markets must satisfy similarly rigorous conditions. All markets must be linked by perfect knowledge of the characteristics of their products or factors.

The basic assumptions of the model inherently connote a lack of realism. Not only are its requirements unattainable, but attempts to avoid unnecessary divergence from its norms cannot be justified without further detailed argument. If some aspects of a system are constrained to non-maximizing levels, there is no a priori basis for asserting that satisfaction of other conditions of optimality will necessarily prove advantageous.[9]

The optimality of competitive equilibrium merely assures efficiency. In general case welfare will not be maximized:

Perfect competition represents a welfare optimum in the narrow sense of fulfilling the requirements of Pareto optimality. . . . An additional difficulty is introduced by the fact that the analysis of Pareto optimal-

214

ity accepts the prevailing income distribution. . . . The problem of finding an optional income distribution is not considered. . . . The analysis of welfare in terms of Pareto optimality leaves a considerable amount of indeterminacy in the solution: there are an infinite number of points . . . which are Pareto-optimal. . . . In order to judge the relative social desirability of alternative points . . . society must make additional value judgments which state its preferences among alternative ways of allocating satisfaction to individuals. Value judgments are ethical beliefs and are not the subject of economic analysis.[10]

Our interest concentrates on the ability of the consumer, assuming satisfaction of other conditions necessary for optimization, to choose from the available goods that combination which, given his income, will yield him the most pleasure. Plot quantities of two desired goods, G_1 and G_2, along the horizontal and vertical axes of Figure 1. Then any point (for example, point A) within the quadrant will denote a unique combination of the two goods having a definite value to an individual. The individual, offered a choice between combinations of goods represented by any two points, will either prefer one to the other or be indifferent as to which he obtains. Ordinarily, we would expect a person to value the combination designated by point B more highly than that of point A, because the former contains more of each good. The locus of all combinations of goods from which the consumer derives equal satisfaction is called an indifference curve. Assuming infinite divisibility of both goods, each point along or between the axes will lie on some indifference curve. Three such curves, I_1, I_2, and I_3, are drawn in Figure 1. The individual will prefer a position on I_3 to one on I_2, and would rather be on I_2 than on I_1.[11]

Limited resources normally prevent the consumer from obtaining satiating amounts of the goods in question. Combinations available to him will be limited to those on or below and to the left of a budget constraint, such as line xy in Figure 1. From the combinations which he can afford the individual will choose that usually unique one which will yield him the greatest satisfaction. If choice is unhampered, he will locate at point A, where budget constraint xy is tangent to indifference curve I_2, the highest indifference curve he can reach.

Since goods are valuable for the enjoyment they yield, it is possible to consider them merely combinations of qualities which themselves form more basic units of personal satisfaction. Consumer behavior, therefore, can be explained with reference to choice among combinations of these qualities in a manner paralleling our analysis of choice among combinations of goods. Thus we can measure quantities of two desired qualities rather than quantities of two desired goods along the horizontal and vertical axes of Figure 1. Assuming perfect information concerning the qualities associated with each good, unrestricted consumer choice will by a now familiar process again yield equilibrium at point A.[12]

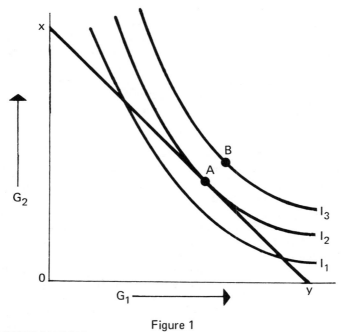

Figure 1

INFORMATION

LEGISLATION

The Fair Packaging and Labeling Act,[13] the product of partially abortive efforts by Michigan's Senator Hart and others to reduce consumer confusion caused by misleading marketing practices, became effective on July 1, 1967. Some indication of the anticipated impact of the regulations as originally formulated can be garnered from the ferocity of industry opposition to their enactment. The Michigan Chamber of Commerce stated:

> Inescapably, one concludes the Hart bill is not really aimed at consumer protection, for that's already available in existing law. The measure is little more than a federal grab for power to make decisions that heretofore have been made by consumers and by business—a power grab based on the fallacious concepts that the consumer is Casper Milquetoast, business is Al Capone, and government is Superman.[14]

A representative of the National Association of Manufacturers argued that "[t]he inevitable effect of the bill will be to roll back the packaging and marketing revolution of this generation. Had we lived in recent years under such a law, we would not buy our products as fresh, as clean, as unbroken or unspoiled, as accurately measured, as easily handled or as cheaply as we do today."[15] Such resulting national disasters as a requirement that the holes in

216

"Life Savers" be filled were predicted.[16] A resolution against passage was adopted by the American Bar Association, whose seven-man Advisory Committee of the Food, Drug, and Cosmetic Division of the Corporation, Banking, and Business Section included several attorneys associated with the food industry.[17]

Section 1451 recites the sources of congressional inspiration:

> Informed consumers are essential to the fair and efficient functioning of a free market economy. Packages and their labels should enable consumers to obtain accurate information as to the quantity of the contents and should facilitate value comparisons. Therefore, it is hereby declared to be the policy of the Congress to assist consumers and manufacturers in reaching these goals in the marketing of consumer goods.[18]

The means used to effectuate this policy, significantly less drastic than those initially proposed,[19] seem hardly calculated to destroy even those surviving fragments of our capitalistic system. The Act subjects to control "consumer commodities," broadly defined by Section 1459 to include:

> any food, drug, device, or cosmetic . . . and any other article, product, or commodity . . . customarily produced or distributed for sale through retail sales agencies or instrumentalities for consumption by individuals, or use by individuals for purposes of personal care or in the performance of services ordinarily rendered within the household, and which usually is consumed or expended in the course of such consumption or use. . . .[20]

Among goods specifically excluded from regulation are meat, poultry, tobacco products, and rat poison.

Section 1454 vests regulatory power in the Secretary of Health, Education, and Welfare, when the consumer commodity is food, drug, device, or cosmetic, or the Federal Trade Commission, if it is not. These authorities are directed by Section 1453 to promulgate regulations providing that:

1. The commodity shall bear a label specifying the identity of the commodity and the name and place of business of the manufacturer, packer, or distributor;
2. The net quantity of contents (in terms of weight, measure, or numerical count) shall be separately and accurately stated in a uniform location upon the principal display panel of that label. . . .[21]

Additional paragraphs seek to avoid consumer confusion through establishing standards of clarity. Thus quantities contained "shall appear in conspicuous and easily legible type in distinct contrast . . . with other matter on the package,"[22] and "shall be so placed that the lines of printed matter . . . are generally parallel to the base on which the package rests as it is designed to be displayed. . . ."[23] In some cases decimal fractions of a pound may not be carried out to more than two places.[24]

If compliance is impracticable or unnecessary, Section 1454 allows the authorities to exempt classes of commodities from requirements of Section 1453. Additional duties include prevention of "non-functional-slack-fill of packages" when "necessary to prevent the deception of consumers or to facilitate value comparisons as to any consumer commodity. . . ." A package is to be considered "nonfunctionally slack-filled" only "if it is filled to substantially less than its capacity for reasons other than (A) protection of the contents of such package or (B) the requirements of machines used for enclosing the contents in such package."[25]

Section 1454(d) states:

> Whenever the Secretary of Commerce determines that there is undue proliferation of the weights, measures, or quantities in which any consumer commodity or reasonably comparable consumer commodities are being distributed in packages for sale at retail and such undue proliferation impairs the reasonable ability of consumers to make value comparisons with respect to such consumer commodity or commodities, he shall request manufacturers, packers, and distributors of the commodity or commodities to participate in the development of a voluntary product standard for such commodity or commodities under the procedures for the development of voluntary products standards established by the Secretary. . . . Such procedures shall provide adequate manufacturer, packer, distributor, and consumer representation.[26]

The absence of penalties for noncompliance assures that standardization programs are truly voluntary:

> (e) If (1) after one year after the date on which the Secretary of Commerce first makes the request of manufacturers, packers, and distributors to participate in the development of a voluntary product standard . . . he determines that such a standard will not be published . . . or (2) if such a standard is published and the Secretary of Commerce determines that it has not been observed, he shall promptly report such determination to the Congress with a statement of the efforts that have been made under the voluntary standards program and his recommendation as to whether Congress should enact legislation providing regulatory authority to deal with the situation in question.[27]

Judicial review of regulations issued pursuant to the Act is authorized in Section 1455. Section 1456 declares misbranded, within the meaning of the Federal Food, Drug, and Cosmetic Act, "[a]ny consumer commodity which is a food, drug, device, or cosmetic . . . introduced or delivered for introduction into commerce'' in disregard of established standards. Similarly, noncon-formity in the packaging of other consumer commodities is to be deemed ''an unfair or deceptive act or practice in commerce'' in violation of Section 5(a) of the Federal Trade Commission Act.[28]

THEORY

Unfortunately equilibrium as depicted in Figure 1 is seldom achieved. Preference patterns which govern purchases are a combination of basic wants and beliefs concerning the characteristics of various products. Product purchases in turn are the means by which basic wants are satisfied. Selection of that combination of goods represented by point A in Figure 1 is axiomatic: argument for any alternative choice normally degenerates to an assertion that the relevant indifference curves should be differently drawn.[29] The problem is that point A generally does not represent an optimum with respect to the satisfaction of underlying desires.

The assumption of perfect information required by the competitive model is obviously unrealistic. In a recent test, 33 young married women with at least 1 year of college and 1 year of regular shopping experience were given nearly 2 1/2 minutes per item to select 20 best buys among items typically stocked by supermarkets. They chose incorrectly 43 percent of the time, spend-ing an average of almost 10 percent more than necessary. Nevertheless, ''the average shopper sweeps past the 8,000 products found in the store and buys 32 items in 15 to 18 minutes. . . .''[30]

The merchant is of course more interested in selling his product than in creating a knowledgeable noncustomer. A. C. Fuller, founder of the Fuller Brush Company stated:

> The American housewife is an intelligent buyer. . . . The great-est safeguard she has . . . is in shopping around from store to store.
>
> This shopping impulse arises the moment she considers buying anything, and the house-to-house salesman *must stifle it*, if he can. He is giving his customer no opportunity to compare values or to postpone buying. ''Do it now,'' he tells her, ''I won't be back this way for a couple of months.'' She buys, when she buys, against an inner voice of discretion which tells her to wait until she can com-pare values.[31]

Packaging is definitely an important instrument of persuasion: ''I'm like a child. If you fix things up pretty, I'll buy them.''[32] Opportunities for manipula-tion are not disregarded: ''[T]hree motivating factors for a successful packaging program are consumer needs, desires and weaknesses. 'Consumer weakness includes the embellishments assigned to a package. . . . They add little or nothing to the functional aspects of the package, nothing to the product, but to a large measure they create the impulse for purchasing.' ''[33]

Unwillingness to seek information before purchase often seems con-demned as almost immoral indifference on the part of the individual.[34] A possi-ble consequence of such an attitude is the assertion that if consumers are foolish enough to purchase blindly they do not deserve legislation which attempts to relieve them of the consequences of their stupidity. Such an approach advocates a needless sacrifice of welfare. Also, it frequently disregards the fact that information, an economic good like any other, can usually be acquired only through relinquishment of some alternative value. Information concerning the optimal level of information one should seek is likewise not costless.[35]

Lack of full knowledge of product characteristics will normally prevent a consumer from acquiring that combination of goods of greatest benefit to him. An error in estimating the characteristics of a product will lead to preference patterns with respect to goods which do not accurately reflect preferences as to qualities. In Figure 2 the individual is shown initially to have achieved an equilibrium with respect to goods identical to that of Figure 1. He has selected that combination of products represented by point A, where indifference curve I^2 is tangent to budget constraint xy. If he is only imperfectly aware of the characteristics of the products, however, he will generally not have succeeded in satisfying his more fundamental desires as fully as his income permits.

The purpose of the Fair Packaging and Labeling Act and similar statutes is to facilitate attainment of a higher level of consumer satisfaction. To accomplish this the government seeks to assure a supply of information which permits an individual to evaluate more correctly the goods available for purchase. Reduction of error in perceiving the qualities associated with various products will transform the preference pattern depicted in Figure 2, resulting in a set of revised indifference curves including, say, I^{R1} and I^{R2}. Point A, now situated on I^{R1}, is no longer an equilibrium position. Now the consumer

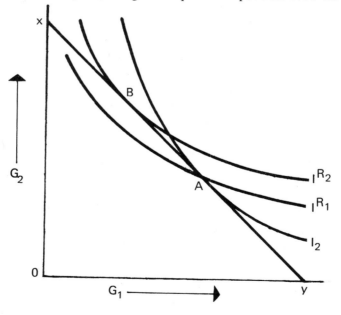

Figure 2

will choose that combination of goods represented by point B, where a higher indifference curve, I^{R_2}, is tangent to the budget constraint. The consumer's welfare has increased, since purchases now more nearly satisfy his basic desires.

CONCLUSION

The Fair Packaging and Labeling Act is an attempt to increase the value of community consumption by restricting the freedom of the producer. As such it is based on reasoning antithetical to the principle of nonintervention of classical economic theory. In this article I have attempted to demonstrate that its effect will be not to impede attainment of ideal equilibrium but rather to increase welfare by tending to correct imperfections in the market mechanism. Thus, it correctly implements the overriding Smithian standard that "[c]onsumption is the sole end and purpose of all production; and the interest of the producer ought to be attended to, only so far as it may be necessary for promoting that of the consumer. The maxim is so perfectly self-evident, that it would be absurd to attempt to prove it."[36]

NOTES

1. *See e.g., Newsweek,* April 10, 1967, at 101.
2. "The ideology of laissez-faire outlived the structural reforms which changed uncontrolled market economy. Indeed, the discrepancy between what many think we ought to do—laissez-faire—and what we in fact are doing—creating a welfare state—has not yet entirely disappeared in the United States." Dalton, "Primitive, Archaic, and Modern Economies: Karl Polanyi's Contribution to Economic Anthropology and Comparative Economy," in *Essays in Economic Anthropology* 1, 9 (J. Helm, ed., 1965).
3. "It can . . . be affirmed that thanks to the nonintervention of the state in private affairs, wants and satisfactions would develop in their natural order. . . . Away, then, with the quacks and the planners! Away with their rings, their claims, their hooks, their pincers! Away with their artificial methods! . . . Let us cast out all artificial systems and give freedom a chance—freedom, which is an act of faith in God and in His handiwork." F. Bastiat, "The Law," in *Selected Essays on Political Economy* 51, 53, 96 (G. de Huszar, ed., 1964).
4. J. Jewkes, *Public and Private Enterprise* 71 (1965).
5. Hamilton, "The Ancient Maxim Caveat Emptor," 40 *Yale L.J.* (1931), 1133, 1135 n. 7.
6. Address by President Johnson, H.R. Doc. No. 220, 88th Cong., 2d Sess. 1 (1964).
7. *See* P. Samuelson, "The Economic Role of Private Activity," in 2 *Collected Scientific Papers* 1419, 1422 (J. Stiglitz, ed., 1966).
8. J. Henderson and R. Quandt, *Microeconomic Theory* 86 (1958).
9. Lipsey and Lancaster, "The General Theory of Second Best," 24 *Rev. Econ. Stud.* 11 (1956).
10. J. Henderson and R. Quandt, *Microeconomic Theory,* at 208. *See also* P. Samuelson, "Modern Economic Realities and Individualism," in 2 *Collected Scientific Papers* 1407, 1410 (J. Stiglitz, ed., 1966).

11. The curves are convex to the origin because acquisition of increasing quantities of a good will normally render it less valuable in terms of other goods possessed in unchanging amounts.

12. See Fels, "Hedonistic Calculus as Seen from a Distance," 91 *Weltwirtschaftliches Archiv* 101, 108 (1963). "Instead of assuming that we have built-in schedules upon which all existing or potential objects are listed in order of preference, let us think of the individual having 'wants.' These 'wants' are not specific, but specific objects and services fulfill them to varying degrees." G. Tullock, *Toward a Mathematics of Politics* 7 (1967).

13. 15 U.S.C. §§1451-61 (Supp. 1967).

14. Michigan Chamber of Commerce. *Federal Legislation Report 2* (1965). "What Salem did for its witches in 1692 may yet become a minute affair in comparison to the trial taking shape for the food industry." A. Mowbray, *The Thumb on the Scale: or the Supermarket Shell Game* (Philadelphia: Lippincott, 1967).

15. Hearings on Packaging and Labeling Legislation before the Senate Subcomm. on Antitrust and Monopoly, 88th Cong., 1st Sess., pt. 2, at 565 (1963).

16. Hearings on Fair Packaging and Labeling before the Senate Comm. on Commerce, 89th. Cong., 1st Sess. 639 (1965).

17. Hart, "Can Federal Legislation Affecting Consumers' Economic Interests be Enacted?" 64 *Mich L. Rev.* 1255, 1266 (1966). The bill which became the Food, Drug, and Cosmetic Act of 1938, 21 U.S.C. §§301-92 (1964), was subjected to vituperative attacks. A spokesman for the Proprietary Drug Association asserted: "The only manner in which the present bill could be properly amended is to strike out all after the enacting clause. . . . I have never in my life read a bill or heard of a bill so grotesque in terms, evil in its purposes and vicious in its possible consequences as this bill would be if enacted." Hearings on Food, Drugs, and Cosmetics before a Subcomm. of the Senate Comm. on Commerce, 73d Cong., 2d Sess. 172 (1933). The Drug, Chemical, and Allied Trade Section of the New York Board of Trade proclaimed: "The 'Tugwell' Food and Drug Bill is anti-NRA. It will seriously affect employment and morale in the industries indicated. It will put thousands of men and women out of work. It will close dozens of manufacturing plants and hundreds of stores. It will hurt thousands. It will help none." Id. at 471. See Hart, *supra* at 1264-65.

18. 15 U.S.C. §1451 (Supp. 1967).

19. "[T]he battle ended in victory for the food manufacturers." A. Mowbray, *The Thumb on the Scale*, at 5.

20. 15 U.S.C. §1459 (Supp. 1967).

21. 15 U.S.C. §1453 (1)-(2) (Supp. 1967).

22. Ibid., §1453 (3) (B).

23. Ibid., §1453 (3) (D).

24. "I remember telling [my mother's mother, Lady Stanley of Alderley] that I had grown 2 1/2 inches in the last seven months, and that at that rate I should grow 4 2/7 inches in a year. 'Don't you know,' she said, 'that you should never talk about any fractions except halves and quarters?—it is pedantic!' " B. Russell, *Autobiography* 33 (1967).

25. 15 U.S.C. §1454(c) (Supp. 1967).

26. Ibid., §1454(d).

27. Ibid., §1454(e).

28. 15 U.S.C. §45(a).

29. The problem is of course much more complex. See e.g., Richter, "Revealed Preference Theory," 34 *Econometrica* 635 (1966). Modern discussions of consumer behavior need not formulate a refutable concept of satisfaction:

"Neoclassical "utility" was a kind of economic ether: an element whose assumed existence was merely a convenient medium for the analytical transmission of the observable phenomena of consumer choice. Since other means have proved capable of yielding the same predictions of these phenomena, the assumption of its existence is simply not needed. To assert this is not to deny that operational theorems about consumer behavior can be obtained from the neoclassical theory, nor that they can be tested against reality. We may merely derive most of these theorems without this subjective ether." R. Kuenne, *The Theory of General Economic Equilibrium* 54 (1963).

Enjoyment as a goal is itself not unobjectionable:
"Suppose that it were discovered that a state of pleasure is always associated with a particular kind of space-time pattern of electromagnetic field, or other physical system, and that we were capable of producing such patterns in the laboratory. . . . Would we be justified in spending a large part of the world's resources in producing pleasure-fields of high intensity? . . . Should we breed billions of rats and supply them each with a pleasure-producing machine?" Good, "A Problem for the Hedonist," in *The Scientist Speculates: An Anthology of Partly-Baked Ideas* 199, 200 (I. Good, ed., 1962). As an alternative to altruistic hedonism that author suggests as a possible goal "that we should maximise the chance that the human race should be immortal." Ibid. at 200.

30. 112 Cong. Rec. 11,507 (daily ed. June 2, 1966). *See ibid.* at 12,169-72. Potato chips may be purchased in packages of 71 different weights, all under 3 1/2 pounds. Barber, "Government and the Consumer," 64 *Mich. L. Rev.* 1203, 1229 n. 76 (1966). "A cursory review of packaged salted nuts in a neighborhood supermarket turned up two brands of different varieties, packed in net weights of 2 1/8, 2 3/4, 3 3/8, 4, 4 1/4, 5 1/4, 5 3/8, 5 1/2, 6, 6 3/8, 7, 7 1/2, 8, and 11 ounces, and all of them priced to end in 'nines'—at 29, 39, 49, or 59 cents a package." C. Bell, *Consumer Choice in the American Economy* (New York: Random House, 1967), p. 335.

Since inspection is normally cursory, advertisers frequently attempt to distinguish their product from those of competitors by stressing as implicitly unique qualities which all brands share.

"Platformate is the ingredient which Shell says puts more mileage into the gasoline gallon. What Shell did not say is that Platformate, or its equivalent, is present in virtually every gasoline refined. When we asked about this, Shell spokesman said only: 'We have never claimed that Platformate was an exclusive ingredient.' " Statement in Program on Gasoline Produced by National Educational Television, Dec. 1966, *quoted in* Sloane, *Advertising: Platformate Fuels German Tiff*, N.Y. *Times*, July 12, 1967, at 53, col. 3.

31. Fuller, "Where Are We Headed in House-to-House Selling?," *Magazine of Bus.* 52 (1927), 703, 705, *quoted in* Note, "Consumer Legislation and the Poor," *Yale L. J.* 76 (1967) 45.

32. Statement by a housewife, *quoted in* Nelson, "Seven Principles in Image Formation," 26 *J. Marketing* 67, 69 (1962), reprinted in *Consumer Behavior and the Behavioral Sciences* 365, 366 (S. Britt, ed., 1966).

33. *Printers' Ink*, Oct. 18, 1963, at 20.

34. "If anyone is so foolish as to enter into an agreement such as this, I do not know that his case can be considered harsh." Statement by a British judge, *quoted in* M. Mayer, *The Lawyers* 283 (1967). Admittedly ignorance frequently appears unwarranted:

Reporter: Twiggy, do you know what happened at Hiroshima?
Twiggy: Where's that?
Reporter: In Japan.
Twiggy: No. I've never heard of it. What happened there?
Reporter: A hundred thousand people died on the spot, all at the same time.
Twiggy: Oh, God! When did you say it happened? Where? Hiroshima? But that's ghastly. A hundred thousand dead? It's frightful. Men are mad."

223

"Seventh Annual Dubious Achievement Awards for 1967," *Esquire* (Jan., 1968), 49, 53.

35. Pathetic examples of consumer inefficiency abound:

Eight years ago, Mrs. Phillips sent a radio to be repaired. The bill came to $8.90. Mrs. Phillips refused to pay—she thought it was going to cost only $1. She sent her 20-year-old son to get the radio back. But, John, an easy mark for a fast sales talk, came home with a new radio, for which he had agreed to pay in $1.25 weekly installments. The radio-shop owner, chubby A.M. Pearson, got Mrs. Phillips to sign the contract.

When Mrs. Phillips fell into arrears on her payments, Radioman Pearson went to court and got a judgment which ordered her to give back the radio and pay him $81.50 in court costs and collection fees.

Mrs. Phillips gave up the radio, but could not pay the rest. In August, 1943, Pearson had the city marshall sell off Mrs. Phillips' assets—her house and lot—to satisfy the court order. Pearson was the only bidder, and he offered $26.50. A year later, as required by law, the marshall delivered the deed to Pearson. During these twelve months, Mrs. Phillips could have kept her home by paying the $26.50 plus a $25 marshall's fee. She says nobody told her that.

Last week Pearson had the unrepaired radio, the "new" radio which he sold her son, a still unsatisfied claim for $55, and the house and lot. (He was willing to let Mrs. Phillips stay on—at $10 a week rent.)

Time, (March 28, 1949), 23.

See also "Luck of Clarence Jackson," *Time,* Sept. 1, 1967, 64.

36. Adam Smith, *An Inquiry into the Nature and Causes of the Wealth of Nations,* Modern Library, 1937, p. 625.

PART SEVEN

*

*Business
and
Consumerism*

INTRODUCTION

Business and Consumerism

USING A systems approach, David Cravens and Gerald Hills analyze the informational flows and interactions among consumer groups, government, and business in the "consumerism system." Although they do not reject the concept of consumer sovereignty they, like Gardner, seem to prefer the concept of freedom of choice which includes subjective as well as objective information sources. By understanding the consumerism system and its informational flows, business can adapt their organizational designs, management involvement, and markets that improve communication and information feedback for not only business but all groups. Business can no longer view consumerism with skepticism and condemnation but, rather, must consider it as a countervailing power in the system. For "not only must business respond, but business must communicate this response to the appropriate parties."

E. B. Weiss also focuses upon the need of business to establish meaningful communications with consumers. He feels that businessmen have failed to do so. "At the moment corporations are beginning to act out their responsibilities as involved members of society, they are simultaneously turning a deaf ear to the individual members of society." While business is aware of the consumerist, it is not "aware of the relationship between consumer legislation and corporate deafness where the individual is concerned." He blames this lack on the limited scope of business and its "traditional concepts of free enterprise."

William Kaye takes a rather pragmatic approach to the question of consumers and business; he looks at the repercussions on profits when consumers fail to respond. By viewing the consumer as a partner as well as a customer, business will find consumerism profitable. Kaye also views the consumer as a source of valuable information whom the firm should work with rather than just paying lip service to. As he says, "Consider, though, the increased business you will reap by giving the consumer his due. Unless your competitor does it first." Business' lack of response could be costly. As Shaffer indicates in his article, dissatisfied consumers are seeking redress through antitrust lawsuits.

Louis Stern wonders whether industry can regulate itself to recognize the consumer's interest, in response to consumer and government demands. His case is that, to be enforceable and meaningful, self-regulation must be industrywide. When standards of industry self-regulation include product standards, promotional practices, and enforcement criteria, they will probably run afoul of the antitrust legislation. He concludes that "consumers do not always fully comprehend the private effects of their wants, let alone their social effects. . . ." To ensure not only consumer protection but also the kind of growth in self-regulation of industry that recognizes its social responsibility, businesses (particularly marketing departments) and government must become responsive to the consumer's needs and interests.

26. MORE ANTITRUST SUITS ARE FILED BY STATES, FIRMS, PRIVATE PARTIES

Richard A. Shaffer

MEET RICHARD and Margo Kline, trustbusters.

They were just another couple until they tried to sell a $42,000 seaside home in Los Angeles not long ago and found it would cost them at least $2,520—a 6% real estate brokerage commission.

"The housing market was weak, so we had to use a broker," Mrs. Kline recalls. "But it made me mad that we couldn't negotiate the sales commission the same way you bargain for the price of a house." So the couple filed a $750 million antitrust class action—seeking damages for themselves and all other home buyers—against all real estate brokers in Los Angeles County for illegally fixing their fees. The defendants have denied any wrongdoing.

Whatever the outcome, the Klines and others like them are rapidly changing the image of trustbusters, once widely visualized as batteries of Justice Department attorneys in pursuit of ruthless tycoons monopolizing huge industries such as oil and steel. These days such legal platoons are outnumbered by non-Justice Department plaintiffs—corporations, city and state governments and even individuals like the Klines.

END OF THE LEGAL RAINBOW

Many are lured by a pot of gold at the end of the legal rainbow—treble damages. The federal government can file civil antitrust suits for damages only when it has been a customer of the defendants, and it can receive only actual damages. But other plaintiffs can receive damages equal to triple the amount lost due to stifled competition. In the last decade, the number of such private lawsuits filed annually has more than tripled, reaching 1,445 cases in fiscal 1971, while federal government complaints have held fairly steady at 50 to 60 a year.

(The private-suit figures don't include thousands of lawsuits filed in the early 1960s against electrical-equipment producers. These suits followed successful federal prosecution of the electrical equipment companies on criminal antitrust charges and thus aren't considered independent actions.)

Plaintiffs seem to be winning more and larger victories, although no one has exact figures because most cases are settled out of court. The impact on the American business scene has been considerable and far-reaching. Corporations have begun erecting myriad protective mechanisms. And although the increase in suits hasn't had much effect yet on the average consumer, it's clearly a boon for lawyers. When Trans World Airlines was awarded triple damages of $138 million against Hughes Tool Co. last year, for example, attorneys fees amounted to $7.5 million.

"This is the golden age of the antitrust bounty hunter," says Washington antitrust attorney John C. Scott. "Today, the private plaintiff packs a harder wallop than either the Justice Department or the Federal Trade Commission.

EXPENSIVE RAMIFICATIONS

Ramifications go far beyond the financial settlements. For instance, in 1969, Shakey's, a chain of pizza parlors, was sued for $49 million by four franchisees who alleged the company violated antitrust laws by requiring them to purchase spices from it. Although the lawsuit was finally settled out of court for only $200,000, the litigation virtually stopped the sale of Shakey's franchises, cost the company a full year of economic growth and "materially reduced earnings," according to Great Western United, Shakey's parent company.

In addition, "these days, private plaintiffs no longer wait meekly in the wings for the government to bring an action and show the way," says Philadelphia attorney Richard G. Schneider. "Now, without hesitation, treble-damage claimants start action even before the government case."

A Justice Department case currently pending against International Business Machines Corp., for instance, was preceded by an antitrust action brought by Control Data Corp., one of IBM's principal competitors. And a recent Justice Department attack on minimum commission rates at the Chicago Board of Trade followed a rising number of private antitrust challenges to historic and fundamental Wall Street practices, including minimum commissions and a ban on institutional membership in the New York Stock Exchange.

Current private antitrust action covers a variety of fields. Libraries are busily suing book publishers, investors are filing against mutual funds, mint growers are taking after makers of chewing gum and mouthwash, and farm workers are hauling lettuce growers into court.

EXTENDING LAW'S EFFECT

And the private plaintiff "seems destined to play an even more prominent role in the future," according to New York attorney Jerrold G. Van Cise. Many other experts agree.

Increasingly, for instance, private plaintiffs are using antitrust law as far more than a remedy for unreasonable restraint of trade in its traditional sense. In professional sports, players are challenging the merger of the American and National basketball associations and asking the courts to outlaw baseball's so-called "reserve system," which prevents a player on one team from bargaining with another for more money. In an Alabama case, the authority of cities and counties in 20 states to enforce model uniform building codes is under antitrust fire. A group of Chicago Negroes used antitrust laws to integrate a neighborhood.

One reason for the volume and scope of this activity is a string of recent federal district court and Supreme Court decisions that warmly embrace the treble-damage action, narrow many important defenses and greatly expand the benefits that private plaintiffs receive from prior government cases against the same defendants. Thanks to changes in the rules of federal court procedure, more cases qualify as class actions these days, allowing small plaintiffs to pool their resources and seek vast sums in damages. And Congress has made it possible to combine dozens of related cases across the country in a single courtroom for pretrial motions and depositions, saving time and money.

States and cities are taking the greatest advantage of this trend, recovering for overcharges on everything from bleachers and plumbing fixtures to rock salt, road oil, antibiotic drugs and children's library books. At least 33 states have antitrust cases pending—Maryland has 14—according to the National Association of Attorneys General. New York and other cities have established separate antitrust legal divisions and some states—among them Kansas, Oregon, Ohio and New Jersey—have created special funds for antitrust work.

There's likely to be even more activity by the states if two cases before the Supreme Court now give a state attorney general the power to sue for antitrust damages to a state's general economy and to represent all its residents as a sort of godfather.

One result of all this is "a mounting anxiety and trepidation among executives," says Richard Posner, an antitrust authority at the University of Chicago law school.

Many large industrial corporations say they are tightening company policy on possible antitrust violations and stiffening penalties for missteps by employees. "A few years ago, the treble-damage case was just another business risk. Plaintiffs rarely collected anything," says a lawyer for a major manufacturer. "But with companies getting sued for billions and having to settle for millions, those days are gone. We used to give very stern warnings around here. But now breaking our antitrust guidelines—even without breaking the law—is likely to get a man fired immediately."

CONCERN AT GE

At General Electric, a spokesman says, "Antitrust considerations are now included as part of most company management courses." Policies are written and "in-depth reviews are conducted at the product department level and at each higher level, with ultimate, final review conducted at the board of directors level.''

(In the early 1960s, General Electric was one of 29 companies fined a total of $1.8 billion for antitrust law violations—including price fixing, bid rigging, and allocating markets—on a number of electrical-equipment products. These federal criminal cases were followed by 2,233 private civil antitrust lawsuits that cost General Electric alone about $200 million to settle.)

Some corporations are sending antitrust experts to industry conferences to serve as alarm systems should dangerous situations develop, even accidentally. Others are warning people in sensitive positions to avoid rump sessions or even social activities at trade association meetings. "In that setting, with competitors all round, a chance remark about prices, for example, could get the company into plenty of trouble, even if it was perfectly innocent,'' says one corporate lawyer.

Irwin Seltzer, president of National Economic Research Associates, a New York consulting firm, says a number of his corporate clients are "so nervous about treble-damage actions that they are asking us to take a close look with a computer at their quantity discounts—or price differentials of any kind—to make sure the pricing policy is rational, not collusive, justified by cost and not even possibly the result of monopoly power.

Still, some critics contend that the private lawsuit hasn't always fulfilled its potential as a deterrent to antitrust violations. "It's possible for a company to break the rules, get caught, get sued, lose and still profit from its crime,'' says Beverly Moore, co-author of a lengthy critique of antitrust law enforcement published recently by Ralph Nader's Center for the Study of Responsive Law.

LONG AND EXPENSIVE

That's largely because antitrust cases are unusually expensive, and thus many plaintiffs tend to settle out of court. With the number of documents, depositions and appeals involved, some cases can last a dozen years if no out-of-court settlement is reached. In the recent price-fixing cases on antibiotic drugs, for example, three attorneys estimate they spent 30,000 to 40,000 man-hours and more than $1 million over a seven-year period gathering evidence and preparing statistical surveys for the 20 states and four cities they represented. In a case involving plumbing fixtures, 34 lawyers appeared in court to begin taking the deposition of one witness. It required 23 days and was scheduled to be followed by 28 other depositions on the plaintiff's side alone.

Even when the plaintiff prevails, courts sometimes copy the damages established by the jury, awarding nominal damages that represent only a fraction of what it cost to prosecute the case. In 1968, for instance, Courtesy Chevrolet Co., a Los Angeles auto dealership, spent $78,496 to win an antitrust award of $19,803 from the Tennessee Walking Horse Breeders Association. (The company was the legal owner of horses shown by its president; it accused the association of arbitrary and unreasonable suspension of membership and refusal to register the company's horses and colts.) Due to financial pressures dictating quick settlements, "far too many antitrust cases are settled for much less than actual damages," says Willard Meuller, a University of Wisconsin economics professor.

A possible solution has been suggested by Thomas Mechling, a Larchmont, N.Y., public affairs consultant and former politician.

A SUING CORPORATION

He's forming a corporation, complete with stockholders, to finance lawsuits in the public interest against other corporations and take its profits from the damage awards. His company, Public Equity Corp., would also conduct courtroom crusades against concerns that allegedly pollute the countryside and cheat the consumer, but Mr. Mechling says those that violate antitrust laws are also likely to be important targets. "That's where the money is," he says.

That's not to say the money is easy to come by. Some private antitrust cases are negated simply on the ground the case would be unmanageable because the plaintiff is suing, say, on behalf of everyone who eats eggs.

And in many more cases, specific damages are extremely difficult to prove to the satisfaction of the court. For example, in the recent plumbing fixtures price-fixing cases, individual consumers had to settle out of court for damages of only $1.8 million, while the middlemen in the fixture business were able to settle for $23 million, the Nader study points out. The court held that the homeowners, even though they may have paid more for houses containing plumbing fixtures, weren't directly injured.

"Such a holding," says Dallas antitrust attorney Jay Vogelson, "is like declaring in a three-car rear-end collision that the first car has no standing to sue because it was hit by the second car that was hit by the negligently driven third car."

27. CONSUMERISM: A PERSPECTIVE FOR BUSINESS

David W. Cravens and Gerald E. Hills

THE CONSUMER self-interest movement will assert itself as a powerful and pervasive influence on business decision making in the decade ahead. The implications of consumerism span virtually every type of firm that produces or distributes consumer goods and services; moreover, firms producing and marketing industrial goods may find that certain aspects of the movement will influence their marketing strategies. Although some of the origins and causes of this movement can be traced back many years, it is more realistic to view it as a product of the sixties.

In general, consumerism expresses itself in efforts to bring pressure on business firms as well as government to correct business conduct thought unethical. Its main thrust encompasses a multitude of group actions concerned with such issues as consumer protection laws, the availability of product and price information, fraudulent and deceptive business practices, and product safety.

Consumer coalitions have focused their actions on the business community, which suggests that major responsibility for the current state of consumer unrest should fall upon business. Although instances of insensitivity of business to consumers may be identified, analysis indicates that the problem is far more complex than the simple failure of firms to respond appropriately to consumer needs and wants. It is clear that all groups—whether consumers, the government, or others—must share with the business community the task of both identifying the issues and problems erupting in our society and carefully formulating and implementing actions for responding to them.

Business leaders must develop appropriate strategies for the decade ahead. Neither panic actions nor violent attack are realistic courses, and unconcern and nonresponse are, at best, naive in view of the growing momentum of the consumer movement. Analysis of the origins of consumerism and an assessment of its nature and scope will provide the businessman with the foundation for developing an objective perspective. Such a perspective must include an

Reprinted from *Business Horizons*, August 1970, pp. 21-28. Copyright 1970 by the Foundation for the School of Business, Indiana University.

examination of social goals, the parties involved, their interrelationships, and identification of the emerging issues.

CONSUMERISM—BACKGROUND AND SCOPE

ORIGINS

Why did the consumer movement come into sharp focus at the end of the sixties rather than before? During the decade of the forties, the nation was preoccupied with World War II. After the war, effects of accumulated demand, reinforced by the economic impact of the Korean conflict, extended well into the fifties. Consumers were primarily concerned with *obtaining* desired goods and services, and their inattention to issues that now underlie the consumerism movement is not surprising. As supplies of goods and services became plentiful in the late fifties, however, other factors began to influence consumer behavior in the market place.

The consumers of the sixties were better educated, more affluent, and had more leisure time than consumers at any other point in the history of the nation. Moreover, they were offered complex assortments of goods and services, one result of postwar technology. Mass communications, particularly television, made the buyer more aware of the proliferation of economic goods as well as, eventually, the existence of problems related to products and services. Although reports of fraud, deception, and disregard for safety were infrequent, the publicity they received invited consumer reactions.

High levels of demand combined with highly efficient production processes introduced and established the mass marketing concept. The attention of firms was focused on utilizing their increased productivity and moving goods and services in unprecedented volumes. Marketing institutions became less labor intensive, and retailing became more impersonal in nature. Consider, for example, the growth of the self-service supermarket and the commercial success of the discount house as alternatives to the neighborhood grocery store and the full-service department store. Similar trends developed in virtually all aspects of retailing.

During this period, an integrated, consumer-oriented marketing effort was advocated by certain leaders in the business and academic communities. In many firms, however, the concept of an integrated marketing effort was never fully implemented. While the consumer was acknowledged as the focal point of the marketing thrust, not enough research was aimed at understanding buyer behavior as a guide to marketing strategy. Much of the consumer dissatisfaction with products and services could have been avoided if marketers had obtained appropriate intelligence from the market place and truly implemented the marketing concept.

As a result of all these factors the sophisticated consumers of the sixties were confronted with a complex, impersonal, and on occasion, deceptive marketing system designed to serve their needs and wants in a highly efficient manner. Clearly contributing to the development of this system was the consumer's increasing demand for goods and services of better quality and at lower prices.

Therefore, the stage was set for an assessment of consumer problems. Rumblings of discontent over business insensitivity to consumers led to formal government recognition of consumers and their role in our economy:

> On March 15, 1962, President John F. Kennedy sent to the Congress a Special Message on Protecting the Consumer Interest. In this message, the first ever delivered by a President on this topic, President Kennedy took note of the important role played by the consumers in the American economy and the challenging problems that confront them.[1]

From this point forward the consumerism movement developed rapidly. Although laws and regulatory actions designed to protect the consumer emerged during the first half of this century, many new aspects of consumer protection were supported in the sixties at both the national and state levels by an increasing number of political representatives. Tight federal budget constraints spurred the search for inexpensive but popular bills. Motives aside, however, certain political figures have contributed significantly to the attention given the consumer's role in our society. Their efforts are perhaps best illustrated by Senator Warren D. Magnuson, chairman of the Senate Commerce Committee and long acknowledged consumer champion on Capitol Hill.

The continuing impact of individual crusades is best illustrated by the highly publicized efforts of Ralph Nader to spearhead improvement, through legislation and public pressure, in such areas as automobile safety standards, pipeline hazards, and radiation standards. In addition to individual crusaders in government and private life, consumers in their role as consumers have become active; coalition formation and demonstration for the purpose of seeking change were popular tactics in the sixties.

A pervasive force underlying the social issues that emerged in the sixties (including consumerism) was a general atmosphere of questioning on the part of many groups. Environment and the quality of life became important issues, and both government and business were criticized. Questioning of the system or the Establishment by intellectuals, popular journalists, and students spread to the man on the street. Many criticisms directed toward large corporations' alleged misuse of power, lack of social responsibility, and the adherence to questionable goals. Social critics like Vance Packard increased public interest and social awareness.

A final accelerating force underlying the development of consumerism in the late sixties was the pace of inflation. This was particularly effective in the development of store boycotts and demonstrations by housewives, who tend to blame retail food stores for high prices.

Thus, the consumerism movement was perhaps an inevitable response to the increasingly complex and impersonal society of our times. Analysis of the contributing factors and accelerating forces suggests that our socioeconomic system is seeking a new level of maturity in moving from a preoccupation with mass needs and wants toward a reassessment of social goals and the means necessary to achieve them.

NATURE AND SCOPE

The developing thrust of consumerism is difficult to describe in terms of specific objectives and issues, but identification and analysis of the myriad of activities under way provide a partial description of the nature and scope of the movement. In addition to the actions of elected officials, consumer boycotts, and consumer crusaders, other activities include:

> The widely publicized efforts of Mrs. Virginia Knauer, President Nixon's Special Assistant for Consumer Affairs.
>
> Product testing and information services such as the Consumers Union; efforts have been expanded beyond product evaluation to include attempts to influence both the business community and government on the behalf of the consumer.
>
> Student involvement with socioeconomic issues (including consumer affairs) reflected in the magazine *Business Today*, published by students for students.
>
> Increased interest on the part of the state and local governments in establishing consumer units and advisory groups, for example, New York City's Department of Consumer Affairs, headed by television personality Bess Myerson Grant.
>
> Popularity of consumer cooperatives and organized groups such as the Consumer Federation of America, which sponsored Consumer Assembly '70, attended by over 600 delegates representing 100 consumer organizations.
>
> The developing interest in consumer affairs by labor unions and related groups as reflected by the consumer education program recently implemented by the Central Labor Council in Washington.

Although the term "consumerism" is increasingly used, it has apparently never been operationally defined. The various actions and concerns associated with the movement provide a basis for defining consumerism—recognizing that it is presently loosely structured and is likely to change as the parties involved develop more explicit statements of their goals and positions. Our definition is that *consumerism is a social force within the environment designed to aid and protect the consumer by exerting legal, moral, and economic pressure on business*.

The fact that private individuals, politicians, and groups engaged in consumerism-related actions to generate public opinion and, ultimately, public pressure makes consumerism a social force. It is also an environmental force in that it is pervasive and surrounds business. Furthermore, the examples that have been cited illustrate attempts to either protect the consumer from business (for example, product safety and cases of fraudulent sales practices) or to aid him in processing information as a basis for allocating his income (for example, the "truth-in-"laws).

Finally, a critical part of the definition is recognition of the tactics employed. Private individuals and groups utilize existing laws as well as generate pressure at all levels of government for new legal constraints. They also apply coalition tactics to generate public opinion and pressure not only on government, but directly on business. This is primarily moral pressure, but it may be translated into economic pressure if customers respond to the negative publicity. The role of government in this process is as both initiator and responder. Individuals within government may generate support in and out of government for issues that may result in legislative action, and government will, of course, respond to issues that have the support of the public.

A SYSTEMS PERSPECTIVE

It is helpful to view the business firm as an element in a large complex system comprised of various organizations, groups, and institutions, all concerned with various aspects of consumer welfare. The accompanying figure shows the primary groups involved in the consumerism movement and the flows of information and influence that bind the system together. Analysis of the movement is complicated by the large number of consumer interest groups and their interrelationships with government agencies, the business community, and the individuals who comprise the markets for goods and services.

GOALS

Apparently, all of these groups hope to advance the welfare of the consumer. Business provides much of the income with which consumers can advance their material well-being; business also produces and distributes the multitude of goods and services which provide the consumer with alternatives for allocating his income. If we assume that the consumer allocates his income to maximize his satisfaction, can we further assume that this objective is achieved the same way by all people? Obviously not. Yet assumptions are implicitly made by many who undertake crusades that all consumers desire more and better information so they can make more "rational" decisions. Although less applicable, the same may be true of certain product safety crusades where the cost is ultimately borne by the consumer.

This is not to condone negligence but rather to suggest that an understanding of consumer decision processes and desires is basic to a true understanding and evaluation of the consumerism movement. The informational needs and desires of consumers vary from person to person. For some, the economic and/or psychological costs of additional information may be exorbitant when related to the "returns." For example, a person who values his time highly and finds the shopping process annoying will be unlikely to incur these "costs" to obtain information that would help him make a slightly better purchase deci-

The Consumerism System—Group and Information Flows

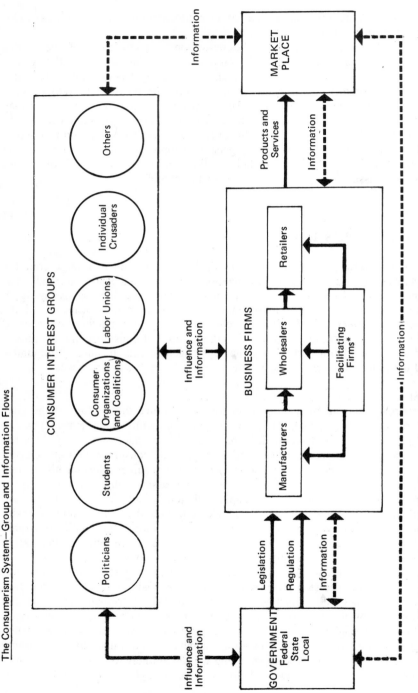

*Financial institutions, transportation firms, and advertising agencies, for example.

sion. A shopper who enjoys the process (no costs) may desire and seek such information.

These questions should be reflected in the actions of consumer interest groups. The obvious issues have gained overwhelming support, but as these are exhausted, it will be necessary to make explicit the costs involved in certain consumer actions. Moreover, curtailment of competition in certain industries could result, which would depress rather than improve the welfare of consumers in society.

The potential impact and possible danger to our society in continuing these fragmented approaches to improving consumer welfare must be assessed. Increased government legislation and control are likely by-products, leading to further constraints for the business decision maker and possibly hampering our pursuit of socioeconomic progress. The flow of new products and services could also be constrained; buyer-seller relationships are likely to become even more impersonal than they are today. In sum, it is clear that if the goal of consumerism is to improve the welfare of consumers, then many factors must be considered. Consumers may be willing to incur more costs for higher levels of satisfaction—but the balance is critical.

INTERRELATIONSHIPS

Flows of information and influence provide the basis for examining inter-relationships between major compontents of the system. The complexity of our socioeconomic system makes the economist's dream of perfect information flows unattainable. Yet development of effective macro-information systems is likely to become a central consideration in helping the consumer voice his opinions and preferences and achieve his goals. Actions taken on his behalf without this intelligence from the market place can easily lead to an imbalance in control and regulation with a possible delay in moving the consumer toward higher levels of satisfaction.

The primary information flows to consumers include promotional efforts of business (as well as varying responses to the consumerism movement); activities of government officials as reported by the news media; communication and interaction among consumers and their "representatives" (both interpersonal and by the media); and the availability of published consumer product ratings. These flows provide the basis for consumers' evaluation of products, as well as for their assessment of the consumerism movement, and indicate the crucial need for effective information flows to and from the consumer. "Noise" and distortion in the system (for example, misleading advertising or unfounded charges by consumer leaders) only serve to impair the ability of the customer to intelligently compare his alternatives.

Government also depends on flows of information and influence. Although government is responsive to voters, many elected representatives are involved in *creating* public opinion; therefore, a two-way flow of information exists. Testimony (state and federal), communications from consumer-interest leaders (as translated by the media), and public opinion polls serve as critical inputs to government leaders. Once again, however, biased and distorted information flowing to and away from government can only serve to impair decision making. Lobbying by business is a particularly influential information flow, which may balance countervailing charges from consumer groups. It also typically reflects the vested interests of certain industries. Rather direct information flows from government include the passage of additional laws and establishment (or strengthening) of regulatory agencies. Unfortunately, these typically reflect the failure of business.

All groups should recognize the desirability of reducing the noise generated by superficial and biased treatment of issues. This is not to suggest, however, that bias can be eliminated from the information flows or that people (consumers, politicians, and businessmen) believe all (or even most) distorted information. Nevertheless, a critical self-examination is in order for all groups, particularly with regard to their role in this system.

IMPLICATIONS FOR DECISION MAKING

Several specific guides to action for business firms have been developed by a task force of business, academic, professional, and association leaders.[2] In addition, more fundamental implications for business decision making are clear.

UNDERSTANDING CONSUMER BEHAVIOR

The rise of the consumerism movement raises serious questions as to the effectiveness of business firms in assessing customer attitudes and preferences; therefore, a better understanding of consumer behavior is a basic requirement for designing effective business response. Over the past ten years, progress has been made in developing both concepts and methods to guide the analysis of buyer behavior, and an increasing number of business firms are beginning to allocate substantial resources to various types of consumer research. Thus, business firms have available or can obtain the assistance needed to increase their understanding of buyer behavior. The question then becomes one of resource allocation.

Product research and development, advertising, and other parts of marketing programs have for many years commanded large amounts of corporate resources. Yet the use of corporate resources for consumer research has been relatively limited. Business managers should carefully assess their need for a better understanding of their consumers.

ORGANIZATIONAL DESIGN

The importance of assembling marketing resources into a coordinated and integrated program aimed at seeking favorable responses in the market place has been emphasized for the past two decades. Although a number of highly successful firms have organized and implemented these resources in terms of the marketing concept, many continue to manage their activities in a fragmented manner.

A proposal has been made that companies establish a position of "vice-president, consumerism'' in order to more closely coordinate strategies.[3] While creation of top-level staff positions for coping with emerging problems and issues fails to recognize many of the more basic considerations in designing effective organizations, the proposal does clearly indicate the need to indentify appropriate responsibility for assessing and responding to the consumer movement. The executive responsible for managing the firm's over-all marketing effort is a logical candidate for this assignment. Of course, the absence of an integrated company marketing effort suggests the need for a more viable marketing organizational design for interpreting issues and determining needed actions.

INVOLVEMENT IN CONSUMER AFFAIRS

Business must look beyond the direct relatonship between the firm and the consumer. Executives can participate through trade associations and industry organizations in various aspects of the consumer movement. Involvement in consumer affairs may require reassessment of the goals and policies of these organizations, including the financial support of needed projects and programs. Jointly funded consumer research studies would enable many small firms to obtain information for decision making. Moreover, measures of attitudes and preferences of consumers will provide these business groups with needed intelligence for more effectively assessing and participating in public policy issues associated with the consumer movement.

Trade organizations also should consider the possibility of social benefit of certain laws—particularly where they would facilitate the compliance of all competitors to certain desirable standards. In addition, more communication within the business community and the strengthening of self-enforcement organizations is in order.

The first response of business to the consumer movement was skepticism and condemnation; increasingly, however, business is acknpwledging this countervailing power. Not only must business respond, but business must communicate this response to the appropriate parties. For some time, in fact, this communication may offer a competitive advantage. Let consumers perceive desirable changes being made before demands are made.

Businessmen should also recognize the commercial opportunities presented by the increasing complexity of purchase decisions and the limited capacity of people to process information. At least one retailer now offers a computer for home installation complete with a standard software (programs) package. Although this alternative is open only to the most affluent, the demand for consumer information services will grow. One company now franchises computerized information centers that provide real estate, automobile, employment, and college search information services.

THE ROLE OF TOP MANAGEMENT

One of the major responsibilities of top management is to chart the course of the enterprise through the uncertain future. This requires an assessment of both the importance and nature of various environmental forces. Middle management, however, given certain achievement targets, is primarily concerned with efficiency of internal operations, yet many of their tasks are performed at the interface between the firm and its consumers.

This is particularly true of persons with responsibilities for various marketing tasks such as advertising, sales force management, pricing, and distribution. In these areas, top management must achieve highly effective communications and feedback with middle management, encouraging careful assessment of both efficiency and customer satisfaction goals. Appointment of a top executive for consumer affairs, suggested previously, recognizes this need.

Active participation by top management in the consumerism movement is needed. The business community can provide an important point of view in developing an appropriate perspective toward the consumer. Moreover, the continuing commentary on the proper balance between business and government demands that businessmen respond to the challenge for leadership.

The problems and issues concerning the consumer that have emerged in the past ten years must be viewed as a challenge rather than as an indication of failure. Careful assessment of corporate goals and required action can provide a strong foundation for moving the business community toward higher levels of social responsibility and achievement.

The need is clear for improved communication and information feedback among all parties involved in the consumerism movement. Debate has been based far too often on superficial response and emotion rather than on an objective assessment resulting from carefully formulated and executed research. Fragmented actions on the part of consumer interest groups without the benefit of information concerning their effects could result in overcontrol and a hampering of the important forces and influences that comprise our socioeconomic system. At the same time, however, all groups should be aware of the potential value of achieving certain consumerism goals. The trade-offs must be weighed carefully for each specific issue and action taken which will tend to benefit both business and consumers over the long run.

NOTES

1. "Consumer Advisor Council, First Report," Executive Office of the President (Washington: U.S. Government Printing Office, October 1963), p. 5.

2. Chamber of Commerce of the United States, "Business and the Consumer: a Program for the Seventies" (1970), pp. 12-13.

3. E. B. Weiss, "Marketers Fiddle While Consumers Burn," *Harvard Business Review* (July-August 1968), p. 51.

28. TAKE IN A NEW PARTNER— THE CONSUMER

William G. Kaye

IF YOU are in the fortunate position of being the sole possible producer of a product with an assured market, you need read no further. Your business probably could benefit from an enlightened consumer affairs program so long as your product is reasonably fit for its intended use and the price is fair enough to discourage a search for an acceptable substitute.

But few are in this position. Most businesses face competition, some of it brutal, and are always looking for means to improve their profits.

This is the very essence of our free enterprise economy and has led to newer, more versatile products, lower prices and the breathtaking technological advances of recent years.

Those advances have changed the entire complexion of the marketplace. It has become increasingly impersonal, complex and confusing and frustrating to consumers. Consumer irritation has led to action—action that can cost a business sales in the short run and profits in the long run if it ignores consumer affairs. Caveat emptor, the entrepreneurial byword of a simpler past, is no longer relevant.

For a businessman, rising to the challenge of awakening consumer interest makes good sense. The results are not measured solely in terms of an amorphous and intangible "feeling of goodwill." They are readily translated into immediate rewards—more sales and larger profits.

Repeat sales and brand loyalty are the hallmark of a satisfied consumer. He becomes an unpaid salesman, seeking to convince his friends and associates of the excellence of his choice.

Conversely, a dissatisfied consumer undergoes a striking transformation. He becomes an anti-customer. He is not satisfied with merely boycotting your product but will, in every way possible, try to influence potential customers against it. He is an active force seeking to reduce your sales and profits.

The more vocal and imaginative anti-customers can destroy much goodwill and consumer acceptance that has been cultivated by costly advertising and

Reprinted from *Nation's Business*, February 1970, pp. 54-57, copyright 1970, *Nation's Business*—the Chamber of Commerce of the United States. Reprinted by permission.

public relations campaigns. (Consider the customer who paints, or would like to paint, lemons all over your product and make sure they are visible to all!)

LIP SERVICE

Most businesses have some staff official who is assigned to handle consumer matters. Too often, however, he has no real authority and no input into the business's operations. He will be introduced at public relations and advertising functions and tucked away in a forgotten corner of the home office when substantive product design, engineering and policy decisions are made.

An enlightened consumer affairs program consists of more than preparing polite form letters to answer all written complaints. It means anticipating consumer complaints, taking consumer advice, giving the consumer a fair shake; in short, accepting the consumer as a knowledgeable partner rather than taking him for granted.

The basic questions to be asked by any businessman are: How important is the consumer to me? And how do I show it?

The answer to the first question is obvious. Without consumers there is no business! They are the one absolutely necessary ingredient to business success.

The answer to the second question seems obvious, too. But is it? Review your business. Is the consumer considered as a customer—a rational human being—or as a cipher whose significance is measured only in terms of end-of-the-month sales figures? Too many businesses will discover, if they objectively review their operations, that consumers are placated—given just enough consideration so that they will not turn to the competition, but ignored when it comes to the important product, engineering and even safety decisions.

In fact, the consumer is a knowledgeable critic who may know more about many facets of your product than you do. Listening to him, and considering his wishes, makes sense in profit terms.

For purposes of simplicity, let us consider two broad facets of the consumer spectrum, namely, the consumer as a customer and the consumer as a partner.

LONG LIVE THE CUSTOMER!

As a customer, the consumer should be king—but what shabby treatment we give our monarchs when it comes to handling their complaints! It is an elemental tenet of psychology that many people have to be upset before even one will complain. Realize, therefore, that for every complaint you receive, there are hundreds, perhaps thousands of anti-customers who will exercise their dissatisfaction by buying your rivals' products next time or ridiculing yours at every chance.

What is your mechanism for handling complaints?

244

How much does it cost? Is it effective? Responsive? Timely? How do you know? What is your follow-up system?

Have you considered alternative methods? Is top management aware of the types of complaints received? Have you personally read any complaint letter recently?

Complaints can cover the full range of your business's operation from your business name to the courtesy of your truck drivers to the price of your product. It would take many pages to consider all possible areas, but let's look at a few.

Your warranties:

Is the extent of coverage and noncoverage clearly stated and immediately understood?

Do the conditions set in the warranty tend to discourage exercising it?

Do your arrangements with dealers or repairmen tend to discourage them from properly honoring the warranty?

Do your warranties support your advertising?

After the advertising and the tinsel have been forgotten, after the purchase has been taken home, put to use and gone Pffft, the customer remembers only your warranty. He is already a potential anti-customer; and now if he can't get proper service without undue effort, if he gets a runaround from the retailer (who is in turn discouraged by the manufacturer's attitude), or if he has to argue the meaning of the warranty's language to get service, you will have created a full-blown anti-customer.

But is it necessary? Can your warranties and warranty service be improved? How much would it actually cost and what would the benefits be? What would an immediate replacement program cost? What would the benefits be?

Your repair and service network:

Are repair facilities conveniently located?

Are they adequate?

Do you have frequent style changes? Are they necessary? Are they explained to repairmen in advance?

Are spare parts and manuals available when new models are introduced?

Do you tell customers of areas of potential breakdowns and how to spot them?

Anti-customers thrive on poor, inconvenient or nonexistent service facilities. They are nourished by a management feeling that service is a necessary evil to be dealt with only when "important" matters have been taken care of. Their legions are filled with those who have to return a product to the factory for service, take a product used in the suburbs to a central city repair location, try to get to a service center with inconvenient midweek business hours, lose the use of the product because spare parts are unavailable, etc. Between purchases, the repair service is the only contact that the customer has with the manufacturer.

It should be used to bolster his faith in the company, not turn him into an anti-customer.

For that matter, consider also your model changes. Are they necessary or have they merely become part of the mystique of the industry? Model changes cause proliferation of parts for repairs and service, and confusion among customers, not to mention among repairmen. They should be made only when there is good reason for them.

Your packaging:

Does the product do justice to the picture on the package?

Does the size of the package promise more than the amount of the product included?

Does your product come in too many or too few sizes? Are they standardized?

Does your package permit easy price-quantity comparisons?

Is all useful material printed on the package and is all the material printed on the package useful?

Does your label include items of current or particular interest, such as calorie count per ounce or relative nutritive value?

Your package represents your business. Of course it should be attractive, but it also should be informative and representative. Customers want information at their fingertips, and it makes good business sense to give it to them.

Safety factors of your product:

What are its inherent safety hazards?

Has it been both laboratory-and-use-tested? Over a long enough period?

Does it meet the industry's standards?

Is the industry's standard-setting mechanism adequate?

Have standards been updated to reflect current technological changes?

Examples of safety failures fill the newspapers (and the *Congressional Record*) every day. Of course, there are standards in almost every industry, but if they were all they should be, there would be no need for a National Commission on Product Safety, for Congressional hearings, for Ralph Nader, etc. Nothing can kill sales quicker than safety failures. Nothing leads to greater losses and legal damages. Nothing causes more heartbreaks. Then why do we pay such little attention to safety factors? Why do we continue making products that prove to be unsafe under foreseeable uses? Why do we continue to talk safety but refuse to encourage adequate, voluntary standards and enforcement?

The measure of business failure in this area can be seen by reviewing the recent history of government regulation and the many current campaigns for regulation in hitherto untouched areas. Safety failures are bad business and should not be permitted by the businessman.

Safety is not limited to shock hazards, sharp edges and brittle parts. In many areas, particularly in the food industry, questions of wholesomeness and sanitation are equally important. Consumers have no choice but to rely on businesses in these matters. Is their reliance well-placed?

Are your food standards adequate in light of today's scientific and technological advances?

Has your production methodology kept pace?

Are your additives necessary? Are you aware of all their effects? Has your product lost its identity under a deluge of additives and preservatives?

Do you make clear to all handlers (and the ultimate consumer) what special care requirements are necessary to prevent adulteration?

Everyone might agree that the horrors catalogued in Upton Sinclair's "The Jungle" were part of an earlier age and have no place in today's economy. But the Congressional hearings that resulted in the recent Wholesome Meat and Wholesome Poultry Products Acts presented some evidence to the contrary. How about your business? Remember, while the permissible margin for error may vary from industry to industry, it is almost nonexistent in the food and drug industries. A low percentage of production error may be acceptable in appliances but could be fatal in foods and drugs.

UNPAID PARTNER CAN PAY OFF

We've considered the consumer as a customer; now let's think of him as a partner—an unpaid partner who may know more about the practical aspects of your product than you do and who will be pleased to have you adopt some of his ideas, anonymously.

Those businesses that have taken the time and spent the effort systematically to review consumer mail have discovered that many consumers are knowledgeable and make positive suggestions. Although consumers may not be graduate engineers, they can be quite creative and imaginative.

Remember, the consumer uses the product. He knows its strong and weak points. But what input does he have in your scheme of product engineering? It may not be too troublesome to devise a method for providing this input. The benefits that could flow from such a system are not limited to lower costs and higher sales.

Either as customer or partner, the consumer should not be kept in the dark. Consumer information and education are integral parts of a comprehensive consumer affairs program and deserve more attention from business than they now receive.

A consumer who believes information is being withheld, or who has no knowledge of the workings of the marketplace, cannot exercise intelligent choices in the market. The resulting frustration breeds suspicion and anger. The suspicion and anger add to the ranks of anti-customers who could have been satisfied customers.

Consumer information and education programs are complements to advertising and marketing programs aimed at creating a positive image for a business.

With proper information, a consumer will know what your product can and cannot do.

Consumer education has a broader function. It is aimed at providing an understanding of the workings of the marketplace and the consumer's position in it. Does your business have either program, and does it accomplish its objectives?

Are your information and education materials prepared with a particular group in mind (the young, the single, the poor, etc.)? Do they reach these groups?

Are your information and education materials consistent with your advertising and marketing materials?

Are your instructions use-tested? Are they concise and understandable?

Is your educational material overly partisan? Have you been objective?

Many more questions could be asked, tailored to your specific business and product or service line. There is no general panacea or ready-made program. Much depends on the individual business, its products, its problems, its consumers, its competition and other relevant matters.

But if your business currently overlooks the consumer, or simply pays lip service to his cause, you may be missing a vast market potential. Chances are that your market will not be greatly affected by continuing your current inactivity—provided your competitors do the same. Consider, though, the increased business you will reap by giving the consumer his due. Unless your competitor does it first.

29. CONSUMER PROTECTION VIA SELF-REGULATION

Louis L. Stern

CONSUMERISM, LIKE marketing, is becoming a broadened concept.[1] It encompasses "health services, public utilities, transportation, and automobile safety, and urging consumer representation, consumer education, and antipoverty programs."[2] The new consumerism includes concern for distortions and inequities in the economic environment and the declining quality of the physical environment.[3] Mary Gardiner Jones expressed it this way:

> What is new today about consumerism is the fact that consumers' concerns today are much more directly focused on the human values and environmental considerations involved in today's economic decisions than they are on the more strictly "economic" problems of obtaining the highest quality goods at the lowest possible price.[4]

Accordingly, it has been suggested that during the 1970s the Federal Trade Commission (FTC) will "by an imaginative, vigorous interpretation of this broad language (Section 5 of the FTC Act) take cognizance of every type of business practice which offends the current social mores."[5]

It is generally agreed that consumerism is here to stay. This is the implicit assumption or explicit conclusion of the business community. In the words of the Chamber of Commerce of the United States,

> But whatever the causes, it is of paramount importance to recognize that the consumer movement is well established and is likely to gain strength in coming years.[6]

Therefore, attention is now turning toward various forms of response to the consumer movement. Indicative of this direction is the creation of the Consumer Research Institute by the business community to objectively study consumer problems and evaluate alternative responses. Listed below are examples

Reprinted from *Journal of Marketing*, Vol. 35 (July, 1971), pp. 46-58, published by The American Marketing Association.

of questions that are being raised concerning organization, techniques, and policies:

1. Is it socially wiser to accept the present state of consumer dissatisfaction than to pay the cost of reducing consumer dissatisfaction?
2. Can industry reform itself without government pressure?
3. Which is likely to be most effective and economical, Better Business Bureaus, trade association complaint bureaus, or corporate divisions of consumer affairs?
4. Should consumers be encouraged toward self-protection through class action suits?
5. Can public policies be market tested?
6. What is the best positioning of consumer representation?
7. Can consumer education suffice to eliminate market abuses?

The following basic issue underlies these questions: What should be the role of private versus government effort to protect consumers? Buskirk and Rothe stated that, "The relative role the government will play, and that which industry should play, is a critical aspect in the resolution of the consumerism issue."[7]

Because consumer issues will be attended to in one way or another, government versus private regulation is a vital subject. This article addresses itself to that subject. It examines the difficulties of private and public regulation and suggests means of improving both. It interprets consumer interests in the broad manner indicated above.

GOVERNMENT REGULATION

There are several objections to government regulation. One objection is that it may lead to further and repressive regulation. Regulations seldom fade away; instead they proliferate. As each refinement or clarification comes into force, business ingenuity probes to discover the minimum requirements necessary for compliance. Then new regulations are formed to close the loopholes which have been found. The process continues with additional and ever more confining rules until innovation is choked and business operating costs are increased. In short, government regulation tends to become progressively intrusive and destructive of incentive.

A second objection to government regulation concerns lack of uniformity of application. Differences from case to case in interpretation of regulations may appear inexplicable and inequitable. Perhaps worst of all, they are unpredictable. On the other hand, uniform application of regulations without consideration of individual circumstances also raises objections, especially from small firms.

Regulations are sometimes unevenly enforced. Because the FTC and the Department of Justice have limited resources, they cannot hope to prosecute all violators of the law. The FTC, which is the principal government agency concerned with consumer protection, receives a small budget ($19.5 million in 1970)[8] in comparison to the job it faces. Moreover, the size of its staff is decreasing relative to the size of the U.S. economy. Merely to keep pace with the growth in disposable personal income since 1962, the FTC would have needed a staff of 2,000 people by 1970 compared to the 1,270 people it actually had.[9] In addition, the FTC has assumed new responsibilities under the Fair Packaging and Labeling Act (1966) and the Consumer Credit Protection Act (1968). The relatively few FTC investigators have time to observe only a small proportion of the total number of firms, products, markets and transactions.

Uneven enforcement is certain to be regarded as unfair if the prosecuted actions were committed in response to competitive necessity. Compound a sense of unfairness with suspicion that government agencies are more interested in developing the dark areas of the law than in enforcing the lighted areas equally, and objection to government regulation is to be expected.

A basic objection to government regulation is that the FTC functions as both prosecutor and judge. Since the commissioners direct the thrust of agency effort and authorize the issuance of complaints, it is unrealistic to expect them to rule impartially when the cases are argued.

There are other criticisms that are being raised. Regulatory actions often take many years to conclude. Sometimes regulatory action is not initiated until the objectionable behavior has been terminated. In addition, the FTC is charged with lassitude, cronyism, and incompetence; with responding only to business and Congressional pressure groups; failure to aggressively detect consumer abuses; and failure to allocate its energies toward really important issues.[10]

Government regulation is a mixed blessing. It serves to represent public ideals. It serves to clarify, define, and make explicit acceptable and unacceptable norms of conduct. It is simultaneously a last resort and a precipitator of action. In addition, it is insensitive, inept, and burdensome. It is fashioned by compromise and twisted by interpretation.

SELF-REGULATION

Self-regulation is an obvious alternative. It is repeatedly called for by businessmen and government authorities.[11] However, what does experience show? Until the passage of the Fair Labeling and Packaging Act (1966), the food industry did virtually nothing to eliminate package-size proliferation or higher-priced large "economy" sizes. The gasoline industry promoted a wide variety of contests or sweepstakes in some of which the winners were controlled geographically or chronologically.[12] The detergent industry had to be forced into developing bio-degradable detergents, and then pressured into removing phosphates and enzymes from their products. The automobile industry produces useless bumpers of variable heights. Sixty percent of the commercial AM and FM radio stations and 35% of the commercial television stations do not support the code of the National Association of Broadcasters.[13]

The record is *not* as one-sided as the listing above. If space permitted, an industry-by-industry analysis might be attempted, but value judgments would still be involved. In any event, it is difficult to discover the whole truth of a company or industry situation. Pollution is a case in point. The public relations field has jumped on the antipollution "bandwagon" to such an extent that a substantial credibility gap exists.[14]

Nevertheless, it can be said that many individual companies and various associations have undertaken pro-consumer activities. These activities range from the proposal of codes "that acknowledge business responsibility to protect the health and safety of consumers, improve quality standards, simplify warranties, improve repair and servicing quality, self-police fraud and deception, improve information provided consumers, make sound value comparisons easier, and provide effective channels for consumer complaints,"[15] to concrete actions to implement such goals.

But voluntary action is seldom adequate. No matter how willingly some companies may observe voluntary guidelines, there are other companies that must be coerced to observe them. The other companies may not pull an industry to their level of ethics, but neither are they so few, or so insignificant, that they can be ignored. In fact, "It isn't just the fringe operators who are guilty, . . . it is too often the nation's most reputable companies."[16]

ENFORCEABILITY

To be meaningful, self-regulation must be enforceable and industry wide. It must punish or prevent violations of regulatory norms. To do so requires collective action in the form of a boycott against the offender (if he refuses to reform). But boycotts in restraint of trade are illegal under the Sherman Act regardless of how meritorious or beneficial the motives or results may be. In fact, the courts are so dogmatic on this point that the Supreme Court of the United States proclaimed:

> Even if copying were an acknowledged tort under the law of every state, that situation would not justify petitioners in combining together to regulate and restrain interstate commerce (in order to prevent copying).[17]

One cannot help but feel that the Sherman Act needs to be amended by Congress or judicial interpretation to permit meritorious restraints of trade. If amended by Congress, the determination of which restraints are meritorious should be left to the FTC and the courts. The procedure would be to require prior approval and periodic reapproval of proposed restraints by the FTC. If, after open hearings, the FTC cannot distinguish between meritorious (from the public's point of view) restraints of trade and self-serving restraints of trade, then surely the restraints are not of much consequence to begin with. If a half-open door policy toward restraints of trade complicates the enforcement task and increases court loads, so be it. That is the price for freeing private energies on behalf of consumer interests. Self-regulation cannot be fully effective with enforcement power.

PRODUCT STANDARDS

One of the most common areas of self-regulation is product standards. Because of recognition of their potential for public gain, several thousand voluntary product standards are now in existence. Product standards may concern safety or healthfulness, size and style variations (thereby reducing production and distribution costs and consumer confusion), or quality or performance. Product standards are least desirable in the latter role since consumer needs and preferences may vary the most in this respect and can alternatively be served by mandatory informative labeling.[18]

The principal danger of product standards is that they may slow product improvement and innovation, or deny reasonable product alternatives to consumers. (In addition, producers may tend to manufacture the minimum quality possible consistent with meeting the standard.) These effects, in turn, may restrict market entry and lessen competition, thus protecting the dominant producers and the status quo rather than consumers' interests. On the other hand, even though product standards are formed solely in the consumers' interests, even safety, they cannot be enforced by collective action. For example, an association of gas pipeline companies, gas distributors, and gas appliance manufacturers adopted a seal of approval for appliances. Safety of operation was a primary criterion in granting the seal of approval. Although the case was clouded by the use of additional test criteria and allegedly discriminatory testing procedures, the court's decision centered upon the refusal of the association to supply gas for use in nonapproved appliances. The boycott was declared illegal (if proved to exist) regardless of consumer peril.[19]

The law bends over backward, so to speak, to protect competition regardless of the immediate consequence to consumers. Accordingly, voluntary standards are only as effective as the willingness of industry members to accept them and the extent to which consumers rely upon them. Naturally, the least ethical producer is least likely to be bound by a voluntary standard, and the industry is more or less helpless to do anything about it. The best the industry can do in concert is to attempt to persuade buyers to accept only products conforming to the standard and to persuade the government to make the standard mandatory. Members of the industry may unilaterally attempt to force the deviant firm into line, but they run the risk of being accused of implicit agreement in doing so.

Is there a way out of the dilemma of trying to protect consumers in the short run while preserving the long-run benefits of freedom? In the writer's opinion, the answer is to: (1) provide maximum consumer involvement in the writing of product standards; (2) provide for automatic review of standards at frequent intervals; (3) permit the sale of products not conforming to the standards provided that the nonconforming products are labeled with the relevant standards and the manner and extent to which they do not conform to those standards; and (4) *permit collective action among firms to boycott any firm whose products conform to neither the industry standards nor the labeling requirement.*

Health or safety considerations might require that some standards be conformed to without exception. In most cases, however, the proposed privilege of deviating from product standards would guarantee the right to innovate. It would also enable firms to better serve specialized market segments for which the standards might be inappropriate. The fact that deviations from product standards would have to be prominently labeled would place some products at a competitive disadvantage for the sake of improved market information. However, the extent of the disadvantage would be limited by the merits of the deviation from the standard and the extent to which consumers felt a need for relying upon the standard.

PROMOTIONAL PRACTICES

Promotional practices are of equal or greater importance to consumer welfare than product standards. Hence, as with product standards, self-regulation is both prevalent and contentious, and the issue again becomes the purpose and effectiveness of such self-regulation.

Promotional practices raise questions of (1) amount (waste, competitive barrier, omnipresence); (2) cultural effects (media control, social values, unbalancing of competition between private goods and social goods); (3) function (to inform or only persuade); and (4) taste. Even the basic principle that the consumer should not be deceived, though readily agreed upon, is disputed in interpretation. For example, how many readers would agree with various members of the FTC that: (1) it is unfair or deceptive to withhold useful information (such as gasoline octane ratings, automobile mileage per gallon, or product test life); (2) irrelevant or emotional appeals are misleading and deceptive; and (3) promotional claims are deceptive unless proven? Three successive presidents of the United States have proclaimed the right of consumers to be informed yet manufacturers do not acknowledge and fulfill a corresponding obligation to provide information—certainly not negative information.[20]

NONPERCEPTION

Aside from being constrained by the Sherman Act, the difficulty of self-regulation of promotional practices is two-fold: On the one hand is nonperception, and on the other is nonresponsibility. The first problem is simply a failure to perceive any injustice in questionable practices. For example, a soap manufacturer may distort a competitor's test marketing program. He may arrange with a wholesaler to buy up a sufficient amount of the test product to inflate the sales measurement. Simultaneously, he may adopt the test product advertising theme and begin to implement it nationwide. As a result, the competitor may be falsely encouraged to "go national" with the new product. Since most of the introductory promotional expenditures will be incurred at the start of the campaign, a large loss will be sustained before it becomes apparent that the product is failing. If the product does succeed, its success will be minimized and undermined by the preemption of the copy theme. The perception problem is that both companies may regard these occurrences as simple competitive gamesmanship.

Another example of misperception (by buyer and seller) is the claim of price reductions or performance advantage "up to" a stated amount. Advertisers are well aware of the legal requirement to be objectively honest in advertising. Furthermore, it is illegal to make statements which by themselves are true, but which when taken as a whole, are likely to deceive.[21] Yet literally true "up-to" statements which probably convey the impression that the price-cut or performance-gain to be expected by the buyer is of the "up to" amount are widespread. Whether such statements are deceptive could easily be resolved through appropriate research. It illustrates the potential value of a government-funded institute to study consumer behavior and the impact of advertising and marketing upon society.[22]

The point is that there are many advertisements and marketing practices in general that are objectionable to many people, but which raise no compunctions among some sellers. Such abuses as the advertisement in poor taste, the unsolicited merchandise, the engineered contest, the shrinkage of package weight, the unsubstantiated claim, and the negative-option sales plan are all defended by sellers who perceive no wrong in them. Their insensitivity may be profit-motivated or philosophical, but in either case it is not conducive to effective self-regulation.

Levitt suggests that a primary reason for businessmen's insensitivity to social responsibility, even though it may be in their long-run interest, is their total commitment to achieving day-to-day profit maximization.[23] The blindness caused by "keeping one's nose to the grindstone" is exacerbated by a steady diet of "chauvinistic patter" from business journals written according to what editors think businessmen want to hear. Other observers have suggested that businessmen's nonperception of the social environment is due to the narrow direction of consumer research toward improving product, package, and promotional appeals; in short, their research has been too sales-oriented.[24]

NONRESPONSIBILITY

The second aspect of the problem of promotional practices is nonresponsibility; that is, sellers recognize the wrong but accept no responsibility for it. A classic case is beer and soft drinks. With society becoming ever more concerned about waste disposal, these two industries are selling more of their product in nonreturnable glass containers. Thirty-six percent of all glass shipments in 1969[25] were for nonreturnable bottles of beer and soft drinks compared with 7.5% of such shipments in 1959.[26] The beverage industries including liquor and wine, but excluding milk, are responsible for 50% of all glass container waste.

When companies are confronted with this abuse of social interest (which is aggravated by consumption of beverages away from home), they reply that they are only serving the public's preference for nonreturnable containers. To their way of thinking, it is the public's responsibility, not theirs. (The cigarette industry uses the same rationale, although additional factors are involved.) Indeed, the responsibility is shared by consumers as individuals and through their governments; however, the first responsibility belongs to the bottlers. Just as producers have a concerted interest relative to consumers in lobbying activities, so, too, producers have concerted responsibilities.

Businessmen who reject the concept of social responsibility may do so in order to maximize profits, or because they feel a lack of mandate from society to take specific actions. That the profit consideration may be declining in importance is indicated by the statement of B. R. Dorsey, president of Gulf Oil Corporation, who declared that " 'maximum financial gain, the historical number one objective' of American business, must move 'into second place whenever it conflicts with the well-being of society.' "[27] The second reason, namely, the lack of public mandate may also be overcome; that is, a concern for democratic process may be upheld via attitude research. However, a deeper question remains: Should the attitudes of an ill-informed and untrained public be controlling?

ALTERNATIVES

Although the line between nonperception of wrong and nonacceptance of responsibility may be difficult to distinguish, the absence of effective self-regulation is clear. Why? One reason is that self-regulation is stymied by the Sherman Act barrier against collective use of pressures upon offenders. Only the removal of the legal barrier to enforceable self-regulation will provide the necessary test of whether enforceable self-regulation can obviate the need for more government regulation.

Resistance to the idea of enforceable self-regulation is based upon fear that self-regulation may be perverted to industry benefit at the expense of consumers or prospective competitors. This fear can be allayed by requiring prior FTC approval of proposed regulations and periodic reapproval. Such fear can be further allayed by including a counter balance to the possibility of business or political influence over the FTC's judgment. This counter balance would include:

1. Separation of the prosecuting and adjudicating functions of the FTC, and placing the latter function under a newly established system of trade courts:[28] and
2. Providing competitors, consumer organizations, and other government agencies the right to seek injunctions from the above trade courts

against any form or application of self-regulation activity which is deemed unfair or socially harmful.

A significantly lesser form of self-regulation would be for trade associations to attempt to prosecute offenses under existing law. This approach might include the initiation of trade practice conferences in order to spotlight questionable activities within the industry and generate trade practice rules or guides. There are three major weaknesses to this approach. First, although the FTC Act broadly prohibits unfair methods of competition and unfair or deceptive acts in commerce, it does not authorize private suits, but applies only to false descriptions or representations in commerce. Second, while Congress would authorize private suits under the FTC Act, neither this Act nor the Lanham Act reaches the potential of enforceable self-regulation for implementing social responsibilities. For example, as currently interpreted, neither law interdicts the sale of hand guns, "high-powered" cars, or telephone solicitation. Third, industries tend to have a "live and let live" attitude. Companies with high ethical standards seldom are inclined to report, much less take action against, the dishonest or offensive members of an industry.

CONCLUSION

The more technology advances, the more deeply will marketing become involved in social issues. The argument that business has no responsibility but to satisfy consumer wants is an open invitation to government regulation. In the short run, consumers do not always fully comprehend the private effects of their wants (witness disbelief of smoking hazards) let alone the social effects of DDT, nonreturnable containers, or private urban transportation. Nevertheless, reality cannot be denied, and wisdom eventually prevails. When business does not accept social responsibility in fact as well as in survey response,[29] public regulation is eventually forced upon it.

Self-regulation cannot repeal human nature, and a free enterprise system cannot survive without a vigorous profit incentive. On the other hand, neither can a free enterprise system remain healthy if "the responsiveness of a firm to the consumer is directly proportionate to the distance on the organization chart from the consumer to the chairman of the board."[30] What is needed is a greater sensitivity to changing public demands upon business.

In order to harness the potential of self-regulatory effort, the Congress, the FTC, and Department of Justice must make enforcement possible when it is clearly in the public interest. However, the opportunity for enforceable self-regulation by no means assures unqualified success for this approach. A continuing threat of increased government regulation will always be necessary to make self-regulation work. Government regulation, in turn, needs consumer advocates to make it function effectively. Hence, consumer protection is a sort of tripod affair. If business is to keep the tripod in balance, self-regulation will have to grow accordingly.

257

The more educated society becomes, the more interdependent it becomes, and the more discretionary the use of its resources, the more marketing will become enmeshed in social issues. Marketing personnel are at the interface between company and society. In this position they have a responsibility not merely for designing a competitive marketing strategy, but for sensitizing business to the social, as well as the product, demands of society.

NOTES

1. Philip Kotler and Sidney J. Levy, "Broadening the Concept of Marketing," *Journal of Marketing*, 33 (January 1969), pp. 10-15.

2. National Goals Research Staff, *Toward Balanced Growth: Quantity with Quality* (Washington, D.C.: United States Government Printing Office, 1970), p. 133.

3. George S. Day and David Aaker, "A Guide to Consumerism," *Journal of Marketing*, 34 (July 1970), pp. 12-19.

4. Address by Mary Gardiner Jones, Federal Trade Commissioner, before the Manufacturing Chemists Association, New York, November 25, 1969.

5. Address by Joseph Martin, Jr., General Counsel, Federal Trade Commission, at a conference sponsored by California Business Seminars, Inc., Los Angeles, California, September 23, 1970.

6. Chamber of Commerce of the United States, Council on Trends and Perspective, *Business and the Consumer—A Program for the Seventies* (Washington, D.C.: Chamber of Commerce of the United States, 1970), p. 10.

7. Richard H. Buskirk and James T. Rothe, "Consumerism—An Interpretation," *Journal of Marketing*, 34 (October 1970), p. 63.

8. From an address by Mary Gardiner Jones, Federal Trade Commissioner, before the Sixth Biennial World Conference of the International Organization of Consumer Unions, Baden/Vienna, Austria, June 29, 1970.

9. Ibid.

10. Edward F. Cox, Robert C. Fellmeth, and John E. Schulz, *'The Nader Report' on the Federal Trade Commission* (New York: Richard W. Baron, 1969). *See also* "The Regulators Can't Go On This Way," *Business Week*, no. 2113 (February 28, 1970), pp. 60-73; and Louis M. Kohlmeier, Jr., *The Regulators; Watchdog Agencies and the Public Interest* (New York: Harper and Row, 1969).

11. Significant articles in this area include Robert B. Hummer, "Antitrust Problems of Industry Codes of Advertising, Standardization, and Seals of Approval," *Antitrust Bulletin*, 13 (1968), pp. 607-618; H. Richard Wachtel, "Product Standards and Certification Programs," *Antitrust Bulletin*, 13 (1968), pp. 1-38; Harvey J. Levin, "The Limits of Self-regulation," *Columbia Law Review*, 67 (March 1967), pp. 603-642; and Jerrold G. Van Cise, "Regulation—By Business or Government?" *Harvard Business Review*, 44 (March-April 1966), pp. 53-63.

12. *See Investigations of "Preselected Winners" Sweepstakes Promotions*, hearings before the Select Committee on Small Business, House of Representatives, 91st Congress, 1st Session, 1970.

13. Maurine Christopher, "Work Added by New Guidelines Strains NAB Codes' Resources," *Advertising Age*, March 15, 1971, p. 93.

14. *See* E. B. Weiss, "Management: Don't Kid the Public With Those Noble Anti-Pollution Ads," *Advertising Age*, August 3, 1970, p. 35; and Stanley E. Cohen, "Anti-Pollution Claims May Prove Pandora Trouble Box for Advertisers," *Advertising Age*, September 14, 1970, p. 110.

15. National Goals Research Staff, *Toward Balanced Growth*, p. 143.
16. "The Editorial Viewpoint," *Advertising Age*, March 30, 1970, p. 14.
17. Fashion Guild v. FTC, 312 US 457, 458 (1941).
18. Louis L. Stern, "Consumer Protection Via Increased Information," *Journal of Marketing*, 31 (April 1967), pp. 48-52.
19. Radiant Burners, Inc. v. People Gas Light and Coke Co., 364 U.S. 656 (1961).
20. For alternative concepts of information *see* National Goals Research Staff, *Toward Balanced Growth*, pp. 139-140.
21. Bennett v. F.T.C., 200 F2d 362; P. Lorillard Co. v. F.T.C., 186 F2d 52.
22. *See* Dorothy Cohen, "The Federal Trade Commission and the Regulation of Advertising in the Consumer Interest," *Journal of Marketing*, 33 (January 1969), pp. 40-44; and "Nobody Understands Marketing Economy, Sen. Moss Says: Proposes a New U.S. Institute," *Advertising Age*, February 15, 1971, p. 14.
23. Theodore Levitt, "Why Business Always Loses," *Harvard Business Review*, 46 (March-April 1968), pp. 81-89.
24. For example, *see* Peter F. Drucker, "The Shame of Marketing," *Marketing/Communications*, 297 (August 19, 1969), pp. 60-64.
25. *Modern Packaging Encyclopedia* (New York: McGraw-Hill, 1970), p. 19.
26. *Modern Packaging Encyclopedia* (New York: McGraw-Hill, 1961), p. 41.
27. Reported by Alfred L. Malabre, Jr., "The Outlook," *Wall Street Journal*, March 22, 1971, p. 1.
28. *See* "FTC's Elman in Parting Shot, Advocates 'Radical Structural Reform of Agencies,' " *Wall Street Journal*, August 12, 1970, p. 4.
29. *See* Arthur M. Lewis, "The View from the Pinnacle: What Business Thinks," *Fortune*, 80 (September 1969), pp. 92-95, and 207-208.
30. Address by Virginia Knauer, Special Assistant to the President for Consumer Affairs, before the Federal Bar Association, Washington, D.C., September 1970.

30. THE CORPORATE DEAF EAR

E. B. Weiss

COMMUNICATION CHANNELS between large corporations producing consumer lines, as well as large retailers, and the individual consumer (where, in fact, channels exist at all) tend to be one-way input systems—woefully clogged. Moreover, this one-way communication system between the individual member of society and the corporative society (to call it a "system" is abominable semantics!) is a half-way communication channel within the corporation itself; it reaches only half-way up the various executive levels. Now computer technology threatens to complete the isolation of corporations from the individual consumer, especially at middle executive levels. The first signs are clearly evident in giant retail corporations, despite the fact that the retailer is closest to the consumer. The continued stultification of the public relations function (the usual end of the tenuous communication link between corporation and consumer) adds the final destructive touch to the already marginal corporative hearing capabilities.

It is ironic that, in this age of amazing technological communication innovation, corporate deafness with respect to the individual customer is in the process of becoming total. (Have you ever tried to complain about a "lemon" to one of Detroit's Big Three, or sweated through an adjustment with a major department store?) It is equally ironic that, in this age of awakened corporate social responsibility, our corporations tend to listen less to individual society members than ever before; yet listening to the individual in our society and reacting promptly, intelligently, and even sympathetically constitute a major corporate social responsibility, particularly in a sophisticated society.

Surely it is as obvious as it is inevitable that individuals, when frustrated, will in due time form into groups (as labor did decades ago) and even stage demonstrations (as the food industry discovered two years ago). And surely it is equally obvious that the frustrated individual will turn to government, where hearing capabilities are extraordinarily acute. I do not refer to communications from the public involving fraud; our large corporations have pretty well stamped out the fraudulent. I refer to those communications from the public representing the "gray area"—situations embracing product, service, and so on that do not violate the law, but which properly raise the hackles of more

Reprinted from *Business Horizons*, December 1968 pp. 5-15. Copyright 1968 by the Foundation for the School of Business, Indiana University.

knowledgeable consumers (whose numbers are clearly multiplying). Consumer legislation does not concern itself with fraud; its objective is to whiten these gray areas of business practice, which an enlightened public finds increasingly irritating.

Top corporate management is now deeply concerned about the corporation as a citizen. Yet my careful reading of thirty-one recent speeches by top management executives on various aspects of the new dimensions of corporate social responsibility fails to unearth a single word on the imperative corporate responsibility for improving communication with the individual consumer. I am not concerned at the moment with corporate *mass* communication with the public on matters of social significance, although both advertising and public relations tend to be painfully amateurish in this area. (Most "image" campaigns are merely self-righteous egotistical exhibitions.) My concern is with the individual who, for any of a variety of reasons (civic, social, critical, or suggestive), decides to communicate with a large corporation by letter, phone, or personal visit. Here, I maintain, corporate management has laid up a solid wall of indifference and even calculated obstruction. All this in an age in which our society is just beginning to reemphasize the supreme importance of the individual.

This was bad enough when the retailer listened willingly to the shopper, but now our giant retailers turn an equally deaf ear to the customer as our giant manufacturers do. Business does listen to the lunatic fringe of our society; a few crank letters, for example, have led to the cancellation of more than one television sponsorship. But business does not listen to the intelligent individual members of our society!

The business community now accepts, with some resignation and less cooperation, the inevitability of consumer legislation, as well as the probability that more is on the way for years to come. But it seems not even dimly aware of the relationship between consumer legislation and corporate deafness where the individual is concerned. As a result, government is clearly in the process of becoming the confidant of the shopping public, which is unquestionably developing the habit of addressing its individual complaints and inquiries concerning products and services to Washington (as well as to state offices and even to local administrators). Politicians are offering individuals what amounts to a wailing wall. Politicians monitor individual grievances, and then act—with consumer legislation, additional regulation, and so on. This does not bode well for the future of the free enterprise system even in its present form (which may or may not be a calamity depending on one's viewpoint).

It is shocking to realize that not one piece of consumer legislation has been initiated by business management. On the contrary, every one of the recently-passed consumer laws was fought—usually bitterly—by business (truth-in-packaging was fought for five years, truth-in-lending for six). Yet, if top corporate management had not been so thoroughly shielded from those individual consumers who tried futilely to communicate, consumer cooperation rather than confrontation would have been the rule rather than the extremely rare exception.

Early this year, W. E. Sturges, vice-president, S. S. Kresge Co., said:

"I predict enormous success for those manufacturers and retailers who find new ways to give the American woman the security in her purchases that she must and will have. The American consumer will become more demanding and more impatient with those manufacturers and merchants who leave her with problems after she gets the merchandise home." Yet there may not be a half-dozen corporations that have laid down a truly modern socially responsible policy of open-channel communication with individual members of our society. Kresge is *not* among the half-dozen!

William M. Batten, chairman of the board, J. C. Penney Co., Inc., addressing himself to this point before the National Retail Merchants Association's annual convention about a year ago, pointedly remarked:

> Meeting competition has long been the primary yardstick which we have used for measuring our performance. But today, *how* we meet competition is under the careful scrutiny of many people in positions of power and of opinion-molding influence. And the results of their scrutiny have broad implications for our operations. . . . In those cases where changes are simply not possible—because of expense, the nature of the product, or the limitations of current technology—can we say that we have no obligation? Don't we then have a duty to inform the consumer as to *why* things are as they are *instead of simply shrugging off her complaints*?

THE SOPHISTICATED CONSUMER

The attitudes of consumers toward business as a social institution become less favorable as public income and education levels rise. Thus the issue is crystal clear: an affluent society of sophisticated consumers—this is the fundamental characteristic of tomorrow's markets—is just beginning to demand new standards from business. Those standards will include respect for the individual consumer. Today's affluent sophisticates control the major share of the nation's disposable dollar; they are marketing's choicest customers. Ultimately, they will represent the major share of the population in numbers; higher education for everyone and social progress make this a certainty. They are exceedingly articulate; they are our political influentials. When government listens to them, it listens at the highest levels, including the Presidency. When corporations listen, even to the typical minimum degree, the listening usually is done by the public relations department. But, as I will analyze in greater detail, public relations does not represent the public, is not responsive to the public, tends to be unaware of or even antagonistic toward the great new social trends, and treats the individual consumer with more cynicism and cold-bloodedness than was ever true of the banker in the days when bankers personified these characteristics.

As a consequence of the growth in affluence and sophistication, we are witnessing the first stages of a revolt of rising expectancy (a phrase that Churchill would have doted on). Customers today expect products to perform satisfactorily, to provide dependable functional performance, and to be safe. This threshold of acceptable performance is steadily advancing. It is precisely this widening revolt of rising expectancy, this steadily rising threshold of acceptable performance, that is the key to the seller's new legal as well as moral liabilities (increasingly, it will be the seller who must beware). The individual consumer will expect—and demand—to be heard by our large corporations and will insist that this is a corporate moral, ethical, and social responsibility.

President George Koch of Grocery Manufacturers of America (which fought truth-in-packaging for five years) acknowledged recently that: "The rise in consumer activities is the end result of a changing, modern era in which the product manufacturer, distributor—and even the retailer—have become *remote to the consumer.*

"She can't take her complaint to her friend at the corner store because he's no longer there. *We must assume more responsibility for communicating with consumers in order to keep ourselves informed of their needs. . . .*"

But, to date, the food industry's dialogs with the public have been puny gestures, and the individual is no better heard in the food industry today despite these noble sentiments. The industry has not yet put its *ear* where its mouth is! The strong response to the messages in the "You have a friend at Chase-Manhattan" campaign and in the early days to A & P's "We care" theme was the tip-off. Here was ample evidence that the public wanted someone who cared in its business contacts. Yet I doubt that the individual depositor finds any more friends at Chase-Manhattan than at any other major bank. I am positive that, in the individual stores of A & P, it was the rare employee who cared. And I doubt that depositors will get a warm reception if they accept Irving Trust's invitation to "Call us Irving."

But whether or not my cynicism is justified (I insist that corporation image campaigns based on largely fanciful images carry the seeds of their own futility), the point is that creative advertising men recognized the public's vast desire for friendliness, for caring, for first-name contacts in its relationship with business. Unfortunately, business management lags far behind the professional image creators in actually bringing the image into real life.

I have stated that this breakdown in individual communication between corporations and the public has been accelerated by the computer. This is almost frightening because the sophisticated uses of the computer in functions that relate to the public are still in the adolescent stage. Quite recently, Gulf Oil admitted its "cold-hearted" computers "couldn't care less" about dissatisfied customers. In a mailer, Gulf tells credit card users that, henceforth, customers' complaints will be answered by "a real, live person who wants you to be satisfied; letters are to be addressed to Jim Insell, 'our listening specialist.' " I rather doubt that Jim Insell will ever duplicate the early performance of General Mills' Betty Crocker. My observations of these programs, presumably planned to reopen a corporate listening post with consumers as individuals, are that: they are merely public relations gestures; they are underbudgeted and understaffed; they become thoroughly automated; and the communications with the public are largely form communications.

The consumer seldom has reason to conclude that anything has really been accomplished; how could this be otherwise when management is not even dimly aware of what transpires in this department and when the department's directives are extremely limited in scope and make no provision for elasticity of policy and practice?

It seems to me inevitable that this yawning chasm between corporation and individual consumer will lead to these portentous developments:

New legislation will give government the authority to arrive at legally enforceable decisions regarding individual consumer inquiries and complaints, thus completing the isolation of our corporations from the individual public.

This legislation will provide for a new type of federal and, possibly, state court, a court that will pass judgment on consumer complaints covering a product's performance and service (as differentiated from fraud).

Additional legislation will provide for still stricter standards covering product performance, safety, defects, and so on.

New legislation will give additional powers to the Federal Trade Commission as well as to the Department of Commerce—powers to act as the consumer's "friend in court" in the gray areas of marketing to which I refer.

The consumer will ultimately be represented by a Cabinet officer, and Betty Furness' department will eventually become huge.

Legal liability of the seller (especially the manufacturer) will be broadened, a trend already evident in recent court decisions.

These developments are not merely probable; each and every one is inevitable. This conclusion seems inescapable when one bears in mind the business community's miserable record of constructive self-regulation in the public interest. I take the position that the total area of free enterprise has been narrowed down more by business' abuse of free enterprise than by government initiative. Business has abdicated to the politician industry's privilege, as well as responsibility, to establish and maintain open and responsive communication channels with the individual consumer. That abdication began before computer technology had begun to leave its mark on our society, even before corporate giantism began to dwarf the individual consumer. Politicians astutely measured the scope of the privilege and happily accepted the responsibility.

A PROGRAM FOR BUSINESS

If business hopes to launch a program that could dampen the political drive for the preceding six developments, it must start with a clear understanding of the pressures within our society that make these sociopolitical and socioeconomic concepts probabilities. First and foremost, business must revise its traditional concepts of free enterprise, of its relations with and obligations to society. If businessmen insist that free enterprise permits them to be indifferent to those qualities on which people put high value, then the public will quite naturally conclude that free enterprise has too much freedom. Accepting, and acting out new dimensions of social responsibility is the essence of the new order of our business society. Business must now become *socially* oriented as well as *profit* oriented (the two concepts, it is now being understood, are not necessarily antithetical). And since it is human to want contact with humans —in a humane way—an increasingly sophisticated society will demand a more personal relationship between seller and buyer, even in a computerized age. This does not imply a return to the days of the country general store, but there is no reason to assume that the public will continue to tolerate a corporate environment in which the individual is treated as an unwelcome intruder.

It is a sad commentary on the widening gap between buyer and seller that Ralph Nader is considering opening a law firm that would represent the public interest in Washington with legal services fully equal to those that business interests are already receiving from leading law firms. Would such a law service be required if the public did not feel totally frustrated in its attempts to communicate with our leading corporations?

Politicians cling to the conviction that it is essential, when campaigning, to "press skin." How many management executives (including even top executives in retailing) ever press skin with shoppers? Is it not a fact that top management's knowledge of the shopper comes from neatly tabulated research reports—research reports that dissect the shopper in the mass rather than individually (and which have been known to be as neatly censored by lower-rank executives as they are neatly tabulated)?

The old-time merchants spent their time on the store floor meeting shoppers. To present-day management executives, the shopper is a numeral on a chart; few manufacturing executives at the management level spend even one day a year in retail stores talking to shoppers; the same goes for retail executives. How many management executives have *ever* had placed on their desks, for just one week, *all* the mail from the public—unedited, and uncensored? Congressmen examine their mail from their constituents carefully, but the management executive who sees even a single uncensored letter from the public is a rarity.

This state of affairs is made still worse by the computer, which "embezzles" the little that remains of the civilized structure of business. This is especially true of mass retailing, where the abuse of the computer is leading many large retailers into precisely the frosty, dehumanized stance that typified banks and bankers years ago. (It is an ironic fact that the computer is pressuring banks toward a somewhat *more intimate* customer relationship, while being permitted to pressure retailing into a remote, detached, uninterested relationship toward its customers.) Actually, this began years ago, long before mass retailers had begun computer installations. It began on the retail floor with salespeople. Then it moved one or two rungs up the retail executive ladder. It became more difficult for a customer to talk to a buyer, or even to an assistant buyer. Today, if a customer does manage to wangle an interview with a buyer, the buyer is inclined to prove to the customer that the salesperson takes second place in the art of frustrating, aggravating, and even insulting the customer.

Now the same attitudes have moved up into still higher retail executive echelons. Indeed, at these executive levels the individual shopper encounters—believe it or not—a total nonresponse. A few months ago, *The New York Times* carried a report on this subject which included the following:

> Department stores, one of the principal offenders in nonresponse, put the blame on computers. Undoubtedly, the complexities of automation have caused problems for many businesses, including many that never should have indulged in the luxury of depersonalizing their establishments. But the letters of complaint are not addressed to the computers; *perhaps, if they were, they would be answered!* The letters are addressed to persons who are paid to do certain tasks, one of which involves the long lost art of soothing dissatisfied customers. But they do not answer these letters, and their secretaries only answer their phones.

The salesclerks' situation will continue to deteriorate; the labor market leaves little hope. More retail executives, at more levels, will become more intolerant of any "interruptions" by customers; unsophisticated computer usage makes this inevitable. But I am positive that even new generations, who have been brought up in an era in which the shopper is always wrong, will not indefinitely accept this state of affairs with docility. The younger generations in particular will rebel; they are not so easily pushed around. As a consequence, mass retailing will find itself increasingly regulated in the public interest. It will be richly deserved!

In the United States in 1960 there were less than 41 million high school graduates, and less than 8 million college graduates. In 1985, each of these impressive figures will have more than doubled—90 million high school and 20 million college graduates. I doubt they will buy goods for long if they are offered in a condescending fashion. I am sure they will not accept ideas or relationships presented in a context of the lowest common denominator. And I am equally positive they will turn to government if industry persists in turning off its hearing aid when they try to communicate as individuals. Management had better beware of our "demonstration-oriented" society; the public has become knowledgeable in planning and executing political and social demonstrations. It has the know-how to mount, almost overnight, a vigorous confrontation with industry. We may not have a renewal of the food demonstrations, but we are almost sure to have a succession of demonstrations, in one form or another, if the public concludes that business has no genuine interest in listening.

Recently, the Washington bureau of *Advertising Age* reported: "We have already pointed out editorially how the food industry bungled truth-in-packaging. There was diligent reform by many individual companies, *but no concerted industry effort to create machinery to deal with customer complaints.*" That is still true of practically all industry. Over the past five years, product lines in most food categories have broadened at an extraordinary rate, which has posed a shopping problem. Some consumers no doubt complained to the major food processors, but did their complaints ever reach top management—unedited? One study disclosed that a typical food supermarket offered fourteen different packages of white rice; not one was in a 1-pound package. The same was true of the six packages of salt, which ran a confusing range from 4/10 oz. to 5 pounds. Imitation maple syrup (seven choices) was available in miscellaneous ounces, pints and ounces, and pounds and ounces. Toilet tissue was packed in rolls of 650, 800, and 1,000 sheets, some single-ply, some double-ply. Of the ten cans of tuna, none was 1 pound or even 1/2 pound. Now the food industry, prodded by the government and using government machinery, is moving to lessen this shopping confusion. But this action followed truth-in-packaging; if industry had listened earlier, it would have escaped governmental hands.

WHAT ABOUT PUBLIC RELATIONS?

No industry has ever undertaken a public relations program until it lost a measure of its freedom. Then it expects the identical policies that led to the public confrontation to become accepted by the public through the magic of public relations! Management must outgrow the belief that a socially acceptable public image can be created by public relations. That may have been feasible occasionally when the public was naive; it will rarely be possible as the public becomes more sophisticated.

I referred earlier to the destructive role that public relations plays in this situation. It is my deep conviction that the public relations fraternity has lost contact with the public. And the combination of top management divorced from the public and of public relations misguided is at the root of the current difficulty.

Gibson McCabe, president of *Newsweek*, talking on this point before a meeting of the Detroit chapter of the Public Relations Society of America, said:

> I think that business leaders—along with scholars, politicians, and educators—are more and more coming to see the need for the private sector of our economy to move more actively toward getting at the roots of social discontent. And, as they do so, they should rightly be able to look to their public counselors for help in establishing goals and putting sound programs into action. But, except in isolated instances, it seems to me that *this is precisely where public relations is at its weakest*—or, at least, has made its poorest showing to date.
>
> In preparation for my meeting with you today, I made an informal survey of *Newsweek*'s top 30 editors. Probably best expressing the general tone of our editors' comments was this statement from a man who has had occasion to deal more regularly with PR people

than some of the others: "Most PR men are okay and helpful on routine matters," he said, "but very few come through in the clinch, when it really counts. Whenever a company is involved in a tense situation, we find the PR man to be of little help, and often more of a hindrance. In short, when the heat's on, don't depend on PR."

All of which brings me to a critical point I want to make—solemnly, emphatically, and, I hope, persuasively: the public relations practitioner today has got to get himself actively and creatively involved in a world of social change. And if the reactions of our editors are an accurate barometer, *it would seem that few of you, to date, are doing so.* It is one thing to be able to report third-quarter financial results, but *quite another to inspire change on a social front.*

How can the public relations industry possibly place management in the mainstream of our new society when public relations itself is still unaware of the existence of a new social order? If public relations strategic planning had anticipated the new mores of our society and had insisted that its strategic concepts be made into company policy and practice, surely truth-in-packaging, truth-in-credit, auto tire standards, safety standards for autos, the drug industry's problems, and, in fact, the entire protect-the-consumer movement would not be staring industry in the face today. Too often, public relations counsel has actually tended to isolate our corporations from the vast changes in our society and from people. Yet, as I mentioned earlier, it is in the public relations department that individual communications from the public tend to wind up.

The public relations programs of our major corporations tend to be:

Inward-looking rather than outward-looking—the factory image rather than the consumer image.

Rather naive and therefore outdated regarding basic assumptions concerning our modern, sophisticated society, and inclined to be unaware of, or unwilling to accept society's mounting demands for broader socially-oriented programs by business.

Reflective of the attitudes of the old guard of business—the U.S. Chamber of Commerce and the National Association of Manufacturers—rather than reflections of the new attitudes of our public.

Still premised on the outworn assumption that a few thousand influentials mold the thinking of our people (actually, we have millions of influentials today, and the total continues to grow).

Lacking in original strategy, failing to guide clients toward creative interpretation and implementation of required new functions.

I have already made clear my conclusion that consumer legislation is directly traceable to the deaf ear industry turns to the individual consumer. With respect to consumerism, I hold these to be incontrovertible truths: consumerism represents *a long-term and powerful* trend, and consumerism will cover most phases of the total marketing function and even now is changing the more modern manifestations of caveat emptor into legislatively compulsory caveat vendor.

Yet, how many top management executives in the major and traffic appliance industry, the entertainment products industry, are really adequately informed about the rising public clamor concerning servicing? Surely it can only be lack of knowledge at the top level that can account for the permissive drift into inevitable truth-in-servicing consumer legislation. (Pressures are mounting even at state and city levels for bills licensing servicemen.)

Last year, the state of New York asked CBS to conduct a survey of the television repair industry. In twenty homes, the third video IF amplifier tube was made inoperative by opening the filament—equivalent to any of the other tubes burning out. Of the twenty servicemen called to repair the sets, seventeen were reported to be dishonest. Including a charge for service and labor, the fee should not have exceeded $8.93. Three servicemen said the tuner needed repair, and the fees ranged from $31.45 to $37.20. One other said the automatic gain control needed service and charged $34.23. In five cases, tubes were needlessly repaired, and the fees ran anywhere from $11.71 to $20.10. The cheating on the service repairs ranged from $4.00 to $30.00, assuming $8.00 as the correct charge.

U.S. News & World Report carried a round-up article on this subject that started this way:

> An affluent America, to the dismay of many citizens, is finding it difficult to keep repaired the gadgets, equipment and conveniences that are supposed to make living simpler in this country today. . . . Families everywhere complain that it takes days—even weeks—to get a serviceman to come to their homes; that the work is often sloppy; that the growing practice of charging a minimum fee for a service call is making simple jobs too costly.
> Actual examples, reported by staff members of *U.S. News & World Report* from across the country, reveal *a rising tide of anger and frustration.*
> How many management executives are really aware of this rising tide of frustration and anger?

Senate Commerce Committee Chairman Warren Magnuson is cosponsor of three pertinent bills on which his committee will hold public hearings; guarantee disclosure and product servicing act to require pinpoint disclosure of the extent of a warranty and its conditions (this bill also would create an advisory council on guarantees, warranties, and servicing to study and report to Congress on the situation); a new-car vehicle guarantee act; and household appliance guarantee act. Both the car and appliances guarantee bills would authorize the Secretary of Commerce, after consultation with the Federal Trade Commission, to set standards for warranties, create an arbitration procedure for settling complaints, allow the Secretary to set standards regulating the manufacturer-dealer relationship in warranties, make clear that ultimate responsibility under a warranty agreement rested with the manufacturer, and assure that dealers are compensated adequately for warranty work.

The proposed advisory council would study and investigate adequacy of performance under guarantees, and the methods of resolving disputes on adequacy of such performance and the extent of difficulty in securing competent servicing of mechanical and electrical products under warranties and guarantees as well as under customary service agreements. It would also study difficulties encountered in obtaining relief for inadequate performance under guarantees and customary service agreements.

Relate the preceding legislative program to the six predictions listed [earlier], and form your own conclusions regarding the validity of those forecasts. It is hardly necessary to draw a final conclusion; the conclusion draws itself. A more knowledgeable, as well as a more affluent, consumer clearly wants someone with whom to communicate concerning purchases. Those communications may include compliments as well as complaints, constructive suggestions as well as adjustments. If business continues to narrow down the already narrow communications channels available for this purpose—and if those communication channels terminate in public relations—then the consumer will turn in still larger numbers to government where communication channels are multiplying and where even top-ranking officials lend an attentive and sympathetic ear.

That can only mean still less freedom for free enterprise. If this is the cause, the end result will be richly deserved. It is the height of irony that at the moment corporations are beginning to act out their new responsibilities as involved members of our society, they are simultaneously turning a deaf ear to the individual members of society. How is it possible to be socially conscious while ignoring the individual?

PART EIGHT

*

Marketing and Consumerism

INTRODUCTION

Marketing and Consumerism

MARKETING IS the focal point between business and consumers. Raymond Bauer and Stephen Greyser point out that a primary reason why business and consumers do not listen to or understand one another is that they talk from two different models of marketing and consumer behavior. Essentially the consumer model is similar to the economist's pure competitive model, and the business model is similar to the economist's monopolistic competitive model. Marketing implications of the two differ in interpretations of the key words: (1) competition, (2) product, (3) consumer needs, (4) rationality, and (5) information. The result is a lack of dialogue between consumer advocates and business.

Bauer and Greyser point out that branded products provide an information source not only to the consumer but also to independent rating services. Because branded products are uniform and identifiable, independent testing services often substitute the brand image for performance evaluation, and evaluation becomes a means of rating the manufacturer. "The problem is that the manufacturer *sells* one thing and the rating services *rate* another."

Philip Kotler observes that consumer sovereignty is not sufficient when the consumer does not have full information and is influenced by advertising. He argues that the marketing concept has to be broadened to the societal marketing concepts. He "calls for a *customer orientation* backed by integrated marketing aimed at generating *customer satisfaction* and *long-run consumer welfare* as the key to attaining *long-run profitable volume*" and he asks that the social and ecological aspects of products and market planning be considered. He feels that consumerism is promarketing and can be profitable by providing the opportunities for creating and marketing new products that not only provide for the consumer's immediate satisfaction but also his long-run welfare. He defines a matrix of salutary, deficient, desirable, and pleasing products for market strategies associated with a societal marketing approach.

Ronald Shafer's article points out how the firm can provide a consumer orientation in its marketing policies. The success of Giant Food stores in adopting such a policy has set a precedent that others in the grocery industry have now adopted.

31. A FOOD CHAIN RECRUITS A CONSUMER ADVOCATE TO SHAPE ITS POLICIES

Ronald G. Shafer

BACK IN the mid-1960s, Esther Peterson was the government's chief advocate of food-packaging regulations and public enemy No. 1 to the grocery industry. Opponents said the plans she favored were "fuzzy, foolish and futile" or would mean "devastating control."

Today she's still pushing grocery reforms, but from inside the industry. And some of her best friends are industry people. "I think the best way to work for change is inside industry," she says. "I'm able to do things I could only talk about before."

For the past year, Mrs. Peterson has been consumer adviser to Giant Food, Inc., a regional supermarket chain based here with 94 stores in Maryland, Virginia, and Washington, D.C. In that time, Giant though only the nation's 20th biggest grocery chain in sales, has become an industry leader in consumerism. It has adopted many of the changes opposed by industry when Esther Peterson was the first White House consumer adviser, under President Johnson, between 1964 and 1967.

Giant's growing basket of consumer aids starts with two items being tried by many other chains: open dating (rather than code numbers) of the shelf-life of perishables, and unit pricing (cents per pound, for instance) besides the total price per package. But Giant goes farther than most; it applies unit pricing to all 7,000 products carried in most of its stores.

AN OLD STANDBY—SOAP

Beyond this, Giant is disclosing on labels of its private-brand products the ingredients of some so-called standardized foods, including cola drinks, and the nutritional values of other foods. For the environmental-minded, it has come up with recycled-paper products and an "old-fashioned," nonpolluting laundry soap that omits both phosphates and phosphate substitutes. The chain now is moving to clarify confusing grade labels on foods. Henceforth, for example, "fancy" fish will be labeled what it is: fish previously frozen and then thawed when it is put on display.

What's more, Giant has begun notifying some manufacturers that it won't carry products it deems to be unsafe or unfairly packaged. A current target: liquid household cleaners packaged with the names, looks or smells of fruits; they could be mistakenly swallowed by children as fruit drinks. If some such products aren't changed, Giant officials hint they may publicize the reasons their stores won't carry them.

Such stands are winning praise from consumer advocates. "The most important thing about Giant's experience is that it can help the organized consumer movement convince retailers in all industries that they can do more to be the buying agents for consumers rather than the selling agents for suppliers," says James Turner, a former aide to Ralph Nader and author of "The Chemical Feast," a Nader report critical of the Food and Drug Administration and the food industry.

Giant's programs also are passing the ultimate test of the cash register; record sales and profits are predicted for the current fiscal year. Some customers appear to be pleased in unexpected ways. Giant's nutritional labeling program, for example, gives high marks to liver. Now some mothers march their children up to big nutrition posters in Giant stores, point and say, "It isn't just me telling you that liver is good for you." And some of the stores report the phenomenon of frequently selling out of liver.

BUT DO CONSUMERS CARE?

Among food producers and other retailers reaction to Giant's efforts is mixed. Generally, the approach is seen as "brilliant merchandising" of consumerism says one industry executive, but there's some skepticism about how meaningful or practical some specific aids are. Some doubters cite industry studies indicating that the average grocery shopper is more interested in, say, the speed of a store's checkout counter than in open dating.

Food-industry officials, however, are cheered that efforts by Giant and other chains have taken some steam out of demands for federal legislation for such things as unit pricing and open dating. Some 75 major chains have gone to unit pricing in some form and 59 have open dating of their own products.

Though Giant tries to meet some of the demands of the consumer movement, company officials insist the company isn't about to become the Ralph Nader of food selling. "We don't want to be an industry maverick or whistleblower," says Joseph B. Danzansky, Giant's 57-year-old president. But as a regional chain, he reasons, the company must be extra-responsive to consumer demands and must get involved in community affairs. (On the latter count,

Mr. Danzansky even has offered to personally help buy Washington a major-league baseball team to replace the departed Senators.)

At first, Mr. Danzansky concedes, he shared the industry's skepticism about some consumer demands. Just last summer, he stated that posting the price of items per unit of measurement was not wanted by customers and would be too costly. He added that open dating for perishables would multiply "throwaway" costs because shoppers would buy only the products with the latest date.

NEW SYSTEMS PAY OFF

In practice, such fears have proved to be "absolutely wrong," Mr. Danzansky says today. Indeed, both unit pricing and open dating have been cost savers at Giant. Unit pricing, for example, cost only $300 to $400 a store to install, and operating costs are offset by improved inventory control, he says. And "it's a great tool for the sale of private labels," which generally are cheaper per unit of measurement than advertised brands.

All in all, Giant's journey into consumerism has been more successful than the moves of some other retailers. Talks with industry and government officials and consumer advocates help disclose some of the ingredients of this success.

The first is credibility. The company took, well, a giant step in this direction by hiring Esther Peterson. As the first White House consumer adviser and a long-time consumer champion, the 65-year-old Mrs. Peterson's consumerism credentials are impeccable. While some friends criticized her move into industry, none doubt her sincerity. The clincher is that while some companies use consumerism rhetoric as "window dressing," Giant "has made some gutsy moves," says David Swankin, Washington representative for Consumers Union.

An extra benefit in Washington of having a former presidential adviser on hand is immediate public attention. Giant was able to announce its nutritional labeling program from a Senate hearing room complete with glowing tributes from an unlikely collection of Senators, industry officials and consumer advocates; the fanfare was arranged with the help of old Peterson allies in the Senate, including Philip Hart of Michigan and Frank Moss of Utah. The presence of Mrs. Peterson generates frequent and favorable news coverage for Giant; Safeway Stores, Inc., the Washington area's biggest food chain (Giant is No. 2), has adopted many similar consumer measures but gets much less publicity.

Another explanation for success is that Giant's consumer efforts are built into the company's power structure. Mrs. Peterson says she had offers from other companies, but "in most I just would have been decoration or for public relations." At Giant, she works directly with a committee made up of the

276

company's 12 vice-presidents, "the power boys" as she calls them. And she has the authority to act.

Mrs. Peterson sometimes uses that authority in unorthodox ways. Last year when beef prices jumped sharply, she had posters put up in Giant stores urging customers to "BUY SOMETHING ELSE." The posters spelled out why prices were rising and suggested cheaper alternatives. "They still kept buying meat, but the complaints went down," she says.

WILLING TO LISTEN

Still another factor is that Giant is willing to listen to outsider's proposals frequently rejected by industry. It was the first company to endorse apetition by a group of George Washington University law students organized as LABEL, Inc. to require the listing of ingredients in the hundreds of food products whose basic materials are standardized by the FDA. The chain's own ingredient-labeling venture is another response.

Giant's nutritional labeling program was devised largely by one of its numerous consumer advisory committees, this one headed by Dr. Jean Mayer, the noted Harvard nutritionist. The plan is one of several being tested by food chains for the FDA. At Giant, labels tell the amount of essential nutrients, such as protein, vitamin C and iron, contained in 10 canned foods; similar information is given on store posters for 48 other foods ranging from bread to watermelon.

So good has been the public response that Giant recently obtained FDA clearance to add 26 more products to its nutrition-labeling project; included are macaroni, ice cream and canned seafood.

SUPPORT AND FOLLOW-UP

The final ingredients in making consumerism work are continuing support by company management and persistent follow-up at the supermarket level. Mrs. Peterson's measures are strongly backed and explained by Giant in full-page newspaper ads and in TV commercials, some of which feature the energetic consumer adviser herself. ("My friends kid me that the first thing I sold was toilet paper," she says.) Mrs. Peterson keeps a close check on stores, frequently sending memos headed, "Are we meeting our commitment?" Employees call them, "letters from Grandma."

The ultimate effect of Giant's efforts remains to be seen. But so far both company executives and Mrs. Peterson seem satisfied. Business has been brisk. In the fiscal half-year ended Oct. 9, sales climbed 13% from a year earlier to over $242 million, and Mr. Danzansky predicts they'll continue to run well ahead of last year's pace.

Profits, too, are up. They have snapped back smartly from a loss suffered in the second quarter last fiscal year after the company began a discount-pricing policy. In the latest half-year, earnings jumped to $3.4 million from $1.2 million a year before, and the Giant president expects a continued uptrend.

For her part, Mrs. Peterson has decided not to return to her former post as legislative representative for the Amalgamated Clothing Workers; she had been on a leave of absence. "I'm very pleased with the response by industry," she says. "People who used to fight me are now my friends." About her only problem, she adds, is getting her own grocery shopping done. "People want to follow me around and see what I'm buying."

32. THE DIALOGUE THAT NEVER HAPPENS

Raymond A. Bauer
and Stephen A. Greyser

IN RECENT years government and business spokesmen alike have advocated a "dialogue" between their two groups for the reduction of friction and the advancement of the general good. Yet, all too often, this is a dialogue that never happens. Rather, what passes for dialogue *in form* is often a sequence of monologues *in fact*, wherein each spokesman merely grants "equal time" to the other and pretends to listen while preparing his own next set of comments. Obviously, this is not always the case; and, if taken literally, it tends to minimize some real progress being made.

Our aim here is to try to facilitate and stimulate that progress by exploring what lies behind the dialogue that never happens and by suggesting what can be done—on both sides—to develop more meaningful and effective business-government interactions.

In this context, we link "government spokesmen" with "critics." Naturally, not all in government are critics of business, and vice versa. However, almost all critics seek redress of their grievances via government action and seek government spokesmen to present their views "in behalf of the public."

Our primary focus will be in the field of marketing—particularly selling and advertising—which is perhaps the most controversial and most frequently criticized single zone of business. Marketing seems to be the area where achieving true dialogue is most difficult and where business and government spokesmen most seem to talk past each other.

Before examining why this takes place, let us look at two comments on advertising that illustrate the lack of dialogue. The first comment is that of Donald F. Turner, Assistant Attorney General in charge of the Antitrust Division of the Justice Department.

Reprinted from *Harvard Business Review* (November-December, 1967), pp. 2-4, 6, 8, 10, 12, 186, 188, 190. Copyright 1967, President and Fellows of Harvard College; all rights reserved.

279

There are three steps to informed choice: (1) the consumer must know the product exists; (2) the consumer must know how the product performs; and (3) he must know how it performs compared to other products. If advertising only performs step one and appeals on other than a performance basis, informed choice cannot be made.[1]

The other comment is that of Charles L. Gould, Publisher, the San Francisco *Examiner*:

No government agency, no do-gooders in private life can possibly have as much interest in pleasing the consuming public as do . . . successful companies. For, in our economy, their lives literally depend on keeping their customers happy.[2]

DOUBLE ENTENDRES

Why do business and government spokesmen talk past each other in discussing ostensibly the same marketplace? We think it is because each has a basically different model of the consumer world in which marketing operates. This misunderstanding grows from different perceptions about a number of key words.

The first word is *competition*. The critics of business think of competition tacitly as strictly price differentiation. Modern businessmen, however, as marketing experts frequently point out, think of competition primarily in terms of product differentiation, sometimes via physical product developments and sometimes via promotional themes. The important thing is that price competition plays a relatively minor role in today's marketplace.

Some of the perplexity between these two views of competition has to do with confusion over a second word, *product*. In the critic's view, a product is the notion of some entity which has a primary identifiable function only. For example, an automobile is a device for transporting bodies, animate or inanimate; it ordinarily has four wheels and a driver, and is powered by gasoline. There are variants on this formula (three-wheeled automobiles) which are legitimate, provided the variants serve the same function. Intuitively the businessman knows there is something wrong with this notion of the product because the product's secondary function may be his major means of providing differentiation (an auto's looks, horsepower, and so on).

Then there is the term *consumer needs*, which the business critic sees as corresponding to a product's primary function—for example, needs for transportation, nutrition, recreation (presumably for health purposes), and other things. The businessman, on the other hand, sees needs as virtually *any* consumer lever he can use to differentiate his product.

Next, there is the notion of *rationality*. The critic, with a fixed notion of "needs" and "product," sees any decision that results in an efficient matching of product to needs as rational. The businessman, taking no set position on what a person's needs should be, contends that any decision the customer makes to serve his own perceived self-interest is rational.

The last addition to our pro tem vocabulary is *information*. The critic fits information neatly into his view that a rational decision is one which matches product function and consumer needs, rather circularly defined as the individual's requirement for the function the product serves. Any information that serves that need is "good" information. To the businessman, information is basically any data or argument that will (truthfully) put forth the attractiveness of a product in the context of the consumer's own buying criteria.

Exhibit 1 summarizes our views of these two different models of the consumer world. We realize that we may have presented a somewhat exaggerated dichotomy. But we think the models are best demonstrated by this delineation of the pure views of contrasting positions, recognizing that both sides modify them to some extent.

Exhibit 1. Two different models of the consumer world

Key words	Critics view	Businessman's view
Competition	Price competition.	Product differentiation.
Product	Primary function only.	Differentiation through secondary function.
Consumer needs	Correspond point-for-point to primary functions.	Any customer desire on which the product can be differentiated.
Rationality	Efficient matching of product to customer needs.	Any customer decision that serves the customer's own perceived self-interest.
Information	Any data that facilitate the fit of a product's proper function with the customer's needs.	Any data that will (truthfully) put forth the attractiveness of the product in the eyes of the customer.

VIEWS OF HUMAN NATURE

A review of our "vocabulary with a double meaning" and the two models of the consumer world shows that the critic's view is based on a conviction that he knows what "should be." In contrast, the businessman's view is based on militant agnosticism with regard to "good" or "bad" value judgments which might be made (by anyone) about individual marketplace transactions.

281

The businessman's view of human nature may be the more flattering, perhaps excessively so. Certainly, the marketer's notion of "consumer sovereignty" compliments the consumer in attributing to him the capacity to decide what he needs and to make his choice competently even under exceedingly complex circumstances. It also sometimes challenges him to do so. This perhaps undeserved flattery glosses over some obvious flaws in the market mechanism. It is rooted in the belief that this mechanism, even though imperfect in specific instances, is better than administrative procedures for regulating the market.

The critic takes a far less optimistic view of human nature—both the consumer's and the seller's. He thinks that the seller often (sometimes intentionally) confuses consumers with a welter of one-sided argumentation. Such information, in the critic's eye, not only lacks impartiality, but usually focuses on secondary product functions and is not geared to consumer needs.

Both sets of assumptions are, we think, at least partially justified. Customers do have limited information and limited capacity to process it. This is the way of the world. Furthermore, there is no reason to believe that every seller has every customer's interest as his own primary concern in every transaction, even though in the long run it probably is in the seller's own best interest to serve every customer well.

All of this disagreement comes to focus on a point where both business and government are in agreement; namely, modern products are sufficiently complex that the individual consumer is in a rather poor position to judge their merits quickly and easily. The businessman says that the customer should be, and often is, guided in his judgment by knowledge of brand reputation and manufacturer integrity, both of which are enhanced by advertising. The critic argues that the customer should be, but too seldom is, aided by impartial information sources primarily evaluating product attributes.

These conflicting views of vocabulary and human nature are reflected in several specific topic areas.

BRANDS & RATING SERVICES

One of these areas is the relationship of national branding to consumer rating services, the latter being a traditional source of "impartial information" for consumers. Somehow the crux of this relationship seems to have escaped most people's attention: consumer rating services are possible *only because of* the existence of a limited number of brands for a given product. In order for a rating to be meaningful, two conditions are necessary:

1. *Identifiability*—the consumer must be able to recognize the products and brands rated.
2. *Uniformity*—manufacturers must habitually produce products of sufficiently uniform quality that consumer and rating service alike can learn enough from a sample of the product to say or think something meaningful about another sample of the same product which may be

282

bought in some other part of the country at some later time. This is a seldom-realized aspect of national branding.

It is generally assumed by both groups that the "consumer movement" is basically opposed to heavily advertised branded goods. The stereotype of *Consumer Reports* is that it regularly aims at shunting trade away from national brands to Sears, to Montgomery Ward, or to minor brands. Yet the one study made of this issue showed that, contrary to the stereotype, *Consumer Reports* had consistently given higher ratings to the heavily advertised national brands than to their competitors.[3]

IDEOLOGICAL BLINDNESS:
What we have here is an instance of the consumer movement and brand-name manufacturers being ideologically blinded by different models of the market world. The consumer movement concentrates on the notion of a product having a definable primary function that should take precedence over virtually all other attributes of the product. True, some concessions have recently been made to aesthetics. But, on the whole, the consumer movement is suspicious of the marketing world that strives to sell products on the basis of secondary attributes which the consumer movement itself regards with a jaundiced eye.

The evidence available to the consumer movement is that, in general, national advertising is *not* accompanied by poorer performance on primary criteria. But the consumer movement fails to relaize that it *takes for granted* the central claim for advertised branded products—namely, that by being identifiable and uniform in quality, they offer the customer an opportunity to make his choice on the basis of his confidence in a particular manufacturer.

But the manufacturers of nationally branded products and their spokesmen have been equally blind. First of all, we know of none who has pointed out the extent to which any form of consumer rating must be based on the identifiability and uniformity of branded products. The only situation where this does not apply is when the rating service can instruct the consumer in how to evaluate the product—for example, looking for marbleizing in beef. However, this is limited to products of such a nature that the customer can, with but little help, evaluate them for himself; it cannot apply to products for which he has to rely on the technical services of an independent evaluator or on the reputation of the manufacturer.

Moreover, except for such big-ticket items as automobiles, consumer rating services usually test products only once in several years. In other words, they rate not only a *sample* of a manufacturer's products, but also a sample of his performance *over time*. Thus, if one "follows the ratings" and buys an air conditioner or a toaster this year, he may buy it on the rating of a product made one, two, or three years ago. Similarly, if one buys a new automobile, he depends in part on the repair record (reported by at least one rating service) for previous models of that brand.

In large part, the consumer rating services are devices for rating *manufacturers!* This is not to say they do not rate specific products. Sometimes they even draw fine distinctions between different models from the same company.

But in the course of rating products, they also rate manufacturers. What more could the manufacturer ask for? Is this not what he claims he strives for?

BASIC DICHOTOMY:

More to the point, what is it that has kept the consumer movement and brand-name manufacturers from paying attention to this area of shared overlapping interests? Neither will quarrel with the exposure either of factual deception or of product weaknesses on dimensions that both agree are essential to the product. This is not where the problem is. The problem is that the manufacturer *sells* one thing and the rating service *rates* another.

The concept of a "product" that dominates the thinking of rating services and the thought processes of those who suggest more "impartial evaluation information" for consumers (e.g., Donald Turner of the Department of Justice and Congressman Benjamin Rosenthal of New York) is that a product is an entity with a single, primary, specifiable function—or, in the case of some products such as food, perhaps a limited number of functions, e.g., being nutritious, tasty, and visually appealing. The specific goal of many proposed ratings—with their emphasis on the physical and technical characteristics of products—is to free the customer from the influence of many needs to which the marketer addresses himself, most particularly the desire for ego-enhancement, social acceptance, and status.

The marketer, oddly enough, tends to accept a little of the critic's view of what a product is. Marketing texts, too, speak of primary and secondary functions of a product as though it were self-evident that the aesthetic ego-gratifying, and status-enhancing aspects of the product were hung on as an afterthought. If this is true, why are Grecian vases preserved to be admired for their beauty? And why did nations of yore pass sumptuary laws to prevent people from wearing clothes inappropriate to their status?

We shall shortly explore what may lie behind this confusion about the nature of products. First, however, let us examine another topical area in which similar confusion exists.

"MATERIALIST SOCIETY"

The selling function in business is regularly evaluated by social commentators in relationship to the circumstance that ours is a "materialist society." We could say we do not understand what people are talking about when they refer to a materialist society, beyond the fact that our society does possess a lot of material goods. But, in point of fact, we think *they* do not understand what they are talking about. Let us elucidate.

At first hearing, one might conclude that criticism of a materialist society is a criticism of the extent to which people spend their resources of time, energy, and wealth on the acquisition of material things. One of the notions that gets expressed is that people should be more interested in pursuing nonmaterial goals.

The perplexing matter is, however, that the criticism becomes strongest on the circumstance that people *do* pursue nonmaterial goals—such as ego enhancement, psychic security, social status, and so on—but use material goods as a means of achieving them. Perhaps the distinctive feature of our society is the extent to which *material* goods are used to attain *nonmaterial* goals.

Now there are many ways in which societies satisfy such needs. For example, there are ways of attaining status that do not involve material goods of any substance. Most societies grant status to warriors and other heroes, to wise men who have served the society, and so on. Often the external manifestation of this status is rigidly prescribed and involves signs whose material worth is insignificant: a hero wears a medal, a ribbon in his lapel, or a certain type of headdress, or he may be addressed by an honorific title.

However, in societies that value economic performance, it is not uncommon for material goods to be used as status symbols. Indians of the Southwest, for example, favor sheep as a symbol even to the extent of overtaxing the grazing lands and lowering the economic status of the tribe. As a practical matter, this might be more damaging to the welfare of the Navaho than is the damage that many low-income Negroes do to their own individual welfares when, as research shows, they insist on serving a premium-priced brand of Scotch.

Many of the things about which there is complaint are not self-evidently bad. Art collecting is generally considered a "good thing." But take the worst instance of a person who neurotically seeks self-assurance by buying art objects. Clinically, one might argue that he would do himself a lot more long-run good with psychotherapy even though, when one considers the resale value of the art objects, he may have taken the more economical course of action. Similarly, it is not self-evident that the promotion of toiletries to the youth as a symbol of transition to manhood is inherently cruel—unless the commercials are especially bad! It is clear, however, that there is no societal concensus that the transition to manhood should be symbolized by the use of toiletries.

What seems to be the nub of the criticism of our society as a materialist one is that simultaneously a great number of nonmaterial goals are served by material goods, and there is no consensus that this should be so. Behind this is our old friend (or enemy): the concept of a product as serving solely a primary function. In the perspective of history and of other societies, this is a rather peculiar notion. Who in a primitive society would contend that a canoe paddle should not be carved artistically, or that a chief should not have a more elaborate paddle than a commoner?

Much of the confusion over the words on our list seems to be a residue of the early age of mass production. The production engineer, faced with the task of devising ways to turn out standardized products at low cost, had to ask himself, "What are the irreducible elements of this product?" This was probably best epitomized in Henry Ford's concept of the automobile, and his comment that people could have any color they wanted so long as it was black. Clearly, Ford thought it was immoral even to nourish the thought that a product ought to look good, let alone that it should serve various psychic and social functions.

285

But all this was closely related to the mass producer's effort to find the irreducible essence of what he manufactured. This effort broke up the natural organic integrity of products, which, at almost all times in all societies, have served multiple functions.

Many writers have called attention to the fact that in recent times our society has passed from the period of simpleminded mass production to that of product differentiation on attributes beyond the irreducible primary function. As yet, however, we do not think there is adequate appreciation of the impact of the residue of the early period of mass production on thinking about what a product is. In that period even very complex products were converted into commodities. Since each performed essentially the same primary function, the chief means of competition was pricing.

PRODUCTS AS COMMODITIES

At this point, we shall argue that the thinking of those who criticize the selling function is based on a model for the marketing of commodities. This factor does not exhaust the criticisms, but we believe it is at the core of present misunderstandings over the concepts on which we have focused our discussion.

On the one hand, to the extent that products are commodities, it is possible to specify the function or functions which all products in that category should serve. It follows that a person who buys and uses such a commodity for some purpose other than for what it was intended has indeed done something odd, although perhaps useful to him (for example, baseball catchers who use foam-rubber "falsies" to pad their mitts). In any event, it is possible both to specify the basis on which the commodity should be evaluated and the information a person is entitled to have in order to judge that product. A person searching for a commodity ought first to find out whether it serves this function and then to ask its price.

On the other hand, to the extent that products are *not* commodities, it is impossible to expect that price competition will necessarily be the main basis of competition. Likewise, it is impossible to specify what information is needed or what constitutes rational behavior. Is it rational for a person to buy toothpaste because its advertiser claims it has "sex appeal"? Presumably people would rather look at clean than dingy teeth, and presumably people also like to have sex appeal—at least up to the point where it gets to be a hazard or a nuisance.

But it does not follow, insofar as we can see, that ratings—or grade labeling—should discourage product differentiation or the promotion of products on a noncommodity basis. If the consumer were assured that all products in a given rating category performed their primary functions about equally well, could it not be argued that those attributes which differentiate the products on other functions would then become increasingly interesting and important? Or, to be more specific, what makes it possible for "instant-on" TV tuning to be promoted—other than a presumed agreement, by both manufacturer and consumers, that the TV set performs its primary function little better or worse than its competition?

This is a facet of competition not appreciated by the opponents of grade-labeling, who have argued that it would reduce competition. Perhaps it would be more helpful if the opponents of grade labeling first gathered some evidence on what has actually happened to competition in countries where grade labeling has been introduced. (The head of one major relevant trade association recently told one of us that he knew of no such research.)

TOWARD MORE INFORMATION

Readers will note that we have indulged in considerable speculation in this article. But most of the issues on which we have speculated are research-able. Relatively little, for example, is really known about how businesses actu-ally see themselves carrying out "the practice of competition," or even about the actual competitive mechanisms of setting prices. Furthermore, in all of this, there is no mention of the *consumer's* view of these various concepts or of his model of the marketing process. To be sure, we can be reasonably certain of some things. For example, we know that consumers do regard prod-ucts as serving needs beyond the bare essentials. Yet it would be helpful to know far more about their views of the overall marketing process.

What we propose as a worthwhile endeavor is an independent assessment of the consumer's view of the marketing process, focusing on information needs from his point of view. Thus, rather than businessmen lamenting the critics' proposals for product-rating systems and the critics bemoaning what seem to be obvious abuses of marketing tools, both sides ought to move toward proposing an information system for the consumer that takes into account *his* needs and *his* information-handling capacities while still adhering to the realities of the marketing process.

For those who have the reading habit, it will be obvious that this proposal is but an extension of the conclusions reached by members of the American Marketing Association's Task Force on "Basic Problems in Marketing" for the improvement of relations between marketing and government.[4] In brief, along with suggested studies on the influence of government policies and pro-grams on corporate marketing decisions, a special study was recommended in the area of consumer-buyer decision making and behavior:

> "It is of the highest importance to investigate the impacts of the host of governmental regulations, facilities, aids, and interven-tions upon the quality and efficiency of consumer-buyer decision making."[5]

The report went on to state that, particularly in light of the generally recognized drift from *caveat emptor* toward *caveat venditor*, "abundant basic research opportunities and needs exist'' in the area of government impact and consumer-buyer behavior.

WHAT CAN BUSINESSMEN DO?

Certainly there is a crying need for more information and, as we have tried to illustrate, for fresh analytic thinking on almost all of the issues on which government and business are butting heads. We have elaborated on the different models of how the marketplace does, and should, work because we think their existence explains the largest part of why marketers and their critics often talk past each other, even when they have the best intentions of engaging in a dialogue. The other part is explained by the relative absence of facts. As we have noted, the consumer's view of the market-advertising process and his informational needs represent an important (and relatively unprobed) research area.

Returning to the "dialogue," we should add a further problem beyond that of business and government spokesmen talking past one another. Inasmuch as many on both sides see themselves as representing their colleagues' views, partisanship becomes mixed with the aforementioned misunderstanding. Since such partisanship is likely to address itself to stereotyped views of "the other side," the comments become irrelevant. That many well-qualified firsthand commentators are regarded as self-serving by their critics is a point aptly made by Denis Thomas. Equally apt is his corollary observation that those "who view business . . . from a suitably hygienic distance lose no marks for partiality even if their facts are wrong."[6]

How then can effective interactions take place? Obviously, the key parts will be played by:

1. Thoughtful business and government leaders.
2. Marketers and their critics who take the time to consider and to understand (even if they do not agree with) each others' premises and assumptions.
3. Those who engage in meaningful dialogue oriented to fact finding rather than fault finding.
4. Those on both sides who address themselves to solving the problems of the real, rather than the presumed, public.

These constructive parts are not easy to play, but there are many who are trying, and succeeding, as these three examples illustrate:

The Department of Commerce has taken a series of measures, including the formation of a National Marketing Committee, to play a positive "activist" role in business-government relations; marketers are involved in what goes on rather than, as has occurred in many previous government situations, being informed after the fact.

William Colihan, Executive Vice President of Young &

Rubicam, Inc., proposed at the University of Missouri's Freedom of Information Conference that marketing undertake a major consumer education job to "make the marketing system benefit the nonaffluent, the undereducated."[7] This 20% of adult consumers represents, he feels, both a public responsibility and a marketing opportunity.

John N. Milne of Toronto's MacLaren Advertising Company Limited spelled out eleven specific major economic, social, ethical, and communications research projects to provide a "factual basis for an objective assessment of advertising, to replace emotional pleas." Business, government, universities, and projects in other nations would serve as sources and beneficiaries of data "so that advertising's usefulness to all segments of society can be assessed and improved."[8]

Beyond the parts played by thoughtful business and government people, we see a distinctive role for schools of business in bringing about meaningful interaction. Business schools are a unique resource both in their understanding of the business system and in their capability to conduct relevant research. Other faculties, at least equally competent and objective in research, generally do not have the depth of understanding of why things are the way they are—a necessary precursor to relevant study. We hasten to add that grasping how something *does* operate implies no consent that this is how it *should* operate, now or in the future.

Both in research and as participants (or moderators) in dialogue, business school faculties can play a significant role.

Business and government should sponsor the necessary research. The particular need for business is to recognize that the era of exclusively partisan pleading must end. In our judgment, the American Association of Advertising Agencies' sponsorship of research on consumer reactions to advertising and advertisements is a splendid model.[9] The findings are by no means exclusively favorable to advertising. But they make more clear where problems do, and do not, lie. And academic "insurance" of the objective conduct of the research and presentation of findings should bring about a degree of governmental acceptance and set the standard for any subsequent research.

We can use more of this, and more of it is beginning to take place. A dialogue is always most profitable when the parties have something to talk about.

NOTES

1. Statement made at the Ninth Annual American Federation of Advertising Conference on Government Relations held in Washington, D.C., February 1967.

2. Ibid.

3. Eugene R. Beem and John S. Ewing, "Business Appraises Consumer Testing Agencies," *HBR*, March-April 1954, pp. 113-126, especially p. 121.

4. *See* E. T. Grether and Robert J. Holloway, "Impact of Government upon the Mar-

ket System," *Journal of Marketing*, April 1967, pp. 1-5; and Seymour Banks, "Commentary on 'Impact of Government upon the Market System,' " Ibid., pp. 5-7.

5. Grether and Holloway, "Impact," p. 5.

6. D. Thomas, *The Visible Persuaders* (London: Hutchinson & Co., 1967), p. 11.

7. *Freedom of Information in the Market Place* (FOI Center, Columbus, Missouri, 1967), pp. 140-148.

8. Speech given at the Annual Conference of the Federation of Canadian Advertising and Sales Clubs, Montreal, June 1967.

9. For a description of the research and a review of the major results, *see* Stephen A. Greyser, editor, *The AAAA Study on Consumer Judgment of Advertising—An Analysis of the Principal Findings* (New York: American Association of Advertising Agencies, 1965), and Opinion Research Corporation, *The AAAA Study on Consumer Judgment of Advertising* (Princeton, 1965); the findings and their interpretation are the subject of the authors' forthcoming book, *Advertising in America: The Consumer View* (Boston: Division of Research, Harvard Business School, on press).

33. WHAT CONSUMERISM MEANS FOR MARKETERS

Philip Kotler

IN THIS century, the U.S. business scene has been shaken by three distinct consumer movements—in the early 1900's, the mid-1930's, and the mid-1960's. The first two flare-ups subsided. Business observers, social critics, and marketing leaders are divided over whether this latest outbreak is a temporary or a permanent social phenomenon. Those who think that the current movement has the quality of a fad point to the two earlier ones. By the same token, they argue that this too will fade away. Others argue just as strongly that the issues which flamed the latest movement differ so much in character and force that consumerism may be here to stay.

In retrospect, it is interesting that the first consumer movement was fueled by such factors as rising prices, Upton Sinclair's writings, and ethical drug scandals. It culminated in the passage of the Pure Food and Drug Act (1906), the Meat Inspection Act (1906), and the creation of the Federal Trade Commission (1914). The second wave of consumerism in the mid-1930's was fanned by such factors as the upturn in consumer prices in the midst of the depression, the sulfanilamide scandal, and the widely imitated Detroit housewives strike. It culminated in the strengthening of the Pure Food and Drug Act and in the enlarging of the Federal Trade Commission's power to regulate against unfair or deceptive act and practices.

The third and current movement has resulted from a complex combination of circumstances, not the least of which was increasingly strained relations between standard business practices and long-run consumer interests. Consumerism in its present form has also been variously blamed on Ralph Nader, the thalidomide scandal, rising prices, the mass media, a few dissatisfied individuals, and on President Lyndon Jonson's "Consumer Interests Message." These and other possible explanations imply that the latest movement did not have to happen and that it had little relationship to the real feelings of most consumers.

In this article, I shall discuss the current phenomenon and what it portends for business. In so doing, I shall present five simple conclusions about consumerism and largely focus my discussion on these assessments. Consider:

1. *Consumerism was inevitable.* It was not a plot by Ralph Nader and a handful of consumerists but an inevitable phase in the development of our economic system.
2. *Consumerism will be enduring.* Just as the labor movement started as a protest uprising and became institutionalized in the form of unions, government boards, and labor legislation, the consumer movement, too, will become an increasingly institutionalized force in U.S. society.
3. *Consumerism will be beneficial.* On the whole, it promises to make the U.S. economic system more responsive to new and emerging societal needs.
4. *Consumerism is promarketing.* The consumer movement suggests an important refinement in the marketing concept to take into account societal concerns.
5. *Consumerism can be profitable.* The societal marketing concept suggests areas of new opportunity and profit for alert business firms.

These assessments of consumerism are generally at variance with the views of many businessmen. Some business spokesmen maintain that consumerism was stirred up by radicals, headline grabbers, and politicians; that it can be beaten by attacking, discrediting, or ignoring it; that it threatens to destroy the vitality of our economic system and its benefits; that it is an anti-marketing concept; and that it can only reduce profit opportunities in the long run.

WHAT IS CONSUMERISM?

Before discussing the foregoing conclusions in more depth, it is important to know what we mean by "consumerism." Here is a definition:

> *Consumerism is a social movement seeking to augment the rights and powers of buyers in relation to sellers.*

To understand this definition, let us first look at a short list of the many traditional rights of sellers in the U.S. economic system.

> Sellers have the right to introduce any product in any size and style they wish into the marketplace so long as it is not hazardous to personal health or safety; or, if it is, to introduce it with the proper warnings and controls.
> Sellers have the right to price the product at any level they wish provided there is not discrimination among similar classes of buyers.

Sellers have the right to spend any amount of money they wish to promote the product, so long as it is not defined as unfair competition.

Sellers have the right to formulate any message they wish about the product provided that it is not misleading or dishonest in content or execution.

Sellers have the right to introduce any buying incentive schemes they wish.

Subject to a few limitations, these are among the essential core rights of businessmen in the United States. Any radical change in these would make U.S. business a different kind of game.

Now what about the traditional *buyer's rights?* Here, once again, are some of the rights that come immediately to mind.

Buyers have the right not to buy a product that is offered to them.

Buyers have the right to expect the product to be safe.

Buyers have the right to expect the product to turn out to be essentially as represented by the seller.

In looking over these traditional sellers' and buyers' rights, I believe that the balance of power lies with the seller. The notion that the buyer has all the power he needs *because he can refuse to buy* the product is not deemed adequate by consumer advocates. They hold that consumer sovereignty is not enough when the consumer does not have full information and when he is persuasively influenced by Madison Avenue.

What additional rights do consumers want? Behind the many issues stirred up by consumer advocates is a drive for several additional rights. In the order of their serious challenge to sellers' rights, they are:

Buyers want the right to have adequate information about the product.

Buyers want the right to additional protections against questionable products and marketing practices.

Buyers want the right to influence products and marketing practices in directions that will increase the "quality of life."

CONSUMER PROPOSALS

The "right to be informed," proposed by President Kennedy in his March 1962 directive to the Consumer Advisory Council, has been the battleground for a great number of consumer issues. These include, for example, the right to know the true interest cost of a loan (truth-in-lending), the true cost per standard unit of competing brands (unit pricing), the basic ingredients in a

293

product (ingredient labeling), the nutritional quality of foods (nutritional labeling), the freshness of products (open dating), and the prices of gasoline (sign posting rather than pump posting).

Many of these proposals have gained widespread endorsement not only from consumers but also from political leaders and some businessmen. It is hard to deny the desirability of adequate information for making a free market operate vitally and competitively in the interests of consumers.

The proposals related to additional *consumer protection* are several, including the strengthening of consumers' hands in cases of business fraud, requiring of more safety to be designed into automobiles, issuing of greater powers to existing government agencies, and setting up of new agencies.

The argument underlying consumer protection proposals is that consumers do not necessarily have the time and/or skills to obtain, understand, and use all the information that they may get about a product; therefore, some impartial agencies must be established which can perform these tasks with the requisite economies of scale.

The proposals relating to *quality-of-life* considerations include regulating the ingredients that go into certain products (detergents, gasoline) and packaging (soft drink containers), reducing the level of advertising and promotional "noise," and creating consumer representation on company boards to introduce consumer welfare considerations in business decision making.

The argument in this area says that products, packaging, and marketing practices must not only pass the test of being profitable to the company and convenient to the consumer but must also be life-enhancing. Consumerists insist that the world's resources no longer permit their indiscriminate embodiment in any products desired by consumers without further consideration of their social values. This "right" is obviously the most radical of the three additional rights that consumers want, and the one which would constitute the most basic challenge to the sellers' traditional rights.

CONSUMERISM WAS INEVITABLE

Let us now consider in greater depth the first of the five conclusions I cited at the outset of this article—namely, that consumerism was inevitable. Consumerism did not necessarily have to happen in the 1960's, but it had to happen eventually in view of new conditions in the U.S. economy that warranted a fresh examination of the economic power of sellers in relation to buyers.

At the same time, there are very good reasons why consumerism did flare up in the mid-1960's. The phenomenon was not due to any single cause. Consumerism was reborm because all of the conditions that normally combine to produce a successful social movement were present. These conditions are structural conduciveness, structrual strain, growth of a generalized belief, precipitating factors, mobilization for action, and social control.[1] Using these six conditions, I have listed in Exhibit I the major factors under each that contributed to the rise in consumerism.

Exhibit I. *Factors contributing to the rise of consumerism in the 1960s*

1. STRUCTURAL CONDUCIVENESS
    Advancing incomes and education
    Advancing complexity of technology and marketing
    Advancing exploitation of the environment

2. STRUCTURAL STRAINS
    Economic discontent (inflation)
    Social discontent (war and race)
    Ecological discontent (pollution)
    Marketing system discontent (shoddy products, gimmickry,
        dishonesty)
    Political discontent (unresponsive politicians and
        institutions)

3. GROWTH OF A GENERALIZED BELIEF
    Social critic writings (Galbraith, Packard, Carson)
    Consumer-oriented legislators (Kefauver, Douglas)
    Presidential messages
    Consumer organizations

4. PRECIPITATING FACTORS
    Professional agitation (Nader)
    Spontaneous agitation (housewives picketing)

5. MOBILIZATION FOR ACTION
    Mass media coverage
    Vote-seeking politicians
    New consumer interest groups and organizations

6. SOCIAL CONTROL
    Business resistance or indifference
    Legislative resistance or indifference

Structural conduciveness refers to basic developments in the society that eventually create potent contradictions. In the latest consumer movement, three developments are particularly noteworthy.

First, U.S. incomes and educational levels, advanced continuously. This portended that many citizens would eventually become concerned with the quality of their lives, not just their material well-being.

Second, U.S. technology and marketing were becoming increasingly complex. That this would create potent consumer problems was noted perceptively by E.B. Weiss: "Technology has brought unparalleled abundance and opportunity to the consumer. It has also exposed him to new complexities and hazards. It has made his choices more difficult. He cannot be chemist, mechanic, electrician, nutritionist, *and* a walking computer (very necessary when shopping for fractionated-ounce food packages)! Faced with almost infinite product differentiation (plus contrived product virtues that are purely semantic), considerable price differentiation, the added complexities of trading

295

stamps, the subtleties of cents-off deals, and other complications, the shopper is expected to choose wisely under circumstances that baffle professional buyers."[2]

Third, the environment was progressively exploited in the interests of abundance. Observers began to see that an abundance of cars and conveniences would produce a shortage of clean air and water. The Malthusain specter of man running out of sufficient resources to maintain himself became a growing concern.

These developments, along with some others, produced major *structural strains* in the society. The 1960s were a time of great public discontent and frustration. Economic discontent was created by steady inflation which left consumers feeling that their real incomes were deteriorating. Social discontent centered on the sorrowful conditions of the poor, the race issue, and the tremendous costs of the Vietnam war. Ecological discontent arose out of new awarenesses of the world population explosion and the pollution fallout associated with technological progress. Marketing system discontent centered on safety hazards, product breakdowns, commercial noise, and gimmickry. Political discontent reflected the widespread feelings that politicians and government institutions were not serving the people.

Discontent is not enough to bring about change. There must grow a *generalized belief* about the main causes of the social malaise and the potent effectiveness of collective social action. Here, again, certain factors contributed importantly to the growth of a generalized belief.

First, there were the writings of social critics such as John Kenneth Galbraith, Vance Packard, and Rachel Carson, that provided a popular interpretation of the problem and of actionable solutions.

Second, there were the hearings and proposals of a handful of Congressmen such as Senator Estes Kefauver that held out some hope of legislative remedy.

Third, there were the Presidential "consumer" messages of President Kennedy in 1962 and President Johnson in 1966, which legitimated belief and interest in this area of social action.

Finally, old-line consumer testing and educational organizations continued to call public attention to the consumers' interests.

Given the growing collective belief, consumerism only awaited some *precipitating factors* to ignite the highly combustible social material. Two sparks specifically exploded the consumer movement. The one was General Motors' unwitting creation of a hero in Ralph Nader through its attempt to investigate him; Nader's successful attack against General Motors encouraged other organizers to undertake bold acts against the business system. The other was the occurrence of widespread and spontaneous store boycotts by housewives in search of a better deal from supermarkets.

These chance combustions would have vanished without a lasting effect if additional resources were not *mobilized for action*. As it turned out, three factors fueled the consumer movement.

First, the mass media gave front-page coverage and editorial support to the activities of consumer adovcates. They found the issues safe, dramatic, and newsworthy. The media's attention was further amplified through word-of-mouth processes into grass-roots expressions and feelings.

Second, a large number of politicians at the federal, state, and local levels picked up consumerism as a safe, high-potential vote-getting social issue.

Third, a number of existing and new organizations arose in defense of the consumer, including labor unions, consumer cooperatives, credit unions, product testing organizations, consumer education organizations, senior citizen groups, public interest law firms, and government agencies.

Of course, the progress and course of an incipient social movement depends on the reception it receives by those in *social control*, in this case, the industrial-political complex. A proper response by the agents of social control can drain the early movement of its force. But this did not happen. Many members of the business community attacked, resisted, or ignored the consumer advocates in a way that only strengthened the consumerist cause. Most legislative bodies were slow to respond with positive programs, thus feeding charges that the political system was unresponsive to consumer needs and that more direct action was required.

Thus all the requisite conditions were met in the 1960s. Even without some of the structural strains, the cause of consumerism would have eventually emerged because of the increasing complexity of technology and the environmental issue. And the movement has continued to this day, abetted by the unwillingness of important sections of the business and political system to come to terms with the basic issues.

IT WILL BE ENDURING

As we have seen, observers are divided over whether consumerism is a temporary or a permanent social phenomenon: some people argue that the current consumer movement will pass over; others argue that it differs substantially from the two earlier movements. For example, the ecology issue is here to stay and will continue to fuel the consumer movement. The plight of the poor will continue to raise questions about whether the distribution system is performing efficiently in all sectors of the economy. There are more educated and more affluent consumers than ever before, and they are the mainstay of an effective social movement. The continuous outpouring of new products in the economy will continue to raise questions of health, safety, and planned obsolescence. Altogether, the issues that flamed the current consumer movement may be more profound and enduring than in the past.

No one can really predict how long the current consumer movement will last. There is good reason to believe, in fact, that the protest phase of the consumer movement will end soon. The real issue is not how long there will be vocal consumer protest but rather what legacy it will leave regarding the balance of buyers' rights and sellers' rights.

Each of the previous consumer movements left new institutions and laws to function in behalf of the consumer. By this test, the victory already belongs to consumers. Sellers now must operate within the new constraints of a Truth-in-Lending Law, a Truth-in-Packaging Law, an Auto Safety Law, an Office of Consumer Affairs, an Environmental Protection Agency, and a greatly strengthened Federal Trade Commission and Federal Food and Drug Administration.

It is no accident that such laws and institutions come into being when the demonstration and agitation phase of the consumer movement starts to dwindle. It is precisely the enactment of new laws and creation of new institutions that cause the protest phase to decline. Viewed over the span of a century, the consumer movement has been winning and increasing buyers' rights and power. In this sense, the consumerist movement is enduring, whether or not the visible signs of protest are found.

IT CAN BE BENEFICIAL

Businessmen take the point of view that since consumerism imposes costs on them, it will ultimately be costly to the consumer. Since they have to meet more legal requirements, they have to limit or modify some of their methods for attracting customers. This may mean that consumers will not get all the products and benefits they want and may find business costs passed on to them.

Businessmen also argue that they have the consumer's interests at heart and have been serving him well, and that customer satisfaction is the central tenet of their business philosophy. Many sincerely believe that consumerism is politically motivated and economically unsound.

The test of beneficiality, however, lies not in the short-run impact of consumerism on profits and consumer interests but rather in its long-run impact. Neither consumerism nor any social movement can get very far in the absence of combustible social material. Protest movements are messages coming from the social system that say that something is seriously wrong. They are the body politic's warning system. To ignore or attack protest signals is an invitation to deepening social strains. Protest movements are social indicators of new problems which need joint problem solving, not social rhetoric.

The essential legacy of consumerism promises to be beneficial in the long run. It forces businessmen to reexamine their social roles. It challenges them to look at problems which are easy to ignore. It makes them think more about ends as well as means. The habit of thinking about ends has been deficient in U.S. society, and protest movements such as consumerism, minority rights, student rights, and women's rights have a beneficial effect in raising questions about the purposes of institutions before it is too late.

Beyond this philosophical view of the beneficial aspects of protest movements may lie some very practical gains for consumers and businessmen. Here are four arguments advanced by consumerists:

1. Consumerism will increase the amount of product information. This will make it possible for consumers to buy more efficiently. They may

obtain more value or goods with a given expenditure or a given amount of goods with a lower expenditure. To the extent that greater buying efficiency will result in surplus purchasing power, consumers may buy more goods in total.

2. Consumerism will lead to legislation that limits promotional expenditure which primarily affects market shares rather than aggregate demand. Consumer games, trading stamps, and competitive brand advertising in demand-inelastic industries are largely seen as increasing the costs of products to consumers with little compensating benefits. Reductions in the level of these expenditures, particularly where they account for a large portion of total cost, should lead to lower consumer prices.

3. Consumerism will require manufacturers to absorb more of the social costs imposed by their manufacturing operations and product design decisions. Their higher prices will decrease the purchase of high social costs goods. This will mean lower governmental expenditures covered by taxes to clean up the environment. Consumers will benefit from a lower tax rate and/or from a higher quality environment.

4. Consumerism will reduce the number of unsafe or unhealthy products which will result in more satisfied, healthier consumers.

These arguments are as cogent as contrary arguments advanced by some business spokesmen against responding to consumerism. This is not to deny that many companies will inherit short-run costs not compensated by short-run revenues and in this sense be losers. Their opposition to consumerism is understandable. But this is not the basis for developing a sound long-run social policy.

IT IS PROMARKETING

Consumerism has come as a shock to many businessmen because deep in their hearts they believe that they have been serving the consumer extraordinarily well. Do businessmen deserve the treatment that they are getting in the hands of consumerists?

It is possible that the business sector has deluded itself into thinking that it has been serving the consumer well. Although the marketing concept is the professed philosophy of a majority of U.S. companies, perhaps it is more honored in the breach than in the observance. Although top management professes the concept, the line executives, who are rewarded for ringing up sales, may not practice it faithfully.

What is the essence of the marketing concept?

The marketing concept calls for a *customer orientation* backed by *integrated marketing* aimed at generating *customer satisfaction* as the key to attaining long-run profitable volume. The marketing concept was a great step forward in meshing the actions of business with the interests of consumers. It meant that consumer wants and needs became the starting point for product and market planning. It meant that business profits were tied to how well the company succeeded in pleasing and satisfying the customer.

Peter F. Drucker suggested that consumerism is "the shame of the total marketing concept," implying that the concept is not widely implemented.[3] But even if the marketing concept as currently understood were widely implemented, there would be a consumerist movement. Consumerism is a clarion call for a *revised marketing concept*.

The main problem that is coming to light rests on the ambiguity of the term *customer satisfaction*. Most businessmen take this to mean that *consumer desires* should be the orienting focus of product and market planning. The company should produce what the customer wants. But the problem is that in efficiently serving customers' desires, it is possible to hurt their long-run interests. Edmund Burke noted the critical difference when he said to the British electorate, "I serve your interests, not your desires." From the many kinds of products and services that satisfy consumers in the short run but disserve or dissatisfy them in the long run, here are four examples:

1. Large, expensive automobiles please their owners but increase the pollution in the air, the congestion of traffic, and the difficulty of parking, and therefore reduce the owners' long-run satisfaction.
2. The food industry in the United States is oriented toward producing new products which have high taste appeal. Nutrition has tended to be a secondary consideration. Many young people are raised on a diet largely of potato chips, hot dogs, and sweets which satisfy their taste but harm their long-run health.
3. The packaging industry has produced many new convenience features for the American consumer such as nonreusable containers, but the same consumers ultimately pay for this convenience in the form of solid waste pollution.
4. Cigarettes and alcohol are classic products which obviously satisfy consumers but which ultimately hurt them if consumed in any excessive amount.

These examples make the point that catering to consumer satisfaction does not necessarily create satisfied consumers. Businessmen have not worried about this so long as consumers have continued to buy their products. But while consumers buy as *consumers*, they increasingly express their discontent as *voters*. They use the political system to correct the abuses that they cannot resist through the economic system.

The dilemma for the marketer, forced into the open by consumerism, is that he cannot go on giving the consumer only what pleases him without considering the effect on the consumer's and society's well-being. On the other hand, he cannot produce salutary products which the consumer will not buy. The problem is to somehow reconcile company profit, consumer desires, and consumer long-run interests. The original marketing concept has to be broadened to the societal marketing concept:

The societal marketing concept calls for a *customer orientation* backed by *integrated marketing* aimed at generating *customer satisfaction* and *long-run consumer welfare* as the key to attaining long-run profitable volume.

The addition of a long-run consumer welfare asks the businessman to include social and ecological considerations in his product and market planning. He is asked to do this not only to meet his social responsibilities but also because failure to do this may hurt his long-run interests as a producer.

Thus the message of consumerism is not a setback for marketing but rather points to the next stage in the evolution of enlightened marketing. Just as the *sales concept* said that sales were all-important, and the original *marketing concept* said that consumer satisfaction was also important, the *societal marketing concept* has emerged to say that long-run consumer welfare is also important.

IT CAN BE PROFITABLE

This last assessment is the most difficult and yet the most critical of my five conclusions to prove. Obviously, if consumerism is profitable, businessmen will put aside their other objections. It is mainly because of their perceived unprofitability that many businessmen object so vehemently.

Can consumerism be profitable? Here my answer is "yes." Every social movement is a mixed bag of threats and opportunities. As John Gardner observed, "We are all continually faced with a series of great opportunities brilliantly disguised as insoluble problems." The companies that will profit from consumerism are those in the habit of turning negatives into positives. According to Peter F. Drucker:

> Consumerism actually should be, must be, and I hope will be, the opportunity of marketing. This is what we in marketing have been waiting for.[4]

The alert company will see consumerism as a new basis for achieving a differential competitive advantage in the marketplace. A concern for consumer well-being can be turned into a profitable opportunity in at least two ways: through the introduction of needed new products and through the adoption of a companywide consumerist orientation.

NEW OPPORTUNITIES

One of the main effects of consumerism is to raise concerns about the health, safety, and social worthiness of many products. For a long time, *salutary criteria* have been secondary to *immediate satisfaction criteria* in the selection of products and brands. Thus when Ford tried to sell safety as an automobile attribute in the 1950's, buyers did not respond. Most manufacturers took the position that they could not educate the public to want salutary features but if the public showed this concern, then business would respond.

Exhibit II. Classification of New Product Opportunities

immediate satisfaction

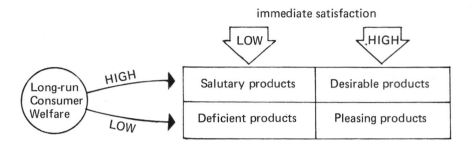

		LOW	HIGH
Long-run Consumer Welfare	HIGH	Salutary products	Desirable products
	LOW	Deficient products	Pleasing products

Unfortunately, the time came but business was slow to respond. Consumer needs and wants have been evolving toward safety, health, and self-actualization concerns without many businessmen noticing this. More and more people are concerned with the nutritiousness of their foods, the flammability of their fabrics, the safety of their automobiles, and the pollution quality of their detergents. Many manufacturers have missed this changing psychological orientation of consumers.

PRODUCT REFORMULATIONS

Today, there are a great many opportunities for creating and marketing new products that meet consumer desires for both short-term satisfaction and long-term benefits.

Exhibit II suggests a paradigm for thinking about the major types of new product opportunities. All current products can be classified in one of four ways using the dimensions of immediate satisfaction and long-run consumer interests. As this exhibit shows, *desirable products* are those which combine high immediate satisfaction and high long-run benefit, such as tasty, nutritious breakfast foods. *Pleasing products* are those which give high immediate satisfaction but which may hurt consumer interests in the long run, such as cigarettes. *Salutary products* are those which have low appeal but which are also higly beneficial to the consumer in the long run, such as low phosphate detergents. Finally, *deficient products* are those which have neither immediate appeal nor salutary qualities, such as bad tasting patent medicine.

The manufacturer might as well forget about deficient products because too much work would be required to build in pleasing and salutary qualities. On the other hand, the manufacturer should invest his greatest effort in developing desirable products—e.g., new foods, textiles, appliances, and building materials—which combine intrinsic appeal and long-run beneficiality. The other two categories, pleasing and salutary products, also present a considerable challenge and opportunity to the company.

The challenge posed by pleasing products is that they sell extremely well but they ultimately hurt the consumer's interests. The product opportunity is therefore to formulate some alteration of the product that adds salutary qualities without diminishing any or too many of the pleasing qualities. This type of product opportunity has already been seized by a number of companies:

> Sears has developed and promoted a phosphate-free laundry detergent which has become a big selling brand.
> American Oil and Mobil Oil have developed and promoted no-lead or low-lead gasolines.
> Pepsi-Cola has developed a one-way plastic soft drink bottle that is degradable in solid waste treatment.
> Various automobile manufacturers are redesigning their engines to reduce their polluting levels without reducing their efficiency.
> Various tobacco firms are researching the use of lettuce leaf to eliminate the health hazards of tobacco leaf in cigarettes.

Not all of these product reformulations will be successful. The new product must incorporate the salutary qualities without sacrificing the pleasing qualities. Thus new low-phosphate detergents must continue to wash effectively, or almost as effectively, as the former high-phosphate detergents. New low-lead or no-lead gasolines must continue to give efficient mileage and performance.

In addition, the company must be skilled at marketing the new products. The company faces difficult questions of what price to set, what claims to make, and what to do with the former product. In the case of low-lead gasoline, initial sales have been disappointing because of several factors, not the least of which is that it was priced at a premium and discouraged all but the most devoted environmentalists from buying it. The environmental appeal is strong, provided that the new product performs about as well as the old·product and is not priced higher.

Salutary products, such as noninflammable draperies and many health foods, are considered "good for the customer" but somehow lack pleasing qualities. The challenge to the marketer is to incorporate satisfying qualities in the product without sacrificing the salutary qualities. Here are examples:

> Quaker Oats has been reviewing desirable nutrients and vitamins, and formulating new breakfast cereals around them.
> Some food manufacturers have created new soybean-based products, in each case adding pleasing flavors that appeal to the intended target groups.
> Fabric manufacturers are trying to create attractive draperies out of new synthetic noninflammable material.

Thus new product opportunities may be found by starting with appealing products and trying to add salutary qualities, or starting with salutary products and trying to add appealing qualities. This will become more important as more people show concern for the environment and demand desirable products.

There is already a sizable market segment made up of environmentalists who are ready to buy any product that has a salutary stamp. The alert company can even specialize in this market by committing itself to creating and assorting products of high environmental appeal.

CONSUMERIST ORIENTATION

A second way to respond profitably to consumerism is to become one of a growing number of companies that adopt and implement a thoroughgoing concern-for-the-consumer attitude. This goes beyond the occasional introduction of a few new products that combine pleasing and salutary qualities. It goes beyond an enlarged public relations campaign to appear as a "we care" company. To be effective, it involves management commitment, employee education, social actions, and company investment. A few companies have moved into a total consumerist orientation and have earned high consumer regard in the process. Here are two illustrative examples:

> Giant Food, Inc., a leading supermarket chain in the Washington, D.C. area, actively introduced unit pricing, open dating, and nutritional labeling. According to a spokesman for the company, "These actions have improved Giant's goodwill immeasurably and have earned the admiration of leaders of the consumer movement."
> Whirlpool Corporation has adopted a large number of measures to improve customer information and services, including a toll-free complaint service and improved product warranties. According to Stephen E. Upton, Whirlpool Vice President, "Our rate of increase in sales has tripled that of the industry. Our interest in the consumer has to be one of the reasons."

Obviously, such companies believe that these measures will increase their consumer goodwill and lead in turn to increased profits. The companies in each industry that adopt a consumerist orientation are likely to earn the early advantage and reap the rewards. If the profits are forthcoming, others will rush in and imitate the innovators. But imitation is often not as effective as innovation. Consumerism may well turn out to be an opportunity for the leaders and a cost for the laggards.

CONCLUSION

Consumerism was born for the third time in this century in the middle 1960s as a result of a complex combination of circumstances, not the least of which was increasingly strained relations between current business practices and long-run consumer interests. To many businessmen, it came as a shock because they thought the economic machinery, creating the highest standard of living in the world, was beyond consumer complaint. But the movement was inevitable, partly because of the success of the economic machinery in creating complex, convenient, and pleasing products.

My assessment is that consumerism will be enduring, beneficial, promarketing, and ultimately profitable. Consumerism mobilizes the energies of consumers, businessmen, and government leaders to seek solutions to several complex problems in a technologically advanced society. One of these is the difference between serving consumer desires efficiently and serving their long-run interests.

To marketers, it says that products and marketing practices must be found which combine short-run and long-run values for the consumer. It says that a societal marketing concept is an advance over the original marketing concept and a basis for earning increased consumer goodwill and profits. The enlightened marketer attempts to satisfy the consumer *and* enhance his total well-being on the theory that what is good in the long run for consumers is good for business.

NOTES

1. These conditions were proposed in Neil J. Smelser, *Theory of Collective Behavior* (New York: The Free Press, 1965).

2. "Marketers Fiddle While Consumers Burn," *Harvard Business Review*, July-August 1968, p. 48.

3. "The Shame of Marketing," *Marketing/Communications*, August 1969, p. 60.

4. Ibid., p. 64.

PART NINE

*

Advertising and Consumerism

INTRODUCTION

Advertising and Consumerism

ADVERTISING HAS been under major attack from consumerists and other groups in society. The basis of the attack has been that advertising distorts, exaggerates, and deceives—that people should have more fact and less fluff. In a unique article, Theodore Levitt argues that embellishment and distortion are among advertising's legitimate and socially desirable purposes. The problem is to differentiate between legitimate distortions and essential falsehoods.

He expands upon the points made by Cohen, Gardner, Craven, and Hills that subjective factors are important determinants of consumer behavior. Levitt says, ". . . the issue is not the prevention of distortion. It is, in the end, to what kinds of distortion we actually want. . . ."

When one thinks of the regulation of advertising, the Federal Trade Commission usually comes to mind. The article by MacGregor is indicative of the new power and thrust of the FTC. Gaylord Jentz points out that the first federal legislation, the Federal Trade Commission Act, "could hardly be called legislation designed to handle the problem of false advertising." Rather the commission's interpretation of Section 5 has extended its scope to the regulation of advertising. Jentz provides an interesting historical perspective on this extension with examples of colorful cases in the development of precedents.

The rather controversial article by Yale Brozen presents the case that the powers of the Federal Trade Commission have been extended to the detriment of business and advertisers. He feels the commission is more concerned with the protection of the consumer than with the preservation of competition. Although he would probably not agree with Levitt's observation that the consumer is an amateur, an impotent midget—and is not king—he does agree with Levitt's analysis of advertising's legitimate functions and the forms it takes.

Brozen feels that many of the claims that the Federal Trade Commission makes against business are unsubstantiated. In particular, he takes issue with the points made in Paul Scanlon's article concerning oligopoly,

308

advertising, and market structures. Scanlon would increase the power of the Federal Trade Commission to the regulation of "oligpoly creating ads." He feels that advertising is a means employed to restrict entry and to increase concentration levels in industries previously competitive.

Jules Backman, in a more traditional analysis, focuses on the allegations of waste, inefficiency, want creation, and distorted information levied against the advertising industry.

34. SKEPTICAL CONSUMERS, TOUGH REGULATORS SPUR A NEW CANDOR IN ADS

James Mac Gregor

BOB DOLOBOWSKY was looking for a gimmick. His ad agency, Warren, Muller, Dolobowsky Inc, landed the account for Stay Dry deodorant last year, and he was worried because "consumers are getting cynical about advertising. They can make fun of commercials, but it's hard to get any other response."

So, says Bob Dolobowsky, "I decided to see what the straight truth would do."

The resulting commercial opens with Mr. Dolobowsky on camera introducing himself. "I'm the president of an ad agency with a client whose product I want you to buy. I think you will, if I simply tell you the truth. It's an antiperspirant with two kinds of drying ingredients, and still it can't keep you dry. No antiperspirant can, not even ours. And that's the truth. The one thing maybe not altogether true is our name, Stay Dry. Probably should be Stay Dry-er—'cause that's what we really help you do. Stay drier. And that's the truth."

If present indications are any guide, you're going to be seeing a lot more ads like that one in coming months. Madison Avenue is under a barrage of critical fire some veteran admen say is heavier than at any time since Vance Packard made "hidden persuaders" a household phrase nearly two decades ago. Consumer advocates are urging, and government agencies are implementing, stiffer regulations of deceptive ads, while studies show consumers increasingly are ignoring or mistrusting much of what advertising is saying.

"OUR LAWYER MADE US PUT THIS IN"

As a result, candor is this season's watchword on Madison Avenue. Grolier Inc., whose encyclopedia salesmen's tactics have drawn regulator's ire, is running ads saying, "After you've said yes to our salesman, you can still say no to the company." Avis Rent-A-Car cutely ends an ad on its policy of always honoring reservations with "P.S. Our lawyers made us put this in," adding that the policy only applies on reservations that Avis has accepted.

Candor, whether substantial or superficial, is only one of the advertising industry's responses to the "truth-in-advertising" crusade. Admen have long preferred to tout their clients and say little of themselves. Now a movement is under way to use advertising itself to improve the industry's credibility quotient; in one such campaign, Time Inc.'s magazines give free space to ad agencies to discuss the industry's strong points.

There's also evidence that advertisers are stepping up efforts to remove controversial ploys from their advertising. Commercials for toys, gasoline and mouthwash, among others, this year appear considerably freer than in years past of strong (and possibly deceptive) claims and gimmicky (and possibly deceptive) techniques of presentation. Several lawyers who specialize in reviewing advertising say their bills to client ad agencies have doubled in the last three years, while a number of copywriters say they're under orders to keep virtually all specific claims out of their work, no matter how strong the supporting evidence appears.

To carry self-policing further, a group of ad industry organizations in September completed formation of the National Advertising Review Board, advertising's first self-regulatory body. It's designed to field and investigate complaints about deceptive ads, and if it can't settle them peacefully it's to take its cases to the public and government regulators.

STIRRING NEGATIVE PUBLICITY

The attackers who have helped provoke these changes are numerous. Consumer advocates ranging from the aggressive Ralph Nader to the cautious Consumers Union have taken to scrutinizing a company's ad claims as well as it products or services; their charges don't always lead to regulatory action, but they can give a company plenty of negative publicity. The Federal Communications Commission, Food and Drug Administration and a host of state and local government agencies are taking increasingly activist stances on advertising; New York City's consumer affairs commissioner, Bess Myerson, for instance, is calling for expansion of broadcasting's "fairness doctrine" to give consumer agencies air time to oppose ads containing allegedly deceptive claims.

In Washington, the Nixon administration's proposal for a consumer protection agency is before Congress. Similar in scope to the existing Environmental Protection Agency, it would bring under one roof many of the government's consumer protection activities. Looming in the wings is the Democrats' effort, a strong "truth-in-advertising" bill sponsored by Sens. Frank Moss and George McGovern; it has been stalled until spring because the Federal Trade Commission thinks its own policies may make the bill unnecessary.

The FTC has, in fact, become the toughest advertising crusader of all.

311

In recent months, it has required most major makers of autos, TV sets, air conditioners and electric razors to furnish lengthy documentation of their ad claims. It has persuaded one advertiser, ITT Continental Baking Co., to devote 25% of its Profile bread advertising for one year to "corrective" ads that specifically point out misconceptions viewers could have gotten from previous ads. The FTC is seeking to apply the penalty to other advertisers as well.

THE ZEREX FIGHT

The FTC isn't infallible. Du Pont Co. and Batten, Barton, Durstine & Osborn Inc. fought FTC charges that ads for Du Pont's Zerex antifreeze were misleading, and last month the FTC withdrew the charges.

But the cumulative effect of governmental attacks—successful or not—has led to a "failure of confidence" that Alex Kroll, executive vice president of Young & Rubicam Inc., says helped produce last summer "some of the worst advertising since World War II. More dull, gray, monotonous, wasteful, flesh-less, derivative advertising than anything in memory." Many admen say the climate isn't much better now.

Proposals for advertising self-regulation have been around for years, but admen say it's no coincidence the National Advertising Review Board was launched just weeks before the FTC began a lengthy round of Washington hearings into advertising practices. "It may not prevent governmental interference," Maxwell Dane, then chairman of the executive committee at Doyle Dane Bernbach Inc., said at the time, "but it will slow it down to the degree that self-regulation seems effective."

How effective can it be? There's some dispute. On the plus side, former U.S. Ambassador Charles Yost and longtime Borden Co. executive William Ewen were named the board's chairman and executive director, giving it credibility outside and inside the ad community. The Council of Better Business Bureaus' national advertising division has been substantially beefed up in manpower and budget for its new duties, which include preliminary substantiation of ad complaints (the complaints it finds valid go to the review board for judgment).

But consumer advocates have frequently charged the Better Business Bureaus with favoritism to big business (a charge the bureaus deny). The 50-man review board itself is liable to charges of conflict of interest, since 40 of its members come from the nation's largest advertisers and ad agencies (the other 10 represent the public). "It's going to be very tricky," says one board member, "sitting in judgment on companies you might want to do business with someday."

This man, like many others, also feels the real challenge to advertising isn't in Washington, but in the shrinking responsiveness of the public to advertising. Survey after survey in recent years has shown the average consumer is steadily becoming less likely to remember any given ad or the product it promotes and more likely to believe it's false just because it's advertising.

One oil company marketing official admits a study of a recent ad campaign found one-third of those who remembered any ad from the campaign associated it with a different brand of gasoline.

ONLY PART OF STORY

Outright deception, ad makers argue, is rare in national advertising, partly because it's bad business, partly because any national ad is heavily screened these days—the agency's lawyers, the client, his lawyers, the network or publisher and its lawyers all review ads. Thus, it's argued, the real deception problem is in local retail ads, which aren't so heavily screened. But others say that's only part of the story.

The last may be the most important. "Television has made advertising so intrusive," says BBD president Tom Dillon, "that its capacity for irritating people is pretty damned great. Print is eclectic; TV is inescapable." Many observers say consumer grumblings about advertising rose sharply a year ago when the TV networks bowed to ad agency urging and reduced their minimum unit of sale to 30 seconds from one minute, effectively doubling the maximum number of ads that can be shoehorned into each TV commercial break. Last fall, some broadcasters began cutting down this "clutter."

Paul C. Harper, chairman of Needham, Harper & Steers, Inc., a major ad agency, attributes the growing skepticism of the buying public to the cumulative impact of professional consumerists, general social unrest, "suspicion of commercial culture among younger segments of the population" and "the sheer volume of advertising, especially in the television area."

"We're an ad agency, not a testing lab," says one agency creative director. "We have to assume the data our clients give us are accurate and that they'll blow the whistle if we misconstrue it. There have been clients who were a little lax in this area, and the FTC's actions recently have given us the club we need to make them document everything. We resigned one small account a while back on just this issue."

In a different sense, Robert J. Keith, chairman and chief executive officer of Pillsbury Co., puts the responsibility for advertising on the manufacturer, specifically its chief executive officer. "The days when a chief executive officer can proclaim personal indignation and promise an investigation into a misleading or dishonest or distasteful advertisement are going fast," he said in a recent speech. "The chief executive officer today must be accountable for the function of advertising" in the same way as in capital appropriations and acquisitions, he said.

Where admen and their regulators don't agree is where the edge of deception lies. Mr. Harper of Needham, Harper & Steers, for instance, makes a distinction between the "gray lie" and "permissible exaggeration." The gray lie, he says, is anything that, while technically true, creates a false impression. Until the recent crackdown on toy ads, clever photography sometimes made tiny toy cars seem veritable Maseratis, big and sleek and speedy. Ecological

313

groups charge some polluters with a similar offense, using indisputable but irrelevant facts to falsely inflate their claims to cleanliness.

DEFENSE OF EXAGGERATION

Gray lies should be exterminated, Mr. Harper says, but he defends "permissible exaggeration," in which something not strictly documentable is used to make an honest, valid point. He cites a recent auto ad in which a small man climbs behind the wheel and seems to grow larger. "Considering the importance of the auto in American life, I think some people do feel just that way," he says.

At FTC hearings on modern ad practices in November, Charles Overholser, research director at Young & Rubicam, called such ads "harmless puffery." But FTC Commissioner Mary Gardiner Jones responded that "there is no such thing as puffery, because if you make a claim, you intend to influence people." Mr. Overholser, who had discussed the intensive research used in making ads, said, "We don't expect metaphors to be believed." Throughout the hearing FTC commissioners maintained that some ad devices are taken more seriously by their audience than their creators intend.

Several ad agency executives say the FTC's hearings have only increased the uncertainty about what will and won't be permissible in future ads, thus increasing the incentive to tone down claims and stress candor. But there's another reason: "Candid" ads seem to work. Mr. Dolobowsky says his Stay Dry deodorant ad hasn't been on the air long enough to see definitive trends, but "we see some signs of the product moving," and he's already planning sequels in the same vein if later reports support his initial impression.

Similarly, there's the enforced candor in the "corrective" ad required of ITT Continental Baking Co. by the FTC. The ad features actress Julia Mead saying "I'd like to clear up any misunderstanding you may have about Profile bread from its advertising or even its name." She goes on to say that Profile won't help anyone lose weight, but that it's a nutritional, all-family bread. A Continental spokesman says future ad plans aren't firm enough to divulge, but ad agency sources say the ad has been well enough received that the company may use it for more than the required 25% of Profile advertising during the period covered by the consent order.

WHAT PEOPLE WANT?

Charles Moss, president of Wells, Rich, Green Inc., thinks anyone who's changing advertising because of the "truth-in-advertising" crusade probably wasn't doing good ads anyway. "I have to laugh at some of the stories I read about the conflict (between advertisers and government). Really, they are in the same business—giving people what they want."

Mr. Moss singles out Wells-Rich's current American Motors "guaranteed car" campaign as an example of giving people what they want. "Other (auto) companies advertise service, but it's the guarantee which makes the ad meaningful to people."

To explain the idea of the guarantee, Wells Rich found it necessary to use 90-second TV commercials instead of 30-second spots, and other admen say the increased demand for documentation and explanation of claims will require longer ads generally, helping to solve the TV clutter problem. Larry Goodman, vice president of the American Newspaper Publishers Association's Bureau of Advertising, is also bullish about the trend's effect on his medium. "We're going to see a continual growth of informational ads," he says, which "can best be run in newspapers."

Mr. Dillon of BBD, though, is worried about how much information will be in the advertising of the future. "The great danger is that truth in advertising will take refuge in utter vacuity," he says. "I have to tell you I see some signs that this is happening already."

If the worst Mr. Dillon feared were to happen, adman Curtis Wright would be ready. Tongue planted firmly in cheek, Mr. Wright, the president of Rock, Bergthold & Wright of San Jose, Calif., has prepared an all-purpose "ad of the future" that, he says, "simply eliminates everything that's ever been attacked in advertising."

The ad consists of a large gray square with the words "For Sale" beneath. Nothing else.

35. THE MORALITY (?) OF ADVERTISING

Theodore Levitt

THIS YEAR Americans will consume about $20 billion of advertising, and very little of it because we want it. Wherever we turn, advertising will be forcibly thrust on us in an intrusive orgy of abrasive sound and sight, all to induce us to do something we might not ordinarily do, or to induce us to do it differently. This massive and persistent effort crams increasingly more commercial noise into the same, few, strained 24 hours of the day. It has provoked a reaction as predictable as it was inevitable: a lot of people want the noise stopped, or at least alleviated.

And they want it cleaned up and corrected. As more and more products have entered the battle for the consumer's fleeting dollar, advertising has increased in boldness and volume. Last year, industry offered the nation's supermarkets about 100 new products a week, equal, on an annualized basis, to the total number already on their shelves. Where so much must be sold so hard, it is not surprising that advertisers have pressed the limits of our credulity and generated complaints about their exaggerations and deceptions.

Only classified ads, the work of rank amateurs, do we presume to contain solid, unembellished fact. We suspect all the rest of systematic and egregious distortion, if not often of outright mendacity.

The attack on advertising comes from all sectors. Indeed, recent studies show that the people most agitated by advertising are precisely those in the higher income brackets whose affluence is generated by the industries that create the ads.[1] While these studies show that only a modest group of people are preoccupied with advertising's constant presence in our lives, they also show that distortion and deception are what bother people most.

This discontent has encouraged Senator Philip Hart and Senator Proxmire to sponsor consumer protection and truth-in-advertising legislation. People, they say, want less fluff and more fact about the things they buy. They want description, not distortion, and they want some relief from the constant, grating, vulgar noise.

Legislation seems appropriate because the natural action of competition does not seem to work, or, at least, not very well. Competition may ultimately flush out and destroy falsehood and shoddiness, but "ultimately" is too long for the deceived—not just the deceived who are poor, ignorant, and dispossessed, but also all the rest of us who work hard for our money and can seldom judge expertly the truth of conflicting claims about products and services.

The consumer is an amateur, after all; the producer is an expert. In the commercial arena, the consumer is an impotent midget. He is certainly not king. The producer is a powerful giant. It is an uneven match. In this setting, the purifying powers of competition helps the consumer very little—especially in the short run, when his money is spent and gone, from the weak hands into the strong hands. Nor does competition among the sellers solve the "noise" problem. The more they compete, the worse the din of advertising.

A BROAD VIEWPOINT REQUIRED

Most people spend their money carefully. Understandably, they look out for larcenous attempts to separate them from it. Few men in business will deny the right, perhaps even the wisdom, of people today asking for some restraint on advertising, or at least for more accurate information on the things they buy and for more consumer protection.

Yet, if we speak in the same breath about consumer protection and about advertising's distortions, exaggerations, and deceptions, it is easy to confuse two quite separate things—the legitimate purpose of advertising and the abuses to which it may be put. Rather than deny that distortion and exaggeration exist in advertising, in this article I shall argue that embellishment and distortion are among advertising's legitimate and socially desirable purposes; and that illegitimacy in advertising consists only of falsification with larcenous intent. And while it is difficult, as a practical matter, to draw the line between legitimate distortion and essential falsehood, I want to take a long look at the distinction that exists between the two. This I shall say in advance—the distinction is not as simple, obvious, or great as one might think.

The issue of truth versus falsehood, in advertising or in anything else, is complex and fugitive. It must be pursued in a philosophic mood that might seem foreign to the businessman. Yet the issue at base is more philosophic than it is pragmatic. Anyone seriously concerned with the moral problems of a commercial society cannot avoid this fact. I hope the reader will bear with me—I believe he will find it helpful, and perhaps even refreshing.

WHAT IS REALITY?

What, indeed? Consider poetry. Like advertising, poetry's purpose is to influence an audience, to affect its perceptions and sensibilities; perhaps even to change its mind. Like rhetoric, poetry's intent is to convince and seduce. In the service of that intent, it employs without guilt or fear of criticism all the arcane tools of distortion that the literary mind can devise. Keats does not offer a truthful engineering description of his Grecian urn. He offers,

317

instead, with exquisite attention to the effects of meter, rhyme, allusion, illusion, metaphor, and sound, a lyrical, exaggerated, distorted, and palpably false description. And he is thoroughly applauded for it, as are all other artists, in whatever medium, who do precisely this same thing successfully.

Commerce, it can be said without apology, takes essentially the same liberties with reality and literality as the artist, except that commerce calls its creations advertising, or industrial design, or packaging. As with art, the purpose is to influence the audience by creating illusions, symbols, and implications that promise more than pure functionality. Once, when asked what his company did, Charles Revson of Revlon, Inc. suggested a profound distinction: "In the factory we make cosmetics; in the store we sell hope." He obviously has no illusions. It is not cosmetic chemicals women want, but the seductive charm promised by the alluring symbols with which these chemicals have been surrounded—hence the rich and exotic packages in which they are sold, and the suggestive advertising with which they are promoted.

Commerce usually embellishes its products thrice: first, it designs the product to be pleasing to the eye, to suggest reliability, and so forth; second, it packages the product as attractively as it feasibly can; and then it advertises this attractive package with inviting pictures, slogans, descriptions, songs, and so on. The package and design are as important as the advertising.

The Grecian vessel, for example, was used to carry liquids, but that function does not explain why the potter decorated it with graceful lines and elegant drawings in black and red. A woman's compact carries refined talc, but this does not explain why manufacturers try to make these boxes into works of decorative art.

Neither the poet nor the ad man celebrates the literal functionality of what he produces. Instead, each celebrates a deep and complex emotion which he symbolizes by creative embellishment—a content which cannot be captured by literal description alone. Communication, through advertising or through poetry or any other medium, is a creative conceptualization that implies a vicarious experience through a language of symbolic substitutes. Communication can never be the real thing it talks about. Therefore, all communication is in some inevitable fashion a departure from reality.

EVERYTHING IS CHANGED. . .

Poets, novelists, playwrights, composers, and fashion designers have one thing more in common. They all deal in symbolic communication. None is satisfied with nature in the raw, as it was on the day of creation. None is satisfied to tell it exactly "like it is" to the naked eye, as do the classified ads. It is the purpose of all art to alter nature's surface reality, to reshape, to embellish, and to augment what nature has so crudely fashioned, and then to present it to the same applauding humanity that so eagerly buys Revson's exotically advertised cosmetics.

Few, if any, of us accept the natural state in which God created us. We scrupulously select our clothes to suit a multiplicity of simultaneous purposes, not only for warmth, but manifestly for such other purposes as propriety, status, and seduction. Women modify, embellish, and amplify themselves with colored paste for the lips and powders and lotions for the face; men as well as women use devices to take hair off the face and others to put it on the head. Like the inhabitants of isolated African regions, where not a single whiff of advertising has ever intruded, we all encrust ourselves with rings, pendants, bracelets, neckties, clips, chains, and snaps.

Man lives neither in sackcloth nor in sod huts—although these are not notably inferior to tight clothes and overheated dwellings in congested and polluted cities. Everywhere man rejects nature's uneven blessing. He molds and repackages to his own civilizing specifications an otherwise crude, drab, and generally oppressive reality. He does it so that life may be made for the moment more tolerable than God evidently designed it to be. As T.S. Eliot once remarked, "Human kind cannot bear very much reality."

. . . INTO SOMETHING RICH AND STRANGE

No line of life is exempt. All the popes of history have countenanced the costly architecture of St. Peter's Basilica and its extravagant interior decoration. All around the globe, nothing typifies man's materialism so much as the temples in which he preaches asceticism. Men of the cloth have not been persuaded that the poetic self-denial of Christ or Buddha—both men of sackcloth and sandals—is enough to inspire, elevate, and hold their flocks together. To simplify the temple in men's eyes, they have, very realistically, systematically sanctioned the embellishment of the houses of the gods with the same kind of luxurious design and expensive decoration that Detroit puts into a Cadillac.

One does not need a doctorate in social anthropology to see that the purposeful transmutation of nature's primeval state occupies all people in all cultures and all societies at all stages of development. Everybody everywhere wants to modify, transform, embellish, enrich, and reconstruct the world around him—to introduce into an otherwise harsh or bland existence some sort of purposeful and distorting alleviation. Civilization is man's attempt to transcend his ancient animality, and this includes both art and advertising.

. . . AND MORE THAN 'REAL'

But civilized man will undoubtedly deny that either the innovative artist or the *grande dame* with *chic* "distorts reality." Instead, he will say that artist and woman merely embellish, enhance, and illuminate. To be sure, he will mean something quite different by these three terms when he applies them to fine art, on the one hand, and to more secular efforts, on the other.

But this distinction is little more than an affectation. As man has civilized himself and developed his sensibilities, he has invented a great variety of subtle distinctions between things that are objectively indistinct. Let us take a closer

319

look at the difference between man's "sacred" distortions and his "secular" ones.

The man of sensibility will probably canonize the artist's deeds as superior creations by ascribing to them an almost cosmic virtue and significance. As a cultivated individual, he will almost certainly refuse to recognize any constructive, cosmic virtues in the production of the advertisers, and he is likely to admit the charge that advertising uniformly deceives us by analogous techniques. But how "sensible" is he?

AND BY SIMILAR MEANS . . .

Let us assume for the moment that there is no objective, operational difference between the embellishments and distortions of the artist and those of the ad man—that both men are more concerned with creating images and feelings than with rendering objective, representational, and informational descriptions. The greater virtue of the artist's work must then derive from some subjective element. What is it?

It will be said that art has a higher value for man because it has a higher purpose. True, the artist is interested in philosophic truth or wisdom, and the ad man in selling his goods and services. Michelangelo, when he designed the Sistine chapel ceiling, had some concern with the inspirational elevation of man's spirit, whereas Edward Levy, who designs cosmetics packages, is interested primarily in creating images to help separate the unwary consumer from his loose change.

But this explanation of the difference between the value of art and the value of advertising is not helpful at all. For is the presence of a "Higher" purpose all that redeeming?

Perhaps not; perhaps the reverse is closer to the truth. While the ad man and designer seek only to convert the audience to their commercial customs, Michelangelo sought to convert its soul. Which is the greater blasphemy? Who commits the greater affront to life—he who dabbles with man's erotic appetites, or he who meddles with man's soul? Which act is the easier to judge and justify?

. . . FOR DIFFERENT ENDS

How much sense does it really make to distinguish between similar means on the grounds that the ends to which they are directed are different—"good" for art and "not so good" for advertising? The distinction produces zero progress in the argument at hand. How willing are we to employ the involuted ethics whereby the ends justify the means?

Apparently, on this subject, lots of people are very willing indeed. The business executive seems to share with the minister, the painter, and the poet the doctrine that the ends justify the means. The difference is that the businessman is justifying the very commercial ends that his critics oppose. While his critics justify the embellishments of art and literature for what these do for man's spirit, the businessman justifies the embellishment of industrial design and advertising for what they do for man's purse.

Taxing the imagination to the limit, the businessman spins casuistic webs of elaborate transparency to the self-righteous effect that promotion and advertising are socially benign because they expand the economy, create jobs, and raise living standards. Technically, he will always be free to argue, and he *will* argue, that his ends become the means to the ends of the musician, poet, painter, and minister. The argument which justifies means in terms of ends is obviously not without its subtleties and intricacies.

The executive and the artist are equally tempted to identify and articulate a higher rationale for their work than their work itself. But only in the improved human consequences of their efforts do they find vindication. The aesthete's ringing declaration of "art for art's sake," with all its self-conscious affirmation of selflessness, sounds hollow in the end, even to himself; for, finally, every communication addresses itself to an audience. Thus art is very understandably in constant need of justification by the evidence of its beneficial and divinely approved effect on its audience.

THE AUDIENCE'S DEMANDS

This compulsion to rationalize even art is a highly instructive fact. It tells one a great deal about art's purposes and the purposes of all other communication. As I have said, the poet and the artist each seek in some special way to produce an emotion or assert a truth not otherwise apparent. But it is only in communion with their audiences that the effectiveness of their efforts can be tested and truth revealed. It may be academic whether a tree falling in the forest makes a noise. It is *not* academic whether a sonnet or a painting has merit. Only an audience can decide that.

The creative person can justify his work only in terms of another person's response to it. Ezra Pound, to be sure, thought that ". . . in the (greatest) works the live part is the part which the artist has put there to please himself, and the dead part is the part he has put there . . . because he thinks he *ought* to—i.e., either to get or keep an audience." This is certainly consistent with our notions of Pound as perhaps the purest of twentieth-century advocates of art for art's sake.

But if we review the record of his life, we find that Pound spent the greater part of his energies seeking suitable places for deserving poets to publish. Why? Because art has little merit standing alone in unseen and unheard isolation. Merit is not inherent in art. It is conferred by an audience.

The same is true of advertising: if it fails to persuade the audience that the product will fulfill the function the audience expects, the advertising has no merit.

Where have we arrived? Only at some common characteristics of art and advertising. Both are rhetorical, and both literally false; both expound an emotional reality deeper than the "real"; both pretend to "higher" purposes,

321

although different ones; and the excellence of each is judged by its effect on its audience—its persuasiveness, in short. I do not mean to imply that the two are fundamentally the same, but rather that they both represent a pervasive, and I believe *universal*, characteristic of human nature—the human audience *demands* symbolic interpretation in everything it sees and knows. If it doesn't get it, it will return a verdict of "no interest."

To get a clearer idea of the relation between the symbols of advertising and the products they glorify, something more must be said about the fiat the consumer gives to industry to "distort" its messages.

SYMBOL AND SUBSTANCE

As we have seen, man seeks to transcend nature in the raw everywhere. Everywhere, and at all times, he has been attracted by the poetic imagery of some sort of art, literature, music, and mysticism. He obviously wants and needs the promises, the imagery, and the symbols of the poet and the priest. He refuses to live a life of primitive barbarism or sterile functionalism.

Consider a sardine can filled with scented powder. Even if the U.S. Bureau of Standards were to certify that the contents of this package are identical with the product sold in a beautiful paisley-printed container, it would not sell. The Boston matron, for example, who has built herself a deserved reputation for pinching every penny until it hurts, would unhesitatingly turn it down. While she may deny it, in self-assured and neatly cadenced accents, she obviously desires and needs the promises, imagery, and symbols produced by hyperbolic advertisements, elaborate packages, and fetching fashions.

The need for embellishment is not confined to personal appearance. A few years ago, an electronics laboratory offered a $700 testing device for sale. The company ordered two different front panels to be designed, one by the engineers who developed the equipment and one by professional industrial designers. When the two models were shown to a sample of laboratory directors with Ph.D.'s, the professional design attracted twice the purchase intentions than the engineeer's design did. Obviously, the laboratory director who has been baptized into science at M.I.T. is quite as responsive to the blandishments of packaging as the Boston matron.

And, obviously, both these customers define the products they buy in much more sophisticated terms than the engineer in the factory. For a woman, dusting powder in a sardine can is not the same product as the identical dusting powder in an exotic paisley package. For the laboratory director, the test equipment behind an engineer-designed panel just isn't as "good" as the identical equipment in a box designed with finesse.

FORM FOLLOWS THE IDEAL FUNCTION

The consumer refuses to settle for pure operating functionality. "Form follows function" is a resoundingly vacuous cliché which, like all clichés, depends for its memorability more on its alliteration brevity than on its wisdom. If it has any truth, it is only in the elastic sense that function extends beyond strict mechanical use into the domain of imagination. We do not choose to buy a particular product, we choose to buy the functional expectations that we attach to it, and we buy these expectations as "tools" to help us solve a problem of life.

Under normal circumstances, furthermore, we must judge a product's "nonmechanical" utilities before we actually buy it. It is rare that we choose an object after we have experienced it, nearly always we must make the choice before the fact. We choose on the basis of promises, not experiences.

Whatever symbols convey and *sustain* these promises in our minds are therefore truly functional. The promises and images which imaginative ads and sculptured packages induce in us are as much the product as the physical materials themselves. To put this another way, these ads and packagings describe the product's fullness for us: in our minds, the product becomes a complex abstraction which is, as Immanuel Kant might have said, the conception of a perfection which has not yet been experienced.

But all promises and images, almost by their very nature, exceed their capacity to live up to themselves. As every eager lover has ever known, the consummation seldom equals the promises which produced the chase. To forestall and suppress the visceral expectation of disappointment that life has taught us must inevitably come, we use art, architecture, literature, and the rest, and advertising as well, to shield ourselves, in advance of experience, from the stark and plain reality in which we are fated to live. I agree that we wish for unobtainable unrealities, "dream castles." But why promise ourselves reality, which we already possess? What we want is what we do *not* possess!

Everyone in the world is trying in his special personal fashion to solve a primal problem of life—the problem of rising above his own negligibility, of escaping from nature's confining, hostile, and unpredictable reality, of finding significance, security, and comfort in the things he must do to survive. Many of the so-called distortions of advertising, product design, and packaging may be viewed as a paradigm of the many responses that man makes to the conditions of survival in the environment. Without distortion, embellishment, and elaboration, life would be drab, dull, anguished, and at its existential worst.

SYMBOLISM USEFUL AND NECESSARY

With*out* symbolism, furthermore, life would be even more confusing and anxiety-ridden than it is *with* it. The foot soldier must be able to recognize the general, good or bad, because the general is clothed with power. A general without his stars and suite of aides-de-camp to set him apart from the privates would suffer in authority and credibility as much as the perfume packaged by Dracula or a computer designed by Rube Goldberg. Any ordinary soldier or civilian who has ever had the uncommon experience of being in the same shower with a general can testify from the visible unease of the latter how much clothes "make the man."

Similarly, verbal symbols help to make the product—they help us deal with the uncertainties of daily life. "You can be sure . . . if it's Westinghouse" is a decision rule as useful to the man buying a turbine generator as to the man buying an electric shaver. To label all the devices and embellishments companies employ to reassure the prospective customer about a product's quality with the pejorative term "gimmick," as critics tend to do, is simply silly. Worse, it denies against massive evidence, man's honest needs and values. If religion must be architectured, packaged, lyricized, and musicized to attract and hold its audience, and if sex must be perfumed, powdered, sprayed, and shaped in order to command attention, it is ridiculous to deny the legitimacy of more modest, and similar, embellishments to the world of commerce.

But still, the critics may say, commercial communications tend to be aggressively deceptive. Perhaps, and perhaps not. The issue at stake here is more complex than the outraged critic believes. Man wants and needs the elevation of the spirit produced by attractive surroundings, by handsome packages, and by imaginative promises. He needs the assurances projected by well-known brand names, and the reliability suggested by salesmen who have been taught to dress by Oleg Cassini and to speak by Dale Carnegie. Of course, there are blatant, tasteless, and willfully deceiving salesmen and advertisers, just as there are blatant, tasteless, and willfully deceiving artists, preachers, and even professors. But, before talking blithely about deception, it is helpful to make a distinction between things and descriptions of things.

THE QUESTION OF DECEIT

Poetic descriptions of things make no pretense of being the things themselves. Nor do advertisements, even by the most elastic standards. Advertisements are the symbols of man's aspirations. They are not the real things, nor are they intended to be, nor are they accepted as such by the public. A study some years ago by the Center for Research in Marketing, Inc. concluded that deep down inside the consumer understands this perfectly well and has the attitude that an advertisement is an ad, not a factual news story.

Even Professor Galbraith grants the point when he says that ". . . because modern man is exposed to a large volume of information of varying degrees of unreliability . . . he establishes a system of discounts which he applies to various sources almost without thought. . . . The discount becomes nearly total for all forms of advertising. The merest child watching television dismisses the health and status-giving claims of a breakfast cereal as a 'commercial.' "[2]

This is not to say, of course, that Galbraith also discounts advertising's effectiveness. Quite the opposite: "Failure to win belief does not impair the effectiveness of the management of demand for consumer products. Management involves the creation of a compelling image of the product in the mind of the consumer. To this he responds more or less automatically under circumstances where the purchase does not merit a great deal of thought. For building this image, palpable fantasy may be more valuable than circumstantial evidence."[3]

Linguists and other communications specialists will agree with the conclusion of the Center for Research in Marketing that "advertising is a symbol system existing in a world of symbols. Its reality depends upon the fact that it is a symbol . . . the content of an ad can never be real, it can only say something about reality, or create a relationship between itself and an individual which has an effect on the reality life of an individual."[4]

CONSUMER, KNOW THYSELF!

Consumption is man's most constant activity. It is well that he understands himself as a consumer.

The objective of consumption is to solve a problem. Even consumption that is viewed as the creation of an opportunity—like going to medical school or taking a singles-only Caribbean tour—has as its purpose the solving of a problem. At a minimum, the medical student seeks to solve the problem of how to lead a relevant and comfortable life, and the lady on the tour seeks to solve the problem of spinsterhood.

The "purpose" of the product is not what the engineer explicitly says it is, but what the consumer implicitly demands that it shall be. Thus the consumer consumes not things, but expected benefits—not cosmetics, but the satisfactions of the allurements they promise; not quarter-inch drills, but quarter-inch holes; not stock in companies, but capital gains; not numerically controlled milling machines, but trouble-free and accurately smooth metal parts; not low-cal whipped cream, but self-rewarding indulgence combined with sophisticated convenience.

The significance of these distinctions is anything but trivial. Nobody knows this better, for example, than the creators of automobile ads. It is not the generic virtues that they tout, but more likely the car's capacity to enhance its user's status and his access to female prey.

Whether we are aware of it or not, we in effect expect and demand that advertising create these symbols for us to show us what life *might* be, to bring the possibilities that we cannot see before our eyes and screen out the stark reality in which we must live. We insist, as Gilbert put it, that there be added a "touch of artistic verisimilitude to an otherwise bald and unconvincing narrative."

UNDERSTANDING THE DIFFERENCE

In a world where so many things are either commonplace or standardized, it makes no sense to refer to the rest as false, fraudulent, frivolous, or immaterial. The world works according to the aspirations and needs of its actors, not according to the arcane or moralizing logic of detached critics who pine for another age—an age which, in any case, seems different from today's largely because its observers are no longer children shielded by protective parents from life's implacable harshness.

To understand this is not to condone much of the vulgarity, purposeful duplicity, and scheming half-truths we see in advertising, promotion, packaging, and product design. But before we condemn, it is well to understand the difference between embellishment and duplicity and how extraordinarily uncommon the latter is in our times. The noisy visibility of promotion in our intensely communicating times need not be thoughtlessly equated with malevolence.

Thus the issue is not the prevention of distortion. It is, in the end, to know what kinds of distortions we actually want so that each of our lives is, without apology, duplicity, or rancor, made bearable. This does not mean we must accept out of hand all the commercial propaganda to which we are each day so constantly exposed, or that we must accept out of hand the equation that effluence is the price of affluence, or the simple notion that business cannot and government should not try to alter and improve the position of the consumer vis-á-vis the producer. It takes a special kind of perversity to continue any longer our shameful failure to mount vigorous, meaningful programs to protect the consumer, to standardize product grades, labels, and packages, to improve the consumer's information-getting process, and to mitigate the vulgarity and oppressiveness that is in so much of our advertising.

But the consumer suffers from an old dilemma. He wants, "truth," but he also wants and needs the alleviating imagery and tantalizing promises of the advertiser and designer.

Business is caught in the middle. There is hardly a company that would not go down in ruin if it refused to provide fluff, because nobody will buy pure functionality. Yet, if it uses too much fluff and little else, business invites possibly ruinous legislation. The problem therefore is to find a middle way. And in this search, business can do a great deal more than it has been either accustomed or willing to do:

It can exert pressure to make sure that no single industry "finds reasons" why it should be exempt from legislative restrictions that are reasonable and popular.

It can work constructively with government to develop reasonable standards and effective sanctions that will assure a more amenable commercial environment.

It can support legislation to provide the consumer with the information he needs to make easy comparison between products, packages, and prices.

It can support and help draft improved legislation on quality stabilization.

It can support legislation that gives consumers easy access to strong legal remedies where justified.

It can support programs to make local legal aid easily available, especially to the poor and undereducated who know so little about their rights and how to assert them.

Finally, it can support efforts to moderate and clean up the advertising noise that dulls our senses and assaults our sensibilities.

It will not be the end of the world or of capitalism for business to sacrifice a few commercial freedoms so that we may more easily enjoy our own humanity. Business can and should, for its own good, work energetically to achieve this end. But it is also well to remember the limits of what is possible. Paradise wasnot a free-goods society. The forbidden fruit was gotten at a price.

NOTES

1. *See* Raymond A. Bauer and Stephen A. Greyser, *Advertising in America: The Consumer View* (Boston: Division of Research, Harvard Business School, 1968); *see also* Gary A. Steiner, *The People Look at Television* (New York: Knopf, 1963).
2. John Kenneth Galbraith, *The New Industrial State* (Boston: Houghton Mifflin, 1967), pp. 325-326.
3. Ibid, p. 326.
4. Ibid., p. 326.

36. FEDERAL REGULATION OF ADVERTISING

Gaylord A. Jentz

ONE OF the most important and fundamental functions vital to the American economy is the mass distribution of goods. The complexities which surround this function have continued to increase as the sale and distribution have become more impersonal and competitive. Within this framework there has developed by all forms of mass communication media an unparalleled dissemination of a variety of information with which the manufacturer, processor, and seller in competition with each other have attempted to influence and affect the consumer's choice of products.

The producer with his technological know-how and engineering skill has found that the ability to produce a product in mass quantities is not his major problem. It is the consumer who decides by his selection what goods will be produced and in what quantities. Therefore the producer's life may well depend upon his getting the consumer acquainted with his product and how effective his persuasion is on the consumer to buy it.

Because of the pressure of competition, the vast means of media available to reach the consumer, and the gullible character of this consumer, truth in advertising, labeling, and packaging became a problem. The mere fact that the expression of words themselves blend so well to half-truths, implications, and double meaning invariably leads to various forms of deception which have as its prey the consumer. The majority of producers, and groups, whose specific trade is advertising (international groups as well), have embraced the concept of truth in advertising. The temptation, however, of a few to gain an advantage and the seemingly endless borderline cases in which one may or may not be engaged in deception have made self-regulation salutary, but obviously not effective in affording maximum protection to the consumer. The need for governmental regulation, particularly on the Federal level, became obvious. It is within the purview of this article to explore only a small segment of the deceptive practices in advertising under Federal regulation, with the full knowledge that on the State and Federal levels advertising is one of the most highly regulated activities in our nation.

Reprinted with permission from *American Business Law Journal*, Vol. 6 (January 1968), pp. 409-427, published by the American Business Law Association.

HISTORY OF FEDERAL REGULATION OF ADVERTISING

The first Federal legislation proposed could hardly be called legislation designed to handle the problem of false advertising. The initial proponents of early legislation were looking for the development of a Federal agency to bolster up the Sherman Act and help procure effective enforcement of these anti-trust laws. In 1914, under the rigorous support of President Wilson, the Federal Trade Commission Act was passed.

The section of this Act which was of major importance was Section 5 which had the following prohibition: "Unfair methods of competition in commerce are hereby declared unlawful."

There is little doubt that the Commissioners themselves felt uneasy about the possible interpretation of their powers. By 1916, however, the Commissioners decided to extend their interpretation of the Act to false advertising and issued their first complaints against false advertising of selling mercerized cotton as "Sewing Silk," cotton goods as "Sun Fast Silks," and cotton thread as "Circle Cilk" and "Embroidery Floss." The first Supreme Court case upholding a cease and desist order against deceptive practices resulting in competitive injury came in 1922. This case involved the manufacturer selling underwear and other knit goods made partly of wool but largely of cotton, labeled as "natural merino," "natural worsted," or "natural wool." The Federal Trade Commission's cease and desist order was upheld. The labeling was held to be misleading to the public and an unfair method of competition as against manufacturers of like garments made of wool and cotton who branded their products truthfully.

In 1931, the Federal Trade Commission was faced with the issue of whether its jurisdiction extended to deceptive advertising which simply deceived the public but which had no adverse effect on *competition*. The case involved a manufacturer of an "obesity cure," through whose publications in newspapers, labels, and other printed matter indicated through scientific research a method of removing excess flesh of the human body in a safe and effective manner without danger to the health of the user. The Commission issued a cease and desist order and the decision was appealed. The Supreme Court held that jurisdiction of the Commission was dependent on three distinct prerequisites:

(1) Methods complained of are unfair.
(2) They are methods of competition in commerce.
(3) A proceeding by the Commission to prevent the use of the method appears to be in the interest of the public.

The Court, in ruling against the Commission's decision, could not find any present or potential competition to have been injured or threatened by the unfair methods complained of.

To some this was felt as a set-back for the Commission but as Weston writing in 24 Fed. B.J. 548, 550-551 (1964) stated, "But in retrospect this decision proves to be a blessing in disguise because it did not seriously hand-

329

icap the FTC and it helped to furnish the stimulus for a major expansion of the Commission's jurisdiction in the Wheeler-Lea Amendment of 1938.''

The Wheeler-Lea Amendment changed Section 5 of the Federal Trade Commission Act to read ''Unfair methods of competition in commerce and unfair or deceptive acts or practices in commerce are hereby declared unlawful.'' The additional words alone gave the Commission authority to protect consumers against deceptive advertising without having to go through the disguise of protecting competitors. This interpretation was clearly brought out in a 1941 case. The case involved the deceptive use of the trade-name ''Remington'' for radio receiving sets. The Court held in referring to the Wheeler-Lea Amendment:

> The failure to mention competition in the later phrase shows a legislative intent to remove the procedural requirement set up in the Raladam case and the Commission can now center its attention on the direct protection of the consumer where formerly it could protect him only indirectly through the protection of the competitor.

The Wheeler-Lea Amendment did more however. It brought false advertisements of food, drugs, medical and veterinary devices, or cosmetics within the meaning of Section 5 of the Federal Trade Commission Act, and generally enlarged the effectiveness of the Commission's decisions. For example, once a Commission order under Section 5 became final, a continued violation would allow a suit in a Federal district court with a civil penalty not to exceed more than $5,000 for each violation. Additional remedies were provided for dissemination of false advertisements of food, drugs, medical and veterinary devices, and cosmetics, such as the use of a temporary injunction pending final determination by the Commission. Criminal proceedings could be brought as a misdemeanor where the product was injurious to the health of the consumer or where there was an intent to defraud or mislead. Through the FTC's own policy statements, the use of these latter remedies have been seldom used but still appear effective deterrents.

In 1939, the Commission's powers were again enlarged with the passage of the Wool Products Labeling Act. Although the FTC already had the power and authority to control false advertising of wool products sold in interstate commerce, the Act extended this authority to include ''informative labeling.'' The percentage of wool and other fibers, disclosure of use of reprocessed or reused wool, and registration number of the manufacturer, among others, were required to appear on the label. The label was required to be on the product until sold to the consumer. The Act was modeled in part after the Food, Drug, and Cosmetic Act and appears to have been effectively used by the Commission.

In 1950, Congress once again enlarged the powers of the FTC. In amending the Federal Trade Commission Act, it was provided that advertisements of oleomargarine or margarine shall be deemed misleading if such advertisment represents that such in any form of fashion is a dairy product. The Amendment also gave the Commission greater penalty power by providing that any violation of a final cease and desist order, *each day* would be considered a separate violation and the offender could be charged not more than $5,000 for each violation. As the Commission continued to gain more enforcement power, the courts also have placed on them more responsibility in the clearness of their order to avoid undue harshness in application of such penalites.

Since 1950, Congress has enacted numerous pieces of legislation designed to regulate false advertising, deceptive labeling, misbranding and deceptive packaging. In 1951, after obvious Commission success with the Wool Products Act, Congress enacted the Fur Products Labeling Act. The Act, as would be expected, closely followed the Wool Products Act as prohibiting false advertising plus requiring informative labeling such as the name of the animal that produced the fur as set forth in the Fur Products Name Guide. This Act provided the Commission with authority to provide guidelines to the fur industry, and set forth the first of a number of Acts calling for "informative advertising." Such advertising is deemed deceptive unless the advertising *includes* required information provided under the Act.

Closely following the passage of this legislation came the Flammable Fabrics Act of 1953, after considerable concern by Congress of serious injuries and death caused by igniting of highly inflammable wearing apparel. The Commission was given authority to establish standards of flammability of fabrics of wearing apparel and to prohibit the manufacture or sale of such that did not meet these standards. Although the standards have been amended, the use and enforcement by the Commission have been a substantial gain for the safety of the consumer.

In 1958, Congress again enacted legislation covering a specialized product area called the Textile Fiber Products Identification Act. This Act is one of the most comprehensive product acts ever written and covers prohibition against false advertising, as well as "informative labeling" *and* "informative advertising."

Congress continues to be active in its efforts to regulate the advertising and labeling of products. Two of their most recent efforts are found in the Cigarette Labeling and Advertising Act of 1965 and the Fair Packaging and Labeling Act of 1966. The labeling requirement of cigarettes has received a great deal of publicity and the requirement on each package, "Caution: Cigarette Smoking May Be Hazardous to Your Health," has been the subject of wide discussion. What is interesting is that no statement relating to smoking and health (informative advertising) is required in the advertising of any cigarettes whose packages contain the above label. The FTC is reponsible for the regulation of this Act but this in no way effects their original authority under the Federal Trade Commission Act as amended over false or deceptive cigarette advertising.

The Fair Packaging and Labeling Act, is not designed as an advertising regulation, but indirectly is effective as such. Labeling and packaging are as much a part of advertising as the direct persuasive use of television, radio, magazines, newspapers, and other forms of mass media. The purpose of this Act is "informative labeling and packaging," referred to as "Truth in Packaging." The Act sets up standards of informing the buying public as to the identity of the commodity, who manufactured or processed such, and sets standards of measurement of net quantities within the package. Any violation comes within Section 5 of the Federal Trade Commission Act as amended.

Perhaps one of the most important functions of the Federal Trade Commission in the controlling of unfair competition in advertising has been its authority to establish industry and general guidelines and regulations within which advertisements must fall. Examples of the above are "Guides Against Deceptive Pricing" and "Tire Advertising and Labeling Guides." Another function of the Commission gaining in popularity is the use of business advisory opinions which has proven effective in combating deceptive advertising practices before they reach the consumer.

The history of Federal regulation in advertising is still far from complete and there awaits in the wings more legislation and controls over the use of words as a means of unfair competition and deception to the consumer.

PATTERNS OF DECEPTION

What is deceptive and what is not deceptive, false, or misleading advertising is not easy to define or determine. The very general broad language of the statutes themselves give flexibility to the Commission to establish guidelines and standards in their determination of what advertising is permissible and that which is not.

The basic rules which have been developed over the years by the Commission which govern all advertising are as follows:

(1) Proof of actual deception is not an essential prerequisite for the Commission to act, only the tendency to mislead or deceive.

(2) Knowledge of falsity and intent by an advertiser is immaterial as the businessmen acts at his own peril.

(3) Deception standards are based upon what would be deceiving to the public, which includes the ignorant, the unthinking and credulous. Whether one or more may not be mislead is not the issue as the Act is designed to protect the consumer and he comes with all sorts of degrees of understanding and intelligence. A phrase used by Judge Augustus Hand in the *General Motors* case and repeated by Judge Pope in the *Stauffer* case sums up this test as:

If the Commission . . . thinks it best to insist upon a form of advertising clear enough so that, in the words of the prophet Isaiah, "wayfaring men, though fools, shall not err therein," it is not for the courts to revise its judgment.

(4) Even the truth may be misleading. Sometimes each segment of the advertisement taken separately may be true, but when the whole is viewed, the advertisement may be misleading. This can also be true when certain factors are omitted as well as the method within which the parts are put together.

(5) It is possible for the same advertisements to convey two meanings. Where such is the case if one such meaning would be false, misleading, or deceptive to the public, the advertisement is prohibited.

It is easy to see that these tests overlap each other and even with guidelines the Commission would have difficulty in applying these to all factual situations. The ingenuity of the advertising business in an atmosphere of strong competition is enough to test how close one can come to the edge of deception without dropping into the crevice.

Deception takes many forms. Among these are deceptive pricing, deception by nondisclosure, deceptive use of product or brand name simulation, deceptive disparagement of a competitor's products, deceptive testimonials or sponsorships, deceptive use of the word guarantee, deceptive representations of composition—character—or source of the product, and deceptive TV mock-ups. For each form numerous cases and rulings can be cited in determining when such an advertisement is deceptive. Time and space only permit a cursory glance at the latter two.

AREAS OF DECEPTION

Numerous cases have been investigated and violations found where there were representations of a product containing certain ingredients, having a certain quality or composition, or coming from a certain origin. Many of these representations were completely false; many however deceive by inference.

COMPOSITION DECEPTION

Deception through false advertising or labeling of the composition of a product has been strictly interpreted by the FTC. The problem becomes most difficult when it is the "brand name" of the product which proves to be the deception in relation to the actual composition of the product. The Commission's attitude is that full disclosure *possibly may* remove the deception and thus the producer may preserve the use of the brand name. The courts have attempted to uphold the findings of the Commission as conclusive if supported at all by the evidence, but also hold that complete excision of a trade name should never be ordered if a less drastic means will accomplish the same result. Thus the conflict becomes apparent.

An excellent illustration of this plight is found in the *Elliot Knitwear Case*. This case involved a label on sweaters containing the trade name "Cashmora." On this label in large script-like letters was also a designation of fiber content —"30% Angora—70% Lambs Wool." The sweaters contained no cashmere and the FTC held that the name "Cashmora" was thus deceptive *per se* and issued a cease and desist order from using the trade name above.

The FTC relied heavily on a number of prior decisions, particularly those in which the courts have held qualifying words are really contradictions and only tend to confuse the public. For example a product was labeled "California White Pine," when in fact the product was yellow pine. The Supreme Court upheld the FTC complete excision of the word "White" because a qualifying phrase such as "not made of white pine" would be completely contradictory. Another example involved goods sold by the Army & Navy Trading Company when in fact few of the items sold in the store were army and navy goods. The court held that the qualifying phrase "we do not deal in army and navy goods" would have been contradictory and confused the public.

The petitioners countered that the Commission had also held that qualifications would cure deception. Two cases were cited as being directly in point. The first is a Commission case involving the use of the trade name "Kashmoor" which contained no cashmere in it. The Commission itself stated:

> If the trade name were "Cashmere" itself, the absolute excision would appear to be inescapable. A complete contradiction of terms such as "Cashmere contains no cashmere" would not clarify the meaning, but would only tend to confuse. However, this is not true of the phrase "Kashmoor—contains no cashmere." While the trade name Kashmoor is a simulation of cashmere and while its use falsely implies a cashmere content in the garments so labeled, it is subject to clarification. An explanation that the garment so labeled is designed to imitate cashmere in appearance and softness, but does not contain any cashmere fibers, is not a flat contradiction of terms, but is a reasonable explanation which would recover the capacity and tendency toward deception inherent in the trade name Kashmoor used alone.

The second case relied on involved a fabric coat labeled "Alpacuna" which contained 50% alpaca, 20% mohair, and 30% wool *but* not vicuna. The Commission ordered the label completely excised. The Supreme Court reversed the Commission, upon learning that the petitioner's labels now read "Alpacuna Coat—contains no vicuna" and specified the fiber of the cloth, stating that nothing should prohibit the use of the trade name if in immediate conjunction there appears clearly a designation of the material of the fibers contained therein.

In reviewing these arguments the court relied heavily upon these last two decisions in holding that excision of the trade name was inappropriate as there was no basis for applying the contradiction doctrine to Cashmora. The court did leave open for the Commission the possible remedy of requiring the petitioner (if he wished to keep this trade name) of adding the phrase to the label—"contains no cashmere." Allowance for qualification to avoid deception is not new.

CHARACTER DECEPTION

Character deception, for our purposes, is misrepresentation or deceptive suggestions of what a product will do when such claims are in fact untrue. The closeness of the question of deception of composition and the variety of claims made, make this area a very broad one with numerous cases and decisions rendered. Since most of these cases follow a similar pattern, only a few are needed for illustrative purposes.

Two cases decided within two years of each other deal with claims of low calorie bread. One involved a bread called "Lite Diet" in which a typical advertisement would read "Who'd believe it could help you control your weight? So try it . . . Lite Diet . . . Lite Diet. . . ." The other case involved national advertisements of a bread called "Hollywood" bread. These advertisements often contained a picture of a beautiful motion picture star, in some instances in a "slender full length pose." The advertisements contained a picture of a loaf of bread bearing the label "Hollywood" and accompanied by such words as "reducing diets," "figure-wise mothers," "dieting," "panther slim," "tigress trim," "stay slender" and others. Practically all advertisements contained a legend stating there are "only about 46 calories in an 18 gram slice" of Hollywood bread. The Commission held that in both cases the inference was definitely that the eating of this bread would reduce weight because of lower calorie content. The truth showed that as compared to other bread, there was no basic difference in calorie content for the entire loaf, but the "Hollywood" and "Lite Diet" breads were cut into thinner slices. Thus, although it was true per slice there was a lower calorie content, the facts taken as a whole would be misleading as to the reduction of weight.

Another case involved the use of the trade-name "Goldtone Studios, Inc." and the advertising of "oil colored portraits," etc. It was discovered that the petitioner was in fact referring to "tinted" photographs as the "oil colored portraits" and was not engaged in using a goldtone process in its photographic reproduction process. The Court upheld the Commission's cease and desist order including the use of the tradename as having a tendency to deceive the public.

A more recent case dealt with a swimming aid device called "Swim-Ezy." The advertisements indicated that through its use the swimmer could become an expert or champion swimmer, and it would prevent the user from sinking. The facts showed some users did sink and when used the user would not look like a champion. The Court upheld the Commission's order.

Lastly, there are the cases that deceive the public into believing a product will measure up to a certain performance for a certain period of time, when in fact the performance will not last that long. A typical case involved "Continental Six Month Floor Wax," which by name and advertisement indicated that the wax would be an effective home floor covering for a period of six months. The evidence showed that the wax protection would not last that long and the Court upheld the Commission's order.

DECEPTION AS TO SOURCE OR ORIGIN

Another variety of similar deception deals with misleading the consumer as to where the product was manufactured or produced. There is always a certain intrigue and a definite selling point when the consumer believes a product is foreign made or has come from a location well known for its particular product. Again most cases of this nature follow a similar pattern.

335

To illustrate, one of the most frequently cited cases deals with boxes of cigars labeled as "Havana Counts." The Commission ruled that the use of the word "Havana" with tobacco products had acquired a special and significant meaning in that at least in part the cigar contained tobacco grown in Cuba. These cigars were made in the United States entirely of domestic grown tobacco. The Court upheld the Commission's ruling. A very similar case is found in which the Commission, upheld by the Court, prohibited the use of words "Grand Rapids" of a furniture manufacturing company, when in fact the furniture was not manufactured in Grand Rapids, Michigan.

Sometimes the Commission requires the source of origin to be stated to avoid deception. In a classic case, the FTC was concerned with labeling and advertising of wood from the Philippine Islands as "mahogany" when in fact such wood was not in the mahogany family. The Commission ruling that using the term "Philippine mahogany" was not deceptive was upheld by the Court.

Occasionally a source of origin acquires a secondary meaning which may be more important than the place of origin itself. A recent case deals with the manufacture and sale of hats under labels and advertisements as "Genuine Milan," "Genuine Imported Milan," and "Genuine Milan, Imported Handblocked." The problem arose in that the hats were not made from "wheat straw" from Italy but were made from Philippine hemp. In the testimony that followed, the word Milan was found to have perhaps two secondary meanings, i.e., hats made out of "wheat straw" (which was far more important as to where such wheat straw was grown), and perhaps connotates even a distinctive weave or braid, which would be more important than either where the product was grown or what it was made out of. Based on these possible interpretations, which could render the use of the name Milan as being non-deceptive, the Court returned the case to the Commission for further findings.

The troublesome problem of secondary meaning is not new to the Commission or the Courts. In 1929 the Court upheld a Commission's cease and desist order of prohibiting the Lighthouse Rug Company from using the word "lighthouse" and depicting a facsimile of the symbol of the Chicago Lighthouse for the Blind. The Court held that the word "lighthouse" had acquired a secondary meaning in a substantial part of the trade, i.e. the rugs were made by the blind in charitable or quasi charitable institutions called lighthouses.

DECEPTIVE TELEVISION DEMONSTRATIONS

In the 1950's, the TV industry blossomed into one of the leading entertainment industries in our nation. With it came new dimensions in the use of movement, voice, and eventually color which all were not found in any other media of advertising. The continued popularity of TV and the dimensions available in reaching a mass audience were naturals for the advertising industry. The ingenuity and imagination available in TV advertising soon brought a series of cases and FTC decisions involving the use of deceptive TV advertising demonstrations.

The use of props and mock-ups as a means of TV demonstrations became a commonplace technique and often a necessity to simulate a real object. This has led to some inherent problems as pointed out in the *Carter Products, Inc.* case of 1963 by Circuit Judge Wisdom.

Everyone knows that on TV all that glistens is not gold. On a black and white screen, white looks grey and blue looks white: the lily must be painted. Coffee looks like mud. Real ice cream melts much more quickly than the firm but fake sundae. The plain fact is, except by props and mock-ups some objects cannot be shown on television as the viewer, in his mind's eye, knows the essence of the objects.

The technical limitations of television, driving product manufacturers to the substitution of a mock-up for the genuine article, if they wish to use what they may regard as perhaps their most effective advertising medium, often has resulted in a collision between truth and salesmanship. "What is truth?" has been asked before. On television truth is relative. Assuming that collisions between truth and salesmanship are avoidable, i.e., that mock-ups are not illegal per se, the basic problem this case presents is: What standards should the Federal Trade Commission and courts work out for television commercials so that advertisers will appear to be telling the truth, consistently with Section 5 of the Federal Trade Commission Act prohibiting unfair advertising practices.

There has been little hesitancy on the part of the Commission or the Courts to strike down mock-ups or props which create false and deceptive facts concerning the performance, quality, or comparative tests of the product. For example, the Commission prohibited the manufacturers of the household detergent "Lestoil" from showing a bottle of "Lestoil" near a burning candle or atop a stove as illustrating its non-combustible qualities, when in fact it possessed a very low flash point. The Commission prohibited the Colgate-Palmolive Company from using their "invisible shield" commercial. This commercial consisted of a transparent glass shield prop, against which a coconut, tennis ball, and the like were thrown with the announcer standing behind it. The object bounced off the shield without reaching the announcer. The Commission held that the advertising of Colgate Dental Cream with Gardol gave the false visual innuendo that decay cannot get to the teeth if brushed with this dentrifice. The Commission also prohibited TV commercials of a toy set called "Giant Blue & Grey Battle Set" which pictorially showed the set included numerous trees and other scenery, components that produced smoke, and toy cannons that fired projectiles which exploded. The problem was that only three miniature trees were in the set and numerous other scenery illustrated did not come with the set. Also, there were no components that produced smoke nor did the toy cannon fire projectiles that exploded.

Other illustrations are the Commission's consent order against the manufacturers of "Blue Bonnet" oleomargarine to cease representing falsely on

TV that moisture drops called "Flavor Gems" (actually magnified drops of a non-volatile liquid for the demonstration) caused Blue Bonnet oleomargarine to taste more like butter than competitive margarines. Another decision involved the use of a boxing glove on which the announcer (Bud Palmer) stroked a competitor's razor across the boxing glove cutting it, but when he repeated it with a "Schick" razor the glove was not cut. The Commission issued a consent order to cease this commercial as purporting to prove that the "Schick" razor was safer than other competitive razors and disparaging the competitors' razors by misrepresenting the harmful consequences of their use.

There are always those cases which involve, through props and mock-ups, deception by distortion of comparative results. One such decision involved a demonstration on TV involving the virtues of "New Super-Strength Alcoa Wrap." The demonstration showed two hams side by side, one wrapped in ordinary aluminum wrap, and the other in the Alcoa Product. The ordinary foil was shown battered and torn with the ham dried out. The "New Super-Strength" foil was not torn and the ham was fresh. The Commission in issuing its order found that the ordinary wrap was deliberately torn and that although a number of hams were purchased and aged the same period of time, the ham which appeared most fresh was then wrapped in the Alcoa foil while the one most dried out was then wrapped in the ordinary foil. Another example of distortion through comparative tests was the attempt by the Mennen Company to show the superiority of the consistency of "Mennen Sof' Stroke" over other competing brands. To show this, a skin diver with a heavy beard dived into six to eight feet of water. While underwater, he demonstrated how competing aerosol shaving creams rapidly dissipated in his hand before being applied to his beard. He then discharged the "Mennen Sof' Stroke" into his cupped hand, applied it to his face and began to shave. The Commission in issuing its order found that the demonstration was not a valid portrayal of the superiority of "Mennen Sof' Stroke" over competing brands because the diver cupped his hand at a sharp angle when using one shaving cream and not the other facilitating the result. Also, the so-called "Sof' Stroke" applied to the diver's beard was actually a mixture of shaving cream and tooth paste.

The crux of the problem came to a head in a classic case decision in 1963. Involved was a television commercial in which "Palmolive Rapid Shave" cream was applied to a piece of plexiglass covered with sand, which the announcer referred to as "sandpaper." The petitioner claimed that the mock-up was necessary because of the inherent difficulties of television in that real sandpaper cannot be distinguished from smooth colored paper. The actor after placing the shaving cream on the mock-up, in one stroke cleaned off the area path of the razor. The commercial continued claiming that "Rapid Shave" would shave the heaviest beards. The Commission held that even fine sandpaper could not be shaved immediately, and that coarse paper could not be shaved until "moisturized" for an hour, thus holding a clear misrepresentation through use of the demonstration. The Commission issued an order which in its initial and later stages was considered very broad as excluding the further undisclosed use of mock-ups. The Court of Appeals, First Circuit, felt that the order was in fact declaring the use of any prop or mock-up deceptive *per se* and in an opinion filled full of analogies entered a judgment setting aside the order of the Commission.

The Supreme Court granted a writ of certiorari and upheld the Commission's order that the mock-up was deceptive. The Court held that it was a material deceptive practice to convey to television viewers the false impression that they are seeing an actual test, experiment, or demonstration which proves a product's claims when they are not because of the undisclosed use of mock-ups. The Court did not conclude that the use of all props and mock-ups was deceptive. In distinguishing between a mashed potato prop as ice cream and the present case the Court held:

> In the ice cream case the mashed potato prop is not being used for additional proof of the product claim, while the purpose of the Rapid Shave commercial is to give the viewer objective proof of the claims made. If in the ice cream hypothetical, the focus of the commercial becomes the undisclosed potato prop and the viewer is invited, explicitly or by implication, to see for himself the truth of the claims about the ice cream's rich texture and full color, and perhaps compare it to a "rival product," then the commercial has become similar to the one now before us. Clearly, however, a commercial which depicts happy actors delightedly eating ice cream that in fact is mashed potatoes or drinking a product appearing to be coffee but which is in fact some other substance is not covered by the present order. ·

The conflict over the use of mock-ups and props is far from over. The *Carter Products, Inc.* case, from which Judge Wisdom stated the problem, involved a TV commercial comparing the virtues of "Rise" as a shaving cream that "Stays Moist and Creamy," while showing that the ordinary lather dried out. The only problem was the "ordinary lather" used in the commercial was not a lather but a mock-up consisting of 90% water and a foaming agent. The mock-up did not contain any soaps or fatty acid salts, which ingredients keep the shaving cream from breaking down. There was no doubt this mock-up was deceptive. A similar decision was reached involving TV commercials to show the superiority of Libbey-Owens-Ford safety glass used in all windows of GM cars over safety glass used in the side and rear windows of non-GM cars. The Commission found that the glass used in the side and rear windows of GM cars was not the same quality as used in the windshields and that in the use of undisclosed mock-ups and props, there was deception by use of different camera lenses, taking a photo through an open window when the viewer would believe it was taken through glass, and even the use of streaks of vaseline to add to the distortion.

These are only a few of the decisions involving TV demonstrations. One truth which seems inescapable is that the use of mock-ups and props will be carefully scrutinized by the Federal Trade Commission.

CONCLUSION

The bulk of Federal regulation of advertising is controlled by the FTC. In 1966, a 1,145 man staff with a budget of approximately thirteen and a half million dollars was needed to cover all of its activities. The complaints involving deceptive practices against consumers were up 45% from 1965. In 1965, 897,609 advertisements in TV, radio, and newspapers and other media were examined of which 34,107 were set aside for further examination.

Statistics do not necessarily tell the complete story, but the power and authority of the FTC over advertising is continually having its effect. The extent of their power and the discretion of their decisions has been the subject of wide discussion and numerous articles. One of the most extensive treatises recently written on deceptive advertising is found in the 1967 March *Harvard Law Review*. The need for Federal regulation in advertising to avoid deception is beyond question. One course is evident, the competitive need for advertising and the ingenuity of the advertising industry will always be an interesting match for any Federal regulation imposed upon it.

37. IN DEFENSE OF ADVERTISING
Yale Brozen

TODAY WE find advertising under attack from many quarters. Many in the life political, whether they be elected or appointed officials, Federal, state or local, are scrambling not merely to be responsive to the attack but to seize the vanguard banners for their own.

Seizing the "vanguard banners for their own" certainly appears true of the FTC. In the words of the commission chairman, Miles Kirkpatrick: "The little old lady of Pennsylvania Avenue [the FTC] has taken off her tennis shoes and has put on cleats."

Prime target of the cleats, it appears, is the face of advertising.

Kirkpatrick has put dozens of ad cases into the hopper, using "novel and imaginative" legal twists that test and broaden FTC's powers. The definition of deceptive claims in advertising has been broadened. Savage penalties have beeninstituted for doing what was previously legal and not regarded as deceptive.

The FTC has come up with the technique of unilaterally deciding what is deceptive, conducting a trial by press release, and demanding that the advertiser run ads admitting the deception. The burden of proving innocence is left to the advertiser, if he can survive the trial by accusation and publicity—a complete turnabout from our judicial system in which an accused is regarded as innocent until *proved* guilty.

We've seen this madness in action. The FTC ferrets out what it perceives as an abuse. Then, with no warning, it levels a barrage of publicity—without, I should add, the substantiation it requires of advertisers.

The victim, reeling from consumer reaction to the attack, scrambles to hold together what is left of the product loyalty and good name he earned in the marketplace. Whatever his counteraction to the FTC's one-sided, *unproven* charges, the advertiser is on the ropes in that product area. What if the FTC was wrong in its charges? No matter! The attitude is that some innocents must be sacrificed to the common good of consumerism.

You remember the FTC's charges against Zerex advertising? The company was publicly maligned for using what FTC charged were deceptive illustrations of the product stopping a leak from a punctured can of Zerex. How many

Reprinted from a lecture presented at the University of Detroit, February 17, 1972, supported by a grant from Earhart Foundation.

sales do you suppose were lost as a result of the FTC's attack on this manufacturer?

Well, you all know the latest chapter in that story. In mid-November the FTC withdrew its charges. It admitted that the ads in question were *not* deceptive. Shades of the Salem witch trials! By what kind of standard have we in this free society allowed the creation and celebration of Star Chamber proceedings? And the company can't even sue for damages. The FTC bears no responsibility for its irresponsible behavior.

Add to this the FTC's "scarlet letter" punishment proposal or so-called corrective advertising which calls for allocating one-fourth of each ad to a public admission of having sinned. The situation is taking on a decidely surrealistic quality.

Now, this is not to say that nothing should be done about misleading or deceitful advertising. Some form of control must be exercised to protect the public and to maintain the usefulness and value of advertising.* Nor is this to say that there are not those who deliberately abuse the advertising medium. But simplistic and sensational rough-housing is not an appropriate remedy. The FTC's clumsy approach to this situation is an example of the cure being more deadly than the disease. That is, unless the motivation is, as some have suggested, not to effect a cure, but to justify its existence. If so, then the FTC is acting wisely in its own interest but not, I contend, in your interest or my interest.

In the past year, the FTC has issued almost a dozen "proposed orders" calling for "corrective advertising." One of the most alarming—because of its broad implication—and one that jolted the advertising industry out of its casual attitude toward these attacks was the recent complaint against Continental Baking ads for Wonder Bread.

Here is the commission's line of reasoning in this particular case. The FTC claimed that by emphasizing Wonder Bread's nutritive value, the company is *implying* its product is unique when, in fact, other enriched loaves have the same nutritive value. The FTC has not claimed that the ads are false. It has not claimed that they misrepresent the product. They simply say that what was claimed was not unique.

For a quarter of a century Wonder Bread has been advertising the nutritional qualities of the product. Suddenly, the FTC is demanding discontinuance of this advertising and the running of "scarlet letter" ads and commercials confessing to sins which were not sins before the FTC's charges. Was Wonder Bread sinning by telling the truth about its product?

In this one formulation, the FTC has raised a pervasive question with respect to future use of product claims. The essence of its allegation is that

---

*One of the main reasons for preventing the appearance and continuance of false or misleading advertising is that all advertising comes under suspicion because of the sins of a few. With all advertising under suspicion—with the public protecting itself by discounting the claims made in every advertisement—this efficient means for conveying information loses its efficiency. Socially valuable expenditures on advertising are not made and some products cannot achieve the success they should achieve.

when you advertise particular aspects of your product, you are *per se* implying that these aspects are unique to your product. So we find the Federal Trade Commission insisting that an advertiser provide no information concerning his product if some other products have the same virtues. Only if he proclaims that other products also do what his does can he advertise the virtues of his product.

There will be a number of consequences to the consumer if this stand is allowed to prevail.

If an advertiser must proclaim that the virtues of his brand are also obtainable from several other brands . . . in other words, if he must say "Wonder Bread Helps Build Strong Bodies 12 Ways and so does Tastee" . . . the effect of his advertising on his sales will be dissipated. He will actually be devoting his ad budget to selling competitive products. I don't think advertisers will do it.

Instead, I think advertisers will reduce the information content of advertising. They will do this in order to avoid the necessity of proclaiming that other brands have similar virtues and in order not to risk being caught in another sudden re-interpretation of advertising game rules.

Furthermore, insofar as the efficiency of advertising in producing sales is lessened, there will be less advertising provided. In either event, consumers will receive less information upon which to base purchase judgments. This means that they must either get information from other sources, which will cost more than the present accessibility through ads and commercials, or make buying decisions on a less informed basis and thus increase the risk of making the wrong decision. All of this will mean an increase in costs to consumers.

The "implied uniqueness" theory is just one of the concepts the FTC is acting on. In its attempt to fill the role of *the* consumer-interest agency in Washington, the FTC is changing regulations and penalties at an unprecedented clip.

We've already reviewed what happened in the FTC's complaint against a DuPont product, Zerex anti-freeze. But did you know that the Commission threatened to remove the product from the market! In other words, kill a product dead. For an agency that is supposed to help keep the market competitive, stopping competition seems to be a very peculiar action.

Another concept being promulgated by the FTC is what has come to be known as "full-disclosure." Whatever that means. Responsible advertisers and ad agencies, of course, do not oppose the proposition that the consumer should be made aware of pertinent facts to assist him in buying a product. The problem is (1) arriving at a definition of what is pertinent and (2) not flooding the consumer with so much information he cannot sift out what is relevant.[1] If we require so much information that ads are not read or become extremely costly, advertising will cease. That is how state pharmacy boards have prevented the advertising of prices of pharmaceuticals by retailers in some states.

Under this "full disclosure" concept, one petitioner—Students Against Misleading Enterprises—suggests the FTC require advertising and labeling of all chemically identical products to carry the disclosure that all products in that field are chemically identical. Initial targets here, presumably, are aspirin and liquid chlorine bleach.

Advertising Age recently offered a few examples of what ad copy could come to under present FTC persecution: "Only Fina Gasoline in all the world is spelled F-I-N-A." "Only Bayer Aspirin comes in the Bayer Aspirin package." Mrs. Baird's Bread is baked fresh—almost every day." "The money you borrow from First National Bank is made by the U.S. Government, for the most part."

How about this? Announcer: "You know and we know that all aspirins are the same and are the acetate of salicyclic acid. We are sorry if we made you believe otherwise but do go to your drugstore and see if you don't think we have the prettiest package."

Now to put a twist on the absurdity of the proposed FTC regulations, Columbia University researchers have found that chemically identical products do not have identical pharmacological effects. Tests on digitalis, a drug used in the treatment of heart disease, were made on lots produced by three different manufacturers. The chemical potency of the three different brands was identical, but the pills produced by one manufacturer had seven times the pharmacological effectiveness of the pills produced by another. Doctors are mystified by the dissimilarity in results from different brands because they can find no chemical or manufacturing process difference among the brands that explains the difference.

Research at Abbott Laboratories has found that there are differences in the pharmacological effects of different brands of aspirin despite their chemical similarity. The Food and Drug Administration has reported differences in the bio-effectiveness of different brands of chloromycetin, but it cannot find any explanation of these differences. A manufacturer who is forced by the FTC to tell consumers that his brand of product is identical with that of other manufacturers because it is chemically similar may thereby be forced to misrepresent his product and those of his competitors and mislead consumers.

The FTC is now calling on advertisers, industry by industry, to file with it documentary proof of all claims. Perhaps the FTC should be forced to substantiate its claims before issuing press releases which greatly mislead consumers. I have already told you about the misleading claims it made about Zerex advertising. It has also made misleading claims about its own virtues in asking for appropriations from Congress.

When the FTC made appropriation requests to Congress for fiscal 1971 and 1972, it released a barrage of publicity about how it could reduce the price of ready-to-eat cereals by 25% by its efforts if it obtained the appropriations it requested. It told the news media that advertising by the industry cost 20% of retail sales (see memorandum of Rufus E. Wilson, dated May 15, 1969). In its budget justification material sent to Congress, it was a bit more discreet, claiming that "advertising expenditures as a percent of sales increased from 4.6% in 1954 to 18.3% in 1966." (Hearings, pt. 6 at 134, 1971.) If the Federal Trade Commission staff had bothered to check the data instead of guessing, they would have found that advertising expenditures for cereals had declined from 11.3% in 1954 to 10.9% in 1970. They would have found that they never exceeded 15.1% in the entire period from 1954 to 1970 much less rising to a high of 18.3% or 20% as claimed. The Federal Trade Commission would be hard put to it to substantiate the claims it has made to Congress and to the public.

Further, their statement that the retail price of cereals would be or could be 25% less if Kellogg, General Mills, and General Foods were broken up cannot be substantiated. One member of the Federal Trade Commission staff told the UPI that "if the cereal business became more competitive, say like the produce section of grocery stores, the consumer might save 25% or at least 15%." (*Detroit Free Press*, June 21, 1971.) According to this FTC staff member, retail markups on cereal are high because major manufacturers suggest retail prices to grocers giving the grocer a markup of 20%.

All I can say is that this is a remarkable display of ignorance which no one could possibly substantiate—not even the FTC. The facts are that the average retail margin on cereals is 14.1% (*Chain Store Age*, July, 1971, p. 62), not 20%. Second, if the cereals carried the kind of markups that prevail in the produce section of groceries, the price would have to go up. The average margin on produce is twice that on cereals—31.0% on produce versus 14.1% on cereals.

Third, if cereals were not advertised, they would be more costly to produce and would carry higher markups—not lower margins at retail—contrary to the FTC's contentions. Ready-to-eat cereals had marked seasonal swings in their consumption prior to the advent of television advertising. December–January consumption rates were little more than half June–July consumption (12.7% of annual consumption in December–January, 21.0% in June–July 1940). With the advent of television advertising, December–January consumption is now only 16% below June–July consumption instead of 40% below. The saving in costs resulting from the smoothing of the consumption pattern by advertising has contributed to keeping the price of cereals low.

Fourth, if cereals were not advertised, the distribution and selling costs to manufacturers would be much higher. Major cookie and cracker companies averaged only 2.2% of sales spent on advertising in 1964 in contrast to 14.9% spent by cereal companies. (*National Commission on Food Marketing*, p. 147.) (See Table 1.) Did this reduce the wholesale cost of cookies and crackers as compared to cereals? The National Commission on Food Marketing found that it did not. In the absence of advertising, cookie companies were forced to spend 19.7% of sales on other selling and physical distribution costs while cereal companies spent only 7.7% of sales on these costs.

Cookie companies provide store-door delivery service, check shelves for out-of-stock items, and help stock store shelves. Cereal companies have found that the increased consumer demand resulting from advertising has caused retailers to correct their "out-of-stocks" themselves. This made it possible for cereal companies to eliminate personal selling and panel truck service to store door, which had been common to the industry prior to 1950, with a considerable saving in cost. Advertising in the cereal industry has been a means enabling the cereal companies to economize on other costs—not simply an addition to cost which was passed on to the buyer.

TABLE 1

CEREAL INDUSTRY AND CRACKER-COOKIE INDUSTRY ADVERTISING AND TOTAL SELLING EXPENSE AS PERCENT OF SALES BY SIZE GROUPS, 1964

	Breakfast Cereals	Crackers and Cookies
	Advertising	
Largest 4 firms	14.9	2.2
Next 4 firms	17.7	0.1
Balance*	19.8	1.0
	Total Selling Expense	
Largest 4 firms	28.0	27.1
Next 4 firms	34.1	23.3
Balance*	40.0	17.6

*Five firms in cereal industry, 12 firms in cracker industry.

Source: National Commission on Food Marketing, *Studies of Organization and Competition in Grocery Manufacturing, Technical Study No. 6* (June, 1966), pp. 206, 210.

Selling and distribution costs for cereals prior to 1940 averaged 35% of sales. With the rise of advertising in the cereal industry, marketing, delivery, and other distribution costs including advertising dropped to 26% of sales in the 1960's. *The FTC should be praising the cereal industry for its successful use of advertising to cut costs* instead of condemning it for its use of advertising.

The FTC also charges the cereal companies with using advertising to bar would-be competitors from the market and thereby monopolize the market. The FTC says that advertising is a barrier to entry by firms new to the market and by new products. This could hardly be more completely at variance with the truth. This claim cannot be substantiated. What can be substantiated is the opposite of this claim.

Advertising is a means of entry—not a barrier to entry. Advertising is a means of competing—not a method of monopolizing. Monopolists don't advertise. Competitors advertise. Where, for example, a single company is granted the franchise to supply both gas and electricity to a town, promotion and advertising expenditures are less than half the level they are when two different companies hold the franchise to supply gas and electricity (Paul S.

Brandon, "The Electric Side of Combination Gas-Electric Utilities," *The Bell Journal of Economics and Management*, 1971) and compete with each other. If there were truly monopoly (or oligopoly) in the cereal industry, advertising expenditures would be much lower than they are. If there were "shared monopoly" as the FTC claims, one of the first things that monopolists would do would be to cut costs and increase profits by agreement to reduce advertising. That is what American Tobacco did in the 1890's after merging 95% of the capacity in the cigarette industry. After American Tobacco was broken up by the dissolution decree of 1911, tobacco industry advertising expenditures doubled (from $13 million a year to $25 million). The level of advertising in cereals indicates vigorous competition. Comes the FTC claiming, with its twisted "logic" and no substantiation, that the level of advertising is evidence of monopoly.

If advertising were a barrier to entry, we would expect low product turnover in industries with high levels of advertising. What we find is exactly opposite (Lester Telser, "Advertising and Competition," *Journal of Political Economy*, 1964). The more intense the level of advertising, the higher the rate of product turnover.

Advertising is used as a means of informing potential customers of the appearance of a new product. It is used as a means for entering a market—not as a means for barring entry, the FTC to the contrary notwithstanding. It is new products which are heavily advertised, not old products. The cereal industry has heavy advertising outlays because it has been introducing new products. If it were not an innovative industry, its advertising outlays would be less.

As is readily apparent, advertising is under heavy attack. If it provides information, it is illegally claiming uniqueness. If it is done by firms which have a substantial share of the market, it is a means of monopolizing. If it doesn't provide information, it has no social value. To advertise at all has become a sin. The FTC is leveling a barrage of unsubstantiated claims against advertising which, if it prevails, may well cause a withering of advertising.

The danger seems clear. Let's look now, for a moment, at what advertising does that is good, that is constructive, and contributory, and at some of the deep and abiding psychological needs it supplies.

The very simple economic basis for advertising is that it allows the advertiser, providing he offers quality and value, to sell more, thus spreading fixed production costs over more sales and reducing the price per unit to the consumer. The more you sell, the lower the price. It's that simple. But let's make one thing very clear. Value and quality are the vital ingredients in this formula. While advertising can persuade a consumer to make the first purchase, no amount of advertising is going to sell the product a second time if the product doesn't deliver. This concept has propelled America, through mass marketing and mass production, into a material position never approached by any other nation.

A second, and less often recognized, economy produced by advertising is a decrease in the cost of distribution with a consequent fall in retail markups. Shelf space in a store is a commodity. Products which have rapid turnover produce more revenue per square foot of shelf space. The store's investment in space can be amortized more rapidly with fast sellers so the store's return on such items need not be as high per turnover as those which stay on the shelf longer. In a study offered in evidence to the Monopolies Commission of Great Britain, a soap company showed that the use of consumer advertising reduced the retail markup on one soap product from 24-26% in 1933 to 16% in the 1960's. Similar differences in markups prevail currently between unadvertised and advertised products. I have already given you the example of the 14% markup on cereals as against the 31% markup on produce. The National Commission on Food Marketing found that, in 1964, markups on non-advertised private label cornflakes and oats averaged 24% while those on the advertised brands averaged 16%.

An analysis of the very much higher cost of retail distribution in Russia compared to the U.S. attributes part of the difference to advertising by U.S. manufacturers and the lack of advertising in Russia. The analysis pointed out that the Russians are beginning to advertise products in order to reduce retail distribution costs.

This information (from the *Journal of Political Economy*, August, 1960) points up a painful irony. While advertising as such is being attacked in the free economy of America, it is being put to fruitful use in the controlled economy of Russia.

Another very important contribution of advertising is its informational function. It is through advertising, in whatever form, that consumers come to know of the availability of a product and the specific advantages if offers. Without advertising, a consumer would have to spend time and sometimes money to get information on which to base a purchasing decision. Either that or make decisions on a less informed basis. Advertising reduces the consumers' cost of search.

In addition to these economies provided by advertising, it is also an economical substitute for other means of marketing products. Lee Loevinger, former head of the Antitrust Division, has pointed out that advertising is a substitute for various forms of personal selling which are more expensive and less efficient. He praises advertising not only for its cost saving aspects but also because it is one of the least coercive techniques for distributing goods. He points out that substitues such as "personal selling . . . would certainly be . . . more coercive." (Statement by Lee Loevinger before the Federal Trade Commission, October 28, 1971.)

These are some of advertising's reasons for being in economic terms and in terms of the personal well-being it has created for the consumer. But does advertising have any philosophical and/or psychological justification?

It does.

In a clear and erudite examination of the morality of advertising, Theodore Levitt, professor of business administration at the Harvard Business School, presents in the *Harvard Business Review* a philosophical treatment of the human values of advertising.

He argues that embellishment and distortion (read emphasis, not deception, for distortion) are among advertising's legitimate and socially desirable

348

purposes. Illegitimacy in advertising consists only of falsification and larcenous intent.

He looks at poetry. Poetry's purpose, like advertising's, is to influence an audience, to affect its perceptions and sensibilities, perhaps even to change its mind. Like rhetoric, poetry's intent is to convince and seduce. It employs—without fear of criticism—all the tools of distortion that the literary mind can devise.

Professor Levitt points out that Keats does not offer a truthful engineering description of his Grecian urn. He offers, instead, a lyrical, exaggerated, distorted description. He does it with exquisite attention to the effects of meter, rhyme, allusion, metaphor and sound. And he is applauded—as are all artists, for doing it successfully.

Commerce takes essentially the same liberties with reality and literality as the artist, except that commerce calls its creation advertising, or industrial design, or packaging.

As with art, the purpose is to influence the audience by creating illusions, symbols, and implications that offer more than pure functionality.

Once, when asked what his company did, Charles Revson, of Revlon, Inc., suggested a profound distinction: "In the factory, we make cosmetics; in the store, we sell hope."

It isn't only cosmetic chemicals that women want, but in addition the seductive charm promised by the alluring symbols with which these chemicals have been surrounded.

A compact carries refined talc, but this does not explain why manufacturers try to make these boxes into works of decorative art. A sardine can, filled with scented powder, would not sell—even if the U.S. Bureau of Standards certified that the contents were identical to those sold in a beautiful, paisley-printed container.

The buyer obviously wants more than scented powder; she desires and needs the promises, imagery, and symbols produced by the advertisements, elaborate packages, and fetching design. She needs the confidence the use of the poetically described and packaged product gives her.

Such a want for embellishment apparently isn't confined to women. A few years ago, an electronics laboratory offered a $700 testing device for sale in two models. One had a front panel designed by engineers who developed the equipment. The other had a front panel designed by professional industrial designers. Otherwise the devices were exactly alike. When the two models were shown to a sample of lab directors with Ph.Ds, the professional design attracted twice the number of purchase intentions that the engineers' design did.

Both the poet and adman celebrate a deep and complex emotion symbolized by creative embellishment—a context which cannot be captured by literal description alone. Advertising is communication and communication can never be the real thing it talks about. All communication is, in some inevitable fashion, a departure from reality.

We select our clothes not only for warmth but for other purposes such as propriety, status, seduction. Natives of isolated African nations—where not the faintest whiff of advertising has ever intruded—encrust themselves with rings, pendants and bracelets. Man continually repackages and molds reality. T. S. Eliot noted: "Human kind cannot bear very much reality."

Comments Professor Levitt: "One does not need a doctorate in social anthropology to see that the purposeful transmutation of nature's primeval state occupies *all* people in *all* cultures and *all* societies at *all* stages of development. . . . Everybody everywhere wants to modify, transform, embellish, enrich and reconstruct the world around him. . . . Civilization is man's attempt to transcend his ancient animality; and this includes both art and advertising."

Professor Levitt goes on: "The human audience demands symbolic interpretation in everything it sees and knows. If it doesn't get it, it will return a verdict of 'no interest.' " He says: "The promises and images which imaginative ads and sculptured packages induce in us *are as much the product* as the physical materials themselves."

In a particularly compelling statement, the professor says: "If religion must be architectured, packaged, lyricized, and musicized to attract and hold its audience, and if sex must be perfumed, powdered, sprayed, and shaped in order to command attention, it is ridiculous to deny the legitimacy of more modest, and similar, embellishments to the world of commerce."

And so the consumer is in an old dilemma. He wants "truth" but he also wants and needs the alleviating imagery and tantalizing associations provided by the advertiser.

Business is caught in the middle. Many a company would go down in ruin if it refused to provide imagery, because very few will buy pure functionality (even the proverbial steak, as good as it is, is better sold by talking about the sizzle). Consumers demand advertising as well as product, and business responds to that demand. It produces the advertising and the product for which people vote with their dollars. It responds to the market ballot box.

Yet, if business uses too much imagery and little else, it clearly is not fulfilling its responsibility to the consumer. The problem is to find a middle way.

Clearly, the FTC's way is not that middle way. It is not even a fair way. The Wonder Bread case is a good example.

For a quarter century Wonder Bread was advertising along nutritive and informational lines. Suddenly, the FTC says, "you can't do this. It is deceitful." This is like changing the groundrules halfway through a game and with no prior notice. We can change the groundrules if we wish, but we shouldn't penalize the players for observing what were the rules of the game. And there is considerable doubt that the FTC's rule change is a useful change.

The action points up a new appropriation of powers by FTC—powers it quite possibly doesn't have under the law!

Assuming it is within the law, why weren't definite and clear guidelines laid out in advance of official action? *Ex post facto* law is the height of tyranny. It was one of the reasons for the American Revolution of 1775. How can such positive action be taken in the *total absence* of any proof of fallacious claims?

To see what the effect of a ban on advertising—or requirements which effectively eliminate advertising as a competitive tool—would be, it is interesting to look at a product where advertising is prohibited in some states. Let us compare its marketing with what goes on in states where advertising of that product is not banned. My colleague in the Center for Health Administration Studies at the University of Chicago, Professor Lee Benham, has examined the marketing of eye glasses and eye examinations. He found that in the two jurisdictions (Texas and District of Columbia) where there was the least restriction on advertising by optometrists, the average price for eye examinations and eye glasses was $29.97. In the two states which completely banned all advertising (California and North Carolina), the average price was $49.87.[2]

Professor Benham's finding on advertising's effectiveness in reducing the price of eye examinations and glasses startled me, to say the least. I had no idea that advertising could produce such a large impact.

I decided to see whether such an effect could be found in any other field. Recently, I began examining the restrictions on retail distribution of pharmaceuticals. We have just had a fracas in Illinois because Osco Drug Stores began posting prices of prescription drugs. I was alerted to the restrictions on advertising in this area because the Illinois Pharmacy Board ruled that this was advertising of drugs and that the law prohibited advertising. It threatened to rescind the licenses of all pharmacists working in Osco Drug Stores unless Osco ceased "advertising."

Looking at the average price of prescriptions in the state which has the most restrictive laws on advertising and retailing of pharmaceuticals (California), I found that it was $4.95 in 1970. The average price of a prescription in the states with the least restrictive laws was $3.52.

Advertising performs a very useful function in minimizing the price of products, in reducing the cost of search, and in making the market competitive. The attacks on advertising must be channeled into more useful areas than those chosen by the FTC or the result may be a less competitive society with a less vigorously growing and innovating economy. That is certainly not a result to be desired. The FTC must be stopped before its anti-advertising zeal stops competition as dead in its tracks as some states have done in the eyeglass industry.

NOTES

1. G. A. Miller, "The Magical Number Seven, Plus or Minus Two: Some Limits on Our Capacity for Processing Information," *The Psychological Review*, March 1956.
2. L. Benham, "The Effect of Advertising on Prices," *Journal of Law and Economics*, forthcoming.

38. IS ADVERTISING WASTEFUL?

Jules Backman

WITH SOME exceptions, economists generally have criticized advertising as economically wasteful. All the criticisms are not so extreme as one widely used economics text which states:

> "Overall, it is difficult for anyone to gain more than temporarily from large advertising outlays in an economy in which counteradvertising is general. The overall effect of advertising, on which we spent $14 billion (actually $15 billion—JB) in 1965, is to devote these productive resources (men, ink, billboards, and so forth) to producing advertising rather than to producing other goods and services."[1]

Most critics do not go this far in condemning advertising. However, they do emphasize that advertising may be wasteful in several ways: by adding unnecessarily to costs, by an inefficient use of resources, by promoting excessive competition, and by causing consumers to buy items they do not need. This article brings together the scattered criticisms of advertising and answers to them and thus presents an overview of the debate in this area. The nature of these criticisms and the significance of waste in a competitive economy are first reviewed. Attention is then given to the vital informational role played by advertising, particularly in an expanding economy. Advertising is only one alternative in the marketing mix, and hence its contribution must be considered among alternatives rather than in absolute terms.

VARIATIONS ON A THEME

The criticism that advertising involves economic waste takes several forms.

COMPETITION IN ADVERTISING

The attack usually is centered on competition in advertising which some critics state flatly is wasteful.[2] Others have been concerned about the relative

Reprinted from *Journal of Marketing*, Vol. 32 (January, 1968), pp. 2-8, published by The American Marketing Association.

cost of advertising as a percentage of sales. Sometimes an arbitrary percentage, such as 5%, is selected as the dividing line between "high" and more "reasonable" levels of expenditure.[3]

Such cutoff points are meaningless, since the proper relative expenditures for advertising are a function of the product's characteristics. It is not an accident that relative advertising costs are highest for low-priced items which are available from many retail outlets and subject to frequent repeat purchases (for example, cosmetics, soaps, soft drinks, gum and candies, drugs, cigarettes, beer, etc.).

Particularly criticized are emotional appeals, persuasion, and "tug of war" advertising where it is claimed the main effect is to shift sales among firms rather than to increase total volume of the industry. For example, Richard Caves states: "At the point where advertising departs from its function of informing and seeks to persuade or deceive us, it tends to become a waste of resources."[4]

In a competitive economy competitors must seek to persuade customers to buy their wares. We do not live in a world where a company stocks its warehouse and waits until customers beat a path to its doors to buy its products. If this is all that a business firm did, we would have economic waste in terms of products produced but not bought as well as in the failure to produce many items for which a market can be created. In the latter case, the waste would take the form of idle labor and unused resources.

INEFFICIENT USE OF RESOURCES

Economists have criticized advertising most vigorously as involving an inefficient use of resources. This criticism has been directed particularly against advertising where the main effect allegedly is a "shuffling of existing total demand" among the companies in an industry. Under these conditions, it is stated, advertising merely adds to total costs and in time results in higher prices. There undoubtedly is a shifting of demand among firms due to many factors including advertising. But this is what we should expect in a competitive economy. Moreover, there are many products for which total demand is increased (for example, television sets, radio sets, cars, toilet articles) for multiple use in the same home. In the sharply expanding economy of the past quarter of a century there are relatively few industries in which total demand has remained unchanged.

It must also be kept in mind that the resources devoted to competitive advertising usually are considered to be wasteful "in a full-employment economy" because they may be utilized more efficiently in other ways. Thus, the extent of "waste" involved also appears to depend upon whether the economy is operating below capacity. This point is considered in a later section.

ADDS TO COSTS

Sometimes, it is stated that if advertising succeeds in expanding total demand for a product, the result is a shift of demand from other products, the producers of which will be forced to advertise to attempt to recover their position. The net result of such "counter-advertising" is to add to costs and to prices.

But all increases in demand do not necessarily represent a diversion from other products. Thus, an expanded demand for new products is accompanied by an increase in income and in purchasing power flowing from their production. Moreover, during a period of expanding economic activity, as is noted later, the successful advertising may affect the rate of increase for different products rather than result in an absolute diversion of volume.

CREATES UNDESIRABLE WANTS

Another variation is the claim that advertising is wasteful because it ". . . creates useless or undesirable wants at the expense of things for which there is greater social need. When advertising makes consumers want and buy automobiles with tail fins, tobacco, and movie-star swimming pools, there is less money (fewer resources) available to improve public hospitals, build better schools, or combat juvenile delinquency."[5] It is claimed that many of these types of products are useless and anti-social. Criticism of advertising is nothing new. In the late 1920s Stuart Chase claimed: "Advertising creates no new dollars. In fact, by removing workers from productive employment, it tends to depress output, and thus lessen the number of real dollars."[6]

These are value judgments reached by the critics on the basis of subjective "standards" which they set up. "What is one man's meat is another man's poison," as the old saying goes. The real question is who is to decide what is good for the consumer and what should he purchase?

In a free economy, there is a wide diversity of opinion as to what combinations of goods and services should be made available and be consumed. Obviously, tastes vary widely and most persons do not want to be told what is best for them. In any cross section of the population of the country there will be a wide disagreement as to what constitutes the ideal components of a desirable level of living. Each one of us must decide what purchases will yield the greatest satisfactions. We may be misled on occasion by popular fads, advertising, or even advice of our friends. But these decisions in the final analysis are made by the buyers and not by the advertisers, as the latter have found out so often to their regret.

COMPETITION AND "WASTE"

The critics of advertising are really attacking the competitive process. Competition involves considerable duplication and "waste." The illustrations range from the several gasoline stations at an important intersection to the multiplication of research facilities, the excess industrial capacity which develops during periods of expansion, and the accumulations of excessive inventories.

There is widespread recognition that inefficiencies may develop in advertising as in other phases of business.[7] Mistakes are made in determining how much should be spent for advertising—but these mistakes can result in spending too little as well as too much.

We cannot judge the efficiency of our competitive society—including the various instrumentalities, such as advertising—by looking at the negative aspects alone. It is true that competition involves waste. But it also yields a flood of new products, improved quality, better service, and pressures on prices. In the United States, it has facilitated enormous economic growth with the accompanying high standards of living. The advantages of competition have been so overwhelmingly greater than the wastes inherent in it that we have established as one of our prime national goals, through the anti-trust laws, the continuance of a viable competitive economy.

INFORMATIONAL ROLE OF ADVERTISING

Advertising plays a major informational role in our economy because (1) products are available in such wide varieties, (2) new products are offered in such great numbers, and (3) existing products must be called to the attention of new consumers who are added to the market as a result of expansion in incomes, the population explosion, and changes in tastes.

The most heavily advertised products are widely used items that are consumed by major segments of the population. This does not mean that everyone buys every product or buys them to the extent that he can. Some of these products are substitutes for other products. For example, it will be readily recognized that cereals provide only one of many alternatives among breakfast foods. In some instances, heavily advertised products compete with each other like, for example, soft drinks and beer. In other instances, additional consumers can use the products so that the size of the total market can be increased (for example, toilet preparations).

Potential markets also expand as incomes rise and as consumers are able to purchase products they previously could not afford. As the population increases, large numbers of new potential customers are added each year. Continuous large-scale advertising provides reminders to old customers and provides information to obtain some part of the patronage of new customers. The potential market is so huge that large-scale advertising is an economical way to obtain good results.

In addition, the identity of buyers changes under some circumstances and new potential buyers must be given information concerning the available alternatives. It has also been pointed out that some of these products are ". . . subject to fads and style changes" and that ". . . consumers become restive with existing brands and are prepared to try new varieties." Illustrations include cereals, soaps, clothing, and motion pictures.[8]

The consumer has a wide variety of brands from which to choose. Product improvements usually breed competitive product improvements; the advertising of these improvements may result in an increase in total advertising for the class of products.

When any company in an industry embarks on an intensified advertising campaign, its competitors must step up their advertising or other sales efforts to avoid the possible loss of market position. This is a key characteristic of competition.

On the other hand, if any company decides to economize on its advertising budget, its exposure is reduced and its share of market may decline if its competitors fail to follow the same policy. Thus, for some grocery products it has been reported that ". . . competition within a sector may have established a certain pattern with regard to the extent of advertising, and any company dropping below this level faces possible substantial loss of market share."[9]

These results flow particularly if the industry is oligopolistic, that is, has relatively few producers who are sensitive to and responsive to actions of competitors. However, as the dramatic changes in market shares during the past decade so amply demonstrate, this does not mean that the companies in such oligopolistic industries will retain relatively constant shares of the market.[10]

The informational role of advertising has been succinctly summarized by Professor George J. Stigler:

> . . . Under competition, the main tasks of a seller are to inform potential buyers of his existence, his line of goods, and his prices. Since both sellers and buyers change over time (due to birth, death, migration), since people forget information once acquired, and since new products appear, the existence of sellers must be continually advertised . . .
>
> This informational function of advertising must be emphasized because of a popular and erroneous belief that advertising consists chiefly of nonrational (emotional and repetitive) appeals.[11]

Elsewhere, Professor Stigler has pointed out that ". . . information is a valuable resource," that advertising is "the obvious method of identifying buyers and sellers" which "reduces drastically the cost of search," and that "It is clearly an immensely powerful instrument for the elimination of ignorance. . . .[12]

Often this information is required to create interest in and demand for a product. Thus, it has been reported:

> . . . to a significant degree General Foods and the U.S. food market created each other. Before a new product appears, customers are rarely conscious of wanting it. There was no spontaneous demand for ready-to-eat cereals; frozen foods required a sustained marketing effort stretching over many years; instant coffee had been around for decades, supplying a market that did not amount to a tenth of its present level. General Foods' corporate skill consists largely in knowing enough about American tastes to foresee what products will be accepted.[13]

Similarly, J. K. Galbraith, who has been very critical of advertising, has recognized that:

A new consumer product must be introduced with a suitable advertising campaign to arouse an interest in it. The path for an expansion of output must be paved by a suitable expansion in the advertising budget. Outlays for the manufacturing of a product are not more important in the strategy of modern business enterprise than outlays for the manufacturing of demand for the product.[14]

We live in an economy that has little resemblance to the ideal of perfect competition postulated by economists. However, one of the postulates of this ideal economy is perfect knowledge. Advertising contributes to such knowledge. Thus, in such an idealized economy, even though advertising may be wasteful it would still have a role to play. But in the world of reality, with all its imperfections, advertising is much more important. Advertising is an integral and vital part of our growing economy and contributes to the launching of the new products so essential to economic growth.

HOW MUCH IS INFORMATIONAL?

In 1966, total expenditures for media advertising aggregated $13.3 billion.[15] It is impossible to determine exactly how much of this amount was strictly informational. However, the following facts are of interest:

Classified advertising was $1.3 billion
Other local newspaper advertising, largely retail, was
    $2.6 billion
Business paper advertising was $712 million
Local radio and TV advertising was $1.1 billion
Spot radio and spot TV advertising was $1.2 billion
National advertising on network TV, network radio, magazines
    and newspapers was $3.7 billion
Direct mail was $2.5 billion

Classified advertising and local advertising are overwhelmingly informational in nature. Certainly some part of national advertising also performs this function. These figures suggest that substantially less than half of total advertising is of the type that the critics are attacking as wasteful;[16] the exact amount cannot be pinpointed. Moreover, it must be kept in mind that a significant part of national advertising is for the promotion of new products for which the informational role is vital.

From another point of view, even if there is waste, the social cost is considerably less than suggested by these data. Thus, in 1966 about $10 billion was spent on advertising in newspapers, magazines, radio, and television; another $746 million was spent on farm and business publications. Without these expenditures, these sources of news and entertainment would have had to obtain substantial sums from other sources. It has been estimated that ". . . advertising paid for over 60% of the cost of periodicals, for over 70% of the cost of newspapers, and for 100% of the cost of commercial radio and TV broadcasting."[17] Thus, advertising results in a form of subsidization for all media of communication. Without it, these media would have to charge higher subscription rates or be subsidized by the government or some combination of both.

ADVERTISING AND EXPANDING MARKETS

Economic growth has become a major objective of national economic policy in recent years. Rising productivity, increasing population, improving education, rates of saving, and decisions concerning new investments are the ingredients of economic growth. In addition, there must be a favorable political climate including tax policies and monetary policies designed to release the forces conducive to growth.

Advertising contributes to economic growth and in turn levels of living by complementing the efforts to create new and improved products through expenditures for research and development. One observer has described the process as follows:

. . . advertising, by acquainting the consumer with the values of new products, widens the market for these products, pushes forward their acceptance by the consumer, and encourages the investment and entrepreneurship necessary for innovation. Advertising, in short, holds out the promise of a greater and speedier return than would occur without such methods, thus stimulating investment, growth, and diversity.[18]

Among the most intensive advertisers have been toilet preparations (14.7% of sales), cleaning and polishing preparations (12.6%), and drugs (9.4%). The markets for these products have been expanding at a faster rate than all consumer spending.

Between 1947 and 1966, personal consumption expenditures for these products increased as follows:[19]

	1947	1955	1966
	(millions of dollars)		
Toilet articles & preparations	1,217	1,915	4,690
Cleaning, polishing & household supplies	1,523	2,480	4,487
Drug preparations & sundries	1,313	2,362	5,062

As a share of total personal consumption expenditures, the increases from 1947 to 1966 were as follows:

Toilet articles and preparations from 0.76% to 1.01%
Cleaning, polishing and household supplies from 0.94% to 0.97%
Drug preparations and sundries from 0.82% to 1.09%

These increases in relative importance are based upon dollar totals. However, the retail prices of these products rose less than the consumer price index during the postwar years.

Between 1947 and 1966, the price increases were as follows:

Total consumer price index	45.4%
Toilet preparations	14.6
Soaps and detergents	2.6
Drugs and prescriptions	22.8

Thus, the increase in relative importance of these highly advertised products has been even greater in real terms than in dollars.

Between 1947 and 1966, the increase in *real* personal consumption expenditures has been:

Toilet articles and preparations from 0.68% to 1.12%
Cleaning, polishing and household supplies from 0.87%
    to 1.05%
Drug preparations and sundries from 0.82% to 1.24%

Clearly, advertising appears to have contributed to an expansion in the demand for these products and to the growth of our economy with the accompanying expansion in job opportunities and in economic well-being. There may have been some waste in this process—although all of such expenditures cannot be characterized as wasteful—but it appears to have been offset in full or in part by these other benefits.

The charge of large-scale waste in advertising appears to reflect in part a yearning for an economy with standardized, homogeneous products which are primarily functional in nature. An illustration would be a refrigerator that is designed solely to be technically efficient for the storage of food. However, customers are also interested in the decor of their kitchens, in convenience and speed in the manufacture of ice cubes, in shelves that rotate, and in special storage for butter. These are additions to functional usefulness which "an affluent society" can afford but which a subsistence economy cannot.

ADVERTISING IN A HIGH-LEVEL ECONOMY

The concept of waste must be related to the level achieved by an economy. Professor John W. Lowe has observed that "Perhaps a good deal of the 'wastefulness' assigned to advertising springs from the fact that a large part of the world's population cannot consider satisfying *psychological wants* when most of their efforts must be devoted to *needs*."[20] (Italics added.)

In a subsistence economy, scarcity is so significant that advertising might be wasteful, particularly where it diverts resources from meeting the basic necessities of life. Such an economy usually is a "full employment economy" in the sense that everyone is working. But the total yield of a full employment subsistence economy is very low, as is evident throughout Asia, Africa, and South America.

Professor Galbraith has noted that "The opportunity for product differentiation . . . is almost uniquely the result of opulence . . . the tendency for commercial rivalries . . . to be channeled into advertising and salesmanship would disappear in a poor community."[21]

In the high level American economy, there usually are surpluses rather than scarcity. The use of resources for advertising to differentiate products, therefore, is not necessarily a diversion from other uses. Rather, it frequently represents the use of resources that might otherwise be idle both in the short run and the long run and thus may obviate the waste that such idleness represents.

THE MARKETING MIX

The concept of waste cannot ignore the question—waste as compared with what alternative? Advertising cannot be considered in a vacuum. It must be considered as one of the marketing alternatives available. Generally it is not a question of advertising or nothing, but rather of advertising or some other type of sales effort.

It is a mistake to evaluate the relative cost of advertising apart from other marketing costs. It is only one tool in the marketing arsenal which also includes direct selling, packaging, servicing, product planning, pricing, etc. Expenditures for advertising often are substituted for other types of selling effort. This substitution has been readily apparent in the history of the discount house. These houses have featured well-advertised brands which were presold and, hence, virtually eliminated the need for floor stocks and reduced the need for space and many salesmen.

Advertising is undertaken where it is the most effective and most economical way to appeal to customers. It is a relatively low-cost method of communicating with all potential customers and this explains its widespread adoption by many companies. To the extent that less efficient marketing methods must be substituted for advertising, we would really have economic waste.

SUMMARY AND CONCLUSIONS

There is wide agreement that the informational role of advertising makes a significant contribution to the effective operation of our economy. There is also agreement that inefficiency in the use of advertising is wasteful, as are other types of inefficiencies that are part and parcel of a market-determined economy. The gray area is so-called competitive advertising, largely national, which is the main target of those who insist advertising is wasteful. Although precise data are not available, the estimates cited earlier indicate that the charge of competitive waste applies to substantially less than half of all advertising expenditures.

Competition unavoidably involves considerable duplication and waste. If the accent is placed on the negative, a distorted picture is obtained. On balance, the advantages of competition have been much greater than the wastes.

Advertising has contributed to an expanding market for new and better products. Many of these new products would not have been brought to market unless firms were free to develop mass markets through large-scale advertising. There may be some waste in this process, but it has been more than offset by other benefits.

Where burgeoning advertising expenditures are accompanied by expanding industry sales, there will tend to be a decline in total unit costs instead of increase, and prices may remain unchanged or decline. In such situations, it seems clear that advertising, while adding to total costs, will result in lower total *unit* costs, the more significant figure. This gain will be offset to some extent if the increase in volume represents a diversion from other companies or industries with an accompanying rise in unit costs. Of course, such change is inherent in a dynamic competitive economy.

Advertising expenditures have risen as the economy has expanded. At such times, the absolute increase in sales resulting from higher advertising expenditures need not be accompanied by a loss in sales in other industries. This is particularly true if a new product has been developed and its sales are expanding. In that event, new jobs probably will be created and help to support a higher level of economic activity generally.

The claim that resources devoted to advertising would be utilized more efficiently for other purposes ignores the fact that generally we have a surplus economy. All of the resources used for advertising are not diverted from other alternatives. Rather, it is probable that much of the resources involved would be idle or would be used less efficiently. Even more important would be the failure to provide the jobs which expanding markets create.

Finally, advertising does not take place in a vacuum. It is one of several marketing alternatives. The abandonment of advertising could not represent a net saving to a company or to the economy. Instead, such a development would require a shift to alternative marketing techniques, some of which would be less efficient than advertising since companies do not deliberately adopt the least effective marketing approach. On balance, advertising is an invaluable competitive tool.

NOTES

1. George Leland Bach, *Economics*, Fifth Edition (Englewood Cliffs, New Jersey: Prentice-Hall, Inc., 1966), p. 437. *See also* Kenneth Boulding, "Economic Analysis," 1, *Microeconomics*, Fourth Edition, 1 (New York: Harper and Row, 1966), p. 513.

2. Nicholas H. Kaldor, "The Economic Aspects of Advertising," *The Review of Economic Studies*, 18 (1950-51), p. 6.

3. Joe S. Bain, *Industrial Organization* (New York: John Wiley, 1959), pp. 390-91. *See also Report of a Commission of Enquiry Into Advertising* (London, England: The Labour Party, 1966), p. 42. The Reith Report defined "substantially advertised products" at 5% or more.

4. Richard Caves, *American Industry: Structure, Conduct, Performance* (Englewood Cliffs, New Jersey: Prentice-Hall, Inc., 1964), p. 102.

5. "Advertising and Charlie Brown," *Business Review,* June 1962, p. 10.

6. Stuart Chase, *The Tragedy of Waste* (New York: Macmillan, 1928), p. 112.

7. Committee on Advertising, *Principles of Advertising* (New York: Pitman Publishing Corp., 1963), p. 34; and Neil H. Borden, "The Role of Advertising in the Various Stages of Corporate and Economic Growth," Peter D. Bennett, Editor, *Marketing and Economic Development* (Chicago, Illinois: American Marketing Association, 1965), p. 493.

8. Lester G. Telser, "How Much Does It Pay Whom to Advertise?" *American Economic Review, Papers and Proceedings* (December 1960), pp. 203-4.

9. National Commission on Food Marketing, *Grocery Manfacturing,* Technical Study No. 6 (Washington, D.C.: June 1966), p. 14.

10. Jules Backman, *Advertising and Competition* (New York: New York University Press, 1967), Chapters 3 and 4.

11. George J. Stigler, *The Theory of Price,* Third Edition (New York: Macmillan, 1966), p. 200.

12. George J. Stigler, "The Economics of Information," *The Journal of Political Economy* (June 1961), pp. 213, 216, 220. *See also* S.A. Ozga, "Imperfect Markets through Lack of Knowledge," *Quarterly Journal of Economics* (February 1960), pp. 29, 33-34, and Wroe Alderson, *Dynamic Market Behavior* (Homewood, Illinois: Richard D. Irwin, Inc., 1965), pp. 128-31.

13. "General Foods Is Five Billion Particulars," *Fortune,* March 1964, p. 117.

14. J. K. Galbraith, *The Affluent Society* (Boston, Massachusetts: Houghton Mifflin, 1958), p. 156.

15. This total excludes a miscellaneous category of $3.3 billion.

16. For the United Kingdom, the "disputed proportion" of advertising expenditures has been estimated at about 30% of the total. Walter Taplin, *Advertising, A New Approach* (Boston, Massachusetts: Little, Brown & Co., 1963), p. 126.

17. Fritz Machlup, *The Production and Distribution of Knowledge in the United States* (Princeton, New Jersey: Princeton University Press, 1962), p. 265.

18. David M. Blank, "Some Comments on the Role of Advertising in the American Economy—A Plea for Revaluation," L. George Smith, *Reflections on Progress in Marketing* (Chicago, Illinois: American Marketing Association, 1964), p. 151.

19. *The National Income and Product Accounts of the United States, 1929-1965, Statistical Tables* (Washington, D.C.: United States Department of Commerce, August 1966), pp. 44-49; and *Survey of Current Business* (July 1967), pp. 23-24.

20. John W. Lowe, "An Economist Defends Advertising," *Journal of Marketing,* 27 (July 1963), p. 18.

21. John K. Galbraith, *American Capitalism: The Concept of Countervailing Power* (Boston, Massachusetts: Houghton Mifflin, 1952), pp. 106-7.

362

39. ANTI-COMPETITIVE ADVERTISING AND THE FTC: A BAN ON OLIGOPOLY-CREATING ADS?

Paul D. Scanlon

ADVERTISING AND "PRODUCT DIFFERENTIATION"

Hon. Miles Kirkpatrick
Chairman, Federal Trade Commission
Washington, D.C. 20580

Dear Mr. Chairman:

In his recent letter to us on the Commission's efforts in the dairy industry, former Chairman Weinberger was kind enough to invite us to offer any thoughts or suggestions we might have for furthering the Commission's effectiveness in terms of consumer benefits from the resources available. Three current matters of some importance occur to us, namely, (1) the consumer losses associated with high-intensity advertising in certain highly-concentrated consumer industries; (2) discounting; and (3) the Commission's recent action in requiring gasoline stations to post their "octane" ratings.

A large volume of economic literature, including the Federal Trade Commission's own recent *Economic Report on the Influence of Market Structure on the Profit Performance of Food Manufacturing Companies* (September 1969), has emphasized the role of high-intensity advertising and of the resulting structural condition called "product differentiation" in the promotion of high degrees of concentration—ultimately higher consumer prices—in a significant number of our important consumer goods industries. At the same time, a great deal of criticism has been directed at the Federal Trade Commission for its difficulties in curbing the advertising practices of our larger advertisers, particularly those that dominate network TV.

Reprinted by permission from *Antitrust Law & Economics Review*, Vol. 3, No. 3 (Spring 1970), pp. 21-29.

MERGERS AND PRODUCT DIFFERENTIATION

It is common ground among economists specializing in the industrial organization field that these two problems are in reality but opposite sides of the same coin, i.e., that they are in fact one problem, not two. Through the device of high intensity advertising, and particularly network TV advertising, markets can be, and many have been, raised to very high concentration levels, without all the consumer losses this condition implies. (Highly "differentiated" consumer products sold by concentrated industries tend to be, on the average 20% higher in price than physically comparable products sold under lesser-known or private label brands. See Dr. Frederic M. Scherer, *Industrial Market Structure and Economic Performance* 331 [Rand McNally, 1970).]

Indeed, much of the current merger movement, as several students of that phenomenon have recently pointed out, is fueled by this lure of potential advertising-created monopoly profits. "A large conglomerate firm skilled in the techniques of saturation TV advertising to dominate particular industries first identifies an industry that is at that time relatively unconcentrated and thus, by definition, relatively unsophisticated in the ways of advertising-induced monopoly power. After acquiring one of the leading firms in this heretofore competitive industry, the acquirer then launches a massive advertising campaign that (1) transfers perhaps 30% to 50% of the industry's total sales volume into its hands, i.e., that converts the industry into a tight-knit oligopoly, and (2) gives it the power to raise the product's *price* by, say, 20% or more (thus recouping, with a handsome profit, the perhaps 10% or so of sales that it had to spend on advertising to *acquire* that price-raising power in the first place). It is precisely this process of transforming previously competitive industries selling undifferentiated (unbranded) products or commodities at low (competitive) prices, into highly-concentrated oligopolies selling differentiated (branded) products at higher-than-competitive prices" that has accounted for the bulk of the increases in concentration in American industries in recent years (most increases in concentration since World War II have occurred since the advent of TV in the 1950's), that is exerting a substantial part of the upward pressure on prices in the American economy, and that will be doing so for years to come if some meaningful action is not taken in this vital area now.

REQUIRE OLIGOPOLISTS TO FILE ADS WITH FTC?

In view of this demonstrated power of uninformative (if not affirmatively misleading) advertising to duplicate the concentration-increasing effects of mergers, a rational public policy in this area along the lines of the Commission's merger guidelines would seem to be highly appropriate. The beginning point, we think, should perhaps be something analogous to the "pre-merger notification" program recently initiated by the agency, one in which certain firms in important consumer goods industries meeting specified structural criteria would be required to notify the Commission a short time in advance of publication (say 60 days) of all planned advertisements. Thus one might propose a rule along the following lines. All advertisements would have to be filed with the Commission no later than 60 days prior to publication where:

1. The sponsoring firm is one of the four (4) largest in an industry in which the four largest firms account for 50% or more of the industry's total sales; or
2. The percentage of the industry's sales accounted for by the four largest firms has increased by 10% or more during the preceding 10 years; or
3. The advertising expenditures of the 8 largest firms exceeds (say) $10 million or 1% of their total sales, whichever is smaller.

DISCLOSURE OF PERFORMANCE CHARACTERISTICS

All advertisements filed under this requirement should then be stringently evaluated, not merely for literal truthfulness under accepted standards of deception but for "informational" content as well. Given the demonstrated capacity of this kind and degree of advertising to promote levels of concentration condemned by the courts in merger cases as offensive to our national public policy, it should be disallowed if it fails to meet reasonable tests of consumer welfare, e.g., if it fails to disclose essential information relating to the product's price, quality, and performance characteristics. If, on evaluation, it appears that the advertisements in question would tend to lessen competition (increase concentration), the advertiser should be advised that it is not acceptable and, if published, is likely to be challenged by the Commission.

"ADVERTISING-PRONE" INDUSTRIES

An effort should be made, in short, to identify those consumer goods industries that are highly concentrated as a result of product differentiation (high-intensity advertising), or that are in the process of becoming concentrated by that means, and then to direct to those industries an enforcement program comparable in resources and sophistication to that the Commission has directed with some success to industries with unfavorable merger records. Product differentiation should be treated with the same amount of concern as "merger-prone" industries. We offer below, in connection with our discussion of the octant-rating matter, a number of other suggestions for dealing with this problem of concentrated, deception-prone industries.

OLIGOPOLY AND "DISCOUNTING"

As you are no doubt aware, the practice of "discounting" is on the rise in the United States in certain industries and, in those industries, has effected substantial reductions in prices paid by consumers. We have recently noted in the press, however, a statement by one of the Commission's officials, Mr. Pitofsky of the Bureau of Consumer Protection, that the Commission is currently developing a broad-ranging program for combating alleged "deception" in this area. If this report is true, we hope the Commission will give the matter a great deal of thought before engaging in any high level of activity in this area. Again we think it is common ground among economists working in the competition-monopoly field that the screw might well be profitably loosened on discounting, not tightened.

PRODUCT DIFFERENTIATION AND COMPETITIVE "SAVINGS" CLAIMS

The problem involved here points up the dangers inherent in any "consumer deception" program that is administered without an acutely sensitive regard for its *anti-competitive* potential. The danger always, as the FTC's critics have emphasized many times, is that one will wind up suing not the firms that are causing the most harm to the consumer, the high-price established sellers that are using their combined oligopoly power to overcharge the consumer for "premium-priced" brand-name (product-differentiated) merchandise, but those whose existence is most vital to the consumer, the sellers of lower-priced *substitutes,* products that have the same performance characteristics but sell for less money. To be sure, new entrants offering lesser-known goods, and the smaller existing firms in our various markets, face an uphill battle against the entrenched oligopolists, in their areas and thus often feel that they have to exaggerate their price savings in order to at least partially offset the enormous advantage accruing to the established oligopolist-sellers in the market from their years of market dominance and high-intensity advertising. They frequently feel—and often correctly so—that, in order to get enough volume to operate efficiently, it is not enough to claim a 15% price savings from the price being charged by their oligopoly-competitors on comparable merchandise (the truth), that they must claim a more spectacular 25% savings ("deceptive").

DISCOUNTERS AND LOWER CONSUMER PRICES

But has the Federal Trade Commission, a public agency with important economic responsibilities, really maximized the effective use of its resources if it spends public money stamping out this kind of "deception"? We think it could better spend its money finding out how the overall *gross margin* of the "discounters" actually compares with that of the local oligopolists and then *publicizing* its findings in that regard so that the discounters will feel less *need* to exaggerate those differences. We think it would be very enlightening, for example, to compare the gross margins or overall storewide mark-ups of, say, S. Klein's and George's in Washington, D.C., with those of Woodward & Lothrop and Garfinckel (these are readily available figures), not to mention a comparison of the prices of these two groups of retailers on a selected "basket" of comparable items. (It is common knowledge in the supermarket trade, for example, that "discounters" earn quite lush profits on gross margins of less than 18%, while the non-discount chain operators generally take a mark-up of up to 23% or more; the big food chains could lower their prices across the board by at least 5% and still be quite profitable if *price* competition in their markets was sufficiently intense to make them give up trading stamps and other such "non-price" gimmicks.) Even where the discounter's price is only moderately lower than his higher-price competitors, however, his "comparative" price advertisements undoubtedly tend to sharpen the consumer's awareness of price as an important element in making purchases and therefore tends to have a distinct pro-competitive effect.

We urge, therefore, a program to *encourage* discounters, not one that will give them and their competitors the impression that the law favors those who maintain high, rigid prices rather than those that shade them.

POSTING GASOLINE "OCTANE" RATINGS—$2 BILLION CONSUMER SAVINGS

Our concern in the "octane" ratings matter centers around the problem of an adequate follow-up to the Commission's highly laudable action in requiring gasoline service stations to post this important piece of information on their pumps.

As the press has noted, some quite vast savings are potentially available to the consumer here. As you know, the so-called "brand name" gasolines of the major refiners sell generally for some 3¢ per gallon more than the price charged for the "independent" or unbranded gasolines *of exactly the same octane rating*. This differential in price would of course be impossible if the motoring public *knew* that there were in fact no significant differences in the performance of these branded and unbranded gasolines. One can predict with considerable confidence, then, that the price of the "branded" gasolines would fall to the level of the "unbranded" gasolines *if* the motoring public could be *effectively* informed of the conclusive significance of the posted octane ratings as a guide to buying gasoline. A drop of 3¢ per gallon in the price of the major refiner's brand-name gasoline would mean, as the press had reported, a decline in the public's annual gasoline bill of some $2 billion. Hence the success or lack of it of the Commission's disclosure effort here will be readily measurable when the ruling goes into effect: if the price of "branded" gasoline falls, it will be clear that the consumer has gotten the message and has, by shifting his patronage to the lower-priced gasoline, forced the majors to lower *their* "branded" prices to the same level; if the 3¢ differential remains, it will be equally clear that the motorist has not accepted the conclusive significance of octane as the test of quality in gasoline.

367

ADVERTISING ATTACK ON FTC RULING?

Since it is fairly reasonable to suppose that the major refiners will not be ecstatic about lowering their gasoline prices by $2 billion, one need not be overly skeptical in order to suspect that they will make every effort to "blunt" the Commission's "octane" message. Extensive advertising campaigns will probably appear designed to convince the viewer that numerous other characteristics of gasoline are much more important than its octane rating and that these other characteristics, all of which are of course possessed in abundance by the sponsor's gasoline, are in fact, so vast that they "swamp" the significance of that numerical octane standard. This will of course be false; there are no such other characteristics, as the Commission is well aware.

There are steps we think the Commission can and should take to counteract this predictable development. First, the Commission should begin an intensive consumer-information and education program designed to fully inform the gasoline-buying public that all gasolines of the same octane rating are of the same motoring utility. Secondly, the Commission should immediately issue an enforcement-policy statement to the effect that it will bring suit against any advertiser that attempts, either directly or indirectly, to persuade the consumer of the falsity of that proposition or to otherwise detract from the effectiveness of the Commission's disclosure effort in the gasoline area. The authority of a public agency to protect the integrity of its rulings from advertising assaults on it ought to be clear enough. Thirdly, the Commission should select an approprate "test" area, make every reasonable effort to inform consumers, in that area of the *significance* of the "octane" ratings being provided them, and then measure the effectiveness of its overall program in that test area.

TESTING EFFECTIVENESS OF "OCTANE" DISCLOSURE—EFFECT ON PRICE

Numerous possibilities commend themselves here. We suggest for example, that the Commission select as a "test area" a community that has relatively "high" gasoline prices (compared with prices in other major cities) *and* that has a relatively vigorous local consumer organization that can be depended upon to help disseminate the necessary information about gasoline. (Since Philadelphia has what we understand is far and away the most aggressive local consumer organization in the country, the Consumer's Education and Protective Association (CEPA), headed by Clarissa Cain and Max Weiner, that City comes immediately to mind here.) With the help of that consumer organization and its members, numerous other local groups should be contacted for further aid. The local media might be willing to help—radio stations, newspapers, local TV stations. Local automobile dealers might be persuaded to help, perhaps even to the extent of putting "stickers" on all new and used cars sold stating the car's octane requirements. (Better still, the Commission might make it mandatory for the country's automobile *manufacturers* to put such a sticker on, say, the gas-tank caps of all new cars coming off its assembly lines.) Commission personnel, accompanied perhaps by representatives of the local consumer organization, might visit the local high schools and enlist the aid of their students in disseminating brochures and other kinds of informative data to the households in the community.

Gasoline prices in the area should be checked before and after this suggested consumer-education program is put into effect. If the test is successful—i.e., if prices fall—consumer groups in other areas could be enlisted to extend it to a wider, national effort.

TAKE OLIGOPOLISTS' ADS OFF TV?

All of these are, of course, piecemeal or secondary solutions to the problem at issue here. What is really required in the gasoline area, as in the other consumer goods industries where anti-competitive advertising messages have successfully misled the consumer into paying "premium" prices for products no better than lower-price substitutes, is a co-ordinated program to stop the deception in question and restore, via the prevention of the anti-competitive advertising itself and reduction of the concentration it spawns, effective *price* competition. We suggest, as a starter, that the Commission having identified the industries that are charging higher-than-competitive prices as a result of misleading TV advertising, take the appropriate steps to either (a) remove all advertising sponsored by those non-competitive industries from the air, or (b) at least secure *equal* time from the networks, as was granted for anti-cigarette advertising, for the disclosure of the *true* performance characteristics of the products being advertised to the injury of the consuming public. If all of these efforts fail to reverse the trend toward concentration and deception in our important consumer goods industries, then the Commission should begin the necessary steps to sponsor a comprehensive *labeling* program in those non-competitive and deceptive industries, one comparable to the meat-labeling and grading program that has virtually ended misleading advertising (and greatly reduced concentration) in the fresh meat industry.

We congratulate the Commission on its efforts in the gasoline octane area and urge it to take equally vigorous action in its follow-up program there and in the other areas mentioned here. We have no doubt that some quite modest expenditures in these three areas would save consumers literally billions of dollars in lower prices and would thus constitute precisely the kind of significant economic policy-making your agency was created to perform.

PART TEN

*

Warranties
and
Product
Liability

INTRODUCTION
Warranties and Product Liability

CONSUMERS HAVE become increasingly dissatisfied with product warranties, and have resorted to the courts for redress. The Shafer article provides examples of class action suits filed by consumerists. The Federal Trade Commission, in its study of consumer complaints with respect to warranties, categorizes the problems in terms of (1) unsuitable products, (2) "the lemon," (3) delay in making repairs, (4) the "orphan consumer," (5) excessive labor charges, (6) failure to honor guarantees, (7) unscrupulous service operators, and (8) the lack of power on the part of the consumer to compel performance.

George Fisk presents a program for business that would dampen consumer complaints and increase the viability of the warranty as a marketing tool. The warranty should be clearly stated. Greater emphasis upon consumer education, particularly at the time of purchase, would have the net effect of reducing claims for warranty service. Fisk presents an interesting marketing strategy with respect to the effect of annual model change-overs on the manufacturer's ability to maintain his warranty. The consumer could register his choice, by the type of program purchased, between the time-tested models under a cost-free warranty and the annual change-over model with a labor service charge for in-warranty service.

The manufacturer's liability for warranties has increased primarily because of judicial decisions with respect to the privity rule rather than because of legislation. Using key cases, David Rados presents an historical perspective on changes in the court's interpretations with respect to product liability. The increase in liability results from the court's striking down attempts to limit liability by the narrow definition of expressed warranties and disclaimers in sales agreements, the decline of privity, and the trend toward the adoption of strict liability in tort.

In response to these changes in manufacturer's liability, management will have to develop positive programs that are aimed at prevention and insurability. As Rados indicates, although consumers have freedom of choice in the marketplace including the freedom to be wrong, they now have less freedom to make an unsafe choice. Consumers must increasingly be protected from the voluntary consumption of unsafe products.

40. CONSUMERS IN COURT

BILLS TO LET CUSTOMERS JOIN TO SUE COMPANIES ARE MULLED BY CONGRESS

Ronald G. Shafer

BEFORE TOO long, the motorist who discovers his new car is a lemon or the furniture buyer who feels cheated by a tricky installment contract may find it much easier to take his complaint to court. Moreover, he may carry a lot more clout when he gets there.

Congressional liberals of both parties, urged on by consumer groups and partially backed by the Nixon Administration, are now about to push bills that would give dissatisfied consumers greatly expanded legal power to seek redress—and would give business new legal headaches. These bills would allow consumers with a common complaint, about a defective product or a fraudulent selling practice to pool their damage claims against a merchant or manufacturer and hire lawyers to file a "class-action" suit in Federal court on behalf of all the plaintiffs.

Such a measure may clear the Senate Commerce Committee within the next two weeks and the House committee not long afterward. Despite stiff resistance from business, a bill authorizing class-action suits may emerge from Congress in some form before this session ends.

"A TERRIFIC TOOL"

A sample of the effect: A relatively small claim of say, $100 could be multiplied to a $1 million lawsuit if it were filed on behalf of 10,000 consumers with similar complaints. Most of the recovery in a successful suit would be divided up among the consumers represented.

Champions of the consumer cause see the class-action lawsuit as potentially one of the most powerful weapons in the consumer protection arsenal. "This is the real stuff; it's a terrific tool," says Ralph Nader. "It's an attempt to say to consumers that from now on your complaints will have access in court as a practical matter, not just on paper. Right now, most individual consumer abuses are too small dollarwise to interest lawyers or too small for consumers to endure the costs" of legal action, Mr. Nader says.

Currently, class actions are barred from federal courts unless each individual claim is at least $10,000, an amount far higher than most consumer claims. Class actions by consumers also are sharply restricted in most state courts. But such suits have begun turning up frequently in some states—California, for instance—where the courts have shown willingness to allow them.

One current California case exemplifies the possible magnitude of consumer class suits. Last August in Los Angeles, two pickup-truck owners filed a class action against General Motors Corp. on behalf of themselves and 200,000 owners of similar 1960 to 1965 GM trucks: they asked $427.5 million in damages. The suit charged GM with refusing to replace without charge allegedly defective wheels on the trucks.

GM'S RESPONSE

In October GM offered free replacement on about 40,000 of the trucks—those equipped with camper units that added to the weight. But attorneys for the two truck owners are seeking court approval to continue the class suit to force the company to replace the wheels on the other trucks. GM has denied any legal obligation and says it is replacing wheels on the camper trucks only "in the interest of reducing the safety hazard resulting from overloading" such trucks.

Consumer groups are advocating bills for class-action suits as "the consumer movement's number one priority legislation," says Edward Berlin, general counsel for the Consumer Federation of America, a coalition of 147 consumer organizations. In particular, they're backing identical measures proposed by Democratic Sen. Joseph Tydings of Maryland and Rep. Bob Eckhardt of Texas that would allow almost unlimited class actions.

Business organizations have lined up solidly against such legislation. "The potential impact of indiscriminate consumer class actions on business is devastating," declares Howard Schiff, speaking for the American Retail Federation. "Because of the great recoveries possible, consumer class actions are a harsh, vindictive remedy which is used not against . . . the so-called hard-core fraud but against reputable businesses," sayd Mr. Schiff, who is president of SCOA Industries Inc., an Ohio-based shoe manufacturer-retailer and department store operator.

ADMINISTRATION PROPOSALS

The U.S. Chamber of Commerce adds that any class-action legislation would be "ineffective, excessive and unnecessary." But if pressed, some business groups say they would at least prefer a bill proposed by the Nixon Administration that would first expand the Federal Trade Commission's consumer-protection authority and then limit any consumer class actions to cases first prosecuted successfully by the Government. The Tydings-Eckhardt measures would require no such "triggering" for the private suits.

The final form of any class-action bills will be worked out by the Senate and House Commerce Committees. One possible compromise currently is under study by the Senate subcommittee, headed by Democratic Sen. Frank Moss of Utah, that handles consumer protection legislation. It would allow class actions, subject to certain limitations, along the lines of the Tydings-Eckhardt bills. But it would also include certain Nixon Administration proposals to expand the FTC's authority; one of these would authorize the commission to obtain preliminary court injunctions to stop suspected consumer frauds quickly.

At this point, the prospects for Congressional action on whatever bills emerge from committee are still rather foggy. Both advocates and opponents of consumer class suits claim support for their views. There is speculation that any vote by Congress may be put off until next year, but consumer spokesmen insist they'll press for a vote before then. If the legislation should fall short of passage this session, there would surely be a new try in 1971.

Despite the controversy over the use of class suits by consumers, this type of legal recourse is nothing new in itself. Class actions long have been used by stockholders, for example, to battle management in corporate fights. But in recent years consumers have begun joining in such suits to try to recover relatively small losses. Otherwise, consumer groups argue, victims of illegal schemes usually haven't any practical way of getting their money back.

A recent antitrust settlement shows how consumers hope to benefit from class actions. In late 1967 a Federal court convicted three drug companies—American Cyanamid Co., Chas. Pfizer & Co. and Bristol Myers Co.—of conspiring to fix prices of tetracycline and other antibiotics between 1954 and 1966. Upjohn Co. and Squibb-Beechnut Inc. were later named as co-conspirators. The judgment paved the way for a battery of lawsuits by state and city governments, hospitals and individuals who had purchased the drugs.

OUT-OF-COURT SETTLEMENT

Lawsuits weren't feasible for the many individual buyers who claimed relatively small overcharges. But David I. Shapiro, a Washington lawyer who represented several states in suits against the five companies, proposed that the public representatives also sue on behalf of affected consumers. The result: When the companies offered cities and states out-of-court settlements totaling

$100 million last year, about $37 million of that was earmarked for direct refunds to consumers who could show receipts for the drug purchases between 1954 and 1966. Tentatively, about $82 million in settlements has been accepted by 43 states and several cities.

The 1967 conviction of the drug companies was overturned April 16 by a Federal appeals court in New York City, which ordered a new trial. But that ruling may not affect the pending settlements accepted by cities and states on the refunds due to go to individuals.

In many state courts, consumer groups contend, class actions by consumers have been blocked by narrow interpretations of the "unity" of their grievances. Last year in New York the National Association for the Advancement of Colored People sought to press a class action against a finance company on behalf of thousands of low-income consumers who had signed installment contracts allegedly printed in tiny type that was illegal. Two lower state courts refused to consider the suit a class action because all the consumers hadn't signed a single contract, even though all the contracts were identical. The suit currently is before a New York appeals court.

Getting into Federal courts is even tougher. For most consumer class actions, the Supreme Court slammed the door shut last year. It ruled that individuals couldn't pool their claims to reach the $10,000 minimum required in such cases heard by the Federal courts.

"SITTING DUCKS"

The bills proposed by Sen. Tydings and Rep. Eckhardt would seek to get around current restrictions in two ways: First, consumer class suits could be filed in Federal courts regardless of the individual amounts involved; second, they could be brought in Federal courts under existing state consumer protection laws. Thus, consumers could take their class suits to state courts where practical but could turn to Federal courts "if state class-action statutes are inadequate and too rigid," explains Rep. Eckhardt.

That approach is much too broad to suit business leaders. They argue that, in practice, such class actions wouldn't be used to help the poor and other consumers against fly-by-night businesses because such operators usually are "judgment proof": that is, they don't have any assets worth suing for. On the other hand, big corporations "would be sitting ducks because they have the money to pay the verdicts," says George Lamb, an attorney for the Association of Home Appliance Manufacturers.

Such critics contend legitimate businesses would be the target of frivolous lawsuits that would cost thousands of dollars merely to defend. The greatest beneficiaries would be lawyers who would prod consumers to file massive claims in hopes of collecting large settlements and fat fees, says George Koch, president of the Grocery Manufacturers of America.

(At least one prominent lawyer shares that concern. President Nixon recently warned some Congressmen that too permissive a bill "might flood the courts with a whole mass of actions which lawyers are perfectly capable of thinking up in the interests of a fee.'')

PREVENTING "HARASSMENT"

The Administration says its proposal to allow consumer class lawsuits in Federal courts only after the Government has obtained a conviction or consent agreement against a company would prevent, "harassment" of legitimate businesses. In addition, such suits could be brought only for 11 specific violations, such as selling a used product as a new, misrepresenting what a product can do or similar deceptive selling tactics.

(Originally, the more liberal approach, without such restrictions, was supported by the President's consumer adviser, Virginia Knauer. But she was overruled by other Administration officials after fierce lobbying by some business interests.)

Consumer groups vigorously oppose the Administration's proposal. "The Administration bill relegates the consumer to a second-class status before the courts," charges Mr. Berlin of the Consumer Federation. "Even as to the very limited kinds of claims that are made actionable, the consumer can seek relief only when the Administration says he may do so. We know of no precedent in the law for this notion, and we consider it to be totally objectionable and insulting.

41. REPORT OF THE TASK FORCE ON APPLIANCE WARRANTIES AND SERVICE

Federal Trade Commission

THIS REPORT is made up of three parts. The first covers the problems of the consumer. Next, the problems of the manufacturer are analyzed. Finally, the third part treats the problems of the retailer.

THE PROBLEMS OF THE CONSUMER

The problems encountered by purchasers of major household appliances in obtaining the benefits of warranties and guarantees in those instances in which the appliances do not function satisfactorily or require repairs during the period they are supposedly covered by a manufacturer's warranty or guarantee are discussed in this part of the report.

The primary sources of the materials used in the preparation of this part were the files of complaint letters in the office of the Special Assistant to the President for Consumer Affairs and in the files of the Federal Trade Commission. There are certain inherent limitations in basing an analysis of these problems on this data. Primarily, the complaint letters give only one side of the story, and at least some of the problems may have been resolved after the letters were written. Further, there is no way of ascertaining the frequency of complaints with respect to the number of appliances sold. However, over 1,000 complaints have been examined and it can be stated that the tenor and apparent objectiveness of the overwhelming majority provide substantial evidence that many are justified and that the purchaser who attempts to exercise his rights under a warranty or guarantee may have considerable difficulty in obtaining satisfaction or redress.

The basic cause of consumer dissatisfaction with service provided under

Reprinted from *Report of the Task Force on Appliance Warranties and Service* (Washington: Superintendent of Documents, January, 1968), 48-91.

a guarantee or warranty is the failure of the manufacturer or the retailer, or both, to fulfill the obligations set forth in the guarantee to the extent and in the manner expected by the consumer. In some instances the cause of dissatisfaction may be based on a misunderstanding on the part of the consumer of the terms of the guarantee. In others it may result from the inability or refusal of the servicing organization to place the appliance in proper operating condition. However, the numerous facets of the problem should be itemized and discussed in order that they may be fully understood.

THE UNSUITABLE PRODUCT

Many described the use of brittle plastic to fabricate moveable parts or parts subject to stresses or strains which resulted in repeated breakages and failures. The use of metal tubes, rather than plastic tubes which are immune to rust or chemical attack, was also identified as a fault of design. There are many others.

A recently purchased refrigerator began to "sweat" inside. Water accumulated on the sides and thoroughly soaked the contents. The owner was ultimately informed that the appliance was defective and that the only solution was to install an additional heater inside the box. The design made it impossible to correct the defect by other means. In one instance, the consumer was asked to pay for the installment of this heater.

Three complaints about the faulty design of television sets made by three large manufacturers are worthy of note. In each case numerous efforts to make the sets function properly were made by the local sellers and in two cases manufacturers' representatives attempted to make the necessary repairs. Despite these efforts none of the sets ever functioned properly. One purchaser was offered a $10 trade-in allowance on the set which he had owned for little more than a year. Another was offered a trade-in allowance amounting to the original cost of the set less 15% on condition that he waive the warranty on the new set.

A casement air conditioner sustained repeated burn outs of the compressor and was repaired three times during the guaranteed period of one year. The owner ascertained that this model was peculiarly susceptible to this type of trouble. As the warranty did not authorize replacement of the appliance, an extended term for design defects, or money back, the owner expects to pay for these recurring failures in the future.

THE LEMON

It is somewhat difficult to determine whether a complaint is attributable to the faulty design of a product or to defects in certain parts and their assembly. Records of the manufacturers or a wide survey of dealers or servicemen might enable one to identify which products of the various manufacturers have design faults. The "lemon" or the machine which is the subject of various

379

and numerous operative failures is constantly referred to in the complaints. Eventually, a number of these appliances are probably made to function properly. However, others continue to have a variety of troubles after the guarantee period has expired. The complaints indicate that there is a very great reluctance on the part of the dealers or manufacturers to replace the "lemon" with a new appliance or to refund the purchase price. While most guarantees contain undertakings to replace defective parts, one which provides for the replacement of a defective major appliance has not been seen.

DELAY IN MAKING REPAIRS

The files are replete with complaints regarding the failure of local service organizations to make the necessary repairs with reasonable promptness. Under this classification are situations in which those responsible for the repairs are apparently willing to make them but do so only after long delays. Such a delay can result in considerable costs to the owner, if for example, a freezer breaks down after it has been filled with food. In a number of instances the dealer or local service facility does not have the necessary parts; in others he does not have sufficient repairmen to schedule the service call without a delay of several weeks.

The unskilled and incompetent repairman is frequently designated as the source of many complaints. Undoubtedly there are many. However, their prevalence and actual role in the failure to perform obligations under a guarantee cannot be accurately assessed. A fully qualified and skilled mechanic cannot compensate for defective design or improper assembly of products.

THE ORPHAN CONSUMER

Most guarantees or warranties place the responsibility for actually making the repairs upon the selling dealer or upon a local service organization. Appliance owners have complained that frequently their warranties are valueless because the local dealer from whom they purchased the product has gone out of business or has stopped carrying the brand of appliance which he sold to them and will no longer repair the kind they purchased. Severance of the seller-customer relationship may also arise if the customer moves from the locality in which the appliance was purchased. In all of these situations the appliance owner may expect to encounter more than ordinary difficulty in obtaining the service authorized by his guarantee. His situation will be more serious if he lives in a small community where service facilities and competition are limited.

According to one complaint, a so-called orphaned consumer was given the option of shipping her appliance 150 miles to the nearest authorized service center or of paying for the repairs herself. In another instance, the original dealer had switched lines, and the consumer was referred to a competitor of the dealer. The competitor treated the consumer with contempt and rudeness and refused to provide the requested service. The factory representative located in a major city some miles distant referred the consumer to still another appliance dealer. This dealer attempted to repair the refrigerator and charged the owner $9.00 for labor and $36.00 for cartage. Almost immediately the refrigerator stopped running. A further appeal to the factory representative was unproductive so the consumer finally persuaded the selling dealer to make the repairs at a charge of $37.58 for "labor." Thus to have his refrigerator, which was still covered by a warranty, repaired the consumer expended $82.58 not counting the cost of the long distance telephone calls. He was also charged an additional $12.36 for a cold control unit which the original dealer advised the owner to purchase and install himself. As this part was covered by the warranty, it should have been provided without charge.

EXCESSIVE LABOR CHARGES

Some guarantees provide that the customer must pay labor and other charges incident to the repairs. The amount and nature of these charges are often aggravating. In one instance the transmission of a washing machine which was covered by a warranty failed. The owner did not object to paying the $5.95 charge for a home call or the $10.95 labor charge but did object to a charge of $13.50 designated as shop labor. This was explained to her as the cost of repairing her old transmission in the shop so that it could be given to another customer whose transmission failed. Another appliance owner complained of a labor charge of $15.95 to replace a thermostat. He stated that it took the serviceman only 15 minutes to do the work and compensation at this rate would amount to over $60.00 an hour. Others complained at having to pay a stated amount ranging from $5.00 to $8.00 for the service call plus an additional amount for labor. These charges would then be repeated if the serviceman had to make another call because he did not have the proper part when he made the first call.

FAILURE TO HONOR GUARANTEES

This leads to the discussion of the failure of a retailer or service organization to honor the provisions of the guarantee regarding the replacement of parts or labor without charge. Frequent examples of this failure of performance arise in those instances where the defect is of a nature which cannot be readily repaired by the dealer. In one instance a refrigerator was delivered with a chipped interior enamel. The seller disclaimed responsibility and refused to repair or replace the refrigerator for which the owner had unfortunately paid cash. After considerable correspondence between the owner and the manufacturer the area distributor called and stated that they would arrange for a replacement. Subsequently an obviously reconditioned refrigerator was delivered. Renewed complaints to the retailer resulted in the offer of a refund of $25.00.

When the picture tube on a recently purchased color television set failed, the retailer stated that he could not replace it because he did not have one in stock. The unusually perceptive owner called the local distributor and found that a large stock of color tubes of the proper make and size was available. Shortly thereafter, the retailer called and stated that he had obtained from a named distributor a tube of another manufacturer which would be suitable if the owner agreed. Subsequently, the owner called the named distributor and learned that the retailer had not ordered a tube from him. It would appear that the retailer intended to install a rebuilt tube in the set.

The files contain many other examples of the failure of dealers to honor the terms of the guarantee by refusing to perform the necessary work, by performing the work in a slip-shod manner, or by attempting to stall until the warranty period expires.

THE DISINTERESTED MANUFACTURER

When the owner of an appliance cannot obtain satisfaction from the dealer or local service organization, he turns to the manufacturer. The complaints establish that the results of such appeals are something less than happy. It is not uncommon for the manufacturer to ignore the appeal altogether and make no response. Some do respond and advise the consumer to contact the dealer about whose conduct she complained. Others recommend contact with a distributor or area service representative. This often leads to what is described as the "run around" with considerable exchange of correspondence, broken appointments, and nothing being done, with the manufacturer, distributor, and retailer, all disclaiming any blame or ability to solve the problem.

THE UNSCRUPULOUS SERVICE OPERATOR

A number of consumers complained that they were treated unfairly by servicing agencies who performed in warranty service on their applicances. Some of these complaints can be attributed to incompetent servicemen. Others indicate a more basic dissatifaction with the business practices of the servicing agency and with the failure of the manufacturer to take effective corrective action.

One independent service company in a major city was a factory authorized service center for a number of major appliance manufacturers. The Commission's files reflect that his activities resulted in over 100 complaints, of which a considerable number were brought to the attention of the manufacturers of the products involved. So far as we know, the company is still a representative for those manufacturers.

In response to a consumer complaint about the unfairness and inefficiency of an independent dealer service facility, the manufacturer replied that it had received many similar complaints about this particular dealer, and that it regretted that it could do nothing about it.

In response to another complaint about excessive labor charges, a manufacturer replied that it furnished its authorized repairmen with a list of suggested charges. However, it added that it could not force them to conform to these charges, and that it was expected that charges would vary in different parts of the country.

As one manufacturer frankly admitted, customers have no guidelines or means of judging or comparing the costs of product repairs. They may be victimized by the illegitimate unscrupulous service operators. There is at the moment no complete defense.

In conclusion it should be noted that the paucity of competent service facilities results in many manufacturers hesitating to give up an outlet in a particular area when there is no alternative available, particularly if such action would make him available to their competitors.

THE ILLUSIVE GUARANTEE

An objective analysis of the warranties and guarantees used in the major appliance industry is set forth in a preceding section of the report. In this part, the views of consumers regarding these guarantees are described.

The failure of guarantee to set forth clearly and in understandable language the nature and extent of the guarantee is a common complaint. A closely related complaint is that the guarantee contains conditions which are unfair and which frequently make the dealer or manufacturer the sole judge of whether a particular defect is covered by the guarantee.

According to consumers, the obligations of the purchaser which are prerequisite to the validity of the guarantee are not clearly disclosed or may be unreasonable. Thus the guarantee may be limited to the original purchaser, e.g., the builder of a new home and not to the purchaser of the home. There may be requirement for presentation of the original sales slip, or evidence of registration of the sale with the manufacturer, or the purchaser may be required to remove and ship a part to the manufacturer, or to pay freight and other transportation costs. Sometimes the actual terms of the guarantee may differ from those advertised.

When unsuccessful efforts are made to repair a defective product during the guarantee period, further complaints regarding the same defect or condition made after the expiration of the guarantee period are answered with the announcement that nothing can be done as the warranty is no longer in effect. In one instance after a purchaser had finally prevailed upon the manufacturer to examine a color television set which had never worked properly, he was informed that the set was completely worn out, and that since the warranty had expired it would cost $300 to have it repaired.

Unreasonable conditions in the guarantee are also troublesome to the consumer. One small shop owner who purchased a window air conditioner was informed that the guarantee was limited so as not to apply if the product was installed in other than a single-family home. Other provisions of guarantees limit the obligation to replace defective parts by use of such phrases as "which are found defective by us." All disclaim responsibility for consequential damages with a few exceptions such as loss of food in the case of a freezer failure.

Another complaint is that the duration of a warranty is unduly limited. Numerous expensive television sets carry warranties of only 90 days—this despite the manufacturers' claims that use of solid state circuitry has eliminated the factor (heat) which is responsible for the most trouble in television sets. The length of other warranties seem to have been carefully determined so that they lapse just before malfunctions may be expected to appear.

LACK OF FORUM

There is no readily available means or procedure by which a consumer can compel performance under a guarantee or be adequately compensated for its breach.

There is no question that the courts have long since departed from their previous policy of erecting protective barriers around the manufacturers and sellers of products. That policy was well described by a judge in these words:

> A wise and conservative public policy has impressed the courts with the view that there must be a fixed and definite limitation to the liability of a manufacturer and vendors in the construction and sale of complicated machines and structures which are to be operated or used by the intelligent and the ignorant, the skillful and the incompetent, the watchful and the careless, parties that cannot be known to the manufacturers or vendors, and those who use the articles all over the country hundreds of miles distant from the place of their manufacturer or original sale.[1]

However, for a variety of reasons the purchaser of an inoperable major home appliance is not inclined to seek redress in the courts for the failure of the manufacturer or seller to conform to the terms of the guarantee. The reasons why they fail to do so are legion—expense, delay, distrust of lawyers, and procedural problems, are perhaps the most common. Action has been taken by the Federal Trade Commission in a number of instances against manufacturers and appliance distributors or retailers who are in commerce and who have violated Section 5 of the Federal Trade Commission Act (15 U.S.C. 41), by deceptive acts and practices involving warranties and guarantees. However, the Commission does not have jurisdiction to reach appliance dealers or service agencies who are not engaged in interstate commerce, or to adjudicate disputes between the manufacturer and retailer on the one hand and the consumer on the other. Therefore the consumer does not really have, at least from a practical standpoint, a forum in which the justness of his claim can be established and which can direct that he be compensated for his damages. The recurring thought expressed in many letters is "I purchased an appliance made by————because I thought they were dependable. I was wrong! Where am I to turn?"

PROBLEMS OF THE MANUFACTURER

This part of the report is based primarily upon information submitted by industry members in response to the oral and written requests of Chairman Paul Rand Dixon. In these requests industry members were asked to describe the warranty service practices and policies of their respective companies, to list what they considered to be the major obstacles to improved warranty service, and to submit suggestions for remedying the problems associated with the warranty of their products. Knowledge of the manufacturers' practices and policies is a prerequisite to an understanding of the problems envisioned by them.

Manufacturers' arrangements for the provision of warranty service to purchasers of their products are not uniform, and many manufacturers employ more than one method. However, the basic arrangements may be categorized as follows:

(1) Service is provided through factory-owned service centers which are managed and staffed by employees of the manufacturers.
(2) Retailers who service as well as sell appliances. These are sometimes franchised.
(3) Factory authorized independent service companies provide service.
(4) Independent or franchised distributors may be responsible for providing service throughout the area in which they sell appliances.

The manufacturers used various means to ascertain whether the service organizations were performing at the required level of efficiency. These included customer sampling, review of invoices, inspections, and related procedures. Supervisory requirements were also imposed upon distributors to supplement the factory efforts, and several manufacturers stated that the distributors were required to assume responsibility for providing service if a dealer or independent servicing organization failed to do so.

Some manufacturers state that they do not prescribe standards for a servicing retailer or for an independent service agency. They point out that in some areas the paucity of really qualified service facilities gives them the choice of providing no service at all or of using a firm which they do not consider qualified. In those areas in which utilities provide service, manufacturers indicated a preference for them, because of the quality of service personnel these organizations employ. It was also pointed out that the conditions throughout the country varied so much that it was difficult to establish uniform standards on a nationwide basis.

Where the community provided a choice of service representatives, manufacturers reported that they attempted to verify the reputation, credit rating, and adequacy of the manpower and equipment of the agency, as well as its willingness to purchase the necessary tools and maintain an adequate technical library.

Several manufacturers now require that distributors, or independent servicing agencies under contract, provide warranty service to purchasers who move in the area with an appliance purchased in another locality. However, others do not and seemingly have made no provision for providing warranty service to such orphaned consumers.

The methods used to determine the amount of compensation to be paid to servicing dealers or agencies for warranty work on appliances are subject to many variables and complexities. One of the simplest, and perhaps the most satisfactory from the standpoint of the consumer, is for the servicing agency to bill the manufacturer for the cost of parts and service at the same rates he would use for his other customers. In fact one manufacturer stated that he expected the amount of this billing to include a reasonable profit for the servicer.

One of the more common practices is for the manufacturer not to pay direct compensation for warranty work because its obligation is restricted to the replacement of any parts used in effecting the repairs. Compensation for the work, i.e., the labor and service charge, is thus dependent upon an agreement between the retailer and the consumer. The dealer may agree to provide warranty service without charge; he may sell the consumer a warranty service policy; or the consumer may pay the labor and service charges on a per call basis.

Those manufacturers which undertake to pay for warranty labor and service may agree to do so at the prevailing rates charged other consumers by the servicing agency, with the understanding that they will only replace the parts the agency used in making the repairs.

Many manufacturers have established detailed schedules showing the amounts they will pay for time spent in diagnosing and repairing various defects in appliances. These schedules will vary from one part of the country to the other because of differences in wage rates and costs. In compiling these schedules, information is obtained from the servicing agencies, who of course must agree to them, and factors such as the anticipated time necessary to make the repairs, the charges made by the agency for its non-warranty work, and the rates paid by other manufacturers are considered. The amount and method of making compensation will be set forth in the agreement between the manufacturer, distributor, or the retailer and the agency which will actually do the work. In some instances a flat rate based on the number of appliances sold in the area will determine the amount of compensation to be paid.

Manufacturers which expect retailers to provide warranty service on a non-reimbursable basis frequently use a method known as "in-boarding." Under this method a specific amount for each model of appliance is "paid" to a retailer who has agreed to perform in-warranty service. This payment is made by means of a deduction from the product price charged to him which is intended to cover the labor costs of the servicing dealer in doing warranty work. Manufacturers favor this arrangement because they believe that it gives the retailer an incentive to avoid unnecessary repairs and at the same time makes it unnecessary for the manufacturer to charge higher prices to cover the cost of factory provided service. If the appliance is sold to a non-servicing dealer, the payment is actually made to a service operator in that locality—this is his flat rate which was mentioned above. Under one variation of the in-boarding arrangement the dealer is simply expected to provide for warranty labor costs out of his margin of profit on the sale of the appliance to the purchaser.

Upon receipt of information that an appliance had a serious defect in its design or manufacture, most industry members stated that they wouldendeavor to locate all such products and repair them at no cost to the purchaser. Sale of the defective units would also be halted until the necessary modifications could be made. Several manufacturers indicated that such defects would be corrected free of charge, even though the warranty period might have expired. Others stated that they had handled those matters in the past as normal warranty type work, with the attendant division of costs between the manufacturer, the retailer, and the consumer. With respect to one defective product the warranty period was extended for an additional year.

More positive action was taken in the case of defects which might result in danger to life or property. In one instance a particular model of appliance was recalled and replaced with another, even though a number had been installed in purchasers' homes. The cost and difficulty involved in locating such units was reported as being of considerable magnitude.

The feasibility of simplifying the language used in appliance warranties was the subject of another question addressed to manufacturers. A surprising number, including some which had the most complex warranty certificates examined, responded that their warranties were written in clear concise language which was perfectly understandable, and that it would not be possible to improve or simplify the terminology used. They also stated that they had received no complaints regarding the clarity of their warranties. Some expressed the fear that simplification or increased brevity would subject them to unjustified claims by consumers. Others noted that as a result of the activities of the President's Committee on Consumer Interests they had undertaken to redraft, shorten, and otherwise simplify the warranties in use. Those who had done so stated that use of the revised warranties had not caused them any additional problems and that on the contrary, use of the revisions had resulted in a more attractive package for the prospective purchaser. Several responses indicated a growing awareness that use of the numerous exceptions was not required and a willingness to go along with industry-wide efforts toward simplification.

Industry members were asked to state what they considered to be the major obstacles to improving the warranty service on their respective products. Their replies give an excellent picture of the problems from the viewpoint of the manufacturer.

All of the replies indicated that one of the greatest problems was a shortage of qualified technicians to repair and service appliances. This shortage is aggravated, as one manufacturer put it, by a tremendous expansion of product offerings and an explosive increase in the number of major appliances in use. The increasing demands on the technical abilities of servicemen because of the greater electro-mechanical complexity of appliances necessitate longer and more comprehensive training programs to qualify persons for entry into this field. The failure of many servicing dealers to take advantage of the manufacturers' training program was noted. The image of the serviceman has not grown in proportion to the knowledge and qualifications which he must have. As a result some customers do not trust a serviceman and are inclined to view his comments and recommendations with suspicion. The demand for service on such products as air conditioners is seasonal. Sufficient personnel to handle promptly service calls at the peak of the season cannot be gainfully employed for the balance of the year. This necessitates some degree of compromise which will result in some consumer dissatisfaction.

The consumers themselves are said to be a major source of difficulties. While they insist on elaborate design and selective operational characteristics, they are unwilling to read and to follow the instructions which outline procedures requisite to the proper functioning of the product. Sometimes this results in damage or malfunctioning for which they blame the manufacturer. Frequently a serviceman is summoned and finds that he need only explain to the consumer how to operate the product. This entails a high cost to the manufacturer or servicing agent and makes it impossible for them to provide services which are justified within reasonable time limits. Consumers have on occasion been unreasonable in their demands for service. One manufacturer reported repeated calls for such services as cleaning a range within the warranty period.

Consumers sometimes attempt to make repairs on appliances and subsequently attribute their lack of success to a defective part or to a serviceman. This results in a number of false claims. A somewhat similar situation arises when a consumer permits an unauthorized service agency to undertake the repairs.

Many dealers will carry more than one line of appliances. This results in several problems for the manufacturer. First, the proliferation of lines makes it impracticable for the retailer to carry an adequate stockage of spare parts. Secondly, the salesmen on his floor generally have difficulty in giving an adequate explanation of the differing features of several lines and in giving competent instructions on how the appliances should be operated. Further this may also result in a misunderstanding on the part of the consumer of the provisions of the guarantee, for the salesman may confuse the guarantee of one manufacturer with that of another. Manufacturers point out that they are unable to exercise effective control over retailers who sell their products. Unjustified promises made by the retailer or his employees are presented to the manufacturer with the expectation that he will fulfill them.

Cost is considered to be a fundamental obstacle to the improvement of warranty service. The shortage of servicemen is said to be symptomatic of this obstacle. Because of the intense competition he faces, the dealer questions his ability to support an adequate service department. Some manufacturers have recognized and accepted the weakness of the retailers and have provided more financial support in the form of increased payments to service agencies which are doing the work. However, other manufacturers do not believe that they can go further than they already have. As one stated,

If we were to offer labor and transportation for replacement parts and service then it would surely mean that we would be called upon to make simple, routine adjustments and to replace parts which were no longer serviceable because of abuse. No one could accurately determine the cost of providing such service, but it is hardly debatable that the cost would be tremendous. In the long run this would mean that people who use their appliances with proper care would be penalized by having to pay many dollars more in purchase price. This would be necessary to enable us to provide service for the less careful users of our appliances.

The varying length of warranty periods also serves to confuse the consumer. When components of a product are warranted against failure for different lengths of time, consumers who do not carefully read the warranty will often misunderstand what is and what is not covered for the extended period.

Another complaint of the manufacturers relates to the difficulty they have, particularly in rural areas, of locating a qualified sercice agency. This problem is more acute for the small manufacturer who cannot afford to establish a network of factory owned facilities.

The final complaint of the manufacturers is that intense competition has made it necessary for them to design appliances having new and complicated features and to offer them for sale at lower and lower prices. This has made it difficult for them to maintain quality control and set aside sufficient reserves to pay for the warranty service costs.

PROBLEMS OF THE RETAILER

In this section of the report, the warranty problems of the servicing dealer and the independent repairman are discussed. The diverse nature of these establishments with respect to size and type makes it difficult to ascribe a common set of problems to them. In addition, the severity of a problem may vary considerably with the relative size of a business. Nevertheless, most retailers apparently share the belief that the major obstacle to providing better warranty service is the shortage of trained technicians to do the warranty work on appliances. Although a detailed consideration of the causes of this shortage is beyond the scope of this report, the more important of the reasons given by the retailers themselves are mentioned in the interest of completeness.

An appliance repairman, and particularly one who works for an independent service organization or for a servicing retailer who handles more than one line of appliances, must be completely familiar with the technical characteristics of a whole range of products. He must be a skilled diagnostician or trouble shooter, who is able to evaluate the symptoms reported by the owner of the appliance, and to ascertain the probable nature of the malfunction by a series of simple tests. After he has found the trouble, he must repair it using the tools carried from job to job, and the limited stock of spare parts carried on his truck. A competent repairman must have all of these abilities and more, for his skills must be developed and enhanced to enable him to keep pace with the demands presented by the novel and more complex appliances which come off the production lines each year.

The conditions under which the appliance repairman works are not among the best. He must ply his trade in the basements and utility rooms of private homes, and work on appliances which have been installed with no thought that access to them should be provided for the repairman. His frequent contact with dissatisfied consumers who complain of delays and question his ability to repair the appliance add to his woes. Finally, he must attempt to collect the charges due upon completion of his work and fill out various forms and repair tickets.

Many retailers recognize that a skilled repairman does not have too much inducement to enter or remain in the field of appliance repair, for the compensation is not particularly good, and in some cases seasonal demand may even put him out of work during slack periods. The proprietors of service establishments contend that their margin of profit on the sale of appliances and the financial support provided by manufacturers do not enable them to pay compensation sufficient to overcome the disadvantages of this work. They point out that job opportunities in factories and shops where the technician will enjoy the benefits of good working conditions, union membership, and better salaries are simply too much for them to overcome.

Some retailers recognize that the real core of the problem is inadequate salaries. However, many of these state that they cannot afford to pay more and must rely on the repetitive training of a rapidly changing work force which does not remain in position long enough to learn to give satisfactory service.

Retailers join with manufacturers in urging Federal and state governments to sponsor training programs in the high schools and vocational schools for appliance servicemen. However, it should be recalled that the manufacturers complained that the retailers do not fully utilize the manufacturer sponsored programs. Several proprietors of private technical schools have also alleged that the manufacturers were reluctant to provide them with training manuals, models, and other forms of assistance in the training of service technicians. Certainly it would appear that more cooperation by all concerned would result in the better utilization of existing training facilities and perhaps make government support unnecessary.

A lack of a readily available source of supply of spare parts is a complaint of a number of retailers. Some have reported that parts orders for even "likely to fail parts" have been delayed for weeks and even months by some manufacturers. Other retailers state that the manufacturers expect them to carry a relatively large inventory of parts on hand, to do warranty was well as ordinary repair work, and that they are financially unable to tie up their limited capital for this purpose. They complain that the manufacturers themselves have displayed the same unwillingness to maintain an adequate stockage of parts, yet since they do not deal directly with the irate consumer, the local repairman receives the blame.

Another of their problems, which the retailers lay at the door of the manufacturer, is poor and insufficient quality control. The retailers point out that major appliances are assembled on a production line and that defects can be eliminated much more cheaply in a factory than they can in a consumer's kitchen or in a neighborhood repair shop. They say it is uneconomical to expect them to correct factory mistakes and shortcomings under the much higher cost conditions that prevail in their part of the industry. Retailers also say that in production and design, ease of servicing should be given more consideration. Access should be provided to facilitate replacement or repair of likely to fail parts. Parts should be marked to permit their ready identification by the repairman.

Unreasonable and unpleasant consumers are also designated as a serious problem for the retailer. They report numerous service calls which result in the skilled repairman merely having to explain to the consumer how to operate the appliance and to repeat information contained in the manual which accompanied the appliance when it was sold. One retailer said that the purchaser who found he could not make timely payments on the appliance was the most difficult to deal with as such a purchaser would falsely allege that his appliance did not work properly. Abuse and discourtesy to servicemen and a failure to keep appointments for service were also noted.

The consumer who attempts to repair or modify his appliance and follows up his failure to do so with a claim that he is entitled to warranty service also presents problems for the retailer. In a somewhat similar category are the consumers who abuse their appliances. While the serviceman can ordinarily detect that such occurrences are the probable cause of the product failure, it is difficult to prove and the retailer feels that in case of doubt he should go ahead and provide service under the warranty with attendant increase in costs.

While many retailers agree that the warranties and guarantees used by major appliance manufacturers are sufficiently clear to be understood by most consumers, they state that a simplification program would be of considerable benefit to the retailer in enabling him to avoid misunderstandings with his customers.

The most serious problem for the retailer, and the smaller he is the more acute it becomes, is the matter of compensation for the warranty service he is called upon to provide. The various methods used by manufacturers to compensate retailers for warranty service were fully described in the section of the report which dealt with the problems of the manufacturers and will not be repeated here. However, under many of those methods the retailer is required to bear a very considerable part of the cost of correcting factory defects. The greater the burden imposed on the retailer, the greater the likelihood that the warranty service he provides will be totally inadequate by any standards.

It is the view of the retailers that they should be paid for warranty service work at the same rates they charge for ordinary service and that such arrangements could be coupled with provisions to provide the manufacturer with protection against exaggerated claims without undue difficulty. Further they believe that the manufacturers should incorporate in the price of their products a sufficient amount to permit the provision of adequate warranty service under the full reimbursement scheme.

The retailers report that no one seems to understand why the cost of servicing appliances is so high. They point out that the standard wage for service technicians is on the order of $4.00 or more dollars per hour. A firm must charge two and one half to three times this rate for service to pay overhead and provide a reasonable profit, and when this is coupled with the cost of providing a repair truck, stocking it with parts, and getting it from point to point the seemingly exorbitant repair charges become more credible. They recognize that steps should be taken to bring these facts to the attention of the consuming public but believe that the ultimate solution rests within the power of the manufacturer to pay all of these expenses.

NOTES

1. Huset v. J. I. Case Threshing Machine Company, 120 F. 865, 870 (A-8, Minn., 1903).

42. GUIDELINES FOR WARRANTY SERVICE AFTER SALE

George Fisk

THE RECENT decision of General Motors to call back 4.9 million cars to check for safety defects was estimated to cost the company 50 million dollars in addition to the time and inconvenience to which GM customers would be subjected.[1] GM's dramatic callback announcement may have been made with an eye to forestalling government controls such as the bills introduced into the Senate of the United States by Senators Magnuson and Hayden calling for truth in warranty legislation.[2]

The GM recall move underscores the fact that everything that moves breaks down sooner or later. With over 800 million traffic vehicles and major appliances in use, individual warranty programs will not follow exactly the same plan because service facilities and consumer use patterns vary from product to product. Nonetheless, there is an urgent need for manufacturers and distributors to try to find warranty guidelines to assure adequate service after sale. This paper is one effort to provide such help.

It is easy to ask, as many indignant consumers do, why manufacturers and their distributors do not provide more adequate warranty services.[3] Walker Sandback, Executive Director of Consumers' Union reports that warranty complaints are among the most numerous and bitter of those received by C.U. He reports over 5,000 letters of complaints annually concerning written warranties. Firms such as Zippo Cigarette Lighters and the Whirlpool Appliance Corporation have attempted to use warranty performance to build solid reputations for quality products. A large number of firms—perhaps a majority—have neither consistent warranty programs nor consistent policies for servicing their products after sale.[4] During his term as president, Lyndon Johnson advised firms holding these views to assure customers that guarantees and warranties meant what they said and said what they meant. He implied that government would act if businessmen did not. Today, the Magnuson and Hayden bill has considerable support from angry consumers who, although they have been

Reprinted from *Journal of Marketing*, Vol. 34 (January, 1970), p. 63-67, published by The American Marketing Association.

winning court cases for a long time, have lacked direct means for protecting their rights as buyers.[5] Mounting support for the consumer movement leads many a businessman to ask what he can do to assure consumers of adequate service in the event that his products fail in the consumer's hands.[6]

A POSITIVE PROGRAM

The programs of firms that have used warranty service to build consumer preferences demonstrate that American industry can convert consumer complaints into successful marketing strategies. To do so will require more than proclamations of intent, however. If for no other reason than to prevent legislative overkill, industry must seek to apply the same intelligence to service after sale that it now applies to wooing the customer in the first place. Four guidelines are proposed here as instruments for meeting the social responsibilities of marketing as well as for assuring a continuing customer interest; warranty integrity, education of the consumer, product quality control, and service on demand. The Whirlpool Corporation, for example, has cut its complaint/sales ratio to a relatively low 20% in seven years using a coherent warranty program based on some of the concepts described here.

WARRANTY INTEGRITY

Most manufacturers and distributors issue written warranties. A majority attempt to live up to the provisions of their warranties but a substantial number of firms use warranties as legal disclaimers of responsibility.[7] To avoid misunderstanding, more attention should be given to the way prospective purchasers interpret written warranties. An unambiguous warranty states not only the details of what is covered but also:

> the name and address of the guarantor,
> the length of time each phase of the guarantee or each major
>   component is covered,
> who can file for a claim,
> what conditions the claimant must fulfill,
> what proportion of the cost must be covered by the person mak-
>   ing the claim,
> what parts and types of damages are not covered,
> when and how the guarantor will fulfill his obligations.

Consumers know that some manufacturers offer stronger warranties than others. Weaker firms tend to offer more comprehensive guarantees than their more successful rivals. Since most businessmen believe that customer satisfaction builds brand loyalty, they are behaving inconsistently if they permit consumer hostility to be directed against an explicit but effectively worthless warranty. The first step in bridging the warranty "credibility gap" is to tell the truth to consumers as they understand it and not as the corporation's legal department would like it to be. If the warrantor fails to deliver according to the customer's expectations, the credibility gap widens, and when large numbers of consumers become aware of the fact that they have suffered the same kinds of losses, the consumer protectionist movement gains support for additional legislation. Consequently, warranty integrity is more than a pious assertion of intent; it is a necessary precondition for customer good will and continued freedom of action in the business community.

"Unconditionally guaranteed," "money-back guarantee," and "lifetime guarantee" are terms often used to conceal the fact that component or accessory parts are not included in the seller's guarantee, that labor costs are not guaranteed, or that the fitness of the product for use is explicitly disclaimed by the seller. Repetition of unsatisfactory experiences based on these kinds of intentional deceptions have led articulate consumers to press for a change in warranty regulations. Even businessmen with the best intentions find it difficult to know how customers will interpret their warranty statements. Therefore, these ambiguous phrases are to be eschewed as vigorously as efforts to include the items previously mentioned in a written warranty are to be encouraged in warranty programs.

The first guideline in establishing warranty policies is to tell as much of the truth as the consumer needs to know to keep his warranty in force, and not as little as he is willing to believe in order to buy. If it is necessary for a seller to include a service contract tie-in to validate a warranty, the buyer has a right to know about this condition before he seeks to file a claim. If the warranty applies to the original purchaser only, subsequent buyers also have a right to this information. If the warranty is intended to apply for the design life of the product, the buyer should be explicitly informed that the *product* life, not the *buyer's* life is the relevant time span. If there are other limiting conditions, the buyer has a right to know them.

CONSUMER EDUCATION PROGRAMS

Perhaps as many as 80% of all consumer claims for warranty service may not be necessary. It is not that consumers are stupid, but they seldom read the operating instructions that accompany their purchases, or obey these instructions faithfully even when they know them. For this reason, some in-warranty service activity should include explicit consumer training in the use of the products purchased. In one instance a housewife complained that her new car would not go. After a 19-mile journey over back mountain roads, the dealer whom she telephoned found that the reason was an empty gas tank. Similar complaints from people who fail to turn on motors, add oil to new engines, or observe other operating instructions, are responsible for needless warranty calls. The pretesting of warranties, using warranty readership analysis can lead to improved operating instructions so that the consumer understands not only her obligations under the warranty but also what is necessary to make the appliance operate effectively.

Since most humans learn by experience rather than by study, an effective warranty education program can capitalize on periods in the use-cycle when the customer is psychologically receptive to suggestion on how to use a product. Housewives are eager to learn how to use equipment when they have just paid for new appliances, but not after self-doubt about the wisdom of their purchase sets in. At the time of purchase it is often possible to use a simple slide film presentation of the product in use. The same film may be repeated when a repair call is needed to restore the product to use the first time. Home demonstrations by public utility representatives, repairmen, or mechanics can be highly effective. Although instruction manuals and decals are helpful, customers frequently fail to read them. Consequently, visual instructions in color may be preferable to an enclosure or to the fine print that adorns the inside wall of a cabinet. The firm that conducts readership tests on its operating instructions and warranty provisions is a rarity indeed, but such studies can be helpful in determining what information customers will attend to, what questions they have that are unanswered by instruction manuals, and what instructions they misinterpret in a way that damages their new purchases.

PRODUCT IMPROVEMENT

Premature failure in use is a prime cause of customer disenchantment with new products. Industry representatives sometimes argue that at the price per pound at which U.S. products are to be sold to compete with imports, multiple inspections for critical parts and sub-assemblies are too costly. Such claims are frequently made without the benefit of cost-effectiveness analysis.[8] Were the tradeoff values of research and development programs, inspection programs, and quality control programs to be compared to the cost of legal defense, customer brand switching, and costly callback programs, the advantages of improved quality control might often be sufficient to offset the increased costs.

From the standpoint of the disenchanted consumer, it is not the price per unit of output but per period of trouble-free use that counts. If, for example, a U.S. tire cost half the price of a European radial tire delivered in the United States, it is not cheaper if it must be replaced in one-third the time while the European product is still safe and delivering excellent gas mileage. The high quality of the products marketed by small foreign firms, which have been eroding the U.S. market share underscores the significance of the loss due to brand shifting in a number of industries ranging from automobile to textiles.[9]

Two avenues of improved quality are especially deserving of closer attention by management: product redesign cycles and assembly inspections. In evaluating the cost-effectiveness of lax quality control against high quality control and redesign, a systems analysis of costs and benefits can improve allocation decisions with respect to the maintenance of parts inventory, the frequency of complaints on performance failures, and the desirability of model change-overs. European manufacturers, for example, are not addicted to annual model redesign. Thus, they are able to stock repair parts even though their production runs are smaller than their American counterparts. Products which are redesigned annually require immense parts inventories compared to products which are redesigned only when a technological improvement warrants change. Annual or biennial redesign also prevents repairmen from discovering and correcting performance defects as rapidly as the designers make new mistakes. For example, a decline in sales of one outstanding electronics product can be traced to the fact that a basic component of this expensive machine is no longer manufactured. This situation developed because under the warranty the component is termed an "unwarranted auxiliary part" for which the manufacturer assumes no liability. At least some consumers are irked by this not uncommon practice even if the producer's interest in cutting cost through reduction of inventory is understandable.

While it is true that the consumer demand for novelty gives dealers something to sell, the tradeoff in many consumers' minds between dependability and variety does not necessarily favor variety to the degree that American marketing men have sometimes assumed. If dependability were not a valued product feature, Volkswagen and Rolleiflex, Wilkinson's Blades, and Electrolux Vacuum Cleaners would not enjoy the American sales they do.

If annual model changeovers are necessary to sustain sales, several choices remain open with respect to warranty policy. A producer can indicate that the warranty coverage is more limited on annually redesigned models, or he can charge a premium for a service contract based upon frequency of repair records and current hourly rates for repairmen. If consumers could register their choice between time-tested models under a cost-free warranty and annual changeover models with a labor service charge for in-warranty service, it might be possible to discover the tradeoff point at which proponents of new design would willingly choose dependable performance in preference to annual model change-overs plus labor charges for warranty services.

Improved assembly and inspection routines can also reduce in-warranty service calls by raising quality. Extending standard assembly times, reinspection of parts and assemblies, reduction of the proportion of allowable defects in parts inspections, setting closer tolerances on moving parts, and using higher quality primary materials are techniques quite well known to industrial engineers.

No socially responsible firm can advocate salability despite social costs such as death and injury on the highways and in the home. (Marketing men need not dictate a level of quality that is detrimental to serviceability if engineering can define for the marketing department an equation for optimality of salability and serviceable quality.) What products businessmen cannot warrant at prevailing competitive prices they are ill-advised to sell. The temper of the times dictates a more prudent social policy than "marketability at any price" on the part of sellers whose volume philosophy has gone unchallenged for many years.

SERVICE

The core of any warranty program ultimately lies in the quality of the maintenance and repair services that can be offered to customers. Inferior post-warranty service calls can induce needless brand switching. In addition, a back-log of uncompleted service calls can depress the level of market penetration for products ranging from television to garbage disposal units. One explanation for unsatisfactory service is inadequate compensation and training of service technicians. It is commonly believed that more repairmen are leaving the retail service field than are entering and that crash training programs to create "tube jockeys" capable only of hit-or-miss replacement tactics are simply adding to the number of unserviced appliances awaiting repair. The BLS estimates that there are 200,000 "appliance repairmen" with an annual attrition rate of 10,000, but the main problem is believed to be quality of service. [10]

To obtain qualified service personnel, industry has to foot the bill although some help is available from government. Recognizing this situation, most trade association apprenticeship proposals for training new appliance technicians depend on Department of Labor funds made available through the Manpower Training Act. However, programs dependent on federal aid could easily col-lapse under the impact of congressional budget cuts. The training of inner city youths in service technician careers will require a sustained level of dedicated cooperation between municipal and state governments on one hand and man-ufacturers and distribution agencies on the other. Uncle Sam cannot deliver the quality and volume of training required to solve industry's appliance techni-cian manpower shortage problem without industry help. Cooperation with the Department of Labor is necessary and desirable for pilot projects, but the domi-nant training role should be assumed by industries whose customers have a right to the service they are promised in written warranties.

Many firms such as RCA, GE, Carrier, and Whirlpool maintain technical training centers where their appliance technicians can periodically update skills needed to assure competent performance. [11] Recruiting and training new service technicians takes a lot of time and money to assure mastery of technically difficult repairs. Refresher courses stressing design changes are also needed for already proficient repairmen. The implied scope of such programs makes it necessary to hire full time service training directors to do the job effectively. In many firms this could force a reexamination of present payroll allocations. However, if business cannot voluntarily provide the quality of repair and maintenance service demanded by the increasingly sophisticated equipment it puts on the market, the government will have little alternative but to impose licensing and inspection programs such as already are in force in Connecticut, Indiana, Louisiana, and Massachusetts.

For example, California has a licensing system under which bill-padding and faulty diagnosis can be traced. New York is considering such a step after tests by Consumers' Union showed wide variations in the quality of diagnosis and in prices for replacing an inexpensive tube in a color TV set. The Louisiana Motor Vehicle Commission requires auto companies to pay the same rate for warranty work as the dealer charges for routine customer service. Since the first step in fair pricing is competent diagnosis and repair, only professional supervision can assure that the quality of repair services will meet these exacting requirements.

Subtle pricing issues also arise in connection with warranty terms. In the first place there is the question whether a producer should be held responsible for replacing components he does not make, such as light bulbs and switches, or whether the consumer should be forced to pay for the manufacturer's assembly and inspection mistakes by paying for the labor required to complete a repair. Reputable manufacturers are in some cases reimbursing dealers at the regular work rate for work performed in fulfillment of warranty contracts.[12]

Sales of separate service contracts with the same characteristics as insurance policies are finding growing markets among producers of complex products such as color TV's and washing machines. If the machine functions properly the customer is out of pocket for the costs of the service contract; if the machine is defective, the dealer charges the manufacturer for routine customer service. If the customer requires such service, she gains by the amount that the service charge exceeds the cost of the warranty contract. The fairness of such a system has been challenged on the grounds that the customer is forced into a lottery in order to enjoy use rights already promised by the warrantor. Some firms therefore are promising to fix anything that goes wrong during the warranty period but including an average warranty service charge in their retail selling price which discounters cannot safely undercut without withholding the warranty as an element of the transaction. If the favorable results attained by these firms were widely duplicated, additional government legislation would be irrelevant.

CONSUMER SATISFACTION: KEY TO SUCCESSFUL WARRANTY PROGRAMS

Customer satisfaction with products in use provides the clue as to the effectiveness of the warranty program. Despite great efforts made in preparing training materials and conducting seminars, classes, and workshops for their service technicians, customer service audits are required to find out how well the training has been applied. Customers seldom complain in a way that commands the attention of top management. In fact, only a fraction of customer dissatisfaction is expressed in complaints: brand switching and store patronage changes are more frequent expressions of dissatisfaction than is letter writing or telephone calls to dealers.

One of the few studies directly attacking the problem of customer satisfaction was conducted by *Better Homes and Gardens*.[13] When asked if they followed the warranty requirements specified by the manufacturer, 84% of the new car owners queried replied in the affirmative. In other words, 16% did not. Of the group that followed warranty requirements, 56% were "generally satisfied" while 34% were partly or not at all satisfied, and 10% had no warranty work performed. Among the 16% of the new car buyers that failed to follow the manufacturer's warranty requirements, a few said it cost too much, but a striking 43% of those that did not follow manufacturer's warranty programs admitted to apathy and indifference by such statements as "didn't remember to take the car in at required intervals," or "too much trouble to keep up warranty." Among these individuals who don't squawk about defective warranties, a surprising proportion are in families in which the household head had done graduate work at a college or university.

The *Better Homes and Gardens* study also showed that consumers distinguish between the manufacturer's warranty and reputation and the dealer's reputation for service.[14] In fact, the reliability of the dealer was chosen as the most influential factor by an increasingly large proportion of consumers in each successively higher age category, possibly reflecting the accumulative effects of experience. If other studies support the *Better Homes and Gardens* data, it could be inferred that while consumers take a long time to become conscious of the warranty programs supporting their use of appliances and durables, they would choose continuous serviceability in preference to initial design advantages.

CONCLUSION

The burdens for servicing goods under warranty are multiplying rapidly. With the rate of increase in automobile population outstripping that in human population, and with over 800 million appliances in use in the United States, the short run advantages of using warranties as a come-on to make sales hardly seems worth the price that industry will be forced to pay as a result of the popular outcry against malpractices. Following the warranty program guidelines outlined here can stimulate repeat sales and word of mouth recommendation by satisfied customers. Such guidelines can aid in designing advertising and promotion campaigns, in pricing repair services, wording the warranties themselves, and making adjustments either at no cost to the consumer or on the basis of a service contract charge. If manufacturers individually and collectively do not recognize the legitimate claims of consumers, there is ample evidence that the Congress, regardless of which political party is in power, may be obliged to do so as the result of mounting public frustration with haphazard warranty service after sale.

NOTES

1. "The Week in Review," *The New York Times,* March 2, 1969, p. 9-E.
2. *The Federal Household Appliance Warranty Act,* U. S. Senate, 90th Congress, 1st session, S. 2728 (December 6, 1967).
3. "Marketing's Credibility Gap," *Sales Management,* 101 (June 15, 1968), p. 25.
4. *New York Times,* June 15, 1964, p. 48, col. 2.
5. *Report of the Task Force on Appliance Warranties and Service,* Special Assistant to the President on Consumer Affairs (Washington, D.C.: U.S. Government Printing Office), January 8, 1969, p. ii.

6. "The Good Is Often Overlooked, So It Is with Appliance Men," *Home Furnishings Daily*, March 5, 1968.

7. *Report of the Task Force on Appliance Warranties and Service*, pp. 4, 39-47. *See also Staff Report on Automobile Warranties*, Federal Trade Commission (Washington, D.C., 1968).

8. Stephen Upton, Walker Sandback, and Fred Prince, "Warranties, Guarantees and Service After Sale," taped dialog, *A New Measure of Responsibility for Marketing*, June 1968 Conference of the American Marketing Association, Philadelphia, Pennsylvania.

9. *Wall Street Journal*, June 5, 1969, p. 1.

10. "The Servicer's Problems: How the Trade Groups are Solving Them," *Merchandising Week*, 100 (July 1, 1968), pp. 8-9, esp. p. 9. Also *Report of the Task Force on Appliance Warranties and Service*, pp. 178-179.

11. *See for example*, Stephen E. Upton, *Customer Services Division, A Serviceways Recap* (Benton Harbor, Michigan: Whirlpool Corporation), n. d.

12. Upton, Sandback, and Prince, "Warranties, Guarantees and Service After Sale."

13. *Better Homes and Gardens Consumer Questionnaire* (Des Moines, Iowa: Meredith Corporation, 1968), pp. 91, 92, and 107.

14. Ibid., p. 107.

43. PRODUCT LIABILITY: TOUGHER GROUND RULES

David L. Rados

In the U.S. economy, the powerful forces of competition and consumer demand compel manufacturers to produce products with a high measure of consumer satisfaction. And, in spite of some legislation and regulation, these forces are still of first importance in guiding the operation of the economy.

But something new has been added. In recent years consumerism has become an important political force. As a result, there have been numerous investigative hearings by national and state governments; many new consumer laws have been proposed, and several important ones already have been passed. Also, the number of product liability suits and the size of the judgments have increased greatly.

More and more the discipline of the competitive marketplace is being buttressed by the discipline of the law. And these new legal forces are particularly important in the field of product liability because, in spite of their threat of considerable expense for the unwary company, they are not well known among executives.

This article will discuss the changing law of product liability and indicate some of the ways in which management can respond. But let us start with a sketch of the climate in which consumer protection has flourished.

NEW CONSUMER CLIMATE

The new attitudes about consumer problems stem from a high level of consumer education and affluence. The consumer knows more and is able to buy more wisely, but he faces bewildering problems in evaluating products. He must judge differences of technology, function, price, and promotion on the basis of commercial as well as noncommercial information that is occasionally misleading, often irrelevant, and always imperfect. The consumer earns

Reprinted from *Harvard Business Review* (July-August 1969), pp. 144-152. Copyright 1969, President and Fellows of Harvard College; all rights reserved.

more and is able to buy a higher standard of living. But he is frustrated because the products he buys do not perform as he has been led to expect.

His awareness of this frustration has been heightened by the considerable publicity given to product safety and effectiveness over the past several years. There have been hearings on automobile, tire, and drug safety. Other industries have either received unfavorable publicity from a product error, like the emission of harmful X rays from TV sets, or are scheduled for investigative hearings, such as those planned for the auto insurance industry. Lengthy and well-publicized debates on consumer protection legislation have added to consumer apprehension about product safety and manufacturers' probity.

The past several years have also seen the passage of bills on truth in lending, truth in packaging, meat inspection, and poultry inspection. Moreover, the correlation between cancer and cigarette smoking continues to receive attention and has recently been the subject of "Stop Smoking" advertising campaigns by the American Cancer Society and the American Heart Association. And the now common ritual by which auto manufacturers call back unsafe automobiles reinforces consumer apprehension about auto safety in general. The rise in consumer expectations and the heightened concern with product safety are more clearly seen in the rise of the consumer protection movement.

PROBLEMS FOR THE MANUFACTURER

The manufacturer is having his difficulties as well. The market that is supposed to influence his products is relatively inarticulate in its quality demands. The product quality offered to the consumer depends on the demand for quality, and this in turn depends on how well informed consumers are.

To make a reasoned purchase, the consumer must be able to state his needs and compare those needs with the offerings in the market. But the amount of technical knowledge alone needed to evaluate, say, a color TV set is formidable. And even if he had the necessary background, the consumer would not have the test and performance data he needs. Thus the technical complexity of products has reduced the number of knowledgeable consumers and therefore has produced a less articulate demand for different levels of quality.

There are still other pressures on the manufacturer. Product complexity raises difficulties in controlling the quality of design and manufacture. There are, of course, many sophisticated quality control techniques, but offsetting pressures encourage the erosion of quality—e.g., the pressure to hold down costs.

Today's markets, moreover, are markets on the move. They must be reached quickly; competitive moves must be matched or bettered; new methods of product differentiation must be attempted. All these factors put pressure on the manufacturer to take less care than he would like. The pressure is particularly pronounced in companies with a strategy of continual product innovation because controlling quality is most difficult during the development and introduction of new products, especially when competitive tactics demand quick reactions.

TOUGHER COURTS

To appreciate the current state of the law, it is necessary to understand how a hypothetical case might have proceeded a decade ago.

In the first place, the manufacturer would not have waited to be sued. Startingat the time of sale, he would have tried to limit his legal liability, using a sales agreement containing disclaimers and narrow express warranties. For example:

The manufacturer of a power lawn mower might have given the purchaser of each of his mowers an express warranty that the machine was free of defects. This warranty would have formed a part of the sales contract and, like all contractual provisions, would have been binding on the producer.

But he would not have stopped at this point. He would first have limited his liability to replacing defective parts and then stated that this was the only warranty being offered (meaning that he would do nothing more than replace defective parts). Under such a limited warranty he would not have been required to pay for, say, injuries caused by a defective part.

But he still might have been sued. Assume a buyer had bought the mower, used it, and been injured by it. In bringing the manufacturer to court, the injured buyer—the plaintiff—could have proceeded either in contract or in tort law. In contract law he might have argued that, regardless of the express warranty, the manufacturer was bound by an implied warranty that his product was reasonably fit to mow lawns and that a mower which can cause an injury is not fit. Thus the manufacturer had broken a provision of the contract and would have to compensate the plaintiff.

The manufacturer would have replied that there was no "privity" (direct contractual relationship) between him and the plaintiff. He would have argued that the plaintiff's business was with the retailer who sold the mower, not with him; and the court would have agreed. In the absence of privity, the plaintiff could not have collected for violation of the contract. He would first have had to sue the retailer, who in turn would have sued the manufacturer.

The plaintiff might also have taken action against the manufacturer in tort (the law of personal injury), arguing that, regardless of whether there was any contract between them, the manufacturer had a duty to prospective users of his mowers to design and produce safe mowers and that he had failed to take reasonable care in fulfilling that obligation. In other words, he would have argued that the manufacturer had been negligent.

But proving negligence is often difficult. If the manufacturer could have proved, for instance, that the product had been designed and manufactured with reasonable care, he would have been held blameless even if the product was actually unsafe. Let us suppose a piece of scrap metal in the housing of the mower had worked loose, flown out of the housing, and caused the injury. If the manufacturer could prove that his production and inspection processes were thorough and performed with care and that part of the production process in which the housing was assembled was highly mechanized, he could be held blameless. The presence of the scrap metal would be treated as an accident, for which no one was responsible. Today, warranties, disclaimers, privity, and negligence still dominate product liability law as legal doctrines, but as defenses against adverse judgments they are much weaker.

WARRANTIES AND DISCLAIMERS

The attempt to limit liability is less successful now than it has been in the past. As one example, claims in advertisements, sales promotion literature, labels, instructions, and oral sales presentations are likely to be held as legally binding on the manufacturer as an express warranty if the purchaser relied on the claims in making his purchase.

The value of disclaimers has also been lower since the landmark Henningsen case:

●In May 1955 Claus Henningsen picked up a new Plymouth from the authorized Chrysler dealer in Bloomfield, New Jersey—Bloomfield Motors, Inc. He and his wife Helen used the car around town for several days, and then on May 19 Mrs. Henningsen drove to Asbury Park.

●On the return trip, while driving along New Jersey Route 36 at approximately 20 miles per hour, she heard a loud noise "from the bottom, by the hood," and the steering wheel spun out of her hands. The car swerved sharply to the right, into a highway sign and then into a brick wall. The car, driven only 468 miles, was a total loss. Mrs. Henningsen sustained painful but not crippling injuries.

What had caused the accident? Mrs. Henningsen had been driving in a safe manner, according to the testimony of a bus driver who had seen the accident. Was Chrysler to blame? The front end of the car was so badly damaged that experts could not say what had gone wrong. One of these experts, an insurance inspector, could only say that "something down there had to drop off or break loose." This meant that it was impossible to prove negligence on Chrysler's part.

The Henningsens sued in contract and won. Chrysler appealed, arguing that when Henningsen bought the car, he had signed a disclaimer that limited Chrysler's liability to the replacement of defective parts. The New Jersey Supreme Court was unimpressed by this argument. Such disclaimers, standard on all automobile contracts, were "a sad commentary on the automobile manufacturers' marketing practices," because customers had no chance to bargain on the point, and yet they signed away any personal injury claims that might arise because of the defects.

"It is difficult to imagine a greater burden on the consumer," the court said. Such disclaimers are so indefensible as to be "inimical to the public good" and therefore invalid as a matter of law. Chrysler could not avoid its

405

legal obligation to make automobiles of good enough quality to serve the use for which they were intended.

The case really turned on whether the disclaimer was the *only* warranty applying. The judge ruled it was not and, in striking down the disclaimer, held that the manufacturer and dealer were obligated (under an implied warranty of merchantability) to market reasonably safe cars.[1]

DECLINE OF PRIVITY

Historically, as the organization of the economy became more complex and the legal ties joining producer with ultimate consumer lengthened, the absence of privity often blocked recovery by injured parties.

The first exceptions to the basic rule (that there can be no recovery in contract in the absence of privity) came in cases involving food and beverage products, then in any products intended to affect human life, such as food, drugs, firearms, and so on. In 1916 came the landmark decision:

● The plaintiff, a canny Scot named MacPherson, was injured when defective wooden spokes on a wheel of his new Buick collapsed. Buick argued that MacPherson had bought the car from a dealer, not from Buick, and therefore that Buick's obligations did not extend to him. But Buick was found to have been negligent in failing to inspect the wheel before mounting it. The judged [sic] ruled Buick was responsible for defects that could be attributed to negligence, regardless of how many middlemen and dealers stood between Buick and the ultimate buyer, that is, regardless of the narrow confines of contract privity.[2]

The Henningsen case, 33 years later, completed the demise of the privity rule. In that case, it was impossible to prove negligence because the front end of the car was too badly damaged to provide the needed evidence. As in the MacPherson case, there was no privity of contract between Henningsen and Chrysler. Again the court overruled the privity argument, but this time in the absence of proof of the manufacturer's negligence.

The significance of these two decisions (and a host of supporting decisions over the years) has been to seriously weaken lack of privity as a defense against product liability suits.

IMPLIED NEGLIGENCE

Perhaps the most radical change in product liability law concerns negligence, as courts move rapidly toward adopting a new doctrine—strict liability in tort—under which an injured plaintiff can recover *whether or not the manufacturer is to blame*. Here is an account of the landmark case:

● A certain Mr. Greenman saw a Shopsmith combination power tool demonstrated in a dealer's store in California. After he had read a promotional brochure, Greenman decided he wanted the tool for his home workshop, and Mrs. Greenman dutifully gave it to him for Christmas. Two years later Greenman bought the attachments that enabled the tool to be used as a lathe. He wanted to make a chalice. After he had worked the block several times without difficulty, it suddenly flew out of the machine and struck him on the forehead, inflicting serious injury.

●Somewhat tardily he hauled both the dealer and the manufacturer, Yuba Products, Inc., into court. Greenman and Yuba were not in privity, of course; for that matter, neither were Mrs. Greenmen and Yuba. This defense was swept aside by the court. Using expert witnesses, Greenman was able to prove that the set screws used to hold the parts of the tool together were inadequate, so that the normal vibration of the lathe caused the tailstock to shift away from the lathe head, allowing the block to fly out. Greenman was also able to prove that he had read the promotional brochure and relied on its claims that the product was rugged.

●With this evidence the jury could decide on the basis either of negligence or of warranty. If it found Yuba had been careless in design or manufacture, it could find negligence; if it held that the promotional brochure represented an express warranty, it could find breach of contract. Like all juries, this one did not reveal how it reached its decision, but it did decide to grant damages to Greenman.

●Yuba appealed to the California Supreme Court, and lost again. But the court added something new. It stressed that Yuba's apparent breach of warranty and negligence were basically irrelevant to Greenman's case. Even if it had not been negligent, Yuba would still be liable. "A manufacturer is strictly liable in tort when an article he places on the market, knowing that it will be used without inspection, proves to have a defect that causes injury to a human being."[3]

The Greenman decision was quickly extended by another California Supreme Court decision, which held that a manufacturer could not escape strict liability in tort by proving its suppliers or dealers were responsible for the defect involved.[4] Moreover, the court also found the *retailer* strictly liable in tort for injuries caused by the defective product.

Since these decisions, the doctrine of strict liability in tort has been adopted by more and more states, particularly many of the influential industrial states, such as New York, New Jersey, Ohio, Michigan, and Illinois. The doctrine has also been applied to new situations, such as leasing, where one rent-a-car agency was held strictly liable in tort for an injury caused by defective brakes in one of its cars.

ONUS ON MANUFACTURER

What does strict liability in tort mean? It has two meanings, one legal, the other social and economic:

The legal meaning is simply that the burden of proving blame or fault has been removed from the plaintiff. Thus it has become far easier to recover damages from manufacturers. Although Yuba was apparently negligent in constructing the Shopsmith, the court did not concern itself with fault. It decided merely who should bear the cost of the injury. This clearly was not to be the "powerless" consumer.

A quote from the Greenman decision illustrates the social and economic meaning of strict liability: "The purpose of [strict liability in tort] is to insure that the costs of injuries resulting from defective products are borne by the manufacturers that put such products on the market rather than by the injured persons who are powerless to protect themselves."

Social conscience today is far more concerned with victims of injury than it was during the nineteenth century, when the basic rules governing product liability were formulated. Strict liability embodies a belief that the cost of accidents should be passed from the few (victims) to the many (consumers) in the form of higher prices and that the agency to accomplish this is the manufacturer. It also reflects the belief that strict liability will encourage greater care by the manufacturer and hence will yield fewer accidents.

OTHER TRENDS

The Henningsen and Greenman cases unquestionably effected a major change in product liability law. Other changes also appear to be taking place, although their significance is not easy to predict.

LOSS OF VALUE:

Greenman sustained an injury. So did Henningsen and MacPherson. What happens when there is no physical injury but just a loss of value? One controversial case gives a hint:

●Mr. Daniel Santor bought a "Grade No. 1" Gulistan rug manufactured by A. and M. Karagheusian, Inc., a well-known rug producer. After being installed, the rug developed a strange line. Santor telephoned the dealer who assured him the line would wear away. But instead of improving as time went on, the situation became worse, and two additional lines appeared.

●Finally Santor decided to take legal action. As the retailer from whom he had bought the rug had moved out of state, Santor proceeded against the manufacturer, with whom, of course, he was not in privity. The court held that strict liability in tort would apply and granted Santor recovery for the loss of value of the rug (i.e., the difference between the rug's present value and its value were it unmarked).[5]

While other courts have reached similar conclusions, particularly in two cases involving poor performance of tractors, the application of strict liability to loss of value cases has not yet been widely adopted. In fact, the California court that ruled for Greenman does not apply strict liability in tort to such cases. Most courts have been reluctant to apply strict liability to loss of value, but some legal scholars urge there is no logical reason to allow recovery for personal injury and deny it for loss of value.

NEGLIGENT DESIGN:

One new cause for action is negligence in design. While strict liability without fault has been emphasized in this article, most product liability cases are still based on allegations of negligence; that is, the plaintiff must prove the product was defective and unreasonably dangerous when it left the manufacturer's hands. This can be difficult to establish, particularly when the product has passed through the hands of several middlemen and has a long life. But if the plaintiff can prove faulty design, at one stroke he proves that the manufacturer was negligent and that the product was unsafe when it left his hands. For this reason, design negligence suits have multiplied in recent years.

ADVERTISING CLAIMS:

Courts have long looked on certain types of claims made in advertising and in labels as express warranties. Thus if a windshield advertised as shatterproof breaks when hit by a pebble, the injured plaintiff may recover even though he and the manufacturer are not in privity. But now the reach of advertising copy is broadening, as this recent case demonstrates:

●A car owner by the name of Inglis proved in court that he had relied on American Motors' advertising claims that his Rambler would be trouble-free, economical in operation, and manufactured with high-quality workmanship. His hopes were frustrated, however. The trunk door was out of line, could not be opened and continually squeaked and rattled; the door handles were loose; the steering gear was inproperly set; the oil pump was defective; the brakes squeaked and grated; the engine leaked substantial quantities of oil; and loose parts inside the car fell out from time to time.

●Unable to obtain satisfaction from his dealer, he took the case to court. The court ruled that where there was difference between the advertising claims and the product's actual performance, there was no "sound reason [why] he should not be permitted to . . . recoup his loss."[6]

Here again, there was no injury, only frustrated expectation. The difference is that the advertising copy was held to be an express warranty, that is, part of the bargain between Inglis and American Motors. Because American Motors did not live up to its end of the bargain, it had to make good the car's loss of value.

EXTENSION OF LIABILITY:

The reach of liability is extending in two new directions. We have seen how the doctrine of privity in product liability has been obliterated, enabling both purchaser and user of a defective product to recover. The Uniform Commercial Code[7] extends these protections not only to the purchaser, but to his immediate family, members of his household, and guests.

Liability is also beginning to reach beyond the manufacturer to his suppliers. Thus:

●When an American Airlines plane crashed because of an allegedly faulty altimeter, the court decided that the cause of action would be against Lockheed, the plane's manufacturer, and not the manufacturer of the altimeter.[8] But the court divided on the issue; and in a subsequent case involving a defective truck part, an Illinois court did extend strict liability in tort to component manufacturers.

So far no advertising agency has been held negligent in the preparation of copy, but such action can be reasonably expected. Even industry associations and testing laboratories, which are organizations remote from the injured consumer, may soon have to face actions. Assume, for example, that a manufacturer markets a product that conforms to standards developed by his industry's trade association. What happens if the product subsequently injures a person because the standard was insufficient? It is probable that, under the right conditions, the trade association will be held liable.

IMPACT AND ACTION

We have seen that several factors have contributed to the fast-growing strength of the consumer movement during the past several years. But the solutions to consumer dissatisfaction are not developing quickly; and as the conditions that have powered the development of consumerism become even more salient, it seems likely that the pressure for more consumer protection will increase.

What is the impact of these changes in the law on business operations? What can management do to minimize the risks of being sued?

The impact of these changes will be greatest on two types of companies:

1. Those who through poor design or careless manufacture have failed to maintain minimum quality standards and consequently are placing unsafe products on the market.
2. Those who are introducing large numbers of new products.

The first is already in danger, for the reasons outlined earlier. *Caveat emptor*, "Let the buyer beware" has been replaced by *caveat venditor*, "Let the seller beware"—or, even better, "The seller must take care."

But, no matter how careful, the company developing large numbers of new products is also in a difficult position. Large firms sometimes have 50 to 100 products in various stages of development. Tight control over the safety of working models and prototypes is difficult. So is quality control of models developed for market tests. Errors in design or manufacture may not in fact show up during short tests, in which case the manufacturer must expose himself by placing thousands or millions of his product on the market before serious flaws are discovered.

Even assuming successful development and performance of test models, the manufacturer must move to pilot plant or full-scale manufacture of the product. Here, the newer the product, the more likely it will be to develop bugs. But even dealing with minor variants of present products does not ensure perfect production from the start.

Hence manufacturers who adopt growth strategies based primarily on product innovation run the biggest risks. What are these risks?

One is the risk of unfavorable publicity resulting from product liability cases or from government investigations. While General Motors will not comment on whether sales of the Corvair suffered from its well-publicized design negligence cases, many executives in the industry believe they have. Such publicity also serves notice to other plaintiffs and encourages them to press their suits.

Second, the cost of developing and introducing new products will increase. Design and preintroduction testing must now be more thorough; advertising and labeling must be tested for clarity and comprehensiveness; and field tests must be monitored closely. These kinds of activities will increase development time and certainly will raise costs.

Third, should the product fail and cause injury there will be costs of litigation and possibly adverse judgments. Since such suits usually are surrogates for a much larger number of possible suits, most are appealed, further raising costs. And while such suits are pending, the acceptability of the product remains in question.

Finally, in the present climate it is clear that any business touched by publicity concerning poor quality of its products will be exposed to the possibility of congressional investigation and regulatory legislation.

But what can management do? That is the crucial question.

SAFETY AUDIT

The first step is to collect information—the diagnostic step.

Management should begin by identifying the products most likely to contain safety-related defects. It can review complaint letters and warranty claims, study problems that competitors have had with similar products, study its own market research about consumer experiences with its products, and review evaluations of its products by outside testing agencies. These steps will help to identify the products on which action should first be taken.

Once potentially unsafe products and lines are identified, an analysis can be made of their safety. Safety engineers should review design and manufacturing procedures to make sure quality control and testing are adequate from start to finish. Careful study should be made of possible ways in which the product can fail, with the aim of correcting serious flaws at the time of redesign. There must be clear, effective communication between the design sections and manufacturing as to acceptable tolerances, drawings, and assembly instructions.

SYSTEMS ANALYSIS

The second, or action, step is to adopt the systems approach that has been so useful in creating safe military products.

This includes the assignment of responsibility for the safety program to a specific individual with responsibility for the safety of the design concept, production and testing procedures, and inspection. He should also be responsible for determining whether safety tests are realistic in terms of consumer use patterns.

Such programs can be expensive, so executive judgment must be exercised to ensure that the trade-offs between added costs and reduced risks of poor design and manufacture are properly made. But such programs do not yield only higher costs. Many businesses that have attempted safety and quality analyses have found they had been overlooking opportunities for low-cost improvements in their products and cheap ways of reducing costs. Thus:

Before it offered its five-year auto warranty, Chrysler Corporation analyzed its engineering, design, and manufacturing procedures with great thoroughness. As a result, significant quality improvements were made in every manufacturing area. The results were wholly beneficial to the company, to say nothing of Chrysler's customers.

The source of a safety-related product defect may lie almost anywhere in the product cycle from initial conception to poor use by the user. Thus in planning the improvement of product safety the responsible executive must not overlook any areas of importance. Here are five major areas.

PRODUCT DESIGN:

Design is a fertile source of product liability cases. Not only is it difficult to control design activities under the best of conditions, but the whole area is relatively neglected to begin with. Moreover, *liability arising from poor design is a business risk which is not insurable.*

What can be done? One obvious move is to check the product against any developed safety standards, either by industry (or trade) group or by government group. The law demands that the manufacturer demonstrate his expertise by producing safe products. If his product has fewer safety features than normal in his industry, this may be used to show failure to exercise the care and skill of an expert.

It is important to anticipate potential hazards and either design them out of the product or warn the user of the hazard and how it can be avoided. This type of check as well as other safety and reliability checks could be performed by formal design review committees—something that many companies have already done. If the proposed product fails to meet their approval, these committees can call for further design checks, such as *failure mode analysis*, a procedure of systematically postulating the most likely ways in which the product can fail, with the aim of reducing or eliminating failures likely to cause injury to users. In many cases it also proves useful to keep complete records on design prodecures, particularly relating to reasons for accepting one design feature and rejecting another.

MANUFACTURING:
Well-run companies take considerable pains to ensure that their products conform to specification and the percent of defectives is held in control. The matter of product liability, therefore, should be a major concern to such companies. This concern impresses on production personnel the need to remedy situations that might lead to unsafe products. Remember also that a company can be held liable for errors of suppliers. (MacPherson was able to collect from Buick although the defective part, the wooden wheel, was purchased from an outside supplier. Buick was negligent in not carefully inspecting the purchased part.) Hence quality control and inspection are important for both purchased materials and materials fabricated in-house.

As with safety analysis, quality control analysis is not entirely a burden; it often uncovers opportunities for companies to do a better job at lower cost. And if the improvement in the product is promotable, the benefits may include a stronger market position.

COMMUNICATIONS:
Designing and producing a safe product is not enough, however. Instructions, labels, advertising copy, and even oral sales presentations must be designed and produced with equal care.

Instructions should be written in clear, simple language; sometimes it will pay to test them for clarity and comprehensibility. Labels affixed to the product itself are important in many kinds of products because original instructions get lost, particularly when the product has a long life. Informative labels, preferably securely attached to the product, with data on potential dangers and basic operating characteristics (load limitations, maximum performance limits, and so on) are useful in such situations.

Advertising and sales presentations must be screened for unwarranted claims. Most large companies already require ad copy to be screened by their legal department. Few take the same pains to ensure that the representations of their salesmen are equally restrained.

Liabilities arising from excessive claims in marketing communications are most serious in the areas of consumer packaged goods and other mass produced goods. (Henningsen recovered in part because of the inequality in bargaining power between himself and Chrysler.) On the other hand, the sale of capital equipment to presumably sophisticated buyers able to protect themselves is far less likely to be challenged because of sales claims that promise too much.

It is possible, however, that even here a plaintiff may recover if he can prove that he relied on sales puffery in making his purchase and operating decisions.

MARKETING RESEARCH:

Marketing executives are becoming more and more aware of the importance of actions that take place after the sale is complete. For example, more attention is being paid to why orders are cancelled and to how the consumer justifies his purchase to himself immediately following the purchase. Also, studies are being conducted to learn how consumers actually use products, in order to generate new ideas for related products and to better satisfy consumer use patterns.

This trend should be reinforced by the demands placed on the manufacturer by product liability. Particularly with a product that is potentially or inherently dangerous, the manufacturer no longer can assume that his responsibility ends with the sale. He must find out how his customers view the product and, specifically, how they are using it. And if there are potential dangers, he must take steps to prevent accidental or even careless use from causing injury.

PRODUCT LIABILITY INSURANCE:

No matter how much care the manufacturer takes to produce safe products, the possibility of product liability cannot be completely eliminated. But product liability insurance can be used to cover the remaining area of risk.

Today's manufacturer usually acts as insurer not only for himself but also for the members of his distribution channels, his consumers, and perhaps even innocent bystanders. As a result, the volume of product liability insurance has increased sharply in the past ten years. While the amount being written is hard to estimate because product liability insurance is usually lumped into a general casualty policy, one estimate is that premiums for such insurance are $60 million annually and climbing fast. Some drug manufacturers are said to carry as much as $100 million of product liability insurance.

Most large companies already have coverage against liability actions, though few top executives know exactly what it covers. Fewer small companies have such insurance; but because adverse judgments could easily wipe out their entire net worth, they now are probably purchasing such insurance at a faster rate than larger companies.

It is particularly important for an executive to understand what such insurance actually covers. Typically it covers injury or destruction of property arising from use of the product. Typically it does not cover:

Business risks, chiefly the failure of a product to perform its intended purpose due to poor design.

The costs of withdrawing a whole class of defective products from the market.

Injury to the product itself, its repair, and its replacement.

Defects which could have been foreseen or detected through proper checking and testing.

414

LET THE SELLER BEWARE

This article has indicated the changes that have occurred in product liability law. The courts have become increasingly impressed by the need to protect consumers from defective products. Both contract and tort law have undergone rapid change in the attempt to satisfy this need. Where contract liability has proved inadequate, it has been supplemented by tort law. This blend of contract and tort law has resulted in the increasing use of strict liability in tort in product liability suits.

It has been argued that consumers should have freedom of choice in the marketplace, including freedom to make the wrong choice. But consumers now have less freedom to make an unsafe choice. Consumers are increasingly to be protected from the voluntary consumption of unsafe products.

The court decisions mentioned in this article illustrate the development of new law and also make clear the message to the producer: Let the seller beware.

NOTES

1. Henningsen v. Bloomfield Motors, Inc., 161 A. 2d 69 (1960).
2. MacPherson v. Buick, 111 N.E. 1050 (1916).
3. Greenman v. Yuba Power Products, Inc., 377 P. 2d 897 (1963).
4. Vandermark v. Ford Motor Company, 391 P. 2d 168 (1964).
5. Santor v. A. and M. Karagheusian, Inc., 207 A. 2d 305 (1965).
6. Inglis v. American Motors Co., 209 N.E. 2d 583 (1965).
7. *See* Edward L. Schwartz, "Uniform Commercial Code" (Thinking Ahead), HBR September-October 1953, p. 23.
8. Goldberg v. Kollsman Instrument Corp., 191 N.E. 2d 81 (1963).

PART ELEVEN

Low Income Groups and Consumerism

INTRODUCTION

Low Income Groups and Consumerism

THE LOW-INCOME consumer has often taken the brunt of the abuses, issues, and problems with which the consumer movement is concerned. Particularly in the ghetto, he has been treated as if independent of marketing strategies and also of consumerism issues. Lee Berton provides examples of the bilking tactics used by sellers in the ghetto and of the government's efforts to stop the practices.

In order to develop policies that will assist the low-income consumer, Louise Richards points out, it is necessary to understand his behavior rather than to use the traditional assumption that he is irrational. As we know, although much of the consumer legislation was designed to protect the low-income consumer, he derives little benefit because he lacks knowledge and skills, and does not appreciate his legal rights to use the legislation for his protection.

The Report of the National Commission on Civil Disorders implies that the structure of the ghetto marketplace and the consumption behavior of the ghetto resident provide the basis and means for exploitative and discriminatory practices. Frederick Sturdivan and Walter Wilhelm conclude, in their study of the Watts riot area, that "the consumer problems in the curfew area are not due to systematic racial discrimination but rather result from the traditional interplay of economic forces in the marketplace, aggravated by poverty conditions." They found that not only were prices higher in low-income area stores, but that there was a consistency of higher prices among the stores in the ghetto areas. The poor in the ghetto be they white, Mexican-American, or black all pay more.

The means of implementing discrimination on the basis of race or ethnicity was through credit practices. "When credit practices are considered, it becomes clear that credit and carrying charges are the devices most commonly used to exercise exploitation," or discrimination aimed at a particular group. In contrast, the Federal Trade Commission's Report showed that in Washington, D.C., credit charges were not noticeably different between the two market areas. The report does agree that disadvantaged minority shoppers do pay more, but particularly in the ghetto.

The Federal Trade Commission's Report also indicates that the marketing system for the distribution of durable goods to low-income consumers is costly. The factors that contribute to the higher cost are (1) the emphasis on door-to-door selling, (2) the ghetto consumer's lack of knowledge of alternatives, (3) the "irrational" shopping behavior of ghetto consumers, and (4) the dependence upon credit as a means of obtaining durable goods.

The ghetto marketplace depends heavily upon the use of credit for its existence. "Insofar as the problem for the low-income consumer is availability of credit, merchants who sell to them focus on this element." Unfortunately, the ghetto consumer pays dearly for the "easy credit" offered to him.

The Federal Trade Commission's Report also emphasizes the need for greater emphasis on consumer education and counseling, if ghetto consumers are to become sophisticated rational shoppers, so that they can benefit from such consumer legislation as Truth-in-Lending.

44. AIDING THE POOR

U.S., STATE OFFICIALS MAP ATTACKS ON SELLERS BILKING GHETTO DWELLERS

Lee Berton

MRS. LOUISE BARRETT, a 42-year-old Negro mother of three, recently discovered that the poor *do* pay more. She learned the hard way.

A "pushy" door-to-door salesman quoted her a "reduced" price of $60 on a Bible and dictionary he said usually went for a total of $80, she relates. But when her bill arrived, it read $77.23—for books she could have bought elsewhere for a total of no more than $45, according to their publisher. She couldn't meet the "small monthly payment," and her modest salary as a supermarket clerk was garnished.

She bought an off-brand TV set from another door-to-door operative, only to have it break down quickly. Fees and interest on her monthly installment contract for the set added up to a rate exceeding 20% a year, well above normal. Also, she had trouble with her back and went to a chiropractor who gave her dozens of treatments. Her back still hurts and she owes the chiropractor $395. He is under Federal indictment for fraud.

Mrs. Barrett, the sole support of her family, admits she has been gullible—though no more so than those Negro and Puerto Rican families in an Upstate New York city who paid $500 each for a set of ordinary cookware because the salesman said its use would prevent cancer. She confesses she knows little about budget-keeping, installment interest rates and the like. She concedes she has spent too much on luxuries in her eagerness to give her family the things middle-class families have, a yearning sociologists say is common in the ghetto. Still, she wistfully wonders why "every crook picks on the poor."

Of course, unethical salesmen don't confine their activities to poor neighborhoods. Many a comfortable suburb has proved fertile ground for the slick seller of "special deals" on aluminum siding or magazine subscriptions.

CRACKDOWN COMING?

Nevertheless, consumer rackets flourish most profusely in the slums, according to anti-fraud experts. Until recently, however, comparatively little was being done about it. Now, however, there are clear signs that Federal, state, and local authorities will be cracking down harder on price discrimination, exorbitant credit rates, sales fraud and other shoddy commercial practices that plague the poor. And ghetto residents themselves are banding together to fight their own battles against those who victimize them.

One of the principal targets is price discrimination. A special House inquiry into consumer-government relationships has heard considerable testimony indicating that many items cost more in the ghetto than elsewhere. A consumer group from the Bedford-Stuyvesant section of Brooklyn, for example, said it paid 6.6% more for 20 grocery items at a chain store in the ghetto than it did for the same items at another outlet of the same chain in a middle-class neighborhood. The price difference climbed to 8.5% the day after welfare checks were distributed, the group reported.

A St. Louis consumer group did some comparison shopping at Kroger Co. supermarkets. It told the House group it found a price differential of 13.6% between a ghetto store and one in a higher-income neighborhood. Walter W. White, manager of Kroger's St. Louis division, denies the chain has deliberately pegged prices higher in the ghetto but adds: "The speed and frequency and volume of price changes create conditions under which inadvertent errors can occur. Certainly we can improve."

A RECURRING PATTERN

Rep. Benjamin Rosenthal, (D., N.Y.), who is heading the House inquiry says that if errors are occurring, "they are all falling into the same inevitable pattern—higher prices in the ghetto." His group is urging the Federal Trade Commission and the Agriculture Department to pressure chain stores into eliminating price differentials. He maintains that the Agriculture Department's food stamps for the poor are being "illegally devalued" 5% to 10% by overcharges and asserts that this alone "justifies Federal action."

Some chain store operators on occasion have conceded that some prices were higher in ghetto stores. In defense, however, they assert that stores in such neighborhoods are plagued by excessive pilferage, high insurance premiums and other abnormal costs that tend to push prices up.

Wherever the truth lies in the pricing argument, ghetto dwellers are acting on their own to get lower prices. Last September six neighborhood clubs in Washington, D.C., formed a consumers' association that has been getting food direct from wholesalers and marketing it to between 100 to 150 families. Mrs. Janie Boyd, association chairman, claims her own food bill has plummeted 50%. She says the association hopes to expand the program to include up to 1,000 families, most of them poor.

In St. Louis, a Catholic church in a Negro area has been busing 25 to 30 neighborhood residents to an open-air market four miles away in a white, middle-class area. "The savings on vegetables alone range from 10% to 15% says Father Robert A. Marshall, associate pastor of the church, St. Bridget's of Erin.

In Harlem, a new cooperative is being formed to operate a supermarket scheduled to open in April; the project is being financed through the sale of $5 shares and $50 debentures which pay 6% and through loans. Cora T. Walker, attorney for the group, the Harlem River Consumer Cooperative Inc., says initial prices at the store will run 5% to 10% lower than those at most other Harlem food stores; co-op members (those who have purchased an interest) will get an annual rebate from any profits, she adds.

Fraud and deceptive lending practices also are under heavier attack now from every government level and from the poor themselves. The poor are particularly affected by shady dealings, according to sociologists and others. For one thing, the poor's lack of sophistication as consumers (many can't comprehend the terms of a sales contract—a handicap shared by some of the more affluent and better educated), coupled with their intense yearning for the material things most other people enjoy, makes them easy marks for glib salesmen. Also, since they lack ready cash to buy items outright, they are heavy users of installment credit.

Often they don't realize how much extra they may be paying in the form of interest, insurance and other added-on-fees. Champions of "truth-in-lending" legislation claim that if they have their way, much of this uncertainty would be removed.

Presently, many installment sellers don't disclose the cost of insurance and other extras to the buyer. They also quote interest rates that don't really tell the buyer exactly how much a year he will have to pay in interest. The 1.5% monthly "revolving credit" offered by some stores doesn't sound like much, for example, but it adds up to an annual interest rate of 18%, more if compounded. Basically, truth-in-lending legislation would force many retailers and other credit sellers to cite the annual cost and to tell prospective borrowers how much would be added to their payments by insurance and other fees. Many retailers have argued that conforming with the requirements of truth-in-lending would be an immensely complex and costly task for them.

The Senate already has passed a truth-in-lending bill, and a House version sponsored by Rep. Leonor K. Sullivan (D., Mo.) has emerged from committee; Rep. Sullivan says the House bill "has an excellent chance of passage late in January."

422

STATE ACTIONS

Some states have moved ahead of the Federal Government in efforts to protect the low-income consumer against misleading credit practices and consumer gyps. A staff member of the consumer affairs subcommittee of the House Committee on Banking and Currency says most large states with urban ghettos have passed laws or established special offices for this purpose within the past three years.

Last year, for example, Massachusetts passed a stiff truth-in-lending law of its own, and Maryland created a state consumer protection office. A national conference, composed of commissioners appointed by each state, is nearing completion of a proposed model code on consumer credit protection. The code would be submitted to state legislatures sometime this year.

Nowhere is there more activity on the consumer protection front than in New York State, where multiple efforts are under way to protect consumers from overpricing, credit deceptions, and fraud. Both Federal and state officials are pressing the attack.

Since last May, for example, the office of U.S. Attorney Robert Morgenthau in New York City has indicted 10 individuals and corporations for bilking low-income families in a variety of swindles. "In some cases, victims were told they could earn enough in commissions to pay for $1,000 worth of household appliances simply by passing along the names of potential customers. We've proven this was impossible," says Richard A. Givens, an assistant U.S. attorney supervising the investigations. "The real sharpies seek out the poor and the minority groups because they're so easily taken in," he adds.

ONE OF THEIR OWN

New York State's 10-year-old Consumer Fraud and Protection Bureau agrees. It handled some 20,000 cases last year, compared with 14,000 in 1966, and most of the 1967 cases involved schemes to exploit the poor. One dodge: The recruitment of Negroes and Puerto Ricans who are then sent out to sell goods of dubious worth at extravagant prices to their own people. "After all," they are instructed to tell customers, "would one of your own people rob you?"

State Attorney General Louis J. Lefkowitz, whose office supervises the Consumer Fraud Bureau also is planning to submit a truth-in-lending measure to the New York legislature this year. Besides the usual provisions for full disclosure of annual interest charges, insurance and other fees, it would also give installment buyers a better chance to escape garnishment of their wages if they fail to meet payments on contracts.

Garnishments are surprisingly common. Martin Kirshbaum, office manager of just one of the 83 city marshals' offices in New York, estimates his office alone serves 8,000 garnishments a year. Lawyers who handle such cases say most people hit by garnishments have low incomes.

Many of them have bought something they belatedly discover they simply can't afford. Some are deadbeats. But sociologists assert that many others have been pressured into buying overpriced goods, under credit terms that have been misrepresented or inadequately explained.

NO COPY OF CONTRACT

Mrs. Barrett, the buyer of the dictionary and Bible, doesn't feel she was fairly dealt with. She claims the salesman quoted her a price lower than the amount on the actual bill, inflated the value of the merchandise to make it appear she was getting a good deal, didn't provide a copy of the sales contract and didn't specify the size of the "small monthly payment."

But Mrs. Barrett has no recourse against the firm that sold the books, Kamin Sales Co., since Kamin has sold the contract to a factor, Regent Discount Corp. Regent obtained the garnishment against Mrs. Barrett's wages. Under New York State law, the assignee of such a contract (Regent, in this case), isn't responsible for the condition of the goods involved or how they were sold.

Under the law, Mrs. Barrett could have lodged a complaint against Kamin within 10 days after its sale of the contract to Regent, but she didn't know about the grace period (Attorney General Lefkowitz wants to raise it to 45 days), and it has long expired.

Regent Discount regrets Mrs. Barrett's plight but sees little remedy for it. "This state of affairs has existed in Harlem for years, and unless these people (the customers) become more educated as consumers, there's nothing we can do about it," says Irving Fineman, secretary.

"I DON'T NEED ANY EXPOSURE"

Steve Kamin, president of Kamin Sales, would rather not talk about the matter at all. "What do I need publicity in the paper for?" he asks. "You know the credit business and how people don't pay up. I don't need any exposure about this."

New York State legislators, eager to reduce the number of garnishments levied agains credit purchasers, are considering a proposal that goes well beyond the grace period extension Mr. Lefkowitz will propose. The joint legislative committee on consumer protection may propose the formation of a state panel empowered to void credit contracts the panel deems unfair.

At the national level, Sen. Warren Magnuson (D., Wash.), has proposed a bill that would allow a buyer to cancel within 24 hours any deal involving $25 or more made with a door-to-door salesman. "Door-to-door sales of expensive items such as TV sets, furniture and clothing are made mainly in low-income areas, where residents welcome the attention they don't ordinarily get in a store, and where they're more susceptible to high-pressure tactics," says a staff counsel of the Senate Commerce Committee. Its consumer subcommittee is scheduled to hold hearings on Sen. Magnuson's bill next month.

TRAINING WARIER BUYERS

Many Federal officials are convinced that giving the low-income consumer more purchasing savvy is necessary, too. An aide to Betty Furness, the President's special assistant for consumer affairs, says her office may add an education director who would be responsible for combating the problem. One possible approach: To raise a warier breed of ghetto consumers of the future by blending buying know-how into school curricula. English students might evaluate ad claims as part of their work, and math students might be taught how to figure credit charges.

Other tactics are being devised by the ghetto groups seeking to aid poor consumers. The recently formed Harlem Consumer Education Council, for example, says it already has helped 10 ghetto residents hopelessly burdened with debt go into bankruptcy thus eliminating their debts, and indicates it hopes to steer at least three or four people a week in the same direction from now on. The Legal Aid Society is assisting the council. Mrs. Barrett, who has been in contact with the council, has been advised to seek bankruptcy.

The NAACP Legal Defense and Educational Fund Inc. has just filed suit against L.B. Spears Furniture Co., a Harlem store, accusing it of overcharging and fraud in the sale of a food freezer to a Negro mail clerk for $1,087. The price included $247.92 in service and insurance charges, says a fund attorney, who puts the maximum value of the freezer at $450. "It was sold to the plaintiff by a door-to-door salesman who used the ruse of bringing lollipops to the buyer's daughter to get him to sign an unconscionable contract," the attorney says.

Godfrey Daum, president of L.B. Spears, says the freezer was sold by someone from a leased department within the store and denies any wrongdoing on his company's part. "We're strictly a one-price house and these people must prove they've overpaid," he declares. "We will contest the suit." The plaintiff is asking $10,000 in punitive damages. The fund says it plans to file "dozens" more such suits "to protect minority and poor people from unscrupulous selling practices."

45. CONSUMER PRACTICES OF THE POOR

Louise G. Richards

To THE economist, being poor means having an income below a certain figure—a figure that represents the minimum amount necessary for a decent life in America today. To the behavioral scientist, being poor means a number of characteristics found to be associated with low income: patterns of family life, health care, education, and general outlook on life. To the poor person himself, however, being poor may mean different things depending on how his money is spent. This report is a summary of research findings on those consumer practices. The report covers not only how money is spent by the poor, but also what kinds of behavior—shopping, methods of payment, and the like—go along with income disbursement.

Few would quarrel with the judgment that an income of $3000 is too low for a family to live on today. Hardly anyone would suggest that even the best consumer practices would solve the problem of poverty. Many would agree, however, that good consumer practices might alleviate some of the worst aspects. Knowledge of actual practices of the poor can suggest new areas for education and action.

One writer on the topic of consumer practices of the poor has concluded that they are irrational in their buying behavior.[1] Some of the evidence for that conclusion is included in this report. To indict poor consumers as irrational is too simple an explanation, however. Moreover, it provides no handles for action. Much of the evidence for irrationality should be considered in the light of other explanations that make equally good sense. The particular social and demographic characteristics of the poor must be taken into account. The inflexibility of low income per se must be kept in mind. And, finally, the possibility that apparent irrationality may stem from the very conditions of poverty must be dealt with. These explanations will be discussed more fully in a later section.

For practices to be labeled as irrational there must be a standard for judging their rationality. Many people would subscribe to the idea that there are

Reprinted from *Low Income Life Styles,* Lola M. Irelan, editor, U.S. Department of Health, Education, and Welfare (Washington: Superintendent of Documents, 1967), pp. 67-86.

good, common-sense rules for stretching income. Many of those who knew poverty during the Thirties, and those who have known severe reverses since then, would avow that such rules helped them keep their heads above water in difficult times.

Most common-sense rules of financial management are applications of the idea that everyone naturally tries to get the best living for the least money. Recent thinking on the topic includes the idea that psychological satisfactions can be added to material ones in arriving at a calculus of values. It is probably true, however, that low-income consumers can seldom afford outlays for emotional satisfactions, except perhaps in choices of low-cost items. Thus, the traditional rules are probably more pertinent today to the low-income consumer's situation than to that of higher income groups with their larger margins for discretionary purchases.

Very simply, the traditional rules for good consumership can be stated as follows:

1. Spend first for necessities and last for luxuries. Although many individuals disagree on how to classify specific goods, few would dispute that food, shelter, basic articles of clothing, and health should have priority over recreation and other categories of expenditure.
2. Buy the best quality of goods for the lowest price. This means that costly extra features—high styles, non-seasonal treats, store services, and above all, the cost of installment buying—should be avoided. In order to follow this rule, a person needs to shop widely and keep up with information about goods, prices, and sources.
3. Another rule stems from recognition of the fact that it is not easy to suppress desires for luxury goods and extra features: Budget small incomes carefully and plan purchases in advance. If possible, one should save for (or insure against) future emergencies to prevent insolvency.
4. Another rule covers the thousand-and-one suggestions for home production of needed goods: Try to get what is needed or wanted without spending money, or by spending only for raw materials. Home preservation of food, home sewing, self-building and self-repairing of homes, are a few of many recommended money saving practices.
5. Take advantage of certain benefits available to persons with limited incomes. Surplus food (and Food Stamps), legal aid, scholarships, day care for children, public housing, and medical and dental clinics are examples of such benefits provided through legislation or private funds.

Most detailed advice to consumers could be put under one of these five rules. Together they provide a backdrop for viewing actual consumer practices of the poor. In reporting the findings, these five rules will be referred to specifically. Before turning to those findings, we need to review what is known about the different kinds of people that constitute the poor population today, and the different kinds of studies that provide the facts.

POPULATION CHARACTERISTICS OF THE POOR

Several writers have pointed out that the poor as a group are neither homogeneous nor strictly representative of the population as a whole.[2] The *majority* of low income families are white, non-farm, and headed by a male between twenty-five and sixty-five years old. Compared with the general population, however, poor families tend to include more non-whites, fewer earners, more families with female heads, larger families, and more old or young persons. The poor more often reside in rural farm areas or in cities (and less often in rural non-farm or suburban areas). Above all, poor people have completed fewer years of schooling than the rest of the population. Almost every family or individual below the poverty line can be characterized by at least one of these facts. These differences between the poor and the general population are important in interpreting research findings about their consumer habits.

SOURCES OF FINDINGS

Two broad areas of research were drawn upon in this report. One area includes the economic surveys of consumer expenditures, savings, and debt made by government agencies and by business—a relatively old and well-established research activity. One continuing survey of this type, the Survey of Consumer Finances[3] has been concerned also with certain attitudes and expectations of consumers.

The second research area includes those studies that examine specific consumer practices, the why's and wherefore's of consumption. The most recent comprehensive study in this area is Caplovitz' *The Poor Pay More.*[4] Caplovitz' study provides information on types of stores used, methods of payment for goods, attitudes toward merchants and installment buying, and aspirations for future purchases on the part of a group of low-income families in New York City. Other studies provide facts about the decision making process, the different sources of consumers' knowledge, and the participation of husbands and wives in financial planning. Also included is a summary of findings from studies of the working-class wife.[5] (Although many working-class families are by no means poor—and vice versa—this summary is the only recent one available on social class differences in taste.)

When possible, we report the practices of families whose incomes are less than $3000, and indicate how their practices differ from families with higher incomes. When available figures were not broken at the poverty line, we report merely the differences between lower and higher income groups.

CONSUMER PRACTICES

Turning now to consumer practices in the framework of the above-mentioned rules for good consumership, here is the evidence:

1. DO LOW-INCOME FAMILIES BUY NECESSITIES FIRST, AND LUXURIES LAST?
For the most part, "Yes." When consumer goods and services are classified according to their survival value (beginning with Food and ending with Recreation), the poor spend more of their income than others do on the basic needs. When goods are classified as durables (automobiles, equipment, furniture, and the like) and non-durables, we find that the poor, on the average, do not buy durables as frequently as higher income families do. When we look at the poor who do purchase one or more durable goods in a given year, however, we find that a startlingly high proportion of their income is spent for those goods.

One weak spot in the poor family's purchasing behavior appears to be this over-spending on durable goods. Since most durable goods are relatively expensive items, it is not hard to see why the purchase of a durable good makes heavy inroads on a small income. Moreover, it is difficult to judge whether or not a given durable good should be considered a luxury for a poor family. (One could argue that an automatic washing machine is not a luxury for a large family in which the mother's time is at a premium.) However, when purchasing families with incomes less than $2,000 spend almost half of their income on durable goods, we need to look for an explanation.

The durable goods that take the largest bites from poor families' incomes are large household appliances and radios, television sets, and phonographs. These are household items that can be considered part of the standard package of American consumption. According to one writer, these home items are especially significant to working-class wives who aspire to the role of the modern, efficient American housewife. Also, of course, much effort and money are devoted to the advertisement of these and other items in the standard package. The poor are no less vulnerable than others are to persuasive selling. Such pressure may be particularly hard for the Negro poor to resist, since traditionally they have been denied access to other forms of social status.

There are other, less subjective factors in the purchase of durable goods than role image and vulnerability to advertising. Young families and those with large numbers of children spend more on durables, regardless of income. Since the poor include proportionately larger numbers of young, large families, we can attribute some over-spending to heavier need in newly formed households with more demand for labor-saving devices. Another factor in some poor neighborhoods is the incidence of merchandizing practices that result in higher prices than those found for the same goods in middle-income shopping areas.

We have made some general statements about how the poor spend their incomes, and have provided some brief explanations of the patterns found. Some of the findings that support those statements are given below.

a. Categories of Spending

Food, shelter, and medical care take larger shares of the poor family's consumer dollar than they do in families with higher incomes, on the average. Clothing and transportation take smaller shares, on the average. Household operation (including furnishings and equipment) and other expenses (recreation, personal care, and education) take about the same share as in higher income families.[6]

The above findings compare average proportions spent annually by different income groups, whether all families in a group made purchases in the category or not. In a given year, most families do buy food, shelter, and at least a few articles of clothing. They probably also pay at least one medical fee. We know from other data that in a given year fewer low-income families make purchases of automobiles, furniture, and household appliances. What is the share of income spent by poor families who do purchase a major durable in a given year?

Among those in the lowest income group (under $2,000) who bought a major durable in 1962, an average of 48% of their income was spent on such purchases. In the next higher income group ($2,000 to $4,999), the share was 28%. These percentages are high compared with the shares of income spent by the poor on "needs," and startlingly high compared with the shares spent on durables by families in other income groups. (In the category that included median family income [$6,000 to $7,499] in 1962, the share spent for durables was only 14%.)[7] The durables that take the largest shares of poor families' income are large household appliances and radios, television sets, and phonographs. High consumption of these same items, and furniture, is reported in Caplovitz' study of low-income families in New York: 95% owned television sets, 63% owned phonographs, and 41% owned automatic washers.[8]

b. Effects of Class and Ethnic Values

The special importance of household appliances, television, and furniture to the working class was discussed in some detail in Rainwater's analysis of the working-class wife. According to that author, appliances and furniture mean something different to working-class wives from what they mean to middle-class wives.[9] The difference in values is a subtle one, but may be an important contribution to over-spending.

Working-class wives' lives revolve around home and housework to a greater extent than the lives of middle-class wives. The working-class wife knows that housework is inevitable, and she dreams of a home (especially a kitchen) that symbolizes the role of the modern, efficient American housewife. She also tends to associate the new with the beautiful. The middle-class wife, on the other hand, is interested in labor-saving appliances that free her as much as possible from the role of housewife so that she may enjoy the social, intellectual, and aesthetic pleasures of upper-middle-class life. These differences suggest that the working-class wife sees household durables as an end in themselves, rather than merely as means to other ends.

One sociologist describes another pattern of spending in terms of the symbolic value of certain products. Negroes underspend in four major areas—housing, automobile transportation, food, and medical care. On the other hand, a number of Negro women are more interested than white women in "high fashion," even in the Under-$3,000 income group. And Negro families report buying Scotch whiskey, a high-status drink, twice as often as white families do.[10] One theorist writing on the subject of "conditions for irrational choices" suggests an explanation: Irrational choice making occurs when "something . . . [is] . . . repressed among a large number of individuals in a specific segment of our society with a distinctive sub-culture."[11]

c. The Effect of Youth and Size of Families

In one analysis of frequency of purchase of selected durables, it was found that the rate for young married couples with incomes under $3,000 increases after the birth of their first child, whereas the rate for couples with incomes over $3,000 decreases.[12] Caplovitz' study also showed that family size among his low-income public housing tenants affects durable goods' ownership (or aspirations for ownership) regardless of the size of income.[13]

These facts and the much cited findings by Caplovitz about high-priced durables in poor neighborhoods provide the evidence for our answer, "Yes, but . . ." to the question on whether the poor spend their incomes on basic needs. We do not want to leave the impression that the poor are profligate spenders on special goods, however.

There is some evidence that they do not have much desire for all kinds of special purchases. In one nationwide study, their desires for "special expenditures" were found to be less frequent than those expressed by middle and upper income families.[14] Although poor families may not dream of as many new purchases as other families do, they do appear to be eager to acquire the standard package.

2. DO LOW-INCOME SHOPPERS TRY TO GET THE BEST QUALITY FOR THE LOWEST PRICE?

Available evidence indicates that the answer is "No." Lower income consumers are not more deliberate in their shopping, more wide-ranging in their search for good buys, more price conscious, nor more informed on the characteristics of products than families with higher incomes. If anything, they are less apt to carry out those practices than others. Neither are low income consumers more apt to buy used articles, to buy "separate items," nor to pay cash for their purchases.

On three counts, poor people do exhibit more economical practices. They tend more often to negotiate special deals on durables, especially through relatives or friends. The *very* poor tend to buy goods on sale more often than others. And, although there is just as much use of credit by low-income families as by others, fewer of the poor have installment or mortgage debt. Among those who do have installment debt, however, the effect on family solvency may be ruinous.

On the basis of strict rationality, one would expect low-income consumers to be more deliberate, searching, price-conscious, and informed than high-income consumers. The low level of education of many poor people goes a long way in explaining why they are not, and indeed, why they fall below other income groups in the frequency of some of these activities. Knowledge of the immense variety of goods on the American market is not easily acquired. Especially in the case of appliances, knowledge of technical features is highly specialized. Knowledge of the intricacies of credit agreements or consumer rights is not easy to acquire, either. The best that a poorly educated person can do, perhaps, is to rely on a known dealer, buy what a relative has bought, or try to negotiate a special deal. These are the very practices that many poor families follow.

Research findings also suggest that shopping practices are affected by length of exposure to urban American ways. The Puerto Ricans are an example of a newly arrived group that prefers traditional, personal stores rather than more bureaucratic, price-competitive outlets, and so do Negro migrants from the rural South. It is reasonable to expect that the longer people live in proximity to modern, depersonalized outlets, and the more they are exposed to knowledge about the urban world (through education or experience), the more often they will conduct wide-ranging searches of stores, and be price-conscious.

One reason for lower frequency of installment or mortgage debt among the poor is their ineligibility for loans under legal credit requirements. It is also possible that some poor families actually prefer not to be in debt. Among those families who are in debt for installment purchases, however, there is a large percentage of young, large families. Again, the pressing needs of this group probably account for some of the extremes of insolvency found among the poor.

The findings that support these views are:

a. Deliberation in Buying

In a nationwide sample of families, the poor were found to be neither higher nor lower than others on a scale of deliberation in durable goods purchases. On three deliberation activities in the scale, however, they were less active than others: They were less circumspect in seeking information, less concerned about the several features of the item and somewhat more dependent on brands. The poor families were no different from others in the extent of their enjoyment of "shopping around," an attitude found to be positively related to high deliberation.

Extent of formal education was more strongly associated with deliberation in buying durables than was income, in the study described above. The higher a person's level of education, the more he or she tended to score high on the deliberation scale. An interesting exception was in buying sport shirts, however: The less well-educated were more deliberate. Thus, the extent of deliberation may be influenced in some groups by the type of purchase.[15]

b. Shopping Scope

Several findings point to the tendency of the poor to use nearby stores rather than distant ones, and to prefer personal buying situations (the peddler as an extreme form), rather than "bureaucratic," impersonal ones. The poorest housing tenants in the New York Study used independent neighborhood stores, chain stores, and peddlers more frequently than department stores or discount houses, for buying durable goods. Among these low-income families, it was the poorest who had the narrowest shopping scope. And it was those who bought from the neighborhood stores or peddlers who paid more for the goods, especially for television sets.[16] In a Chicago study, the personal buying situation also was found to be more appealing to the upper-lower-class than to the lower-middle and upper-middle classes.[17]

In a study of urban families in Wisconsin, the preference for independent and neighborhood stores (rather than chain stores) was related to motives concerning the store and its personnel, rather than to motives concerning price, and was more typical of rural migrants to the city than of natives or urban migrants.[18] Caplovitz also found narrow shopping scope more typical of those who had been a short time in New York or any other city, and more typical of those with less education. He found, for example, that the Puerto Ricans in the study were narrower in shopping scope than Negroes or whites.[19]

Another factor in shopping scope, according to Rainwater, is the discomfort felt by working-class women in "downtown" stores:[20] ". . . [Clerks] . . . try to make you feel awful if you don't like something they have told you is nice and they would certainly think it was terrible if you told them you didn't have enough money to buy something."

c. Information about Products

According to several studies, formal education appears to be the key characteristic of the informed consumer. Income is slightly related to use of consumer rating magazines (the poor use them less often), but education is strongly related.[21] Education is also clearly related to consultation of any kind of reading material (including advertisements) as a source of information about products.[22]

These are formal channels of communication about products, and it is not surprising that those with skills and experience in formal communication are more active. Those with little education do make more use of relatives (though not necessarily more use of all other people) as a source of information about durable goods. Relatives were found to be a fruitful source of information for poorly-educated people in decisions on a model for a subsequent purchase of a durable. Other interesting differences between those with lower and higher levels of education have been found. In one study, the latter tended to buy a different model from the one seen at someone's house, whereas the former more often bought the same model.[23] In another study, high-income persons were found to be more critical of features of goods, including obsolescence.[24] Education apparently induces a more critical attitude and less reliance on reference groups in the choice of consumer goods.

d. Purchase of Used Goods and Separate Items

The tendency of low-income families in New York to buy new appliances and furniture (especially sets) was mentioned by Caplovitz,[25] but no nationwide data are available to confirm this finding. The only nationwide figures found on the purchase of new vs. used items concern automobiles; the evidence is clear that the poor tend less often to buy new autos and more often to buy used ones.[26]

On the topic of buying sets of furniture and other items sold as pre-selected groupings, one unpublished study indicates that low-income households purchase living room suites less often than higher income households. No difference was found in frequency of purchase of other kinds of sets by income group. There was a slight tendency for low-income respondents in that study to *prefer* suites, and some other types of sets, however, compared with respondents in higher income households.[27]

If lower-class consumers do tend consistently to prefer sets of furniture to separate pieces, two factors may be at work; one cultural, and one economic. There may be a true class difference in taste for the strictly harmonious room: More interest on the part of the working class.[28] It is possible also that low-priced sets may be more numerous than separate items in furniture outlets located in poor neighborhoods.

e. Use of Credit and Installment Buying

Half or more of the poor families over the nation use consumer credit of some kind. (eighty-one percent of the New York City tenants in Caplovitz' study used it.)[29] Poor families nationwide who had installment debt in 1962, however, were a smaller proportion—between one-fourth and one-third of all families below the poverty line. This proportion can be compared with half or more families with higher income who had installment debt in 1962.[30]

Mortgage debt is also carried by a smaller proportion of the poor than of higher income families over the nation—only about one-fourth of the former owed on mortgages in 1962, compared with half or more of families in higher income brackets. Another kind of debt—money owed to doctors, dentists, and hospitals—was owed by a small proportion of poor families (about 17 percent), and this proportion is similar to that reported for families with higher incomes.[31] It is not so much whether poor people buy on credit, however, as what it does to their financial situation that interests us. The ratio of debt to annual income is considerably higher for the poor than for others—about twice as high as the ratio among better-off families.[32] (Also, debt is clearly responsible for a shaky financial status in many poor families, as described in the section below.)

There is conflicting evidence on whether the poor actually prefer buying on credit. On the one hand, findings from a nationwide study show that in general low-income consumers do approve of installment buying.[33] On the other hand, the majority of Caplovitz' respondents said they thought that credit is a bad idea, although some felt that buying on time is easier than trying to save cash for large purchases.[34]

Only persons with high income or a college education are well informed on the real cost of credit, according to one nationwide study.[35] Added to this fact are two others reported in the New York City study: (1) Credit costs were higher for goods bought in the very sources that many poor families use—ped-dlers and neighborhood dealers; and (2) A majority of the families did not know where to go if they should be cheated by a merchant. Thus, many factors seem to converge in making installment debt an especially pressing problem for the poor.

3. DO LOW-INCOME FAMILIES BUDGET THEIR INCOMES AND PLAN THEIR PURCHASES?

One proof of good financial management in families—whether or not they manage to stay solvent—suggests that poor families do not score very well. Few have many assets, and a sizable minority have negative net worth. (In other words, these families' debts exceed their assets.) Poor families who are insolvent are not complacent about it, however.

As a group, the poor save very little and are not often covered by insurance. Moreover, when they do save or invest, they tend to be less "modern" in their pattern of saving than higher income groups. Also, their views on the value of life insurance are more traditional.

The central place of installment debt in many poor families' insolvency was described earlier. Regardless of kind of debt, cultural factors may affect this proclivity to be in debt. Solvency as a moral obligation is not strong in all cultures. Thus, we might expect differences among ethnic groups in tightness of control over family finances. We might also expect changes in ethnic groups' state of solvency as they acquire education and higher-status occupations in the American setting.

Again, education is an important factor in explaining low efficiency of planning among the poor. Education can affect not only the amount of knowledge one has about financial matters, but also one's mode of thinking about money. The ability to think of money as a long-range, abstract value, rather than as concrete visible amounts, may allow educated consumers to weigh purchases and income more effectively. For the concrete thinker, it is easy to "Buy now" with a small portion of the weekly paycheck, and hard to see in advance how difficult it will be to "Pay later."

Hardly anyone would expect families on $3,000 or less income to save or buy insurance. Furthermore, since there are high proportions of families with no major earners among the poor (as high as 72 percent in the Under-$1,000 group), savings and insurance plans supported by employers or unions are often out of reach.

Below are some of the facts behind this general picture:

a. Insolvency
In 1962, 17 percent of those in the lowest income quintile had negative net worth. In these families, debts exceeded assets, whether those assets were savings or merely the value of their own houses and autos.[36]

Negroes and Puerto Ricans in the New York City study were more often insolvent than whites, regardless of age and family size and good or poor consumer practices. Among Negroes, the debt component of the debt-income ratio was greater in the highest income group, while the opposite was the case for whites and Puerto Ricans. When those same groups were classified according to occupational groups, however, the racial difference decreased in importance. Negroes in white collar jobs or in business were more likely to be out of the red than those in unskilled or semi-skilled jobs.[37]

Low income families are not unconcerned about money or about the state of the family's finances, however. In the New York City study those families who were relatively insolvent were much more likely to mention financial worries than solvent families, and more likely to mention financial worries than other types.[38]

b. Efficiency Of Planning

In a Minneapolis study of planning, income per se was found to be less important than education in predicting "planfulness of actions" and efficiency in decision-making, in eight areas of family life. Also related to these qualities of consumership were certain attitudes characterized as developmental, modern, manipulative, prudential, and optimistic. On this basis, we would expect persons who are non-developmental (i.e., more material, traditional, fatalistic, impulsive, and pessimistic) in viewpoint to be less efficient. Among those same families, successful consumership was also related to good family agreement on roles, and good communication in the family.[39]

A certain kind of efficiency is practiced by many working-class wives, but it may not be the best method in the long run. According to Rainwater, the wife in the working-class family tries very hard to exert control over the outgo of cash income.[40] Her style of control often resembles the old "sugar bowl" method, in which small amounts are doled out until the cache is gone. One workingman's wife described the process as follows: ". . . if I have a little extra money then I buy something. If I don't have any money, I just don't buy clothes for that time, or nothing extra. I like it that way. I always know where I am."

c. Savings and Insurance

The nationwide figures on extent of saving show that nearly 50 percent of those in the Under-$3,000 income group had no savings in 1962, compared with 28 percent or less of those in higher income groups.[41] In the New York City study, 68 percent were found to have no savings.[42] Low-income persons in general are also less often covered by insurance, either medical, hospital, or life insurance.

The kind of saving most often preferred by low-income families is the low-risk, non-investment type that can be easily liquidated. Those who think of investing at all think of real estate, farms, or business, rather than stocks, bonds, or insurance. Low-income persons who consider life insurance think of it as a source of funds for terminal medical and burial expenses, in addition to support for dependents in case of death.[43]

The avowed purposes in saving differ for low-income families. Their reasons resemble the traditional view that one should try to secure the future against emergencies. Poor families who save, or would like to save, usually mention one reason—they want to save for old age or retirement. Although middle-income families mention this reason too, they also say that they want to save for purchases such as vacations or autos.[44]

5. DO LOW-INCOME FAMILIES MEET SOME NEEDS THROUGH HOME PRODUCTION?

Evidence on home production by the poor is sparse, but what there is points to less, not more, production in two areas: food growing, and home repairs. However, since these types of home production are also affected by the extent of home ownership (known to be lower among the poor), these facts about the effect of income must be considered tentative.

In the one study consulted, it was interesting to note that those with the highest average amount saved through home production had training beyond high school (though not a college degree). Those with twelve grades of school or less, and those with a bachelor's degree or more, were below average in amounts saved through home production.[45]

Those findings bear out our hunch that many home production activities will not be attempted, nor be successful, unless someone in the family has had special training or experience in these skills. Often, expensive tools and understanding of technical instructions are necessary for the success of a home project. This means that the poor, and the poorly educated, may be unable to improve their situation very much through this means.

5. DO LOW-INCOME FAMILIES TAKE ADVANTAGE OF CONSUMER BENEFITS AVAILABLE TO THE POOR?

The existence of many successful programs in legal aid, medical and dental clinics, and similar facilities, testifies to the variety of ways the poor could cut their cost of living if they took advantage of them. A summary of evaluations of so many diverse programs cannot be included in this report. Many experienced workers would agree, however, that there is need for greater coverage or utilization. The unmet health needs, the legal predicaments of the poor, and the great educational losses of poor children, are cases in point.

Whether coverage is adequate or not, the lack of full success by established programs often is justifiably attributed to apathy on the part of the people who need them most. Apparently, it is not enough to offer the service. It has to be carefully planned to conform to attitudes, schedules, and locales of potential recipients. Also, the availability of the service has to be communicated directly and simply, and the preliminaries have to be carried out quickly and smoothly. Thus, we must conclude that the poor do not use these resources to the full for easing their income situation.

ADDING THE SCORE

How do consumer practices of the poor compare with the recommended rules of financial management? On almost every count, we have found that the poor fail to use what many would call the rational solution:

1. Although they spend most of their income on basic needs, those who buy durable goods make serious inroads on their incomes.
2. Most do not use more deliberation, consult more sources, or shop more widely, to get the best buys. Instead, many depend on known merchants or relatives for judgments of what to buy.
3. Few have savings of any size; most do not have life insurance; and only about half are covered by medical insurance.
4. It is doubtful whether many carry out home production activities to supplement cash purchases.
5. Many probably do not make full use of the programs established to provide services and goods free or at reduced rates.

Explanations of some of these apparently irrational consumer practices can be found in the special needs and characteristics of concentrated sub-groups of the poor. We have mentioned the concentration of young, large families, in connection with the problems of durable goods purchases, heavy installment debt, and insolvency. We have also mentioned the concentration of recent migrants (from within or outside the United States), in connection with findings about narrow shopping scope and preference for personal treatment in stores. A third group, one that undoubtedly includes many more of the poor, consists of those with little formal education. The lack of education shows up as an important factor in low level of knowledge about the market and the economy, and in inadequate conceptual tools for planning and making decisions.

Other kinds of explanations point to objective conditions (in sociological terms, to the social structure) that account for existing consumer practices by the poor. Three examples of such conditions are: the credit system, with its risk-cost formula and inexorable penalties that work against the poor; merchandising practices in some low-income area stores; and the fluctuating nature of employment in occupations followed by many low-income earners.

One purely economic explanation also deserves attention: the effect produced by low income, per se. The size of an income determines to some extent whether any "economies of scale" can be employed by a family. A small income has to be disbursed in smaller amounts than a large income, regardless of the different ways families now spend incomes. Thus, low-income families can less often take advantage of low prices for quantity purchases. On the other hand, some products and services are available in standard units that cannot be divided into smaller ones. Thus, large outlays (such as one month's rent in advance) are greater disturbances to a small than to a large income.[46] Since there is less possibility for flexibility in the disbursement of a small income, there is more possibility of imbalance.

Finally, we come to the psychological explanations proposed by a number of writers for explaining consumer practices of the poor. Among the traits or values that are said to dispose the poor to behavior different from the middle and upper classes are: an attitude of fatalism; a preference for immediate gratification of impulses; a low level of aspiration and low need to achieve; an unclear view of the higher social structure; a concrete style of thinking; and over-concern with security.

Often the psychological differences attributed to the poor are discussed as if they were "givens,"[47] in much the same way as the idea of irrationality seems like a "given." However, these same differences are discussed by other writers as possible outcomes of objective social and economic conditions of the lower class.

One set of research findings indicates, for example, that a child's preference for immediate gratification is related to the absence of a father in the home. Another finding indicates that continued delay in reward can induce this same preference in children.[48] In a like vein, it has been said that "splurges" by lower-class people are natural reactions to past deprivation and insecurity about the future.[49] Still another writer argues that low ambition in the lower class is more apparent than real: Lower-class people have ambition, but since it is unrealistic for the poor to aspire to the same goals as the middle class, their goals only seem less ambitious.[50] Thus, we have explanations that range from the social characteristics of the poor, through purely economic and purely psychological factors, and finally back to the environment of the poor. What does all this mean for planners of programs to improve their consumer practices?

At first glance, the problem seems to be so severe, and the explanations so deeply rooted in far-reaching social problems that it may seem futile to attack it at all. It is instructive, however, to look at some consumer programs that have been successful, and at some recommended programs based on the New York study. Examples of recent successful programs are described in some detail in the 1965 report of the President's Committee on Consumer Interest, "The Most For Their Money."[51] Recommendations based on the New York study are found in the final chapter of Caplovitz' book.[52]

In general, the successful programs and the recommended actions employ unorthodox, "backdoor" methods that capitalize on the very differences in the poor that we have described. They may use informal methods of education carried out locally in poor neighborhoods. They may attack problems of financial management indirectly through appeals to material interests rather than by teaching abstract principles. They may provide for intervention at the top in dealing with problems that stem from rigidities in the market itself. Finally, they may concentrate efforts on special groups of the poor who seem particularly vulnerable to buying mistakes or insolvency.

If the apparent irrationality of poor consumers can be dealt with in these realistic ways, we have some hope of softening the worst effects of a hand-to-mouth existence.

NOTES

1. Pierre Martineau, "Social Classes and Spending Behavior," in Martin Grossack, ed. *Understanding Consumer Behavior* (Boston, Massachusetts: Christopher Publishing House, 1964).

2. Jean L. Pennock, "Who Are the Poor?" *Family Economic Review* (Consumer and Food Economics Research Division, Agricultural Research Service, U.S. Department of Agriculture, March 1964).

3. George Katona, Charles Lininger, and Eva Mueller, *1963 Survey of Consumer Finances,* Monograph No. 32 (Ann Arbor: The University of Michigan, Survey Research Center, Institute for Social Research, 1964).

4. David Caplovitz, *The Poor Pay More* (New York: The Free Press of Glencoe, 1963).

5. Lee Rainwater, R. Coleman, and G. Handel, *Workingman's Wife* (New York: Oceana Publications, 1959).

6. Emma G. Holmes, "Expenditures of Low-Income Families," *Family Economic Review* (Consumer and Food Economics Research Division, Agricultural Research Service, U.S. Department of Agriculture), March 1955; also LIFE, *Study of Consumer Expenditures: A Background for Marketing Decisions,* vol. 1 (New York: Time, Inc., 1957).

7. George Katona, Charles Lininger, and Richard Kosebud, *1962 Survey of Consumer Finances,* Monograph No. 32 (Ann Arbor: University of Michigan, Survey Research Center, Institute for Social Research, 1963); also, Katona, Lininger, and Mueller, *1963 Survey of Consumer Finances,* 1964.

8. Caplovitz, *The Poor Pay More,* 1963.

9. Rainwater, *Workingman's Wife,* 1959.

10. Raymond Bauer, "The Negro and the Marketplace," paper read before the American Psychological Association, Los Angeles, California, September 1964.

11. Arnold M. Rose, "Conditions for Irrational Choices," *Social Research,* 30, no. 2, Summer 1963.

12. Martin H. David, *Family Composition and Consumption* (Amsterdam: North Holland Publishing Company, 1962).

13. Caplovitz, *The Poor Pay More,* 1963.

14. George Katona, *The Mass Consumption Society* (New York: McGraw-Hill, 1964).

15. Eva Mueller, "A Study of Purchase Decisions," in Lincoln Clark, ed. *Consumer Behavior,* Committee for Research on Consumer Attitudes and Behavior (New York: New York University Press, 1954).

16. Caplovitz, *The Poor Pay More,* 1963.

17. Gregory Stone, "Sociological Aspects of Consumer Purchasing in a Northwest Side Chicago Community," (Master's Thesis, University of Chicago, Chicago, Ill., 1952).

18. John Harp, "Socio-economic Correlates of Consumer Behavior," *The American Journal of Economics and Sociology,* 20, no. 3, April 1961, pp. 265-270.

19. Caplovitz, *The Poor Pay More,* 1963.

20. Rainwater, *Workingman's Wife,* 1959.

21. Hugh W. Sargent, *Consumer-product Rating Publications and Buying Behavior,* University of Illinois Bulletin No. 85, Urbana, Illinois, 1959.

22. Mueller, "A Study of Purchase Decisions," 1954.

23. *Ibid.,*

24. Katona, *The Mass Consumption Society,* 1964.

25. Caplovitz, *The Poor Pay More,* 1963.

26. Katona, Lininger, and Mueller, *1963 Survey of Consumer Finances*, 1964.
27. Unpublished data from the author's study, "Cognitive Structure and Consumer Behavior," under a grant from Consumers Union, Mt. Vernon, New York, 1961-1962.
28. Rainwater, *Workingman's Wife*, 1959.
29. Caplovitz, *The Poor Pay More*, 1963.
30. Katona, Lininger, and Mueller, *1963 Survey of Consumer Finances*, 1964.
31. *Ibid.*
32. *Ibid.*
33. George Katona, *The Powerful Consumer* (New York: McGraw-Hill, 1960).
34. Caplovitz, *The Poor Pay More*, 1963.
35. Katona, *The Mass Consumption Society*, 1964.
36. Katona, Lininger, and Kosebud, *1962 Survey of Consumer Finances*, 1963.
37. Caplovitz, *The Poor Pay More*, 1963.
38. *Ibid.*
39. Reuben Hill, "Judgment and Consumership in the Management of Family Resources," Sociology and Social Research, 47, no. 4 (July 1963), pp. 446-460.
40. Rainwater, *Workingman's Wife*, 1959.
41. Katona, Lininger, and Kosebud, *1962 Survey of Consumer Finances*, 1963.
42. Caplovitz, *The Poor Pay More*, 1963.
43. Katona, *The Powerful Consumer*, 1960.
44. *Ibid.*
45. James Morgan, Martin David, Wilbur Cohen, and Harvey Brazer, *Income and Welfare in the United States* (New York: McGraw-Hill, 1962).
46. Charles V. Willie, Morton O. Wagenfeld, and Lee J. Cary, "Patterns of Rent Payment Among Problem Familes," *Social Casework*, October 1964, pp. 465-470.
47. Martineau, "Social Classes and Spending Behavior," 1964.
48. Walter Mischel and Ralph Metzner, "Preference for Delayed Reward as a Function of Age, Intelligence, and Length of Delay Interval," *Journal of Abnormal and Social Psychology*, 64, no. 6, 1962, pp. 425-431.
49. Paul Lazarsfeld, "Sociological Reflections on Business," in Martin Grossack, ed. *Understanding Consumer Behavior* (Boston: Christopher Publishing House, 1964).
50. Suzanne Keller and Marisa Zavallone, "Ambition and Social Class: A Respecification," *Social Forces*, 43, no. 1 (October 1964), pp. 58-70.
51. President's Committee on Consumer Interest, *The Most for Their Money*, A Report of the Panel on Consumer Education for Persons with Limited Incomes (Washington, D.C.: U.S. Government Printing Office, 1965).
52. Caplovitz, *The Poor Pay More*, 1963.

46. EXPLOITATION OF DIS- ADVANTAGED CONSUMERS BY RETAIL MERCHANTS

Report of the National Commission on Civil Disorders

MUCH OF the violence in recent civil disorders has been directed at stores and other commercial establishments in disadvantaged Negro areas. In some cases, rioters focused on stores operated by white merchants who, they apparently believed, had been charging exorbitant prices or selling inferior goods. Not all the violence against these stores can be attributed to "revenge" for such practices. Yet it is clear that many residents of disadvantaged Negro neighborhoods believe they suffer constant abuses by local merchants.

Significant grievances concerning unfair commercial practices affecting Negro consumers were found in 11 of the 20 cities studied by the Commission. The fact that most of the merchants who operate stores in almost every Negro area are white undoubtedly contributes to the conclusion among Negroes that they are exploited by white society.

It is difficult to assess the precise degree and extent of exploitation. No systematic and reliable survey comparing consumer pricing and credit practices in all-Negro and other neighborhoods has ever been conducted on a nationwide basis. Differences in prices and credit practices between white middle-income and Negro low-income areas to some extent reflect differences in the real cost

Reprinted from *Report of the National Commission on Civil Disorders* (New York: Bantam Books, 1968), 274-277.

of serving these two markets (such as differential losses from pilferage in super-markets) but the exact extent of these differential real costs has never been estimated accurately. Finally, an examination of exploitative consumer prac-tices must consider the particular structure and functions of the low income consumer durables market.

INSTALLMENT BUYING

This complex situation can best be understood by first considering certain basic facts:

(1) Various cultural factors generate constant pressure on low-income families to buy many relatively expensive durable goods and display them in their homes. This pressure comes in part from continuous exposure to commercial advertising, especially on television. In January 1967, over 88% of all Negro households had TV sets. A 1961 study of 464 low-income families in New York City showed that 95% of these relatively poor families had TV sets.

(2) Many poor families have extremely low incomes, bad previous credit records, unstable sources of income, or other attributes which make it virtually impossible for them to buy merchandise from established large national or local retail firms. These families lack enough sav-ings to pay cash, and they cannot meet the standard credit require-ments of established general merchants because they are too likely to fall behind in their payments.

(3) Poor families in urban areas are far less mobile than others. A 1967 Chicago study of low-income Negro households indicated their low automobile ownership compelled them to patronize primarily local neighborhood merchants. These merchants typically provided smaller selection, poorer services, and higher prices than big national outlets. The 1961 New York study also indicated that families who shopped outside their own neighborhoods were far less likely to pay exorbitant prices.

(4) Most low-income families are uneducated concerning the nature of credit purchase contracts, the legal rights and obligations of both buyers and sellers, sources of advice for consumers who are having difficulties with merchants, and the operation of the courts concerned with these matters. In contrast, merchants engaged in selling goods to them are very well informed.

(5) In most states, the laws governing relations between consumers and merchants in effect offer protection only to informed, sophisticated parties with understanding of each other's rights and obligations. Consequently, these laws are little suited to protect the rights of most low-income consumers.

443

In this situation, exploitative practices flourish. Ghetto residents who want to buy relatively expensive goods cannot do so from standard retail outlets and are thus restricted to local stores. Forced to use credit, they have little understanding of the pitfalls of credit buying. But because they have unstable incomes and frequently fail to make payments, the cost to the merchants of serving them is significantly above that of serving middle-income consumers. Consequently, a special kind of merchant appears to sell them goods on terms designed to cover the high cost of doing business in ghetto neighborhoods.

Whether they actually gain higher profits, these merchants charge higher prices than those in other parts of the city to cover the greater credit risks and other higher operating costs inherent in neighborhood outlets. A recent study conducted by the Federal Trade Commission in Washington, D.C., illustrates this conclusion dramatically. The FTC identified a number of stores specializing in selling furniture and appliance to low-income households. About 92% of the sales of these stores were credit sales involving installment purchases, as compared to 27% of the sales in general retail outlets handling the same merchandise.

The median income annually of a sample of 486 customers of these stores was about $4,200, but one-third had annual incomes below $3,600, about 6% were receiving welfare payments, and another 76% were employed in the lowest paying occupations (service workers, operatives, laborers, and domestics)—as compared to 36% of the total labor force in Washington in those occupations.

Definitely catering to a low-income group, these stores charged significantly higher prices than general merchandise outlets in the Washington area. According to testimony by Paul Rand Dixon, Chairman of the FTC, an item selling wholesale at $100 would retail on the average for $165 in a general merchandise store, and for $250 in a low-income specialty store. Thus, the customers of these outlets were paying an average price premium of about 52%.

While higher prices are not necessarily exploitative in themselves, many merchants in ghetto neighborhoods take advantage of their superior knowledge of credit buying by engaging in various exploitative tactics—high pressure salesmanship, bait advertising, misrepresentation of prices, substitution of used goods for promised new ones, failure to notify consumers of legal actions against them, refusal to repair or replace substandard goods, exorbitant prices or credit charges, and use of shoddy merchandise. Such tactics affect a great many low-income consumers. In the New York study, 60% of all households had suffered from consumer problems (some of which were purely their own fault), about 43% had experienced repossession, garnishment, or threat of garnishment.

GARNISHMENT

Garnishment practices in many states allow creditors to deprive individuals of their wages through court action without hearing or trial. In about 20 states, the wages of an employee can be diverted to a creditor merely upon the latter's deposition, with no advance hearing where the employee can defend himself. He often receives no prior notice of such action and is usually unaware of the law's operation and too poor to hire legal defense. Moreover, consumers may find themselves still owing money on a sales contract even after the creditor has repossessed the goods. The New York study cited earlier in this chapter indicated that 20% of a sample of low-income families had been subject to legal action regarding consumer purchases. And the Federal Trade Commission study in Washington, D.C., showed that retailers specializing in credit sales of furniture and appliances to low-income consumers resorted to court action on the average for every $2,200 of sales. Since their average sale was for $207, this amounted to using the courts to collect from one of every 11 customers. In contrast, department stores in the same area used court action against approximately one of every 14,500 customers, assuming their sales also averaged $207 per customer.

VARIATIONS IN FOOD PRICES

Residents of low-income Negro neighborhoods frequently claim that they pay higher prices for food in local markets than wealthier white suburbanites and receive inferior quality meat and produce. Statistically reliable information comparing prices and quality in these two kinds of areas is generally unavailable. The U.S. Bureau of Labor Statistics studying food prices in six cities in 1966, compared prices of a standard list of 18 items in low-income areas and higher-income areas in each city. In a total of 180 stores, including independent and chain stores, and for items of the same type sold in the same types of stores, there were no significant differences in prices between low-income and high-income areas. However, stores in low-income areas were more likely to be small independents (which had somewhat higher prices), to sell low-quality produce and meat at any given price, and to be patronized by people who typically bought smaller-sized packages which are more expensive per unit of measure. In other words, many low-income consumers in fact pay higher prices, although the situation varies greatly from place to place.

Although these findings must be considered inconclusive, there are significant reasons to believe that poor households generally pay higher prices for the food they buy and receive lower quality food. Low-income consumers buy more food at local groceries because they are less mobile. Prices in these small stores are significantly higher than in major supermarkets because they cannot achieve economies of scale, and because real operating costs are higher in low-income Negro areas than in outlying suburbs. For instance, inventory "shrinkage" from pilfering and other causes is normally under 2% of sales, but can run twice as much in high-crime areas. Managers seek to make up for these added costs by charging higher prices for good quality food, or by substituting lower grades.

445

These practices do not necessarily involve "exploitation," but they are often perceived as exploitative and unfair by those who are aware of the price and quality differences involved, but unaware of operating costs. In addition, it is probable that genuinely exploitative pricing practices exist in some areas. In either case, differential food prices constitute another factor convincing urban Negroes in low-income neighborhoods that whites discriminate against them.

47. POVERTY, MINORITIES, AND CONSUMER EXPLOITATION

Frederick D. Sturdivant and Walter T. Wilhelm

A NUMBER of reports, ranging from informal studies by journalists to carefully researched investigations, have provided evidence that residents of ghettos pay more for their consumer goods than do other Americans.[1] For example, David Caplovitz' study of 464 families living in three New York settlement houses revealed a consistent pattern of high prices, poor quality, high interest charges, and unethical merchandising techniques. He concluded that "The problems of low-income consumers stem from the same set of forces that have created that special system of sales-and-credit—the quasi-traditional economy—catering to their wants."[2] In California, The Governor's Commission on the Los Angeles Riots tended to reinforce this view. Following three months of investigation into the causes of the Watts riots, the Commission reported, "Our conclusion, based upon an analysis of the testimony before us and on the report of our consultants, is *that consumer problems in the curfew area are not due to systematic racial discrimination but rather result from the traditional interplay of economic forces in the marketplace, aggravated by poverty conditions.*"[3] (Emphasis added.) These studies suggest, therefore, that the market system works to the disadvantage of the poor because they are poor—not because of race of ethnicity. Any correlation between minority group status and exploitation is, according to these studies, attributable to the high incidence of poverty among minorities rather than some insidious form of discrimination.

The studies reported to date, however, have not provided adequate proof to support this conclusion. The California Commission, for example, reached its conclusion without conducting a series of comparative shopping analyses between ghetto and non-ghetto stores and utilizing shoppers of various racial and ethnic backgrounds. Instead, staff consultants and their reserach assistants

Reprinted from *Social Science Quarterly* (December, 1968, pp. 643-650, by permission of the Southwestern Social Science Association.

"spot checked" prices in various locations throughout central Los Angeles.[4] Caplovitz did analyze certain of his data utilizing the variable of minority group status. His findings in this area, however, were unclear. On the one hand he noted, "The amount paid for appliances differs greatly among the racial [sic] groups. Whites pay the least, Puerto Ricans the most, with Negroes in between."[5] However, Caplovitz then noted that nonwhites tended to pay lower prices when the purchase is for cash. In fact, his data suggested that nonwhites paid less than whites when buying on credit in large stores outside the ghetto. This conflicting evidence was derived from the shopping experiences of the 464 cooperating families. The variables of method of payment, minority group status, and type of store were considered. However, *brand and model variations were not taken into account*. Thus, one does not know whether whites generally selected more expensive models and brands or if this shopping behavior was characteristic of either the Negroes or Puerto Ricans studied. Unless the variable of product brand and model is held constant, meaningful price comparisons cannot be made unless one subscribes to the rather risky assumption that brand or product quality selection is randomly distributed among the various ethnic and racial groups. In essence, the statement that exploitation in the marketplace is a function of economic status rather than minority group status is still untested.

RESEARCH DESIGN AND METHODOLOGY

The study was conducted in Los Angeles and involved the use of three couples and three shopping areas. The three couples represented the major populations of the city—Negro, Mexican-American, and Anglo-White. The shopping districts were the predominantly Negro south central section of Los Angeles (which includes Watts), the Mexican-American section of east Los Angeles, and Culver City, a middle-class, Anglo-White community.

The criteria used in selecting the couples included not only minority group status, but also comparable "credit profiles." The similarity of their profiles was designed to neutralize any price or credit differentials based on alleged risk. The characteristics of the shoppers' credit profile are noted in Figure 1.

Family Status	Married, 1-2 children
Age of Head of Household:	25-30
Employment:	Employed full time for 1-2 years on present job
Gross Income:	$2,850 to $3,250
Savings:	$0 to $100
Total Assets:	$300 to $450
Indebtedness:	$200 to $500
as % of gross income:	6.6% to 16%
as % of assets:	67% to 111%

Figure 1. Shoppers' Credit Profile.

The stores selected for comparative shopping in the Negro and Mexican-American sections were determined, in part, on the basis of detailed studies of consumer shopping patterns in those areas. Appliance and furniture stores in the two areas were arrayed on the basis of shopping frequency patterns determined from nearly 2,000 consumer interviews conducted in an earlier study of Watts and East Los Angeles.[6] Stores were then either included in the sample or eliminated from the list depending on the presence or absence of the same brands and models available in the control area. Culver City was selected as the nonpoverty shopping area because the composition of its retailing community and price structure typified shopping conditions for suburban Los Angeles area communities.

The attrition rate for stores to be included in the study was rather high because of the difficulty of finding the same brands and models in the disadvantaged areas versus Culver City. Comparative pricing analyses involving poverty areas and more prosperous sections in a city are very difficult because of variations in merchandise. When national brands are carried by a ghetto appliance dealer, he generally stocks only the lower end of the line. Retailers in higher income areas usually concentrate on the middle and upper price ranges of the product line. Furthermore, off-brand merchandise tends to make up a substantial part of the ghetto dealer's stock. Since these lines generally are not carried in other areas, direct price comparisons are impossible. Among the stores frequented by the residents of the two poverty areas, therefore, only six carried brands and models capable of direct price comparisons with stores in the outside community. The stores selected in the outside area were comparable to the ghetto stores in terms of size and estimated sales volume.[7]

The shopping procedure involved the selection of a 19-inch, black and white, portable TV set by each couple in each of the nine stores. Each couple (the order was determined randomly) selected a predetermined TV set and did everything necessary to obtain price data, except sign the contract. The shopping trips to each store were separated by a minimum of three days to avoid any suspicion by the sales clerks or management. The shopping was conducted during the last two weeks of July and the first week of August, 1967. A final briefing was given the similarly attired couples before they entered each store to make certain they selected the correct model. A typical dialogue in the store might be described as follows:

Salesman: May I help you?
Shoppers: Yes, we would like to see your portable TV's.
Salesman: They are right over here. Did you have anything special in mind? Color?
Shoppers: No, we want a black and white set. (The shoppers look at several sets and then ask about the preselected set.)
Shoppers: This is a nice set. It is the type we had in mind.
Salesman: It is a very nice set. We could deliver it today. (Salesmen often attempted to get the shoppers interested in a more expensive model.)
Shoppers: How much does it cost?

Salesman: (quotes the price)

Shoppers: How much would it run us a month?

The salesman figures out the credit terms. The couple specify that they want the smallest down payment and the lowest possible payments. Upon being told the monthly payment figure, the wife says they should think it over and asks the salesman to write down the credit terms. (Only one store refused this request saying that such information was "confidential and not allowed out of the store.")

In sum, the method included the selection of six of the most frequently used furniture and appliance stores in the two major poverty areas of Los Angeles for comparison with three stores selected on the basis of brand and model availability from an average suburban community. Fundamental to the method was the use of three disadvantaged couples, representing the three major population groups in the area, with basically the same credit characteristics. The three couples dressed in basically the same mode, shopped in the same stores, and priced exactly the same products. Thus, the only relevant variable not held constant was minority group status.

FINDINGS

In the process of testing for discrimination in the marketplace, data were collected which again confirm the presence of higher prices in ghetto stores. Ignoring the question of minority group status for the moment, Table 1 indicates that the average price asked the three couples for a given product was always higher in the disadvantaged area stores than in the control area (Culver City). The total cost or the credit price (shown in parentheses), averaged higher in the poverty areas as well.

While there were notable differences in prices between areas, there was an observable consistency in retail prices within the stores.[8] Among the prices recorded in Table 2, 19 of the 24 retail prices asked for the four models of TV sets were the same, regardless of minority group status. The prices asked the couples in the three Watts area stores were identical. In the control area, Store No. 1 increased the price by $10 for both the Negro and Mexican-American couples. In this case, the Negro couple shopped the store first and was asked $119 for RCA Model AH0668. Four days later, the Anglo couple was offered the same set for $109. After a wait of another three days, the Mexican-American couple shopped the store and was asked $119 for the set. The other six shopping trips in the control area produced identical prices for all three couples.

The Mexican-American area showed the greatest variation in prices. In part, this practice may be attributable to cultural patterns in the Mexican-American community where higgling and haggling is more common. There was no pattern of discrimination. In Store No. 1 the Mexican-American couple was asked the highest price while in Store No. 3 the Mexican-American and

Table 1. Average Retail and Credit Price for Portable TV Sets
by Area and by Brand

Product	Average Price[1]		
	Watts Area	East L.A. Area	Control Area
Zenith X1910	$170 ($194)	-	$130 ($190)
Olympic 9P46	$270 ($448)		$230 ($277)
RCA AHO668	$148 ($174)	-	$115 ($154)
Zenith X2014	-	$208 ($251)	$140 ($190)

[1]Prices are averages computed from the shopping experiences of the three couples in each of the stores selected. Retail prices refer to the price asked for the product before adding on credit charges. Credit prices, *shown in parentheses*, are the total of retail prices, sales tax, and interest charges.

Negro couples were charged a slightly higher price than the Anglo couple. When credit prices are considered, however, it becomes clear that credit and carrying charges are the devices most commonly used to exercise exploitation. In the East Los Angeles stores, for example, the Anglo-White couple was not quoted the highest retail prices, but they were charged the highest credit price in both stores. In all nine cases in the control area there were differences in credit charges even though the retail price differed in only Store No. 1. The most blatant case of discrimination occurred in Culver City Store No. 1. While the legal limit on interest is 10 percent on a twelve-month installment contract in California, the Mexican and Negro couples were asked to pay 42 and 44 percent respectively.[9] The Anglo couple was asked the legal rate. In Store No. 3 in Culver City, the two minority group couples were also charged a higher (and illegal) rate of interest. In Store No.2 all three couples were charged an illegal rate with the Anglo couple being charged the highest amount.

In the predominantly Negro area stores, where all three couples had been asked identical retail prices in the three stores, only one store charged the same legal rate of interest on its eighteen-month installment contracts. There were minor variations in the charges assigned by Store No. 2, with the Negro couple charged the highest amount and the Mexican shoppers the lowest. At Store No. 3 the retail price was quoted at $270 before tax. Adding tax at 5 percent

TABLE 2. Retail[2] and Credit[3] Prices Portable TV Sets by Area, Store, Brand, and Race

Area & Store	Zenith-X1910			OLYMPIC-9P46			RCA-AH0668			ZENITH-X2014		
	Negro	M-A	Anglo	Negro	M-A	Anglo	Negro	M-A	Anglo	Negro	M-A	Anglo
East L.A.												
Store 1												
Store 2[1]				$200 ($265)	$240 ($281)	$230 ($284)						
Store 3										$210 ($245)	$210 ($250)	$204 ($258)
Watts												
Store 1	$170 ($194)	$170 ($194)	$170 ($194)									
Store 2							$148 ($178)	$148 ($169)	$148 ($174)			
Store 3				$270 ($412)	$270 ($507)	$270 ($418)						
Culver City												
Store 1							$119 ($172)	$119 ($169)	$109 ($122)			
Store 2										$140 ($183)	$140 ($183)	$140 ($203)
Store 3	$130 ($145)	$130 ($152)	$130 ($140)									

[1]The model preselected for this store was sold before the experiment was completed.
[2]Retail prices refer to the price asked for the product before adding on interest charges.
[3]Credit prices, *shown in parentheses*, are the total of retail prices plus interest.

the total retail price before financing should have been $283.50. Deducting the required minimum down payment of $15.80, the total to be financed was $267.70. At the legal rate of 15 per cent for an eighteen-month contract interest charges would have amounted to $40.16 for a total price of $322.66. However, the total price to the Anglo and Negro couples was approximately $420, or an interest rate of nearly 50 percent. The total cost to the Mexican couple was $506.62 with charges of 82 percent.[10]

SUMMARY AND CONCLUSIONS

In spite of the difficulties associated with finding identical products in ghetto and non-ghetto stores, this study has attempted to determine the basis of price discrimination experienced by disadvantaged shoppers in the market-place. The research question was, "Is exploitation in the marketplace a function of low income or minority group status?" By selecting three pairs of disadvantaged shoppers whose only significant difference was their race and ethnicity and having these couples shop in the same stores for identical merchandise, the research design attempted to answer this question.

The findings demonstrate that installment purchases, which especially characterize the purchasing behavior of the disadvantaged produce major variations in the prices paid by the poor. Although no perfect pattern of discrimination based on minority group status emerged from the study, it should be noted that it was common for the couples to be charged higher credit costs when shopping outside of their own areas. In East Los Angeles, the Anglo couple received the highest charges. In the Watts area, the store charging the highest and most varied prices asked a substantially higher price of the Mexican couple. In two of the non-ghetto stores the minority shoppers were charged higher and illegal amounts.

The findings indicate that merchants find credit charges an excellent vehicle for exercising economic and racial or ethnic discrimination, but Table 2 demonstrates that however substantial and illegal many of these charges may be, they are not as significant as price variations between disadvantaged and prosperous areas. While the minority couples were subjected to discriminatory pricing in two of the three control area stores, in no case did they pay more than they would have paid in ghetto stores for the same merchandise. In most instances the prices were substantially less. It might be concluded that disadvantaged minority shoppers pay more, but especially in the ghetto.

The presence of high business costs, parasitic retailers, and the dominance of inefficient "mom-and-pop" firms in the ghetto underline the importance of comparative shopping by the disadvantaged. At the same time, the willingness of certain "outside" retailers to take advantage of the poor, especially members of minority groups, suggests that the disadvantaged are still subject to economic exploitation even when shopping beyond the boundaries of the ghetto.

Notwithstanding the difficulties of designing a test of minority groups and economic exploitation (a parallel study of automobile prices had to be abandoned in this project), additional studies should be undertaken. Experiments involving this phenomenon in other major American cities would provide a more complete understanding of these practices. Doubtless, this situation is not unique to Los Angeles, and the extent to which it is reflective of a national pattern of discrimination against the minorities and the poor it is deserving of further analysis and correction.

NOTES

1. For examples of the former *see*, *Wall Street Journal*, August 16, 1966; *Women's Wear Daily*, July 6, 1966; *Los Angeles Times*, October 8, 1967; *Los Angeles Herald Examiner*, October 11, 1966.
2. David Caplovitz, *The Poor Pay More* (New York: The Free Press, 1963), p. 179.
3. The Governor's Commission on the Los Angeles Riots, *Violence in the City: An End or a Beginning* (Los Angeles, December 1965), p. 63.
4. Interview with Gerald L. Rosen, Staff Attorney, The Governor's Commission on the Los Angeles Riots, January 18, 1966.
5. Caplovitz, *The Poor Pay More*, pp. 90-91.
6. Frederick D. Sturdivant, "Better Deal for Ghetto Shoppers," *Harvard Business Review*, 46, no. 2 (March-April, 1968), pp. 130-39.
7. Initially, the reader may be disturbed by the small size of the sample. However, it should be noted that *every* television dealer in the low-income areas that met the comparability criteria for the test was included in the study. The comparability criteria could have been relaxed and thus the sample size increased, but such a step would have made it impossible to test the hypothesis.
8. This consistency in retail prices was not attributable to the presence of price tags. In five of the six ghetto stores and one of the control area stores the customers had to rely on sales personnel for price information.
9. The Unruh Retail Installment Sales Act sets the maximum rate a dealer may charge on time contracts in California. A dealer may charge less, of course, but no evidence of this practice was found in the study. For most installment contracts under $1,000 the maximum service charge rate is 5/6 or 1 percent of the original unpaid balance multiplied by the number of months of the contract. In revolving charge accounts, such as those used by most department stores, the legal limit is 1-1/2 per cent per month on the first $1,000 and 1 percent per month on the balance over $1,000.
10. The model Olympic TV set wholesales for $104. Thus, with a retail price of $270 the dealer was already profiting from a markup of 160 per cent.

48. ECONOMIC REPORT ON INSTALL-MENT CREDIT AND RETAIL SALES PRACTICES OF DISTRICT OF COLUMBIA RETAILERS

Federal Trade Commission

THIS REPORT presents the results of a survey of installment credit and sales practices involving household furnishings and appliances in the District of Columbia. The purpose of the survey was to obtain a factual picture of the finance charges, prices, gross margins and profits, legal actions taken in collecting delinquent accounts, and the assignment relationships between retailers and finance companies. The survey covered those D.C. retailers of furniture and appliances having estimated sales of at least $100,000 for the year. The 96 retailers providing data had combined sales of $226 million, which represented about 85% of the sales of furniture, appliance, and department store retailers in the District of Columbia.

USE OF INSTALLMENT CREDIT

Sixty-five retailers with combined sales of $151 million indicated regular use of consumer installment sales contracts. The remainder sold only for cash or on a regular or revolving charge account basis. This report focuses primarily on retailers using installment contracts. These retailers were classified into two groups: those appealing primarily to low-income customers and those appealing to a more general market.

District of Columbia stores varied widely in their use of installment credit.

Reprinted from *Economic Report on Installment Credit and Retail Sales Practices of District of Columbia Retailers* (Washington: Superintendent of Documents, 1968), ix-xvi and 1-24.

Some general market discount appliance stores made very few sales on credit. At the other extreme, a number of low-income market retailers sold entirely on installment credit.

Installment credit was used much more extensively by retailers selling to low-income consumers than by retailers selling to other consumers. Low-income market retailers used installment credit in 93% of their sales. The comparable figure for general market retailers was 27%.

CUSTOMER CHARACTERISTICS

A sample of installment sales contracts and credit applications was analyzed to identify the customer characteristics of low-income market retailers. The analysis revealed substantial differences between customers of the low-income market retailers and all residents of the District of Columbia. The average family size was larger—4.3 persons compared to an average 3.5 persons for the District of Columbia. Almost half of the families of customers in the sample had five or more members. The median family income of the same customers was $348 per month. This is very low considering the larger than average size of the families. The Bureau of Labor Statistics recently estimated that the maintenance of a moderate standard of living for four in Washington, D.C., requires a monthly income of $730.

Most customers were engaged in low-paying jobs. The largest proportion, 28%, were Service Workers. such as waitresses and janitors. Second in importance were Operatives (including such occupations as taxi drivers and laundry workers). Laborers and Domestic Workers also represented a significant share of the sample. Together, these four major occupational groups accounted for 75% of the customer sample. In comparison, only 36% of the general population in the District was classified in these low-paying occupational groups. There were 31 welfare recipients in the sample, accounting for 6% of all customers in the sample. There were also a number of customers in the sample dependent on social security, alimony, support payments, and income received from relatives.

A review of credit references noted in the 486 contracts subjected to detailed analysis revealed that 70% indicated no credit references or references with low-income market retailers only. Only 30% of the customers of this retailer, therefore, had established credit with general market retailers.

GROSS MARGINS AND PRICES

The survey disclosed that, without exception, low-income market retailers had high average markups and prices. On the average, goods purchased for $100 at wholesale sold for $255 in the low-income market stores, compared with $159 in general market stores.

Contrasts between the markup policies of low-income and general market retailers are most apparent when specific products are compared. Retailers surveyed were asked to give the wholesale and retail prices for their two best-selling models in each product line. These price data are typical of the large volume of products sold by each class of retailer.

For every product specified, low-income market retailers had the higher average gross margin reported. When similar makes and models are compared, the differences are striking. For example, the wholesale cost of a portable TV set was about $109 to both a low-income market and a general market retailer. The general market retailer sold the set for $129.95, whereas the low-income market retailer charged $219.95 for the same set. Another example is a dryer, wholesaling at about $115, which was sold for $150 by a general market retailer and for $300 by a low-income market retailer.

OPERATING EXPENSES AND NET PROFITS

Despite their substantially higher prices, net profit on sales for low-income market retailers was only slightly higher and net profit return on net worth was considerably lower when compared to general market retailers. It appears that salaries and commissions, bad-debt losses, and other expenses are substantially higher for low-income market retailers. Profit and expense comparisons are, of course, affected by differences in type of operation and accounting procedures. However, a detailed analysis was made for retailers of comparable size and merchandise mix to minimize such differences.

Low-income market retailers reported the highest return after taxes on net sales, 4.7%. Among the general market retailers, department stores had the highest return on net sales, 4.6%. Furniture and home furnishings stores earned a net profit after taxes of 3.9%, and appliance, radio, and television retailers were the least profitable with a net profit of only 2.1% on sales.

Low-income market retailers reported an average rate of return on *net worth* after taxes of 10.1%. Rates of return on net worth varied considerably among various kinds of general market retailers. Appliance, radio, and television retailers reported the highest rate of return after taxes, 20.3% of net worth. Next in order were furniture and home furnishings retailers with 17.6% and department stores with 13% on net worth.

ASSIGNMENT OF CONTRACTS

Low-income market retailers typically held their installment contracts and did not assign them to finance companies or banks. Only one-fifth of the total contracts were assigned by low-income market retailers. Among general market retailers, appliance stores assigned almost all (98%) of their contracts to finance companies and banks. General market furniture stores assigned somewhat more than half of their contracts (57%). Among the retailers surveyed, only the department store category involved no contract assignment.

FINANCE CHARGES

There is considerable variation in the finance charges of D.C. retailers of furniture and appliances, particularly among the low-income market retailers. Most of the retailers surveyed determined finance charges in terms of an "add-on" rate based on the unpaid cash balance. When calculated on an effective annual rate basis, finance charges of general market retailers varied between 11% and 29%, averaging 21% when contracts were assigned and 19% when retailers financed their own contracts. Finance charges by low-income market retailers imposing such charges ranged between 11 and 33% per annum, averaging 25% on contracts assigned to finance companies and 23% on contracts the retailers held themselves.

One low-income retailer made no separate charge for installment credit. All of his finance charges were, in effect, included in the purchase price. Other low-income market retailers kept finance charges below the actual cost of granting credit. This practice of absorbing credit costs can give the illusion of "easy" credit, but the customer may be paying a great deal for such installment credit in the form of much higher prices.

JUDGMENTS, GARNISHMENT, AND REPOSSESSIONS

One of the most notable facts uncovered by the study relates to the frequency with which a small group of retailers utilized the courts to enforce their claims with respect to installment contracts. Eleven of the 18 low-income market retailers reported 2,690 judgments. Their legal action resulted in 1,568 garnishments and 306 reposessions. For this group, one court judgment was obtained for every $2,200 of sales. In effect, low-income market retailers make extensive use of the courts in collecting debts. While general market retailers may take legal action as a last resort against delinquent customers, some low-income market retailers depend on legal action as a normal order of business.

CONCLUSION

Installment credit is widely used in marketing appliances and home furnishings to low-income families. Often these families purchase durable goods, such as furniture, television sets, and phonographs, through the mechanism of "easy" credit. Low-income market retailers specialize in granting credit to consumers who do not seek or are unable to obtain credit from regular department, furniture, or appliance stores. As a group, low-income market retailers made about 93% of their sales through installment credit.

The real cost of this "easy" credit is very dear, however. Primarily it takes the form of higher product prices. Credit charges, when separately stated, are not notably higher than those imposed by general market retailers. Though some low-income market retailers imposed effective annual finance charges as high as 33%, others charged much less or nothing at all. Markups on comparable products, however, are often two or three times higher than those charged by general market retailers.

The findings of this study suggest that the marketing system for distribution of durable goods to low-income consumers is costly. Although their markups are very much higher than those of general market retailers, low-income market retailers do not make particularly high net profits. They have markedly higher costs, partly because of high bad-debt expenses, but to a greater extent because of higher salaries and commissions as a per cent of sales. These expenses reflect in part greater use of door-to-door selling and expenses associated with the collection and processing of installment contracts.

The high prices charged by low-income market retailers suggest the absence of effective price competition. What competition there is among low-income market retailers apparently takes the form of easier credit availability, rather than of lower prices. Greater credit risks are taken to entice customers. Insofar as the problem for low-income consumers is availability of credit, merchants who sell to them focus on this element.

The success of retailers who price their merchandise on such a high markup in selling to low-income families leads inevitably to the conclusion that such families engage in little comparative shopping. It would appear that many low-income customers lack information or knowledge of their credit charges and credit source alternatives, or of the prices and quality of products available in general market retailing establishments. To the extent that door-to-door sales techniques are utilized, such families frequently make crucial purchases without leaving the home and without seeing the products they commit themselves to buy. The fact that low-income market retailers emphasize the use of door-to-door salesmen both reflects and encourages such behavior. The Commission is well aware that door-to-door selling, as well as home-demonstration selling, provides an opportunity for deceptive and high-pressure sales techniques. Moreover, such selling methods are also very high-cost methods of distribution. It would appear, therefore, that the low-income consumers who can least afford mistakes in their buying decisions face two serious problems when they are confronted with a door-to-door or home demonstration sales approach—(1) the high cost of this sales technique will ultimately be borne by the purchaser, and (2) the opportunity for high pressure or deceptive selling is great, thus discouraging comparative shopping and enhancing the probability that the consumer will agree to purchases he would otherwise not want.

While public policy can help solve the problems of low-income consumers, legislation alone may not be sufficient. Legislation aimed at disclosure and regulation of finance charges will help low-income as well as other consumers make more rational buying decisions. Intensified programs on both state and Federal levels to eliminate all deceptions and frauds in the advertising and oral representations of the terms of sale and credit charges will also help to endure that their money is spent advantageously. The poor, to a considerable extent, however, are not sophisticated shoppers. Many cannot afford the luxury of "shopping around" because their potential sources of credit are limited.

Others, because of inadequate consumer education or lack of mobility, simply do not engage in comparison shopping.

Thus, in attempting to deal with the phenomenon of the poor paying more for consumer goods, every effort should be made to improve consumer counseling. Many customers continue to buy from low-income market retailers even though they have sufficient income to qualify for credit at stores selling for less. Greater community effort in consumer education is needed.

Beyond the matter of education is the question of credit availability. Many low-income families are quite capable of making regular payments. They should have the option of making payments on reasonably priced merchandise. Local community effort in the development of effective credit sources could contribute materially to freeing individuals from dependence on "easy" credit merchants. Moreover, perhaps general market retailers can take steps to make it easier for low-income families to apply for and receive credit. Some retailers have already found that they can do so economically. Various community business organizations might consider ways of more actively encouraging low-income families to seek credit from retailers selling for less.

Increased competition for the patronage of low-income consumers would go a long way toward resolving many of the problems confronting them in the low-income market. Public policy should consider the various ways by which new entrants could be encouraged into these markets to increase the competitive viability of these markets.

While the availability of credit is perhaps the major reason why low-income families purchase from the low-income market retailers, it is only logical to conclude that the sales techniques of these retailers are also an important factor. Low-income market retailers have every incentive to continue these techniques since their risk of loss is substantially reduced by their virtually unopposed access to judgment and garnishment proceedings to enforce payment or secure repossession. The 2,690 actions taken by eleven low-income market retailers suggest a marketing technique which includes actions against default as a normal matter of business rather than as a matter of last resort. At present, in the face of default, creditors can seek both repossession and payment of the deficiency, including various penalties. It may be appropriate to require creditors to choose one or the other of these legal remedies, and not to have the option of pursuing both courses simultaneously. Repossession would then fully discharge the merchant's claim. It is equally necessary to ensure that purchasers receive *actual* notice of any such proceedings and have legal counsel available to defend them in court. Perhaps, consideration should also be given to some form of negotiation before a court-appointed neighborhood referee as a compulsory prelude to a default judgment.

It is apparent that the solution to the problem of installment credit for the poor requires a variety of actions. A requirement that finance charges be clearly and conspicuously stated is a necessary but not a sufficient solution to the problem of installment credit for those consumers who are considered poor credit risks and are unsophisticated buyers. Among the complementary steps which might be considered are the following: (1) make reasonable credit more accessible; (2) provide counseling services which will encourage customers to practice comparison shopping; (3) equalize the legal rights of buyers and creditors in installment credit transactions; (4) encourage additional businesses to enter the low-income market; and (5) intensify consumer protection activities on both Federal and local levels to eliminate all fraud and deceptions in the advertising and offering of credit.

INDEX*

A & P Company, 131-32, 263
Administrative Conference of the United
  States, 75
Advertising, 90, 212, 243-44, 261, 308-69
  and consumer sovereignty, 7, 9-10,
    272
  and deception, 35, 48, 151, 444,
    459, 461
  and government regulations, 91,
    105, 116-24, 125-33, 144, 149,
    194, 255, 294, 308, 310-15,
    328-40, 363-69
  as marketing technique, 2, 33, 40,
    43, 47, 68, 240, 242, 248, 254,
    279, 288-89
  and warranties, 245, 400, 405,
    409-10, 413
Advertising Alert, 121, 266, 344
Advisory Council on Executive Organi-
  zation, 69, 71
Alabama, 230
Alderson, Wroe, 202
American Airlines, 410
American Association of Advertising
  Agencies, 289
American Bar Association, 90, 98-101,
  102-15, 217
American Chemical Society, 47
American Marketing Association, 287
American Motors, 314, 409
American Newspaper Publishers Association,
  315
American Retail Federation, 374
American Society of Mechanical Engineers,
  47
American Society of Safety Engineers, 47
American Spice Trade Association, 87-88
Antitrust, 44, 46-47, 227, 228-32, 355,
  375-76
    the FTC and, 95, 98 passim, 104,
      107, 113, 125, 329
    Senate Subcommittee, 188. *See also*
      Department of Justice

Antitrust Law & Economics Review, 93-94
Archer, Frank, 191
Arizona Consumers Council, 26
Association of Home Appliance Manu-
  facturers, 376
Automobile, 57, 147, 302
  insurance, 42, 47, 54, 62-63
  safety legislation, 39 passim, 79,
    84-85, 268, 297, 301, 403
Automobile Information Disclosure Act of
  1958, 84
Automobile Manufacturers Association, 164

Backman, Jules, 309, *352-62*
Batten, Barton, Durstine & Osborn Inc.,
  312, 313, 315
Bauer, Raymond A., 272, *279-90*
Beilenson, Anthony, 57
Benham, Lee, 351
Bentham, Jeremy, 165
Berton, Lee, 418, *420-25*
Better Business Bureaus, 16, 20, 29, 40,
  62, 162, 250, 312
Better Homes and Gardens, 399-400
Birmingham, Robert L., 186-87, *212-21*
Boat safety, 42, 65-66
Bostwick v. *Cohen,* 146
Bralove, Mary, 54, *86-88*
Brozen, Yale, 308, *341-51*
Burditt, George M., 187, *208-11*
Bureau of Automotive Repair (California),
  57
Bureau of Behavioral Studies (FTC), 118,
  123
Bureau of Competition (FTC), 73
Bureau of Consumer Protection (FTC), 73,
  366
Bureau of Economics (FTC), 73, 100, 118
Bureau of Federal Credit Unions, 83
Bureau of Field Operations (FTC), 119
Bureau of Labor Statistics, 456

*Inclusive page numbers of author's articles are in italics.

House of Representatives *(cont'd)*
    Foreign and Interstate Commerce
    Committee, 156, 188-89, 196,
    375
Housing and Urban Development Act of
    1968, 83
Humphrey, Hubert H., 41
Hutt, W. H., 3-4

Illinois, 156, 160, 351, 407, 410
Income
    distribution, 6, 237
    real, 21-22, 39. *See also* low income
        groups
Indiana, 57, 398
Inflation, 14, 27, 33, 67, 235
Institute of Life Insurance, 164
Insurance, 48, 170, 399, 414, 421, 435-36
    auto, 42, 47, 54, 62-63
    life, 26, 141, 436, 438
Interest, *See also* credit
    limitation laws, 165, 171, 175,
        177-83
    rates, 26, 137, 422
International Organization of Consumers
    Unions, 26
Interstate Commerce Commission, 41, 83
Interstate Land Sales Disclosure Provisions
    of 1968, 54-55, 83

Jentz, Gaylord A., 308, *328-40*
Johnson Administration, 41, 49, 54
Johnson, Lyndon B., 27, 41, 54, 117, 195
    consumer messages of, 25, *60-67*,
        195, 213, 291, 295, 393
    and Special Assistant to the President
        for Consumer Affairs, 25, 192-93,
        274
Jones, Mary Gardiner, 249, 314
Jordan v. *Montgomery Ward & Co., Inc.,*
    146
Journal of Marketing, 177
Jungle, The, 25, 54, 247

Kansas, 230
Kaye, William G., 226, *243-48*
Kefauver, Estes, 25, 295
Kellogg Company, 129, 196, 345

Kelsey, Frances, 25
Kennedy, John F., 25, 34, 54, 235, 293,
    295
Kirkpatrick, Miles W., *98-101,* 341, 363-69
Knauer, Virginia H., 22, 25, 31, 236, 377
Koch, George, 196, 263, 376
Korean War, 22, 234
Kotler, Philip, 272, *291-304*

Labor Unions, 22-23, 26, 292, 296, 390
Land fraud, 42, 61, 83
Lanham Act, 105, 257
Lefkowitz, Louis J., 423-24
Levitt, Theodore, 255, 308, *316-27,* 348-50
Loevinger, Lee, 348
Louisiana, 57, 398
Louisiana Consumer League, 26
Low income groups, 27, 418-61
    and Caplovitz study, 26, 159, 428
        passim, 447-48
    and credit, 120, 136-37, 150, 157-60,
        166, 174, 376, 418 passim
Lowe, John W., 359

MacGregor, James, 308, *310-15*
Magazine Publishers Association, 212
Magnuson, Warren D., 42, 44, 153, 156,
    195, 197, 200, 206, 235, 269, 393,
    424-25
Main, Jeremy, 186, *192-99*
Maine, 147
Malthusian theory, 295
Management, 15, 33, 241-42, 245, 261
    passim, 299, 303, 324
    and health and safety issues, 28, 35
    and warranties, 35, 372, 402, 411
Mannes, Mary, 193
Marketing concept, 2, 14, 30-34, 272,
    299-300
Marketing research, 293, 414
Maryland, 230, 274, 423
Massachusetts, 57, 398, 423
Mayer, Jean, 277
McGovern, George, 311
Measurement of Social Welfare, 6
Meat Inspection Act of 1907, 80, 291
Metcalf, Lee, 49
Michigan, 407
Minnesota, 178-79

466